Pierre Albert-Birot

Pierre Albert-Birot

A Poetics in Movement, A Poetics of Movement

Debra Kelly

Madison • Teaneck
Fairleigh Dickinson University Press
London: Associated University Presses

Associated University Presses
440 Forsgate Drive
Cranbury, NJ 08512

Associated University Presses
16 Barter Street
London WC1A 2AH, England

Associated University Presses
P.O. Box 338, Port Credit
Mississauga, Ontario
Canada L5G 4L8

The paper used in this publication meets the requirements
of the American National Standard for Permanence of Paper
for Printed Library Materials Z39.48–1984.

Library of Congress Cataloging-in-Publication Data

Kelly, Debra.
  Pierre Albert-Birot : a poetics in movement, a poetics of movement
/ Debra Kelly.
    p.   cm.
  Includes bibliographical references and index.
  ISBN 0-8386-3625-X (alk. paper)
  1. Albert-Birot, Pierre—Criticism and interpretation.
  2. Poetics.   I. Title.
  PQ2601.L315Z67   1997
  841'.912—dc20   96-28000
                                                              CIP

PRINTED IN THE UNITED STATES OF AMERICA

Dedicated to the memory of my mother
Muriel Joyce Kelly

et Grabinoulor s'assit d'ébahissement de ce que tant d'hommes depuis si longtemps aient pu croire à la mort et se soient complu à imaginer pour leur désespoir un monde mort en face du monde vivant comme si vraiment la chose était possible et Grabinoulor vit bien que sa mère était la rose qui s'épanouissait à côté de lui la forêt qu'il traversait les oiseaux qui volaient les enfants qui jouaient les amoureux qui passaient la lumière qui les éclairait et alors il eut beaucoup de joie et admira le monde
—"Grabinoulor cherche l'Empire des Morts,"
Les Six Livres de Grabinoulor, I, 6

("and Grabinoulor was knocked sideways by the thought that so many men over such a long time had been able to believe in death and had been pleased to drive themselves to despair by imagining a dead world opposite the living world as if such a thing were really possible and Grabinoulor saw very clearly that his mother was the rose blooming beside him and the forest he was walking through and the birds flying the children playing the lovers passing by the light illuminating them and then he was filled with joy and he admired the world")
—"Grabinoulor Goes to Look for the Empire of the Dead,"
The First Book of Grabinoulor.

Contents

Preface

Les premiers temps je croyais qu'il fallait être un homme tout
à fait extraordinaire pour écrire un livre, un homme pas du tout
comme les autres, pas du tout comme moi, mais à force d'en
voir et d'en feuilleter je me suis habitué et j'ai fini par penser
que les livres sont des choses comme les autres et que faire un
livre est un travail qui peut être fait par un homme ordinaire,
voire par moi.

—Rémy Floche, employé

("At first I thought you had to be a really extraordinary man to
write a book, a man not at all like others, not at all like me,
but by looking at them and flicking through them I got used to
them and I ended up thinking that books are things just like
anything else and that making a book is something that can be
done by an ordinary man, indeed by me.")

—Rémy Floche, employee.

THE presentation of a lifetime's work by a writer whose work has been
neglected by the academic establishment and that remains largely unknown by the general reading public presents both problems and pleasures. A text that has been, quite literally, little read offers a different set
of challenges and demands a different approach from that of a text that
has already generated multiple readings. A body of critical research develops by rewriting itself; it is self-generating through repeated contact
with the original texts to which it must respond and which, in turn, reveal
more and more of their possible readings. This study, therefore, appears
at a particular point in the development of the critical framework. A
number of articles and a significant monograph have been published, and
here I am seeking to understand the originating moment of a poetics to
provide a focus from which to view the work as a whole—together with
some necessary questioning of previous responses that are already apparent. The principal aim here is to uncover the matrix of a poetics, to offer
a reading of a selection of both poetry and prose generated from that
matrix, and to explore the processes of a poetics in its multiple forms.
The general critical framework is that of the visual arts and of the dis-

9

course of the visual arts, not as imagery or theme but as structure—an exploration of the functioning of a set of basic structures on canvas, in poetry, in narrative. This is a generative rather than a reductive process, for these fundamental elements then once again ceaselessly recombine in the alchemical process that is poetry. From the distillation of a potentially infinite number of elements in the vast poetic universe created by Pierre Albert-Birot, a residue is left that may serve as a base for analysis.

It is my hope that I will provide the reader of Albert-Birot with an entry into his complex universe. This artistic universe is the expression of a multifaceted quest for knowledge and an unwaning belief in the value of the human constructed in the consciousness of the elusive nature of· truth and meaning. Albert-Birot, the poet/painter, constantly reevaluates the creative act on canvas and in numerous poetic and narrative forms. This book attempts to offer a global reading of his production as a whole as well as a detailed reading of certain key elements. A choice of texts has necessarily been made from the wealth of material available, both published and unpublished. It is also to be hoped that it will serve as an inspiration for other scholars to discover and offer new readings of those works discussed here and the many others to which I have only alluded.

Chapter 1 establishes the initial problematic of individual and artistic identity and goes on to analyze the major canvas *La Guerre* painted in 1916, reading this simultaneously as an ideological, historical, artistic, and autobiographical statement. The underlying structures of this non-figurative oil on canvas are examined, and the painting is read in its historical, artistic, and individual context as an originating moment in the poetics of Albert-Birot. *La Guerre* is shown to be fundamental to an understanding of the construction of Albert-Birot's poetic universe, and it is clearly established that the critical framework of the visual arts is essential to the reading of the entire oeuvre. The notion of "movement" is defined here not only as a series of experiments between artistic tradition and new forms but also as a poetics that seeks to express the ever-changing relationship between the Self and the Universe. It is here that the initial problematic of individual and artistic identity is first given expression.

Chapter 2 examines the advent of Albert-Birot to a particular concept of modernity in 1915–16 and seeks to understand his role as founder-editor of the avant-garde literary and artistic review *SIC* published from 1916 to 1919. This includes an assessment of the degree of interaction between Pierre Albert-Birot and the prevailing theories and general artistic climate of the period and an exploration of the way the individual functions in the collective space as he or she strives to establish an artistic identity and to find a voice.

Chapter 3 deals with the early period of Albert-Birot's poetic development, analyzing the first major poetry collection *La Lune ou le livre des poèmes,* printed by the poet himself in 1924. Comprised partly of poems that appeared first in *SIC, La Lune* is the material and intellectual inheritor of *SIC* and the expression of the painter turned poet/typographer, exploring his new material in all its aspects to produce this first "manual." Here the poet discovers all the processes of poetic creation: the visual, the verbal, the physical, and the meta-physical. From traditional versification to the limits of pure sound and vision, *La Lune* is a project for a linguistic Utopia.

Chapter 4 examines the intensely introspective *Poèmes à l'Autre Moi* (1927), considered by the poet to be his most important collection. This is self-portrait and self-narrative in poetic form. It is an exploration of the relationship between the individual of everyday experience and the Self made sublime through the mediation of the poetic act—not opposites but two perceptions of the same experience. This time language is explored for its role in the creation of identity and in the confrontation of self with Self. The poet confronts the dilemmas of human existence. *L'Autre Moi* is not, however, a narcissistic text. Rather it opens up from the individual to the universal and in the process reveals the same underlying structures already read in the originating moment of Albert-Birot's poetry.

The final chapter offers a reading of the masterpiece of Albert-Birot's universe, the six-volume "épopée", *Grabinoulor.* Begun in 1918 and continued until the early 1960's, it is the metatext and pivotal point of Albert-Birot's entire production. A number of aspects of this vast, non-punctuated narrative are considered: the status of "epic"; the discourse of the visual arts and their importance for the structure of this "chaos géométrique"; the discourse of excess and the process of "ever-becoming"; the divine status of the poet and of artistic creation; and the sacred and spiritual quest of the narrative striving toward an understanding of the possibilities of the creative act itself. This analysis allows a further consideration of the notion of movement and a discovery of Albert-Birot's understanding of the act and processes of artistic creation.

The conclusion comments on the place and status to be accorded the work of Albert-Birot within the panorama of twentieth-century artistic production. I end by offering a questioning for new readings of *Grabinoulor,* of the theater—which in itself deserves a full-length study—and of the poetry and other prose works to which I have alluded in my attempt to present the work as the continuous whole to which it strives.

Albert-Birot's artistic production covers the whole range of possible modes of expression: figurative paintings and sculptures, still lifes, landscapes, cubist and abstract canvases, experimental forms of *la peinture absolue,* traditional versification, punctuated and nonpunctuated poetry and prose, sound-generated poetry, visual poetry or "poésie plastique," translation, linear narrative in more ambiguous form, theater, and autobiography. The reeditions of the major poetry collections and the complete theater by Rougerie, of *Les Mémoires d'Adam* and *Rémy Floche, employé* by the Editions de l'Allée, the facsimile edition of *SIC* and the first integral edition of *Les Six Livres de Grabinoulor* by Jean-Michel Place (see bibliography for details) have made his work more accessible over the last ten years. The theater is better known both on radio and on stage. Although absent from the majority of literary anthologies of the twentieth century, *SIC* is a point of reference for art historians. Albert-Birot's canvas *La Guerre* has been exhibited in exhibitions covering the avant-garde of the First World War and the development from cubism to abstraction. The selection of works chosen for analysis here—*La Guerre* (oil on canvas, 1916), *SIC* (1916–19), *La Lune ou le livre des poèmes* (1924), *Les Poèmes à l'Autre Moi* (1927), and *Grabinoulor* (1918–early 1960s)—reveals the development of a poetics and an attitude toward poetic creation. The matrix of the poetics identified in the opening chapter returns again and again in myriad and multiple forms, allowing the way in which the processes of creation function to be analyzed and reflected upon.

Grabinoulor, begun in 1918 and worked on more or less continually for the fifty years of poetic creation that followed, is the key to the universe created by Pierre Albert-Birot. Although we examine this work closely only in the final chapter of this study, we work toward a reading of it from the outset. It is constantly present, simultaneously informing and informed by the other texts within its orbit, a process in constant movement rather than a fixed point of reference. It is the product of the application of theories of the poetics of creation and a theory in the process of being created, a work that is both structuring and perpetually being constructed. Previous readings of Albert-Birot's work have tended to focus on *Grabinoulor,* and these have provided a number of basic thematic and structural approaches to this enormous, proliferating work.[1] It is also essential to understand the relationship of Pierre Albert-Birot to the two artistic movements with which he has readily been associated—futurism and surrealism—and the extent of his involvement will be discussed through the exploration of the literary and artistic magazine *SIC,* published monthly from 1916 to 1919.[2] *SIC* has frequently been labeled a mouthpiece of futurism in France, and certainly Albert-Birot's meeting with its ideas in the person of Gino Severini in 1915 had an enormous influence on the poet's sudden advent to modernity.[3] In *SIC,* Albert-Birot published early work by Tzara, Aragon, and Soupault and thereafter followed the common tendency to qualify as "surrealist" anything contemporary with Breton's movement that explores the realm beyond the everyday. This misinterpretation was reinforced by Gallimard's marketing of the 1964 edition of *Grabinoulor* (comprising selections from Volumes I, II, and III) as "un classique du surréalisme." What concerns us in the present study is the challenge that the paradoxical position of Albert-Birot, with regard to the artists and poets surrounding him and to the prevailing concepts of modernity and of the avant-garde, immediately sets up—a paradox continually apparent in the enigmatic status of a literary oeuvre that, while lying at the very heart of twentieth-century artistic preoccupations, continues to deny rupture with the past (sine qua non of the avant-garde). Resisting facile categorization and mechanical theorizing, its complexity and density stimulate a questioning into the nature and processes of all artistic creation.[4]

Unless indicated by a reference and acknowledgment, all translations are my own. It should be noted that these are either literal translations or a translation simply to convey meaning and are in no way meant to be a definitive or creative equivalent. The aim is only one of information for the reader who requires some help with the French original.

Acknowledgments

FIRST thanks must go to Pierre Albert-Birot for a lifetime of creation. Working with such richness has been a constant source of pleasure. I would like to thank Denise Morton who provided a supportive friendship and many hours of valuable conversation in the early stages of the thesis on which this book is based. My thanks also to my husband, Gary Clare, for his support in innumerable ways during the final stages of the project. It is with the most heartfelt gratitude that I thank Jenny Hawkes, who prepared the original typescript with infinite patience and great understanding and remained on "standby." In the often problematic translation process I must thank Natalie Byrne for her contribution, and particularly Sue Rose, who worked with great interest and creative integrity on Albert-Birot's key poetic work. A word of thanks also to the masters and doctoral students of Birkbeck College, who provided a stimulating atmosphere and supportive network in which to work, and to colleagues at the University of Westminster, who have been equally encouraging. The Sir Edward Sterne Studentship from the University of London provided the financial support, and I thank the committee for selecting me. I take this opportunity to extend my respects to Professor Malcolm Bowie and Professor Margaret Davis, who examined the thesis and made valuable suggestions for publication. Most of all I wish to acknowledge the "trinity," without whom this work would have been impossible— Madeleine Renouard, whose sustained support and critical perception are unfailingly generous; Arlette Albert-Birot, who opened her home and her heart to me; and Barbara Wright, whose translation of Book 1 of *Grabinoulor* inspired this study and who remains a great friend of PAB.

> Trinité je reçois tout l'univers dans ma solitude
> (*Poèmes à l'autre moi*, Trente-troisième poème)

> ("Trinity I receive the whole universe in my solitude")

I have dedicated this book to my mother, who was unable to see it through to completion but who continues to be my inspiration.

Pierre Albert-Birot

1

Identity, *La Guerre,* and the Structures of a Poetics

Donc passez vos jours à vivre bien en rond, cultivez la courbe,
c'est ma ligne, je n'en comprends pas d'autres; je te le dis Adam,
aie peur de la droite, ligne affreuse et d'ailleurs impossible.
                              —*Les mémoires d'Adam,* p. 79)

("Therefore spend your days living circularly, cultivate the
curved line, it is my line, I understand no others; I tell you
Adam, fear the straight line, a terrible line and what is more,
impossible.")

THE ENTRY INTO A POETIC UNIVERSE: CONTINUITY AND RUPTURE

ALBERT-BIROT, the sculptor, painter, and occasional poet, had lived
alongside the adventure of modernity, seemingly unmoved by the artistic
revolution of cubism and untouched by the poets who were to become
the contributors to *SIC*, until his meeting with Gino Severini in 1915 and,
through him, Apollinaire. Out of this paradox has been spun a web of
personal mythologizing, as well as a selection of anecdotes retold in more
or less similar form by the poet in interviews and in his short autobiography, which conceals much more than it reveals.[1] It is not our intention
to rework the biographical details of Albert-Birot's advent to the forefront
of the Parisian avant-garde in 1916 from a position of total obscurity and
of confusion and ignorance regarding the development of what is generally termed "modernity" in art and literature. To provide a contextualiza-
tion, a "background" to our initial questioning, however, it remains
necessary to comment briefly on certain features of the period leading
up to 1916 where this study will begin and to offer a schema of the fifty
years of poetic production that constitute Albert-Birot's life's work, to
set those works chosen here for analysis against a more general overview.

A reading of the most detailed and best-researched account of Albert-

Birot's early years allows a series of recurrent themes in the poet's personal and creative itinerary to be established, which suggest a number of basic conflicts, both personal and artistic, and which contain the germ of the creative impulse, its evolution, and its development. Two of his sculptures, *La Veuve* and *Les Ames simples,* were exhibited in the 1903 "Salon des Artistes Français" and received favorable critical notice (among nearly nine hundred exhibits) from the establishment of the day.[2] The theme of the *veuve* and of solitude is a recurrent one in early poems, sketches and canvases.[3] Examining the *moi naissant* of Albert-Birot, Lentengre reads the period as one of a constant battle for identity.[4] Here we will limit ourselves to the formulation of our initial set of problematics concerning the individual and identity:

- the image of the self and the place of the other
- the individual functioning in/with/against the collective
- the quest for self-affirmation and a voice with which to speak the self
- the quest for self-perpetuation in the experience of rupture and fragmentation[5]

The self-reflective adventure of Proust and of writers since him—Leiris, Michaux, Perec, to name but three who suggest an immediate comparison with Albert-Birot—will not be analyzed in detail here. It suffices to point out that this quest for an enduring selfhood, the problem of the subject and of experiencing subjectivity, is one of the most recurrent driving forces of twentieth-century writing. Albert-Birot is to be placed immediately in the development of both the modern narrative and modern poetry.

The opposition between Self and Other takes numerous forms in both early and later work, oscillating between a quest for a self-affirmation that would be an ideal state, and an absolute complete unto itself, and the need for an affirmation of the self by the other, an experience that remains in a state of flux, open to uncertainty. Between the two is the search for a more comfortable relationship between the Self and the World around it, for a place in the world. The various manifestations of these conflicts will become clear as we follow Albert-Birot's itinerary from *SIC,* through *La Lune,* and most intensely in *Les Poèmes à l'Autre Moi* and *Grabinoulor.* What is certain is that from his arrival in Paris at eighteen, Albert-Birot seeks to establish an identity that is at this stage uncertain although already bound up with artistic creation, until a group of events and meetings come together and act as catalyst. Until this point the sculptor/painter cannot become the poet of the next fifty years. Of these early attempts at self-expression and self-affirmation, two forms

Autoportrait, P. Albert-Birot, 1903. Oil on canvas.

must be stressed here: self-portraiture and the numerous projects for literary magazines that precede *SIC*.

The repeated attempt to affirm self-by-self is a basic element of the poet's quest and once again manifests itself in numerous forms. For this study in particular, the number of self-portraits of Albert-Birot and portraits of his wife Germaine provide an essential key in the reading of his work, once again thematically and for the uncovering of the structures that generate its form(s).

Throughout Albert-Birot's artistic production, he painted self-portraits, from a sketch dated around 1896 when the artist is twenty years old to the *Autoportrait* of 1935 when the poet is nearly sixty. In 1915 he painted the large figurative portrait of Germaine, followed the next year by a major cubist portrait of her. These portraits mark the rupture between the artist still seeking himself and the poet finding a new creative potential.[6] In the 1927 collection *Les Poèmes à l'Autre Moi*, the preoccupation with the representation of the self is returned to when the self becomes text rather than canvas. A number of questions are therefore raised concerning not only his own artistic development but each medium that is, what "changes" take place in the representation of self on canvas to self in language? The process would indicate a testing of the limits and the possibilities of both forms of expression and stresses the relevance of an approach to Albert-Birot's work that focuses on these formative years, when his advent to an expression of his creativity comes both practically and theoretically by way of the visual arts. In the change of material from paint and color to words, Albert-Birot begins an exploration of language that starts physically as he typesets and prints his own collections (particularly *La Lune ou le livre des poèmes)*, the creative act still tangible despite its different form, the painter becoming poet-artisan. The change of medium represents also this rupture between old and new, for it is on canvas that the revelation of the nature of a modern creativity comes to the artist:

> Mais plutôt que par étapes, la mutation s'accomplit par bonds successifs. Voici le meilleur exemple: en 1915, Pierre Albert-Birot entreprend un nouveau portrait de Germaine. Elle est assise sur une chaise basse, les jambes allongées, les pieds reposant sur un pouf. C'est une très grande toile (110 x 200) qu'il prend, reprend sans arriver à rendre tout ce qu'il sait de sa femme et qu'il voudrait transmettre. Alors brusquement, il plante là toile et modèle, puis, dans l'allégresse, il peint le *Grand portrait cubiste de Germaine*. Rue des Saints-Pères, il avait accroché les deux toiles face-à-face, la première jamais terminée, comme témoin d'un passé à jamais révolu, la seconde éclatant de la joie de ses lignes, de ses quadrillages, architecture bouleversée et recomposée, exploration de l'âme même de son modèle, cubisme analytique. "Si vous saviez combien le portrait cubiste est plus ressemblant," affirmait-il.[7]

("But rather than in stages, the change was accomplished in successive leaps. This is the best example: in 1915 Pierre Albert-Birot undertakes a new portrait of Germaine. She is seated on a low chair, legs stretched out, her feet on a stool. It is a large canvas (110 x 200) which he works and reworks without managing to portray what he knows of his wife and what he wishes to convey. Then suddenly he sets up his canvas and his model and, with great exhilaration, he paints the *Large Cubist Portrait of Germaine*. In the flat in the Rue des Saints-Pères, he had hung the two paintings opposite each other, the first never finished, a witness to a past vanished forever, the second bursting with the joy of its lines, its squares, an architecture disassembled and reassembled, the exploration of the very soul of its subject, analytical cubism. 'If only you knew to what extent the cubist portrait is the greater likeness,' he used to say.")

The existence of these two paintings that became symbolic to the poet of his old and new self imply a number of problematics essential to the reading of his work proposed here. It is significant that the acknowledgment of the change in artistic expression comes in the representation of the Other, which at that time gave back the clearest and strongest reflection of himself. It is in the visual arts that the realization takes place. It is thus the visual that provides the initial impetus for a modern expression of Albert-Birot's creativity.[8]

The gestation period of *SIC*, which includes the changes from earlier projects for a literary and artistic journal to the early issues of the magazine produced in 1916, reflects the same quest for an identity as the repeated self-portraits and now also for a voice with which to speak that identity. As early as 1904 there were plans to found a literary journal with his friend Maurice Gignoux (known as Saint-Chamarand), and in 1905 *La Poétique* appeared edited by Saint-Chamarand alone, although with contributions by Albert-Birot. Between the end of 1904 and early 1905, the two of them had proposed several titles: "L'Elan Littéraire Universel"; "Le Flux—publication mensuelle de littérature française et étrangère"; "L'Ardeur Littéraire—publication mensuelle d'oeuvres françaises et étrangères"; "L'Elan Littéraire—publication mensuelle d'oeuvres françaises et étrangères"; "L'Oeuvre Idéaliste." One might see the embryo of *SIC* in the dynamic of such titles, yet there is nothing to substantiate the fact that Albert-Birot was at this stage sure of what would develop into *SIC*. What is clear is the influence of the philosophy and ideals of a vitalism, originating in the works of Spencer and of Bergson, with which Albert-Birot had come into contact during his attendance at public lectures in literature and philosophy at the Collège de France and the Sorbonne. He was especially impressed by the teaching of the sociologist Alfred Espinas, rationalist philosopher and disciple of Spencer.[9] It is within this dynamic, optimistic, vitalist perspective and in the positive role accorded the human will that Albert-Birot's own philosophy and poetics would develop.[10]

In 1909 he produced two ideas for covers of the magazine to be called "Le Bois sacré et les Heures Littéraires," subtitled "Philosophie, beaux-arts, poésie, roman." The most advanced project for a literary journal was *1915,* immediately preceding *SIC* yet far from iconoclastic. It was intended to be a "luxury" review, and the proposal, although bearing some resemblance to that of *SIC,* reveals a very different attitude, still looking to the past and to continuity with it:

> Pour nous, qui ne sommes pas sur le front, nous combattons seulement avec notre plume, non pas en polémiste, mais en artiste. Tous nos désirs tendent à ce que *1915* soit un journal résumant tout ce qui caractérise l'esprit français et constitue ce charme particulier qui séduit si fortement tous les peuples: le goût, l'élégance, la simplicité, la clarté. (*1915,* "Communiqué")[11]

> ("For us, who are not at the Front, we are fighting only with our pen, not as polemicists, but as artists. All we wish is that *1915* will be a review that resumes everything that characterizes the French spirit and constitutes that particular charm that all nations find so seductive: taste, elegance, simplicity, clarity.")

During the whole of 1915, there were numerous magazine projects before this more advanced version, and it seems this was the moment when the quest for identity was at a particularly crucial point—ready for a meeting with the public space, awaiting a catalyst. How does Albert-Birot come, therefore, from *1915* to *SIC?* Through a necessary rupture— a rupture that at that moment appears definitive between the past and present, between the searching, uncertain, and as yet insular self to an affirmed personal and public creative identity. The historical and political timing of this self-affirmation cannot be underestimated. Despite the very marked awareness of the "avant" and "depuis" in the "PREMIERS MOTS" of *SIC,* which expresses the desire for change, for the new, there is the continuity between the two projects generated from a patriotic energy, characteristic of these war years in other writers. Yet the new dynamic is present, and the fundamental structures that we will explore in Albert-Birot's canvas *La Guerre* are an expression of a psychological moment, a moment when historical, artistic, and personal events coincide.

The opening words of the first issue of *SIC* (January 1916) differ certainly in form and tone from the communiqué of *1915,* which we have previously quoted. They accept a rupture with the past, yet are still searching: "Venez avec nous, regardons, voyons, entendons, cherchons." ("Come with us, let us look, see, hear, seek.") In the same rubric of the second issue, the editorial has found what it is looking for, perhaps not

PREMIERS MOTS.

Notre volonté:

Agir. Prendre des initiatives. ne pas attendre qu elles nous reviennent d'Outre-Rhin.

Notre désir:

Regarder, voir, entendre, chercher, et vous emmener avec nous.

Aimer la vie et vous le dire; la vivre et vous y convier.

Un jour vous ne compreniez pas telle chose que vous comprenez aujourd'hui; rappelez vous combien cette chose était inexistante pour vous AVANT, et combien elle existe DEPUIS; rappelez-vous, rappelez-vous, et ne dites pas: je ne comprends point telle chose, donc elle n'est pas.

Venez avec nous, regardons, voyons, entendons, cherchons.

SIC

"Premiers Mots," *SIC*, n° 1, January 1916. Facsimile, Editions Jean-Michel Place, p. 2.

yet the form of its expression, but the declarations "SOYONS MOD-ERNES," "A CHAQUE TEMPS SON ART," ("LET US BE MODERN," "TO EACH TIME ITS ART") are bold and the voice stronger and louder. This meeting with modernity through the person of Severini and ostensibly therefore through futurism has tended to influence the reading of *SIC* and of Albert-Birot's early work.[12] To understand Albert-Birot's expression of "modernity," the issue is more complex than a simple "borrowing" of futurist technique and inspiration, for those areas of the search for a personal identity and of early philosophical influences that we have previously uncovered are inextricably linked to the development and direction of *SIC*.

There was certainly an intuition, a creative impulse at work during the first decade of the century, but it was coupled with an uncertainty and a confusion concerning the value of the "new," which prevented Albert-Birot from developing his positive potential. There is an awareness of what is not wanted in artistic creation but a lack of formulation concerning how to set about creating what is desirable, a frustration with being involved in creations that did not convey the intensity of an energy and an enthusiasm fueled by his philosophical readings.[13]

In Albert-Birot's writings prior to his sudden revelation of modernity, there is a belief in the continuity of artistic tradition:

> Certes l'artiste ne doit pas perdre de vue les chefs d'oeuvre du passé, mais ils ne doivent être pour lui qu'un point de départ; il doit savoir rejeter ce qui, en eux, tient aux temps, à l'époque, au milieu dans lequel il vit; le maître n'imite pas ses maîtres, il les continue.[14]

> ("Of course the artist must not lose sight of the great works of the past, but they should only be a starting point for him; he must know how to reject in them what belongs to the times, to the age, to the milieu in which he lives. The master does not imitate his own masters, he continues their work.")

This then is a concept of modernity that reveals a close relationship to that of Baudelaire and certainly to Apollinaire.[15]

There are, therefore, two forces within the poet: one desiring continuity as protection from the uncertainties of rupture with the past; the other seeking an experience as expression of a dynamism as yet unnamed, present, but unformed, invisible, unspoken—the "invisible," the "indicible" of the poem that opens his first collection, *Trente et un poèmes de poche:*

> Que vas-tu peindre ami? L'invisible.
> Que vas-tu dire ami? L'indicible
> Monsieur car mes yeux sont dans ma tête.
> —N'ayez-pas peur, c'est un poète.

> ("What are you going to paint friend? The invisible
> What are you going to say friend? The unsayable
> Sir because my eyes are in my head.
> —Fear not, he's a poet.")

In these four lines are contained the history of a coming to artistic expression, a grasping of the present moment of creation, and a future program, a promise of the manifestation that is as yet invisible, unutterable, the poetic universe that the poet has to convey, the first affirmation of the voice of a poetic self whose creation would continue for fifty years. Although Albert-Birot himself preferred to insist on his sudden "rebirth" with the "birth" of *SIC*, the reality of the situation reveals a slowly unfolding series of events and a long gestation period for the journal. In his autobiography Albert-Birot insists on the dramatic change of everyday circumstances offered him by the war and the sudden clearer insight into the type of journal he wished to produce after several abandoned projects. Yet the meeting with the modern is a more complex encounter and one most significantly that brings about rupture—rupture with the past, both personal and artistic; rupture with the self; and the point of rupture that marks Albert-Birot's entry into the avant-garde. In the archeology of the poetics we have so far attempted to excavate, we reach the anterior state, the fundamental opposition, the conflict that initially motivates a creative force and generates other dialectics:

- the necessity of rupture and the desire for continuity, the dilemma of the notion of modernity and personal dilemma for Albert-Birot
- the anguish of the self that is death-bound and the desire of the self for immortality, the opposing forces of Thanatos and Eros
- the structures of continuity and discontinuity, of wholeness and of fragmentation

It is in the adventure of the avant-garde set within the discourse of modernity as a whole (or of the avant-gardes, alternately accepting and refusing their common front), the avant-garde intensely aware of the historical moment, actively seeking rupture with what precedes, that both the personal and the public voices of Albert-Birot are to be heard clearly for the first time. Yet contrary to the driving force of the avant-garde, the will remains in the work of Albert-Birot to reassimilate that rupture into the greater whole. He experiences a slow coming to an awareness of what the artistic self is seeking as represented by the twin portraits of Germaine and the sudden shock of the modern through the meeting with Severini. The isolated and hesitant individual abruptly moves to a position in the collective adventure of the avant-garde with a public voice expressed through *SIC*. Before examining the form and content of *SIC* as both personal expression and as a literary and historical document of the period, we will explore these twin forces of continuity and rupture, which lie at the heart of Albert-Birot's poetic expression in his major canvas *La Guerre*. First coming to the modern aesthetic through the visual arts in his own work on portraiture and the productions of Severini, this moment of historical, artistic and personal rupture is originally expressed through line, shape and color.

THE ARTIST EXPRESSES THE PRESENT MOMENT

La Guerre: the very title of the canvas propels the composition into its historical and artistic moment.[16] The date of its creation is included with the title, 1916. The world is at war, and Albert-Birot himself is at war, waging it on behalf of the modern and his own artistic identity. This scenario is the artist's challenge, an aesthetics and an ethics, a quest for a mode of living and of creating. At this moment the artist takes his stance in the history of humanity, of ideas, of art, to live and to speak the conflict, the violence, the beauty, the jubilation of that present moment and of life itself:

> on y trouve douceur et violence amour et haine laideur et beauté et des tas de choses et même impalpabilité peut-être peuvent-ils les manifester et les poser sur une toile au moyen des sept couleurs et les deux lignes mères la droite et la courbe.
>
> *Grabinoulor,* V, 6, p. 637

> ("There is gentleness and violence love and hate ugliness and beauty and lots of things and even impalpability perhaps they can be shown and put on a canvas by the means of the seven colors and the two mother lines the straight line and the curved line")

In the general introduction to Albert-Birot's corpus and poetic universe, we have particularly stressed the rupture that marks his coming to an understanding of the modern aesthetic. *La Guerre* is the expression of this precise moment in the poet's personal and artistic itinerary. Furthermore the subject confronts here the moment of fundamental historical and social cleavage. *La Guerre* informs all Albert-Birot's work, constructing as it does a scenario that is not only a historical reality but the form of an existential truth, the knowledge of life and death. In the structures and colors of *La Guerre,* the necessary opposites that generate meaning, creation, and life are given form, the impalpable made palpable, the as yet unsaid now expressed—here with touch and sight, means of expression that remain fundamental in Albert-Birot's poetry. These fundamental oppositions at work in the structure of *La Guerre* may be uncovered again and again throughout his work and are essential for the construction of *Grabinoulor,* the reiteration of rupture and fragmentation set against the continuity and desired state of absolute, which may be

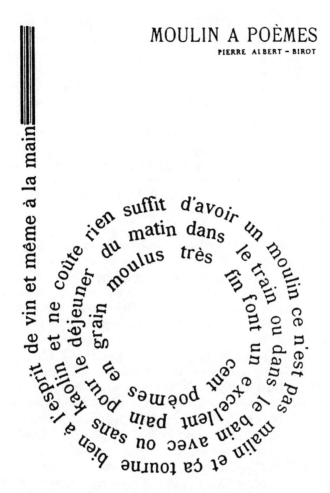

MOULIN A POÈMES
PIERRE ALBERT – BIROT

"Le Moulin à Poèmes," P. Albert-Birot, *Les Amusements Naturels*, p. 107.

achieved through artistic creation and which is the constant of the poet's quest:

> Ce double mouvement avait trouvé sa représentation visuelle, celle de la pointe et du cercle, dès les premières oeuvres abstraites du peintre comme *La Guerre* de 1916, avant de devenir cette dialectique de la sphère et de la percée qui est celle de l'oeuvre poétique.[17]

> ("This double movement had found its visual representation, the point and the circle, as early as the painter's first abstract works, like *War* painted in 1916, before becoming this dialectic of the sphere and the breach, which is that of the poetic works.")

The way in which the poetry is generated from this same original moment and constructed in these same forms, "ces deux lignes mères," is everywhere apparent: obvious in the visual poetry of *La Lune ou le livre des poèmes* (1924) and *Les Amusements naturels* (1945, and see reproductions), a constant in the construction of space and knowledge in the *Mémoires d'Adam* as Adam comes to a consciousness of the world, frequently discussed in *Grabinoulor* in innumerable forms and fundamental for its construction, poignant in *Les Poèmes à l'Autre Moi* (1927) and *La Panthère noire, poèmes en 50 anneaux et 50 chaînons* (1938), both at the projected meeting point of the human and the eternal.[18]

It is Albert-Birot's expression in the visual arts that first gives form to the problems to which he will constantly return. In exploring this form of expression, we can establish a "visual poetics" with which not only to analyze the surface and underlying structures of this abstract—or perhaps a more apt term is nonfigurative—canvas but also to prepare a way of reading the space and structure of the other poetic and prose texts selected in this study. Such an approach obviously raises questions concerning the relationship between painting and writing, a question of particular pertinence here personally for Albert-Birot and generally in the artistic climate of the period. It is Apollinaire seeking to express and validate the painterly discourse of cubism in words, setting up a dialogue in poetry with the paintings of Delaunay, the troubled polemics regarding "poésie cubiste, poésie plastique," Reverdy, Max Jacob, Apollinaire again, Albert-Birot himself, the aesthetic and philosophical problem of rendering the simultaneity of experience in image and in words, and here we can add the names of the futurist poets and painters, Marinetti, Severini, Carrà, and Balla. And beyond the preoccupations and debates of the period, as artist and writer attempt to understand and produce an expression of the modern world, are eternal questions concerning the process of artistic creation in paint or in words. How does as artist or writer or poet find the expression of the energy, of the flux, of the movement of the creative act, of the impulse of the work of art, of life itself in the fixed space of the canvas or of the printed page? How is the ephemeral, the impalpable, given form, for "des tas de choses et même impalpabilité" (previously quoted) must be given composition on the canvas and on the page. Does this "fixing" of the myriad components of the artistic object isolate it in time, condemn it to the past, the already done, or can the passage of time be halted in such a way as to preserve an eternal present moment—perpetual movement within a moment that is itself perpetually present—the processes of creation, the poetic/artistic act revealed in the contemplation, reading, speculation on the apparently "finished" object offered up? In exploring the construction and functioning of other aspects of Albert-Birot's poetry and prose, an answer to

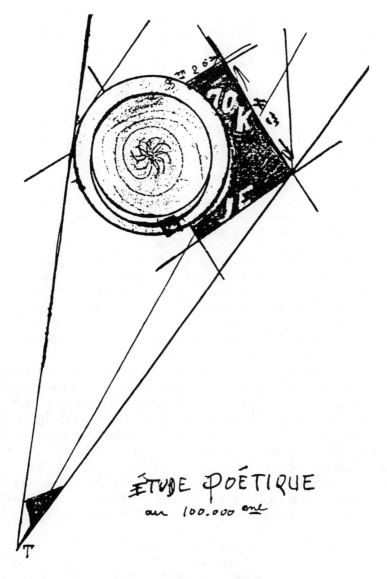

"Etude poétique au 100.00^{ème}," P. Albert-Birot, *Les Amusements Naturels*, p. 121.

this is sought.[19] First, however, Albert-Birot's almost trivialization of the change in mode of expression from painting to poetry needs some commentary. Serving to elaborate once again the poet's personal myth, Albert-Birot relates the sudden abandoning of the visual arts for a life dedicated to Poetry, a decision made after the execution of *La Guerre:*

> Un soir je me suis dit, pourquoi ne ferait-on pas de la peinture avec des formes géométriques comme le musicien compose avec des notes? J'ai réalisé un tableau abstrait sur la guerre, "essai d'expression plastique," et le lendemain j'ai tout vendu, chevalet, tubes de couleurs et pinceaux.[20]

> ("One evening I said to myself, why not make a painting with geometric forms just as a musician composes with notes? I completed an abstract painting on the war, 'attempt at plastic expression,' and the next day I sold everything, the easel, the tubes of color and the brushes.")

La Guerre is then a final statement—but on what exactly? Is this another manifestation of the rupture between the "old" artist and the "new" poet? An expression of the rupture and the healing of it? The creations that follow *La Guerre* manifest exactly the opposite. Creatively *La Guerre* is opening statement rather than conclusion. Theoretically also it is in the discourse of the visual arts that Albert-Birot expresses his aesthetics most consistently.

Like the projects for *SIC,* the theme and form of the painting that would become *La Guerre* of 1916 evolved slowly and had preoccupied the painter in sketches, drawings, and finally oils, for more than a year leading up to its completion in 1916. The early issues of *SIC* and these preliminaries for *La Guerre* are chronologically and artistically linked, for it is in the notebooks in which Albert-Birot prepared these issues of *SIC* that the sketches of spirals, helixes, triangles, and circles, which would eventually give form to the completed oil on canvas, are first to be found, interspersed with a number of aphorisms, not used in *SIC,* but of significance for the creative process here coming into being:

> N'obéir qu'à sa sensibilité
> = Anarchie. Or
> l'ordre est conséquence d'ordres.[21]

> ("Obeying only one's sensibility
> = Anarchy.
> Order is the result of orders.")

From potential chaos creation is a process of ordering through both intuition and intellect. Form is given through a structure that does not restrict

La Guerre by Pierre Albert-Birot. Photograph by Jacqueline Hyde, Paris. Reproduced courtesy of Madame Arlette Albert-Birot.

Sketch, P. Albert-Birot, Notebooks. Collected in *Pages Sans Titre*, editions hors commerce.

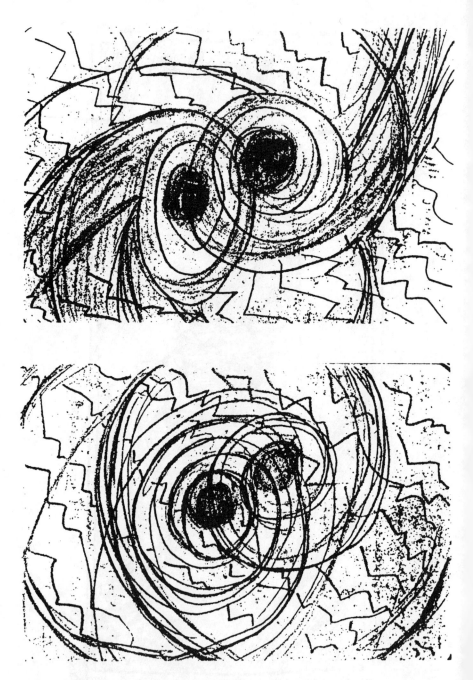

Sketches, collected in *Pages Sans Titre*, editions hors commerce.

(Style = Ordre) = Volonté

Art Ægyptien qui t'a fait? <u>VOLONTÉ</u>
Art Grec qui t'a fait? <u>VOLONTÉ</u>
Art Gothique qui t'a fait? <u>VOLONTÉ</u>
Arts Italien, Flamand, Espagnol qui vous a faits? <u>VOLONTÉ</u>

 Art Français qui t'a fait?

<u>VOLONTÉ</u>

Or que nous apportent la guerre et l'avant-garde cubiste et futuriste?

<u>VOLONTE</u>

𝒟onc:

guerre + cubistes + futuristes = volonté = (ordre = style)

guerre + cubistes + futuristes = style = art

guerre + cubistes + futuristes + x = <u>PROCHAINE</u>

<u>RENAISSANCE FRANÇAISE</u>

c. q. f. d.

"(Style = Ordre) = Volonté," *SIC*, nº 5, May 1916. Editions Jean-Michel Place, p. 34.

the dynamics of the original impulse, an attitude close to that of a maxim of Kandinsky: "La création est un libre jeu de forme et de moyens d'expression à l'intérieur de règles strictes.[22] ("Creation is a free game of form and of modes of expression inside strict rules.") *La Guerre* is not the final statement that Albert-Birot seems anxious to suggest, it is the beginning of every lesson of creation, a discourse on the conflict necessary in creativity—intuition and intellect, sensibility and workmanship, the marvelous and the everyday, the subconscious and reason, the unknown and the known, the intangible and the tangible.

La Guerre is war in every form, then—historical reality, moment of human conflict encapsulated on canvas with an underlying political, social, and ideological discourse. A personal challenge as the individual confronts his or her moment in history, in art, and in personal development, the setting up of a program of artistic creation at a moment of acute self-awareness, *La Guerre* is a key moment in Albert-Birot's creation and in contemporary culture. Where should the emphasis lie in our reading of it? In the course of this study, the relevance of this canvas shifts—for the reading of *SIC* the historical, ideological, and artistic statement of *La Guerre* takes precedence as Albert-Birot stands surrounded by his contemporaries and their debates. As the study develops through the poetry from *La Lune* to the *Poèmes à l'Autre Moi*, *La Guerre* must finally be read as a personal program, the moment of expression of artistic consciousness and self-awareness to which we are constantly returned. The moment is that which segregates one moment from the continuity of eternity and to which the poet constantly returns.

The Viewer Confronts the Canvas

To understand the structure and functioning of a set of complex, proliferating texts (as is the case for *Grabinoulor*) or of the complexity of an abstract canvas, the reader is faced by the same problems of hesitancy and ambiguity. Necessarily implicated in the object's re-creation, the reader/spectator must make a preliminary set of decisions concerning that object: "On a peint pour notre sentiment, on a peint pour nos sens, pourquoi ne peindrait-on pas pour notre intelligence?" ("We have painted for our feeling, we have painted for our senses, but why couldn't we paint for our intelligence?") (Notebooks for *La Guerre*). Albert-Birot here stresses the importance of the visual in all cognitive processes. The eye and the mind link the visible to the establishment of meaning, prefiguring Merleau-Ponty's *L'Oeil et l'esprit*, and returning us to creation as the establishment of order in potential chaos. The first task of the reader/viewer is, therefore, to define the object of analysis in a less ambiguous way (ambiguity being the mark of the modern artistic object in painting, poetry, and music). We propose to do this through what we have loosely termed a "visual poetics," the implication being that such a framework belongs not only to the theory and practice of the visual arts, for just as the boundaries between the arts have been breaking down since Romanticism onwards, so, too, must ways of approaching them.[23] A poetics is therefore understood as a theory of the way in which a text or canvas functions, though the visual here should not be understood in a mimetic sense—that is, that the text or canvas reflects "reality" or that we are primarily concerned with "imagery" here. A visual poetics here is one that reveals the structure of the text or of the canvas and the way in which meaning is constructed and produced.

In the analysis of *La Guerre,* we will be considering the coming into being of an individual imaginative space, and in more general terms the parallel artistic adventure of a modern space that will be revealed in Albert-Birot's painting, poetry, and narrative. The adventure of both painting and poetry throughout the first quarter of the twentieth century follows a route where the two constantly interact. In the techniques of deconstructing and reassembling *(analyse-synthèse),* in the presentation of the experience of simultaneity, in the attention to the effects of musical composition, and the privileging of the material over the object (originating in the poetry of Mallarmé particularly, systematized by painting and finally given back to poetry), these mutual concerns are worked over and over.[24]

The reception of any nonfigurative canvas poses an enigma from the outset. Albert-Birot's *La Guerre* obviously invites speculation on a possible narrative, given the thematic and ideological associations of a painting with such a title produced in 1916 by an artist/poet who had openly claimed to have found a new personal artistic freedom due to the political and historical situation:

Alors quand la guerre a éclaté ç'a été une grande révolution pour moi car instantanément, naturellement, du jour vraiment du jour au lendemain, je me suis vu libre . . . j'étais donc libre de moi-même, j'étais seul avec moi-même. . . . Pendant un an je me suis regardé, je me suis cherché, et j'ai été là en face de moi.[25]

("So when the war broke out it was a total revolution for me because instantaneously, naturally, from literally one day to the next, I found myself free . . . I was therefore freed from myself, I was alone with myself. . . . For a year I contemplated myself, I went in search of myself, and I was there face to face with myself.")

Nonetheless the presence of such a heavily connoted title directs the viewing/reading of such a message within common, shared human experience before any individual considerations. Theoretically the war becomes the first part of the equation that will establish the regeneration of France and of French art particularly (see page reproduced from *SIC*, n° 5, May 1916). Such a title also interacts with a myriad of other artistic creations celebrating or denigrating war in all its manifestations. The personal impact on Albert-Birot of Severini's exhibition "L'Art plastique de la Guerre" is undeniable. For the purpose of this study, we will, however, consider the connotations, both general and personal, of the work following the analysis of the structures of the work to provide as clear a reading of the work itself as possible. If "abstraction" is intensely subjective, the expression of this subjectivity can be apprehended only by rigorous analysis, just as true creation necessitates an ordering and *règles strictes*. These "rules" of creation and analysis are in no way limiting or stifling. Rather they allow both the creator and the reader/viewer a way of apprehending the conditions of creation. In the reception, as in the production, of such a work, Cendrars's formula of *analyse-sythèse* must function. We see here how the procedures elaborated by semiotics may prove revelatory in the apprehension of the modern work of art, ways to "decipher" and to posit possible "meanings," to offer a path for the cognitive processes.[26] However, possible meanings are attributable to the canvas by its title, its "name" signifying its presence in the historical moment. Albert-Birot's naming of it provides it with an artistic and cultural identity. Yet the reading of its "meanings" does not end there, for the reception of the work of art raises further questions on this relationship between naming and meaning, on painting and meaning, on painting and naming—on the relationship between *La Guerre* and the writing, both poetry and narrative, which are to follow it. The ways in which the semiotic procedure reads the work are fundamental to the approach adopted here and throughout this study of Albert-Birot's work:

On voit que la sémiotique visuelle ne fait pas sienne une lecture linéaire et continue des tableaux ou des photographies mais qu'elle essaie de mettre en place des procédures d'établissement du texte plastique en s'interrogeant sur la nature sémiotique des différents types de contiguïté (les "lisières" ou les "bords") ou de non-contiguïté (les "sauts anaphoriques" produits par les récurrences plastiques du même et de l'autre qui peuvent constituer une trame sur toute la surface plane du tableau). Ces organisations syntagmatiques peuvent ainsi rendre compte et des lectures orientées partielles et des saisies simultanées des formants ou des termes opposés d'une même catégorie dans le cas des contrastes.[27]

("It will be seen that visual poetics does not embrace a linear and continuous reading of paintings or photographs, but that it attempts to put in place ways of establishing the visual text by questioning the semiotic nature of different types of contiguity [the 'borders' or the 'edges'] or of noncontiguity [the 'anaphoric jumps' produced by the visual recurrences of the same figures and of other figures that may make up an interweave on the entire surface of the picture]. These syntagmatic organizations may therefore take into account readings of the forming figures or of the opposing terms of the same category in the case of contrasts, which are both partially oriented and simultaneous initial reaction.")

Contiguity and noncontiguity, linear and simultaneous reading—this method is applicable not only to the visual composition *La Guerre* but, as we will discover in the final chapter of this study, to the narrative form of *Grabinoulor.* Geometry plays a crucial role not only in the visual expression of cubism and abstraction but in writing as it seeks to express the enigma of the real and the problems of representation. Both the artist and the writer need forms and structures to transpose the apprehension of the real. Geometry also allows the structuring of the space of desire.

We will return to these ideas in our consideration of the imaginary space constructed in *Grabinoulor.* It is not our intention to analyze *La Guerre* as if this were a narrative.[28] Neither is it the aim of this chapter to present a technical semiotic analysis but rather to read *La Guerre* as an originating moment of a poetics when personal, historical, and cultural events coexist and come together to produce a work of art. Therefore while working within the framework offered by Floch, we intend to emphasize this canvas as a space where the program of this poetics is inscribed, a type of *mise en abyme* of the oeuvre as a whole.

THE CONSTRUCTION OF A POETIC SPACE: "AU MOYEN DES SEPT COULEURS ET DES DEUX LIGNES MÈRES LA DROITE ET LA COURBE"

We will begin our analysis of this space by focusing on the way in which the canvas is divided up by line (shape) and color. An initial division may be made between the right- and left-hand sides of the painting, with an important focal point in the upper center. The space can be divided into the visual oppositions of shape and the direction of these shapes: the large circular shape in the top center; the elongated triangular shapes pointing across and up that originate on the left-hand side; and the broader, flatter triangles that originate on the right. Further divisions are made by the series of bold, curved lines that reverberate across the canvas from the right, suggesting if not concentric, then certainly overlapping, circles. There is thus opposition between straight and curved lines, and this division is made more complex by three straight lines that divide the canvas into four unequal parts and radically fragment the lines and shapes within them. The whole, therefore, emerges in disruption and movement from the outset. An initial opposition is set up between rapid fragmentation and the more whole figure suggested by the large circular mass of gray in the top center, which contrasts most strongly with the sharp bright angles of the left-hand side triangles. There is movement in color as well as structure, with vibrant primary yellows, reds, and bright blues dominating this left-hand side, moving to dark blues, greens, browns, and finally grays and blacks on the more muted right-hand side. These are not blocks of color, but each shape is subdivided into complementary shades of that color, adding density to what would otherwise be flat planes. Each space is worked and reworked. The presence of the material, of matter, is the palpable expression of something more intangible.

An initial dynamism is motivated by these shapes (circular and triangular), which are not fully enclosed within the space of the canvas: The circles are not complete. The triangles appear to issue from an outside source, suggesting that the space of the painting is a point of convergence of elements originating from a space outside the canvas, rather than the canvas being offered as a closed, hermetically sealed, self-generating, and self-referential space. There is dialogue with and propulsion from outside sources. The initial opposition in shape, then, is between circle and triangle, between straight and curved lines, a geometrical representation that speaks of something other than itself. In color, too, there is an opposition between color and "noncolor" (gray, black, white), between a chromatism and an antichromatism, which also organizes the space of the painting, giving substance to the initial geometrical division. The initial impact, however, is that of a striking colorfulness—even more so when compared with other canvases of the period. This initial segmentation based on a binary opposition between forms allows us, then, to identify a primary set of units—right, left, and center—which are each themselves made up of smaller signifying units.[29]

The central section of the canvas where these forms meet is more troubling for this line of inquiry, because what appears to be a train of smoke, a recognizable figurative element, is introduced at the crucial point of contact and interaction between the abstract forms. This figurative element thus poses questions concerning the modes of representation and signification within the canvas. This is an essential challenge not only for this painting but for the way in which Albert-Birot constructs his entire poetic universe form this point onward. The initial hypothesis is that this space is a signifying whole and that the contrasting organization identifiable through the co-presence of opposing visual categories allows us to discuss a textual structure—in other words, that there is something to "read" beyond the initial apprehension of circle and triangle, curved and straight line. It is not only the meaning of a canvas that we are reading here but the main characteristics of Albert-Birot's work—the way in which the "poetic" space of *La Guerre* is constructed, assembled with the precision of geometry, and with the whole range of color from the primary colors and their mixtures, to the "noncolors" of black and white and their only outcome, gray, abstract and figurative expression, intense subjectivity and rigid logic, interaction between *l'imaginaire* and the real, the way poetry and prose in every form possible will be generated.[30]

If we compare *La Guerre* directly with the narrative of *Grabinoulor*, the structures of the two modes of expression initially appear to be totally incompatible, indeed, diametrically opposed. *La Guerre* is composed of divisions and limits, of fragments, of parts, hyperstructured without constructing a whole. *Grabinoulor* is an enormous and proliferating whole, constructed rather as a series of concentric circles that ripple out from the body of *Grabinoulor* to encompass the world, the universe, and beyond in space and time. Yet despite the absence of punctuation and the apparent opportunity for completeness, nondivision, the narrative is rigorously structured, a linear narrative, with chapters, chapter headings, volumes, rigorous syntax, and division upheld within its wholeness and "circularity." Furthermore, *Grabinoulor* is a continual juxtaposition of disparate elements, and it may be read through the functioning of the contiguity and non-contiguity of these elements, just as in the structures of *La Guerre*. The hypothesis, therefore, is that the tools of analysis for a visual structure will permit us to read a linear text and its unfolding space, and that a comparison between the two modes of expression may tell us something about the way in which the pictorial and the verbal function: straight line and circle—figures of the visual, figures of the narrative.

". . . LA DROITE ET LA COURBE"

Although one must insist on the autonomous nature of each canvas, the work must also be considered as one moment within the totality of the output of the artist during a certain period of his creativity.[31] The implication is that certain ways of working, certain problems or desires, certain ways of thinking of the world and its representation/re-creation, may traverse a number of paintings within a given time span.

The canvas under analysis here is created at a significant turning point in the history of Albert-Birot's artistic production. As has been previously pointed out, several of Albert-Birot's notebooks contain sketches, which reveal the amount of work that went into the structure of the final composition of *La Guerre* in oils. It has also previously been suggested that the dialectic between straight line and circle will also be a generator of dynamism in Albert-Birot's poetic constructions. In addition to the general symbolism of the masculine/feminine opposition and interaction, the forms are highly suggestive within the specific cultural and artistic framework of this moment in history. The Parisian skyline had been dominated since the last decade of the nineteenth century by the Eiffel Tower, and throughout the first years of the twentieth century a dialogue had been established between poetry and painting around this monument. For the 1900 Universal Exhibition, the Tower was joined by the "La Grande Roue." Thus circle and triangle interact in a physical, geographical space, and in a mythical space that is the Paris of poets and painters. This confrontation between *la droite et la courbe* is operating, therefore, in the poet's personal creative economy but at a limit of interaction with the cultural and historical moment. The obvious examples are the paintings of Robert Delaunay, who repeatedly turned to the Tower to explore his own medium, and some of whose paintings figure the Wheel and the Tower together. Of the poems, those by Apollinaire and Cendrars are particularly noteworthy. Around the Tower the battle of Old versus New rages, and it becomes the very symbol of modernity. The problem of capturing the essence of the Tower leads both poets and painters to reflect on the nature of the material and methods of creation, and *painting* the Tower and *writing* the Tower are revealed as very distinct practices despite the constant dialogue between the two.

Futurist theory had particularly explored the use of the simultaneous contrast of lines, planes, and forms, and Severini's 1913 Manifesto discusses these in the production of a "constructive interpretation in order to achieve a dynamic composition open in all directions towards space."[32] An obvious comparison can be made between the work of the futurist painters and Albert-Birot (see reproductions and references in the index of artworks reproduced). The dialectic between acute and obtuse angles and circles had been formulated by Carlo Carrà in his 1913 "Plastic planes as spherical expansion in space":

A pictorial composition constructed of right angles cannot go beyond what is known in music as plainchant (canto fermo). The acute angle, on the other hand, is passionate and dynamic, expressing will and a penetrating force. And the obtuse angle, as a geometrical expression, represents oscillation, the diminution of this will and force. Finally, a curved line has an intermediary function, and serves, together with the obtuse angle, as a link, a kind of transitional form between the other angles.[33]

This "language of lines," of forms, structures Albert-Birot's canvas, both a "surface" structure and, as we will discover, the expression of a deep structure underlying this canvas and the poetic production to follow.

The numerous sketches for *La Guerre* specifically and others dating from this same period clearly show the extent of Albert-Birot's fascination for spirals, *tourbillons*, helixes, and triangles, and an examination of these together reveals one of the methods of working that the painter/poet explored. Obviously the large canvas in oils is the culmination point of this "working out" of problems of the expression of form and theme. Among these sketches are pieces of a more complete nature: two ink drawings whose composition differs interestingly from the final oil canvas, and one of which appeared in *SIC* n° 5, May 1916 (JMP, p. 37) (see reproductions). The dating of these drawings can be made precise through reference to the notes made for the compilation of *SIC*. The figures here, particularly of the spiral, are taken up throughout Albert-Birot's creative production and function particularly as the expression of a dynamism that recurs in his work with insistent frequency.[34]

These "preliminary" sketches hold an equal status with the "finished" composition when considering the context of the work and are not to be considered as simply preparatory work. To constitute this "corpus" for the purpose of our analysis here, we have narrowed down the time span and the range of sketches to cover only those from the first notebook (*SIC* 3–7, ending in July 1916). The analysis of the sketches and ink drawings provides a possible reading of the "language" of the abstract canvas and facilitates an analysis of the deeper formal structures that function below the surface. The similarities and differences between the canvas and the two most complete ink drawings help to elucidate some of the ambiguity of the dialogue between triangle (obtuse and acute) and circle. A program can, therefore, be established to define both the construction of the space within the canvas and its focal point, which in turn organizes the flux and movement of the composition, allowing the viewer to follow the trajectory of the painting. In both drawings the nature of the circle is less ambivalent than on the canvas, a world in space occupying again the top center of the sketch. A number of triangles, half blank, half shaded, constitute the right-hand side, while one larger triangle of mainly plain surface and wider angle occupies the left. The meeting point (point of combat?) between the two sides of the drawings takes place in a space slightly below the circle, which appears in a more independent position within the dynamics of the forms. In drawing no. 1 (see our labeling), the element of "smoke" is to be found around the edge of the space, thus containing it. This sketch is on the whole of a more "figurative" tendency—clouds of smoke parting to reveal the drama between opposing forces as they move across the background of a black void to meet. The language of forms created here is not a complex one and offers itself to an immediate apprehension by the observer. In drawing no. 2, where the forms are more stylized, the most obviously figurative and referential element is replaced by a zigzag line (although perhaps still connotative of lightning), which suggests rather a dynamic force with more emphasis on this formally. The key to the composition of the forms themselves lies in sketches that precede these more complete expressions. One sketch particularly denoted by Albert-Birot as "En tristesse" is composed of flat, broad, obtuse triangular shapes similar to those found on the right-hand side of the ink drawings. In direct opposition, "Gaieté" is expressed by a sunlike circle radiating long, curling waves of energy in the sketches reproduced here.

The circle shape in the ink drawings has no such irradiating qualities—suggesting once again an analogy with the earth as opposed to the sun. However, these wavy lines are present here in the triangles. The long masses of wavy lines are to be found on one side of the acute, elongated triangles on the left-hand side, each one being composed partly by a flat, plain surface and partly by these densely interwoven lines. If *tristesse* is expressed by broad, flat, plain forms, and *gaieté* or energy in the form of such curling lines, then the acute triangles contain a paradox to some extent: a cohabitation between negative and positive forces. They are at once dynamic energy and a possible denial of that energy. Similarly on the oil canvas, the triangles are made up of colors that simultaneously suggest life, energy, positivism, and their opposites. The color opposition takes place between the sides of the canvas, the far right-hand sides being varying shades of gray, and within the forms themselves, each made up of bright and muted color, contrasting tones.

In both ink drawings, the obtuse triangle is largely composed of a plain white surface with less and less defined lines on the top part. Its composition and shape suggest a less dynamic presence than the acute, densely drawn forms on the left. In drawing no. 2, the more stylized formation, these shapes moving in from the left reach the central part of the sketch and begin to move across into the right-hand section as in the final canvas. The void so apparent in the first, more figurative sketch is virtual obscured by these forms. This is also true of the canvas where the space is composed entirely of these fragmented triangular shapes. It may be suggested, therefore, that the left-hand side of the sketches promotes a dynamic, life-giving, positive force, which nonetheless exists only in counterbalance to its opposite—the triangles having each a dual nature within themselves, each one being a microcosm of creation and

Sketch for *La Guerre*, P. Albert-Birot (AM1927642), Notebooks. Collected in *Pages Sans Titre*, editions hors commerce. India ink, 30 x 13 cm.

Sketch for *La Guerre*, P. Albert-Birot (AM1977650). Collected in *Pages sans titre*, editions hors commerce. Also reproduced in *SIC*, n° 5, May 1916. Editions Jean-Michel Place, p. 37, entitled "Essai d'Expression Plastique," "Guerre".

of life itself. These forms seek to oppose forms where the negative aspects of their existence are almost solely in evidence, filling as they do so the void of nothingness, noncreation, nonexistence.

We have identified in the sketches an opposition not immediately discernible on the canvas where the dialectic between acute and obtuse is less defined structurally but exists, initially articulated by color. These forms are not whole, but fragmented and delineated by brown and black/white lines and are, therefore, separate blocks of color, the canvas being constituted not only by this formal structure but by chromatic construction also.

". . . LES SEPT COULEURS"

Albert-Birot's concern with the chromatic structure of the canvas places him within the current of modern art from the Fauves onward. Color had been the preoccupation of the Fauves in an attempt to render not an imitative use of color but an expressive one, a use of color that would cause a reaction between spectator and canvas. Color continues to have a "suggestive" function, a symbolic, connotative function, but its use also becomes structural.[35] Art criticism has, however, tended to neglect the structural aspects of color, its "présence concrète," and to concentrate on its symbolism. Yet it is in color that we seize most closely the very gesture of the painter:

> La couleur est en effect l'ultime constituant de la peinture. *C'est en elle que prend naissance l'acte de peindre.* Considérée de tout temps comme inséparable de *l'expérience du peintre,* elle a été néanmoins de tout temps marginalisée dans la lecture du tableau.[36]

> ("Color is in fact the ultimate constituent of painting. It is in color that the act of painting is born. Always considered inseparable from the painter's experience, it has nonetheless always been marginalized in the reading of paintings.")

The experience of the creative artist and the act of creation are constantly worked and reworked throughout Albert-Birot's poetry and narrative. *La Lune* is the product of the poet/artisan. *Les Poèmes à l'Autre Moi* is an exploration of the creative self and the moment it is made sublime in the poetic act. Adam seeks to understand the new creation by which he is surrounded, incessantly in *Grabinoulor,* proliferating in its quest for knowledge of the ultimate act of creation: "chaque tableau sera un temps de la création du monde en création perpétuelle."[37] ("each painting will be a moment of the creation of the world in perpetual creation.") We might add that every text, every poem, will be a world in perpetual creation.

André Lebois has indicated the place of color in Albert-Birot's poetry and, in particular, as the title suggests, in *La Joie des sept couleurs* (1917), where a kaleidoscope of colors, of light and life, are celebrated in the joy of creation.[38] Jean Follain also stresses the luminescent quality of Albert-Birot's work, the effect of light being perhaps more evident than an attention to color: "Prose et poésie chez Albert-Birot ont l'apparence plus lumineuse que colorée: les couleurs souvent ne s'y affirment pas trop violemment, mais se conjugent, se fondent dans l'émerveillement de la lumière.[39] ("In Albert-Birot's work prose and poetry have an appearance that is more luminous than colored. Colors are often not defined too violently, but combine, fuse together in the wonder of light.") The use of color in Albert-Birot's theater frequently performs a symbolic function, for example, in *Matoum et Tévibar* where Matoum "le vrai poète" diffuses light and color when he speaks his poetry. Many of Albert-Birot's indications for decor, costumes, and staging directions rely on the effects of light, particularly important for creating the atmosphere of the drama rather than imposing "realistic" sets and thereby conferring a mimetic value on dramatic production.

It is the sensitivity to the effects of color and light that places Albert-Birot's artistic sensibility closer to the Orphism of Delaunay than to the more analytical cubism of an early Braque or Picasso and invites an analogy once more with Severini and Balla. Dora Vallier explores the "code" of the cubist palette usually neglected in the attention given to form by art critics: "Sans la couleur il n'y aurait pas de forme, et il faut ajouter, la forme est avant tout couleur.[40] ("Without color there would be no form, and it must be added, form is above all color.") She goes on to argue for the meaning of color in the choice of the limited palette of Braque and Picasso, particularly, and the attention paid to space in their canvases—black, white, gray, allowing a "fixed" space whereas the "mobile" combinations of the primary colors and their mixes are not stable: "J'ai senti que la couleur pourrait donner des sensations qui troublent un peu l'espace et c'est pour cela que je l'ai abandonnée."[41] ("I felt that color could render sensations that slightly trouble space and that is why that I abandoned it.") There is sensation and movement, mobility, "la joie des sept couleurs." Albert-Birot's construction through line and shape follows cubist analytical technique—but far from being troubled by the sensations produced by color, it is this that is desired. Delaunay's approach to simultaneity was based on his work with color, and essentially color stands at the border between the external and the internal world:

Pour Delaunay, le simultané était en même temps son inspiration, sa perception de la vie, mais aussi le métier, ce avec quoi il travaillait, les couleurs et les contrastes. Dans ce jeu de substitution image (perception sensuelle)—couleurs, il y a évidemment la possibilité de toutes sortes d'interactions entre le monde intérieur du poète. . . . Tout le jeu miroitant de leurs contrastes reflètent le sens d'une rencontre de deux simultanéités, celle infinie du monde, et celle, qui essaie d'en être le microcosme, de la subjectivité du poète.[42]

("For Delaunay the simultaneous was at once his inspiration, his perception of life, but also the craft, that with which he worked, colors and contrasts. In the game of image (sensual perception)—color substitution, there is evidently the possibility of all sorts of interactions between the internal world of the poet. . . . The whole shimmering game of their contrasts reflecting the sense

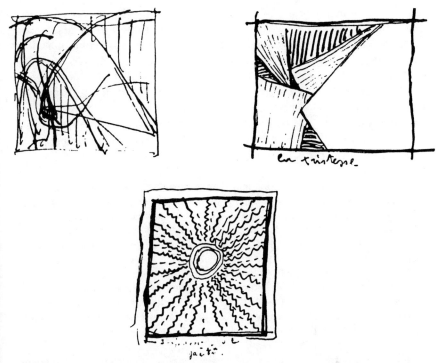

Sketches, P. Albert-Birot, "En Tristesse" and "Gaieté," Notebooks; collected in *Pages Sans Titre*, **editions hors commerce.**

of a meeting between two simultaneous moments, that of the infinity of the world, and of that which tries to be its microcosm, the poet's subjectivity.")

In Delaunay's work color introduced a modern lyricism. Color is not only an element of a symbolic nature, it also structures the universe of the work of art as it functions at the borderline between the internal and the external. We return to the "bords," to what happens at the limits. If Matoum is the true poet, it is because he is able to stand at the border between the two while his poetic vision is conferred on all those around him. Matoum's poetry confers light and life, and he is painter as much as poet, transforming all around him, as does the poet in Albert-Birot's own "poème-affiche" (see reproduction from *La Lune ou le livre des poèmes*, p. 204). Form is color, then, and color is painting, for painting is the observation of the relationships between colors just as the relationships between words are the material of the poet: "Il n'y a pas de couleur fixe, tout est couleur par contraste, tout est couleur en mouvement, tout est profondeur."[43] ("There is no fixed color, all is color by contrast, all is color in motion, all is depth.") Such a declaration brings to mind the description of the kaleidoscope offered by André Lebois in his discussion of Albert-Birot's work to which we previously referred. In echo, in reflection of the art of the period, *La Joie des sept couleurs* and *Grabinoulor,* in turn, are never still, and such a dynamism runs through all of Albert-Birot's creation. Thus *La Guerre* stands as the basis of, the reflection of, and the constant visual point of reference to the poetic work. Within the canvas the seven colors of the spectrum—the field of perception of the human eye—are present: red, orange, yellow, green, blue, indigo, and violet, the colors with which it is possible to create:

> Chacune correspond à une longueur d'onde d'après sa saturation lumineuse et toutes ensemble délimitent le champ perceptif. En deçà du rouge et au-delà du violet, l'oeil ne voit rien, et comme la disposition de ces couleurs à l'intérieur du spectre est invariable et hiérarchique—allant de la plus lumineuse (le rouge) à la moins lumineuse (le violet)—le champ perceptif tout entier renvoie d'une part vers la lumière et de l'autre vers l'obscurité, c'est à dire vers la qualité différentielle première, celle-là même qui se réduit aux traits + et − , et à travers ce double renvoi, la gamme chromatique tout entière indique la place respective du blanc et du noir, tout en les excluant. Ainsi se dessine une dichotomie fondamentale chromatique—achromatisme, couleurs—non couleurs, qui précise le principe de spatialisation agissant dans la peinture.[44]

> ("Each color corresponds to a wave length according to its light saturation and all together they make up our field of perception. On this side of red and on that side of violet the eye sees nothing, and since the disposition of these colours inside the spectrum is invariable and hierarchical—going from the brightest (red) to the least bright (violet)—our entire field of perception goes on the one hand from light and on the other to darkness, that is to say from the fundamental quality differential, that which can be reduced to the symbols + and − , and through this double return, the whole chromatic range indicates the respective places of black and white, while at the same time excluding them. This is how a fundamental chromatic dichotomy—achromatism, colors—non-colors, which is the principle of spatialization acting in painting, comes into being.")

The range of colors and the human capacity to perceive them, the limits of human knowledge, light and dark, the limits of human experience, known and unknown—the quest of Albert-Birot's poetic project is here inscribed. Every color of the rainbow, and therefore all possibilities together, with black, white, and gray all present, basic material of creation, matter, is to be given form and expression.[45] Is the gray of the circle of *La Guerre* to be transformed to pink by the poet, as in the "poème-affiche"? Having explored the presence of this color system, we must now try to understand its language, its meaning within the constructed universe of the painter/poet: "La peinture étant un langage beaucoup plus formalisé, beaucoup plus matérialisé, les constituants du sens y sont d'autant plus saisissable: ils sont visibles dans le fonctionnement de la couleur."[46] ("Since painting is a language which is much more formalized, much more material, the constituents of meaning are much more readily grasped. They are visible in the way color functions.")

READING THE CANVAS: THE ESTABLISHMENT OF A POETICS

The analysis of the constituent units of the whole work leads to the essential apprehension of a manifestation of thematic content, which together make up the expression of the work of art. The identification of shape and color in the composition provides a number of categories with which to read the work: curved/straight; acute/obtuse; plain/shaded (wavy line in the ink drawings); bright/muted colors; bright/gray chromatic categories; wholeness/fragmentation, which all function to constitute the deep level of expression. At this point we may extend our reading beyond the limits of the object under analysis to an exploration of the ways in which the artist, either in the visual arts or in literature, arrives at a language that expresses the most intense moment of that creation, the expression of a subjectivity.[47] *La Guerre* is to be considered as an autobiographical statement, an expression of the self that constantly will be explored by Albert-Birot in his poetic creation.

Our investigation has been concerned so far with the "surface" level of the work, the relationships and combinations of the forms between themselves. On the deeper structural level, the functioning of the forms, these sharp-edged, acute shapes, suggests discontinuity, division; their pointed, penetrating shape is of the immediate, the instant, the triangles susceptible to further and further fragmentation in the broad lines of the canvas's construction. Color also is applied in segments, again connoting fragmentation and discontinuity and making that fragmentation tangible. The circle and the curved lines that reverberate repeatedly across the canvas are the largest single form, and the presence of the curved line looms vast, an imposing continuous presence. In linear terms, in the opposition between the short, straight lines of the segmented elements and the continuous, curved line that constitutes the circle, there again appears to be a correlation between discontinuous and continuous, the immediate moment and the eternal, the incessantly fragmented and that which constantly endures.

The central part of the canvas is the meeting place of the circle and the triangles "moving in" from right and left. The spectator's eye is drawn initially to this point of convergence, large, solid, concrete gray, texturized, the material worked and reworked. This is one of the two figures that may be "read" immediately, the other being the trail of dense gray/ green smoke that stretches across this central section. The title of the painting and the dating of it incorporated into the canvas justify an initial reading of its being somehow "representative" symbolically of its histori- cal period, the canvas being a product of the first truly global war. The representative nature of these two figures implies a connection with the immediate connotations of the title and a first "meaning" for the work as a whole, a mode of representation of the external world in its historical moment. Alternatively, this may be read in a more abstract way, repre- senting a figure of rupture in the canvas.

In his analysis of Kandinsky's composition, Floch identifies a struggle between "negative" and "positive" forces as a structuring element func- tioning within the canvas. In a general cultural/historical context, a read- ing of Albert-Birot's canvas within these opposing terms is the one that springs most readily to the mind of an observer situated near the close of the twentieth century. Particularly from our historical viewpoint, with the knowledge of the destruction of two World Wars and living with the threat of nuclear war and global conflagration, Albert-Birot's composition would suggest an articulation of both a personal and a universal discourse, a confrontation between positive and negative forces at work in human existence. Yet there is a constant ambivalence with *La Guerre*, which precludes any easy deciphering. There is, for example, no precise color or form opposition between the forces of the two sides of the canvas.[48] The colors are mainly bright, and it is the circle, connotative of the world, that is uniformly gray. The initial division of the canvas has thrown up a series of possibilities: oppositions between shapes, some color opposi- tion, elements of a figurative reference, and elements of an abstract lan- guage of ambiguous nature. The triangle itself is an ambivalent figure in Albert-Birot's work. Inverted it may be a symbol of female sexuality— for example, in the "Poèmes à la chair" in *Grabinoulor*. In *La Guerre* it suggests dynamic, penetrative, aggressive masculine forces.[49] In his analysis of Kandinsky's expression, Floch identifies a mythical discourse and a "discours visuel ancien" belonging not solely to the artist's particu- lar created universe. Certainly the forms used by Albert-Birot in *La Guerre* are ones that resonate with a symbolism rooted in human con- sciousness. There is a thematic discourse and a plastic, visual discourse of line and color, and it is between the two that the poetic discourse may be apprehended. To understand how this discourse functions, the semiotic manifestation of its dynamics should be analyzed, the differences and the relations between opposing elements, and therefore the movement in the "text." The initial articulations of meaning within a semantic universe may be made visible by the use of the semiotic square.[50] The suggestion is that there is a narrative at work within the abstract composition, which may be read, having apprehended its language, not as a "comme si" reading by reference to the external but as its internal meaning.

If we consider Albert-Birot's canvas through the opposing poles of life and death (as suggested by the curved line/straight line opposition and as implied by the title) and their converse positions nonlife/nondeath, it is possible to establish a narrative that constructs such a semisymbolic term of reference for this personal artistic moment. It has previously been suggested that the opposition between discontinuity/continuity and immediacy/duration allows us to place the work within a perspective of the dynamism of the present moment, which is to be celebrated as creation comes into being in that moment of movement and speed. Yet a greater artistic goal would be the recuperation of that present, to make it endure as an eternal moment. This double-focused relationship with time is upheld by the artist's own attitude toward the new, the dynamic, and the energy of the avant-garde's experimentation to achieve simultaneity of expression and to render the multiplicity of their modern life experience. On the other hand, the presence of the circle indicates a yearning for a transcendence of the moment, which is thereby rendered eternal. The forces of the immediate and the eternal produced visually here will become the very basis of Albert-Birot's poetics, as we will discover particularly intensely in the *Poèmes à l'Autre Moi* and in *Grabinoulor*. The canvas, an enclosed space whose elements are simultaneously perceptible for the viewer, allows us to juxtapose in space and time this meeting of opposites. The dynamics of a creation that may be intuitively felt and that is frequently commented on in the poetry is here made visible. This is where the dialogue between poetry and painting becomes most pertinent and most essential.

To return to a circuit of life/death opposites and converses, a further symbolic reading may be deciphered moving on from, or rather deeper into, this time opposition, between duration and fragmentation. *La Guerre* may also be read as the visible manifestation of Albert-Birot's own artistic moment, coinciding, of course, with artistic trends of the time, but the canvas is foremost an autobiographical statement. The semiotic square provides a representation of our hypothesis:

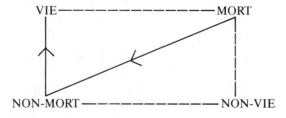

The circuit we have proposed is a classic one of revolt.[51] Albert-Birot has been artistically "dead" during the early years of the twentieth century, unable to find an outlet for his creative desires, unreceptive to new ideas, cut off from the artistic circles where such ideas are generated. Gradually through the contact with others (particularly Germaine and then Severini), he moves to the position of "non-mort," not yet fulfilling his capabilities, but experiencing an awakening. We should remember the title of his first long poem *De la mort à la vie*. It is significant that while painting the two portraits of Germaine that he "comes to life." In the final movement and through the painting of *La Guerre* as an historical event and a personal artistic expression, and then in the creation of *SIC*, he is brought fully to life. The affirmation of the title of the literary review is literally that of life, his (re)-birth to which he constantly refers, a moment of intense artistic, emotional, and social activity. *SIC* and *La Guerre* both proclaim positivity over negation, life over death, and the elements of the canvas and their relationships within it are the founding moment of a poetics, the origin of this fundamental dialectic over whose chasm the poet will continue to leap. The visual expression of this dialectic allows a crystallization, a definition of a mixture of impulses that finally combine at this particular historical and personal moment. These intellectual and physical (poetic, painterly, artisanal) drives are given an embodiment that is at once corporeal and immediate while making a statement on the eternal nature of Art.

We have, therefore, arrived at a reading of the narrative underlying this "abstract" composition, although, as has been demonstrated, the term "abstract" is a misleading one. Indeed Albert-Birot himself expressed his dissatisfaction with the label. His own understanding of such paintings was one of the intensification of the presence of the subject. Therefore it is a contradictory term. A better description here certainly is nonfigurative. A denial of imitation and of mimetic impulses in artistic creation is close to Albert-Birot's early maxims in *SIC* and to his general theorizing on the visual arts.[52]

The search for the expression of movement and the apprehension of the present moment in Albert-Birot's canvas may be perceived as more than a futurist-inspired attempt to render a dynamism. Albert-Birot's "poetic motivation" is articulated on two levels. The analysis of *La Guerre* returns us to, and reinforces, therefore, our initial intuitions concerning this visual expression of an intense personal moment of self-definition as an artist, and a program for a lifetime of poetic creation, to answer the dilemmas here articulated.

FROM *LA GUERRE* TO *SIC* AND INTO A POETIC ADVENTURE

The consideration of this deeper structure of the work offers some readings of the ambiguities we have perceived at the surface level. The immediacy of the moment, which we have suggested is the deeper-level significance of the triangular form, is double-sided between energy and inertia and existence and the void. The present moment injects a dynamism into the course of time—it may then be destroyed and lost. It enters partially the eternal circle but does not pierce or destroy it. Rather the dynamic moment may be recuperated by the enduring. The concentric circles that move across the canvas subsume the immediate moment. No matter now many times repeated, it becomes finally part of the duration. Therefore on the surface level and in a perspective offered by the title, the relationship between the forms is one of opposition, combat, and conflict. A reading with a reference to a social and historical reality outside the canvas may be effected as may be a reading of the nature of the evolution of art itself and, in particular, the trajectory of all avant-gardes.

At the deeper level, the spatial structure of the canvas reveals a construction, structuralization in time. It remains, therefore, in our analysis of Albert-Birot's poetry and prose work to discover whether spatial forms function in a similar way and whether there is a correlation to be made between the functioning of time (present moment/the eternal) on the canvas and its expression in the written word, before we can read *La Guerre* as a founding moment in Albert-Birot's creative adventure and as a complex expression of his attitude toward the nature of the work of art and of art itself.

We would suggest that *La Guerre* is an expression of time in a visual composition working within the poles of duration and fragmentation, the limits of a poetic discourse. The composition expresses the dynamics of the present moment, both in the historical context of the war and in the artistic expression of that moment, the two an instant in history. The moment is at once a part of the unfolding, eternal movement of time and a break in that movement. The eruption of the war into history and of the avant-garde into artistic history injects a dynamism into the course of events. In 1916 it is a breaking point, a possibility for regeneration, and it occupies the foreground of the canvas. In the course of time, it is a moment assimilated into a greater totality, suggested by the reverberations of the circles that move across and encompass the dynamic shapes. The canvas is at once a celebration of the moment, of its energy and possibility, and an awareness of its nature as fragmentary, a fleeting moment in eternity. The dual nature of time and of events either historical or artistic is presented visually in their structures of continuity and discontinuity.

The canvas equally presents through its "motivation poétique" the entrance of the individual human moment that is the artist/poet into time. The self enters the flux of history; the poetic self enters into an enduring artistic history. We would suggest that Albert-Birot's quest, no different from that of other writers, is to make his individual mark endure, to give both his moment in time that interrupts the duration and the fragmented temporality of his existence a positive value. At the same time, he embarks on a personal and artistic adventure, again constantly reiterated by writers and painters, toward a discovery of his origins, the acceptance of and assimilation into an archaic past that is made eternally present by the work of art. Thus the ambiguous nature of innovation within any experimentation by the avant-garde is revealed. *La Guerre* already intimates that after the frenzied, outward, social activity of the war years, the poet will turn inward to explore a sense of self and a personal conception of divinity and the eternal in the *Poèmes à l'Autre Moi* and in *Grabinoulor.*

Albert-Birot has a keen sense of his historical and artistic moment.[53] And we arrive within this awareness of history and of the passage of time, at a basic principle of his poetics, that is, how to confer a lasting value on this present moment. A fragment of existence must be assimilated into the whole and yet retain its individuality. This is the experience that commentators on Albert-Birot have tended to identify as a desire to make the present moment eternal, describing the "perpetual movement"—for example, in the narrative of *Grabinoulor*—as an attempt to resist the fixing of the moment in time. Our reading of the deep structure of *La Guerre* suggests a more complex relationship to time, and this is one we will explore further in our reading of the movement of that prose narrative in our final chapter.

Within a poetics of dynamism, energy, optimism, and exuberance, as Albert-Birot's work is frequently described, the constant movement within the text of *Grabinoulor,* the dynamism of a present moment that is perpetually renewed, is then made "eternal" through its expression in artistic form. Yet this relationship between creator, work, and time appears facile within a reading of the deeper structure of continuity and discontinuity that has been uncovered. Furthermore the relationship between creator and creation is complex. Albert-Birot, constantly reworking his personal creation myths, assumes a moment within his own poetic universe, which is then set against time. In this perspective his quest is more Proustian than a futurist-inspired celebration of the present. Similarly the *Poèmes à l'Autre Moi* and *Grabinoulor* project a poetic self within the time of the work, which is projected into and yet protected against human time—again a Proustian quest.

The canvas is "creation" made visible, the "invisible" and the "indicible" are given an embodiment; "impalpabilités" are given form. *La Guerre* makes manifest an artistic striving to create—its original impulse. The process of creation itself also is explored; a new creation is produced and inserted into the movement and into history. From its position in the present moment, it summons its origins and looks to the future simultaneously. The date, 1916, is that which Albert-Birot sets for his own mythological rebirth. *La Guerre* is also the birth of Albert-Birot's myths of creation. A world has come into being: "chaque tableau sera un temps de la création du monde en création perpétuelle." An artistic identity has come into being to create perpetually. Creation and identity—the adventure of the individual—unfolds as a whole universe comes into being and the processes of that creation are further revealed. Because identity is in flux, so is the creation that strives to give it form within time also in flux. Albert-Birot's poetic adventure is one in movement between artistic tradition and new forms of expression. It is equally a poetics of movement constantly seeking to render the being of the individual and the nature of his relationship to the universe.

2

Pierre Albert-Birot, *SIC*, and the Avant-Garde: Collective Adventure and Voyage of Self-Discovery

On commence à comprendre la nécessité du moderne, mais c'est l'avant-garde qu'il faut.

—Pierre Albert-Birot, Notebooks (unpublished)

("We are beginning to understand the necessity of the modern, but what is needed is the avant-garde.")

L'avant-garde en art c'est revenir aux principes de base. Ils sont très simples et peu nombreux. Déplaisent aux gens qui se piquent de science.

—Robert Pinget, *Du Nerf*

("The avant-garde in art is a return to basic principles. These are very simple and few in number. And rather disagreeable to those who think they are very learned.")

SIC AS PERSONAL PROGRAM AND SOURCE DOCUMENT

PREVIOUS studies have, as a matter of course, included reference to *SIC* either as a theoretical and creative outlet for Albert-Birot or as a voice of the avant-garde of the First World War period, particularly as a disseminator of futurist ideas in France.[1] On the whole, however, these references to *SIC* have remained just that—reference to, rather than a deeper questioning of the importance of, the magazine as a starting point for Albert-Birot's literary output and its relevance both historically and artistically in the wider context of the period. This chapter is concerned with Albert-Birot as founder and editor of this literary journal, published regularly from January 1916 to December 1919 and comprising fifty-four issues.[2] It is our intention here to outline some of the major aspects of the journal that we consider essential for a reading of the development of Albert-Birot's creative output from painting to poetry. It is in *SIC* that the early poems and the first chapter of *Grabinoulor* find their audience; it is in *SIC* that the poet finds his poetic voice and a mode of speaking with which to communicate with the world outside himself; and it is in *SIC* that the poet/editor establishes a role with which to function in the collective space and seeks an integration with the artistic adventure of the period. *SIC* is fundamental in the establishment of the identity of Albert-Birot at this time, an identity carried forward into fifty years of poetic creation. The journal is equally instrumental in the establishment of the poet's more theoretical concerns and allows him to contribute critically and analytically to the debates of these years. *SIC* therefore permits us to situate its creator more clearly within the pervading artistic climate and in relation to the activities of the avant-garde while simultaneously outlining the beginnings of his intensely individual creative production.[3]

However, in addition to its status here as a personal program, any literary journal is a communicative medium in its own right and is for literary analysis an authentic source document.[4] Thus it necessitates a different approach to its content from that of an analysis of those same poems and paintings grouped together within a collection. Theory, creation, reflection, review, and criticism are generated side by side. There is continued interaction between a multiplicity of artistic objects and the reactions they engender rather than their isolation in a collected works by one creator. The production of a literary journal involves energies from many directions. The reception, the reading experience, is therefore also a very different one: the reading, looking at, handling of these creations by diverse poets and painters allows a participation in a piece of cultural and literary history. The interaction from page to page between poetry, reproductions of paintings and woodcuts, musical compositions, theoretical considerations, interviews, and so on allows a very different perception of the notion of synthesis between the arts, which was a major tenet of "modernity" and of "l'esprit nouveau."[5] The dynamic *action* of these creations is displayed here with much greater impact than any amount of theorizing on the aims of the futurists or the cubists.[6] It is a focusing on the *act* of creating an artistic program by making, fabricating an object that comes into being periodically, constantly changing shape and tone, constantly dialoguing with itself and the exterior. Poets, painters, sculptors, and musicians contribute both creative pieces and critical comment. Most importantly, *SIC* provides the opportunity to study these short works in terms of their context, thus providing a solution to the problem of re-creating the ideological environment necessary for an understanding of such texts.[7] Its program is a statement on the arts during this period and a contribution to its moment in history. Albert-Birot's

choices as editor reveal a general aesthetic discourse. *SIC* allows an interaction between all the arts—poetry, painting, theater, music, sculpture
("sons, idées, couleurs, formes," the program of its title).

We have previously discussed the gestation period of *SIC*, the changes
from earlier projects to the first issues of *SIC*, and Albert-Birot's birth in
modernity with the journal. This sudden revelation and "rebirth" has, as
we have already said, served Albert-Birot's personal myth, celebrating
the dramatic change of direction and the entry into the modern world.
The reality of the situation reveals a slowly unfolding series of events,
although Albert-Birot's later accounts constantly reiterate the importance
of *SIC* for his identity at the time.[8] An analysis of the "life" of the journal
permits us to trace the development and self-affirmation of the poet/
editor, the concerns of *SIC* reflecting the parallel development of an individual artistic/poetic production within the collective. An assessment of
the role of the journal allows us also a consideration of Albert-Birot's
contribution to twentieth-century literary history and opens up a questioning on the nature of "modernity," a simplification applied to multifaceted concepts and productions. Yet it is difficult to find an adequate
discourse and a theoretical framework with which to provide such an
assessment. A set of criteria developed to consider types of theoretical
documents by both artists and critics as source material is used here as
a guideline for the study of the literary review since the points made
appear to be applicable. Such documents should be studied with the following in mind:

1. The general cultural context of the age and, in particular, those ideas
   and theories of greatest interest to the artist, whether they come
   from science, history, literature, or social theory, or from other
   periods of art.
2. The specific ideological milieu in which the writer formulated and
   tested his own ideas and thoughts, such as his circle of friends and
   acquaintances and his contacts with critics, poets, and writers.[9]

The first of these criteria we have broadly outlined in our presentation
of Albert-Birot's development up to 1915 and the contacts he made then.
Some comment must be made on the effect of the war on the art of the
period and on the intellectual and moral climate in which it was produced.
However, because it is not our aim here to discuss the avant-garde as a
concept from a theoretical or historical viewpoint, this will be kept to
the minimum necessary for an understanding of certain aspects of *SIC*'s
discourse. The influences from 1916 onward will become clear in our
analysis of the contributors and contributor/collaborators of *SIC* and of
the group around Albert-Birot at the time involved in such events as the

staging of *Les Mamelles de Tirésias*. The further possible criteria for the
analysis of a source document continue:

3. The medium through which the ideas were transmitted insofar as
   is considered the intellectual and emotional attitude the writer
   assumed in addressing a specific audience: his choice of language,
   his logicality or absence of it, and perhaps even the kind of
   ideas chosen.
4. The writer's personal qualification as a theoretician, as they (his
   ideas) may be conditioned by both his education and his past
   experience with ideas, and his present attitude toward the written
   or spoken word as a means of conveying intentions.[10]

The medium of the magazine allows Albert-Birot such an "intellectual
and emotional" response both to what he considered to be the journal's
needs and aims and those of his own creativity. *SIC* and the early work
engender and nurture each other in turn. The rhetoric of the early issues,
certainly revealing in the visual style and choice of language a reading of
futurism newly discovered, loudly addresses his Parisian audience and
those at the front with patriotism and belligerence. *SIC* is in every sense
originally a review of combat, on the front line of the defense of modernism from the right-wing backlash given ammunition by historical events,
and at the forefront of promoting a new French art, which, it was believed,
would emerge vigorous from the conflict.[11] Nonetheless after these early
issues, the choice of creative contributions, ideas, and tone, and indeed
appearance, serve to underline the changing role of the magazine. Finally,
SIC reveals an Albert-Birot who is a less convincing theoretician than
creative artist. Apart from a talent for aphorisms that he was able to
work into his poetry from time to time, his theorizing is often naive
and lacking in true critical perception. Certainly his education and past
experience had not equipped him for the elaboration of a critical discourse, and his relationship to art is best communicated in his creative
productions themselves. It is the creative activity of *SIC* that we hope to
explore here, and while working within its avant-garde label, to avoid the
dogmatism such labeling often gives rise to. *SIC* is thus Albert-Birot's
expression of and contribution to "modernity" within the context of the
avant-garde,[12] and his approach to this idea of the value of the modern is
more complex than the early polemical tone influenced certainly by the
futurists and by the general climate of the war, which had roused patriotic
feelings among the French avant-garde as much as in the discourse of the
establishment. The first issues do, however, situate Albert-Birot in relation to the forms of artistic expression that marked the beginnings of the
century. The role of *SIC* is, therefore, multiple. It is the manifestation of

a critical discourse finding its way, a personal thought process in movement, considering, accepting, and refusing the artistic ferment around it, an artistic production in movement seeking principles and forms, accepting or refusing, and above all beginning to create. The journal is the crystalization of the talent of the sculptor, painter, and nascent poet, the jubilation of the multifaceted artist that allows him to find an identity and to situate himself with relationship to others, the exploration of the multiplicity of possible forms of expression. *SIC* is the place of beginnings, of an artistic life and, therefore, of conflicts, but above all of potential in all senses, of life force, and of possibilities. If *La Guerre* is the founding expression of a poetics, then *SIC* documents the profusion of creativity born of it.

The interest of this "contextualist" approach becomes apparent here, for it allows us to chart how Albert-Birot's personal aims, originating in a different perspective from that of the dominant ideological context of the avant-garde of the period, begin to run parallel, converge, and finally diverge once again with the rise of the surrealist movement coinciding with the consolidation of his individual identity as a poet.

FINDING A VOICE: THE VOYAGE OF SELF-DISCOVERY

The Title and Cover of *SIC*

The title of *SIC* provides an initial insight into an understanding of Albert-Birot's entire poetic project from this point onward. In later interviews the poet was explicit about its significance: "Cela veut dire que c'est 'ainsi,' c'est le cri absolu, ce sont les initiales bien sûr, de *s*on, *i*dée, *c*ouleur, mais le vrai sens, c'est un désir d'affirmer quelque chose."[13] ("It means that it is 'thus,' it's the absolute cry, of course the initials stand for sound, idea, color, but what it really means is a desire to affirm something.") "Il y a une volonté de puissance dans le 'SIC' latin: Ainsi c'est ainsi. Mais pour moi, c'était surtout un son, une idée de couleur."[14] ("There is a will to power in the Latin 'SIC': thus it is thus. But for me, it was above all a sound, an idea of color.") The title is, therefore, indicative of Albert-Birot's philosophical position and of his perception and relationship to the world around him at the time. It is revelatory, too, of his artistic relationship to word and image. In his own account of *SIC*'s gestation and birth, Albert-Birot is categoric on the constructive aspects that he continued to consider the propelling force behind the journal. This emphasis on the positive, on the constructive nature of his aesthetics, and on the evolution of artistic principles will bring him into conflict with other forces in the avant-garde:

Quant au texte, j'ai pris immédiatement position sur le plan positif, constructif, je n'avais absolument pas l'intention que ma revue fût une entreprise de démolition, la guerre était là qui se chargeait de détruire, j'estimai qu'au contraire le temps exigeait qu'on ne pense qu'à construire et d'autant que du point de vue de l'art quand on apporte des nouvelles tendances, les vieilleries disparaissent d'elles-mêmes. Le système de "la table rase" est très bon en philosophie mais ne s'impose pas en art.[15]

("As far as the text was concerned, I immediately took up a positive, constructive position. I absolutely never intended that my journal should become a demolition site. We already had the war that had taken on the job of destroying everything. I believed, on the contrary, that the times demanded that we thought only of constructing and all the more so from the point of view of art, since as new tendencies come to the fore, the old ones disappear of their own accord. The system of tabula rasa works very well in philosophy but is not imperative in art.")

We will be returning to this in our evaluation of Albert-Birot's position within the avant-garde and the conflict between the dynamics of his vitalism, the will to rupture within the avant-garde, and the pressures of a new conservatism encouraged by the war. Albert-Birot himself gives an exact description of the motif of *SIC* (see reproduction):

Je suis parti de l'idée d'affirmation en réaction contre tout négatif, tout de suite je m'orientai vers le "SIC" latin dans lequel je voyais un "oui" catégorique et en même temps le signe des généralités auxquelles la revue était consacrée: c'était SONS, c'était IDEES, c'était COULEURS, et je gravai sur bois un grand "SIC" central dont l'encadrement était fait à peu près de deux "F," ce qui donnait le OUI central, plus SONS—IDEES—COULEURS, le tout contenu dans la FORME.[16]

("I began with the idea of an affirmation in reaction to all negations. Immediately I oriented myself toward the Latin "SIC," in which I saw a categorical "yes" as well as the sign for the general concepts to which the journal was devoted: it was SOUNDS, it was IDEAS, it was COLORS, and I made a wood engraving of a huge central "SIC," surrounded, like a frame, by two "F"s which gave the central YES, plus SOUNDS—IDEAS—COLORS, the whole thing contained within the FORM.")

The title clearly functions on several levels and not the least within the basic dialectical opposition between the individual and the collective, which we identified in chapter 1.[17] The title of *SIC* is an intensely personal interpretation of a cultural heritage mapped onto a statement of modernity and a direct, energetic response to life and art that directly addresses the prospective reader.[18]

SIC thus provides an entrance into Albert-Birot's poetic universe, the poet insisting on the convergence between life and art, taking *SIC*'s program as "le programme de ma vie,"[19] ("the program of my life") while simultaneously claiming a role in the collective adventure around him, a voice with which to articulate his theoretical and creative position in the clamor of other voices and in the flux and ambiguity of the adventure. It is particularly within the perspective offered by a belief in the synthesis between the arts, and especially the interaction between poetry and painting that prevails during the period that the individual and the collective converge: "C'était là se réclamer de l'unité fondamentale de l'art dans ses diverses manifestations, principe non seulement défendu, mais mis en application par l'avant-garde de 1912–1914."[20] ("It was to reclaim the fundamental unity of art in all its diverse manifestations, a principle not only defended but put into practice by the avant-garde of 1912–1914.")

The original cover, which appears throughout 1916 (issues 1–12), undergoes a series of subtle changes during the four years of the journal's development. The choice of woodcut and of Gothic lettering for the very stylized insignia of *SIC* is certainly not "innocent" and suggests a relationship to a favored medium of textual illustration of the time as well as to Apollinaire's *Les Soirées de Paris*.[21] January 1917 saw changes in the cover (see the reproduction of the four different covers): the *SIC* insignia has become more stylized and smaller, the words indicated by the initials moved to the side to make room for the table of contents (issues 13–24). However the third year of existence (issues 25–36) saw the most changes, as the magazine's program is firmly established. The *SIC* insignia is now printed black on white (a reversal of the original woodcut print of white on black), and, although retaining the original form, it is no longer a woodcut but printed from a drawing. It is smaller, having moved to the upper left-hand corner and incorporating "Sons, Idées, Couleurs, Formes," its foundation date, and Albert-Birot's name as director within its circle. The journal's complete birth certificate firmly establishes its identity. The table of contents is retained but has moved up to the top of the page to make way for the reproduction of a sketch. The cover confirms *SIC*'s adherence to visual impact, which has been apparent within its pages from the first issue onward. The other issues of 1918 feature either the reproduction of a sketch or a woodcut, a poem (twice) or a piece of music (once) on the cover.[22] The final year (issues 37–54) sees the motif completely changed. The Gothic lettering has disappeared to reveal black roman capitals, printed white on black and in a small block in the center of the page. The table of contents remains above it, and in the top right-hand corner in another block of print are its foundation date and founder's name. The insignia used for the cover throughout 1918 has moved to the center of the back page. There is no explanation of "Sons,

E T C ...

PEINTURE. — SIC ne peut faire autrement que de s'élever contre le primitivisme-image que plusieurs artistes cherchent à remettre au jour. La guerre ne porte pas en soi une marque de barbarie et d'ignorance; il y a eu des guerres dans les temps barbares, dans les temps civilisés, dans les temps modernes, il y en aura aujourd'hui, il y en aura d'autres dans l'avenir; la guerre est une chose inévitable puisque la vie ne naît que des contrastes, c'est une chose humaine, naturelle, cosmogonique qui durera autant que les mondes : les formes changent, la chose demeure. Par suite ne pensez pas mieux représenter la guerre de 1914 en vous fabriquant la mentalité d'un imagier du XVe siècle, nous sommes au XXe, pensez-y un peu, écrivez vos épopées en français, non en roman.

SCULPTURE. — Et que devient la sculpture ? Elle ne devient pas, elle reste. Il est indiscutable qu'elle se trouve sur un plan beaucoup moins avancé que la peinture et la poésie. Les sculpteurs les plus « jeunes » n'en sont encore qu'à la déformation. Serait-ce, comme le pensent quelques uns, que la sculpture ne peut cesser d'être objective sans cesser d'être sculpture ? Ce n'est pas notre avis, les recherches de Boccioni et d'un ou deux autres nous permettent de penser que des jeux de masses et de plans peuvent très bien ne pas être de l'architecture, et nous voulons espérer que quelques sculpteurs le penseront aussi.

S I C se trouve dans les maisons suivantes:

Art Contemporain — *Bd Saint-Germain, 188.*
Boutique Verte — *Rue Notre-Dame de Lorette, 34.*
Charbo — *Bd du Montparnasse, 96.*
Chéron — *Rue la Boëtie, 56.*
Librairie Crès — *Bd Saint-Germain, 115.*
   — Delesalle — *Rue Monsieur le Prince.*
   — Ferreyrol — *Rue Vavin, 1 et 3.*
Galerie Grandhomme — *Rue des Saints Pères, 40.*
Librairie Lutetia — *Bd Raspail, 66.*

Galerie Marseille — *Rue de Seine, 16.*
Martine — *Fg St-Honoré, 83.*
Librairie Monnier — *Rue de l'Odéon, 7.*
Galerie Marguy — *Rue de Maubeuge, 11.*
Librairie Nicot — *Bd Raspail, 224.*
Le Parthénon — *Rue des Écoles, 54.*
   — — *Bd Haussmann.*
Pasquini — *Avenue de Wagram, 43.*
Galerie Weil — *Rue Victor Massé, 25.*

De plus notre Revue étant aux *Messageries Hachette* on peut se la procurer dans toutes les Bibliothèques des Gares et du Métro.

✳   ✳

Les numéros 1 et 2 étant épuisés, nous avons fait en sorte d'en réunir un certain nombre d'exemplaires que nous tenons à la disposition de nos lecteurs aux prix de 0,75 le № 1 et 0,50 le № 2.

SIC **SE PROPOSE DE FAIRE DE L'EDITION**
LIVRES, BROCHURES, ALBUMS, MUSIQUE.

SIC publie des poèmes, de la musique, des dessins, des reproductions de tableaux, des croquis d'architecture, de meubles, etc....

ABONNEMENTS

La série de 12 Nos	3.00	Tirage de luxe limité à 10 exempl.	
Province.	3.50	sur Japon	50 Fs.
Étranger.	4.50		

Un numéro spécimen sera envoyé à toutes les adresses qu'on nous communiquera.
(Service régulier à tous les mobilisés qui en exprimeront le désir)

Imprimerie RIRACHOVSKY, 50, Bd St-Jacques, Paris.   Le gérant Pierre ALBERT-BIROT

Back cover of *SIC*, n° 8/9/10, August-September-October 1916. Editions Jean-Michel Place, p. 80.

Idées, Couleurs, Formes" on the cover; the identity and program of the magazine was firmly established for Albert-Birot and for his readers. It is time for Pierre Albert-Birot to channel his energy elsewhere: "Cette revue a duré quatre années entières, revue d'avant-garde et de combat dans toute l'acceptation du mot, elle fut le point de départ de tout le re-nouveau d'après-guerre, on peut retrouver dans ses pages toute la conception littéraire qu'est en pleine activité aujourd'hui."[23] ("This journal lasted four whole years, a journal of the avant-garde and of combat in all senses of the word. It was the point of departure for all the postwar

JE VOUS DIS

QUE CE GRIS

EST ROSE

COMME UNE FÊTE

EMPORTEZ-LE

IL EST A VOUS

DON
DU POÈTE

"Poème Affiche," P. Albert-Birot, *La Lune ou le livre des poèmes, Poésie 1916–1924, Rougerie.* p. 437.

Prix 0,20

Paraît une fois par mois

Janvier 1916

N° 1

SONS
IDÉES
COULEURS
FORMES

Adresser tout ce qui concerne
•SIC•
à Pierre ALBERT-BIROT, Directeur
37, Rue de la Tombe-Issoire — Paris.

 Desireux de faire connaissance avec tous ses amis, reçoit:
le Samedi soir à partir de 8 h. ‖ le Mardi de 5 à 6 h.
37, Rue de la Tombe-Issoire ‖ 11, Rue de Maubeuge

Cover of *SIC*, January 1916. Editions Jean-Michel Place, p. 1.

SONS
IDÉES
COULEURS
FORMES

Pierre ALBERT-BIROT, Directeur

DANS CE NUMÉRO :

Deutschland über alles................... ***
Vibrisme........................ Dessin de   J. RU ROUSSEAU.
Quai aux Fleurs..:............. Poème...   PIERRE REVERDY.
Ayes pitié. .... ***
« Sic Ambulant ».......................... ***
Paris et Lacédémone..................... ***
Nature morte........... ...... Poème...   FRITZ R. VANDERPYL.
Les Nouveaux Rois..................... ***
ETC. — LETTRES : Autres poèmes durant la guerre, PAUL CLAUDEL. — La guerre au Luxembourg, BLAISE
            CENDRARS. — La lucarne ovale, PIERRE REVERDY. — Almanach des Lettres et des
            Arts. — Le manuel de la volonté, B. DANGENNES. — Une nouvelle revue italienne.
    PEINTURE : Exposition des Secessionistes à Rome.

Pᴵ 0,30   Adresser tout ce qui concerne   N° 13
Étranger 0,45   la Revue   Janvier 1917
Paraît une fois par mois   37, Rue de la Tombe-Issoire. — Paris.   Deuxième Année

(SIC reçoit le mardi de 16 à 18 heures, 11, rue de Maubeuge, Galerie Marguy.)

Cover of *SIC*, January 1917. Editions Jean-Michel Place, p. 97.

renewal. In its pages can be found the entire literary conception that is flourishing today.")

SIC achieves a visual impact from the outset and communicates through form and content simultaneously. The relationship between the arts is stated both explicitly and through the design of the review. Pierre Albert-Birot insisted on the importance of the typographical arrangement of its pages: "Du point de vue typographique, j'ai tout de suite adopté des dispositions 'visuelles,' ma première page, par exemple, a été conçue pendant longtemps comme une affiche."[24] ("From the typographical point of view, I immediately adopted 'visual' arrangements. For example, my front page was conceived, for a long time, as a poster.") The personal program again feeds into and from the artistic preoccupations of the period. Albert-Birot was to carry the idea of the "poster" page into the creative production of his "poèmes-affiches" and "poèmes-pancartes."[25] The appearance of a magazine such as *SIC* had a broader role to play in the furthering of the close relationship between poetry and painting: "*SIC, Nord-Sud*, etc., parviennent à une présentation exemplaire, avec une mise en page concertée, des dispositions typographiques inédites. . . . Ces recherches indiscutablement liées à celles que mènent les artistes plastiques constituent un chapitre important de l'histoire du cubisme."[26] ("*SIC, Nord-Sud*, etc., achieve an exemplary presentation, with a strictly planned layout and innovative typographical arrangements. . . . This research, indisputably related to that being carried out in the visual arts, constitutes an important chapter in the history of cubism.")

As indicated by the changes in the appearance of the cover, *SIC* changes and develops throughout its existence, and these developments can be followed in three main ways.[27] The first, is through the examination of the "editorial"-type interventions by Albert-Birot himself. Although these are not editorial columns in any traditional way, he does voice his opinions in various sections of the magazine. The early issues use the "poster" and manifesto format to transmit the objectives of the magazine and are the proclamations of the editor's and (presumably) of the contributors' values and attitudes. These are less frequent, except in a few significant places, in the later issues. The editorials then tend to come in the shape of Albert-Birot's reviews and assessments, particularly in the rubric "Etc.," which deals with recently published books and especially other literary journals. Having established itself, *SIC* can proceed to survey from its own angle other contemporary research and issues rather than solely discussing its own objectives. The composition of some issues would seem to indicate the magazine and its editor "taking stock" of the position so far reached.[28] Thus the editorial of *SIC* latterly remains implicit but consistently well defined in the magazine's compilation.

The second way is by considering the evolution of Albert-Birot's creative contributions and the nature of these. The poet/editor contributes consistently with both poetic and artistic productions, although the frequency with which he inserts his own new material varies. The creation of the "Editions SIC" permits the organizing of his material into print. *SIC* also serves therefore to prepare readers for the creative output.

The final way is by looking at the nature and frequency of contributions by other poets and painters. The frequent contributions of a number of varied creative artists and poets is equally a defining element of *SIC* and the revelation of editorial choice. Once again the inclusion of work by these contributor/collaborators, and by other sporadic contributors, varies widely.[29]

Thus the nature and position of *SIC* within the avant-garde of the war years, from its early polemical stance as advocate and defender of modernism to its establishment within literary history, may be evaluated. To define the voice of Albert-Birot, we will first consider the role of the poet/editor.

Pierre Albert-Birot as Poet/Editor

In an article in the *Times Literary Supplement* on "The role of the literary magazine,"[30] George Steiner proposes four broad rules for the literary review, which are exemplified to a greater or lesser extent by the better-known reviews of the twentieth century:

> Firstly they may serve to expound, to publicize or to exemplify the style or ideology of a literary movement, coterie or school.
> A second purpose is that of the commemoration or dissemination of works, often from the recent past, which have not yet gained widespread acceptance which run the risk of falling silent.
> A third function is therapeutic . . . to keep the house of literature in good order, to purge it of false gods, to discriminate between the vital and the cancerous.
> A fourth purpose is a more diffuse one. A number of important intellectual literary reviews have set out to build bridges between different disciplines and literary styles.

Although *SIC* was originally one of the most consistent outlets for the diffusion of Italian futurism in France, it does not promote one ideology to the exclusion of all else. Once established its voice is rather that of a more general *esprit nouveau* in the style of Apollinaire, publishing the early surrealists along with the work of other French and foreign poets and painters and, although continuing to attack outdated attitudes to art, assimilating Albert-Birot's own cultural heritage. The position is nonetheless a courageous one in the chauvinistic and, to a large extent, xenophobic atmosphere of Paris during the war. Cubism particularly, never accepted by the artistic establishment, was viewed with suspicion as undermining truly French artistic and cultural values. Albert-Birot defends the modernist *état d'esprit,* yet his own inclination is at the same time in keeping with the new mood of the avant-garde, who, although not totally abandoning innovation, begin to return to a certain "order" in their artistic principles. The dissemination of experimental works (particularly those of Albert-Birot himself but also, for example, those of Tzara) remains, however, a major aim of *SIC,* and the promotion and staging of *Les Mamelles de Tirésias* in uproar, bringing it to the attention of all of

Paris, secures its notoriety inside and outside the avant-garde, as does its celebration of *Parade,* which had scandalized bourgeois Parisian society.

The third category poses more of a critical dilemma than the previous two, for although Albert-Birot immediately seizes on the innovative genius of Apollinaire and Reverdy, some of the contributions are of less obvious stature, although this is, of course, in the nature of such an experimental enterprise. The early issues particularly testify to an editor whose own critical perceptions are not as refined as, say, those of Reverdy himself in *Nord-Sud.* This is not a major role for *SIC,* which rather accumulates pell-mell the diverse creative forces around it. However the magazine accommodates more comfortably Steiner's final category, the bridging of disciplines being a fundamental concern, and the inclusion of very diverse literary styles stressing the impossibility of such easy labels as *cubisme littéraire* and the exclusive influence of futurism; on the whole the value of this outweighs its lack of discrimination.

The nature of a literary journal is dependent on numerous factors. The choice of the contents is obviously dictated by the editor, and as such Albert-Birot is both an intellectual and a creative presence, organizing, managing, commissioning, and contributing himself. However, there are other considerations also at work in the creation of such an enterprise. The way in which a review is funded, either independently or with the support of other organizations, will obviously influence editorial policy. *SIC* was self-funded and its identity that of one editorial direction.[31] According to Steiner the journals that have best reflected the spirit of their age have been "the explicit manifestos of a single editorial presence."[32] For Albert-Birot the journal allows him to enter into artistic life and to explore his own inner creativity. *SIC* provides an immediate outlet for his creations and simultaneously provides the possibility to design, to organize, to orchestrate a material object in all its dimensions. The experience of this will never leave the poet. The outcome of this will be, on a practical level, the personal printing of *La Lune,* and more abstractly, a particular relationship to the material of poetic creation.[33]

The final, but not least important, feature that influences the nature of such a magazine is the relationship between editor and contributors. There is evidence to suggest autocracy on the part of Albert-Birot, and certainly his own creative output increases as the magazine establishes itself, suggesting that his openness to a diverse group of poets and artists is in proportion to a growing confidence in his own ability. The uneven quality of *SIC* might be due less to the questionable critical perception of its editor than to the poet's growing confidence that this would not be his only mark on the world and legacy to posterity. Thus *SIC* may be open rather than definitive. Furthermore the war had disrupted the personal and artistic lives of the major protagonists of modernism, and, although many continued to create while at the front, the impact on daily conditions was not conducive to any coherence in artistic development. It is likely that Albert-Birot found it increasingly difficult to find consistent collaborators, as artists and poets followed divergent paths and new allegiances were formed.[34]

Having only a small number of very regular contributors places the magazine in the danger and limitations of a clique. In this perspective the final issues of *SIC*—divided between the triumvirate of Roch Grey, Léopold Survage, and Albert-Birot—are an indication of its imminent demise. This is in direct contrast to the period of *SIC*'s most intense activity, when Albert-Birot not only included a diverse selection of creative contributors but also included the critical opinions of other writers, each contributing to the nature and form of the journal.

OTHER VOICES: COLLABORATORS AND CONTRIBUTORS TO *SIC*

There is clearly a distinction to be made between occasional contributors and what may be termed the magazine's "collaborators," because their frequent contributions give form and tone to *SIC*, interacting with Albert-Birot's own productions, the whole filtered through his choices as editor. Our own choices here have been determined by frequency and by the impact of their inclusion in the development of the nature of *SIC* and for the more general literary and artistic context of the period.[35] *SIC*, with its parade of naïvetés, authoritarian pronouncements, and narcissistic indulgence, together with its status as a very real platform for experiment and combat, is a place of action and a voice of the avant-garde during the turbulent period of the war. The scope for the analysis of the literary journal in this light is potentially enormous, and this study will limit itself to brief comments on other contributions. For although the interaction between Albert-Birot and these other voices is an essential component in his evolution, we are focusing here on his work alone.

On the outbreak of war, there was no decisive artistic or literary movement, and with the upheaval in everyday life and the departure of artists and poets to the front, this state would continue for the next two years. The war years provide, then, a type of watershed. The research of the cubists and futurists had peaked and then found itself in a difficult social and artistic climate. By 1916, however:

Or, dans le courant de 1916 le retour de certains après l'épreuve de la mobilisation et du Front et surtout le besoin de combler l'absence de manifestations artistiques et culturelles vont susciter des initiatives qui, dans le Paris d'alors, auront des retentissements relativement considérables.[36]

("Furthermore in the course of 1916, the return of certain artists after the experience of mobilization and the front, and above all the necessity of replenishing the absence of artistic and cultural production, would give rise to initiatives which, in the Paris of that time, would have relatively considerable repercussions.")

The various literary journals of the time were essential *points de ralliement* (*Le Mot, L'Elan, SIC, Nord-Sud,* for example) for the dispersed avant-garde under attack from conservative forces, and their content reveals rather the divergence between their individual research rather than any concerted "movement," an early sign of the divergent paths the key figures of the prewar period would lead after the end of the conflict.[37]

The identity of the magazine was forever changing and was never an adherent of one particular movement. Certainly it stood at the crossroads of futurism, dadaism and surrealism, but it was formed and directed by individual voices. What is initially striking is that, although *SIC* is frequently considered a mouthpiece of futurism in France, the actual number and impact of futurist contributors is far less than that of the individual poets Apollinaire and Reverdy (and also of the critical input of Aragon). Second it becomes clear that amidst the diverse nature of *SIC* and the clamor of these many voices, the voice and presence of Albert-Birot himself becomes more and more firmly established.

The first of these other voices is that of Severini. The Italian painter had, of course, played a role in the initial shaping and rapid changes of tones that took place in the early issues, and the effect of his exhibition and lecture is certain.[38] Albert-Birot publishes his own type of manifesto in issue nº 3 after his frequentation of Severini, and he is enthusiastic about Severini's work:

Il y a là tout un monde nouveau qui fait paraître évidemment bien petit le monde objectif; élancez-vous, futuristes, vers cet attirant inconnu, votre enthousiasme, seul, déjà, est de la beauté, votre foi est bienfaisante; nous devons vous tenir pour de précieux générateurs d'activité intellectuelle, vous aimez *l'inconnu,* vous aimez *la vie,* vos projets sont *illimités,* pour tout cela nous devons vous aimer. (JMP, p. 15)

("Here there is a whole new world that obviously makes the objective world seem very small; hurl yourselves, futurists, toward this enticing unknown. Your enthusiasm alone, already, is beauty, your faith is refreshing; it is our duty to hold you up as the precious generators of intellectual activity. You love the *unknown,* you love *life,* your projects are *limitless,* and for all this we must love you.")

However, the actual nature of the influence of futurist thinking on Albert-Birot is more complex than assumed by certain critics of the period. This reading of futurism by Albert-Birot is very compatible with his own philosophical training and inclination toward vitalism. His later stance in *SIC* is, of course, more critical of futurism, as we will discuss later.[39] Severini, in fact, contributes to three issues only in the first year of *SIC*. Although the weight of futurism is certainly felt through his name and the inclusion of his work, it should also be remembered that he was the most Parisian of the Italian futurists, having lived in the French capital for several years, and of the futurist painters he is the most influenced by cubist techniques and the preoccupations of the French avant-garde.[40] The futurist label applied to *SIC* is an oversimplification even in these early issues, and Albert-Birot's attitude toward the "ism" (and indeed to any "ism") is ambiguous from the outset. Commenting on *Parade* as the collaboration between cubists and futurists, he notes: "Ce sera une occasion de plus pour les ignorants de qualifier SIC de revue futuriste, nous n'y pouvons rien, avec ou sans épithète *SIC* continue" (issue nº 17, May 1917, JMP, p. 130).[41] ("It will be one more occasion for the ignorant to label *SIC* a futurist journal. There's nothing we can do about it. With or without epithets, *SIC* goes on.")

The number of futurist contributions in total is actually very small, and the majority of these are futurist design and experimentation in the theater. It is, in fact, in Albert-Birot's own ideas on theatrical construction that futurist thought is most evident, although he certainly followed to some extent the techniques advocated by Marinetti in particular for his multiple-voice poems and typographical experimentation and those favored by Severini and Balla in his paintings. However, the influence of futurism is not the whole story of their genesis and construction, and Albert-Birot's exploration of language in particular differs radically from that of Marinetti, as we will explore in the following chapter.[42] There is in futurism an attempt to restructure poetic language and to introduce new literary techniques, dissolving the barriers between life and art, and to establish a new criterion for poetry.[43] It is undeniable that it had some effect on the way in which the artist/poet Albert-Birot began to look at the world and its ideas, spreading as they do from painting, sculpture, and poetry to theater, architecture, stage design, music, ballet, photography, cinema, furnishing, and fashion, incorporating, therefore, all those areas that *SIC* initially sets out to explore.

In terms of a chronological survey of contributors/collaborators, Guillaume Apollinaire would appear immediately after Severini, through whom Albert-Birot met the poet. In terms of impact for Albert-Birot personally, his is undoubtedly the most essential set of contributions. Apollinaire's first contribution, the poem "L'Avenir," appears in issue nº

4, April 1916, placed opposite Severini's "Recherche nouvelle—Dans le Nord-Sud" (JMP, pp. 28–29). From there until his death, his contributions are frequent and very much at the heart and of the spirit of *SIC*. The charisma of Apollinaire was heralded by his peers and is celebrated in the opening words of Pierre Reverdy's *Nord-Sud:*

> Quoi d'étonnant que nous ayons jugé le moment venu de nous grouper autour de Guillaume Apollinaire. Plus que quiconque aujourd'hui il a tracé des routes neuves, ouvert de nouveaux horizons. Il a droit à toute notre ferveur, toute notre admiration.

> ("It is hardly surprising that we have decided that the time has come to group ourselves around Guillaume Apollinaire. More than anyone else at the moment he has marked out new paths, opened up new horizons. He deserves all our fervor, all our admiration.")

The influence of Apollinaire also attracted other contributors to *SIC*. Philippe Soupault, for example, recounts how it was through the intermediary of Apollinaire that his first poem, "Départ," came to be published in *SIC:*

> Après la publication de mon premier poème dans *SIC* de Pierre Albert-Birot, grâce à l'intervention d'Apollinaire dont j'admirais les poèmes, j'ai décidé d'aller le remercier. Apollinaire était très accueillant et il m'a reçu amicalement, j'allais dire chaleureusement. Il aimait qu'on l'admire et qu'on l'aime. Et moi, je l'admirais visiblement. C'était une première rencontre. Je l'ai revu ensuite regulièrement.[44]

> ("After the publication of my first poem in Pierre Albert-Birot's *SIC,* thanks to the intervention of Apollinaire whose poems I admired, I decided to go and thank him. Apollinaire was very welcoming, friendly, I was going to say warm. He loved to be admired and liked. And as for myself, I visibly admired him. That was our first meeting. After that I saw him again regularly.")

Apollinaire was also experienced in producing a magazine himself, taking over the direction of *Les Soirées de Paris* with Serge Férat in November 1913. The journal was established in February 1912 and had been suspended for the five months leading to this second series, continuing until June 1914. Serge Férat himself became a very regular contributor toward the end of *SIC*'s existence, along with his sister Roch Grey, La Baronne d'Oettingen, who had financed her brother's review. The example of *Les Soirées de Paris* certainly provided a model for *SIC,* not the least in its espousal of the cause of the visual arts.[45] Apollinaire was aware of the enduring gap between cubism and the public appreciation of it. He had sought to redefine the work of art, with regard, for example, to the

37, Rue de la TOMBE-ISSOIRE — PARIS

P^x 0,50

3ᵉ ANNÉE

JANVIER 1918

Paraît une fois par mois

Nº 25

DANS CE NUMÉRO :

Dessin de Léopold SURVAGE

Tirage sur chine : 6 exemplaires

Cover of *SIC*, January 1918. Editions Jean-Michel Place, p. 185.

techniques and material of cubist collage, which had appeared to devalor-
ize the work in the attempt to revolutionize the perception of the representation of "reality." Apollinaire's experience, both creatively and
critically, is an example for Albert-Birot of the poet/editor, consolidating
a position within the avant-garde. His creative generosity allows him to
gather around him other poets and painters with a literary and artistic
journal as a pivotal point. Apollinaire is an individual creator functioning
successfully within the collective, a position toward which Albert-Birot
is striving at this time. Albert-Birot looked to Apollinaire in the first year
of *SIC* for indications of the direction the magazine and indeed the poet
himself should be taking. In the interview published in *SIC* nº 8/9/10,
Albert-Birot reveals his own uncertainty concerning "Les Tendances
Nouvelles," and the attitude of Apollinaire will be very much that of *SIC:*
"Le présent doit être le fruit de la connaissance du passé et la vision de
l'avenir" (JMP, p. 58). ("The present should be the fruit of the knowledge
of the past and the vision of the future.") However it should be added
that this is very much in line with Albert-Birot's thought, which is nonetheless at this point still unformulated either theoretically or creatively.
The questions he puts to Apollinaire are the same questions he is asking
himself, working toward the answers through his dialogue in *SIC* and in
his own creative experimentation. Apollinaire legitimizes Albert-Birot in
his capacity as poet/editor. He acknowledges his individual work, in his
"poèmepréfaceprophétie" for the *Trente et un Poèmes de poche,* perceiving the essence of a complex creativity worked into simple expression
and form.[46]

Among the contributions by Apollinaire are "Il pleut" and "Pablo Picasso" (to which we will return). Both are poems of particular relevance
in the development of the simultaneous visual expression sought in the
"calligrammes," key texts around which both cubist and poetic research
were revolving. It is, however, the staging of *Les Mamelles de Tirésias*
that is the apex of *SIC*'s literary activity. The whole of issue nº 18, June
1917, is devoted to a *compte rendu.* Its importance occupies the major
part of both this issue and the following one, which features selections
from the critical reaction in the press.[47]

The facsimile edition of *SIC* provides in its "Documents" the reproduction of the program for the play—a sketch by Picasso on the cover, poems
by Max Jacob, Jean Cocteau, Pierre Reverdy, and Albert-Birot, and a
woodcut by Matisse (JMP, pp. 469–76).[48] The program is indicative of
how it is, particularly with the collaboration of Apollinaire, that *SIC* assumes its position at the forefront of the avant-garde, although closer to
the *esprit nouveau* of the author of *Calligrammes* than to any one group
or movement. Apollinaire appears in his lecture on the "Esprit Nouveau"
to remove himself from the proliferating "isms" around him. He advo-

Paraît le 15 et le 30 de chaque mois

N° 40 et 41

28 Février et 15 Mars 1919

4me ANNÉE
REVUE FONDÉE
EN JANVIER 1916
PAR PIERRE
ALBERT - BIROT

DANS CE NUMÉRO :

37, RUE DE LA TOMBE-ISSOIRE
PARIS (XIV°)

Ce Numéro double : 1,20

Abonnement pour toute la Terre
10 francs
à partir de Janvier 1919.

Tirage sur Chine : 4 exemplaires.
Exemplaire N°

Cover of *SIC*, February-March 1919 (the January issue had been dedicated exclusively to the memory of Apollinaire). Editions Jean-Michel Place, p. 313.

Recherche nouvelle de GINO SEVERINI.

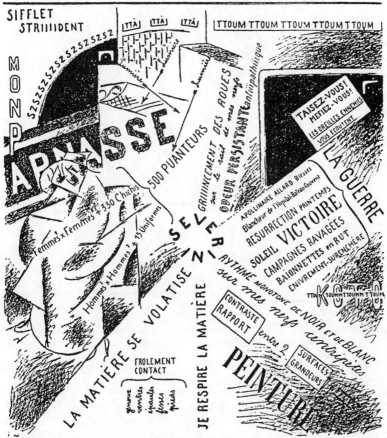

"Dans le Nord-Sud," *SIC*, **n° 4, April 1916. Editions Jean-Michel Place, p. 28.**

cates the elaboration of a creative attitude, which, at the same time as acknowledging its artistic heritage, continues the research into new forms of expression—a continued striving for synthesis between the arts and above all the quest for truth in art. His attitude is not the foundation of any specific "movement" but a general artistic and literary current encapsulating all the schools of thought from symbolism onwards. The

PIERRE ALBERT-BIROT

"MANIFESTATION SIC"

DU 24 JUIN 1917

Un dessin de Picasso

27, RUE DE LA TOUR-D'AUVERGNE
PARIS

Il a été tiré de ce programme :
10 exemplaires sur Japon signés par l'auteur de la pièce avec encartage d'un bois original de Georges de Chirico, sur Tochi, numérotés de 1 à 10
20 exemplaires sur Japon numérotés de 11 à 30

EXEMPLAIRE N°

Cover for the programme of the production of *Les Mamelles de Tirésias*, June 24, 1917, sketch by Pablo Picasso. Editions Jean-Michel Place, p. 469.

concept of the "esprit nouveau" had become widespread during this period. It was indicative of a socially, artistically, and morally reconstructed France, which would survive the war and emerge stronger. Even after his death, Apollinaire is very much present in *SIC*. A special commemorative issue was dedicated to him in January/February 1919 (n° 37/38/39), with contributions from many sources, including Aragon, Cendrars, Cocteau, Paul Dermée, Max Jacob, Picabia, Reverdy, André Salmon, and Tzara. Albert-Birot's own contribution, "Ma Main amie," is included in the collection of *La Lune ou le livre des poèmes*. Also included is "Offrande," a poem of typographical innovation, in which the poet on earth dialogues with Apollinaire, "la nouvelle étoile qui vient de s'allumer" ("The new star that has just lit up.") (see reproduction).

By 1918 Albert-Birot's own thinking and expression were clarified.

Through the intermediary of Apollinaire, Albert-Birot's editorial and personal program becomes clear, and the sculptor becomes the architect of a poetic universe:

> Mais, Bon Dieu, la vie toute entière est à l'art, à l'artiste, et la vie toute entière doit être dans l'oeuvre d'art, et la vie pleure, rit, chante, et gémit, souffre et jouit, la vie est noire et blanche et rose et bleue et verte et rouge, simple et complexe, logique et folle, bête fatale lyrique épique élégiaque tragique dramatique comique douce brutale délicate grossière fantaisiste excessive restreinte particulière générale mondiale universelle.

> ("But, my God, the whole of life is for art, for the artist, and the whole of life must be in the work of art, and life weeps, laughs, sings, and groans, suffers and enjoys, life is black and white and pink and blue and green and red, simple and complex, logical and crazy, silly fatal lyrical epic elegiac tragic dramatic comic sweet brutal delicate crude whimsical excessive restrained particular general earthly universal.")

It is December 1916. Albert-Birot is writing *SIC* (JMP, p. 96) about, not his own *Grabinoulor* begun only in 1918, for which this would be an apt attempt at a description, but about Apollinaire's *Le Poète assassiné*—revelatory nonetheless of what is to come. This is a creator's statement on painting, literature, music, an elaboration of Albert-Birot's own "sons, idées, couleurs." It is equally a philosophical declaration on the human condition, a way of thinking at once complex and childlike, and above all one that heralds the expression of excess, which we will consider in the final chapter of this study.

Pierre Reverdy is the other individual collaborator on *SIC* who should be commented on.[49] Reverdy is, of course, a poet/editor himself, founding *Nord-Sud* in March 1917 (a quotation from the inaugural issue began our section on Apollinaire above). This journal was shorter-lived than its comrade in arms, although it usually received greater attention in the chronicling of the period than *SIC*. Reverdy begins contributing to *SIC* at the beginning of 1917, and in April 1918, issue n° 16, Albert-Birot greets *Nord-Sud* enthusiastically in the rubric "Etc":

> En France il y avait jusqu'ici 333,777 journaux pour faire dormir les gens et 1 pour les éveiller, vraiment c'était un travail surhumain—car ils dorment bien— et c'est avec plaisir que nous saluons le courageux qui vient nous aider: désormais contre 333,777 nous serons 2: *SIC* et *Nord-Sud*, s'il en vient seulement encore un ou deux autres nous serons tout à fait en force. (JMP, p. 128)

> ("In France there were, until now, 333,777 journals to make people fall asleep and one to wake them up. It really was a work of superhuman effort—because

they are fast asleep—and it is with pleasure that we salute the brave one that
has come to help us: from now on we shall be two against 333,777: *SIC* and
Nord-Sud. If only one or two more would come along, we would be up to
strength.")

The tone is indicative of the avant-garde at the time—an elitism in what
is considered to be "true art," a militantism with regard to the dissemination of theories and experimental creation, a disparaging attitude to art
that does not respond to the needs of the moment. The seeds of the type
of inclusion/exclusion program operated by the surrealists are apparent,
but above all there is the desire to present this "common front" against
the critics and artists of a reactionary backlash.[50]

Throughout the period of *Nord-Sud,* Reverdy is occupied with his own
magazine, but he returns to *SIC* in issue n° 31, October 1918, and from
then until October 1919 his presence is very much at the forefront of *SIC.*
It is his prose pieces particularly that reveal a closeness between the
thinking of the poet and his editor, with regard to those who refuse to
recognize the revelations of modernity, a damning indictment of the gap
of incomprehension and ensuing rejection of the new poetry and painting
by a public led by reactionary critics ("Vociférations dans la clarté," *SIC,*
n° 31, October 1918, JMP, pp. 236–37; "Certains avantages d'être seul,"
SIC, n° 32, October 1918 [2ème n° d'octobre], JMP, pp. 242–43). Reverdy
continues with an exploration of the nature of creator and true creation.
Again he is very close to Albert-Birot, particularly when encompassing
the position of the whole of the avant-garde:

> Pour celui qui crée, l'étrangeté de cette création n'existe pas: c'est un fait, le
> seul admissible et passionnant. Il en résulte seulement une indifférence insur-
> montable pour le reste. . . . Une oeuvre d'art ne peut se contenter d'être une
> *représentation;* elle doit être une *présentation.* On présente un enfant qui naît,
> il ne représente rien. Une oeuvre d'art représentatif est *toujours* fausse. (JMP,
> p. 242)

> ("For him who creates, the strangeness of this creation does not exist: it is a
> fact, the sole admissible and fascinating fact. The result of this is only an
> insurmountable indifference to everything else. . . . A work of art cannot con-
> tent itself with being a *representation;* it must be a *presentation.* One presents
> a newborn child, the child does not represent anything. A representative work
> of art is *always* false.")

After a series of poems and additional prose pieces, Reverdy's major
contribution is the serialization of the novel *L'Imperméable* in four issues
of 1919 (40/41, 42/43, 45/46, 47/48) from February to June. This last issue
has four pages given over to Reverdy.[51]

Reverdy's work highlights the individuality of the poets working within the *esprit nouveau*. It is immediately different from that of Apollinaire and Albert-Birot, far removed from the thrust of futurism, yet working within that modern tendency, or rather tendencies, all subsumed by the cubist *état d'esprit*.[52] It was in cubism's (re)construction of a new, more intense, subjective reality, a kind of "sur-reality," that poetic minds as diverse as those of Apollinaire, Albert-Birot, and Reverdy found their inspiration. *SIC* is the presence of just such a *lieu commun* between poetry and painting and between the minds of poets and painters working diversely, yet all integral to the development of the modern aesthetic.

Our criteria in choosing individuals and more general movements to comment on here have been numerical frequency and impact on artistic history and evolution. Three contributors in particular place *SIC* at the crossroads of futurism and cubism with what was to follow. Those contributors are Tristan Tzara, Louis Aragon, and Philippe Soupault, heralding the advent of Dada and surrealism.[53]

The spirit of Dada is present in *SIC* from n° 21/22, September 1917, onward in theory and practice, with a prose piece by Tzara, "Note 6 sur l'art nègre," whose sentiments could not fail to please the Albert-Birot whose research was leading him toward a primitivism of expression in the "Poèmes à crier et à danser" and "La Légende":

L'art fut dans l'enfance du temps, prière. Bois et pierre furent vérité. Dans l'homme je vois la lune, les plantes, le noir, le métal, l'étoile, le poisson. Qu'on laisse glisser les éléments cosmiques, symétriquement. Déformer bouillir. La main est forte grande. La bouche contient la puissance de l'obscur, substance invisible, bonté, peur, sagesse, création, feu. (JMP, p. 158)[54]

("In the infancy of time art was prayer. Wood and stone were truth. In man I see the moon, plants, darkness, metal, stars, fish. Let the cosmic elements slip away, symmetrically. Distort, boil. The hand is immensely large. The mouth contains the force of the obscure, invisible substance, goodness, fear, wisdom, creation, fire.")

As with Reverdy's *Nord-Sud,* Albert-Birot acknowledges in "Etc. . ." under "NAISSANCES": *"Dada:* cahiers d'art d'une tenue et d'une sobriété sympathiques, publié à Zurich par le poète roumain Tristan Tzara et le peintre Janco. *Dada 2* va paraître incessamment" (JMP, p. 167) ("BIRTHS: *"Dada:* an art journal of a sympathetic nature and sobriety, published in Zurich by the Rumanian poet Tristan Tzara and the painter Janco. *Dada 2* will appear shortly.") Despite French resistance to ideas from beyond her borders encouraged by the war, Dada quickly became important in the avant-garde combat, international in its perspective and its development. Although using typographical innovation and the strategies of the *soirée futuriste,* there is a radically different interpretation of the role of the artist and a real subversive element in the experience of Dada.[55] Its rupture with the past is, however, alien to Albert-Birot's own views on both life and art, and yet he places *Dada 3* second only to Picabia's *391* in *SIC*'s *thermomètre littéraire,* and there is no doubt that he supported the endeavor to create an expression that would be "pure": "Dada me semble vraiment du bon grain, votre broyage de la substance verbale me sembe devoir se résoudre en poésie pure. Je pense à cela depuis longtemps moi-même."[56]

("Dada truly seems to me to be good seed. Your grinding of the substance of words must, it seems to me, end in pure poetry. I have been thinking of this myself for some time.")

The exchange between *SIC* and *Dada* was reciprocal, and Albert-Birot dedicated the first "poème à crier et à danser" as "Pour Dada," the poem appearing in *Dada 2* (December 1917), whereas "Rasoir mécanique," "Crayon bleu," and a section of *La Joie des sept couleurs* were published in *Dada 3* (December 1918), and "Catastrophe" and "le poète ne mettra pas d'objets. . . ." (later inserted in *Grabinoulor* I, 8) in *Dada 4–5*. Albert-Birot also signed the first Dada manifesto, but typically he kept his distance from the movement despite an evident personal sympathy between himself and Tzara. In later years he clarified his position with respect to the subversion, rupture, and destruction of Dada:

Dada est parti avec la volonté bien arrêtée de démolir à tout prix . . . tandis que moi je suis parti avec la volonté bien arrêtée de construire. . . . Tzara n'aurait pas dû m'y inviter car il savait mieux que quiconque à quel point nous suivions des chemins divergents.[57]

("Dada set out with the firm intention to demolish at any price . . . whereas I set out with the firm intention to construct. . . . Tzara should never have invited me along because he, better than anyone, understood the point to which we were following diverging paths.")

With hindsight Albert-Birot identifies the divergent paths inherent in and the ambivalence of every avant-garde project, as the individual and the collective engage in the dialectic between construction and destruction, rupture with and assimilation into the past.

The contributions of Philippe Soupault all concern the cinema, a medium in which Albert-Birot was himself interested at this time, alerted to the creative potential of this new technique. (Albert-Birot's own productions will be discussed later.) Soupault contributes both creative pieces comprising a series of miniscenarios and critical pieces on how cinema should be used creatively and above all poetically. In Soupault's "premier poème cinématographique" (JMP, p. 187), the future conception of surrealist filmmaking can already be discerned—using distorted images and generated from the interaction between the unconscious mind and exterior "reality."

In the "Note 1 sur le cinéma," Soupault writes of the necessity of making a distinction between potential methods of creating for the screen as opposed to creating for the stage and of his belief that the cinema should be the realm of the poet:

> Dès maintenant apparaît pour ceux qui savent voir la richesse de ce nouvel art. Sa puissance est formidable puisqu'il renverse toutes les lois naturelles: il ignore l'espace, le temps, bouleverse la pesanteur, la balistique, la biologie, etc. . . . Son oeil est plus patient, plus perçant, plus précis. Il appartient alors au créateur, au poète, de se servir de cette puissance et de cette richesse jusqu'alors negligées, car un nouveau serviteur est à la disposition de son imagination. (JMP, p. 187)

> ("From this moment on, the richness of this new art will be apparent to those who have vision. Its force is formidable because it turns all the natural laws upside down: it ignores space and time, it overturns gravity, ballistics, biology, etc. . . . Its eye is more patient, more piercing, more precise. It is, therefore, up to the creator, the poet, to make use of this force and this richness that have been neglected up until now, because a new servant is at the disposal of his imagination.")

There follows Soupault's first "scénario" dated December 1917, entitled "Indifférence," which uses these elements to recreate the type of surreality born of a liberation from everyday experience:

> Je me lève et tous disparaissent, je m'installe à la terrasse d'un café, mais tous les objets, les chaises, les tables, les fusains dans les tonneaux, se groupent autour de moi et me gênent, tandis que le garçon tourne autour de ce groupe avec une rapidité uniformement accélérée. . . . Je suis sur un toit en face d'une horloge qui grandit, grandit tandis que les aiguilles tournent de plus en plus vite. Je me jette du toit et sur le trottoir j'allume une cigarette.
> "Indifférence." Poème cinématographique. (JMP, p. 188)

> ("I stand up and everyone disappears. I sit down on the terrace of a cafe, but all the objects, the chairs, the tables, the charcoal drawings in the barrels group around me and get in my way, while the waiter swivels around this group with a uniformly accelerated rapidity. . . . I am on a roof facing the clock tower while the hands are turning faster and faster. I hurl myself off the rooftop, and on the pavement I light a cigarette.")

Louis Aragon's contribution to *SIC* is of particular interest because it takes the form of critical and review pieces rather than creative productions, and as such it does indeed become the expression of *SIC*'s opinions, from this author's first contribution in March 1918 (issue 27), throughout 1918, to the final piece in February/March 1919 (issue n° 40/41). The first contribution is his "compte-rendu" of the performance of *Les Mamelles de Tirésias* to commemorate the publication of the play in the "Editions *SIC*." In May 1918, issue n° 29, Aragon and Breton jointly publish a poem "Treize Etudes" (JMP, p. 219; see also errata, p. 226), and his review of Reverdy's *Les Ardoises du Toit* (JMP, pp. 222–23) sets the precedent for Aragon as a type of resident "literary critic," in a series entitled "Les Oeuvres littéraires françaises. Critique synthétique," which begins in October 1918, issue n° 31.[58] These are a type of poetic review covering Apollinaire's *Calligrammes* (issue n° 31, October 1918), Paul Claudel (issue 33, November 1918), Léon Bloy, Walt Whitman, Blaise Cendrars, Emile Dermenghem, Fernand Divoire (n° 35, December 1918), Max Jacob, and Jean Giraudoux (n° 40/41).

The importance of Aragon's critical contributions as a voice of *SIC* during these months is to be measured by the (non)appearance of Albert-Birot's own review section "Etc. . . ." The rubric appears only in n°s 36 and 40/41, and here it is concerned with other literary journals—otherwise it does not appear at all. In contrast the issue prior to Aragon's critical contributions contains a particularly long "Etc. . .," including reviews of both books and other journals. In the final issues, after Aragon's participation, "Etc. . ." is spasmodic, veering between the nonexistent and the very long—notably issue 49/50 containing an "Etc. . ." of four pages in length, with a mixture of books and journals reviewed.[59]

In this final year Albert-Birot's energies would appear to be already turning elsewhere, and he is willing to allow the voice of *SIC* to be determined by others, critically if not creatively. That the most prominent of these voices should be one of the later surrealists places *SIC* at a point of departure for the postwar period.[60] We have situated *SIC* and Albert-Birot with regard to futurism, the cause and discourse that *SIC* is usually labeled as supporting, and we have suggested other readings. The "other voices" of *SIC* ends on that of the surrealists. By way of further consideration of *SIC*'s place in twentieth-century artistic history, a little more needs to be discussed regarding Albert-Birot's position vis-à-vis the movement that will mark every domain of artistic production in this century.

The representation of Dada and surrealism figure strongly and frequently, particularly throughout 1918 and early 1919. It reveals an artistic and creative sympathy, with new research on Albert-Birot's behalf. Despite his reluctance to adhere to any one particular movement and despite division and disparities, there are certain "states of mind" and attitudes toward poetic creation that cut across barriers between individuals and "isms." Nonetheless, Albert-Birot's position with regard to surrealism as a movement needs some clarification and indicates some of the reasons for his slow fade into obscurity as surrealism grows in strength. This in turn sheds light on his own relationship to the creative.[61] Albert-Birot's proximity to the surrealist movement is that, like them:

P. Albert-Birot dénounce un monde cerné par les limites du possible, par les habitudes, par les interdits. . . . La raison, barbelée d'antinomies, prétend comprendre mais "la vraie intelligence sur-comprend." L'absurde dont parle P. Albert-Birot a quelque chose qui n'a pas de limite, c'est le champ du possible et de l'impossible mêlés. L'imagination donne figure d'être à l'irréel et crée le surréel. Elle ne se borne pas à reculer les frontières du réel; elle offre une vie sans frontières.[62]

("P. Albert-Birot denounces a world defined by the limits of what is possible, by habit, by prohibitions. . . . Reason, spiked with antinomies, claims to understand, but 'true intelligence goes beyond understanding.' The absurd about which P. Albert-Birot talks has something which has no limit. It is the field of the possible and the impossible mixed-up together. The imagination gives form to the unreal and creates the surreal. It does not limit itself to pushing back the frontiers of the real; it offers a life with no frontiers.")

Essentially for Albert-Birot, the surreal is what poetry should strive to convey, and he refuses the intermediary voice of a "movement" to express himself: "De tout temps le poète a cherché à entrer en contact avec ses formes cachées, avec son moi quasi-divin . . . mais quand ça devient un 'isme,' c'est du truquage, c'est du faux. D'ailleurs si loin qu'on regarde, aucun grand poète ne fut jamais un 'iste,' Mallarmé, Rimbaud."[63] ("Since the beginning of time the poet has sought to enter into contact with his hidden forms, with his almost divine self . . . but when it becomes an 'ism,' it's faked, it's false. What's more, as far back as you go, no great poet was ever an 'ist,' Mallarmé, Rimbaud were not.") Albert-Birot's disgust with the surrealist movement and its methods, its "truquage," is evident in "Mon bouquet au surréalisme." His own "surréalité" is a transposed reality where poetry resides.[64]

Vouloir faire neuf est bien, ne pas pouvoir ne pas faire neuf est beaucoup mieux. L'isme est un peu comme une loupe, il grossit le point précis examiné mais on ne voit plus rien de ce qui est autour et ce point est tellement grossi qu'il attire: on se jette dedans, il vous avale, et on va passer sa vie là-dedans, consacré au service de l'isme, je ne sais pas pourquoi je pense à un eunuque.[65]

("Wanting to introduce new ideas is good, being unable not to introduce new ideas is much better. The ism is a bit like a magnifying glass. It magnifies the precise point under examination, but you can no longer see anything around it, and this point is so magnified that it attracts: you throw yourself into it, it swallows you up, and you end up spending your life inside, devoted to the service of the ism. I don't know why it makes me think of a eunuch.")

It is certainly difficult not to see here a criticism of the attraction and dangers of the greatest "ism' of the 1920s, whose influence would extend far beyond, while Albert-Birot remains firmly on the side of individuality: "Le temps est venu où nous devons être entier. Il n'y a pas tel isme et tel autre, il y a ECRIRE, il ne s'agit pas d'être . . . iste ou . . . iste, mais d'être ECRIVAIN."[66] ("The time has come when we must be complete. It's not a question of this ism or that ism, it's a question of WRITING. It's not a question of being an . . . ist or an . . . ist, but of being a WRITER.")

The voice is decided, strong and individual, no longer in a supporting role in the drama of futurism, cubism, dadaism, and early surrealism.

Having considered the appearance of *SIC* and Albert-Birot's role as its founder/editor, and having provided a short survey of its major contributors, let us now consider its program as inscribed in its title, a program of the magazine and a program for a continuing creativity.

AN EXPLORATION OF THE PROGRAM OF *SIC:* "SONS, IDÉES, COULEURS"

"Sons"—The Music and Sounds of the Modern World

Although music is not frequently a feature of *SIC*, its presence is an important one, together with "sound" in a wider application, including the harmonies and dissonances of the experiments of *bruitisme* and the use of sounds in poetry. The techniques of simultaneity had called upon an analogy with musical form, and in turn there had been experimentation to reproduce music representative of the sounds and lifestyle of the modern age. The futurist painter Russolo had instigated a musical program "The Art of Noises," in 1913, addressed to the "great Futurist composer" Pratella and inspired by Marinetti's position on language:

Ancient life was all silence. In the nineteenth century, with the invention of the machine, Noise was born. Today Noise triumphs and reigns supreme over the sensibility of men. For many centuries life went by in silence, or at most in muted tones. The strongest noises which interrupted this silence were not intense or prolonged or varied. . . . Today music, as it becomes continuously more complicated, strives to amalgamate the most dissonant, strange and harsh sounds. In this way we come ever closer to noise-sound. THIS MUSICAL EVOLUTION IS PARALLELED BY THE MULTIPLICATION OF MACHINES which collaborate with man on every front. . . .[67]

The familiar futurist celebration of the noise and rhythms of the modern world is apparent but equally is the need for a transposition of the noises into a creation analogous to poetry:

The new orchestra will achieve the most complex and novel aural emotions not by incorporating a succession of life-imitating noises, but by manipulating fantastic juxtapositions of these varied tones and rhythms. Therefore an instrument will have to offer the possibility of tone changes and varying degrees of amplification.[68]

Certainly Albert-Birot's wife Germaine de Surville shows some futurist influence in her compositions, which comprise the majority of the musical pieces published in *SIC*. Germaine's application of *bruitisme* is apparent in her "Réflexion sur la danse" in *SIC* n° 28, January 1918:

Elle [la danse] peut et doit s'accompagner de chants et de cris suggérés par le rythme même. . . . L'orchestre sera formé d'un ensemble d'objets de bois, différents de FORME, de VOLUME et de QUALITE. (JMP, pp. 188–89)

("It [dance] can and must be accompanied by songs and cries that are suggested by the rhythm itself. . . . The orchestra will be made from an ensemble of wooden objects of different FORM, VOLUME AND QUALITY.")

Structurally Germaine places the orchestra in the center of the stage, the "materialism" and presence of the total artistic creation, again as advocated by Marinetti but influenced no doubt by Albert-Birot's own ideas on dramatic production and his project for "un théâtre nunique" in *SIC* n° 8/9/10, October 1916, and the sketch published in *SIC* n° 21–22, September/October 1917. Equally in her musical accompaniment to Albert-Birot's *Matoum et Tévibar* reproduced in *SIC* n° 42/43, March/April 1919, there is an element of primitivism in her work, which clearly aligns her with her husband.[69]

La danse par excellence ce sont les enfants qui sautent en riant, qui font une ronde en chantant, ce sont les paysans qui claquent leurs sabots en rythmant la bourrée ou autre; ce sont les sauvages, les sauvages surtout, criant, hurlant, gesticulant, trépignant, exprimant frénétiquement de tout leur être l'émotion rythmique (JMP, p. 188)

("Dancing par excellence is children jumping and laughing, dancing in a circle while singing, it is peasants clicking their clogs to keep the rhythm of a bourrée

un bois de Henri-Matisse

For the programme as above, a wood engraving by Matisse. Editions Jean-Michel Place, p. 472.

or some other traditional dance; it is tribal people above all, shouting, shriek-ing, gesticulating, stamping their feet, frenetically expressing themselves with all their rhythmic emotion")

The music published in *SIC* is frequently the musical accompaniment to a dramatic production,[70] experimental theater and music working closely, and moving, of course, to the forefront of avant-garde research with Stravinsky, Satie, and Les Six. Blaise Cendrars and Sonia Delaunay, in whose joint creation poetry and painting interact most closely, dedicate "La Prose du Transsibérien" "aux musiciens," thus acknowledging the synthesis of the arts and the importance of music for the concept of simultaneity.

In parallel fashion musicians included everyday noises in their music, just as the painters and poets included elements of daily life: "Les musiciens ont une démarche analogue à celle des peintres: on célèbre la machine, puis on produit de la musique grâce à elle et dans un troisième mouvement on compose pour elle."[71] ("Musicians proceed in an way analogous to painters: the machine is celebrated, then music is produced, thanks to the machine, and in a third movement music is composed for the machine.") The music produced by Erik Satie for *Parade* was a type of sound collage, earning him the label "le Picasso de la musique," but the real turning point for musical research had been in 1913 with Stravinsky's *Sacre du Printemps*. In *SIC* n° 17, 1917, Stravinsky's music is the focus of some attention in this issue devoted to the Ballets Russes, with the publication of an article translated from an Italian journal *La Voce*:[72]

> Stravinsky inaugure un nouveau cycle, une sensibilité nouvelle par-dessus tout rythmique. C'est un primitif et non un décadent et son art a des primitifs l'ingénuité, la simplicité, malgré son apparente complication, l'absence de sentimentalité—non d'humanité—et surtout la fraîcheur; il ressemble à l'art fatigué de Strauss ou de Debussy, comme une aurore ressemble à un crépuscule. (JMP, p. 131)

> ("Stravinsky inaugurates a new cycle, a new sensibility that is above rhythmics. He is a primitive, not a decadent, and his art has from the primitives the artlessness, the simplicity, despite its apparent complexity, the absence of sentimentality—not of humanity—and above all the freshness; it resembles the tired art of Strauss or Debussy as dawn resembles sunset.")

The decor and costumes reproduced in this issue are for Stravinsky's "Le Feu d'artifice" and "Le Chant du rossignol," and the following issue (*SIC* n° 18) contains the reproduction of a manuscript for "Une oeuvre nouvelle" by Stravinsky. Of all the arts, music is, however, the least represented in *SIC*, and it is not until n° 44, April 1919, that Erik Satie is brought to the readers' attention by Perez-Jorba:

> "Musique en effet qui vit et qui a un corps et qui a une tête et qui a des jambes et qui s'enroule souvent dans son cache-nez. Musique qui volis nolis subit une volonté formidable de création et dont seul le Maître est le maître. Musique d'Erik Satie" (JMP, p. 362).

> ("Music that indeed lives and has a body and that has a head and that has legs and that often snuggles down into its muffler. Music that willy nilly undergoes a formidable will of creation and of which only the Master is master. The music of Erik Satie.")

Musical instruments had, of course, been frequently included in cubist painting and collage, and several artists had been particularly sensitive to the structural effects of music, particularly as their own composition moved toward abstraction.[73] The interplay between poetry and music works on several levels. In terms of composition, music may show the way to new poetic creation. Music is at once the most expressive and least mimetic of the arts, rendering internal evidence visible and external, and thus fulfilling a poetic quest. Unburdened with semantic weight, it is nonrepresentational and is instantaneously perceived.[74]

An apparently more prosaic interest in sound is evident in Albert-Birot's poems for several voices and obviously in the "Poèmes à crier et à danser," which are composed of sound and rhythms exclusively. These are closely allied to futurist techniques and to Apollinaire's "Poèmes-conversations." Yet inherent in this use of the voice is a fundamental research into the very structure of poetry, as we shall discover in our later analysis of Albert-Birot's use of sound in these and other types of poetry. The use of onomatopoeia announces the failure of discursive rhetoric, using sounds alone as an access to the senses, an experiment reiterated in the sound poetry of the 1960s and an essential component of any exploration of language. These poems will be explored in detail in chapter 3.

"Idées": Theoretical Expression

To return to the first words of *SIC* n° 1 (January 1916), Albert-Birot expresses his *volonté* and *désir* and inaugurates a dialogue, with his readers certainly, but it is impossible not to read this as equally a dialogue between the old and new Albert-Birot:

> Un jour vous ne compreniez pas telle chose que vous comprenez aujourd'hui; rappelez-vous combien cette chose était inexistante pour vous AVANT, et combien elle existe DEPUIS; rappelez-vous, rappelez-vous, et ne dites pas; je ne comprends point telle chose, donc elle n'est pas. Venez avec nous, regardons, voyons, entendons, cherchons. (JMP, p. 2)

> ("There was a day when you did not understand something that you understand today; remember how much this thing was nonexistent for you BEFORE, and how much it exists SINCE; remember, and do not say I do not understand such a thing at all, therefore it does not exist. Come with us, let us look, let us see, let us hear, let us seek.")

The editor announces his intentions, the poet begins to find his voice, a quest for knowledge has begun. Albert-Birot is assuring himself of the changes in his intentions as much as addressing his prospective readers, the "regarder, voir, entendre, chercher" being equally a program for his own poetic creations and his searching for a direction at this point.

There are various sections of the review, some short-lived, some enduring through most of the magazine's existence, in which the poet/editor chooses to express himself directly: "**REFLEXIONS**," which appears during the first year only, revealing Albert-Birot's aptitude for aphorisms, a talent used in some of his poetry; and "**ETC. . .**," which announces as its intention the charting of the fortunes of modern literature, music, theater, architecture, sculpture, painting, furniture, and fashion,[75] the last two soon fading out of *SIC*'s horizons but the first being represented by reviews of books and especially of other literary journals, throughout the next four years, heralding innovation and criticizing reaction; "L'opinion d'un Pékin," a type of comment in poetic form, which disappears after issue n° 3, but which is indicative of Albert-Birot's delight in verse and humor; and the very important "Dialogues Nuniques," where "Z" provides the road to enlightenment for "A" on the subject of modern art. During the first year, Albert-Birot also uses full-page posterlike notices to express artistic ideas and the direction of *SIC*. It is these manifesto-like pages of bold typographical impact that have earned *SIC* its futurist description. However, it is more the position of "ETC. . .," which allows greater insight into Albert-Birot's attitudes and which is more indicative of the enduring direction that the magazine takes.

There are changes in emphasis despite an overall continuity in content, and the cover changes we have noted are an outward sign that Albert-Birot gives of these subtle changes in direction and approach from year to year. Although the final two issues have few contributors and this less diverse nature announces its demise, the energy and variety of the journal are continued up to October 1919 (n° 49/50), issues 47/48 and 49/50 witnessing Albert-Birot's return to rhetoric in his demand for the opportunity for mass participation in the poetic act.[76] Throughout 1916 we may count as themes in these various rubrics poetry and painting (the mainstays of the journal), music, some sculpture, the theoretical concerns of the avant-garde, and the poet's own concept of "nunisme" and "modernity" in general. Significantly consideration is given to the influence of the war on the artists.[77] The war continues until 1918, of course, but the questions posed by Albert-Birot in the early issues do not reappear. It would appear that, once he has worked out the principles creatively (his canvas *La Guerre*), his attention in *SIC* moves on to something else. However a nationalistic fervour is evident in Albert-Birot's "Premiers mots," and from the first issue he opens up a questioning on the effect of the war on the arts. From issue 3 he publishes the replies and finds his own endeavor applauded.[78]

Following on from Apollinaire, Albert-Birot reiterates the idea in

"Etc. . ." that the war is a source of energy for the arts, not barbaric but "une chose inévitable puisque la vie ne naît que des contrastes, c'est une chose humaine, naturelle, cosmogonique qui durera autant que le monde: les formes changent, la chose demeure" (JMP, p. 80). ("An inevitable thing since life is born only of contrasts, it is a human, natural, cosmogonic thing which will last as long as the world—its form changes, the thing stays the same.") Thus typical of his period, Pierre Albert-Birot places *SIC* as avant-garde in every sense of the term, and the magazine is his arm of combat, defender of the modern and of French patriotism. The final issue of 1916 (19 December 1916) includes one of the large poster-type pages entitled "L'Esprit Moderne," again linking war and modernity and acknowledging Guillaume Apollinaire. The first two issues of 1917 continue in this style and register, but they mix undoubtedly futurist-inspired rhetoric, calling on "Ingénieurs! Généraux!.," with a more personal program:

> *Cherchez autre chose*
> *toujours autre chose*
> *encore autre chose*

(JMP, p. 106)

> *("Engineers! Generals!") ("Seek something else*
> *always something else*
> *again something else.")*

Albert-Birot's own canvas *La Guerre* has been extensively considered here as a foundation movement of his poetics. That it is equally a statement on the historic and artistic present is, of course, undeniable, interacting with the work of other artists and poets naturally preoccupied with the upheaval and what changes it would bring. In issue n° 5, May 1916, when Albert-Birot begins his "dialogues nuniques" on modern art, he offers his equation of the elements of artistic energy, a page to which we have previously referred in our analysis of the canvas:

guerre + cubistes + futuristes = volonté = (ordre = style)
guerre + cubistes + futuristes = style = art
guerre + cubistes + futuristes + x = *PROCHAINE   RENAISSANCE*
                                                                    FRANCAISE

(JMP, p. 34)

("war + cubists + futurists = will = (order = style)
   war + cubists + futurists = style = art
   war + cubists + futurists + x = NEXT FRENCH RENAISSANCE")

This is a clear indication of Albert-Birot's alignment with the other forces of modernism and the artistic regeneration of a victorious France, the curious allies we have already noted. War is an artistic catalyst, seen as the release of vital energy, not as a destructive power.[79] In the statements and productions of Dada, its absurdity, destruction, and futility would be questioned and rendered artistically. Albert-Birot's personal education had inclined him already to a development and not a rupture in the evolution of art. That this became a more general consideration of the artistic climate brings a coincidence of individual and collective temperament. Finally, Apollinaire's "L'Esprit Nouveau et les poètes" will be closer to Albert-Birot than the aggressive rhetoric of the futurists.[80]

Of Albert-Birot's personal statements on modernity, the most important and sustained is "le nunisme" as expressed both in his "dialogues nuniques" and in his theory on the theater. The term's etymology as Albert-Birot explains, is from the Greek: "NUN, maintenant, à présent" (JMP, p. 43), ("NUN, now, at present.") providing another classical root for the journal whose name derives from Latin. "Nunisme" is, as we have previously suggested, Albert-Birot's expression of modernity: "La volonté n'est-elle pas en effet chère à tous les esprits forts qui constituent ce qu'on nomme le mouvement moderne, le mouvement nunique" (JMP, p. 103). ("Is not will indeed dear to all the strong minds which constitute what is called the modern movement, the nunic movement.")

Apart from the design for the "théâtre nunique" in n° 21/22, September/October 1917, and a brief allusion in the preceding note to Soupault's text on the cinema (n° 25, January 1918), which will be considered later, allusion to nunisme ends after issue 13. The final "dialogue nunique" (which actually takes the form of a "monologue nunique") also appears in n° 21/22, with the "RIDEAU" literally falling on these dramatic dialogues. Conceived ostensibly between two interlocutors, they are rather representative again of the "old" and "new" Albert-Birot, whose past and present are finally reconciled and integrated within his poetic creation by the end of 1917.[81] The adjective *nunique* first appears without explanation in issue 5, May 1916 (JMP, p. 38), and is explained in the following issue:

Un "isme" qui doit survivre à tous
  Le nunisme est né avec l'homme et ne disparaîtra qu'avec lui.
  Tous les grand philosophes, les grands artistes, les grands poètes, les grands savants, tous les flambeaux, les créateurs de tous les temps ont été, sont, seront nunistes.
Nous tous qui cherchons, soyons d'abord nunistes.
Hors le nunisme point de vie
Etre nuniste ou ne pas être.

                                                                (JMP, p. 43)

("An "ism" which must survive all others
  Nunism was born with man and will only disappear with him

>   All the great philosophers, the great artists, the great poets, the
> great scholars, all the leading lights, the creators from all ages
> were, are, will be nunists
> All of us who seek, let us be first nunists
> Outside nunism there is no life at all
> To be nunist or not to be.")

This is an assimilation of all modern tendencies, therefore, together
with Albert-Birot's maxim *chercher* and emphasis on life energy and vitalism without neglecting the artistic heritage. In issue 11 Albert-Birot
celebrates the great works of the past. His is a modernism that creates
the new without a denial of what has preceded. In the eight "dialogues
nuniques" and one "monologue nunique,"[82] Albert-Birot reveals his understanding of modern painting but more especially his sensitiveness to
the *état d'esprit* of cubism. He shows also an understanding of the way
abstraction would develop through creative subjectivity: "Aucune des
oeuvres du passé n'est une représentation purement objective" (JMP,
p. 39), and similarly "L'image complexe contiendra la réaction du sujet
pensant . . . le sujet réagit sur l'objet" (JMP, p. 46); "Une part du sujet
est indispensable; l'image objective ne devient représentation d'art
qu'après avoir été recréée par le sujet. En d'autres termes l'art commence
au sujet" (JMP, p. 55). ("None of the works of the past is a purely objective representation.") ("The complex image will contain the reaction of
the thinking subject . . . the subject reacts upon the object.") ("A part of
the subject is indispensable; the objective image becomes artistic representation only after having been recreated by the subject. In other words
art begins with the subject.") Albert-Birot goes on in this dialogue to
explain modern art in terms of nunisme:

> A   Je comprends maintenant notre tort vis-à-vis des cubistes et des futuristes,
>   nous voulons toujours retrouver l'objet.
> Z   . . . tandis qu'ils n'en ont pris que certains éléments constitutifs, suivant
>   en cela la loi nunique qui tend au minimum d'objectif et au maximum
>   de subjectif.
>
>   (JMP, p. 55)

> (A: "I now understand our error with regards to the cubists and the futurists,
> we always want to recognize the object. Z: . . . whereas they took only certain
> constitutive elements, thereby following the nunic law that tends toward the
> minimum of the objective and the maximum of the subjective.")

In the two dialogues "Autour du monde" et "Continuent" issues 8/9/
10 and 11), Albert-Birot exhibits his knowledge of cubist analytical techniques but draws attention to the point that "un tableau n'est pas une

planche d'histoire naturelle pour école primaire, un tableau n'est pas un film parce que les états ne sont pas successifs, mais simultanés"[83] (JMP, p. 79). ("A painting is not a natural history plate for primary schools, a painting is not a film because its states are not successive but simultaneous.") The continuation in issue 11 underlines this indication of a position on modern art close to Delaunay's simultaneity, termed "orphisme" by Apollinaire, as the painter moves closer to abstraction: "Le maximum de connaissance permet le maximum d'émotions esthétiques. A cela nous gagnons donc déjà plus de richesse en émotivité et plus de réalité. . . ." (JMP, p. 87). ("Maximum knowledge allows the maximum of aesthetic emotions. With that we then already gain more richness in emotionalism and more reality.") Analysis and subjectivity, then, are Albert-Birot's expression of Cendrars's formula of analysis and synthesis.[84] It is here that he gives the most complete definition of his "ars poetica":

> Et c'est alors que va se concevoir l'oeuvre d'art, car avec ses éléments de connaissance l'artiste va *construire* une oeuvre comme un architecte fait une maison avec des pierres, des fers, des bois; de ses multiples émotions pétries, amalgamées, distillées, ordonnées, il va créer un tout, un ensemble, une forme, non pas représentation visuelle de l'objet cause de modification du sujet, mais représentation en quelque sorte de cette modification elle-même; vous voyez donc qu'ici comme ailleurs, l'analyse mène à la synthèse et que ce faisant l'artiste, en toute liberté, devient plus que jamais le créateur qu'il doit être. (JMP, p. 87)

> ("And it is then that the work of art will be conceived, because with elements of his knowledge the artist will *construct* a work just as the architect builds a house with bricks, iron, wood; with his multiple emotions molded, amalgamated, distilled, ordered, he will create a whole, a form, not a visual representation of the object, a cause of the modification of the subject, but a representation to some extent of this modification itself; you see, therefore, that, here as elsewhere, analysis leads to synthesis and that by doing this, the artist, in all freedom, becomes more than ever the creator he must be.")

The analogy with architecture is one that is followed through explicitly and implicitly in Albert-Birot's creative activity, both in *Grabinoulor* and in his poetry. The construction of the work of art is both manual and mental. The poet is artisan and creator in all senses, transposed to divine status by his or her creation.[85] This emphasis on architecture, on structure, on the act of construction of a work of art, and on its process of structuralization will be examined as we proceed from our initial analysis of the structure of *La Guerre* to Albert-Birot's own *poésie plastique* in all its forms and finally to the creation and creating process of *Grabinoulor*.

The "dialogues" of 1917 continue on the essential element of synthesis:

et comme nous disons à l'instant la vie est ou n'est pas, nous devons dire l'art
est ou n'est pas, il n'y a qu'une différence de conception esthétique qui va là
aussi du simple au complexe et il me semblerait assez logique de penser que
nous allons nécessairement vers un art plus complexe qui serait synthèse des
sentiments esthétiques un peu comme l'être humain est synthèse de la vie
organique. (JMP, p. 111)

("And as we are saying just this instant life is or is not, we must say that art
is or is not, there is only a difference of aesthetic conception that goes from
the simple to the complex, and it would seem to me quite logical to think that
we are necessarily going toward a more complex art, which would be the
synthesis of aesthetic feelings, rather as the human being is the synthesis of
organic life.")

The final dialogue ends with a parallel between the poet/artist and the
"divine creator," first touching on the place of the everyday in the work
of art: "L'esthétique hellénique trouve que la nature se trompe toujours
et l'esthétique moderne trouve que la nature ne se trompe jamais; esthé-
tiquement les défauts *n'existent pas,* tout ce qui EST EST MATIERE DE
BEAUTE, le rôle de l'artiste est justement de créer, avec cette matière,
l'oeuvre" (JMP, p. 143). It continues on to the nature of the creation and
its relationship to the creator: "De plus, encore une fois, l'artiste n'a pas
à s'occuper de refaire la nature, l'oeuvre d'art est chose humaine et non
pas divine, la vie, toute la vie est là, nous n'avons qu'à prendre et créer
un monde essentiellement humain qui ne révèle aucune tendance à se
mettre en parallèle avec le monde divin: c'est de cette manière que nous
en approcherons le plus. . ." (JMP, p. 143). ("Hellenic aesthetics considers nature as always wrong, and modern aesthetics considers that nature
is never wrong; aesthetically faults *do not exist.* All that IS IS THE
MATERIAL OF BEAUTY. The role of the artist is precisely to create,
with this material, the work of art.") ("What is more, once again, the
artist should not spend his time remaking nature. The work of art is a
human and not a divine thing. Life, all of life, is there. We only have to
take it and create an essentially human world that shows no tendency to
put itself in parallel with the divine world—it is this way that we will
come closest to it.") This statement on Albert-Birot's own will to creation
and the nature of this art that can in its turn become "divine" begs further
investigation. The role and nature of the creator and myths of creation
are a constant within Albert-Birot's work. What concerns us here is that
it is from a reflection on the visual arts that Albert-Birot comes to an
understanding of the creative act and of poetic creation. These dialogues
on modern painting lead to a questioning of the nature of artistic creation
in general[86] and as such are fundamental to any appreciation of the poetry
of Albert-Birot considered in its entirety.[87]

Albert-Birot's other main theoretical statements in *SIC* revolve around the theater and the cinema. Although it is not our major intention within this study to discuss the poet's theatrical concerns and dramatic productions in depth, some reference is unavoidable because Albert-Birot's conception of poetry was bound up with that of drama since the outset.[88] The question of the modern theater is one to which Albert-Birot turns his attention early on in *SIC*. In the first issue, he expresses some hope in the "Vieux Colombier," though he adds that this is certainly not the best that can be hoped for. By issue 9 his position on what is needed is clearer, but how to go about it is still vague: "Un théâtre moderne au sens absolu du mot. Ce théâtre-là n'existe pas. Mais il nous semblerait nécessaire qu'il existât: si dès maintenant nous y pensions" (JMP, p. 22). ("A modern theater in the absolute meaning of the word. This theater does not exist. But it would seem to us necessary that it exist—what about if we think about it from now on.") However the situation is not ameliorated with any rapidity. Albert-Birot laments the lack of "CRE-ATEURS" in the theater, for the theater, like the other arts, "ne peut être de l'imitation" (JMP, p. 48). He reiterates the first "Réflexion" to appear in *SIC:* 'L'art commence où finit l'imitation" (*SIC* n° 1, JMP, p. 3). ("Cannot be imitation.") ("Art begins where imitation ends.") The theater is, of course, its own synthesis of "sons, idées, couleurs, formes," and Albert-Birot's theatrical creations contain indications for decor, lighting, costumes, and musical accompaniments. The poet/dramatist is always conscious of the totality of the effect. Indeed it is surprising that the theater did not become more of a vehicle for the *mise en scène,* literally, of the program of *SIC,* as Albert-Birot's interest continued throughout the 1920s.

By issue n° 8/9/10, Albert-Birot is ready to put forward his own ideas: "A propos d'un théâtre nunique." It is interesting to note that in the interview with Apollinaire in the same issue the theater is the one area upon which the poet is reluctant to be drawn:

Question trop compliquée peut-être. Le théâtre de chambre ou de scène aura moins d'importance qu'autrefois. Peut-être qu'un théâtre de cirque naîtra plus violent ou plus burlesque, plus simple aussi que l'autre. Mais le grand théâtre qui produit une dramaturgie totale c'est sans aucun doute le cinéma. Cette opinion n'est pas seulement la mienne au demeurant et Léon Daudet l'a déjà développée maintes fois et excellemment. (JMP, p. 59)

("Too complicated a question, perhaps. Auditorium and stage theater will be less important than before. Perhaps a circus theater will be born that is more violent and burlesque, simpler also. But the great theater, which produces total dramatic art, is without any doubt the cinema. This is not only my opinion, incidentally, and Léon Daudet has already developed it several times and excellently.")

Given the hesitation of Apollinaire, it would indeed appear to be the impetus of Albert-Birot in particular that brings *Les Mamelles de Tirésias* to the stage in 1917.

Albert-Birot's own ideas revolve around *naturellement*—the suppression of the three unities of time, place, and especially action:

> L'action principale n'aura pour ainsi dire pas plus d'importance que les autres actions ou fragments d'actions qui la compénètreront; on ne reculera devant aucun contraste, aucune diversité, aucun inattendu, acrobaties, chants, pitreries, tragédie, comédie, bouffonnerie, projections cinématographiques, pantomimes, le théâtre nunique doit être un grand tout simultané, contenant tous les moyens et toutes les émotions capables de communiquer une vie intense et enivrante aux spectateurs. Pour ajouter encore à cette intensité les multiples actions se dérouleront sur la scène et dans la salle. Pour atteindre à un réalisme plus profond on dédoublera certains des personnages de manière à montrer les actes et les pensées, si souvent en contradiction. (JMP, p. 64)[89]

> ("The main plot will not have, as it were, any more importance than the other plots or parts of plots with which it will be shot through; we will not shrink from any contrast, any diversity, anything unexpected, acrobatics, songs, tomfoolery, tragedy, comedy, buffoonery, cinematic projections, pantomimes. Nunic theater must be a great simultaneous whole, containing all the means and all the emotions capable of communicating an intense and intoxicating life to the spectators. To add even more to this intensity, the multiple plots will take place on the stage and in the auditorium; to attain a deeper realism, certain characters will be split in two so as to show their acts and thoughts, so often in contradiction with each other.")

He continues with ideas for decor, a structural innovation with the public in the center, and the spectacle taking place on a turning platform. A sketch for this latter idea is published a year later in issue 21/22. By April 1918, however, Albert-Birot has changed his mind concerning this relationship between audience and stage, preferring a strict division and considering his previous position as "mauvais conseil au détriment de l'art lui-même. . . . L'art est un monde créé par l'homme et l'homme doit le contempler à distance" (JMP, p. 211). (". . . bad advice to the detriment of art itself. . . . Art is a world created by man, and man should contemplate it at a distance.") His initial statement concerning simultaneous and diverse action is one that he carries out in *Larountala* to great effect. Yet this later position is one that underpins the difference in the relationship between the creator and his or her creation and the spectator/reader to that creation.[90]

The cinema was the creative medium that Apollinaire had considered to be one of the future paths of poetic creation in "L'Esprit Nouveau et les poètes." It is in issue n° 25 that an article by Philippe Soupault appears, as we have previously discussed. Albert-Birot himself, however, had referred to the potential of the new artistic form as early as October 1916 in his ideas on the "théâtre nunique," where he considered it to be a mode of expression through which it would be possible to produce "la réalisation de l'ultraréalisme" (JMP, p. 187). Albert-Birot uses the term *ultraréalisme*, rather than Apollinaire's *surréalisme*, although the concept of a creation that extends beyond surface realism would appear to be close both in theory and practice.

It is in a much later issue (49/50, October 1919) that Albert-Birot publishes his own theory and creative production exploring this new artistic and poetic medium.[91] His position reveals his sympathy with Soupault's earlier ideas:

> Il apparaît que le cinéma est un art de la vue, il doit donc entièrement exprimer par le mouvement, par la forme, par la couleur. Je vois là par définition la suppression de toute projection de texte. De plus le cinéma permettant de réaliser depuis longtemps déja un grand nombre de surréalités je le vois tout naturellement sujet du poète. . . .
>
> J'ai CHOISI un sujet aussi banal, aussi dépourvu d'intérêt, d'imprévu, que possible, voulant prouver par là que ce n'est pas par l'étrangeté du sujet, par l'imprévu des situations, par les horreurs tragiques que l'intérêt doit être suscité, mais que nous avons bien à portée de notre sensibilité poétique une possibilité d'expression nouvelle qui nous permet d'exprimer d'une manière neuve par conséquent intéressante n'importe quel sujet, n'importe quelle rengaine rabâchée depuis 3 mille ans. (JMP, p. 414)

> ("It appears that the cinema is an art of sight, it must therefore be entirely expressed by movement, by form, by color. I see there by definition the suppression of textual projection. What is more, since the cinema has allowed for a long time the realization of a great number of surrealistic things, I see it naturally as a subject for the poet. . . .
>
> I CHOSE a subject as banal, as bare of interest, of the unexpected as possible, wanting to prove by that that it is not through the strangeness of the subject, through the unusualness of the situations, through tragic horrors that interest must be fueled, but that we have in the reach of our poetic sensibility a possibility of new expression that allows us to express in a new and consequently interesting way any subject, any old hackneyed expression that has been repeated again and again for the last three thousand years.")

His term *ultraréalisme* has changed to the Apollinairean *surréalité*. His "Première étude de drame cinématographique," "2 + 1 = 2," follows the theory of taking the classic eternal triangle—wife, husband, and lover—

and projecting the equation visually. The husband shrinks in size when the lovers are together, until, after time has passed, husband and lover merge into one another. The theories of Albert-Birot on the cinema and those of the young surrealist Soupault are akin. This similarity indicates that the early forms of surrealism were more in keeping with the conception of Apollinaire's *surréel* as Albert-Birot understood it. In his theoretical piece as quoted above, there is an insistence on the visual and on movement in the cinematic medium where text, and therefore voice, is silenced. Albert-Birot would explore this aspect of poetic language in his visual poetry, where the eye provides a privileged modes of access to the world, to beauty, to poetic creation, to knowledge.

Cinematic form is allied to the domain of painting, and in Albert-Birot's scenario the visual impact of the cinematographic technique interacts completely with that of the visual arts:

> Puis ils se stylisent, et deviennent, ainsi que le salon, une composition de peinture, successivement un tableau fait dans l'esprit de Chardin, de David, de Manet, de Rousseau, de Picasso et enfin un tableau appartenant à ce que Guillaume Apollinaire nomme très justement l'Orphisme, tous ces tableaux bien entendu sont animés et non pas fixes. (JMP, p. 418)

> ("Then they become stylized and become, like the living room, a pictorial composition, successively a painting done in the style of Chardin, David, Manet, Rousseau, Picasso, and finally a painting belonging to what Guillaume Apollinaire calls quite rightly Orphism. All these paintings are, of course, dynamic and not fixed.")

The cinema becomes, then, another artistic form, and the *super-reality* its techniques are capable of producing makes it primordially the material of the artist and of the poet. A medium of the poetic visual that has the capacity to change constantly before the viewer's eye could not fail to please Albert-Birot, although he later became disillusioned with the cinema's ensuing predilection for the representation of "reality." Nonetheless the exploration of other media leads to a constant regeneration of the poetic form. It is significantly again the visual that provides a mode of transposition from "real" to "surreal"—a way of making seen that which would otherwise remain invisible, Albert-Birot's original and unending poetic quest.

"Couleurs": The Visual Arts

To consider the range of the plastic arts represented in *SIC*, we will extend the boundaries of *couleurs* to include all the visual arts, because, by necessity of the printing process, the reproductions in *SIC* are mainly of woodcuts and engravings or sketches.[92] This marriage between the poem and the visual arts is the consistent feature of *SIC*. Albert-Birot is sure of this direction from the first issue, when he places a reproduction of his sketch "Le Bracelet" opposite the first of his published poems "La Kouan'inn bleue." The final issue in December 1919 has Albert-Birot's long poem "La Légende," accompanied by a woodcut by Léopold Survage illustrating the central figure of this "poème narratif entrecoupé de poèmes à crier et à danser."[93]

Although Albert-Birot's artistic training was as a sculptor, he affords very little attention to this form of expression within the pages of the magazine despite the developments in, for example, the work of Picasso or Boccioni for the futurists. In Picasso's work particularly, there is a constant dialogue between sculpture and painting, and sculpture remains a privileged mode of expression for the artist. Furthermore the use of form and space in cubist collage certainly reveals a legacy to sculpture. For Albert-Birot, however, the scant interest paid to such developments would indicate that sculpture, and notably all of his own sculptures, are representational figurative works, belonging for him to the past. As has been noted in the introductory section on Albert-Birot as sculptor, his work was heralded for its "realism" and "exactitude." "L'esprit *SIC*" is directly opposed to such an art, and Albert-Birot's quest for "truth" in art has nothing to do with such exact imitation: "L'Art commence où finit l'imitation."

SIC's first issue is concerned about the type of war memorial to be imminently produced in honor of France's fallen: "Un socle, le Droit devant, le Devoir derrière, un soldat tombant dans les bras de la France dessus. Je vous en prie. . . . Nous ne méritons pas ça et EUX non plus. . . ." (JMP, p. 7) ("A pedestal, Right in front, Duty behind, a soldier falling into the arms of France above. Please. . . . We don't deserve that and neither do THEY.") Following on from his previous acclaim as a sculptor able to convey emotion in stone, Albert-Birot could well have been one of those commissioned to execute such a monument. The actual monuments did indeed reflect the "return to order" of the war years. The concern with modern sculpture remains just there, however, with no coverage of the developments in technique or of how he envisages future tendencies. It is not until issue 15 that Albert-Birot publishes "Quelques mots sur la sculpture." He had been taking an interest especially in the work of Chana Orloff; the text is a résumé of a talk given by him at her studio. He considers the legacy of only three sculptors—Rude, Carpeaux, and Rodin—"qui ont amorcé une conception d'esthétique nouvelle," ("have started a conception of a new aesthetics") and the others simply worked within a disguised Greek, Gothic, or other defunct style. After ten years of cubism and futurism, he sees no progress despite some *tentatives*

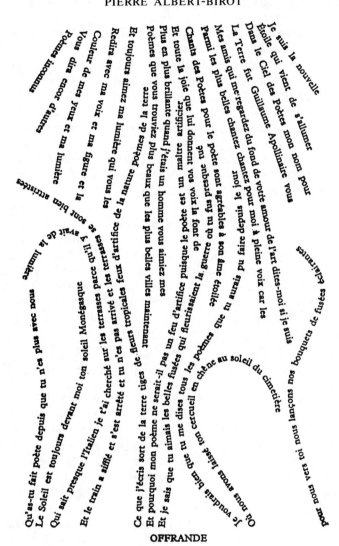

OFFRANDE

"Offrande," P. Albert-Birot, *La Lune ou le livre des poèmes,* in *Poésie 1916-1924,* Rougerie, p. 213.

intéressantes by Boccioni, and he expresses his hope that Chana Orloff will follow poets and painters toward "la réalité pensée" and not "la réalité de vision." In Albert-Birot's view sculpture has not surmounted this too narrow relationship to reality. He hopes that future sculptors "eux aussi feront des compénétrations d'objectif et de subjectif, d'intérieur et d'extérieur, de réalisme et d'idéalisme . . . leurs oeuvres ne seront plus la représentation apparente et isolée de l'objet, mais sera ce quelque chose de beaucoup plus vaste qu'on pourrait peut-être nommer un centre plas-tique" (JMP, p. 115). ("They also will make interpenetrations of the objec-tive and the subjective, of inside and outside, of realism and idealism . . . their works will no longer be the apparent and isolated representation of the object but will be this something that is vaster that could be called the plastic center.") Thus sculpture must follow the direction that leads, in Albert-Birot's view, to true creation. Yet although he returned to paint-ing in a research toward "la peinture pure," he never himself worked on such an expression in sculpture.

In the final years of *SIC*, sculpture is nonetheless present in the collabo-ration and enduring friendship with Ossip Zadkine, whose research breaks through those limits of realistic representation to achieve abstract, subjective, and poetical expression in the sculptured form. *SIC* publishes a photograph of a Zadkine sculpture (issue 40/41). Issue 45/46 includes a text by the sculptor on an African art exhibition, in which he expresses the belief that "le jeune sculpteur d'aujourd'hui puisera surtout dans les oeuvres d'art nègre la conception évidente de la spontanéité de la vraie liberté pour en arriver à l'EXPRESSION' (JMP, p. 369). This is, of course, the nature of the cubist interest in African and Oceanic art. Zad-kine continues: "Le sculpteur noir était prêtre. Il obéissait aux rites, aux lois, qui lui dictaient les attitudes, les poses. Mais il apportait aussi toute sa croyance au divin et son désir admirable de vouloir créer l'IMAGE, l'ICONE" (JMP, p. 369). ("The young sculptor today will above all draw from African works of art the obvious conception of spontaneity of true freedom to attain EXPRESSION.") ("The black sculptor was a priest. He obeyed the rites, laws, which dictated the attitudes, the poses. But he also brought all his belief in the divine and his admirable desire of wanting to create the IMAGE, the ICON.") Zadkine thus reveals his understanding of the expression of the absolute in art, close to Albert-Birot's conviction concerning the role of the poet. In general, however, sculpture appears to be linked, for Albert-Birot, with reality in all senses of the word—reality in the context of earning his living as well as in the sense of the realistic representation of exterior reality.

The impact of innovation, research, and true creation in contemporary painting, however, is noted by Albert-Birot from the first issue of *SIC*. Here it is less criticized than the other forms of artistic expression that *SIC* is setting out to explore and to promote, and there is no doubt that the interaction between poet and image is a salient feature as Albert-Birot plans the layout of the magazine: "Dans ce n° 4 en regard du poème d'Apollinaire, je publiai sur une grande page une recherche nouvelle de Severini: 'Compénétration simultanéité d'idées-images,' une composition très curieuse de formes et de textes."[94] ("In issue n° 4 opposite Apolli-naire's poem, I published on a large page some of Severini's new research: 'Interpenetration simultaneity of ideas-images,' a very curious composition of forms and of texts.") The poet/editor is aware of the visual impact of a poem entitled "L'Avenir," placed opposite an experimental composition of word and image combined (see reproduction). The text of the poem interacts with the collage-type structure of Severini's production incorporating snatches of posters and newspapers, one piece proclaiming "APOLLINAIRE ALLAIRE Blessés" (JMP, p. 28). The dynamism of Severini's composition seeks to produce a myriad of sensations, both visually perceived and heard, and the immediacy of that present moment in time is continued across the two pages of *SIC*, as the reader's eye wanders from visual composition to poetic text.

The importance of the visual arts as an essential element in *SIC*'s overall character cannot be overstressed. After Albert-Birot's completion of the first issue single-handedly, the first contribution is not a text but a reproduction of Severini's "Train arrivant à Paris." It is a work representative of futurist research into the re-creation of velocity on the canvas, revealing his sympathy with Balla's conception of the penetration of planes.[95]

As previously indicated Albert-Birot's first critical text in the second issue of *SIC* (February 1916) concerns Severini's exhibition "L'Art plastique de la guerre." His comments reveal his reaction to and understanding of futurist techniques, particularly their endeavor to represent movement:

Chez les futuristes, chez vous [Severini] en particulier, l'idée évoque un ensemble de formes en mouvement, tandis que chez les autres peintres une ou plusieurs formes isolées et immobilisées évoquent une idée. Or je me dis que l'association d'idées est en quelque sorte un infini, et par suite il me paraît que pour être logique avec vous-même, vous devez envisager la compénétration des idées, réalité de la compénétration des plans. . . .

Il n'est donc que deux moyens à choisir: ou une forme isolée et fixée volontairement en dehors de tout, représentative plastique conventionnelle de l'abstraction: c'est ce que l'on a fait jusqu'ici; ou un infini de formes *vivantes* représentatif de l'absolu: c'est ce que vous voulez faire aujourd'hui. (JMP, p. 14)

("In the work of the futurists, and in your [Severini] work in particular, the idea evokes an ensemble of forms in movement, whereas in the work of other painters one or several isolated and immobilized forms evoke an idea. Now I say to myself that the association of ideas is to some extent an infinity, and therefore it seems to me that to remain logical in your own thoughts, you must envisage the interpenetration of ideas, the reality of the interpenetration of planes. . . .

There are therefore only two ways to choose: either a form that is isolated and voluntarily fixed outside everything else, a conventional plastic representation of abstraction, which is what has been done until now; or an infinity of *living* forms, representative of the absolute, which is what you want to do today.")

This idea of "un infini de formes vivantes représentatif de l'absolu" is the goal toward which futurist techniques should work. It is equally a divulgence of Albert-Birot's own creative preoccupations, a communication of Infinity and the Absolute through an art in perpetual movement, the creation of a Poetic Self and a Poetic Universe through the *Poèmes à l'Autre Moi* to *Grabinoulor,* a dynamic, self-perpetuating Creation. Again it is in the initial theorization of the visual arts that Albert-Birot comes to the understanding of the very essence of his poetic quest. Albert-Birot's sensibility to the experience of time with futurist research is clear: "En résumé on peut dire que jusqu'ici un tableau était une fraction dans l'étendue, et qu'il devient avec vous une fraction dans le temps." ("In short we can say that until now a painting was a fraction in space, and that it becomes with you a fraction in time.") What follows is revelatory of his own creative process, insisting as he does on the subjectivity at work in such a creation: "Je crois donc qu'il serait intéressant de pousser jusqu'au bout les conséquences des principes des réalisations subjectives, de viser au maximum possible d'intégralité, afin que vous tendiez à plus de réalisme encore" (JMP, p. 15). ("I think, therefore, that it would be interesting to push to the limits the consequences of the principles of subjective realizations, to aim for the maximum possible whole, in order that you aim to attain even more realism.") The enigma of what it is the artist/poet should reveal is here presented ("l'invisible," "l'indicible"). What exactly is shown and is seen is the very question that the art of the twentieth century poses as the artist approaches human perception from every angle: "Depuis le cubisme notre oeil et notre cerveau se sont familiarisés avec une superposition des plans sur la toile et dans l'imaginaire."[96] ("Since cubism our eyes and our brain have become familiar with a superimposing of planes on the canvas and in the imagination.") It is in such a composition that true poetic creation is to be perceived. Finally it is the visual language elaborated by cubism rather than the innovations of futurism to which Albert-Birot will adhere.[97]

Albert-Birot's own contributions to *SIC* in the realm of the visual arts mainly consist of a series of reproductions of woodcuts and wood engravings (including the *SIC* motif itself that is a woodcut). The early ones tend to be of a more figurative nature, but in issue 8/9/10 there appears an abstract piece "Femme nue dans une salle de bain." In the same issue Severini's "La Modiste" reveals Albert-Birot's own research into abstract form to have developed further than that of the Italian. To complete the emphasis on the visual arts in this particular issue, Severini pays tribute to the futurist painter and sculptor Boccioni, who was killed at the front, and Albert-Birot begins his "Dialogues nuniques" on the principles of modern painting, as previously discussed. Very importantly it is during this first year of the magazine's existence that one of Albert-Birot's most developed sketches for *La Guerre* appears (one of the two most complete sketches that predate the large oil on canvas in 1916). It is published opposite the futurist poet Luciano Folgore's poem "Carrousel."

The final issue of 1916 (n° 12, December) places two different forms of "plastic expression," one literary, one a sketch, side by side: Apollinaire's "Il pleut," where the expression of the poetic text is reinforced by its visual form, and Albert-Birot's own study "Intimité." This particular production is a mixture of abstract forms, collage (the *SIC* motif), and the figurative, a hand holding a pen at the very center of the picture. Word, figurative image, and subjective abstract creation fuse together in a visual synthesis.

True to its endeavor to present new research, *SIC* begins its second year with the reproduction of an example of J. Rij Rousseau's "Vibrisme," although it is difficult to see what the technique offers that futurism and cubism have not already explored. The May 1917 issue is devoted to the Ballets Russes and the collaboration between cubists and futurists. The plastic arts are here presented in their interaction with dramatic production—Balla's decor for Stravinsky's *Le Feu d'Artifice,* and the costumes by Depero for the same composer's *Chant du Rossignol.* Here also is a further attempt to present the interaction between poetry and painting in Apollinaire's "Pablo Picasso," which is framed and constructed like a cubist painting and which provides one of his most lyrical accounts of the work of the painter: "Voyez ce peintre il prend les choses avec leur ombre aussi et d'un coup d'oeil subliminatoire" (JMP, p. 133).[98] ("See this painter, he takes things also with their shadow and in a look that makes them sublime.") Albert-Birot's "Dialogues nuniques," as already discussed previously in "Idées," progress toward subjective abstraction in artistic creation. His own thinking appears to be stretching far beyond the reproductions actually in *SIC* by other artists and particularly those by the futurists.

Throughout its third year (1918), the visual arts continue to take a predominant position in *SIC.* The majority of the covers feature the reproduction of a woodcut or a sketch. January 1918 (n° 25) begins the magazine's year with a sketch by Survage (with whom a close collaboration begins). February's issue has Serge Férat's cover for *Les Mamelles de Tirésias.* The play has just been published "aux éditions *SIC*." This number also includes Férat's sketches of Lacouf and Thérèse Tirésias.

The interaction between *SIC* and the books published "aux éditions *SIC*" is obviously close. The magazine serves as launching pad and advertising space for Albert-Birot's more ambitious editorial projects. The col-

THÉATRES NUNIQUES

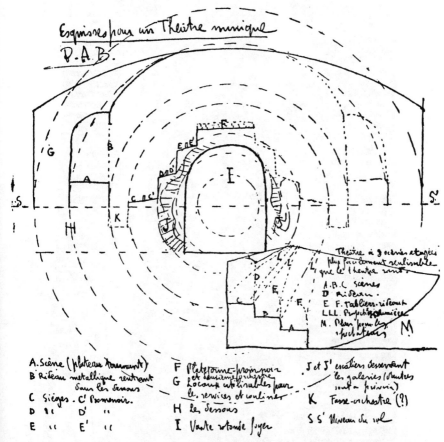

Sketch for the "théâtre nunique," P. Albert-Birot, *SIC*, n° 21-22, September-October 1917. Editions Jean-Michel Place, p. 166.

laboration with Survage and Férat brings about a change in the nature of *SIC*, as Albert-Birot's distancing himself from futurism becomes evident. By issue 28 "Etc. . .," on a recently published "plaquette consacrée à Carrà," Albert-Birot writes of the painter "qui nous paraît le plus sympathique d'entre les Futuristes, justement parce que'il semble s'éloigner d'eux" (JMP, p. 216). ("Small volume dedicated to Carrà.") ("who seems to us the most sympathetic among the futurists precisely because he seems to be distancing himself from them.") Yet remaining true to the aim of presenting all new tendencies, the interest remains. In issue 34, November 1918, "comme nous ne devons rien ignorer des recherches qui

LA STATUE
GRAVURE SUR BOIS DE LÉOPOLD SURVAGE

"La Statue," Léopold Survage, wood engraving, *SIC*, nº 54, December 1919. Editions Jean-Michel Place, p. 451.

gravure sur bois

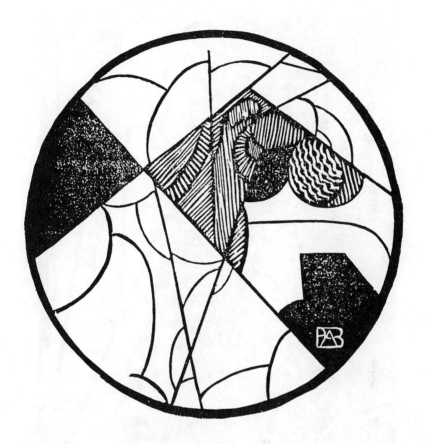

Femme nue dans une salle de bain

"Femme nue dans une salle de bain," P. Albert-Birot, n° 8/9/10, August/September/
October 1916. Editions Jean-Michel Place, p. 74.

se font autour de nous il nous a paru bien de signaler ces essais de
futuristes" ("As we mustn't ignore any of the research taking place around
us, it seemed right to signal these futurist attempts.") (JMP, p. 258). He
publishes two marionnettes from Depero's "Ballet plastique" on the cover
and inside a piece by Settimelli. The tone has changed, however, from an
enthusiastic embracing of all that is, even most superficially, innovative,
and *SIC*'s interest is guarded, especially because the performance has
not been personally seen. Albert-Birot has established himself and car-

Le premier bois de GINO SEVERINI

(Septembre 1916)

LA MODISTE

"La Modiste," Gino Severini, SIC, n° 8/9/10, August/September/October 1916. Editions Jean-Michel Place, p. 60.

"Il pleut," Guillaume Apollinaire, *SIC*, nº 12, December 1916. Editions Jean-Mischel Place, p. 92.

ried out his own experimentation in both poetry and painting, and the wholehearted espousal of all that is new has disappeared from *SIC*. There is a more objective view of what is happening around him and a more definite line in editorial policy. From this vantage point, Albert-Birot begins tentatively to suggest a kind of "taking stock" of the avant-garde's campaign this far. In issue 26 in "Etc. . .," he calls on critics to begin to elaborate a more definite distinction between cubism and futurism (JMP,

Étude au fusain.

INTIMITÉ

"Intimité," P. Albert-Birot, charcoal drawing, *SIC*, n° 12, December 1916. Editions Jean-Michel Place, p. 93.

p. 200). If it is futurism that has acted as the catalyst in enabling Pierre Albert-Birot's creativity to break through into modernity, it is cubism that prevails. The move toward abstraction inherent in both techniques influences him most markedly. There seems to be evidence to suggest that in Albert-Birot's changing attitude towards futurism, and in his desire to make more clear its distinctions with cubism, there is a yearning for "something more." It is in cubism that he perceives an exploration of the creative act and a research into the absolute of the work of art.[99]

The changes in his attitude are revealed also by his decision not to stage *Larountala* and *Les Mamelles de Tirésias* once again. This project has been proposed in issue 26, but by number 30 he writes: "Comme je n'ai pas à faire oeuvre de guerre au sens étroit du mot mais oeuvre d'art, j'ai estimé que les circonstances n'étaient pas favorables pour la meilleure

Dessin du Peintre Futuriste Giacomo BALLA
Tiré de sa scène plastique pour la Symphonie de Strawinsky
" LE FEU D'ARTIFICE "

Balla's decor for Stravinsky's *Le Feu d'artifice*, *SIC*, n° 17, May 1917. Editions Jean-Michel Place, p. 132.

réalisation possible des manifestations" (JMP, p. 227). ("As it is not my job to create war in the strict sense of the word but to create a work of art, I thought that the circumstances were not favorable for the best possible realization of these manifestations.") Between this and the issues of 1916, rallying literally to an "avant-garde" position and rejoicing in the energy and potential for artistic expression released by the war are two years of reflection and creative endeavor. There is certainly ambiguity in the statement. It is possible to read between the lines that the poet is more concerned with his own creativity than with the desire constantly to push toward the public manifestation of modernity, although both the artistic and social climate were certainly not propitious for the restaging of the avant-garde spectacle.

The position of taking stock through the medium of the visual arts continues throughout the early issues of 1919. In issue 42/43 a huge project of critical appreciation (which never completely materializes) is proposed. Prefacing a critical piece by Paul Dermée on the aesthetics of

Costumes pour le ballet de Strawinsky " LE CHANT DU ROSSIGNOL "

Créés et réalisés par le Peintre Futuriste DEPERO

	Jaune		Rouge
I° (Dame de la cour)	Bleu	II° (Mandarin)	Noir
	Vert		

Depero's costumes for Stravinsky's *Chant du Rossignol*, *SIC*, n° 17, May 1917. Editions Jean-Michel Place, p. 134.

Metzinger, Albert-Birot announces the project according to cubist principles: "L'analyse avant la synthèse! Et d'abord l'attitude esthétique individuelle de chacun des peintres cubistes . . . Puis la recherche de ce qui leur est commun à tous—de ce qui constitue essentiellement le Cubisme" (JMP, p. 345). Thus finally it is cubism that endures and subsumes other considerations in *SIC*, as it does in Albert-Birot's creative production. "Ensuite ce sera le même travail pour les littérateurs d'esprit nouveau et la mise en lumière de l'esthétique générale qui inspire aujourd'hui tout un ensemble d'effets dans les arts et dans les lettres" (JMP, p. 345) ("Analysis before synthesis! And first the individual aesthetic attitude of each of the cubist artists. . . . Then the research into what is common to all of them— into what essentially constitutes cubism.") ("Next it will be the same work to be done for the literary hacks of the Esprit Nouveau and the shedding of light on the general aesthetics which today inspires a whole lot of effects in art and literature.") Albert-Birot explicitly adopts the term *esprit nouveau* to cover modern poetry, and it is cubism's own techniques of analysis and synthesis that will allow a critical appraisal of the period. The various "isms" of the period will dissolve their apparent barriers into a final synthesis.

The proposal of this analytical and synthesizing project is important on two levels. First it would indicate the primary position of research in the visual arts, implying that Albert-Birot believes that an understanding of the plastic arts is a necessary preliminary to any analysis of the literature of the period. Second it is indicative of the poet/editor now sure of his own position. Compared with the "searching" tone of the adolescent *SIC*, a more mature tone is established. It is in this same issue that *SIC*'s "Thermomètre littéraire" is published, grading other magazines and publications. In issue 45/46 a text by M. Raynal on Severini, proposed in the critical survey series, is critical of the Italian's lack of subjectivity: "Il devrait peindre un peu plus à la première personne. Le temps est passé où la connaissance de formes abstraites devait être uniquement définissable; il faut désormais qu'elle soit intuitive. Et, dans un rigoureux examen de conscience, l'artiste doit reconnaître ce qui dans son oeuvre répond à sa propre intuition" (JMP, p. 308). ("He should paint a little more in the first person. The time has gone when the knowledge of abstract forms had to be uniquely definable; from now on it must be intuitive. And, in a rigorous examination of conscience, the artist must recognize what in his work responds to his own intuition.") We have already established that the insistence on the role of subjectivity within the creative act is close to Albert-Birot's own thinking at this time, and, finally, futurism is found lacking in this perspective. Yet, ultimately, Albert-Birot never quite relinquishes the original spirit of *SIC* and the inclusion of the experimental. Issue 47/48, the last issue that contains a diversity of contributors, includes the reproduction of Prampolini's costumes for the production of *Matoum and Tévibar* in Rome and Albert-Birot's demands for the mass participation in modernist spectacle in "Les Jeux," where the creative artist may dialogue not only with himself and with other artists but with the crowd.

However, his own creative activity is in full production: *La Joie des sept couleurs, Larountala,* and the *Poèmes quotidiens* have recently been published "aux Editions *SIC*," and the atmosphere of the final issues of *SIC* reveals a project reaching its conclusion. The interaction between the text and the visual remains, however, as the life of the journal comes full circle, and Survage's woodcut accompanies "La Légende." The complexity of Survage's work and Albert-Birot's poem fully demonstrate the journey from January 1916 and his "Kouan'inn bleue" and "Le Bracelet."

The importance of the visual arts in the development of *SIC* and in Albert-Birot's personal evolution is manifold, from the obvious impor-

37, Rue de la TOMBE-ISSOIRE — PARIS

Pᴿ 0,50

3ᵉ ANNÉE

FÉVRIER 1918

Paraît une fois par mois

N° 26

Tirage sur chine : 6 exemplaires
EXEMPLAIRE Iᵉ

LES MAMELLES DE TIRÉSIAS. (Couverture).
Dessin de Serge FÉRAT.

Cover of *SIC*, nº 26, February 1918, reproduction of Serge Férat's cover for Apollinaire's *Les Mamelles de Tirésias*, recently published 'aux Editions SIC'. Editions Jean-Michel Place, p. 193.

tance of the visual for the magazine's impact to the most sustained of his critical and theoretical enquiries. From his early training as a sculptor, the familiarity with the tactile nature of artistic creation will find other modes of expression in painting and eventually poetry. For Albert-Birot the sculptor, manipulator of the material with his hands, molding form in space, the step to painter and then creator of visual poetry is a short one. The dialogue between sculpture, painting, and poetry revolves around space, making space a perceptible, tangible, created reality. The physical formation of the material is transposed into the manipulation of letters, and Albert-Birot's fascination with typographical experimentation and his dexterity in such a process testifies to an enduring physical contact with his material and with form in space. The sculptor becomes poet-typographer in *La Lune*, which we will explore in the following chapter. It is, however, into *Grabinoulor* above all that the energy and knowledge accumulated in *SIC* is transferred, and it is there that the enduring presence of the visual arts for all Albert-Birot's creation becomes increasingly apparent.

THE WAY FORWARD AND THE AFTERLIFE OF *SIC*

The aim of this chapter has not been to discuss the avant-garde as a concept from a theoretical or historical viewpoint but to cover in a narrower sense the "Naissance et Vie" of *SIC*. The discussion has, of course, generated some reflection on the context of the magazine's production, since any vital literary review must essentially champion a cause, propose a reading of art, and initiate a discourse around its own productions.[100]

The essential nature of *SIC* is one of a foundation for Albert-Birot personally and for his position in his century. The interest in a reading of the journal is this very mixture. All its frequent naïveties, weaknesses, and pomposities allow us to breathe "l'air du temps" for a better understanding and to appreciate a selection of works as they jostle each other and shout to make themselves heard, far removed from "la paix du livre."[101] ("The peace of the book.") There is in *SIC* excitement, innovation, and experimentation. *SIC* certainly stands at the crossroads of futurism, dadaism, and surrealism. Yet Pierre Albert-Birot's personal characteristics, built on his desire for construction, his vitalism, and his understanding of what the "poetic" is give *SIC* its special nature. The long gestation period counterbalances any passionate embracing of the modern for its own sake, despite early enthusiasms. An analysis of the magazine reflects the position of the poet/editor at the various stages of his creative development. Thus as Lentengre suggests, *SIC*'s "sons, idées, couleurs, formes" are very much a personal program, and *La Lune* in particular is generated from "L'esprit *SIC,*" as is *Grabinoulor* itself.

Yet its program is also a general statement on the arts during this period. Albert-Birot's choices as editor reveal more general aesthetic concerns than those at work in any personal poetics. *SIC* allows an interaction between all the arts—poetry, painting, and theater in particular—and this is its contribution to its moment in history, fulfilling the conception of synthesis between the arts.

To determine exactly the mark of *SIC*, let us briefly return to the criteria set out in the introductory section of this survey. Certainly, *SIC* has "expounded, publicized and exemplified the style and ideology," or at least aesthetic discourse, of the general literary movements of the period and served as a showcase for various "schools." Its role of "commemoration and dissemination" is obvious, and its promotion of the new young poets is one of its most vital roles. The "therapeutic" or "cleansing" function is less in evidence for the general context, the journal publishing as it does a disparate selection of contributions. On a personal artistic level for the poet/editor himself, this is, however, an essential role, his avid desire to know eventually becoming more discriminating as he finds his own position and voice. "Building bridges" between "disciplines and literary styles" is perhaps the function *SIC* fulfills best, welcoming the work of creators whose artistic and intellectual adherences varied widely and whose voices would only dialogue in dissent elsewhere. This is the cubist *état d'esprit* to which we have previously referred. Cubism's principles of analysis and synthesis had led to a dismantling and re-creation, a subjective interpretation of the visual world. The liberation of the material of creation and of its form from perspective paralleled the liberation of the artist's imagination and subjectivity, placing the cubist movement as the originating force of modern artistic expression. Cubism is a state of the modern mind and the attempt to elaborate a language with which to explore and speak of the problematic nature of humankind's changed perception of the world. As an artistic technique, it at once is influenced by and exerts an influence over poetic procedure, engaging in a constant dialogue with poetry. *SIC* came into being and sustained itself in such an atmosphere. The energy of *SIC* is transferred into the creating of poetry, and above all into *Grabinoulor,* whose own spirit is nourished from these experiences, as Albert-Birot recognized: "Ils [les livres] sont la suite de ma revue, et vont je crois bien au-delà." ("They [the books] are the continuation of my journal, and go, I believe, far beyond it.") And on *Grabinoulor* he adds: "Ce livre est le prototype de l'esprit *SIC.*"[102] ("This book is the prototype of the spirit of *SIC.*") Through the trials that cubism endured during the period, Albert-Birot remained committed to its original concepts.

Albert-Birot's most frequently quoted statement on the end of *SIC*, "Les revues d'avant-garde doivent mourir jeunes" ("Avant-garde journals must die young.") tells really only part of the story and is a typical "myth-making" conclusion to the magazine's activity. Certainly the artistic scene at the end of the war did not please him personally: "D'abord *SIC* était une revue de guerre, née en pleine guerre; arrivée dans le temps de paix, elle n'était plus dans son atmosphère. Ensuite . . . elle ne m'amusait plus, une revue conduite quatre ans c'est une rude charge et je commençais à vouloir m'occuper de moi-même."[103] ("First *SIC* was a war journal, born in the midst of war; when peacetime came, it was no longer the right atmosphere for it. Then . . . I no longer enjoyed it. Directing a journal for four years is a heavy burden, and I was beginning to want to take care of myself.") The last sentence would appear to be the truer statement because, as we have shown, although the nature of *SIC* had changed considerably from its original "revue de guerre" stance, it could certainly have attracted new contributors to work with Survage and Férat, for example. However Albert-Birot's passage from old to new is completed. Choices had been made and the magazine and Albert-Birot's own creative ability had flourished in unison; the poet is now sure of himself and ready to develop further his own artistic creation. Once again personal and historical events contribute to the nature of the production of that creation: "Et enfin les grossières et vaines gueuleries qui commençaient à péter sur le Parnasse confirmèrent mes intentions de me retirer sous ma tente, ou mieux de m'enfermer dans mon antre."[104] ("And finally the vulgar and vain squabbles that were beginning to break out on Parnassus confirmed my intentions to retire to my tent or rather to shut myself in my lair.") A personal taste for solitude and a mistrust of literary movements begin a period of artistic isolation. At the end of the article by George Steiner, there is an essential question: "A good editor must always ask himself: is my next issue necessary?" By the end of 1919, Albert-Birot could only answer, "No."[105]

In a 1966 BBC interview, Pierre Albert-Birot gives a self-analysis full of insights: "En somme, c'est moi qui en ai profité le plus de ma revue, c'est d'être à la tête de cette revue qui m'a obligé à me creuser moi-même et à me découvrir de plus en plus"[106] ("All in all, it's me who profited most from my journal. It was being at the head of this journal that made me dig down inside myself and discover myself more and more.") Albert-Birot offered the "real meaning" of his chosen name for *SIC* as the affirmation of something that he does not go on to define. After this reading of the magazine, a definition of it could be that of an affirmation of the self. Albert-Birot begins by affirming his new self against the old one entrenched in the ideas of the nineteenth century. By the end of 1919, he is ready to affirm his individual creativity against the further ruptures of the avant-garde. One set of artistic battles over, new artistic horizons and adventures present themselves. The voice of *SIC* is the voice of Pierre Albert-Birot, engaged in a dialogue with the other creative artists of the period, but above all with himself, striving toward a self-discovery and a self-affirmation as a poet:

> A quoi reconnaît-on alors le véritable artiste?
> L'artiste est son meilleur critique—s'il dialogue avec son oeuvre, c'est un artiste, s'il dialogue avec le public, c'est probablement un imposteur.[107]

> ("How do you recognize the true artist?
>   An artist is his own best critic—if he dialogues with his work, then he's an artist; if he dialogues with the public, then he's probably an imposter.")

To examine the poet, we will proceed to a consideration of the poems of *La Lune,* many of which had already appeared in *SIC*—continuity rather than rupture in the creative process. *SIC* is a landmark in cultural, collective history. It is yet another "territory" of the creative explored by Albert-Birot. The conflicts of human relationships and of the creative process are once again given form as in the structure of *La Guerre. SIC* is another canvas that reveals the conflicts necessary for the dynamism, for the movement in all senses of the work of art.

3

La Lune Ou Le Livre Des Poèmes:
The Manual of a Poetics

> Voici l'ombre à côté de la lumière
> Voici l'espace à côté du corps
> Voici le monde est fait
> . . . .
> Avec la gauche avec la droite
> Avec le dos avec la face
> Avec le mètre avec l'équerre
> L'espérance et l'infini
> Le feu la haine et les anges
> Thèbes Babylone et Athènes
> Rome Paris Versailles et New York
> Voici le monde est commencé
> Bel ouvrage
>
> —Extract from "La Lune au plafond," in
> *La Lune ou le livre des poèmes*

> ("Here is shadow by the side of light
> Here is space by the side of the body
> Here the world is made
> . . . .
> With the left and the right
> With the back and the front
> With the meter and the square
> Hope and infinity
> Fire hate and angels
> Thebes Babylon and Athens
> Rome Paris Versailles and New York
> Here the world is begun
> A beautiful piece of work")

THE DESCENDANT OF *SIC*

THE poem "La Lune au plafond," chosen as an epigraph to this chapter
and reiterating the title given to the first major collection of Albert-Birot's

poetry (first published in 1924), narrates here its own coming into being, the coming into being of a world, the generation of the poet's own "bel ouvrage." The poem is an important one, not only echoing the title but serving as illustrative text for the whole collection as it renders visible the process of its own creation. The poems included in the collection date from as early as 1903, although precise dating is difficult, with the majority being produced around the period of the First World War and covering, therefore, Albert-Birot's involvement with the avant-garde of those years. Poised between the old and new methods of creation at his disposal, the sculptor and painter completes his metamorphosis into poet here. *La Lune* is a pivotal point and above all a testing ground for the creator's new material, allowing him to explore poetry in all its forms.

The collection is a fascinating one for several reasons, and any reading of it must take into consideration its own composite and disparate nature. Its importance for the development of Albert-Birot's poetry is apparent once again on a personal level and in the general context of the age in which it was produced.[1] The greatest emphasis should be placed here on the fact that materially and intellectually *La Lune* is the direct descendant of *SIC*. All the early poetry is nourished by "l'esprit *SIC*," but it is above all *La Lune* that is the true inheritor.[2] The previous collections are contemporaries of the literary journal, feeding into and off it. However, Albert-Birot declares at the end of 1919, "Les revues d'avant-garde doivent mourir jeunes." ("Avant-garde journals must die young.") He states his direction in turning from *SIC* as one that leads to a voyage of self-discovery. It is by way of *La Lune* and the *Poèmes à l'Autre Moi* (to be considered in the chapter that follows) that the poet fulfills his creative potential. The *Trente et un poèmes de poche* (1917) serves in many ways as a "preface" to *La Lune* and already contains all the elements of Albert-Birot's poetics, revealing his relationship toward his craft and placing his work at the heart of the modernist adventure under the patronage of Apollinaire's "poèmepréfaceprophétie," which opens the collection.[3] The first poem of the "Thirty-one" is that to which we constantly return as foundation stone of a poetics, its four lines containing a future program:

> Que vas-tu peindre ami? L'invisible.
> Que vas-tu dire ami? L'indicible
>   Monsieur car mes yeux sont dans ma tête.
>   —N'ayez pas peur, c'est un poète.

> ("What are you going to paint friend? The invisible.
> What are you doing to say friend? The unsayable
>   Sir because my eyes are in my head.
>   —Fear not, he's a poet.")

The thirty-first and final poem is equally a statement on Albert-Birot's conception of his productions:

> La nature n'a pas de point
> Le jour n'est pas séparé de la nuit
> ni la vie de la mort
> les ennemis sont unis par la haine
> Vae soli
> Pourquoi? Puisqu'il n'existe pas
> Ce livre n'est pas
> séparé
> de ceux qui le suivront
> et de point
> je n'en mets point

> ("Nature has no full stops
> Day is not separated from night
> nor life from death
> enemies are united by hate
> Vae soli
> Why? Since it does not exist
> This book is not
> separated
> from those which will follow it
> and as for full stops
> I'll stop putting them.")

Literary creation thus joins the eternal cycle of life and death, and the nonuse of punctuation extends beyond the poetic form to a metaphysical consideration of the relationship between humankind and the cosmos. This final poem of the *Trente et un poèmes de poche* sets out the difficult relationship between language, the material of poetry, and the nature of poetic expression, what exactly it is that poetry seeks to express, a relationship that will be explored in diverse ways in *La Lune*. The importance of this small collection is that it lays down the basis of a creative attitude as early as 1917. In the thirty-one poems, Albert-Birot states his position within the contemporary artistic discourse and provides a glimpse of the production yet to appear. The variety of the later poetry is already discernible, and by the second year of *SIC*, Albert-Birot is already (re)born as poet, sure of his direction, no longer innovating for its own sake, and already seeking an individual discourse in the chorus of the collective.

It is, however, from the very process of composition of *SIC* that *La Lune* is born. Albert-Birot, for whom the visual is the original element of creativity, could not fail to be fascinated by the process that produced the object *SIC*.[4] His first attempt at producing poetry himself from conception to publication was the "Quartre Poèmes d'amour," published in the Editions SIC in 1922. There were forty copies in all, hand-printed by Pierre and Germaine Albert-Birot and eventually included in *La Lune*. This collection was completed in September 1924 after a year's work by the poet/typographer[5] and is testimony to his mastery of typesetting and to imagination and dexterity combined. The process of the physical production of a work has repercussions for the reception of the text. The tangibility of a poetry that has been literally handled and composed by the poet himself, turned over in the hand as well as in the mouth, deliberately visualized, calls equally for a corporeal reaction on the part of the reader who, while enjoying the *divertissement* of certain aspects of the visual poetry, is awakened to deeper responses and must also engage physically with the object. The material presentation, the materiality of the text in a very concrete sense will provide an important focus of this study as we explore the generation of the poem between the visual and sound. Albert-Birot is an artisan manipulating the blocks of letters on the space of the page; he is poet manipulating language and the poetic object in the greater spaces of the world and of the imagination. His dedication to the printing of *La Lune* during a whole year is no mere quirk of an individual personality or passing interest. It is a commitment to the construction of an artistic and cultural object, and his work should be literally viewed as such. *La Lune* is both the descendant of *SIC* and the inheritor of the theory and practice of the visual arts.[6]

The relationship between the poetic object and the poet/typographer cannot be overstressed. Yet poetry is generated also through sound and its production and reception, and the two cannot be isolated. For the purposes of the study here, however, we will examine separately how the two generating forces of poetic production function, sometimes closely, sometimes poles apart. The disparate nature of the collection precludes any type of global approach, and the various threads that lead to poetic creation must be followed separately. The problems of analysis that arise offer some ways of reading the collection and uncovering its importance as "foundation text," just as we have read *La Guerre* as the expression of an originating moment of a whole poetics. Here that moment is anticipated, expanding out and furnishing a broad base for a fertile creativity to build on. This chapter will therefore look at the structure in a multi-dimensional manner: to consider the "sections" proposed by Albert-Birot as he constructed the collection from poems of diverse nature and to consider these poles of sound and of vision to reach a better understanding of the creative act itself. The "Poèmes à crier et à danser" stand at one pole of creative possibility, where voice and body are convoked to celebrate the movement of the poem. Paradoxically, the next step could only be total inarticulation, silence. At the other limit are the intricate typographical constructions such as "Dentelle," where the voice is silenced as the eye searches across the poem. At one limit is the poem that is lifted from the support of the page, revitalized by the breath and voice of the reader, the poem that leaves behind it a blank page. At the opposite limit is the poem that exploits the page that supports it, which cannot exist without the interaction between space and type that the page allows. Between the denial of the written word and its exaltation is inscribed a poetics with which to read these creations, and above all the *process* of their creation. In *La Lune*, Albert-Birot's poetic creation works in the space between the poles of sound and vision with various stages between the two:

THE POEM

'Poèmes à crier et à danser'		"visual" poems e.g., "Dentelle"
SOUND	SOUND AND VISION	VISION
voice		eye
movement		hand

THE BODY

Albert-Birot's poetry makes discernible the limits between which all poetry functions. The idea that poetry divulges its own poetics is not a new one and is certainly not an individual feature of the work of Albert-Birot. The poetic imagination tends to move towards its "meanings," not solely in the light of the avowed "intentions" of the poet, but especially in the poems themselves:

> Of course it would be an exaggeration to suppose that every poem is the deliberate illustration of an "ars poetica" (though works do exist which have been carefully constructed in accordance with a strict theoretical blueprint). What I am suggesting is that when poets come to write, they do so under the influence of certain inbuilt presuppositions about the nature of the process in which they are engaged. Whether consciously or unconsciously, the poet has a lively sense of what the poetics is, and what the status the words he is putting together have in relation to the world beyond the text. I believe that there is, so to speak, a phantom poetics which hovers in the writer's mind as he works, a powerful though indistinct paradigm.[7]

We are suggesting that the "phantom" in Albert-Birot's case is far from indistinct but remains an elusive object of desire. For the motivation

LES ANCIENS

Oui Madame, oui Monsieur,
les Anciens ont fait
des chefs-d'œuvre

NOUS LES CONNAISSONS

et c'est parce que nous les connaissons

que nous sommes

CUBISTES, FUTURISTES, SIMULTANISTES, UNANIMISTES,

+ ...ISTES, + ...ISTES, en un mot NUNISTES

et c'est parce que

vous ne les connaissez pas

que vous ne l'êtes pas.

CE SONT EUX, LES GRANDS AIEUX

qui nous ordonnent

d'être JEUNES

APPRENEZ A LES CONNAITRE

ILS VOUS DIRONT

DE NOUS AIMER

Page from *SIC*, n°11, November 1916. Editions Jean-Michel Place, p. 82 showing the attention to typographical setting out that fascinated Albert-Birot and that he would use himself in *La Lune ou le livre des poèmes*.

behind his production is not simply the manifestation of the poem and its poetics, but it is a quest for knowledge concerning the nature and process of the Act of Creation: How does Being come into existence from Nothingness?

Rien
Comme sur l'écran pendant l'entracte
Ni haut ni bas
Comment marcher
Le blanc avec le blanc

La lumière avec la lumière
Ame de Saint dans l'infini
N'était-ce pas commencé
Etait-ce fini
   Voici l'ombre à côté de la lumière
Voici l'espace à côté du corps
Voici le Monde est fait
           —"La Lune au plafond," *La Lune,* p. 171

("Nothing
Like on the screen during the intermission
Neither top nor bottom
How to walk
White with white
Light with light
Saint's soul in infinity
Had it not begun
Had it ended
   Here is shadow by the side of light
Here is space by the side of the body
Here the world is made.")

The same questioning is reiterated:

RIEN

Oh pardon c'est quatre lettres de trop
Pas même rien
Et c'est encore trop
Il faudrait commencer l'Histoire
Avant son commencement
Qu'on veuille bien croire qu'elle commence en effet
Dans le blanc qui précède ce rien

(NOTHING

"Oh sorry it's four letters too many
Not even nothing
And it's already too much
History needs to be begun
Before its beginning
Whether you want to believe or not that it in fact begins
In the whiteness which comes before this nothingness.")

In the opening lines of *La Belle Histoire* written in the summer of 1957 and published in 1966, only one year before the poet's death, we find him still seeking the limit beyond the opening "rien" as in *La Lune.* He is still seeking the absolute knowledge of the process of all creation, the certitude of beginning before the beginning, to create truly, the continuing preoccupation of contemporary writers in a world of multiplying discourses and an excess of communication.

THE MYSTERIOUS NATURE OF *LA LUNE*

The title of the collection is enigmatic, but a number of clues lead us into the text through its mysterious and half-hidden ways.[8] "La Lune au plafond," which echoes the title, and on which we have previously focused, confirms within it the elements that are already and will continue to be essential to Albert-Birot's entire creation. The poem is generated from nothingness through the poet's perception of the world, through the senses—from the small enclosed space of his garden to the great ancient and modern cities of the Earth, through joy and sorrow, through love and death, through illusion and truth, through the elements of the everyday and the eternal questioning of humankind. As the poem explores the very nature of its own creation, touch and sight and sound work in unison:

> Il y a au bout des doigts
> Des souvenirs et de l'espoir
> Et les doigts savent des mélodies qui prennent
> Il y a quelque chose de doux qui s'enroule
> Et l'on dit oui
> Et les yeux de l'homme s'enrichissent
> De tout ce qu'on leur donne
> Et de tout ce qu'ils voient
> Ils sont très riches les yeux
> Car tout ce qu'ils voient est à eux
> —"La Lune au plafond," *La Lune*, p. 171

> ("At the end of the fingers there are
> Memories and some hope
> And the fingers know some melodies which catch on
> There is something gentle which coils around
> And you say yes
> And man's eyes are enriched
> By everything which is given to them
> By everything they see
> Eyes are very rich
> Because everything they see is theirs")

The erotics of the creative act become evident here, as they are in the first volume of *Grabinoulor* with the very visual "Poèmes à la chair." The hand and the tongue caress language, and the mind enjoys the fruit of this physical contact:

Les mots sont tièdes comme la chair et ondoyants comme une femme nue
. . . .
Et l'esprit comme un mouleur moule ce que les mains prennent les mains
qui aiment les mains humaines qui donnent en prenant
—"La Lune au plafond," *La Lune*, p. 171

("Words are warm like flesh and undulating like a naked woman
. . . .
And the mind like a molder moulds what the hands take the hands
which love the human hands which give while taking")

From its initial impulse, the creative act vibrates in all its complexity. The creative act is physical in every way, artisanal, sensual, erotic. It is an exchange, a reciprocal action, giving and taking, an act of mutual generosity. The body is at once active and passive, a creative force, perceiving and creating, and space where sensations play.

Returning to the title of the collection, a reference to the moon will necessarily evoke in the reader dreams of an archaic past, the moon as object of mystery and of worship, the symbol of the eternal feminine. Furthermore the connotation of Pierrot is certainly not displeasing to Pierre the poet.[9] However, the actual references in "La Lune au plafond" are not to its mysterious nature nor fueled by a romantic yearning. It is claimed here as a metaphor for artificial light, a human creation. Moreover the planet itself may be attained through humankind's scientific knowledge. In "Cage" (p. 113), a further insight is provided by the "mangeur de cavorite," "cavorite" that allows space travel in H. G. Wells's *The First Men on the Moon:* "Substance opaque à la gravitation, manufacturée au moyen d'un alliage compliqué de métaux et d' 'hellium.' Nouvelle justification, mais secrète, du titre du recueil."[10] ("An opaque substance which gravitates, manufactured by means of a complicated alloy of metals and 'helium.' A new justification, but a secret one, of the title of the collection.") The title here obliquely establishes it within its literary period and the modernity of *SIC*, the spirit of which would embrace welcomingly such technological and scientific advances, which allow, here in the imagination only, the conquest of humankind's "final frontier," where human replaces God with empirical knowledge of the universe. Such a title then places it symbolically within a poetic tradition while laying claim also to the prevailing climate of modernity, and indeed raising the problem of the status of god and of humans in the universe, which will be one of the dominant themes of *Grabinoulor*.

ÇA NE SE FAIT PAS

AVANT, en France,
vous demandiez un vêtement pas comme les
autres:

ÇA NE SE FAIT PAS.

Un instrument pas comme les autres:

ÇA NE SE FAIT PAS.

Un papier, une étoffe pas comme les autres:

ÇA NE SE FAIT PAS.

Une machine pas comme les autres:

ÇA NE SE FAIT PAS.

Un artiste présentait une œuvre pas comme
les autres:

ÇA NE SE FAIT PAS.

Or maintenant la France réveillée

S A I T

que tout "CE QUI NE SE FAIT PAS"

PEUT SE FAIRE

et se **FERA**

Inside cover of *SIC*, n° 7, July 1916. Editions Jean-Michel Place, p. 50.

As we shall discover, *La Lune* is above all a manual of poetic creation. The nature of the creative act is intensely practical:

Le poète . . . a le don de développer cet instinct jusqu'à une formulation quasi monstrueuse, et lui, le poète, ce n'est plus alors un gentil petit monde imité qu'il va construire pour son usage personnel, *il ne va pas, comme on le dit trop facilement, chercher à vivre "dans la lune,"* mais au contraire, il va sucer, pomper, accaparer, dévorer toute la vie.[11]

("The poet . . . has the gift of developing this instinct to an almost monstrous formulation, and it is not then a nice little imitative world that the poet is going to construct for his personal use, *he is not going, as is flippantly said, seek to 'live in the moon,' but on the contrary, he is going to suck out, suck up, absorb, devour the whole of life."*)

Poetry is not, according to popular (mis)conception, removed from the world and the basic needs of human desire but is vital and nourished by the reality of the everyday. Poetry is not other worldly, mysterious, and prey to romantic outpourings but is concrete, palpable, and necessary. Read in this way, the title of *La Lune* is as ironic as that of *SIC*, a Latin word in Gothic lettering for a review that celebrates every innovation of the avant-garde.

Beyond the myriad connotations of *La Lune*—archaic, modern, personal, collective, divine, and human, the subtitle is less ambiguous in nature. Arlette Albert-Birot perceives this as rather the first clue to the true nature of the collection: "La première indication nous est glissée dans le sous-titre, 'ou le livre des poèmes.' Association de l'article défini qui rend l'objet unique, sinon sacré, et tout le vague 'des poèmes,' nécessité grammaticale du génitif, certes, mais aussi volonté d'une expression vague et globalisante.[12] ("The first indication is suggested to us in the subtitle, 'or the book of poems.' The association of the definite article renders the object unique, if not sacred, and the vague 'of poems' is certainly made grammatically necessary by the genitive, but it is also the will to use an expression that is vague and globalizing.") There is, then, a sacred element in this book of poetic origins, and as such it relates the myth of its source and lays down its poetic laws. It is important to note that this is a book "des poèmes" and not "de poésie." Certainly it is a globalizing form, as Arlette Albert-Birot indicates, yet so would be "poetry." Rather it testifies once again to the disparate nature of the diverse "poèmes," at once a totality and each one of singular, individual nature. In "La Lune au plafond," Albert-Birot is exploring what is essentially the suggestion of the collection's subtitle: as the various elements of creation are woven together, the construction of the poem is revealed, and the "book" comes into being. The "des" suggests equally an arbitrary collection in the way a medieval text might have been assembled. The emphasis on the "poem" situates Albert-Birot's production within the evolution of poetry from its original uses as humankind's "memory" in myth, ritual, religion, epic, in the accumulation of knowledge, the charting of passing time, and the establishment of a history to a creation in its own right. Poetry passes from being the "mémoire du langage" to the "miroir du langage," reflecting its own creation:

Il suit que les ouvrages en vers se raréfient. Il ne reste que les poèmes, c'est-à-dire des morceaux de longueur parfois considérable, mais qui atteignent rarement les dimensions d'un volume. Le volume de vers est alors un recueil qui contient plusieurs poèmes. Ceux-ci sont d'autant plus soignés qu'ils sont courts. L'evolution qui conduit la peinture de la fresque au tableau de chevalet semble également valoir pour le poème.[13]

("It follows that works in verse become rarer. There are only poems, that is to say, pieces of a sometimes considerable length, but which rarely reach the dimensions of a volume. The volume of verse is then a collection that contains several poems. These are all the more carefully formed since they are short. The evolution that takes painting from the fresco to the easel seems to be equally true for the poem.")

An exploration of the various "sections" of *La Lune* as constructed by Albert-Birot and the "titles" he gives to each one will reveal the poet indeed to be following poetry from its original commemorative, ritualistic, epistemological, and didactic uses to a modern exploration of poetic language and form for its own sake:

Et tout l'art, depuis Racine jusqu'au surréalisme, paraît avoir été de rechercher les concentrations toujours plus élevées de cet élément spécifique de toute poésie, trop dilué pour un goût de la poésie qui devenait de plus en plus conscient de sa recherche. Par l'élimination de toute finalité didactique, de toute finalité rhétorique et de toute finalité mnémotechnique, la poésie est devenue de plus en plus la poésie.[14]

("And the aim of all art, from Racine to surrealism, appears to have been to seek higher and higher concentrations of this specific element of all poetry, too diluted for a taste in poetry that became more and more conscious of its own research. By the elimination of any didactic end, of any rhetorical end, and of any mnemonic end, poetry became more and more poetry.")

A new understanding of the world, of the poet's role, of language itself leading to a new intelligence celebrates and reactivates the ancient uses of poetry. The process of poetic creation of all types and the nature of poetry itself are explored. The term "poem," at once global and individual, transcends the categorization imposed on it from the exterior, enjoying its interior multiplicity. As we follow this journey from the archaic to the modern, so the nature of *La Lune* will be revealed, and here are laid the foundations for a lifetime's production.

To cover the collection as a whole, after a general consideration of the first two sections, we will examine in detail one representative poem from each of the forms included in the long "Poèmes" section. Although there are interesting variations to which we will refer, not all of them can be done justice here.

"CHRONIQUES ET DIVERS POÈMES DU MÊME GENRE": THE FIRST USES OF POETRY

The opening section of *La Lune* is composed of sixteen poems, thirteen of which had already been published in *SIC*. The first poem, "Chez Paul

Guillaume," had appeared in the December issue of 1917.[15] This particular set of poems thus formed a major part of Albert-Birot's own creative contribution to *SIC*, notably during the years 1918–19. The link between *La Lune* and *SIC* is established on a factual basis, and this relationship between the two invites a reading of these poems on several levels. Within the collection we may read them as a type of personal "diary," a form of autobiography, the "chroniques" serving once again as a form of Albert-Birot's personal "mythologizing." In the context of *SIC*, the reader responds more readily to the poems as a form of chronicling of literary history, as a historical perspective opening up to include the literary journal and the artistic activities in which it was involved. Opening out still further to the wider perspective of the history and development of poetry itself, Albert-Birot returns poetry to one of its original functions. It celebrates both the everyday and events of special significance, the rituals of daily life recalled through rhythm and repetition, great deeds committed to posterity through the repeated telling of them:

> Il n'est pas sûr du tout que la poésie soit née de par le monde, en tant que poésie. C'est plutôt le contraire qui tendrait à l'être, si l'on se mettait à rassembler les éléments qu'on a sur les origines les plus lointaines des poésies les plus diverses. On trouve des formules rituelles, des généalogies de dieux ou de héros, des chronologies, des encyclopédies orales. Le premier caractère commun de ces types les plus archaïques de "poésie" c'est d'avoir une finalité nettement définie, non esthétique: magique, historique, juridique, didactique. Et le second caractère commun de ces mêmes types archaïques c'est d'atteindre cette finalité (conservation des rites, des généalogies, des connaissances agricoles, nautiques, juridiques, etc.) par le moyen de techniques très apparentes, techniques de la mémoire orale; c'est-à-dire des mnémotechniques. Ce que nous appelons poésie n'est pas né comme plaisir, mais comme outil. Toute l'histoire ultérieure de la poésie sera l'histoire des changements d'usage et de destination de cet outil.[16]

("It is not certain that poetry was born in the world as poetry. If one were to begin to put together the elements that we have on the most distant origins of poetry of the most diverse types, the opposite would tend to happen. One finds ritualistic formulas, the genealogies of gods or heroes, chronologies, and oral encyclopedias. The first characteristic these most archaic types of 'poetry' have in common is to have a clearly defined aim that is not aesthetic but magical, historical, judicial, didactic. And the second common characteristic of these same archaic types is to achieve this aim (the conservation of rites, of genealogies, of farming, marine, judicial knowledge, etc.) by means of very apparent techniques, the techniques of oral memory, that is, by mnemonics. What we call poetry is not born as a source of pleasure but as a tool. All the ensuing history of poetry will be the changes of the use and of the destination of this tool.")

As we have already suggested, *La Lune* is not only a personal manual of a poetics. It follows also the destiny of poetry itself from the ancient to the modern, as we shall discover when we follow its composition.

As a celebration of events, the "chroniques," particularly those dedicated to various artistic events, exhibitions, poetry readings, and the like, reveal a great deal about Albert-Birot's attitude to his moment in history. Apollinaire, as would be supposed from the direction of *SIC*, is frequently a focal point:

> Ensuite Apollinaire a touché
> la poésie non les poètes
> Et nouvel Homme-Feu
> il nous a révélé tous les secrets des Dieux
> Qui le tutoient
>   —"Chez Paul Guillaume," *La Lune*, p. 21

> ("Then Apollinaire touched on
> poetry not poets
> And new Fire-Man
> he revealed to us all the secrets of the Gods
> Who speak to him as a friend")

A reading of "Il pleut" follows the music of Auric and of Satie at an artistic event held after the death of the poet:

> Et puis on a peut-être un peu pleuré je ne sais
> Quand Cendrars à la place des siens
> Vint dire LE JET D'EAU ET LA COLOMBE POIGNARDEE
> Poème de Guillaume Apollinaire
>   —"Chronique d'automne," *La Lune*, p. 33

> ("And then we perhaps cried a little I don't know
> When Cendrars instead of his own
> Came to read THE JET OF WATER AND THE STABBED DOVE
> Poem by Guillaume Apollinaire")

Within these literary chronicles, the actors, decors, values, and debate of the time are constantly evoked. In "Vernissages," Cendrars, Soupault, Severini, and Max Jacob are assembled, and Albert-Birot reflects on cubism in a way reminiscent of his "dialogues nuniques" in *SIC*:

> Et je me suis dit
> La peinture à l'huile
> C'est bien difficile
> Surtout la cubiste

Car point d'apparence là-dedans
Qui puisse nous mettre dedans
Le peintre seul est là dans chaque cadre
Et s'il n'a rien dans la peau
Il n'y a rien dans le cadre
O cubiste sois beau
Ou ne sois pas

—"Vernissages," *La Lune,* p. 23

("And I said to myself
Oil painting
Is very difficult
Especially cubist oil painting
For there is no appearance in there
Which can put us inside
The painter alone is there in each frame
And if he has nothing under his skin
There is nothing inside the frame
O cubist be handsome
Or don't be at all")

There is humor evident in the tiny details recorded, written with a wink at the future reader he is constantly implicitly convoking.[17]

Et comme ma chronique
Doit être véridique
Je suis bien obligé de dire
Qu'à Madame André Lhote
Les coques ont donné la colique

—"Vernissages," *La Lune,* p. 23

("And since my chronicle
Must be true
I am obliged to say
That Madame André Lhote
Got the runs from the cockles")

This concern also for the relationship to the events of the everyday is a constant throughout Albert-Birot's work, from the early short collection *Poèmes quotidiens,* through such poems as the "poèmes domestiques" later in *La Lune,* to the fantastic adventures of *Grabinoulor* generated from the elements of ordinary daily life. The observation of detail is a source of humor in artistic, historical, and personal events:

Et Satie
Le 16 février 1919

Les jambes allongées
Assis sur une banquette
La tête sous son chapeau
Sa main gauche appuyée sur son parapluie
Suçait son pouce droit à 5h 20
Pendant qu'on jouait "Parade"
                —"Chronique d'hiver," *La Lune*, p. 44

("And Satie
On the 16th of February 1919
With his legs stretched out
Sitting on a bench
With his head under his hat
And his left hand resting on his umbrella
Was sucking his right thumb at twenty past five
While 'Parade' was being played")

The retaking of Soissons merits only one line. More interesting is the American marines' baseball match, and above all:

Mais j'oubliais le principal
    Le matin vers midi moins le quart
J'avais vu toute seule sous une tente
Une femme éplorée
Qui regardait le trou
Qu'elle avait à son bas
Je ne sais pas ce qu'elle est devenue
        —"Chronique des marins américains," *La Lune*, p. 42

("But I forgot the most important thing
    In the morning at quarter to twelve
I saw all alone under a tent
A tearful woman
Who was looking at the hole
That she had in her stocking
I don't know what became of her")

Memory and remembering, an original and ancient form of poetry, is used to stage the modern age, a "mise-en-scène" of this moment of the twentieth century. Such attention to the place of the everyday alongside the great events of human history is neither new nor paradoxical. It has constantly been used to great effect in the literature of our century, where the two run parallel and interplay, both the apparently mundane and the supposedly significant material of artistic creation.[18]

Within the chronicles there is frequent reference to *SIC*, Albert-Birot's voice in the multitude of voices around him:

> Sur la table à l'entrée
> Les revues de Paris
> De Rome et de Barcelone
> Revues à coeur ou mécaniques
> S'offraient à l'amitié
> Mais *SIC* qui fait toujours
> Un peu l'ours
> S'était soigneusement dissimulé
> Sous les autres
> > —"Vernissages," *La Lune*, p. 23

> ("On the table in the entrance
> The journals from Paris
> From Rome and from Barcelona
> Heartfelt or mechanical journals
> Were offering friendship
> But *SIC* which is always
> A little at odds with the world
> Had carefully hidden itself
> Under the others")

The slight irony here is prevalent in the poet's attitude toward his self-prescribed task of editor of a literary journal:

> Car que faire en ce monde
> A moins que l'on ne fonde
> Une Revue
> Profonde
> Qui confonde
> Ceux qui confondent
> Espoirs se fondent
> Et se fondent
> Ça fait toujours dans le Cosmos
> Quelques Directeurs de plus
> C'est pourquoi Pierre Albert-Birot
> A grand désir de prendre l'air
> Et de suspendre pour un temps
> Ses visites chez l'imprimeur
> > —"Chronique d'été mais pourtant véridique,"
> > *La Lune*, p. 30[19]

> ("For what to do in this world
> Unless you found
> A Journal
> A profound one
> That confounds

Those who confound
Hopes found themselves
And merge together
That always makes in the Cosmos
A few more Editors
That's why Pierre Albert-Birot
Has a great desire to get some air
And to suspend for a while
His visits to the printer")

Albert-Birot appears here to take up a self-imposed mission, the ful-fillment of a vocation to record the moment for posterity. Yet he retains also a distance, an ironical stance. The "diary" becomes art as the poem moves from "journal" to book. The instant becomes eternal:

Quant aux oeuvres
Ce que j'en pense m'appartient
Et n'a rien à faire ici
Chacune est ou sera livre
Un oeil noir les attend
L'oeil est moins poire que l'oreille
Même quand il est vert
                           —"Vernissages," *La Lune*, p. 23

("As for the works themselves
What I think is my business
And has no place here
Each one is or will be a book
A dark eye awaits them
The eye is less of a mug than the ear
Even when it's green")

In the "chroniques" the battle with time has begun. The deprecatory tone of these poems implies, however, that the "chronicling" of life is only one, and not the most exalted, function of poetry. Slowly a definition of the poet's role is undertaken, a role that will be explored more pro-foundly when the poet makes the journey from exterior to interior, from the observer of the fleeting moment outside himself to the seeker of the enduring moment within himself.

In this section of *La Lune*, a series of "didactic" poems also revitalizes another archaic poetic function, one that Albert-Birot would certainly have been aware of, given his knowledge of classical and medieval litera-ture. These poems are significant also for their indications of his attitude to poetry and to the theater.[20] His advice to young poets is that the poem is constructed simultaneously of imagination and of observation:

Pour faire un poème
Pardonnez-moi ce pléonasme
Il suffit de se promener
Quelquefois sans bouger

Regardez dehors et dedans
  Avec toutes les cellules
  De votre vous

Et voici que vous êtes riche
  —"Aux Jeunes Poètes," poème genre didactique,
  La Lune, p. 56

("To make a poem
Excuse me for this pleonasm
It is enough to take a walk
Sometimes without moving

Look outside and inside
  With all the cells
  Of your self

And there how rich you are")

The treasure must then be placed in the hands of the artisan:

Travaillez façonnez polissez assemblez
  Tous ces immatériels matériaux

("Work fashion polish assemble
  All these ethereal materials")

The composition of *La Lune* itself is thus detailed and explained with clarity. The *impalpabilités* are given form on the canvas. In the poem the *immatériel* becomes material. True creation is born through reciprocal exchange between the world and the poet through language that allows artistic transposition:

Maintenant
Que vous avez reçu le monde en vous
  Portez le monde qui va naître

· · · · · · · ·

  Et vous serez aimés
  Des mots des sons des rythmes
Qui s'ordonneront pour vous plaire

("Now
That you have received the world in you
Bear the world which is going to be born

. . . .

And you will be loved
By words by sounds by rhythms
Which will follow in order to please you")

The nature of such a process of creation must necessarily imply the divine nature of the creator himself:

Soyez triple comme un dieu
Ou plutôt comme une mère
Et naîtra le poème

("Be triple like a god
Or rather like a mother
And the poem will be born")

Human and divine, the poem comes into being. In the *Poèmes à l'Autre Moi*, we will discover in its most intense incarnation Albert-Birot following his own advice, seeking the poem within himself as the simplicity of the creative exercise reveals its most complex component:

Copiez copiez
Religieusement
La Vérité que vous êtes
Et vous ferez un poème

A condition que vous soyez poète

("Copy copy
Religiously
The Truth that is you
And you will make a poem
As long as you are a poet")

The didactic treatise for actors appeals to them not to "interpret" poetry, for by so doing they change its nature. Once again the most archaic of the applications of poetry is the truest of all:

Un poème est une prière

. . . .

Ne soyez pas une vieille dévote
Soyez un saint

Mais quand je vous parle
De messe et de prière
Ne pensez pas à nos religions
De tristesse et de mort
Qui parlent bas dans une crypte sombre
Mais à quelqu'un
De ces cultes païens
Qui aiment le Soleil
Surtout n'oubliez pas que poème est vérité
—"Aux Comédiens," *La Lune*, p. 58

("A poem is a prayer
.   .   .   .

Don't be a churchy old woman
Be a saint
But when I speak to you
Of mass and of prayer
Don't think of our religions
Of sadness and of death
Which talk quietly in a dark crypt
But of someone
From those pagan cults
Which love the Sun
Above all don't forget that the poem is truth")

Poetry is prayer, and the poem is revelatory of the truth of the poet, human existence and experience, and the act of creation. The opening section of *La Lune* is composed of poems with a self-avowed purpose. Albert-Birot, aware of his historical moment, seeks to fix it in its artistic and everyday detail. He explores also his theories of poetry, nascent theories as yet, for the nature of his material has not yet been fully explored. Dialoguing here with the reader and with different kinds of potential readers, Albert-Birot continues to dialogue with himself as in *SIC*.

"Jeu-Imitation" and "Petites Proses": Between the Ancient and the Modern

The ironic tone of "Soyez Bons," which begs an indulgence to the *passéistes* ("the devotees of the past") in their misguided innocence ("elle est plus bête que méchante") ("it's silliness rather than nastiness") is placed before the final poem of this *chroniques* section. In contrast to the *passéistes*, this final "Poème Anecdotique," subtitled "pour servir à l'histoire de notre temps," ("to be used for the history of our times") is dedicated to Apollinaire. The placing of these two poems side by side at the close of the *chroniques* invites a reading of the poems as another form of the leave-taking of the old Albert-Birot and a greeting to the new one. The meeting of the old and the new is the structure that underlies the following section of *La Lune*. Albert-Birot's intentions in "Jeu-Imitation" have been variously interpreted. What seems to be clear is that this is the marking of a passage. Old ideas are gently "ironized" out of existence and new ones pushed to the fore.

In the preface to the Gallimard edition of *La Lune*, André Lebois considers them to be parodies and offers texts whose form they could be satirizing. Yet he also remains open to the ambiguity of the whole enterprise, unable to help coming to the conclusion that these "parodies" may not be what they appear: "N'y aurait-il pas mystification à double entente? Des vers sincèrement écrits par notre poète très jeune n'auraient-ils pas été insérés, dès *La Lune*, avec l'intention de laisser le lecteur perplexe? Secrets de l'humour."[21] ("Is there mystification with a double meaning here? Have not verses written sincerely by our poet when very young been inserted, from *La Lune* onward, with the intention of perplexing the reader? Secrets of a sense of humor.") Arlette Albert-Birot's note to the collection upholds this idea, particularly because the original title for the section was "Antiquailles," crossed out on the original list of what was to be included in the collection.[22] The new title invites the reader to consider them as merely parodic and shows Albert-Birot to be master of all poetic forms. Yet there would appear to be, certainly in part, some willful deception at work here. Just as the two portraits of Germaine hung on the poet's walls opposite each other, so the old and the new Albert-Birot must confront each other and cohabit within this collection of poems. This procedure, suggests Arlette Albert-Birot, "permet à Albert-Birot de dissimuler ouvertement la liquidation de son passé poétique. . . . Les six poèmes qu'il veut nous faire prendre pour des parodies n'en étaient pas à l'origine. Ils furent sans doute écrits entre 1903 et 1912, et on peut les lire comme une chronique secrète des années d'apprentissage de la poésie."[23] ("allows Albert-Birot to dissimulate openly the liquidation of his poetic past. . . . The six poems that he wants us to take as parodies were not so originally. They were undoubtedly written between 1903 and 1912, and they can be read as the secret chronicle of the years of apprenticeship in poetry.") Certainly these are part of Albert-Birot's apprenticeship. However, we have earlier also suggested that in *La Lune* the poet deliberately traces poetry to its sources and explores its original place in the development of humankind's intellectual progress. The titles of the six poems in this section overtly claim their legacy to the celebration of past deeds and emotions, which became the domain of poetry: "Vieille épistre à des jeunes gens," "Genre sentimental," "Genre élégi-

aque," "Genre heroïque," "Genre patriotique," and "Genre magnifique."
The poet assimilates his own poetic past to that of the evolution of poetry.

The position of the "Petites proses" between the "Antiquailles" and
the modern "poèmes" is another bridge, a passing place between old and
new. For the poems date from around 1912–13 and were originally written
in Esperanto. Albert-Birot's interest in the "universal" language dates
from about 1911 and is one of his first steps toward modernity. There was
much discussion and debate from the beginning of the century onward
concerning the need for such a form of communication.[24] Albert-Birot's
enthusiasm led him to conceive of the beginnings of a literature for the
new language as yet without a literary form or discourse:

> Il comprend vite que l'absence d'une littérature freint l'expansion de la langue
> universelle. Il se met donc à l'ouvrage avec l'ardeur du néophyte, et, de janvier
> 1912 à septembre 1913, il écrit une trentaine de "petites proses" en espéranto
> toujours accompagnés du texte français. C'est dans ce lot qu'il puisa les onze
> textes qu'il décida d'ajouter au recueil.[25]

> ("He quickly understands that the absence of a literature is hindering the
> expansion of the universal language. He sets to work therefore with the ardor
> of the neophyte, and, from January 1912 to September 1913, he writes around
> thirty "little proses" in Esperanto, always accompanied by the French text. It
> is from this batch that he draws the eleven texts that he decided to add to
> the collection.")

That the "petites proses" open up the way to modernity for Albert-
Birot is evident from their position here, and from the fact that the first
of them, "La Kouan'inn Bleue," was the poem that inaugurated *SIC*. Most
importantly through the experience of Esperanto and through the use of
a poetic prose, Albert-Birot begins to seize poetry in its modern incarnation, as an experimentation and exploration of language itself.

Thus from the beginning of the collection to the point where we join
the major section of *La Lune*, entitled simply "Poèmes," we have simultaneously traversed the evolution of poetry across its most ancient and
enduring forms, through myth, religion, teaching, philosophy, the recounting of daily life, the celebration of significant moments, and the
expression of human emotion and experience. In the final section Albert-
Birot explores the essence of his art, and an examination of the individual
poems contained therein not only reveals the sources of his poetics but
allows the reader to touch the very generation of the poem and to understand its "raison d'être":

> Nous avons vu la poésie, langage de la mémoire, devenir pour des multiplies
> raisons un art du langage. . . . Car la poésie n'est pas un fait culturel mystér-
> ieux et secret. Elle est un produit de l'homme destiné à des hommes[26]

("We have seen poetry, the language of memory, become for multiple reasons an art of language. . . . For poetry is not a mysterious and secret cultural fact. It is a product of humans destined for humans.")

"Poèmes": The Exploration of Language

Poetry and Sound, Poetry and the Visual

There are seventy-six "poèmes" in this main section of *La Lune*. The first thirty-one cover more or less the four years of *SIC*'s existence. The poems from the early issues of the journal are grouped together, each one generating others of a similar kind and constantly broadening the exploration of a poetry conceived in sound and vision. For the forty-five others, written between 1918 and 1924, the chronology is more or less respected.[27]

SIC had allowed Albert-Birot to present his most advanced research, providing an opportunity for innovation and for an interaction with the work of other poets and painters. Certainly, presenting a number of the poems in the context of *SIC* is different from presenting them in isolation within the pages of the collection. The poems published in collections during the review's lifetime are less overtly experimental than many of the poems eventually collected in *La Lune*. However, these—*Trente et un poèmes de poche* (1917), *La Joie des sept couleurs* (1919), and *Poèmes quotidiens* (1919)—are equally important in any analysis of Albert-Birot's original conception of a poetics and will be frequently referred to here.

The rate of the poet's creative contributions fluctuated throughout the four years of *SIC*'s existence. The issues of 1916 reveal the paucity of his production up to this point, with several of them not containing a single poem by the journal's founder-editor. From early 1917 until the beginning of 1919, the experimental poems appear with regularity. From this point on, however, Albert-Birot's contributions become once again less frequent. In chapter 2 we suggested that, with the poet now sure of his creative direction, the personal need for *SIC* becomes less important. Yet the "chroniques" continue in 1919 as testimonial to the magazine's activity. A pattern of production is set up which will be that of Albert-Birot's life's work: a search for a mode of expression among a multiplicity of possibilities, an exploration of the medium that ensures "true" creation, the self-affirmation of the poet and of an individual voice and a testimonial sequence.

The difficulties concerning a reading and an understanding of the experimental nature of many of the poems of *La Lune*, and particularly those whose existence depends on the generation of sounds, continue to be a source of discussion in later interviews with Albert-Birot. Each time a certain disarray is apparent on the part of those seeking to bring these poems into being according to the poet's intentions, while Albert-Birot himself clearly continues to enjoy the effects created and to endorse the validity of such experimentation.[28] As for the visual poems, they are considered here as an integral and essential part in the formation of the poetry of Albert-Birot. They present a counterargument to the charge of the merely ornamental and entertaining nature of such poetry, which is frequently used to dismiss a wide variety of visual poetry. The "categories" of sound-generated and visually generated productions we propose for analysis are divided thus:

- the visual and the verbal functioning together
- a midpoint with the visual providing information for or reinforcing the verbal production, or with the visual signs stressing the message to be communicated
- the emphasis on pure sound, with the poem having to be produced aloud to exist
- the visual disrupting the verbal message and addressing principally a viewer

The poems move from a midpoint where sound and vision function together in some way (this can take a number of forms—with the visual providing information for verbal production as in the "Poèmes à voix simultanées" or with visual signs reinforcing the communication of the poem) to one limit where the voice dominates and to the other where the eye takes precedence and the verbal message is secondary. Within these three dimensions, further subdivisions operate, with eye and voice working to a greater or lesser degree in each "category." Here, then, we are moving to the way in which the poem comes into being when received— that is, we are analyzing the poetics at work here, not from the point of production but from that of reception.

Sound and Vision

"Derrière la fenêtre" is the first poem featuring what might be termed typically "modern" techniques to appear both in *SIC* (n° 3, March 1916) and in *La Lune* (p. 311). The technique of "mots collés" suggests futurist inspiration. Although it is not overtly a "sound" poem in the way the later simultaneous poems are, it is reliant on sound for the generation of its effect, as the tram, a feature of the modern city prevalent in much of the poetry of the period, rushes through the rain:

Pluie de gris de pluie
Mugissementtournantdeferfrotté
Pierresquitremblent
Untramwaytourneaucoin
—"Derrière la fenêtre," *La Lune,* p. 99

("Rain of grey of rain
bellowingfrictionedironbend
Stoneswhichshake
atramturnsthecorner")

Albert-Birot explains his technique of "mots collés" in a way that reveals a sympathy with the futurist principle of the penetration of planes that had been developed first as a painting technique and had been one of the aims of Marinetti's attempts to render multifaceted modern experience through his "words-in-freedom." Albert-Birot explains this interpenetration of experience thus: "C'est quand je sens la nécessité de mélanger exactement les choses, les idées . . . qui peuvent entrer l'une dans l'autre, alors le mot collé met l'idée dans cette situation par l'oreille."[29] ("It's when I feel the need to precisely mix up things, ideas . . . that can become part of each other, then a stuck-together-word places the idea into this situation through the ear.").

Yet his perception and use of the technique is not solely futurist-inspired: "Les idées dans l'esprit ne sont pas toujours bien rangées dans l'ordre où nous les écrivons et bien souvent plusieurs viennent ensemble. C'est cette sorte de 'fouillis' que j'ai cherché à rendre en ne faisant qu'un mot de plusieurs mots, et même quelquefois plusieurs lignes d'une seule pièce."[30] ("Ideas in the mind are not always nicely arranged in the order in which we write them down, and very often several appear together. It's this sort of 'jumble' that I've sought to render by making just one word from several words, and even sometimes several lines of one continuous piece.") The "mots collés" recall in their inspiration, as explained here by the poet, a use rather akin to the "stream of consciousness" and the techniques of Joyce. The techniques would also appear to be an intensification, and the logical conclusion of the belief in the "nonseparateness" of poetic production, which led to the nonuse of punctuation for Albert-Birot.

"Derrière la Fenêtre" explicitly contrasts the old, slow modes of transport with the speed and exhilaration of the modern, the experience of which opens up the way towards infinity and the absolute:

Terresmersespaceprofondeurs
Journuit
Pluiesoleil

Infini
Absolu
Un che-val-tour-ne-au-coin
Vieille mécanique
                Pluiegrisdepluie
Untramwayélectrique

("Landsseasspacedepths
Daynight
Rainsun
Infinity
Absolute
A hor-se-tur-ns-the-cor-ner
Old mechanism
                    Raingreyofrain
Anelectrictram")

The contrast between the "tramwayélectrique" and the 'vieille méca-nique' also implies a contrast between the techniques of poetry now considered outmoded and the search for what were considered more fitting ways to express the modern world. There is thematically and technically futurist influence,[31] but the title widens its relationship to include more general preoccupations of the poetry and painting of the period as well. The observation of the city from the window is a privileged theme of the modern experience. Cendrars declares "Les fenêtres de ma poésie sont grand'ouvertes sur les boulevards. ("The windows of my poetry are wide open onto the boulevards"). Delaunay paints his "Fenêtres" series, and Apollinaire responds with his own "Les Fenêtres."[32] Yet the experimental form and the experience of the poem are also a personal adventure. Placed as the opening poem to the modern section of *La Lune*, the old and new Albert-Birot once again face each other. The "vieille mécanique" of "Jeu-Imitation" is now placed behind him, as the conviction of the poet is turned definitively toward the present moment of the avant-garde, defending itself from the conservative backlash of the war period.

The poem is at this first limit of Albert-Birot's work on sound-generated poetry. For its effects to be rendered, the poem must be read aloud, but the visual impact is of equal importance. The typographical setting out is significant. The lines of the "mots collés" expand and shorten, with the words "infini" and "absolu" in spatial isolation.[33] Of the other poems that use this technique, "Un homme qui passe" uses alliteration and assonance, inviting the reader to read out loud and to reproduce the sounds of a poem where the experience of interpenetration is less thematic and more lyrical than that of "Derrière la Fenêtre."[34] The eye is drawn to those words that are capitalized. It is the first poem to incorpo-

———————— DENTELLE ————————

```
IL  FAUDRAIT  TROUVER
ΛΛΛΛΛΛΛΛΛΛΛΛΛΛΛΛΛΛΛΛΛΛΛΛΛΛΛΛΛΛΛΛΛΛΛΛ
U·⚘·N·.·,·.☉·.·.·A·⚘⚘·U·⚘·T ·⚘ :R· ⚘ : E
CCCCC      I    EEEEE     L
C   C      I    E   E     L
C          I    E         L
C          I    E         L
C          I    EE        L
C          I    E         L
C   C      I    E   E     L   L
CCCCC      I    EEEEE     LLLLL
CELUI·⸀·'-'·⸀CI⸀·.·⸀EST·;·T ROP·⸀·.·⸀BAS
ON⸀(⁚⁚)'LE'(⁚⁚)'TOUCHE⸀(⁚⁚)'AVEC⸀(⁚⁚)⸀LA⸀(⁚⁚)⸀MAIN
M⸀A⸀I⸀S⚘I'L⚘E·S·T⚘E'N⚘P·A·P·I·E·R⚘D⸀E⚘S·O·I·E
ΛΛΛΛΛΛΛΛΛΛΛΛΛΛΛΛΛΛΛΛΛΛΛΛΛΛΛΛΛΛΛΛΛΛΛΛ
C/O/M/M/E'/./·/UN·/./·/CER.CEAU·/./·/D'É/C/U/Y/È/R/E
ΛΛΛΛΛΛΛΛΛΛΛΛΛΛΛΛΛΛΛΛΛΛΛΛΛΛΛΛΛΛΛΛΛΛΛΛ
I:L::.,⚘:,.::S:U:F:F:I:T:⚘::D:E:⚘:::D:I:R:E
HH     HH     OOOOOOO     PPPPPPPPP
HHHHHHH       OO    OO     PPPPPPPPP
HH     HH     OOOOOOO     PP
P*O*U*R⸀«»:«»PASSER«»«:»«»AU«»:«»⸀T*R *A*V*E*R*S
HH     HH     OOOOOOO     PPPPPPPPP
HHHHHHH       OO    OO     PPPPPPPPP
HH     HH     OOOOOOO     PP
```

"Dentelle," *La Lune ou le livre des poèmes*, p. 214.

rate capitals in *SIC* and *La Lune*, although this had been used from the second of the *Trente et un poèmes de poche* onward). With "VASTITE-LUMINEUSE" the poetic self simultaneously opens out to the experience around him and incorporates within himself the totality of what he perceives, and "LES IDEES COLOREES" are expressed through the medium of the poem. This poem in particular begins to reveal Albert-Birot's sensibility to the experience of space, both within the poem and outside it, internal space in its "vastité lumineuse" meeting with the "hors de moi." Through the *Poèmes à l'Autre Moi* and *Grabinoulor*, the meeting point of these spaces will be explored intensely.

CAGE

Saute ¡
Sautille i i
Jaune
Dans ta cage verte
Et chambre rouge
Des barreaux
Quand on est oiseau
Qu'on chante et qu'on vole
Mais tout cet enfer
Est en fil de fer
Ravengar
Icare
Mangeur de cavorite
Je vous quitte
Enfer
En fil de fer
Comme une note
Quitte
Sa corde
orde

"Cage," *La Lune ou le livre des poèmes*, **p. 113.**

In "Jardins Publics" the space outside the self comes to meet the poet. The poem uses various techniques—"mots collés," capitalization, and a type of "collage" of sounds and repeated snatches of conversation—to suggest the multiplicity of sights, sounds, and sensations perceived by the poet. The poem is constructed using the techniques of both painting and especially the cinema:

Arbresalléschaisesbancs
COULEURSMOUVANTES EN VERTSOLEIL
Petitbassin petitsbateaux jetd'eau
—"Jardins publics," *La Lune*, p. 102

("Treespathwayschairsbenches
MOVINGCOLORS IN GREENSUN
littlepond littleboats waterjet")

This opening shot widens its perspective to incorporate the noises and sights of the various activities, then gradually draws back to end as it began. The lower case "mots collés" describe the elements of the scene, the capitals emphasize the visual sensation and the "COULEURSMOU-VANTES." It is Delaunay's technique of simultaneity that Apollinaire named Orphism which is called to mind, the whirling forms of contrasting colors in light.[35]

The middle section is a dense poetic "mass," and it is a preliminary indication of a form used throughout Albert-Birot's poetic production, and which he termed "poèmes en masse." There are several like this in the earlier collection *La Joie des sept couleurs*. There, these sections of vertical or horizontal blocks are interspersed with the regular linear form of the poem. These poetic "masses" are reminiscent also of the density of the prose of *Grabinoulor*. The "reporting" of overheard conversations recalls Apollinaire's own "poèmes-conversations." This technique makes the poem into a type of "collage," incorporating elements of the everyday in their recognizable form, but in a newly created context.[36] The poem thus inherits the techniques of cubism and Apollinaire's application of these within poetic form. Once again, however, we guard against the use of the word "influence." For the attempt to render a simultaneity and a multiplicity of experience in a verbal mass is Albert-Birot the "pyrogène," as Apollinaire called him, at work once again. The technique/idea used previously is sparking off in him his own innovation. A prose "block" invites not a linear reading but a juxtaposition of all the elements. The poem presents the observed elements of the everyday with the universal themes of life and death. Just as the swirling colors of the "enfantsroses" contrast with the "femmesennoir," so the childish games of winning and losing remind us of the stakes of war.

The color that shouts from the page among the others is ROUGE, and the eye is immediately drawn to the repeated "LA GUERRE LA GUERRE" in capitals of the same size. As we have discussed in our analysis of *La Guerre* and in our treatment of *SIC*, the war is a fundamental element in the birth of Albert-Birot's modern consciousness, at a moment when modernism was under attack from the conservative establishment, encouraged by the conflict to attack such disruptive forces. In *SIC*, Albert-Birot had initially proclaimed, like the majority of the avant-garde at this point in the war, a belief in the energy of war to be a prevailing force for French art, and for the nation's cultural self-definition, bringing avant-garde and conservation superficially in line. This poem signals a more ambivalent attitude, with the consequences of war placed in their very human context. As for the reception of the poem, it is clear that this stressed visual sign in the text must also be heard. It is a poem where

UN HOMME QUI PASSE

Me voici arrivé

en moi

VASTITÉLUMINEUSE

Palais ? Non

Ateliercirculaireassourdissantauxyeux

Vapeurpistonsbiellescourroiesrouesengrenagessifflementsgrin-
cementsretentissements

silencieux   Couperforgerriver

Embrassementsbaisersétreintes

Forces irradientesascensionnelles

s'incorporentéperdument

LES IDÉES COLORÉES

Hors de moi   dans l'espace

J'entends un homme qui passe

"Un homme qui passe," *La Lune ou le livre des poèmes*, **p. 101.**

sound and vision work in unison, where shades of light and dark must be
perceived visually and rendered audibly.

The Poems "à voix simultanées": Midpoint of Sound and Vision

"Crayon bleu" initiates a series of poems subtitled "à voix simultanées." Although it is the only one composed for three voices, it is not
the most difficult technically. The poem did not appear in *SIC* but significantly appeared in both *Procellaria* and *Dada*.[37] The poem is composed
of lyrical elements for the first voice:

"il fait beau dans mon coeur"
"ô diaphanes réalités"
"Luminosités"
(etc)

—"Crayon bleu," *La Lune*, p. 103

("It's fine in my heart
Oh diaphanous realities
Luminosities")

This is shot through with types of onomatopoeic noises represented in italics, which incorporate elements of the everyday into the body of the poem:

pan—pan—pan   pan—pan—pan—pan
krii   krii
Atchou
(etc)

The third voice adds, in smaller lettering—which would perhaps indicate that this is to be rendered more softly, perhaps more distantly—a few snatches of conversation:

                              merci bonsoir
        je lui dirai
        Jean viens ici

                              ("Thank you good evening
        I'll tell him
        Jean come here")

   The voice of the poet, the sounds of the world around him, and the world of everyday life are re-created simultaneously. The materials that the poet "chante à pleine pâte," are all around him to be seized and transformed. Here the typographical disposition provides the phonetic indications, suggesting variations in tone and speed for the various simultaneous voices. Here we are at the midpoint of these sound-generated poems: visual presentation is important but less for its autonomous visual impact than for the information it provides concerning the verbal production of the poem.

   Albert-Birot's work on language here is one that elicits an active response from his reader, for the poem is not confined within the bounds of a logical sequence. It is the production of a new order of understanding of the world and of the poem. The visual impact immediately demands an active participation, and such a presentation of sounds calls for a reader-speaker, a producer of those sounds rather than a silent consumer. This, in turn, becomes a communal action, because one reader alone cannot render the three voices simultaneously. In this insistence on participation and communication, the poem becomes in every sense a drama, echoing the social, collective practices of the theater. These sound-generated poems are more than avant-garde experimentation. They are indicative of an exploration into the status of the voice and, by implication, of the expression of the presence of the self.[38] Furthermore in a collection in which, as we have already suggested, Albert-Birot explores the nature of poetry at its origins, poems that demand to be spoken out loud again convoke the presence of the tradition of an oral past, when poetry was passed from mouth to ear to mouth and was essential in providing a way for the collective to express itself.

The first of these simultaneous voice poems to appear in *SIC* was "Le Raté" (n° 8/9/10). It follows a similar technique to the previous poem analyzed, though it has a more complex structure. The two voices are indicated typographically by italics and roman letters. The presence of the voices varies between alternation and simultaneity, and the poem is composed of complete words (one voice expressed only with "mots collés") rather than pure sounds. Albert-Birot insisted on the timing of the poem in a musical sense to make apparent the differences in speed that must be rendered when it is spoken. The word PLOMB is capitalized, and the difference between the "mesure lente . . . chronomètre extra-plat" and the "irrésistiblemouvement" must be perceived: "La volonté, c'est l'opposition des deux vitesses, la lenteur et la rigidité."[39] ("What is wanted is the opposition between two speeds, slowness and rigidity.") The final poem "à voix" is different again in structure, a dense mass of type in the center representing the "thoughts" of the outwardly observing and self-reflective subjectivity around which are the fragmented sights and sounds of the poet's journey. Such a composition instantly recalls both cubist and futurist techniques in the visual arts yet insists on the voice for its production. "Métro" is the most complex of this set of poems, revealing Albert-Birot's understanding of both the cubist perception of the world and its transposition into art, and the differences inherent in poetic creation where the voice participates. It is revelatory, too, of his perception of the place and role of the artist/poet at a central point in the world around him, a point through which these elements pass, and at the centre of his creation:

> toute la terre
> aime le centre   cet amour a fait la
> Terre la Terre
> —"Métro," *La Lune*, p. 112

> ("the whole earth
> loves the centre   this love has made
> the Earth the Earth")

This idea had been taken up in the *Trente et un poèmes de poche* and in the "Poème Promethée" in *La Lune*, which will be discussed later.

"Poèmes à crier et à danser": The limit of Pure Sound

With the first of the "poèmes à crier et à danser," "Chant I," here subtitled "essai de poésie pure," we move to the other limit of the sound

JARDINS PUBLICS

Abresalléeschaisesbancs
COULEURSMOUVANTES EN VERTSOLEIL
Petitbassin petisbateaux jet d'eau
Aiguillepiquée centredecercle

Gazons fleurs pigeons moineaux Petits! Petits! non pas
toi gourmand tu leur manges tout Petits! Petits! Cerceauroulant
garçoncourant hep! hep! Cerceaujuponvoitured'enfant non non
Guignol pas par-là voici le gendarme hi hi hi hi hi odeurvanillée
gaufres! les belles gaufres! courserotativeenmusiquedeschevaux
deboisimmobilesporteursd'enfantsrosesivresd'airenrond tourner
tourner femmesennoir la guerre la guerre mon fils est mort si si
ce n'est pas de jeu tu triches c'est moi le vainqueur balle ROUGE
roule rouououle hop! entre mes jambes

Petitbassin petitsbateaux
Rumeurlégère
En notes claires
D'enfantsoiseaux
LA GUERRE LA GUERRE
Arbresalléeschaisesbancs
COULEURSMOUVANTES EN VERTSOLEIL

"Jardins publics," *La Lune ou le livre des poèmes*, p. 102.

poems, where the attempt to create this "pure poetry" finds its accomplishment in pure sound. The disposition of the poem on the page regulates ·the rhythm and length of the sounds, but this serves only as an indication of how to produce the poem vocally. The poem was published in *Dada 2* (December 1917) with the title "Pour Dada," and this title is added in black pencil to the manuscript written in blue ink.[40] In the righthand margin is the title that appeared in *La Lune*. There are only three of these poems, but the technique is employed also in the extended poem "La Légende," subtitled "poème narratif entrecoupé de poèmes à crier et à danser." In that poem the crowd expresses itself solely through sounds that convey excitement, delight, wonder, and the like. The poem ends in a celebration: "dans un mouvement accéléré qui finit en tourbillon" ("A narrative poem interspersed with poems to shout and dance" . . . "in an accelerated movement that ends in a vortex.") Albert-Birot's directions for the poem indicate it to be conceived as a dramatic production, to be produced orally and physically. This small number of poems has excited a great deal of comment from critics, moving them to place Albert-Birot within both the futurist and dadaist movements. The poems

CRAYON BLEU

Poème à trois voix simultanées

Il fait beau dans mon cœur
pan - pan - pan   pan - pan - pan - pan

des mondes va
toc-toc   toc-toc
tu dors

cinémadempensécquejetournenenpleinair
krii   krrii
merci bonsoir

des soleils va
zzzzzzzzzzzz

Je pars et je suis revenu

ô diaphanes réalités

des forêts des forêts des forêts
Atchou
je lui dirai
de l'autre côté

c'est un ballon captif
whou — whou —— whou — whou

luminosités
si tu veux

des monts des mers des villes
pron - pron - pron   drrrr   Jean viens ici

des étés
clac clac

que je ne puis-je aboyer un poème
Les 3 voix
à l'unisson } WHOU — WHOU — WHOU
(imitatif)

allons va va mais va donc
rououououououon

où avez-vous été
vrrrrom — vrrrrrrom — vrrrrrom

des monstres va
vendredi

donnez-moi de la matière
veux-tu te taire

que je chante à pleine pâte
Elgar

que mon poème ait une âme
houi — houi — houi

Ah ma pauv' dame
offensive

et des tripes

"Crayon Bleu," *La Lune ou le livre des poèmes*, p. 103.

MÉTRO

POÈME A 2 VOIX

Mercerou	Dupleix	Grande Roue	Thermogène	il y une place
qu'il est laid	lumière verte		ce manteau ne va pas avec le chapeau	
une lanterne	choir c'est aimer le centre êtres et			un pompon
commissariat	choses aiment le centre toute la terre			rouge sur
	aime le centre cet amour a fait la			
Zénith	Terre la Terre Mobilité la roue			un bonnet bleu
Du onnet	quel coup de génie mon gant droit à			ce coup de
Dubonnet	l'envers peut très bien être mon gant			
	gauche descendre est aussi monter			sifflet
les femmes	quand il fait jour il fait nuit fourrures			
à gosses	mousseline ombrelle parapluie le			main
encore un	bleu du ciel les nuages les orages les			soldes
	ouragans sont peut-être la masse des			
bonhomme	pensées humaines			où faut-il
sale devant moi	que je n'oublie pas mon chapeau			descendre
sortie amandre		Ah il est parti		correspondance
le type du délégué socialiste		une collection de vieilles têtes		
Bon Marché				del Orso

"Métro," *La Lune ou le livre des poèmes*, p. 112.

inspired the Rumanian Isidore Isou to create Lettrism, and the exponents of sound poetry have always claimed him as a precursor.[41]

Albert-Birot stated his intention explicitly as an attempt to render his desire to imagine a poetry made by primitive humans:[42] "reconstituer cette fraîcheur de la poésie des premiers hommes" in his belief that "le mouvement, le cri, je pense que ça a été le premier poème de l'humanité" ("reconstitute this freshness of the poetry of the first men" . . . "movement, shouts, I think that was humanity's first poem.") Thus his attempt to explore the origins of poetry takes him back explicitly to an archaic past, when "language" is movement, sensation, and sound and humans' relationship to the cosmos was less complex, more direct. The exploration of a "primitive" art form in an attempt to capture the very essence of artistic production had been a feature of cubism. For the poets it is above all the exploration of sound and of rhythm that allows this dialogue with the past. Poetry also allows a communication with our innermost being.[43] It is a journey that Albert-Birot would make again in the later collection *Silex, poèmes des hommes des cavernes*, where he once again explores his conception of what humans' first poetry would have been.

POÈME À CRIER ET À DANSER

Chant II

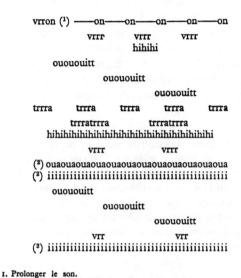

1. Prolonger le son.
2. Mettre la main en soupape sur la bouche.

"Poème à crier et à danser," Chant II, *La Lune ou le livre des poèmes*, p. 117.

With the "poèmes à crier et à danser," we reach the extreme limit of Albert-Birot's sound-generated poetry. He himself recognizes it as such a limit: "Ça c'est à peu près ma dernière limite, je crois que je n'ai pas été plus loin, *parce que pour aller plus loin, il n'y avait plus qu'à garder la feuille blanche.*"[44] Our emphasis. ("That's about my final limit, I believe I didn't go any further, because to go any further, would have been to keep the blank page.")

We are at the limit of Albert-Birot's experimentation, at the limit of human creative history, at the limit of the poem's contact with the page, at the limit of the spoken with the written, and at the opposite limit of "poésie plastique," which forms the other major part of Albert-Birot's modern adventure, at the opposite limit of *SIC*, printed material and visual artifact, at the opposite limit of the dense text of *Grabinoulor*. Here is presented the necessity of taking the poem from the printed page, from the textual body, to reinsert it into its original space, the human body, to be generated by the human voice. The exhortation is to remove the poem from the printed fixity of the page, the restitution of the reciprocal giving of life between poem and human body: the human being is suffused with the rhythm and sound of the poem, and human breath in turn vitalizes the poem. It is a first indication of the divine qualities with which Albert-Birot ceaselessly accredits both the poem and the poet.

It becomes more and more evident on reading these early poems and making a parallel with later work (here, for example, between the "poèmes à crier et à danser" and *Silex*) that a consideration of Albert-Birot's experimentation solely in the light of, let us say, futurist poetics may be an initial revelation, but is finally a superficial reading and one that does not do justice to these later creations. The futurist attitudes to and aims in (re)producing sounds are fundamentally different from those of Albert-Birot:

> S'opposant à l'idéalisme symboliste au nom de la sensibilité pragmatiste et anti-psychologique du monde moderne, Marinetti avait assumé des positions d'un matérialisme absolu; inspiré par le naturalisme et le positivisme il avait ainsi préconisé l'emploi des onomatopées dans les mots en liberté Futuristes, en tant que mimésis de la vie et de la matière: "le bruit qui naît du frottement et du choc des corps solides, liquides ou de gaz en vitesse est devenu un des éléments le plus dynamique de la vie futuriste. Le bruit est le langage de la nouvelle vie humaine mécanique."[45]

> ("Opposing symbolist idealism in the name of the pragmatic and antipsychological sensibility of the modern world, Marinetti had assumed the position of an absolute materialism. Inspired by naturalism and positivism, he had therefore advocated the use of onomatopoeia in futurist words-in-freedom, as mimesis of life and matter: "the noise that is born of the friction and the shock of solid bodies, liquids, or gases moving quickly has become one of the most dynamic elements of futurist life. Noise is the language of the new mechanized human life.")

This position leads to a discussion of its development by Russolo, in particular with his 1913 "L'Art des Bruits," and to "le bruitisme," as we have previously alluded to in our section on *SIC*. Situating Albert-Birot within this perspective, the commentary continues: "Chez Albert-Birot cette idée est traduite de façon exemplaire. Ses "poèmes à crier et à danser" conjuguent dans une même performance l'explosion vitaliste et le matérialisme. La canalisation de l'émission vocale, qu'il préconise, rend à celle-ci son statut physique d'énergie jaillissante et de voix qui reste ancrée dans un corps."[46] ("In Albert-Birot's work this idea is translated in an exemplary way. His 'poems to shout and dance' bring together vitalist explosion and materialism in the same performance. The canalization of the vocal emission, which he advocates, gives this its physical status of gushing energy and voice that remains anchored in the body.") Certainly here we are closer to the corporeality of the reaction that the poems incite, but with Albert-Birot's use of sound we are far away from the "langage de la nouvelle vie humaine-mécanique" (Marinetti) of futurist endeavour. It is significant that the title of "L'Avion" was suppressed in favor of a more general and less representational one, "Chant II," although the "vronn" and "traa" sounds place this particular poem closest to futurist technique and mechanical noises.[47] The "Chant I," published in *Dada*, works within a more Dadaist perspective of a language stripped of all meaning and certainly invites a comparison with Hugo Ball's phonetic poems.[48] Albert-Birot's research is into the primitivism of expression rather than mechanical reproductions of the "modern" sounds. It is the exploration of a language discharged of its semantic weight, a language devoid of referential meaning, an attempt at pure expression.[49]

Through sound Albert-Birot explores emotion, sensation, the incantatory power of sound. The voice, the ability to generate sound, is analogous to life itself, and even the word "mort" may be (re)vitalized by its sound made in the mouth and spoken by the voice: "Beau dans sa brillante sonorité mais justement cette sonorité si lumineuse ne correspond pas du tout au silence noir que le mot représente ceux qui l'ont inventé sont sûrement des peuples nés avec l'immortalité dans la tête." ("Beautiful in its brilliant sonority but precisely this luminous sonority does not correspond at all to the black silence that the word represents those who invented it are surely peoples born with immortality in their heads") *Grabinoulor*, V, 14.

If for Albert-Birot sound is the sign that the human body is filled with a life force, that the machine is running properly, his delight in the sounds of language is closer to Barthes's "bruissement de la langue" than to the futurists' "bruitisme":

> Or, de même que les dysfonctions du langage sont en quelque sorte résumées dans un signe sonore: le bredouillement, de même le bon fonctionnement de la machine s'affiche dans un être musical: le bruissement.
>
> Le bruissement, c'est le bruit de ce qui marche bien. Ce sont les machines heureuses qui bruissent.[50]

("Just as the dysfunctions of language are to some extent summed up in a sonorous sign: spluttering, so the smooth running of the machine is given musical form: murmuring. Murmuring is the noise made by something that is working well. Happy machines murmur.")

However, there are problems concerning language's capacity to "bruire":

Parole, elle reste, semble-t-il condamnée au bredouillement; écriture, au silence et à la distinction des signes: de toute manière, il reste toujours trop de sens pour que le langage accomplisse une jouissance qui serait propre à sa matière.[51]

("The spoken word, it seems, is condemned to spluttering; writing, to silence and to the distinction of signs. In any case, too much meaning always remains for language to accomplish an enjoyment that would be appropriate to its matter.")

We are reminded here of Albert-Birot's stated intention to "alléger la poésie" and to suppress the semantic weight of words, "parties lourdes des mots," which leads to the unison of sound with movement in order to express the essence of poetic emotion.[52] What follows in Barthes's account would appear to be a description of just such a language freed of its semantic content and therefore its "trop de sens":

Mais ce qui est impossible n'est pas inconcevable: le bruissement de la langue forme une utopie. Quelle utopie? Celle d'une musique du sens; j'entends par là que dans son état utopique la langue serait élargie, je dirais même *dénaturée*, jusqu'à former un immense tissu sonore dans lequel l'appareil sémantique se trouverait irréalisé; le signifiant phonique, métrique, vocal, se déploierait dans toute sa somptuosité, sans que jamais un signe s'en détache (vienne *naturaliser* cette pure nappe de jouissance), mais aussi—et c'est là le difficile—sans que le sens soit brutalement congédié, dogmatiquement forclos, bref, châtré. Bruissante, confiée au signifiant par un mouvement inouï, inconnu de nos discours rationnels, la langue ne quitterait pas pour autant un horizon de sens: le sens, indivis, impénétrable, innommable serait cependant posé au loin comme un mirage, faisant de l'exercice vocal comme paysage double, muni d'un "fond"; mais au lieu que la musique des phonèmes soit le "fond" de nos messages (comme il arrive dans notre Poésie), le sens serait ici le point de fuite de la jouissance.[53]

("But what is impossible is not inconceivable. The murmuring of language forms a utopia. What sort of utopia? That of the music of meaning; I mean by that that in its utopic state language would be broadened, I would even say *denatured*, to the point where it forms an immense sonorous web in which the semantic apparatus would find itself unrealized. The phonic, metric, vocal signifier would unfold itself in all its sumptuousness, without a sign ever detaching itself (let this pure sheet of enjoyment *be made natural*), but also—and this is where the difficulty lies—without the meaning being brutally dismissed, foreclosed, in a word, castrated. Murmuring, given to the signifier by a movement unheard of, unknown to our rational discourses, language would not, nevertheless, leave behind the horizon of meaning. Meaning, undivided, impenetrable, unnameable, would, however, be placed far away like a mirage, making of the vocal exercise a sort of double landscape, furnished with a 'background.' But instead of the music of phonemes being the 'background' of our messages (as it is in our poetry), the meaning would be here the vanishing point of enjoyment.")

Albert-Birot's "poèmes à crier et à danser" would appear to have as their goal the type of linguistic Utopia described here by Roland Barthes.[54] Such a parallel raises the question of Albert-Birot as a precursor, of an Albert-Birot not only at the heart of an avant-garde and of a collective adventure at the beginning of the twentieth century, but as a poet-creator whose work announces and prefigures later experimental texts and individual creative questionings that were to follow. The position of Albert-Birot within the developments of the twentieth century can only be approached with a more definite and complete view after an appreciation of *Grabinoulor*. We will offer our suggestions in the concluding remarks of this study. At this point in the development of our analysis, this is merely an indication that once his situation within the avant-garde movements of the early twentieth century is established, this is only a beginning. The way is opened up for fifty years of continued creativity, a quest toward an understanding of self, of the world, and of literature.

As we work toward a conclusion of this section, which has been a short survey of the poet's exploration of sound, Barthes's concluding paragraph to the article we have quoted is particularly fitting, especially given the Albert-Birot of classical literature and philosophy who has simultaneously sought modern modes of expression:

> Je m'imagine aujourd'hui un peu à la manière de l'ancien Grec tel que le décrit Hegel: il interrogeait, dit-il, avec passion, sans relâche, le bruissement des feuillages, des sources, des vents, bref le frisson de la Nature, pour y percevoir le dessin d'une intelligence. Et moi, c'est le frisson du sens que j'interroge en écoutant le bruissement du langage, de ce langage qui est ma Nature à moi, homme moderne.[55]

> ("I imagine myself today rather like the ancient Greek as described by Hegel. He questioned, he says, passionately, relentlessly, the murmuring of the foliage, the springs, the winds, in a word the quiver of nature, to perceive there the design of an intelligence. And for me, it's the quiver of meaning that I am questioning in listening to the murmur of language, of this language which to me, a modern man, is nature.")

Albert-Birot is ancient Greek and modern human being. His entire project is encapsulated here. This handful of poems is essential for an understanding of his work as a whole.[56]

The poem is for Albert-Birot a physical embodiment of the creative act. His poetry constantly inscribes the story of its creation in its relationship to the human body, as we shall discover also in the following section covering the impact of the visual in the construction of the poem. The sound poems are meaningless until revived, revitalized, reinspired by the human voice and breath, reactivated by the body. These poems are sound and movement. Such a poem is the place of an intense subjectivity for both creator and reader, revealing the search for the origins of humanity, poetry, and an individual.[57] The varying speeds, sensations, and emotions lie inert until stimulated by the receiving body, and the exchange is reciprocal, for the body perceiving the poem on the support of the printed page is habitually passive and inert while reading until urged to movement by the poem. At its origin the creator breathes life into his creation. At its reception the reader recites and reciprocates.[58] The poem is made present by the voice; the voice is the expression of the human subject. It is equally the link to the divine and the sacred through its sources of incantation and of magical force. The poet instinctively touches the wellspring of the power that the word had or has in oral cultures: "The fact that oral peoples commonly and in all likelihood universally consider words to have magical potency is clearly tied in, at least unconsciously, with their sense of the word as necessarily spoken, sounded, and hence power-driven."[59] It is the advent of the Logos to which we will return in our reading of *Grabinoulor*.

Spoken words are therefore "power-driven," dynamic, as Walter Ong indicates in his study of the passage of the word from mouth to print, for oral utterance comes from inside "living organisms." At our point in the history of the printed word, we tend to ignore this fact: "Deeply typographic folk forget to think of words as primarily oral, as events, and hence as necessarily powered: for them, words tend to be assimilated to things, "out there" on a flat surface. Such "things" are not so readily associated with magic, for they are not actions, but are in a radical sense dead, though subject to dynamic resurrection."[60] Thus the spoken and the written word have a different relationship to "reality," and this is of primary importance to the sacred:

> The interiorising force of the oral word relates in a special way to the sacral, to the ultimate concerns of existence. In most religions the spoken word functions integrally in ceremonial and devotional life. Eventually in the larger world religions sacred texts develop, too, in which the sense of the sacral is attached also the written word. Still, a textually supported religious tradition can continue to authenticate the primacy of the oral in many ways.[61]

The claim to orality in *La Lune* thus revives poetry's links to its archaic past in multiple ways, further establishing it as a foundation text in a sacred sense. It is a manual and a guide, to be spoken and heard, a founding moment that must endure. Furthermore for a poet who constantly returns to the importance of communication between the poet and the crowd, between creator and those who receive his creations, the message cannot fail to assume a sacred significance.[62] *La Lune* calls to the archaic, to the sacred, to the origins of literature, and to the experiments of the avant-garde.[63] The text of pure sound is a "texte-limite."[64] Albert-Birot's knowledge and understanding of the poetic impulse are inscribed and given voice in *La Lune*. Its subtitle *"le livre des poèmes"* is intensely revelatory of its nature. It is sacred text, The Book, that reveals the origins and nature of creation and of poetic communication.

The voice, we have already suggested, is also the intense moment of a subjectivity. Each voice speaks a self, and through the articulation of sounds the self comes into being. As Albert-Birot's creation develops, so the self will be made visible, manifest. The voice is a medium of communication. Yet prior to this it is a reaching into an interior space, a communication with the self. It is this inner dialogue that will be developed in the *Poèmes à l'Autre Moi*. In *La Lune* the poet has not yet reached this intense apprehension of self. Sound is a way of apprehending the external and of positioning the self with regard to it.[65] At this point the voice is the center of the self that seeks to meet with the external. The graphic illustration of this we have seen in the poem "Métro."

Already in *La Lune,* Albert-Birot presents the poet firmly at the center of his existence, assimilating, directing, and reassembling the myriad sensations he encounters. Richly suggestive, given the process of creation we have proposed as a constant of Albert-Birot's productions, is Ong's development of the idea of the position of the individual in relation to the universe around him:

> The centering action of sound (the field of sound is not spread out before me but is all around me) affects Man's sense of the cosmos. For oral cultures the cosmos is an on-going event with man at its centre. . . . Only after print and the extensive experience with maps that print implemented would human beings, when they thought about the cosmos or universe or "world," think primarily of something laid out before their eyes . . . a vast surface of assemblages of surface (vision presents surfaces) ready to be "explored."[66]

What we are suggesting is that with Albert-Birot's investigation of the limits of language and sound, and his perception of the poet firmly at the center of the universe, the poet enters into an archaic dialogue and a perception of human existence, which is perhaps nostalgic—nostalgic for an oral past and the security of an existence at one with that universe at once inside and outside. The "modern" view of humankind and its inventions had restored humanity to the center of creation but had left an existential void and a fear as well as excitement in the possibilities of the modern world. The acclaimed "joy," "optimism," "oui à la vie" of Albert-

Birot's poetry, reiterated by every commentator, is founded on his belief in the power of poetic creation through which the poet may retrieve a lost relationship with the cosmos and at the same time elevate humankind to divine status.

The idea that it is through rhythm and repetition that the poet reaches some kind of apprehension of infinity, of an absolute, is one to which we will return in the study of *Grabinoulor*. Yet sound itself is not enough, What of the other limit of poetry, the realm of the visual? The voice may speak of and enter into a dialogue with infinity, but it cannot appropriate a lasting moment, an eternal:

> All sensation takes place in time, but sound has a special relationship to time unlike that of the other fields that register in human sensation. Sound exists only when it is going out of existence. It is not simply perishable but essentially evanescent, and it is sensed as evanescent.[67]

In an oral culture, the sounds of poetry endure through repetition. The modern poet must commit his words to paper to acquire for them the status of the eternal. A paradox thus arises, for such fixing of the word may be linked to death rather than to life, the words condemned to silence.[68] The modern poet must explore the medium of the written, isolating, unspoken perhaps, but with the chance of "salvation" because it is enduring.

Albert-Birot situates his poetry between the two extremes of the human apprehension of language, both of which take place in the body: the archaic impulse of an oral culture to commit to communal memory, to follow the rhythms of the body and the cosmos, and the perception of the written word in modern technologized society, isolated, silent, closed on and in the page, a private exchange between the individual and the word. The commitment of the word to space on the page fixes it, and although related to the world of sound, in print an extra dimension is added. Furthermore writing makes words appear to be similar to the things we see around us. Words may be seen and touched. They are objects, they "belong" to us. They are externalized and eternalized. A new space is created, a new relationship between body and word.[69]

Poetry and the Visual

Through his own mastering of the printing process, Albert-Birot fully realized the implications of the written, and above all the printed, word and its mode of functioning compared to the spoken word.[70] The marks on the page allow an exploration of the space of the page that supports them and beyond that of the mental space that perceives them. There is an immediate perceptual and theoretical problem presented by any speculation on the poem's physical embodiment, or the form of its typographical arrangement on the page, as this entails separating these elements from the rhythmic and phonic elements.[71] In this study we attempt to analyze these elements together where possible and separately where necessitated by the form of the poem.

We have previously proposed in our discussion of the "sound" poems of *La Lune* that Albert-Birot's work is generated from and oscillates between two poles—the intensely visual and pure sound, between the silent manifestation of a creation and the vociferous celebration of that creation with a midpoint where the eye and the voice work together to embody the creation physically and vocally. Within the "visual" poems a similar course may be charted to that of the previous section, from an initial moment where sound and vision work in unison, to a place where the visual signs stress the message to be communicated, to a point where the emphasis on typographical disruption interferes with the reading process, displacing the vocal elements and preferring to present a direct visual impact. This is equally true of the obvious comparison to be made in the poems of Apollinaire in *Calligrammes,* where visual form may emphasize verbal content—for example in "Il pleut"—or where typographical disposition demands each time a new approach to reading, a challenge taken up by a number of critics who offer various ways of approaching these often different poetic constructions.[72] The questions concerning the status of the linguistic sign, the poet's attitude toward it, the functioning of the poetic creation in space and the reception of the text by the reader are the areas that have provided the most fruitful and thought-provoking criticism.[73] As Anis points out, it is particularly since the theories and experimentation of the twentieth-century avant-garde, reinforced by developments in both semiotic methods of investigation of text and image and the consideration of the place of the reader in the generation of the written text, that such texts have lost their "innocence": "Pour l'ensemble de ces courants de recherches, l'espace graphique ne se réduit jamais à une transparence, à un médium neutre."[74] ("In all these trends in research, the graphic space is never reduced to being transparent or just a neutral medium.") This is the perspective in which we have elaborated our theoretical procedure, which is based on the conferral of new status on the "support" of the written text as validated by the creative procedure of the avant-garde and the theoretical procedure of semioticians.[75]

The lack of an adequate critical term to serve as description and perceptual interpretation of such poetry is testimony at once to its varying manifestations and to our disarray when confronted by it. In their analysis of the graphic space that characterizes the various types of "visual" poetry, Anis and Puech propose the term "poème paginal,"[76] inspired by

a passage from Mallarmé's preface to "Un coup de dés," itself an introduction to the concept and its conception, which remains essential for
any explanation of the functioning of the poem in space.[77] To some extent
the term limits the scope of the poetry of Albert-Birot in that much of
his creation rather exhibits a desire to leave the support of the page than
to exploit the space of its support—that is, to function in a universal
space rather than in the space of the page. Again it brings our creator
close to the figure of reference to which we constantly return. Apollinaire
also creates a personal, mythical space in such poems as "Coeur couronne et miroir" and "Lettre-Océan," poems that function certainly on the
space of the page yet elaborate the space of the poet's imaginary into
which the reader may enter.[78] "Poésie cubiste," "poésie plastique," "poésie visuelle," "poème paginal"—none of these labels adequately describes
the multiple functioning of such poetry.

The question remains as to how the reader does exactly perceive, see,
read these constructions, and the problem is one to which we will return
after our consideration of Albert-Birot's productions. Certainly there is
a comparison to be made between his works and those of his contemporaries, Apollinaire, Reverdy, and Cendrars, in particular. Our intention
here, however, is not to cover in any depth the comparison between
various techniques and conceptions but rather to focus as exclusively as
possible on the nature of Albert-Birot's work alone and on the place of
a visual poetics within the framework of his larger poetics of creation.[79]

Visual poetry is at the limit of two perceptual languages: "au carrefour
de la lisibilité et de la visibilité,"[80] exploiting the visual properties of
written language and the semantic possibilities of visual form.[81] In a type-
written article in the Fonds Albert-Birot on Roch Grey's "Les Chevaux
de minuit," the poet reveals to what extent the multiple facets of the
visual are essential to poetic creation and for his own poetics:

> Au premier regard jeté sur cet admirable livre on 'VOIT' par la très particulière
> disposition typographique du texte . . . une forme visuelle. . . . Je pense qu'il
> faut voir là un double désir: d'abord traduire par le mouvement graphique
> quelque chose qui correspond au mouvement de l'esprit qu'il est en train de
> composer et en plus, un désir de jouer, de s'amuser, de se donner au plaisir
> des yeux en écrivant qui ensuite sera un plaisir pour les yeux du lecteur.

> ("With the first glance at this admirable book, you 'SEE' through the very
> particular typographical arrangement of the text . . . a visual form. . . . I think
> that a double desire should be seen therein: first, to translate by the graphic
> movement something that corresponds to the movement of the mind, which is
> in the process of composing, and, in addition, a desire to play, to have fun, to
> give oneself to a visual pleasure, which will then be a pleasure for the eyes of
> the reader.")

The visual allows the expression of a new intelligence of the world ("mouvement graphique/mouvement de l'esprit") and a full exploration of the creative act and of the possibilities and limits of poetic creation. As with sound the body of the poet, and of the reader, is called on to participate, to celebrate. The visual is pleasure, a game that allows the creator to give form to his desire: "Nous entendons le chant de joie du Créateur devenu fabricant et qui donne à son oeuvre la forme exacte qu'il souhaitait."[82] ("We hear the song of joy of the Creator turned manufacturer and who gives his work the exact form he desired.")

The Visual Reinforces the Verbal Message

The first in the series of poems to utilize typographical experimentation in a visual way, rather than to indicate sound or rhythm patterns, as we have previously explored, is "Les Eclats," which is placed in *La Lune* immediately after the third "poème à crier et à danser." Thus two typographical processes, perceived very differently by the reader, are placed literally side by side. "Les Eclats" first appeared in *SIC* n° 28 (April 1918) with the subtitle "poème-idéogrammatique," an "explanation" that was not reproduced in the collection of *La Lune*. Within the context of *SIC*, such a title would again suggest that Albert-Birot's research is situated in the orbit of Apollinaire's own experiments.

Situated thus in a pivotal position, the poem has received some critical attention (G. Lista, for example, suggests that the typographical disposition is that of a "bouquet de fleurs").[83] Given the title and the scattered visual disposition that reinforces this verbal image, together with the date (1918) printed in *SIC*, the poem would rather suggest its link to the theme of war, and such a fragmented form is doubly rich in suggestions, given our own analysis of the canvas *La Guerre*. The typographical disposition of "Les Eclats" is literally that of an explosion, the particles of the shell proclaiming their destination. Such a poem invites also a physical manipulation of the poem, the placing of the poem horizontally, rather than on its initial vertical plane, suggesting also the blast from a gun. The words of love in the upper left-hand side are printed in tiny letters in a direction contrary to that of the thrust of the main body of the poem, a timid, fragile refutation of the more aggressive delivery of the poem. Their slightly curved appearance, recalling the continuity/discontinuity dialectic of *La Guerre*, invites us to read them as words of life and hope, belonging to that which is eternal. Read in such a perspective, the thrusting vertical/horizontal shapes jutting into space, elongated and sharp, express the dynamism of the ambiguous present moment and the ambiguity of war itself. The first of Albert-Birot's visual poems, therefore, functions within the visual language he has previously created on canvas. For

LE RATÉ

poème à deux voix

Mesure lente — arabesque grise —
temps similaires
lac mauve — chronomètre extra-plat —
cuivre — zinc — étain — PLOMB —

Irrésistiblemouvementenformedeforceclaire
ensemble { à l'assautdespuissancesnoires
{ *Mesure lente — arabesque grise — lac mauve*

Épanouissementdeclartémâlegénératrice —
(desmondeslyriques
(*Arabesque grise*

Rutilementcolorédespulsations
(vitales
(*Arabesque grise*

Harmoniesimprévuesdes
(dissonancesdutemps
(*Mesure lente — chronomètre extra-plat*

Soulèvementsrythmiquesdes
(complexitéssonores
(*Cuivre—zinc—étain—PLOMB*

Vertigecélestialdesimmensitésspatiales
Amour — délice — et orgue — tic-tac tic-tac tic-tac

"Le Raté," *La Lune ou le livre des poèmes*, p. 106.

POÈME IMAGÉ

Deux voix simultanées
(Lire de bas en haut).

PIERRE ALBERT-BIROT.

"Lundi," "Poème Imagé," *SIC*, nᵒ 24, December 1917. Editions Jean-Michel Place, p. 181; *Poésie 1916-1924*, p. 111 without image.

the purposes of our analysis, it also sets up a first "subdivision" within our typology of Albert-Birot's visual poems, where the verbal message is reinforced by visual form and where the dialogue between poetry and painting, between Albert-Birot/poet and Albert-Birot/painter, is made explicit through typographical disposition.

The second of the visual poems in *La Lune* is "Reposoir," which suggests a similar research, although the poem is more adventurous typographically and the reading of it presents more of a problem.[84] The disposition recalls that of a small area of ground: sand, small stones, leaves, and grass in lowercase letters, the capitals following the flight of "un oiseau qui passe." The eye is attracted in particular to four movements of the poem—two lines disposed normally, "de l'herbe fatiguée" and "couleurs anciennes," and two of unusual disposition that echo each other: "feuilles mortes," "feuilles sèches." Thus in the initial distribution of the print on the page, the passing of time and the presence of death are indicated in the background of the "landscape." The four concluding lines, disposed conventionally, confirm the message received through the visual impact of the poem. They again place the poem thematically within Albert-Birot's poems of the war period and formally within our scheme of continuity and discontinuity. Within the ambiguity of the present, which may bring death, there is hope and belief in the renewal and continuation of life:

> Mais là-bas le vert est plus jeune
> et l'herbe remue
>
> —"Reposoir," *La Lune,* p. 125

> ("But over there the green is fresher
> and the grass is waving")

The poem is juxtaposed between a visual typographical setting out and a more conventional one. However the disposition places it within the same "division" as "Les Eclats," where the visual echoes, reinforces, makes explicit the verbal, particularly here as the movement of the bird, at once incorporated into and external to the "scene" of the poem, cuts through the fixity of the image on the printed page. Yet the movement of the young, green grass is created as a verbal rather than a visual image. There is a visual/verbal interaction in "Les Eclats" and "Reposoir," and we must read the poems in terms of Albert-Birot's own poetic language. In earlier manifestations of "la poésie plastique," in *La Joie des sept couleurs,* the visual poem is a "poème-dessin," where the interaction between word and image is generated mimetically.[85] Concrete images of an imaginary space—such a creation is more familiar to the poetry of the nineteenth century than the twentieth. Here Albert-Birot maintains a belief in meaning. This first naive equation between the visual and the verbal (the attempt to make signifier and signified coincide, as Timothy Mathews describes the futurist project) situated in the celebratory *La Joie des sept couleurs* is Albert-Birot's initial creative position. Yet just as Albert-Birot/painter moves from the figurative, through cubism to abstraction, so, too, does the relationship of Albert-Birot/poet to language become more complex, more analytical, and more self-reflective. It is in *La Lune* that this change takes place.

LES ÉCLATS

Je
t'
ai
me

Je veux le cœur d'une vierge
Je veux les seins d'une nourrice
Pourquoi n'irais-je pas jusqu'à Dieu
Je préfère un saint du paradis et des âmes en prière
J'aurai un bras
Moi je tuerai les pierres
J'aurai une tête

"Les Eclats," *La Lune ou le livre des poèmes*, **p. 121.**

The Visual and the Verbal Function Together—the Midpoint of the Visual Poems

The poems that follow "Reposoir" lead the way into the "poèmes-pancartes" and "poèmes-affiches," which are the previously most commented on of Albert-Birot's visual poetry. "Exposition de Toilettes d'été" first appeared in *SIC* n° 40/41 (February/March 1919). The title was repeated in fragments or complete throughout the poem, suggesting the incorporation of an advertising poster into the poem. The words glimpsed in the outside, everyday world enter the imaginary space of the poem and create a passageway between external and internal worlds. The technique is reminiscent of that of cubist collage, where elements of the everyday are literally the material of art, a technique whose impact would reverberate throughout the creation of all artistic objects, canvases, and texts of the twentieth century.[86] Apollinaire commented on the use of lettering particularly within the cubist canvas: "Picasso et Braque introduisaient dans leurs oeuvres d'art des lettres d'enseignes et d'autres inscriptions, parce que dans une ville moderne, l'inscription, l'enseigne, la publicité, jouent un rôle artistique très important et parce qu'elles s'adaptent à cette fin."[87] ("Picasso and Braque introduced in their works of art letters from signs and other inscriptions because in the modern city, writing, signs, and advertising play a very important artistic role and because they lend themselves to this end.") The poet thus seizes upon the importance of the word. From the painter's point of view, it is the contrasting colors that speak: "Cette affiche jaune ou rouge hurlant dans ce timide paysage, est la plus belle des raisons picturales nouvelles qui soient; elle flanque par terre tout le concept sentimental et littéraire et elle annonce l'avènement du contraste plastique."[88] ("That yellow or red poster screaming in this timid landscape is the most beautiful of the reasons for new pictorial form. It puts paid to the entire sentimental and literary concept and announces the coming of visual contrast.")

This type of recuperation of anonymous inscriptions is utilized, for example, in Apollinaire's "Lettre-Océan." The relationship between these and the "poèmes-conversations" is an immediate one. Fragments of conversation are used in a type of "sound collage," and the everyday once again enters directly into the work of art.[89] Albert-Birot expresses the difficulty of any direct apprehension of the world of language, however, and this poem begins:

> Les paroles sont des petits ballons de toutes les
> couleurs qui nous échappent et vont doucement
>   danser au plafond
> et quelquefois le plafond crève le ballon et quelquefois
>   le ballon crève le plafond
>   —"Expositions des toilettes d'été," *La Lune*, p. 126

> ("Words are little balloons of every
>   colour which escape from us and gently go
> to dance on the ceiling
> and sometimes the ceiling bursts the balloon and sometimes
>   the balloon bursts the ceiling.")

Language is used up and swept away, disposable material of the twentieth century:

c'est pour cela que tous les
matins dans les maisons les domestiques ont à balayer beaucoup de paroles crevées

("and that's why every
morning in houses maids have to sweep up
lots of burst words.")

Language is living and therefore may die. The seizing of words, the apprehension of the world through language is fraught also with danger: "Il y a aussi des gens imprudents qui saisissent le fil d'un petit ballon." ("There are also rash people who grab the string of a small balloon.") Belief in the poetic act endures, however, and finally poetic transposition is possible:

Et puis les plus belles
Montent jusqu'au Ciel
De la Terre et d'ailleurs on les voit presque toutes les nuits

("And then the most beautiful
float up to the Sky
from the Earth and what's more we see them nearly every night.")

The transposition of the everyday into art allows a fixing in the eternal to which the poetic quest ceaselessly returns.

The following poem "Girouette" also comprises what would appear to be an advertising poster for "C. Beroit, Chicory Fabricant," glimpsed as poet and poem take the metro, becoming incorporated at that moment into the creation of the poem (*La Lune*, p. 128). The impact of these elements of the everyday, the references to reality, go far beyond the merely anecdotal. Within the canvas, the incorporation of letters raises questions concerning the space of the painting:

Ces lettres constituaient une information supplémentaire sur l'espace du tableau et sa profondeur, par leurs dimensions, mais aussi par la dynamique propre
à la lettre ou mot, d'indiquer des directions gauche-droite, haut-bas, ou l'inverse, selon qu'elles étaient placées horizontalement ou verticalement; dynamique désignant par contraste la profondeur du tableau et la redoublant *dans un
espace imaginaire, qui est celui de la lecture sonore ou visuelle.*[90]

("These letters constituted through their dimensions extra information on the
space and depth of the painting, but also through their dynamics, which are
the feature of the letter or word and which indicate directions right and left,
top and bottom, or vice versa, according to whether they were placed horizontally or vertically. A dynamics which shows by contrast the depth of the paint-

ing, a depth which is intensified *in the space of the imagination, the space of visual or sonorous reading.*")

In the cubist canvas, the perception of perspective was questioned by the use of lettering. Obviously the poetic preoccupations are different. Yet the underlying premise is the same—to make visible the poetic/artistic process of transformation from the observed everyday to creation. It is an art that is no longer imitation, a poetry that is no longer merely lyrical or the expression of sentiments, but an art—visual or literary—that presents concretely our relationship to the real. In "Girouette" the outside world calls out to the poet and demands the apprehension of its sounds:

> Holà poète
> C'est-le-son-d'une-clochette-qui-traverse-le-mur-sans-qu'on-le-
> voie-vient-s'enfoncer-dans-mon-oreille-et-me-ressort-au-bout-
> des-doigts dididing
> > —"Girouette," *La Lune,* p. 128

> ("Hey poet
> It's-the-sound-of-a-bell-coming-through-the-wall-without-anyone
> seeing-it-embeds-itself-in-my-ear-and-comes-out-through
> my-fingertips ding ding.")

The poet's task is to transpose those sounds into the poem. He carries the poem within him during his metro journey. When the everyday calls him this time with its sights, the visual begins to truly be, as the fragmented perceptions become part of a created whole:

> Boîte vase ou palais
> Je vous donne la vie quand mes yeux vous ont vu

> ("Box vase or palace
> I give you life when my eyes have seen you")

These two poems in particular, making manifest the creative process itself, are situated at a midpoint where sound and vision work together. They remind us of the similar midpoint position within the sound-generated poems we have previously discussed. The "poster-poems" of the four "poèmes-pancartes" and the five "poèmes-affiches" are at once visual and verbal—visual in their impact, verbal in their message. These are not like the "poèmes-dessins" of *La Joie des sept couleurs.* The "affiches" are more complex in design. The third, using a single letter *A,* is reminiscent of the large capital *A* that begins *La Joie des sept couleurs*—

REPOSOIR

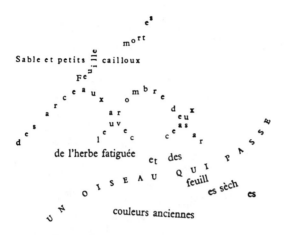

"**Reposoir**," *La Lune ou le livre des poèmes*, **p. 125.**

the large, bold *A*, the beginning of the alphabet and the vowel that demands the mouth wide open, the beginnings of both sound and vision, of verbal and visual communication, the voice and the eye working together. Albert-Birot imagined, indeed intended, these posters to interact with the urban space, recalling also Apollinaire and Léger, as previously quoted:

> Albert-Birot imaginait ces poèmes sur les routes placardés comme des affiches publicitaires. . . . Il voyait poèmes-affiches comme une poétique dans la ville. De moindre dimension que les pancartes, ils évoquent un temps de la vie urbaine que l'affichette avait ainsi retenu et souligné.[91]

> ("Albert-Birot imagined these poems along the roadside stuck up like advertising billboards. . . . He saw the poem-posters as poetry in the city. Being of smaller dimensions than the boards, they evoke a moment of urban life that the small poster had retained and emphasized.")

PIERRE ALBERT-BIROT

EXPOSITION
DE TOILETTES D'ÉTÉ

Les paroles sont des petits ballons de toutes les couleurs
qui nous échappent et vont doucement danser au plafond
et quelquefois le plafond crève le ballon et quelquefois le ballon
crève le plafond

TOILETTES D'ÉTÉ

c'est pour cela que tous les
matins dans les maisons les domestiques ont à balayer beaucoup de paroles crevées

EXPOSITION DE TOILETTES D'ÉTÉ

et puis il y a aussi celles qui
se jettent par les fenêtres et vont s'abimer dans les rues de
la ville grand embarras pour les voitures et les piétons hélas

TOILETTES D'ÉTÉ

causes d'effroyables accidents et
puis il y a aussi des gens imprudents qui saisissent le fil d'un
petit ballon ou bleu ou jaune ou rouge ou blanc et s'y suspendent
et pour beaucoup de ceux-ci le fil casse ou le ballon éclate
et ils tombent et se font parfois très mal il y en a d'autres qu'on
n'a jamais revus
Et puis les plus belles
Montent jusqu'au Ciel
De la Terre et d'ailleurs on les voit presque toutes les nuits

EXPOSITION DE TOILETTES D'ÉTÉ

"Exposition de Toilettes d'Eté" *La Lune ou le livre des poèmes*, p. 126.

Here we see the poeticizing and mythologizing of the city, another
preoccupation of twentieth-century discourse. There is then to be a reciprocal exchange between the everyday and poetry—the everyday providing the material of poetic creation and receiving back its own transposed
reflection; raw material and creation interact and divulge something of
their respective nature and composition.

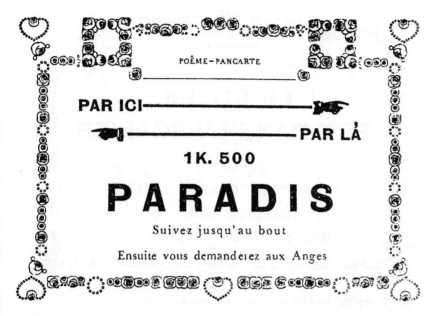

"Poème-Pancarte," *La Lune ou le livre des poèmes*, p. 181.

The Visual Disrupts the Verbal Message

We arrive now at the final limit of Albert-Birot's poetry, where visual impact takes precedence and where the visual presentation of the poem disrupts the verbal message, requiring the application of a different reading process. The poem "Ode," placed almost at the end of *La Lune*, is one of Albert-Birot's most experimental forms. It was originally displayed on a rotating column, with the single letters arriving by chance and depending on the position of the viewer.[92] The poem is an object to be seen, the letters acquiring a movement and a dimension in space very different from the perception we have of them on the printed page. The "event" of the poem incorporates an element of chance, as the reader's/spectator's eyes fall upon them at random. Albert-Birot, therefore, literally puts into action the intention of Mallarmé in "Un coup de dés." The date 1922 in the poem suggests a greeting to the New Year. The poem as a whole is composed of twelve letters, five of which may be rearranged to spell the word "POEME" and the remaining HIRRERY is evocative of a cheering, a shout of jubilation, although this element of the vocal is totally disrupted, arranged in such a way that the eye takes precedence over the voice.

Of the remaining poems of visual impact, "Fleur de Lys" and "Rosace"

POÈME-PANCARTE

LE SOLEIL
EST DANS L'ESCALIER

POUR TOUS RENSEIGNEMENTS
S'ADRESSER PLUS LOIN
CHEZ LE MARCHAND DE VIN

"Poème-Pancarte," *La Lune ou le livre des poèmes,* p. 182.

are perhaps more open to the charge of being merely "ornamental," although they once again trace the coming into being of the poem. As the reader's eye follows the unfurling of the lines, the poem becomes, comes into being: "Mon poème devient." Even in such "decorative" pieces, more serious creative preoccupations are at work, between the hand of the poet and the eye of the reader. Hand and eye are explicit in "Rosace": "Vous verrez les os de ma main." Head and heart are also convoked for the physical generation of the poem. With "Regardez et vous verrez" four times repeated, the reader/spectator must look and look again for the poem to come into being.[93] From such a perspective, "Dentelle" equally invites closer attention. Its content is certainly a recurrent theme in Albert-Birot's work, the ability of the poet to pass into another world where the dimensions are more suited to the poetic self. Formally the poem is a visual tribute to the beauty and skill of such an endeavor: "Un pur hommage à la typographie, prouvant l'habilité du poète à monter une page et à la caler: caractères retournés, couchés, décalés, utilisation détournée des signes et jeu suprême où les mots sont composés uniquement avec les lettres qui les forment."[94] ("A pure homage to typography, proving the skill of the poet to set and make up a page using characters in unusual alignments, turned around, laid down, shifted about, an unexpected use of signs and a supreme game in which words are solely composed of the letters that make them up.") The connotation of lace, fabricated by hand, becomes a metaphor for the typographer's/

━━━ POÈME-AFFICHE ━━━

ATTENTION

DÉFENSE DE FUMER

A

CE CHEMIN MÈNE AU CIEL

A

ATTENDEZ

LE POÈTE

A A A

VIENT LE VOICI

"Poème-Affiche," *La Lune ou le livre des poèmes*, **p. 204.**

poet's art, the human manufacture of an object of beauty through knowledge, patience, and skill. The reference to the circus, "un cerceau d'écuy-
ère," implies also the ludic and the element of pleasure inherent in such
a process, where skill is dissimulated as "divertissement."

The poem is also perceived as a block of print on the page, and this
leads into another "category," another form of Albert-Birot's visual

"Ode," *La Lune ou le livre des poèmes*, p. 216.

poems, and a consideration of the impact of such a block of type on the page. In "Dentelle" the block of print is manipulated, fragmented; in "Poème Prométhée" there is a more rigorous application of such a technique. "Poème Prométhée" first appeared in *SIC* n° 30, June 1918, and it is evidently a type of matrix for poetic creation: "Albert-Birot attachait une certaine importance à ce poème du télégraphe qui allait marquer une nouvelle étape de son écriture. Quatre fois quatre carrés parfaits, autrement dit 16 vers, lui semblèrent la forme accomplie du poème."[95]

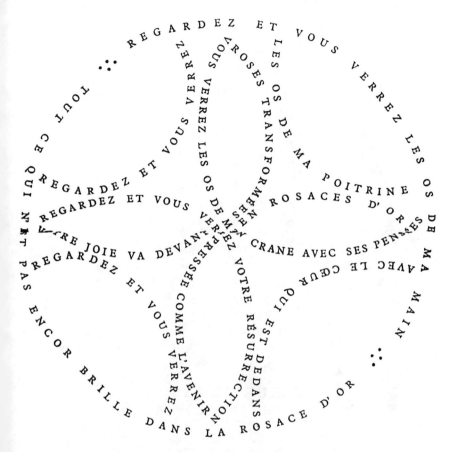

"Rosace," *La Lune ou le livre des poèmes*, **p. 200.**

("Albert-Birot attached a certain amount of importance to this telegraph poem, which would mark a new stage in his writing. Four times four perfect squares, in other words, sixteen lines, seemed to him to be the accomplished form of the poem.") The symbolic and mythological connotation of the title leaves the reader in little doubt as to the poem's centrality to the problematics of creation and the ambiguities of any quest for knowledge. In an artistic perspective, a comparison with the techniques of analytical cubism is irresistible. Even though the poem's content is more concerned with the sounds of the outside world, its form provides the impact. The elements of reality are perceived, analyzed, synthesized, and given back re-formed as on a cubist canvas.

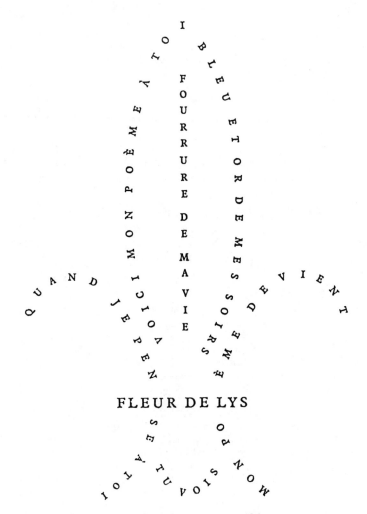

"Fleur de Lys," *La Lune ou le livre des poèmes*, p. 196.

The principle of the sixteen-line poem identified by Arlette Albert-Birot is evident in the tribute to Apollinaire, "Ma Main Amie," that follows, but without the rigor of the sequence of nine poems later in the collection: "Les Corbeaux" (p. 167), "Le poème sans nom" (p. 168), "Fox Film" (p. 208), "De l'est à l'ouest" (p. 215), "Retour" (p. 222), "L'Avenir joue" (p. 223), "Poème Rose" (p. 220), three sections of "Les Jours" (p. 217), and the final part of "Le Feu" (p. 183), all composed in rectangular blocks. The technique had also been used to great effect, inserted

POÈME

PROMÉTHÉE

LES MOTS QUI COURENT OÙ VONT-ILS

Je vois	Le pote	Sonori	Gent m
passer	au n'est	té des	ais l'ou
rires et	pas très	cloc h	rs gris
pleurs	d r o i t	es d'ar-	est l a s

Tac tac	Reviens	z s z s z s	Verts c u
tactactac	ne peuẍ	z s z s z s	ls de bou
tactactac	me pas-	z s z s z s	teilles à
tactactac	ser de	z s z s z s	l'envers

Fil d'a-	T u n'as	Le globe	De mots
m o u r	pas l e	est u n	et m o i
fils d'ar-	p a s s o	gros pe-	j e s u i s
g e‚n t	ur d o u	l o t o n	le chat

S p a t i a	Tactactac	Tac tac	Est m o r
lité san	tac tac	où est le	te je sui
s i n c o	tac tac tac	chatnotr	s pris da
n n u e s	mademoi	e Jeanne	ns les fils

P I E R R E   A L B E R T - B I R O T

"Poème Prométhée," *La Lune ou le livre des poèmes*, **p. 131.**

periodically, within the narrative-type structure of *La Joie des sept couleurs.*

The "Poème-Prométhée" is a type of matrix that concretizes the poem. Although in a literal, graphic sense it might be called a type of "poésie cubiste," its intentions extend beyond visual representation. The formation of the written word into blocks of print issues both from painterly techniques and from the work on the material of language. Most notably it is into the "Poème Prométhée" that Albert-Birot works his own name, not yet at the center of the creation, as did Apollinaire in "Coeur couronne et miroir," but as frame, limit, border, the self at this intermediary point between two universes, one external, one internal. The principle of the

JE ME SUIS AUSSITÔT RÉPANDU COMME UNE LUMIÈRE
ON PARLAIT DERRIÈRE LE MUR QUI N'ÉCOUTAIT PAS
IL Y A DES VERS DANS LE PIED DE LA TABLE ET DESSUS
MUSICALITÉ ASCENDANTE DU BLEU UNE CULOTTE UNE CHEMISE
AVEC UN HOMME DEDANS ET DE LA JOIE QUI SE FROTTE LES MAINS
NOTRE BEL AUJOURD'HUI EST AMOUREUX DE NOUS ON A
CHANTÉ LA MARSEILLAISE MAIS C'ÉTAIT UNE VOIX DE
IL ENTRE UN CHANT PLUS BEAU QUE LA MARSEILLAISE
QUAND ON OUVRE SA FENÊTRE LE MATIN LA ROBE
ROSE ROSE EST ÉTENDUE SUR LE CIEL ET SUR LE DIVAN
ET JE DIS QUE LE MONDE EST LE CERCLE DES POÈTES
QUE CELUI QUI N'AIME PAS NE SE RÉVEILLE PAS
LA TRISTESSE EST HORIZONTALE LA JOIE EST VERTICALE
AVEZ-VOUS BIEN DORMI MADAME VELINA ET VOUS MERCI
CHAQUE JOUR AUJOURD'HUI EST AMOUREUX DE NOUS
QUAND IL NOUS VOIT PARAÎTRE À LA FENÊTRE

"La Joie des sept couleurs" (section), *Poésie 1916-1920*, Rougerie, p. 140.

poet as "telegraph pole," center of communication, and intermediary for the relaying of human intelligence, recalls the early "poème de poche": "Je suis le poste central où tous les fils aboutissent" ("I am the central receiver where all the lines end up" VIII, p. 19). Apollinaire placed himself at the center of the mirror of language that reflects artistic creation: Albert-Birot at this stage is the point of convergence, not yet sure of the identity of his creative self. The game in the "Poème Prométhée" is one of serious dimensions. The poet/painter may be able to play with the multiplicity of existence and of language, even with infinity, by exercising a rigorous set of constraints ("la règle du jeu"), playing a part of the totality in order to attain the whole, taking a section of the infinite with which to play infinitely: "Comment dirai-je la joie du Monde maintenant que me voici tout seul je la dirai mathématiquement"[96] ("How shall I speak of the joy of the World now that I am all alone I will say it mathematically.")

This proclamation of intent in *La Joie des sept couleurs* is followed by two "blocks" each composed of sixteen lines. These "blocks" of print of dramatic visual impact are thus very different from the "contour"-type "poèmes-dessins" or the visual and verbal message of the "poèmes-affiches"[97] The poems are a visual working out of a type of analytical and creative problem: how to present the disparate elements that generate the created construction in an adequate form. The final consideration in this type of poem, where the visual takes precedence over the verbal, brings us to the "Poème-Rébus" (p. 202) and demands another type of deciphering via the visual. "Le 'poème-rebus' se lit tantôt en clair, en déchiffrant la typographie, tantôt comme un rébus, en tenant compte de la graphie, des caractères employés, de la disposition des lettres."[98] ("The

Les fleurs dans leur vase

       n t

o   l
         '

    e t a
    o   i
    ê b r   petit meurent

l
a   u
R   d s   D   Q U E
o   u   a   N   V
s   e pose l   E   O
e   i   o   T   U
e a u m i l   n   T I U L S
                 A   D
                 E   I S I
OÈME-RÉBUS   L   E
                 L   Z
                 E   Q U'

"Poème-Rébus," *La Lune ou le livre des poèmes*, **p. 202.**

'poem-rebus' can be read both obviously by deciphering the typography, and as a puzzle, taking into account the graphic form, the characters used, the placement of the letters.") In *Discours Figures*, Lyotard devotes a section to the way in which the rebus works in a discourse: "le rébus est un discours travesti d'un objet visible."[99] ("The rebus is the disguised discourse of a visible object.") Such a puzzle functions within the discourse, within the graphic space of the text, rendering the plastic aspects of that space visible.[100]

The confusion arises around the substitution of the visual element for the linguistic one within the context of the written text. For Lyotard the rebus presents the "figural" at work in the discourse, functioning differently from the purely linguistic poem and from the "calligramme": "Le poétique est au moins la présence du figural dans le discours. Y parle-t-on encore par choses? Oui, mais les choses ne sont plus seulement sur le papier. Où sont-elles? Dans l'esprit, comme image? C'est aller trop vite."[101] ("The poetic is at least the presence of the figural in discourse. Does one still speak there through things? Yes, but the things are no longer just on the page. Where are they? In the mind, in the form of an image? We are running ahead of ourselves. . . .") Once more Albert-

Birot's exploration of the visual is another facet of the exploration of the creative process and of the perception of the created object. In the rebus a verbal message is slowly constructed from the visual signs. And yet the poem, whether "poème-dessin," "poème-affiche," "poème-rébus":

> travaille exclusivement avec du signifiant linguistique. Même quand le texte se lit sur un calligramme, le contour de la 'colombe poignardée.' Le lisible n'est jamais répudié. Paradoxe du figural venant se faire héberger par le texte sans le détruire.[102]

> ("works exclusively with the linguistic signifier. Even when the text is read on a 'calligramme,' like the contour of the 'stabbed dove.' The legible is never repudiated. The paradox of the figural is when it comes to lodge itself in the text without destroying it.")

This is certainly true of Albert-Birot's visual productions. The visual "pattern," even when privileged, is finally subordinated to the linguistic communication. The initial visual impact and the trajectory from total to parts in sequence and back to total make visible both the creative process and the process of our perception of it. In his visual poetry Albert-Birot continues to its logical conclusion his exploration of language and the nature of the poetic object. For the poet it is in the manipulation of the letters on the page that more of the facets of language and of the objects it creates are revealed. In the reception of the text, the practice of reading is equally revelatory.[103]

THE MANUAL OF A POETICS: "QUE VAS-TU DIRE, AMI? L'INDICIBLE / QUE VAS TU PEINDRE, AMI?—L'INVISIBLE"

The artist, who in his or her painting and drawing comes to an understanding of the creative act and produces a microcosm of creation through the form and space of the canvas, applies himself or herself as poet to the concrete dimensions of the poem to produce a construction that is at once visual and verbal. Thematically personal joy and a vitality, a celebration of the creative force, fuel Albert-Birot's experimentation. Structurally, the visual form of that creation leads the reader to the origins of literary creation, to the place where his typographical experimentation invites us:

> Toutes les directions qu'il assume sont, celles d'une typographie neuve, d'une imprimerie à créer, d'une composition à inventer, d'un espace à habiter, d'une écriture à faire, d'une valeur phonémique à trouver, et il devient le digne compagnon de la création, réalisant le contenant et le contenu.[104]

("All the directions he takes are those of a new form of typography, a way of printing to be created, a composition to be invented, a space to inhabit, a form of writing to create, a phonic value to be found, and he becomes the worthy companion of creation, realizing the container and the contents.")

The space of the page is the space at work in the poetic imagination, present in the human psyche. It is this that makes an understanding of Albert-Birot's visual poetry an essential component of an appreciation of his work in its totality. The fact that he mastered the printing process and printed *La Lune* himself at the near-beginning of his poetic output cannot be reiterated often enough. Creation does not only take place in the mind of the poet, it is received not only in the mind of the reader: creation is concrete, the poem is an object. The printed space is a practical, functional, and mechanical one. The poet/reader replaces it with a "literary or aesthetic space," an imaginary space.[105] Here mechanics and aesthetics fuse to create a space that is at once imaginary and material. According to the testimony of Arlette Albert-Birot, the poet worked directly from manuscript composition to the typographical composition. In *La Lune* the printed page is as much the place of a creation as when the poet first picked up his pen:

> La plume à côté du papier
> Attend que le poète
> Les unisse.
> —Haï-Kaïs, n° 6, *La Lune*, p. 152

("The pen at the side of the paper
waits for the poet
to unite them.")

The intensity of Albert-Birot's visual poetry lies partly in the pleasure of corporeal contact for both the typographer/poet/creator and the spectator/reader/receiver. The superficial visual delight belies deeper bodily sensation just as the sound poems explore the archaic noises and rhythms of poetry. This is not experimental poetry for its own sake nor merely playful audacity in breaking the rules, being willfully "modern." It is not a sterile artistic practice in search of something even more "new." The relationship between the body of the poet and the body of the poem is fundamental to Albert-Birot's work as a whole. Here it assumes its place in the modern aesthetic as a questioning of the processes of creation and of the place of the self in that creation. In the later collections, *La Panthère Noire* and *Silex*, the sophistication of the game with time and space takes on greater intensity. However it will not be in the construction of a "plastic" space on the page that Albert-Birot will continue his prolonged questioning into the relationship between the space of the page and the imaginary space. The final "blocks" of poetry that close *La Lune* look back and forward, as their titles ("Retour" and "L'Avenir joue") suggest, and the realization that the effect of cubist expression may be written linearly without losing its poetic intensity becomes apparent:

Il y a là-bas qui me prolonge et ici que je tiens et ailleurs
il y a le dos la face le profil mais je suis toujours devant
—"Les Jours," *La Lune*, p. 217

("There is over there which prolongs me and here which I hold and elsewhere there is the back the front the profile but I am always at the front")

On part et l'on revient et c'est toujours le même jour et la même heure et la
    même main
Maintenant est éternel il n'y a pas de tout à l'heure à bientôt ni d'avant ni
    d'après
—"Poème Rose," *La Lune*, p. 220

("You go and you come back and it's always the same day and the same time
    and the same hand
Now is eternal there is no later soon nor before nor after")

As Albert-Birot composes these lines, Grabinoulor, eternally present himself, has already made his appearance into his poetic universe. He is born of the perception of a world as seen through the eyes of the cubist artist. He is created by a poet who has tested the limitations and possibilities of his material.

At the end of *La Lune* between "Retour" and "Avenir," Albert-Birot at once subsumes his own past and his future:

Et voici qu'on parle tout seul et qu'on tend réellement la main à la main
    souvenir
On ne sait plus combien de temps on est revenu on n'a plus rien à se dire
A-t-on déjà mangé tout son bel héritage et faut-il encore s'en aller
—"Retour," *La Lune*, p. 222

"(And here you talk to yourself and you really hold out your hand to the
    remembered hand
You no longer know how long you've been back you have nothing more to
    say to yourself
Have you already used up all your fine inheritance and must you go away
    again")

The short line that ends "Retour" is answered by the opening of "L'Avenir joue":

Il regarde et il voit la maison qui s'en va et l'Avenir joue
                          —"L'Avenir joue," *La Lune,* p. 223

("He looks and he sees the house that is leaving and the Future plays")

Far from being condemned to silence ("on n'a plus rien à se dire"), the dialogue with the self will begin with new intensity in the *Poèmes à l'Autre Moi,* and the step toward a perpetual dynamic movement and an eternal moment taken in the company of Grabinoulor. Finally it is not through a simultaneous visual impact that Apollinaire's vision of past, present, and future may be merged and held in a poetic moment. It is not through the assemblage of type on the page but in a linear narrative created originally in the cubist "state of mind."[106] This will form our approach in the final chapter. The revelation of cubism had been the perception of the multiple facets of the object, and its major contribution to artistic expression the elaboration of a visual language in which to express multiple perceptions, with which to view, think, and render the object and our perceptions of it in its complexity. Eye, ear, and mind work simultaneously—an intense moment when receiver and creator, reader and poet, spectator and artist are bound together in the creative moment, in the act of creation.[107]

The visual poems of *La Lune* may be to a certain extent "set pieces," but they remain part of a greater whole. The prose narrative may be set, fixed linearly in print, but its dynamism must still visually and rhythmically function and be perceived from a multiplicity of angles. Returning to Roger Caillois's point that the evolution of artistic form has been one from fresco to individual canvas, from poetry to poem, we may simultaneously perceive in the work of Albert-Birot the opposite journey, a desire to return to those origins, to a poetic universe of completeness. *Grabinoulor* is epic and fresco, and although the power and force of the individual poem is never denied, rupture of any kind is fought against. A will to continuous communication, to the process of creation, to the dynamic movement inherent in the process of an oral literary tradition leads Albert-Birot to attempt to "write himself out of" the paradox of the printed word. The artist/poet in him may delight in the aspect of the page, but the philosopher/poet is troubled by its closure, isolation, and implied lifelessness. The poet is trapped by the necessity of print into a metaphysical drama: his creation is a way of "escaping," denying time, eternalizing creator and creation in enduring form, while at the same time that creation may be condemned to a nonlife on the page:

One of the most startling paradoxes inherent in writing is its close association with death. This association is suggested in Plato's charge that writing is inhuman, thing-like and destroys memory. . . . The paradox lies in the fact that the deadness of the text, its removal from the living human lifeworld, its rigid visual fixity, assures its endurance and its potential for being resurrected into limitless contexts by a potentially infinite number of living readers.[108]

Albert-Birot enters into the practice of typographer half as game, half in seriousness, exploring the limits of the effects of language. As for Apollinaire typographical experimentation, whether emphasizing the visual or the phonic, allows an exploration of the dynamics of language, allowing the act, the action, creation to be made visible while rendering manifest simultaneously the processes of the creative self and the role of the reader/spectator/speaker. Yet the innovations of Albert-Birot never reach the sophistication of Apollinaire in "Lettre-Océan," which exploits all his varying techniques. Despite an obvious pleasure in the artifact he has created, a kind of metaphysical malaise has set in, making him suspicious of solely printed works. Albert-Birot is seduced, like many other poets, into making an attempt to make object and word coincide, but the experiment is abandoned without taking it toward any attempt at exhaustivity, as he had done with pure sound.[109]

In *La Lune,* foundation text of a poetics, Albert-Birot activates language from both limits, giving volume to both sound and vision: words must be present both audibly and visually. Visual poetry is not a denial of sound but an exploration of another dimension of language:

Concrete poetry plays with the dialectic of the words locked into space as opposed to the sounded, oral word which can never be locked into space (every text is pretext), that is, it plays with the absolute limitations of textuality which paradoxically reveal the built-in limitations of the spoken word too.[110]

Albert-Birot, arriving at the medium of language after exploring the visual arts, tests the limits and capacities of his material. Sounds provide an excess, a superabundance of language; the visual space on the page may present a way of closing off a section, which may be polished and offered as a complete object. Having tested his material and its functioning in external space, the poet turns to the way it may function in his own internal space. What has become evident through the writing and printing of *La Lune* is that the poet can never present in a totality an imaginative space in the typographic space. After the introspection of the *Poèmes à L'Autre Moi* and the consolidation of self, the narrative of *Grabinoulor* will open more and more onto that imaginative space in an attempt to encompass the very body and spirit of creation, physical and spiritual presence, in a textual body without the closing off, the setting up of limits, which imply lifelessness rather than a dynamic creation.

La Lune shows the development of an individual creativity. Each of its disparate elements is a reflection on the freedom and constraints of language as a creative material. Each is an adventure in language on which the reader embarks with the poet, hallmark of a modernism that will ceaselessly expose its own illusions through the work of very different writers and poets. In the poetry of Albert-Birot, each element, each poetic unit is the moment from which a universe is built and expands, the endless moments of a poetic logic that is the foundation and continuing force of *Grabinoulor*. This is finally what brings Albert-Birot's poetics closer to cubism than to any of the other experimental forms he has tried out—the synthesis of simultaneous realities, a poetic unity, a perpetual movement of/in the multifaceted object, which may perhaps, through the skill of creator, be held in an eternal present made sublime. *Grabinoulor* will achieve in an apparently linear narrative a "chain" of poetic instances.[111] *La Lune* is the work of the artisan who has laid his material out before the eyes (and ears) of those who will receive it, as the material is tested, hammered, and molded into shape. The poems are the products of a craftsman: 'Tout ce qui est dans la tête, sa tête, il le réalise avec sa main.'[112] ("Everything that is in his head, he realizes with his hands".) For the reader, for the *reception* of the text, the poem demands a corporeal response. Through the body passes the musicality of the poem, sounds, rhythms, impulses, the breath, the life force of the spoken word. Through the visual also comes a corporeal response, pleasure in the object, a reflection on space, on the place of the artistic object and its relationship to the human. Functioning with and through the body, the poem is itself physical embodiment. In *La Lune* there is privileged contact between reader and poem, reader and poet. The physical engagement of the reader through voice and touch and eye is ascertained, for the viewing of the poems cannot be passive, the poem must be engaged physically. The body of the text and the body of the reader fuse in the way in which all poetry demands, a demand we sometimes find obscure or difficult, for here also is the meeting place between self and other, a space fraught with uncertainty, fragmentation, fragility, but a space that the poet demands of the reader to come to. *La Lune* is a manual of poetics. The reader is asked to look at, to touch, to hear, and to vocalize, to read Poetry. It is in *La Lune* that we may first uncover a process of creation, how a creativity takes form, how the ineffable ("l'invisible," "l'indicible") may be expressed. At varying speeds and intensities, in various forms, Albert-Birot's poetry sends out its messages, and both poet and reader come to touch the core of poetic creativity.

The production of *La Lune* with eye, ear, voice, body, and mind renders the world at once visible, audible, tactile, and intelligible—the poem and the world that is the poem. The present of the poem is the presence of the poet, the two bound up together in a poetic moment that subsumes past, present, and future. If there is a physical presence of poet, poem, and reader, there is also metaphysical presence. The rhythm, the musicality of the spoken word, is the "musicalité de la pensée,"[113] the rhythm of thought, of all human activity, the rhythm and breath of the universe. The poem is the space where these relationships between individual and universal may be explored. It is the space where the limits and capacity of the self may be explored. The poem is metaphysical reflection and a quest for knowledge. This questioning of the processes of artistic creation questions the processes of all creation: How does Being come into existence from Nothingness? The experimental nature of the poems of *La Lune* has led the poet far beyond the collective discourse of the avantgarde to the place of an individual questioning the production of a new order of understanding of the poem, the self, and the world.

Outside, within, and finally against the artistic movements of the period—futurism, cubism, and surrealism—Albert-Birot has affirmed himself as artist/poet/creator, imitating, innovating, and finally finding his own voice and way, propelled forward by an instinctive vitalism, an enduring belief in the force of artistic creation that will allow him to resist any compromise in the elaboration of the huge enterprise that is *Grabinoulor.*

The artist/poet has worked the present moment, has situated a personal creative moment within literary and artistic history, juxtaposing through canvas and page a past, present, and future. Yet that personal moment must be worked more intensely, with a greater subjectivity, that the hitherto fragmented might assume a place of continuity, of duration. The poems that close *La Lune* move closer and closer to *L'Autre Moi* and to *Grabinoulor.* It is not through pushing language to pure sound or to the limit of silence that further exploration can be made:

> Me voici respirez-moi l'Avenir lui tourne le dos l'Avenir se retourne et sourit
> Me voici et le sourire anéantit le temps perdu et vient tout droit jusqu'ici
>   l'Avenir joue
>
>   .   .   .
>
> Et L'Avenir est parti à bientôt je regarde il a laissé la couleur de ses yeux
>   —"L'Avenir joue," *La Lune,* p. 223

> ("Here I am breathe me the Future turns its back to him the Future turns
>   back again and smiles
> Here I am and the smile abolishes lost time and comes straight here the
>   Future plays
>
>   .   .   .
>
> And the Future has gone see you soon I look and it has left behind the
>   color of its eyes")

This last line is the concluding line of the collection. The way forward is in the exploration of the self and in the coming to an understanding of the transposition of that self to Poetic Self: the dialogue with the self begins.

4

The *Poèmes à L'Autre Moi*: The Reflection on/of the Self

Mais quoi, l'autre? Ce n'est pas un autre, c'est toujours moi, je suis en deux parties, voilà tout, une qu'on voit et l'autre qu'on ne voit pas, mais qu'est-ce que ça fait, elle n'en est pas moins là, et moi je pense qu'avec cette partie invisible de moi je vais faire des choses encore plus magnifiques qu'avec mes gros bras et mes rudes mains. Et tout cela est naturel.

—*Les Mémoires d'Adam*

("But what does that mean, the other? It's not an other, it's still me, I am made of two parts, that's all, one part that can be seen and the other part that cannot, but what difference does it make, that part's no less present, and I think that I'm going to do even more magnificent things with this invisible part of myself than with my big arms and my rough hands. And all that's completely natural.")

Et que l'on peut offrir à soi-même et à quelques autres dans un poème qui a l'air d'être fait de lettres assemblées en mots ordonnés sur du papier mais qui prend la forme du poète et de son infini

—"Huitième poème," *Poèmes à l'Autre Moi*

("And which you can present to yourself and to several others in a poem which seems to be made of letters combined in words ordered on the page but which assume the shape of the poet and his infinity")

AN ARCHAEOLOGY OF THE SELF

In *SIC* the discourse is one of a search to define a field of knowledge; knowledge concerning artistic creation and life itself; an ontological quest that explores the human subject, the individual and collective; and the beginning of a journey to explore self, other, and the world. In *La Lune* the poet invited his reader to explore the processes of creation—artisanal, emotional, intellectual, between silence and sound, between the spoken word and the visual. In the *Poèmes à l'Autre Moi,*[1] the poet reveals some of the processes of the poetic imagination, the source of a mythical space, and the space of creativity. He invites us to witness and participate in the movement of the transposition of the Self, a self made sublime, self to Self through the mediation of Poetry and through the presence of the Word. This desire in Albert-Birot's work for an extraordinary Self living an extraordinary existence in an extraordinary universe has been recognized by several critics previously: "Un moi sublimé en moi universel offre aux autres son éternel."[2] ("A self made sublime as universal self offers to others a status as eternal.") Jean Follain writes of the "transposition émerveillée des actes usuels de l'existence" ("marvelous transposition of the usual acts of our existence") and Albert-Birot's intent as he pursues "l'ajustement de soi-même à l'univers"[3] (the adjustment of the self to the universe"). Throughout his creations Albert-Birot continues "la quête incessante et magnifique de soi"[4] ("The never-ending and magnificent quest for the self").

> Aussi la solitude d'Albert-Birot sera réduite par les doubles qu'il suscite. Cette orchestration du double apparaît dans toute sa force avec ses *Poèmes à l'Autre Moi* qui s'élargissent d'autant et effectuent leur montée lyrique dans cette forme du verset qu' Albert-Birot leur donne. Pour les faire soudre, il lui a fallu descendre dans l'intime le plus profond et se réconcilier avec son visage, avec lui tout entier.[5]

> ("Albert-Birot's solitude will furthermore be reduced by the doubles that he creates. This orchestration of the double appears in all its strength with the *Poems to the Other Self* which spread themselves and fulfill their lyrical rise in this form of verse that Albert-Birot gives them. To make them fuse together, he had to descend down into the innermost depths of himself and reconcile himself to his face, to his entire self.")

Such an insight provides a foundation for any study of *L'Autre Moi.* For Follain, Pierre Albert-Birot the man effects this internal journey and returns Pierre Albert-Birot the poet. Like Jean Follain, André Lebois writes with comprehension and passion on Albert-Birot's desire and potential for self-exaltation and provides several instances throughout the work,[6] celebrating Albert-Birot's certainty in the power of creation, yet always with the vague and disturbing background of writing against something, like Rémy Floche who writes "pour ne pas être transformé en bureau."[7] ("so as not to be tranformed into a desk"). Max Pons, tireless promoter of Albert-Birot's work, writes of "le génie du poète qui refait le monde à sa dimension."[8] ("the genius of the poet who remakes the world to his own dimension"). Without denying the exaltation and joy in the possible fulfillment of the potential of the self, none of these commentators seek to explore the implications of such a quest as we have set out to do in our reading of the *Poèmes à l'Autre Moi* or to consider the reasons for these immediate responses to the texts. In her preface to Albert-Birot's play *Matoum et Tévibar*, where the question of the true poet and his alter ego the false poet Tévibar is explored in a light-hearted and farcical manner, Germana Orlandi begins to uncover more complex issues at work: "Le poète discerne en lui-même le cercle des forces contraires qui l'enserrent et l'obsèdent."[9] ("The poet discerns in himself the circle of opposing forces that surround him and obsess him.") Whatever the form this other of the self, positive or negative, may take, it is indispensable for the creative process here at work: "Le Moi semble ne pouvoir exister sans la co-présence antagoniste et complémentaire de l'Autre Moi avec lequel il entretient un dialogue libérateur."[10] ("The self seems to be unable to exist without the antagonistic and complementary copresence of the other self with whom it holds a liberating dialogue.") The concept of the double of the self is an essential generating force of *Grabinoulor*, who in volume III meets Furibar, his most constant and most antagonistic companion and whose dialogues form a large part of the narrative. The exploration of the self leads not only to divine transposition but equally to a more mundane self-knowledge. Nonetheless it is from self-knowledge that the possibility of the sublime comes into being: "Un monde se forme dans notre rêverie, un monde qui est notre monde, et le monde rêvé nous enseigne des possibilités d'agrandissement de notre être dans cet univers qui est le nôtre."[11] ("A world is formed in our reverie, a world that is our world, and this dreamed world teaches us the possibility of the enlargement of our being in this universe which is our own.") Critics have also, perhaps too easily, read Albert-Birot's desire for the Other Self, and indeed other selves, because both thematically and structurally there is a recurrence of doubles in all his work as a type of "autobiography." "Notre auteur a besoin de cette fiction du double, il en joue, il en fait une sorte d'autobiographie simulée où le regard-miroir de l'introspection suit les péripéties d'un moi de plus en plus authentique."[12] ("Our author needs this fiction of the double, he plays with it, he makes of it a type of simulated autobiography where the introspective look in the mirror follows the ups and downs of a more and more authentic self.") One of the reasons for this ready acceptance of the symbiotic relationship between Albert-Birot and his creation lies again in the poet's personal mythology; his friends and close associates often called him "Grabinoulor."[13] Jean Follain writes:

On en vient à appeler Albert-Birot du nom de son héros, mythique projection de lui-même dans sa longue vie imaginative, traversant aisément le temps et l'espace, se mouvant dans la plus énorme fantaisie et il y a un Grabinoulor qu'on voit, un autre qu'on ne voit pas. Ce double se manifeste tantôt chez *Adam* "le premier homme sous le ciel," tantôt chez *Rémy Floche*, tantôt chez cet autre soi-même pris à partie dans le recueil intitulé *Poèmes à l'Autre Moi.*[14]

("Albert-Birot came to be called the same name as his hero, the mythical projection of himself in his long imaginative life, traveling easily through time and space, moving in the most enormous fantasy, and there is a Grabinoulor that can be seen, another which cannot. This double manifests itself as much in *Adam* 'the first man beneath the sky' as in *Rémy Floche* and as in this other self taken to task in the collection called *Poèmes à l'Autre Moi*.")

As Arlette Albert-Birot remarks, bringing a very real knowledge of Albert-Birot's life with poetry to her observation, poetry is:

La projection de soi: elle est le double animé que l'on interroge dans les *Poèmes à l'Autre Moi* ou bien le personnage de Grabinoulor. . . . Albert-Birot s'essayait, au sens où l'entendait Montaigne, son ami de toujours, à travers lui-même devenu Grabinoulor, Rémy Floche, Adam, du premier au dernier poème, il veut créer un chant d'amour qui serait ininterrompu.[15]

("The projection of the self: it is the animate double questioned in the *Poèmes à l'Autre Moi* or in the character of Grabinoulor. . . . Albert-Birot, was testing himself, in the sense Montaigne his lifelong friend meant, through himself transformed into Grabinoulor, Rémy Floche, Adam, from the first to the last poem, he wants to create a song of love that would be uninterrupted.")

The reader readily makes the assimilation between creator and creation. The double—the other self identified in the small critical corpus—reflects as much the desire of the reader as that of its creator. Readings reveal the need in all of us to communicate with some absolute outside ourselves, which may simultaneously be assimilated into the self. Here we intend to explore the collection within the framework of a general questioning of the notion of the subject before offering any comment on the particular approaches of Albert-Birot as he reformulates a problematic worked time and time again since Montaigne. Narcissistic quest it may be, but narcissism as an acknowledgment of a universal desire and one that will perhaps not offer the consolation of an exalted self but will certainly explore the human condition: our mortality but equally our potential. What concerns us here initially, therefore, is not the reception of the text but its production. Both thematically and structurally, the notion and constant use of the double is part of Albert-Birot's uninterrupted creative production, a quest for continuity and permanence that reaches its fulfillment in *Grabinoulor,* an attitude to his creativity which is equally true of his poetry, making the extended work of prose and his shortest poem inseparable. Beneath the exaltation of the poems, a metaphysical uncertainty is nonetheless evident and in the light of the diverse "autobiographical" projects of other writers and the critical discourses that have explored these, a deeper, revelatory questioning takes form:[16] "Les *Poèmes à l'Autre Moi* se situe à la racine de ce mouvement double par lequel tout écrivain se dédouble, faisant naître en lui un autre moi et visant à embrasser du même coup la totalité."[17] ("The *Poems to the Other Self* are situated at the root of this double movement by which every writer makes himself double, giving birth to another self inside himself and attempting to embrace totality in the same stroke.") This reading of the Other Self as writer, creative artist formulating a language with which to face questions of his own identity, to explore the other in the self in his relationship to others, to confront his own body and its mortality, questions of being, articulates the problematic of the writing of the twentieth century: the fundamental problem of finding a language with which to think (and express) the self and the world. When Albert-Birot confronts his own face, his own body, he confronts the dilemmas of humankind's existence. The critic is able to formulate a series of questions with which to initiate an analysis of this collection:

- How does the writer construct a self in language, a material that has been tried and tested by the Poet-Artisan in *La Lune*? Does such a material have the potential to effect a transposition to the sublime, to express the absolute?[18] The writer explores the source of both self and language. The construction of the self entails a quest for origins.
- What is the relationship of self to other? A multifaceted dilemma— what is the relationship of the individual to society, to the collective? What is the relationship of the singular to the universal? What is the relationship of self to the other in the self? When the poet confronts his identity in language, in poetic creation, he necessarily confronts this "Autre Moi" to embrace a totality. What finally, or rather where, is the place of the reader, who is solicited by the writer-self? Desired, feared, and necessary, the reader is other.
- What are the consequences of such a face to face with the self? The human face is the trace of its history and memory of the origins of the individual and of humanity itself. The self-portrait situates the individual in the passage of time. In the mirror we are face to face with our mortality. What then is the status of the written word? Can the writer secure an eternal moment in the flux of time? We return to the dilemma of language, a material of difference and lack.
- Finally what is the value of such a poetic creation? What is the value

of self-exploration and self-expression, the questioning of the complexities of human existence in a world where meaning continues to retreat? The dialectic between action and creation, acting in a political, social sense and reflecting, exploring the self for a better understanding of man is a fundamental dilemma of twentieth-century literature. How does the individual justify a choice in this conflict?[19] What is "le faire poétique"?[20]

La Guerre is the space in which an archaeology of a poetics may be uncovered and where we read both division and fragmentation and the will to unity and continuity. The search for origins continues in the archaeology of the self, layer upon layer is explored in a dialogue as the poet digs deeper and deeper down into himself, this dialogue staging the division necessary to seek unity, and the fundamental condition of narrative, applicable also to poetry:

> Tout récit se modèle sur l'écoute d'un Autre, se développe en face d'une réponse toujours déjà là et sur/avec laquelle il est nécessaire de compter/conter. Le sens du discours narratif est le produit d'une relation qui fait éclater l'unité du sujet parlant, "responsable" de son récit, en une position fondamentale dialogique.[21]

> ("Every narrative is modeled on the listening of an other, is developed in response to a reply that is always already there and on/with which it is necessary to count/recount. The meaning of narrative discourse is the product of a relation that makes the unity of the speaking subject, who is 'responsible' for his narrative, burst open into a fundamental dialogic position.")

BETWEEN THE ACT OF VISUAL CREATION AND THE ACT OF WRITING

To continue the process we have begun of reading Albert-Birot's work through the parallel modes of expression of writing and painting,[22] let us first remind ourselves of a statement by Albert-Birot himself on the act of creation that is the painting:

> Il ne s'agit plus, avec la peinture, de "peindre" quelque chose, mais bien de peindre la peinture, le tableau va représenter la peinture VIVANT, c'est-à-dire la matière je suis tenté de dire "cosmique"—en pleine évolution. Le peintre en quelque sorte va se mêler à la matière, et c'est tous les deux parfaitement unis, associés, même mariés, qu'ils vont, comme dans la Nature, s'ordonner dans le désordre, chaque tableau sera un temps de la création du monde en création perpétuelle.[23]

("It is no longer a question in painting, of 'painting' something, but rather of painting painting, the picture will represent LIVING painting, that is to say the matter which I'm tempted to call 'cosmic'—in the midst of its evolution. The painter will, to some extent, become mixed with the matter, the two of them perfectly united, associated, married even and, as in nature, become ordered in disorder, each painting will be a moment of the creation of the world in perpetual creation.")

This statement pinpoints Albert-Birot's own relationship to the creation of the artistic object, whether painting or poem. Typically of his own "critical discourse," he expresses his position most clearly with regard to the visual arts. It is here that he places himself truly within the discourse of modernity; it is no longer the case to "paint something" with paint, or to "represent something" with words: Albert-Birot has a modern consciousness of the artist/writer's relationship to his material.[24] Throughout *La Lune* he has experimented and tested the limits of language, to some extent treating his material as an object outside of himself to be explored, manipulated, and molded. During the twenties, a time of isolation and increasing solitude for the poet now withdrawn from the collective adventure of the avant-garde, he explores the relationship between language and self. The opposition that the poet makes between "dire/faire" in poetic creation has already led us to discuss a modern sensibility that places him very much as inheritor of Mallarmé and indicating the way in which symbolism opened the way toward the preoccupations of the avant-garde despite their very different productions. In the *Poèmes à l'Autre Moi* Albert-Birot explores, as the title suggests, the nature of the self in writing and consequently the nature of writing itself. This quest initially begins as a continuation of a personal mythologizing characteristic of the period in *SIC*:

> En signes humains je dirai
> Moi qu'on représente à volonté par Pierre Albert-Birot
> —"Premier Poème," first lines

> ("Using human signs I will tell
> Of myself whom people describe ad lib as Pierre Albert-Birot")

A mythologizing that expands into the narcissistic quest of the poet and a writing that is increasingly conscious of itself:

> Et voici je te mets dans un livre tel peut-être qu'on ne
> t'y a jamais mis et je continuerai à t'y mettre à

toutes les pages toi mon sublime moi réalité de
mon image dans la réalité du poème
                    —"Huitième Poème," concluding lines

("And look I am putting you in a book in a way perhaps that no one
ever has and I will continue to put you in
every page you my sublime self reality of
my image in the reality of the poem")

A movement follows illustrating moments of intense introspection, which
at times celebrates the exalted moment, transcendence of the human, and
embracing of the divine:

Moi aussi j'ai fait jaillir l'eau du Rocher je le sais dans
tel poème et tel autre et tel autre il y a un miracle
qui s'ouvrira et se refermera sur quelqu'un
comme il s'est refermé sur moi et celui-là me
retrouvera dans ce mystère où je veille ma vie
éternelle
                    —"Trente-troisième poème"

("I have also caused water to gush from the Rock I know in
one poem or another and another there is a miracle
which will open and close on someone
as it has closed on me and they will
find me in this mystery where I watch over my eternal
life")

Yet he finally concludes within human limitations, implying necessarily
uncertainty, the precariousness of the poetic quest, the position of the
reader as other, and ultimately death itself:

Tout moi poème
    Mais vient-il jusqu'aux lèvres parlantes
        Qui ne l'ont jamais vu
        Ont-elles forme pour lui
Ou lèvres hélas lui font corps
    Lèvres font vie de vie
    Mais plus loin lèvres tuent
                    "Trente-quatrième poème"
                    —(concluding lines of the final poem)

("All myself poem
    But is he framed by eloquent lips
        That have never laid eyes on him
        Do they assume a shape for him

Or do lips alas form one body with him
          Lips create life from life
      But further on lips can kill.")

The *Poèmes à l'Autre Moi* are generated from the basic opposition between life and death, from the dialectic of the single moment and the
eternal moment that we have uncovered as underlying the structure of
La Guerre, between the reality of human existence and its being made
sublime. The dialogue between self and other, already explicit in the title
of the collection, invites us to consider these limit experiences within the
discourse of the myth of Narcissus, which haunts modern writing. In
this respect Albert-Birot's other symbolist precursor, Paul Valéry, proves
enlightening reading: "N'est-ce point penser à la mort que se regarder au
miroir? N'y voit-on pas son périssable? L'immortel y voit son mortel. Un
miroir nous fait sortir de notre peau, de notre visage. Rien ne résiste à
son double."[25] ("Is not looking at oneself in the mirror to think about
death? Do we not see our perishable state there? The immortal sees his
mortality there. A mirror makes us leave our skin, our face. Nothing
resists its double.") Albert-Birot's intention is indeed to explore self and
other in the mirror:

Je ne savais pas et j'ai voulu savoir et j'ai dit
          je vais me mettre face à face
Et j'ai mis au bout de mon désir mes yeux et mes
          doigts chercheurs de secret
                              —"Douzième Poème," opening lines

("I did not know and I wanted to know and I said
          I am going to look myself in the eye
And my eyes and my fingers on a quest for secrets I placed
          at the far end of my desire")

The poet advances then not only to explore self and other but also the
Narcissus-self and the Narcissus-writer, cleaving identity further still yet
thereby coming closer to discovering what exactly is the process of creation.[26] The narcissistic quest is the quest for the absolute:

Narcisse face à l'eau, l'écrivain face à la page blanche, confrontent tous les
deux des absolus sur lequels ils désirent s'imprimer (Narcisse par l'image,
l'écrivain par le langage), afin de pouvoir rejoindre ces absolus par la trace qui
les définit (tout en provoquant leur perte). Le texte narcissique (la tentative
de récupération du langage par le sujet) est la résultante de ces deux aliénations
(la deuxième présupposant la première)[27]

("Narcissus facing the water, the writer facing the blank page, both of them
confront absolutes on which they wish to imprint themselves [Narcissus by

means of image, the writer by means of language], to be able to join these absolutes by the means of the trace that defines them [while at their same time causing their loss]. The narcissistic text [the attempt to recuperate language by the subject] is what results from these two alienations [the second presupposing the first].")

Valéry referred to his chosen theme of Narcissus, which accompanies him throughout his literary production as "une sorte d'autobiographie poétique,"[28] a description appropriate also to Albert-Birot's *L'Autre Moi* and other texts, including the prose works *Rémy Floche, Les Mémoires d'Adam,* and the ubiquitous *Grabinoulor.* Further statements by Valéry also send vibrations through a reading of the collection of *L'Autre Moi*: "Entre tous les objets, ce toi-moi. L'origine a un point symétrique. Loi du Narcisse. On abstrait le mirage. Alors il y a un Autre. Quel est celui-ci? qui fait voir ce qui voit."[29] ("Between all objects, this you-me. The origin has a symmetrical point. The Law of Narcissus. The image is isolated. Then there is an Other. Who is this? Who makes he who sees see?") This "toi-moi" is introduced in the first poem; Albert-Birot addresses his "rêve autre moi," "toi moi cher silence—dieu." ("dream other me") ("you me dear silence—god") "L'Autre" is inscribed from the first into the title.[30] Valéry, intensely and intuitively modern in his perception and relationship to language, is sensitive to the problematic that will obsess twentieth-century literature and indeed other areas of questioning, most essentially psychoanalysis—for the problem of the subject is the problem of language, the two painfully and revealingly bound up together and leading to a self-reflective literature in our century:

> Si nous interrogeons l'histoire de la littérature depuis une centaine d'années, ce qui nous frappe d'abord, c'est la complexité et l'ambiguïté d'une telle aventure, sensible dans le fait qu'à un nouvel espace littéraire, à une entente et à une communication profondément modifiées, s'ajoute une réflexion qui prend place à l'intérieur de certains textes et les rend comme indéfiniment ouverts à partir d'eux-mêmes[31]

> ("If we examine literary history from about a hundred years ago onward, what is most striking is the complexity and ambiguity of such an adventure, which makes itself felt in the fact that a way of thinking is added to a new literary space, to a profoundly changed understanding and communication, a way of thinking that takes place inside certain texts and makes them indefinitely open from themselves outward.")

In this act of self-reflection is humankind's desire to seize that part of himself that the very act of thinking has posited as object, to unite the "other" with the "self," wherever that self may be considered to be: "Une dualité du sujet et de l'objet, rupture insurmontable, que par la suite, de milles manières, toutes les religions et philosophies vont tenter de surmonter ou d'approfondir."[32] ("A duality of the subject and the object, an insurmountable rupture that subsequently, in a thousand ways, every religion and philosophy will try to surmount or to deepen.") There is an objectivity that recognizes and affirms mortality and a subjective vision that attempts to deny and to transcend human mortality. Albert-Birot's *Poèmes à l'Autre Moi* are an attempt to unify objective and subjective visions, a consciousness of the internal rupture of modern man, to unite them in a transcendence, a victory of life over death, of Eros over Thanatos. The affirmation of life, begun as a shout of joy in *La Joie des sept couleurs*, seeks its origins in *L'Autre Moi* and raises complex and painful questions that necessarily must turn around language itself, at once a system of lack and of plenitude, but still the most complete one person has to explore and represent from within:

> Nous estimons qui'il est surtout important de reconnaître que le texte moderne se définit non simplement par le fait d'être vu ou ressenti comme langage (exigence à laquelle pourrait satisfaire une critique purement linquistique), mais surtout par sa conscience d'être soi, ou d'être langage. C'est la conscience qui crée (qui est) véritablement la brèche. Pour le texte moderne, il faudra donc, en fin de compte, lire la conscience du texte ou lire la rupture inscrite dans le texte, rupture qui en constitue véritablement le sens.[33]

> ("We believe that above all it is important to recognize that the modern text is defined not simply by the fact of being seen or felt as language (a requirement that a purely linguistic criticism could satisfy) but above all by its awareness of being itself, of being language. It is awareness that truly creates (which is) the breach. For the modern text, it is necessary, finally, to read the awareness of the text or to read the rupture inscribed in the text, a rupture which truly constitutes its meaning.")

It is in this perspective that we will read the narcissism of Albert-Birot's *L'Autre Moi* as a foundation also for reading *Rémy, Adam, Grabinoulor*—not in any pejorative sense that the poet produces a self-obsessed and self-adoring literature but as an awareness of the human subject, language, and literature itself.[34] There follows a detailed analysis of a selection of the poems, situating the collection within modern concepts of the self, the position of the subject in the discourse of modernity, the self and its relationship to language, considering both the singular nature of Albert-Birot's literary creation and the more universal aspects of his work as a twentieth-century poetic discourse. It is in an exploration of *L'Autre Moi* that we may begin to decide the effects of the experience of the avant-garde on the later development of his work and begin to define more exactly Albert-Birot's position in the modern aesthetic.

THE *POÈMES À L'AUTRE MOI* AND SELF-PORTRAIT: PARALLEL DISCOURSES

Throughout Albert-Birot's artistic production, he painted a number of self-portraits, from a sketch dated around 1896 when the artist is twenty years old to the *Autoportrait* of 1935 when the poet is nearly sixty, as we indicated in chapter 1.[35] In the *Poèmes à l'Autre Moi*, the self becomes text rather than canvas and thereby raises a number of questions concerning not only Albert-Birot's artistic development but each medium itself. What "changes" take place in the representation of self on canvas to self in language? The process would again indicate a testing of the limits and the possibilities of both. In the change of material from paint and color to words, Albert-Birot carries on his exploration of language begun in *La Lune*. The change of medium represents to some extent the rupture between old and new (never forgetting that it is on canvas that the revelation of the true nature of creation comes to the artist/poet). Yet between "autoportrait" and "autobiographie poétique" (Valéry), which we might label the poems of *L'Autre Moi*, the desire remains the same, the artist-poet asking "Who am I?"[36]

To raise questions concerning these parallel discourses on the self, we intend to take up some of the points made by Philippe Lejeune, turning his attention from autobiography to self-portraiture and of particular relevance for this study.[37] Lejeune makes a fundamental analogy between the expression of self-portrait and autobiographical texts. The term autobiographical is full of uncertainties and suspicions, raising questions on the status of both autobiography and of fiction, aspects of which we will develop. What interests Lejeune is the perplexity that these give rise to in the spectator/reader. Such remarks are particularly pertinent here, as is apparent from our introductory remarks on the poems of *L'Autre Moi*, which move from a dialogue between the "toi-moi" to leave the fate of the Narcissus-self and Narcissus-writer, in the hands, or rather on the lips, of the unknown reader. Where, we might ask, is the spectator or reader standing while Narcissus contemplates his own image in the mirror? This is a problem of which our poet is intensely aware, one eye on himself and one eye on the reader, anxious concerning the reception of his creation, for it is the other who holds the door to Eternity ajar, if not wide open.

Lejeune asks two simple questions, which initially appear self-evident and naïve: "A quoi reconnaît-on un autoportrait? Quel intérêt spécial peut-il y avoir à regarder un autoportrait?"[38] ("How do you recognise a self-portrait? What special interest can there be in looking at a self-portrait?") For the first, the importance of the title of a painting becomes evident. What apart from the written word allows us to distinguish a self-portrait from the portrait of someone else? There is nothing in paint in itself to express self from other, at least not perhaps for the viewer.[39] The second question is the same we might ask of the fascination that autobiography holds over its readers and indeed that of any literature we "suspect" to be largely autobiographical. What do we hope to discover about (an)other and why? What is the special need/pleasure we experience when reading such texts? What is essential in our apprehension of a self-portrait (and indeed of autobiographical writing) is that we accommodate our looking/reading with respect to the directive of the "title" and the name of the author/artist. Lejeune identifies those changed interpretations we make concerning whether the portrait is of a self or of another as the story of reading a painting.[40] In this light what is the process of reading that takes place within the pages of *L'Autre Moi*, whose title the reader may initially seize as an address made to himself, only to find himself excluded in the first poem as the poet dialogues internally: "Cet autre moi qui fait de moi nous de face de profil et de dos" ("Premier poème") ("This other self which makes me us face on in profile from the back.")

The fundamental problem of the self-portrait is whether this is a mirror-image, or whether it is painted as (the artist imagines) others see him. Self and other, other in self—the game with mirrors reflects a myriad possibilities. And who does the self-portrait look out upon: self or other? Furthermore by painting a self-portrait, as Albert-Birot did several times, the artist dialogues not only with (him)self, a dialogue that takes place at fixed moments in the life-span, but also with painterly tradition, creating what Lejeune terms an "inter-texte" generated through other famous (and not so famous) self-portraits.[41]

Our uncertainty as to the status of (self)-portrait reinforces our desire to invest in the proper name: "Une identité, c'est une relation établie entre une image, et un nom propre."[42] ("An identity is a relation established between an image and a proper name.") Albert-Birot's collection of self-portraiture in writing begins:

> En signes humains je dirai
> Moi qu'on représente à volonté par Pierre Albert-Birot
>
> ("Using human signs I will tell of
> Myself whom people describe ad lib as Pierre Albert-Birot")

The self-portrait immediately provides it label, leaving its reader/spectator in no doubt as to whom he is facing. The human signs here are language by means of which we constantly reiterate our human obsession with human identity: "Car le portrait ne marche qu'avec ce présupposé: cet individu a une valeur sociale, et, plus fondamentalement: l'homme a une valeur."[43] ("For the portrait only works with this presupposition, that this individual has a social value and, more fundamentally, that man has a value.") Indeed it is from this investment in the human that all representations take their value: "Ne marchent que comme signes de l'homme."[44] ("Only work as signs of man.") In the second poem of *L'Autre Moi*, the question of the way in which the name functions is posed, and the differences between such an easily "labeled" identity for the everyday world and the more elusive identity of the self are made poignant:

> L'hiver est pour ceux qui ont une date de naissance
> pour eux et pour moi
> Mais ni pour toi ni pour nous au-delà d'image qui me
> fait chaque jour une image
> Où vit mon nom mais toi qui est moi tu ne sais pas le
> nom que porte mon image

—"Deuxième Poème"

> ("Winter is for those who have a date of birth
> for them and for me
> But not for you nor for us beyond the image
> which creates me daily an image
> In which my name lives but you who are myself you do not know
> the name taken by my image")

Lejeune, whose exploration of autobiography has led him to approach the very heart of the act of writing and the implications of the autobiographical text for all literature, conjectures that it is in self-portraiture that we touch upon the essence of Art itself. It is here that our assimilation of the poems of *L'Autre Moi* to the quests of autobiography and of self-portraiture is complete and validated:

Je vois alors l'autoportrait comme une situation particulière, un tantinet biscornue, où fait brusquement irruption au milieu du genre le plus codé (le portrait) une étincelle (qui n'est parfois que dans l'esprit du spectateur) donnant à voir de manière vertigineuse l'essence de l'art: l'auto-représentation de l'homme (et non la représentation du monde), l'autoportrait devenant allégorie de l'art lui-même.[45]

("I therefore see the self-portrait as a particular situation, a tiny bit odd, in which a spark [which is sometimes only in the mind of the spectator] suddenly erupts in the middle of the most coded genre [the portrait] showing in a vertiginous way the essence of art—the self-representation of man [and not of the world], the self-portrait becoming the allegory of art itself.")

The narcissistic quest of the self-portrait is in no way self-limiting, self-delimiting. Rather it invites the reader/spectator to uncover the process of its creation, as does that of any text of autobiographical status. As we have already explored, Albert-Birot's relationship to his art is one of intense subjective investment both physically and intellectually. As the reader uncovers the relationship between creator and creation, a space opens up into which he is invited. This is not a narrow two-way relationship between Narcissus and his image as it may initially be perceived. When we approach the *Poèmes à l'Autre Moi* via the routes of self-portraiture and indeed of autobiography, we come to a realization of the poems as the continuation of the poems of *La Lune*. Superficially we may read the collection as the turning-inward of a poet who has given up, lost, misplaced his position within the sociopolitical adventure of the avant-garde. In one context this offers a valid reading. However this turning inward has other implications for the writing process. Our reading of *La Lune* has revealed the generating forces of its poetics, of its processes which function with the eye, mind, ear, mouth, hand, and heart of the spectator/reader. It demands from us a physical, emotional, intellectual response and a part to play in the game of creation. In the *Poèmes à l'Autre Moi*, we are invited to play an even more serious games. Lejeune makes the analogy between entering into the act of painting and the act of writing explicit.[46]

In the exploration and representation of the self, therefore, the artist opens up to the other, and in a movement from the singular to the universal (a journey explored in the *Poèmes à l'Autre Moi* that we will examine later), the self of the other is also glimpsed. The game is thus one with mirrors, whose images perpetually reflect each other, but as the spectator/reader is invited to approach a subjectivity at work and in the process of a discovery of itself, so this other must turn to look at itself also:

Si j'imagine que la toile est miroir, elle disparaît comme peinture. L'autoportraitiste voyait dans son miroir un tableau (à faire); moi je vois dans son tableau (fait) un miroir. Le tableau est comme une glace sans tain: le peintre est derrière (de l'autre côté par rapport à moi), et moi je le surprends en train de se regarder. Du coup nous devenons . . . contemporains.[47]

("If I imagine that the canvas is a mirror, it disappears as painting. The self-portraitist saw in his mirror a painting [to make]; I see in his [made] painting a mirror. The painting is like a mirror without any silvering—the painter is

behind [on the other side in relation to me], and I surprise him in the process
of looking at himself. We become . . . contemporaries.")

Through the communication of two subjectivities who look at the other
to look at themselves, the passage of time is transcended into an absolute,
an eternity for Albert-Birot:

> Voici de l'éternité celui qui m'aura trouvé en aura
>   puisque j'en ai tout autour de moi voici je donne-
>   rai de l'éternel à celui qui m'aura trouvé je donne-
>   rai mais vous n'avancerez pas les mains vous ne
>   remuerez pas les lèvres ce serait la résurrection
> —"Trente-troisième Poème"

> ("Here is eternity the one who finds me will have it
>   since I am surrounded by it here you are I will give
>   eternity to the one who found me I will give
>   but you will not hold out your hands
>   you will not move your lips this will be the resurrection")

From the self-portraits of the earlier years of artistic activity, through
the intense subjective investment in the abstraction of *La Guerre*, the
beginnings of *Grabinoulor* to the *Poèmes à l'Autre Moi*, Albert-Birot's is
an expression that is a self-narrativity. Yet this self-narration never closes
in upon itself, but rather turns outward to include the other into the
activity of creation. For the creator this is at once a generous movement
and one that is selfish, one of self-glorification, and in this it is a moment
when the human approaches the divine: "Car l'autoportrait est vraiment,
au sens religieux, une apparition. L'esprit créateur's incarne dans une
des figures de sa création. S'*en*visage, et se dévisage."[48] ("For the self-
portrait is really, in the religious sense, an apparition. The creative mind
is incarnated in one of the figures of its creation. Is *en*visaged and looked
hard at.") Already in *La Lune* the poet has placed himself at the center
of his created universe; the quasi-religious imagery and incantatory of
L'Autre Moi bring with them an ecstasy at once unique and all-embracing:

> Et nous sommes heureux d'avoir des mots sur
>   les lèvres des mots divinités des lèvres
>   des lèvres roses déesses de mots
> Et voici que dans notre chaleur d'être nous avons
>   encor créé ces vers image d'équilibre
>   qui nous ressemble davantage
> Ils ont mon corps et notre espace mais ils n'ont
>   pas ses limites et partout comme nulle
>   part ils sont encore où il n'est plus

Verbe sans visage ils sont paysage et sa lumière
   chaleur sans feu homme et Dieu mystère
     du mouvement dans l'immobilité
                   —"Vingt-sixième Poème"

("And we are content to have words on
   our lips word deities of the lips
     lips pink goddesses of words
And in the heat of being we have
     again created these lines an image of equilibrium
       which looks even more like us
They have my body and our space but they do not have
   its limits and everywhere as nowhere
     they are still there where it is no longer
Words without a face they are landscape and its light
   heat without fire man and God mystery
     of movement in stasis")

It is in the poem that we come closest to the divine nature of creation. The poetic text allows a creation in movement that is less obvious in self-incarnation on canvas. Here we arrive at the heart of Albert-Birot's desire: the nature of the creator is to create, and this must be a process in perpetual movement, for beyond the process of creation is nothingness.[49] The self-portrait has its mortal aspect, an image fixed in time, a death mask, while the poem passes physically from body to body, a cycle of perpetual reincarnation. It is from the tension between life and death, Eros and Thanatos, that the *Poèmes à l'Autre Moi* are engendered, as are all self-reflective writings, whether on paper or canvas: "Tout écrit autobiographique, et cette quintessence de l'autobiographie qu'est l'auto-portrait, se trouve être un monument funéraire, que l'on se dresse à soi-même."[50] ("All autobiographical writing, and this quintessential autobiography which is the self-portrait, is a funeral monument, which one erects to oneself.") Albert-Birot, sculptor, cannot fail to make the analogy, making of his name both material and finished monument:

Si j'étais pour quelque mémoire
Pierre sculptée à la douleur
Sur un vieux tombeau sans couleur
Palais du temps ultime armoire
                —"Troisième Poème"

("If I were for some memorial
Stone carved in grief
On an old colorless tombstone
Palace of time final closet")

As Lejeune also notes, the sculpture is closer even to death than self-portrait: "Des autosculptures? Des autobustes? Oui, mais plus mortuaire encore que l'autoportrait."[51] ("Self-sculptures? Self-busts? Yes, but even more of a mortuary stone than the self-portrait.") This exclusion of the viewer confronted by the solidity of a finished product makes sculpture an impossible choice of medium of self-narration for Albert-Birot. Nonetheless these poems present a paradox not often explored in the work of a poet readily celebrated as the "poète de la vie," of joy, of exaltation in nature, of vitality. Here in only the second major collection, the poet already deals with his own death. The artist/poet who has (re)awoken to life is intensely aware of the value of the moment.

Through the *Poèmes à l'Autre Moi*, the poet explores again the limits and possibilities of visual and verbal language. The portrait runs the risk of remaining a fixed moment in time and is thus death-bound; the self-portrait is an illusory access to the self, and to truth:

C'est une peinture qui à la fois produit, exprime et traduit son auteur. Elle nous dit donc—croit-on—d'où elle vient; on suppose qu'elle nous livre son essence, son origine, sa vérité. De là sans doute, procède l'illusion commune selon laquelle l'autoportrait constituerait une voie d'accès privilégiée vers la vérité, sinon de l'art, du moins de tel ou tel artiste.[52]

("It is a form of painting that simultaneously produces, expresses, and translates its author. It tells us then,—we think—where it comes from; we suppose that it gives up its essence, its origins, its truth to us. Whence no doubt, comes the common illusion according to which the self-portrait constitutes a privileged access to the truth, if not of art, at least of such and such as artist.")

The poet seeks truth as text, as poem, despite the ambiguities inherent in any such quest, particularly of an autobiographical nature. Grabinoulor also will be brought up against the enigmatic nature of truth and the possibility of its inexistence, the absolute truth of which the Creator has kept for himself: "Quant à votre désir de la vérité il peut vous paraître louable mais il convient que vous ne la possédiez que très approximativement."[53] ("As for your desire for truth it may seem laudable to you but it is right that you should only possess it very approximately.") These words would go some way toward expressing our uncertainty in the century of relativity and of existential doubt; awareness is written into our literature of the illusory nature of any attempt to represent the truth of oneself. The self represented in the poem may fall victim to the same dilemma, yet for Albert-Birot the poem demands more forcefully, more hopefully, a continuation into the infinite and toward a truth, as the section of the poem we chose as epigraph to this chapter suggests.

The revelation of *L'Autre Moi* is that finally, despite the ecstasy, exaltation, and divine status of poetic creation, identity can only be conferred, formed in human terms, through human communication, a communion through human language and through the human body, despite its imperfections and failings:

> Saveur d'humain me fait
> Comme humain m'a fait mon humain fera
> Graine fruit et graine
> J'ai mis mon sentiment humide sur mes lèvres
> Goutte à goutte me voici
> Tout moi
>
> . . . .
>
> Tout moi poème
> Mais vient-il jusqu'aux lèvres parlantes
> Qui ne l'ont jamais vu
> Ont-elles forme pour lui
> Ou lèvres hélas lui font corps
> Lèvres font vie de vie
> Mais plus loin lèvres tuent
> —"Trente-quatrième Poème" and final poem incipit/excipit)

> ("The sweet taste of humanity creates me
> as humanity has created me my humanity will create
> Seed fruit and seed
> I wore my moist feelings on my lips
> Drop by drop here I am
> All myself
>
> . . . .
>
> All myself poem
> But is he framed by eloquent lips
> Do they assume a
> shape for him
> Or do lips alas form one body with him
> Lips create life from life
> But further on lips can kill")

Immortality, as the quest of the writing of *L'Autre Moi,* cannot be conferred by an absolute. Rather the identity, the self that is the poem, is in the hands and between the lips of another human being. It is only in the potential power of the self that is creator to motivate the body of another, that the self may achieve its infinity, its eternal, its absolute. It is uncertain, but it is the only chance of salvation. As the Creator informs Grabinoulor, we must content ourselves with a relative absolute: "La Création doit rester à ma disposition ne comptez que sur une immortalité relative d'ailleurs en toute chose ne comptez que sur le relatif je garde pour moi

l'absolu."[54] ("Creation must remain at my disposition only count on a
relative immortality what's more only count on the relative in all things
I keep the absolute for myself.")

In the *Poèmes à l'Autre Moi,* Albert-Birot explores the only possible
knowledge one can have of oneself, of the present of the self within the
flux of history, a moment infinitely small, a particle, a fragment set against
the curve of eternity as in *La Guerre.* The ultimate goal, which remains
ever precarious in its outcome, is to transcend the personal and reach a
universal, where the self is the only mirror which may reflect the world,
but in whose reflection it is possible to see ourselves mirrored:

> Trinité je reçois tout l'Univers dans ma solitude et tout
> l'Univers me parle quand je me mets ma main sur
> ma poitrine c'est tout l'Univers que je tiens . . .
> . . . .
> Voici de l'éternité celui qui m'aura trouvé en aura
> puisque j'en ai autour de moi voici je donne-
> rai de l'éternel à celui qui m'aura trouvé . . .
>
> —"Trente-troisième Poème"

> ("Trinity I welcome the whole universe in my solitude and the
> whole Universe speaks to me when I place my hand
> over my chest I have the whole Universe in my hand . . .
> . . . .
> Here is eternity the one who finds me will have it
> since I am surrounded by it here you are I will give
> eternity to the one who found me . . .")

A READING OF THE POEMS

The analogy between modernity and the narcissistic text is one that
considers not only the self-reflective nature of the subject but that of the
text.[55] There is a double movement of objectivation and of a literature
aware of itself as literature, intensely subjective. Within this literature,
which has lost its certainty in the direct relationship between language
and representation of the world, between language and "reality," between
language and a representation of the self, there is a distinction to be made
between a "variante faible" and "variante forte" for all narcissistic texts.[56]

Nous situerons dans la variante faible tout texte qui fait partie de la modernité
dans son ensemble, c'est-à-dire tout texte conscient de soi comme littérature
et dont la 'fonction' prédominante et l'objet principal est de s'exposer en tant
que tel. Face à cette variante faible, nous pouvons définir une variante forte:

le texte où la conscience de soi comme littérature en devient véritablement le sujet. Dans ce genre de texte, la fonction poétique atteindrait son paroxysme, puisque l'auto-référence y atteint son plus haut degré. Barthes (*Le Degré zéro,* p. 123) a pu dire que l'oeuvre moderne est 'impossible'—impossible, parce que comme le Narcisse mythique, elle se cherche et essaie en vain de s'appréhender.[57]

("We will situate in the weak variant any text that is part of modernity as a whole, that is to say, any text aware of itself as literature and whose predominant 'function' and principal object is to show itself as such. Facing this weak variant, we are able to define a strong variant—the text in which the awareness of itself as literature becomes its true subject. In this type of text, the poetic function would attain its paroxysm, because self-reference attains its highest level there. Barthes (*The Zero Degree of Writing*, p. 123) could say that the modern work is 'impossible,' because like the Narcissus of myth, it seeks itself and tries vainly to seize itself.")

In the quest to attain the "impossible" object, we recognize the quest Pierre Albert-Birot has set himself from the first of the *Trente et un poèmes de poche:*

> Que vas-tu dire, ami?—L'indicible
> Que vas-tu peindre, ami?—L'invisible

> ("What are you going to say, friend?—The unsayable
> What are you going to paint, friend?—The invisible")

After our analysis of *La Lune* and a general reading of *L'Autre Moi,* we may begin to understand just where such a poetic quest may lead:

Dans ces cas extrêmes, où la recherche de soi devient l'essence de l'expérience littéraire, le texte vacille entre se dire et se taire dans son désir de saisir sa propre parole, tout comme Narcisse vacille entre l'être et le non-être lorsqu'il tente de rejoindre son image. Faut-il ajouter que cet état est paradoxal, bien entendu, puisque le texte nous parle de son incapacité de se dire, mais il est aussi commun à toutes les tentatives d'appréhension d'un absolu.[58]

("In these extreme cases, where the seeking of the self becomes the essence of the literary experience, the text vacillates between speaking of itself and saying nothing of itself in its desire to seize its own word, just as Narcissus vacillates between being and nonbeing when he tries to join his image. Must it be added that this state is paradoxical, of course, since the text speaks to us of its incapacity to speak itself, but it is also common to all attempts to grasp an absolute.")

We have already referred in passing to a number of paradoxes in the course of the collection from the first attempts to speak the self, through failure and exaltation and eventually ending in uncertainty. What we will hear in *L'Autre Moi* is the reiteration of a perpetual quest, a cyclic movement, not a linear one, the circle that has already been established as a fundamental figure in Albert-Birot's poetics.[59] What is more the reader is familiar with this narcissistic cycle, recognizing these universal and fundamental elements of the human psyche:

> Cette reconnaissance, ou sensation de retrouver les éléments primordiaux dans la psyché, vaut pour le lecteur aussi bien que pour le poète. Si la génération de l'oeuvre est en quelque sorte prédéterminée par un nombre limité de structures universelles de la psyché, l'appréhension de son sens le sera de la même façon. . . . Retour sur soi et circularité: le lecteur investira de sens certaines structures essentielles et universelles du texte—mais qu'il n'a pu reconnaître que parce qu'elles préexistaient et "résonnaient" déjà en lui.[60]

> ("This recognition or sensation of finding the primordial elements in the psyche holds good for the reader as well as for the poet. If the generation of the work is to some extent predetermined by a limited number of universal structures in the psyche, the apprehension of its meaning will be so in the same way. . . . A return to the self and circularity—the reader will invest with meaning certain essential and universal textual structures—but that he could only recognize because they already preexisted and 'resonated' in him.")

Both psychoanalytic discourse and the process of reading adopted by semiotics read the surface structure and underlying structure ("deep" structure) of the text. Just as semiotics works on the material of the text, so does psychoanalytical discourse. Both read "otherwise" and bring our attention to the implicit discourse. It is in this deep, underlying structure of the text that we may apprehend the meaning(s) of the text, the dynamism of the writing, and this is the structure toward which our reading moves. In our reading of a narcissistic text, we would expect the fundamental element of the narcissistic cycle, the opposition, tension between life-drive and death-drive to provide the motivating force of the text. We return to the basic binary opposition that we uncovered in our reading of Albert-Birot's *La Guerre* as illustrated by our diagram of the semiotic square to clarify such a reading. To read *L'Autre Moi*, we need to pass between the two levels of the text:

> Si le texte narcissique a comme structure profonde la tension vie/mort (le cycle narcissique) la surface peut-être considérée comme marquant cette structure première. Elle devra donc être réduite afin de retracer et d'isoler les instances de cette tension oppositionnelle qui est générée par le cycle.[61]

("If the narcissistic text has as a deep structure the tension between life and death (the narcissistic cycle), the surface can be considered as marking this first structure. It will need, therefore, to be reduced to retrace and to isolate the instances of this oppositional tension which is generated by the cycle.")

This fundamental opposition engenders a number of other binary oppositions which, despite their disparity, return to this original structure.[62] In our reading of the *Poèmes à l'Autre Moi*, we will read these binary oppositions as the structure of the text is uncovered.

The reading of the poems will follow a double movement, a "reduction" of the surface level of the text into a series of oppositions along the paradigmatic axis and the "amplification" of these oppositions in the narcissistic cycle, a type of integration, "resolution" of these oppositions, recuperated into an "explanation":

On peut également dire que dans un texte dont la surface présente un certain degré d'illisibilité, il faudra en quelque sorte déconstruire un sens au niveau de la profondeur du texte. Autrement dit, la lecture de la chaîne syntagmatique ne permet pas de rejoindre le cycle. Ce sont les séries paradigmatiques établies en relation avec les tensions oppositionelles engendrées par le cycle qui permettent de "percer" la surface et de retrouver, dans un deuxième temps, un nouvel axe syntagmatique ou logico-linéaire de la lecture, en l'occurrence, la lecture du cycle narcissique.[63]

("It equally can be said that in a text whose surface presents a certain degree of illegibility, to some extent a meaning has to be deconstructed at the level of the deep structure of the text. In other words the reading of the syntagmatic chain does not allow the cycle to be joined. It is the paradigmatic series established in relation to the oppositional tensions engendered by the cycle that allow a 'piercing' of the surface and a retrieval, at a second stage, a new syntagmatic or logico-linear axe of reading, in this case, the reading of the narcissistic cycle.")

This reading will be necessarily marked by a number of *a priori* assumptions informed by readings of other texts, of Albert-Birot's works already examined here, by the initial indications of the collection's title as explored in our introductory section, and by the reading of the first poem with which we open this analysis. That such a perspective is validated we hope to have justified by the conceptual framework set up in these preliminary remarks.

"Premier poème": The Initiation of a Quest for Identity

The nature of the quest is clearly set up as one in language and therefore human:

En signes humains je dirai
Moi qu'on représente à volonté par Pierre Albert-Birot

("Using human signs I will tell of
Myself whom people describe ad lib as Pierre Albert-Birot")

It is one that will explore the subject designated in social discourse ("on")
by name, whose true identity is yet to be explored. The relationship
between self and other is delineated also. The exploration of the subject
is not only the relationship between self as perceived by self, but as the
self believes others perceive him, a fundamental problem of any self-
portraiture whether literary or visual. The quest is articulated, therefore,
in what might be termed an autobiographical project, a desire to speak
the self, a desire to know who is this "I" who speaks in human communication and through the poem. Who is this "I" who creates? Who is this
"I" who functions in everyday existence? What is the relationship between "I" and the body that provides a place to "be"? Language, the
medium through which the quest is to be fulfilled (or attempted to be), is
immediately posited as a system of signs. Thus we are confronted with
the dilemmas and paradoxes of a modern awareness of language as an
arbitrary system of signs, characterized by difference and lack, a system
demanding interpretation that can be only temporary and incomplete. At
this point in the quest, however, the material presents no such problem
for the poet:

Moi tandis que je suis assis et que je parle un langage et
une langue qui peut me ressembler

("Myself when I am sitting down and when I speak a language and
a tongue which may look like me")

The poet perceives himself to be at the center of his own discourse. In
the perspective adopted in our analysis, a Lacanian reading through a
linguistically informed approach to the problem of identity, the quest of
origins through language will be revealed as having a more complex relationship to the subject locked in a search for origins and for his identity:

Moi qui n'ai pas été moi avant d'être et qui ne serai pas
moi après

("Myself who was not myself before I existed and who will not be
myself afterwards")

We have a basic initial problematic:

- language
- identity
- self
- other
- being (and nonbeing)

Albert-Birot is articulating the question of the subject, of being, approached in a myriad of ways by human discourse, philosophical, scientific, poetic—all posing the enigma of human existence. Such a problematic is set within the human time of the present moment:

> Et qui suis en train de vivre plus de dix-neuf siècles
> après le Crucifié

> ("And who is living over nineteen centuries
> after Jesus Christ")

and within the eternal time of human history:

> Plus de cinq mille ou cinq cent mille peut-être après la
> mort des premiers yeux sur la Terre

> ("More than five thousand or five hundred thousand years perhaps after
> the death of the first eyes on Earth")

Each duration ("en train de vivre") is but an instant when strung out back to the origins of human existence.

The quest is also situated in a specific place:

> Dans Paris qui vit avec moi et me donne l'élan de ses
> milles rues et de ses millions d'habitants

> ("In Paris who lives with me and gives me the impetus
> of its thousand streets and its millions of inhabitants")

Each isolated individual experience is also part of a greater collectivity, the place of the individual is one of interaction ("qui vit avec moi") and simultaneously of solitude.

> Toi lui et tous ils sont un chacun comme moi-même

> ("You him and everyone are an individual like myself")

The initial problematic thus extends to include:

• the position of the self in time, personal history, and history (we may recall our reading of *La Guerre* as the articulation of a personal, artistic and historical moment within time)
• the place of the individual in space as well as time; the position of the individual with regard to others; the individual and society.[64]

The quest for the origins and identity of the individual subject is simultaneously a quest for the origins of the human race and for an understanding of the functioning of human society. The singular attempts to embrace the universal, an action that is cyclic:

> Je me hâte de me prendre et de me dire mot à mot à
> > l'autre moi
> Et faisant le grand tour par les autres hommes qui vont
> > et viennent

> ("I hurry to catch hold of myself and tell of myself word by word
> > to the other self
> And taking the long way round via the other men who come
> > and go")

Here, articulated for the first time, is the concept of "l'autre moi" which in this initial elaboration of the poet's quest remains of an ambiguous nature. This "other" has remained hidden:

> Je n'avais pas aperçu l'autre moi que j'enveloppe ou
> > bien qui m'enveloppe

> ("I had not glimpsed this other self that I envelop or
> > else who envelops me")

There would appear to be a physical relationship between them that has not yet been identified. To reach some understanding the communication between the self and this other will take the form of a dialogue which is the poem:

> . . . me dire mot à mot à
> > l'autre moi

The dilemma is whether this self, moi, is actually other, autre:

> Mais cet autre moi est-ce bien encore moi
> Lui qui pourtant n'est pas un autre et qui est là quand je
> > suis seul

("But this other self is it still actually me
He who however is not another and who is there when I
        am alone")

The enigma lies in the nature of this other self, addressed as "un autre moi," "mon cher silence-dieu," in a semireligious discourse with overtones of guilt and supplication:

    Pardon d'avoir voulu te faire entrer avec moi dans les
                    jours qui se comptent
    En images-mères . . .

    ("Forgive me for wanting to bring you with me into
                    the days which are numbered
    In mother-images . . .")

This other self is of mysterious, quasi-divine nature, some kind of absolute within the self not subject to the law that governs all human, mortal life, the law of time, and thus necessarily of death. Therefore the basic dynamism of the poem is structured between a desire to know, a drive that we may identify as a life-drive, that of Eros, a knowledge that is necessarily accumulated within the only certainty of the human, which is death, Thanatos, which governs, paradoxically, life. We may begin to perceive other oppositions at once deriving from and subsumed by the tension between Eros and Thanatos and already set out in our initial problematic of language and identity, self and other, being and nonbeing:

Eros	Thanatos
Absolute	Human
(outside time)	(subject to time)
(outside space)	(situated in space)
Toi (of enigmatic nature at this point in the quest)	Moi (of known social discourse)
Object (of desire)	Subject
Unity	Separation
Continuity	Limits (therefore fragmented)

Between the tension created by the opposites
            are two

images

Image/Eros	Image/Thanatos
Ideal	Consciousness of self
Perfection	Imperfection
Presence (desire fulfilled)	Absence (lack)

which reflect each other

Self

image-desire-life	image-mirror-death

CYCLE OF
NARCISSUS

Toi	Moi

Self as other

Immortal	Divine	Mortal	Human

The movement of the poem is exactly this, from the "Moi" of line 2, to the "Toi" of the final word. The dilemma of the quest is inscribed within the poem. Initiated by the look ("apercevoir," "toi qui as mes yeux et mes lèvres"), it begins in silence. The image that begins as absence for others "et que pourtant on ne voit pas quand on me regarde" must be written in words to take form, to be. Thus we would expect an equivalence between Eros, the desire, and language, yet the desired absolute is addressed as "cher silence-dieu," that which cannot be articulated in human language to express this consciousness of an absolute, which is inexpressible ("l'indicible"). The poet is brought immediately up against the paradox of language, the disparity between the poem that articulates the awareness, the consciousness of self, and the basic impossibility of forming this in the material that is available to him. The poet faces the chasm between an awareness of the self and the (im)possibility of expressing the self. We are brought back again to the initial question and answer that generates the whole of Albert-Birot's poetic production:

Que vas-tu dire, ami?—L'indicible

The capacity of the poet, of the word, of language is put to the test by the act of attempting to create the poem. The hollow between language and existence, which opens up when the self begins to articulate itself, is the space into which the poet writes himself. It is the space of creation that fascinated Albert-Birot, the space between God the absolute and Adam, creature of language, caught in a system of division and lack.[65] In *La Lune* the poet has already gained an awareness of the limits of language pushed to the edge of silence. Yet in the continuation of his poetic quest, he is compelled to take up once again the material he knows to be flawed in the exploration of his subjectivity and in the hope for the assimilation of self to an absolute to escape the inevitability of the human: "C'est la confrontation avec l'absolu qui engendre la division mais qui engendre le désir de la transcender."[66] ("It is the confrontation with the absolute that engenders the division, but which engenders the desire to transcend it.") The poet in search of an understanding of the self is also in search of a language, and the text continues to be written as the perpetual quest unfolds. From the initial problematic set out in the first poem develops the entire collection, the dialogue that expands in an attempt to answer the mysteries and enigmas and gives form to the thirty-three poems. A further set of questions may be elaborated to shape our reading:

- What is the nature of the "rêve-autre moi," the "cher silence dieu" who remains hidden?
- Who is the "I" of everyday existence? Who is the "I" who creates?
- How can the self be expressed in language? What is the nature of this system of signs?
- What is the space of creation and how does it function? Once formed, filled, does it contain within it the answers to the above?

Through the recurring themes, dominant figures, and specific elaborations of these questions, we will explore through the poems of *L'Autre Moi* the journey of this quest of identity and creation.

"Deuxième Poème": The Poet Considers the Name

In the first lines of this second poem, the poet turns outward to the reader who resembles himself and will therefore recognize the quest of the poem:

> Je laisse mon contour à ceux qui viennent avec une
> bouche et une main

> ("I leave my contour to those who come with a
> mouth and a hand.")

The poem must be received from body to body for the quest to continue. The physicality of the poem and of its reception provides a foundation for all Albert-Birot's poetry as we have discussed in our reading of *La Lune*. These corporeal reactions to the poem are urged as the reader uncovers the process of the poetics at work. In the *Poèmes à l'Autre Moi*, this reciprocal relationship between creator/poet and re-creator/reader is made manifest. The poet's gamble is that, particularly in the intense subjective investment made here, the reader will recognize himself and participate in a creation of his own identity in the the poem and simultaneously a re-creation of that of the poet. As André Green has pointed out, works of art are "transnarcissiques," as poet, artist, novelist, and reader, viewer are able to overcome fundamental feelings of lack in the temporary certainty of being addressed, needed by the other:

> L'objet d'art vise à s'offrir comme une construction dont l'effet doit être de constituer un double narcissique du créateur. En lui doit se trouver la perfection à laquelle aspire le narcissisme. . . . Ce programme est réalisé par la fabrication de cet objet de médiation—dont la réussite sera assurée s'il parvient à créer la même impression chez le consommateur de l'oeuvre. C'est en quoi nous proposons d'appeler l'objet d'art un objet transnarcissique.[67]

> ("The art object aims to offer itself as a construction whose effect must be to constitute a narcissistic double of the creator. In it the perfection to which narcissism aspires must be found. . . . This program is realized by the making of this mediatory object whose success will be assured if it manages to create the same impression in the work's consumer. This is why we propose to call the art object a transnarcissistic object.")

The final lines of the collection reiterate this desire, but in less certain mood:

> Tout moi poème
> Mais vient-il jusqu'aux lèvres parlantes
> Qui ne l'ont jamais vu
> Ont-elles forme pour lui . . .
> —"Trente-quatrième Poème"

> ("All myself poem
> But is he framed by eloquent lips
> That have never laid eyes on him
> Do they assume a shape for him")

The essential problematic of *L'Autre Moi* is the presence of the subject in his representation in language. As such the reader recognizes it as his own desire and lack also, recognizing his own narcissistic desires, and the quest, both powerful and fragile, will find some sort of resolution, not in a fulfillment but in a continuation:

> Saveur d'humain me fait
> Comme humain m'a fait mon humain fera
> > —"Trente-quatrième Poème," opening lines

> ("The sweet taste of humanity creates me
> as humanity has created me my humanity will create")

In this second poem, therefore, the ultimate goal is already delineated, yet the adventure in language will follow its course of disappointments and of exaltations before leaving the collection in the hands and mouth, before the eyes of the reader.

The realms of self and of other, of the everyday and of that which lies beyond human experience, run their parallel intersecting and diverging courses. The world of the human is one of changing seasons, of time, of birth, and therefore of death:

> L'hiver est pour ceux qui ont une date de naissance
> > pour eux et pour moi

> ("Winter is for those who have a date of birth
> for them and for me")

Most significantly this realm is also that of those who have a name:

> Mais ni pour toi ni pour nous au-delà d'image qui me
> > fais chaque jour une image
> Où vit mon nom mais toi qui est moi tu ne sais pas le
> > nom que porte mon image

> ("But not for you nor for us beyond the image
> which creates me daily an image
> In which my name lives but you who are myself you do not know
> the name taken by my image")

In the first poem, the second line stated clearly the identity of this self in the poem, and Albert-Birot's relationship to his name marks his work, writing himself into *La Lune* in "Poème Prométhée" and into *Grabinoulor.*[68] This fascination with the name is an element of the narcissistic quest for a knowledge of identity:

Le nom est un bastion solide du narcissisme, du savoir et du pouvoir. On veut laisser un nom après la mort. On préfère parfois la mise en place d'un nom

sur une tombe, au dos d'un livre, que de vivre avec d'autres personnes des
échanges qui ne laisseraient aucune trace écrite. Entre le nom et la mort du
corps, il y a la parole qui n'est pas entendue.[69]

("The name is a solid bastion of narcissism, knowledge, and power. We want
to leave a name behind after death. We sometimes prefer the marking of a
name on a tomb, on the cover of a book, to living exchanges with other people
that would not leave any written trace. Between the name and the death of
the body, there is the word which is not heard.")

Within the dialectic of Eros/Thanatos which we have set up the name
has ambiguous status, since although attached to mortal man, it has the
capacity to endure after death. Yet the "other self" to which the poet
aspires has no need of the name:

> . . . ô pardon je te
> parle de moi de mon corps et de mon visage
> Laissons la face et le profil laissons la neige mon nom
> et mon image . . .

> (" . . . Oh forgive me I am speaking
> to you about myself about my body and my face
> Let's leave aside the face and the profile leave aside the snow
> my name and my image . . .")

In the opposition set up here, there is no name, for this is the "true" self,
the name being placed on the side of Thanatos:

Eros	**Thanatos**
Unnameable	Name
(Idealized self complete	(Mortal man
unto itself, beyond mortal	in time)
time and space)	

The name as the identity of the self in time stands at the very border of
the two realms. The self is in the world of man, of cold, of winter, of
bodily needs, of passing time; the self transcends the division between
the two:

> Et je ne serai jamais que moi tant que je ferai une
> différence entre le jour et la nuit
>
> (concluding lines of this poem)

> ("And I will never be anyone else but me as long as I
> differentiate between day and night")

Day and night, a fundamental and heavily connotated division, is written into the poem, one of the basic oppositions that make up human existence. Human experience is one of limits, differences, light and darkness, day and night, and life and death. To transcend this is to perceive existence as a continuum:

> La nature n'a pas de point
> Le jour n'est pas séparé de la nuit
> ni la vie de la mort
> —Poème XXXI, *Trente et un poèmes de poche*

> ("Nature has no full stop
> Day is not separated from night
> neither is life from death")

The desire for unity expressed in poetic creation had been written into Albert-Birot's first collection as an artistic validation of the nonuse of punctuation. In the *Poèmes à l'Autre Moi* and essentially in *Grabinoulor,* it is a metaphysical necessity for the poet.

To know the nature of the "rêve autre moi," the poet must come to an understanding of the known and unknown, the named (nameable) and the unnamed (the unnameable). Writing is a constant refiguration:

SELF	OTHER SELF
body	intangible
name	unnameable
divided	complete

The quest for identity is the quest of a creativity—the empty space of the self is the space of creation. Although the self is divided and one part of it unknown, the opposition that engenders the tension from which the first poem is generated will continue as "moi" strives toward unity with "autre moi," and to fill that "empty space," not a void but a creative potential. The *impalpabilités* expressed on canvas must now be given form on the page.

"Troisième Poème": The Poet Contemplates His Reflection

The second poem has ended as a formulation of the enormous difficulties of the quest, one which, in a search for identity, necessitates tremendous powers of the imaginary. For the quest to continue, the self must be unified in another realm; the poet must activate a different apprehension of (non)existence. Before this is possible, the human self must be examined in its detail to effect some reconciliation between the body and the reflective self that contemplates it.

This third poem presents "cette histoire de mon visage," a self-portrait in words, as the poet contemplates his image in the mirror:

> Que disent mes yeux à mes yeux

> ("What do my eyes say to my eyes")

and repeated more affirmatively in the final verse:

> Et mes yeux disent à mes yeux

> ("And my eyes say to my eyes")

The self here is in a physical confrontation in an unambiguous presentation of the quest of identity as a narcissistic repetition. The rhyming structure of the poem places both the thematics and the form of the poem into a classical heritage. Following on from the insistence on the name in the previous poem, the poet plays on the associations of his name:

> Si j'étais pour quelque mémoire
> Pierre sculptée à la douleur
> . . . .
> Pierre allume une cigarette

> ("If I were for some memorial
> Stone carved in grief
> . . . .
> Pierre lights a cigarette")

and focuses on the "solitude" of the poet which has been noted by several of Albert-Birot's commentators[70] as a foundation of his poetry and on the problem of the continuing existence of the work of art:

> Pierre aimé tu n'as pas d'ami
> A qui donc livres-tu ton livre

> ("Beloved Pierre you have no friends
> So to whom will you consign your book")

The first verse places the poem firmly on the side of Thanatos, the last, after the reconciliation with his physical appearance, firmly on the side of Eros—*tombeau* to *vie,* a reversal of human experience, the same movement followed as in his early elegiac poem "De la mort à la vie." In Albert-Birot's first *drame, Matoum et Tévibar,* light is symbolic of poetry, the head of the "vrai poète" Matoum being illuminated as he speaks his verses and restores life where there was death. This collection seems also to be an early attempt at denying his own death by writing it (an attempt brought to its intensity in the 1953 collection *Le Train bleu*). It is here we may read the particular nature of Albert-Birot's narcissism, for in the faithful repetition of the myth, unity of self with self can only be accomplished in death. The impulse of Albert-Birot's poetic creation appears to be aimed at the projection of the self into a Self where such paradoxes of human existence might be overcome:

> Le mythe de Narcisse exprime donc, à son niveau le plus fondamental, la condition paradoxale de l'homme: vivre dans un état d'aliénation sans jamais pouvoir prendre conscience de l'état idéal qu'est la mort. On peut conclure que le narcissisme constitue le lien précaire et ambivalent entre la *vie* (la conscience de soi) et la *mort* (l'abolition de la conscience), qui détermine l'état conflictuel inhérent à la condition humaine.[71]

> ("The myth of Narcissus expresses then, at its most fundamental level, man's paradoxical position—living in a state of alienation without ever being able to become aware of the ideal state which is death. It can be concluded that narcissism constitutes the precarious and ambivalent link between life (self-awareness) and death (the abolition of consciousness) which determines the conflictual state inherent to the human condition.")

The desire of self, perceived as other, may provoke the desire for death, where the impossible fusion may be achieved.

In the *Poèmes à l'Autre Moi*, Albert-Birot explores and offers a type of "poetic spirituality," a kind of possible salvation through the work of art. With the knowledge of the origins of the self and of his desires he may transcend them. Thus to equate "l'autre moi" with a soul, some kind of divine or immortal being can only be part of the quest of this subject in language and in his desire. It is only through the intermediary of the other that the self may attempt to seize its identity. The "stade du miroir" is not a temporary state to be evolved from, but it is the state of the subject. It is at once the beginning of the subject's awareness and its structure:

> A la fois lieu de naissance et structure définitive, il représente la caractéristique propre de l'être humain: la séparation que Lacan analysera plus tard sous les termes d'"aliénation" et de "refente," en mettant en rapport cette constitution et cette séparation. Par leur commun rapport avec le mot latin le "pars" (partie), dit-il, "separere," séparer, se termine en "se parere," s'engendrer soi-même, si bien que "c'est de sa partition que le sujet procède à sa parturition."[72]

> ("At once the place of birth and a definitive structure, it represents the particular characteristic of the human being—the separation that Lacan will later analyze under the terms of 'alienation' and 'refente' ('cleaving'), bringing to-

gether this constitution and this separation. Through their common link to the Latin word 'pars' (part), he says, 'separere,' to separate, ends in 'se parere,' to beget oneself, so that 'it is from its partition that the subject proceeds to its parturition.'")

We might read Albert-Birot's *L'Autre Moi* then as another birth, an exploration of a subjectivity thrown back on itself, returning to a solitary position after an adventure in which both self and other were found lacking, incompatible, divided after an initial exaltation and the fleeting impression of the individual finding its artistic identity as the new poet shakes off the old Albert-Birot. As we read with a discourse exploring the drama of the subject in language, we uncover the activity of the seeking of the self. This poem is an initial and finally unsatisfactory passage to the state of the half-way point of the poem:

> Ces deux témoins privés d'image
> Dont je suis forcé d'abuser
> Qui me content sans s'amuser
> Cette histoire de mon visage[73]

> ("These two witnesses deprived of images
> Whom I'm compelled to misuse
> Who tell me without making fun
> The story of my face")

In his analysis, which brings together disparate aspects of Lacan's work to synthesize the formation of the analyst's concept of the subject, Bertrand Ogilvie provides a suggestive reading for this poem conscious of the illusory nature of its apprehension of the self in the mirror:

Car telle est la discordance entre le je et sa propre réalité que la manière dont il se saisit en s'apparaissant pour la première fois à lui-même est d'emblée fictive. Le sujet dès le départ se cherche et se trouve, se constitue dans quelque chose de radicalement "autre": la forme anticipée de ce qu'il n'est pas mais dont il n'a pas d'autre possibilité sinon de croire qu'il est.[74]

("Because the discordance is such between the I and its reality that the way in which it grasps itself by appearing to itself for the first time is immediately fictitious. From the beginning the subject seeks itself and finds itself and constitutes itself in something that is radically "other"—the anticipated form of what it is not but of which there is no other possibility than to believe that it is.")

The poem follows closely what Lacan viewed as the general scenario of this development that never ends and that seeks to fill this lack with a perpetual movement forward, "à travers la série des identifications secondaires et la prolifération du langage,"[75] ("That is through the series of secondary identifications and the proliferation of language") which is actually the cause of the lack. The circle of Narcissus is a vicious one that provides its own temporary pleasures:

> Mais mon visage est un ami
> Tout changeant comme un paysage
>
> Et voici que j'aime aujourd'hui
> Comme dans un grand paysage
> A voyager sur mon visage
> Avec mon amitié pour lui
>
> ("But my face is a friend
> Unpredictable as a landscape
>
> And what I like doing today
> As in a vast landscape
> Is exploring my face
> Showing friendship for him")

In the "story" of his face confronted by his face, the subject may find a temporary reconciliation and read what was previously unreadable, as well as unite what was irrevocably divided:

> Tu vois je me réconcilie
> Avec moi tout entier merci
> Et merci veux-je dire aussi
> A la lumière qui nous lie
>
> ("You see I am making my peace
> With myself completely thank you
> And I also want to say thank you
> To the light which unites us")

The temporary reconciliation is preferable to an awareness of division and death: "Ce à quoi le sujet s'identifie est ce qu'il veut être et donc aime tout autant qu'il le hait d'être autre justement."[76] ("The subject identifies himself to what he wants to be and therefore loves as much as it hates to be other.") Yet in the unity is implied the permanent reconciliation in death:

Mais cette réciprocité propre à l'imaginaire convertit aussitôt ce désir de mort en une crainte du désir de mort venant de l'autre, crainte de la castration, de la mort pourtant indissociablement désirée, puisqu'elle est l'horizon même de la "précipitation" du sujet.[77]

("But this reciprocity proper to the imagination immediately converts this desire for death into a fear of the desire for death coming from the other, fear of castration, of death nonetheless indissociately desired because it is the very horizon to which the subject 'hastens.'")

By an act of will, the poet attempts to transcend the death-drive and convert its dynamism into one of life:

> Et mes yeux disent à mes yeux
> Quand je regarde la rosace
> De ces deux maîtres de l'espace
> Que ma vie est belle avec eux

—(concluding lines)

> ("And my eyes say to my eyes
> When I look at the rose window
> Of these two masters of space
> That my life is beautiful with them")

If the self can remain within a self-created, self-perpetuating time and space, which is invested by a language spoken between self and other, then the lack may be fulfilled, yet the only language available is that which divides the subject and divides the subject from "reality." Albert-Birot's poetic quest is to remove the self from this realm to that of a "réalité de mon image dans la réalité du poème" ("Huitième Poème"). After the exaltation of man's place in nature in *La Joie des sept couleurs*, it is as though after the experience of language as conducted in *La Lune*, the poet is severed from the outside world in *L'Autre Moi*. Or rather that his consciousness of being divided within in his contact with the everyday and his desire for another realm of existence is thereby made acute. For the subject to realize himself completely, he must be cut off from all possible relationship with the "real" into the space between the eye of self and the eye of the other in the self, where the look can master its own created time and space:

C'est la brèche séparant l'homme de la nature qui détermine son manque de relation à la nature, et suscite son bouclier narcissique, avec son revêtement nacré, sur lequel est peint le monde dont il est séparé pour toujours: mais cette même structure est aussi le spectacle où son propre milieu s'implante en lui, c'est-à-dire la société de son petit autre.[78]

("It is the breach separating man from nature that determines his lack of relation with nature and gives rise to his narcissistic shield, with its iridescent covering, on which is painted the world from which he is forever separated. But this same structure is also the spectacle where his own environment is established in him, that is to say, the society of his other.")

Through the poetic will the image moves from Thanatos to Eros (and compare our earlier analysis):

Eros	Thanatos
Image-ideal	Image-consciousness
	of self and other
Unity	Division
Presence	Absence
"Que ma vie est belle avec eux"	"Malgré cet ennui qui la tue"

The final verse of this poem (previously quoted) emphasizes the look as origin and motivator of the expansion of the self. Albert-Birot, the "visuel" as he has previously been defined, effects his transposition through the look, and in our fundamental opposition the look would be placed on the side of Eros. However it is here we may discern the ambiguous nature of such a poetic enterprise. Albert-Birot's reconciliation of self with self is perhaps illusory, for the gaze locked in the mirror is rather death bound: "Voir est un acte dangereux . . . à force de vouloir entendre la portée de son regard, l'âme se voue à l'aveuglement et à la mort."[79] ("Seeing is a dangerous act . . . through wanting to understand the scope of its look, the soul dooms itself to blindness and death.") Nonetheless in Albert-Birot's schema, the look is desire, dynamism, the motivation of the artistic work; through the look self and exterior are united. The poet creates with an eye turned inward and an eye turned outward. Starobinski's following remark places the nature of the look as one of excess and as such provides a suggestive starting point for a reading of *Grabinoulor* within the perspective established here: "le regard qui assure à notre conscience une issue hors du lieu qu'occupe notre corps, constitue, au sens le plus rigoureux, un excès."[80] ("The look that guarantees our consciousness a way out of the place occupied by our body constitutes, in the strictest sense of the word, an excess.") In the fundamental oppositions we have set up as structuring the *Poèmes à l'Autre Moi*, the position of the look remains ambiguous and a subject for further reflection:

Eros	Thanatos
The look-desire	The look-image in mirror
life-force	death
"à voyager sur mon visage"	"cet ennui qui la tue"
Perfection of the Absolute	Human imperfection
"ces deux maîtres de l'espace"	"ma gueule pointue"

We return ceaselessly to the cycle of Narcissus set up in the first poem.

The Dialectics and Reconciliation of Time and Space

The quest as defined in these first three poems is the problem of identity in language, and specifically the status of the named and unnameable, the image of the other of the self. The poems that follow, leading to a first "exaltation," a transposition of self to Self in the eighth poem, are an expression of the obstacles to the fulfillment of the quest and the relationship between the physical and the meta-physical, "moi" and "rêve-autre-moi."

The underlying structures in Albert-Birot's poetics, which we identified in *La Guerre*, are the "courbe et droite" which return explicity to close the fourth poem:

> La blancheur de ma chair
> Veut que je coure après mon espace
> Et que je m'unisse encore à mes lèvres
> Restez avec moi
> Elles et toi
> Courbe et droite
>
> —"Quatrième Poème"

> ("The whiteness of my flesh
> demands that I chase after my space
> And join together again with my lips
> Stay with me
> Them and you
> Curve and straight line")

In the analysis of *La Guerre*, we made an analogy between the expression of the circle as one of eternity, and of the straight line as the moment, the instant. Here the circle would be identified as a figure of Eros and the continuation of life, the straight line as one of Thanatos. The quest of these poems is hereby set within the time dialectic that provides a foundation structure for Albert-Birot's work as a whole. In the apprehension of an absolute which incorporates death and life, we uncover the impulse of a poetic creation that celebrates both the eternal moment and the fleeting one of which the eternal is paradoxically comprised. The adventure of the quest oscillates between these impulses as does all human life; the act of creation may subsume the two. The fifth poem continues the physical/meta-physical dialectic in its opening lines:

> J'ai dit j'étendrai le bras et l'index et je serai au-
> delà de mon doigt

("I said I will stretch out my arm and index finger and I will be
  on the other side of my finger")

The effort of such a transposition is fraught with difficulties of comprehension and for the poet's capacity:

> Mais au-delà c'est encore ici le numéro seul
>   est changé avecque moins ou davantage
> Pour faire croire et là-bas parle d'ici comme ici
>   parle de là-bas belle histoire
> —"Cinquième Poème"

("But on the other side is still here only the number
  has changed with less or more
To make believe and over there speaks of here as here
  speaks of over there is that all")

It is perhaps easier to make do with illusion rather than truth. The everyday and the realm of the absolute run side by side; the question is how
to cross the limiting barrier:

> Ne serai-je donc plus au-delà de mesures que
>   prend mon tailleur avec son mètre souple

("So will I no longer be beyond measurements
  taken by my tailor with his versatile tape measure")

into the place, into the space where:

> Tu n'auras plus d'années ni de contours ni haut
>   ni bas ni oui ni non ni coeur ni visage

("You will have no more years nor outlines nor top
  nor bottom nor yes nor no nor heart nor face")

the space where conflicts and tensions are unified:

> Alors toi qui as dit parfois jamais pour un ins-
>   tant te voici dans toujours l'immobile

("So you who said sometimes never for a second
  here you are in forever stasis")

The double face of the narcissistic quest and the ambiguous nature of
Albert-Birot's poetry, too simply read as one of life-drive only, are re-

vealed in their complexity.[81] The confrontation with the absolute provokes a division but initiates also the desire to transcend it. The ideal is the fusion of self with Self, of Eros with Thanatos, the abolition of the relationship of dialectic opposition, yet this union of opposites as an ultimate realization is fraught with danger. This will be the essential problematic of our reading of *Grabinoulor* in the next chapter. Just as we have read the dynamics of looking as moving between Eros and Thanatos so, too, does the desire of the poet. The "absolute" of the Self in poetry is paradoxical by nature, unifying and transcending oppositions, but retaining its double nature. The absolute of the poetic goal may be opposed to Thanatos as a finality and rupture with the perpetual quest and to Eros when this is assimilated to human desire:

Eros	**Thanatos**
Absolute	Finality, end of human life, end of human desire
Life as imperfect, human desire marked by mortality	Absolute

The poetry is created within a tension that at once repulses and invites death. As suggested in our introduction to Albert-Birot's formative years, his affirmation of life over death is an affirmation of will in a subjectivity unsure of its identity, desiring and fleeing the other simultaneously:

> Le silence a peur des lèvres enrichies de mots le
> silence n'est jamais las du silence
> Ni dos ni face ni avant ni après voici et la lu-
> mière n'a pas besoin de lumière
> —"Cinquième Poème" (concluding lines)

> ("Silence is afraid of lips rich with words
> Silence never wearies of silence
> Neither back nor front nor before nor after here it is and
> light has no need of light")

The desire is ambiguous because to apprehend absolute knowledge of the self, the only true fulfillment of the quest, is the abandoning of it to silence:

> La situation existentielle de l'écrivain, conscient de cette impuissance du langage à véhiculer la vérité, se fait extrême: comme Narcisse, qui oscille entre la vie (la conscience de son désir) et la mort (le retour dans l'indifférencié) dans le désir de se rejoindre, l'écrivain oscille entre la parole et le silence dans le désir de se dire.[82]

The existential situation of the writer, aware of this powerlessness of language to convey truth, becomes extreme. Like Narcissus who oscillates between life (the awareness of his desire) and death (the return into the undifferentiated) in the desire to unite himself, the writer oscillates between words and silence in the desire to speak himself.")

The mortal risk that the poet runs oscillating between his two mortal desires is reiterated in the sixth poem, where "l'Ange" provides the inspiration and way to the "other self":[83]

> L'Ange est toujours là mais on ne peut plus lui
> > prendre la main avec les mains non
> Et non ce tombeau s'ouvre et vous invite à tom-
> > ber dans ses profondeurs ange ange
> > > > > —"Sixième Poème"

> ("The Angel is always there but you can no longer
> > clasp his hand with your hand no
> and no this tomb gapes and tempts you
> > to fall into its depths angel angel")

The search for the absolute in the company of the angel is rejected for the everyday which, despite its banality, is the desired state, away from mortal danger:

> Mais le klaxon m'a fait sortir de l'angle où je
> > commençais à mourir d'un rêve d'ange
> Et je vais téléphoner dire comment allez-vous et
> > prendre deux tasses de thé

> ("But the horn made me move from the corner where I
> > was starting to die of a dream of angels
> And I am going to phone say see how you are
> > and drink two cups of tea")

The objects of the everyday have also the potential to propel the imaginary, the trivial as access to the sublime:

> Et puis on lit l'Intran pour faire le tour du monde
> > avant dîner et puis on s'en-
> > dort enveloppé de je serai[84]

> ("And then you read the Intran for a trip around the world
> before supper and then you drop off to sleep
> enveloped in I will be")

The following poem takes up these elements of the everyday and places them in the unrelenting passage of time, opening and closing with the same lines, emphasizing the repetition:

> Le jour heureux d'être aujourd'hui ne sait plus
> qu'il a dans le dos le passé gueule
> qui regarde sans bouger

—"Septième Poème"

> ("The day happy to be today no longer knows
> that it has behind it the past an ugly face
> that watches motionless")

This is the everyday of human existence, not as a safe harbor from risks of the quest, but as the everyday as imprisoning without access to any realm beyond itself. It is repetition and monotony where desire remains unfulfilled:

> Les désirs glissent et font des courbes allongées
> pour se croiser sans toucher
> les gens qui sont assis entre eux

> ("Desires slide and form long curves
> so they can pass each other without touching
> the people who are sat among them")

The repetition of the everyday is the tragedy of human existence inserted without recourse into time, as the days pass:

> On s'en va quand même avec eux tant on est
> habitué à s'en aller et l'on arrive à
> l'heure puisqu'on est forcé d'aller droit
> Dans ce couloir à sens unique qui s'allonge ent-
> re hier et demain bonjour comment vas-tu

> ("Nevertheless you go with them you are
> so used to going away and you arrive
> on time because you are forced to travel in a straight line
> In this one-way corridor which stretches
> between yesterday and tomorrow hallo how are you")

In this series of three poems, we may again identify a constant desire for and refusal of life and of death in these ambiguous forms we have uncovered:

Eros	Thanatos
Absolute	Everyday human existence;
unlimited imagination;	physical and mental prison;
conflicts resolved	linked with passage of time,
	therefore movement

Therefore here the relentless movement of existence is death bound, compared with the realm of an absolute presented as an idealized immobility: "te voici dans toujours l'immobile" ("Cinquième Poème"). Yet once again the oppositions may constantly shift, for to be immobile is to be dead:

Eros	Thanatos
Movement; life-force,	Immobility; inertia, in Freudian
classic Freudian life-	terminology the desire of all
drive, origin of desires	mankind to return to its original
	state

In this dialectic it is the everyday that is desired, the small dramas of the everyday preferred to the nothingness of nonexistence. The perpetual dilemma of human existence, where the nonlife of the banal everyday filled with trivia, is more desirable than an absolute that may be a void.[85]

The eighth poem brings about an initial reconciliation between human time and space, a transcended time and space made accessible through the poem. This is the poet's feat of imaginative power that allows him a victory over the dangers of the narcissistic quest in which he is engaged and is apparently unable to break out of. The poet begins locked into the present moment:

> Il semble que le passé ne me reconnaisse pas et que
>   l'avenir ne m'ait pas encor vu derrière ce n'est
> déjà plus moi et devant pas encore et tu ne m'as
>   pas reconnu

> ("It seems that the past does not recognize me and that
>   the future has not yet caught sight of me behind I am
>   already no longer myself and not yet in front and you did not
>   recognize me")

Taking up the physical elements of the earlier poem, the quest is reiterated, but this time self is unified with self, and the identity remains intact and unimpaired by the everyday:

> J'étais au bout de mes doigts j'étais au bord de mes lèvres
>   J'étais sur toute la surface de mes vête-
>   ments et bien au-delà et je savais que c'était encor
>   moi autour de moi

("I was at the tips of my fingers I was on the edge of my lips
I covered the entire surface of my clothes
and even beyond that and I knew it was still
myself surrounding myself.")

The self is amplified:

Et comme un cortège on entre dans la maison entouré
de soi

("And like a funeral procession you go into the house surrounded
by yourself")

and exalted:

Et caché au milieu de soi on assiste à la fête qu'on se
donne on y chante et l'on s'y saoule de lisse et de
toujours

("And hidden in the heart of yourself you attend a party you
are throwing yourself you sing and you get drunk on smoothness
and on forever")

The division is apparent in the early lines:

. . . marcherais-je
toujours vers moi que je veux et ne m'atteindrais-
je jamais

("Could I walk
always toward myself whom I want and would I never reach
myself")

and has been unified. Yet this is only a partial fulfillment of the quest for
an identity. For here identity is not conferred by self on self, but by other
on self. At the point of the keenest perception of lack and division, a
recognition is bestowed from outside the self by social discourse:

Et pourtant quelqu'un m'a dit c'est toi Pierre comment
vas-tu et je l'ai cru et j'ai tendu la main et souriant
je me suis trouvé debout au milieu de moi très
bien merci et toi

("And yet someone said to me it's you Pierre how
are you and I believed him and I held out my hand and smiling

I found myself standing in the middle of myself
very well thank you and you")

It is here that Albert-Birot writes with the greatest simplicity and the greatest emotion on the basic lack at the very origins of human identity and the drama he plays out in this collection is the drama of all human existence, which places his work at the heart of a modern literary problematic as through an act of poetic will he attempts to confer an enduring identity on his subjectivity. This is an ambivalent project. The poet is grateful, relieved at times to take refuge in the temporary salvation of the other, at others fleeing the other as threat to the subject, while all the time working toward a lasting reconciliation of the divisions of the self, a self with the potential to be made sublime through poetic creation.

The unity of identity offered temporarily by the other outside the self provides a salvation in space and time and the poem comes to be written:

> Et l'on a une montre dans sa poche et même un
>   calendrier qu'on va retrouver quand la bouche
>   affaissée on reviendra de l'éternité maternelle ce
>   poème dont se souvient le poète

> ("And you have a watch in your pocket and even a
>   calendar which you will find again when the entrance
>   collapsed you came back from maternal eternity this
>   poem remembered by the poet")

The poet, previously fooled into thinking he would attain an absolute by a *rêverie* on the other-worldly in art—"étoiles," "ciel," "anges"—now acquires negative descriptions: "mondes lourds," "feux provisoires," "prison," "vieux tableaux." He is able to create truly:

> Et l'on commence avec les mains l'infini que l'on finit
>   avec l'esprit ce cher compagnon qui sait tout faire
>   jusqu'à nous-même . . .

> ("And with your hands you begin the infinite which you finish
>   with your mind that dear companion who can do anything
>   even ourself . . .")

This affirmation of true poetic creation is that of the poetics we have uncovered in *La Lune* where hand and mind combine to make the poem. Human time and space are transcended, and the poet reaches the desired state and is able to communicate it:

> Et que l'on peut offrir à soi-même et à quelques autres
> dans un poème qui a l'air d'être fait de lettres
> assemblées en mots ordonnés sur du papier mais
> qui prend la forme du poète et de son infini

> ("And which you can present to yourself and to several others
> in a poem which seems to be made of letters
> combined in words on the page but
> which assume the shape of the poet and his infinity")

The words inscribed on the page with the hand: "et l'on commence avec les mains l'infini" take on a sublime and eternal form rescued from silence: "et quand j'écoute mes mots c'est toi qui places ceux qui sont toi toi infinitif que les mots tuent." They are restored by the act of poetic will "que l'on finit avec l'esprit," until the transposed self takes on a higher reality:

> Et voici je te mets dans un livre tel peut-être qu'on ne
> t'y a jamais mis et je continuerai à t'y mettre à
> toutes les pages toi mon sublime moi réalité de
> mon image dans la réalité du poème

> ("And look I am putting you in a book in a way perhaps that no one
> ever has and I will continue to put you in
> every page you my sublime self reality of
> my image in the reality of the poem")

The poet attempts to overcome the paradox of the written word, silent and thus linked to death, placing language restored to life firmly on the side of Eros.[86] Yet the double nature of language becomes apparent, as does that of the paradox of the body, necessary and mortal:

Eros	Thanatos
LANGUAGE	Silence
The Body	(still, unarticulated)
(mouth, voice)	
Thought	LANGUAGE
L'esprit	écrire
The meta-physical	The Body (physical)

We are reminded here of the initial quest of Albert-Birot's poetry, the articulation of "l'indicible" within the limits and potentialities of language. If language remains the mere reflection of the poet's thoughts, it is doomed to silence. The poet's task is to represent "la réalité du poème" on a different level and requires an expression that will ensure his existence. Therefore at this point in the poetic quest, we are at an initial stage of accomplishment that must continue. The exaltation of the concluding lines qualifies:

> je continuerai à t'y mettre à
> toutes les pages . . .

Of the poems that build up to a reiteration of the initial quest in the twelfth poem, the tenth constructs an eroticism around the nature of this adventure, while poems nine and eleven provide a humorous element reminiscent of *La Joie des sept couleurs* and certain poems of *La Lune* and the early *Trente et un poèmes de poche*.

The ninth, addressed to the "petit clown-nombril" may appear somewhat contrite. What is most interesting is the emphasis on the reciprocal physical communion between body and universe, a recurrent idea in Albert-Birot's poetry, whether as the pleasure in the natural in *La Joie des sept couleurs* or in *Grabinoulor* whose relationship with the surrounding universe knows no barriers. Here when the body is able to be uncovered to the sun, such a communion takes place:

> Je m'empresse de te montrer le zénith
> Et passons ainsi tous les deux
> A visage découvert
> Soit face à face
> Soit face au bleu de l'espace
> Des existences planées

> ("I am losing no time in showing you the zenith
> And so let us both go on
> Frankly
> That is face to face
> That is facing the blueness of space
> Of polished existences")

As opposed to the dialogue elsewhere in *L'Autre Moi*, here the poet addresses his own body; the introspection opens up as vast spaces just as does the intellectual dialogue with the Other:

> Car à contempler ton petit visage au milieu de mon ventre
> Des grimaces que tu me fais je ris
> Et prends autant d'espace
> Qu'à regarder le ciel
> Cher petit clown

("Because gazing at your little face in the middle of my belly
The faces you pull for me I laugh
And take up as much space
As watching the sky
Dear little clown")

The eleventh poem takes up several of the dynamics of *La Joie des Sept Couleurs* and *La Lune,* particularly the form of a "block" of poetry of the type previously discussed, the use of onomatopoeia, and an attention to a visual typography in the final "moI," the capital I insistant upon its physical and spoken presence.

However it is the tenth poem that intensifies and eroticizes the nature of this narcissistic quest. The poet here celebrates the eroticism of the look, desire, appropriation, a reciprocated possession and assimilation, the "coït à double face." The look then works in two directions, laying the self on all that surrounds it, and giving those things to the self. The look here is not the death bound one of Narcissus but is generator of life and movement:

Que de pierres d'arbres et de cieux
Que de gens
M'ont fécondé
Tandis que je les animais
Le monde entier vit de nos regards et de nous-mêmes

("So many stones trees and skies
So many people
Have impregnated me
While I gave them life
The whole world lives by our looks and ourselves")

The look is a desire that is sexual and powerful, a desire literally made concrete, a physical creativity:

Les murs naissent quand nous les regardons

("The walls come into being when we look at them")

Here we read the full impact of Albert-Birot's poetics of desire; his is a world that comes into being through the body of the human, through the eyes, ears, mouth, and hands. We read also in the closing lines the weight against which his poetry moves, against the old and decaying, that which lives off youth and taints it with negativity, with death that remains unspoken here:

Vieilles putains je suis trop beau pour vous
Agrippeuses de jeunesse
prometteuses pointues d'idéal défoncé
Je n'irai point vous donner mes couleurs

("Old tarts I am too handsome for you
Snatchers of youth
Shrill temptresses of broken-down ideals
I am not going to give you my colors")

This would appear to be a cry against the inevitable extreme of Narcissus's desire. Here the look is not between self and self, but between self and world from where creation springs. Nonetheless the poem unambiguously opens the way to an understanding of the driving force of creation within Albert-Birot's universe. In the transposition of the self, there is transposition of the universe where the individual and the rest of creation are at one, for each individual is creator:

Eros	**Thanatos**
The look	The look
Energy (positive)	Destruction
"coït à double face"	"vieilles putains" etc.
individual at one	isolated individual, prey
with the universe	to disillusion
"couleurs"	"gris"
positivity, life	negativity, death
CREATION	SILENCE

"Douzième Poème": The Exaltation of the Self

A third of the way through the collection, we arrive at the first poem of exaltation, a restatement of the quest and a celebration of the possibility for the fulfillment of human desire. The first four lines provide not only a reiteration of the initial quest set out in the first poem but also an expression of the dynamics of the poetic act, the desire for knowledge, the confrontation with the self, an act by nature a sensuous one of looking and touching:

Je ne savais pas et j'ai voulu savoir et j'ai dit
        je vais me mettre face à face
Et j'ai mis au bout de mon désir mes yeux et mes
        doigts chercheurs de secret

("I did not know and I wanted to know and I said
        I am going to look myself in the eye
And my eyes and my fingers on a quest for secrets I placed
        at the far end of my pleasure")

The eroticism of the quest is continued with the verbs *prendre* and *toucher*, which follow. Elements of previous poems are taken up, the obstacles to fulfillment that were presented are now overcome:

> Etait-ce le jour était-ce la nuit peut-être le jour
> m'attend toujours dans ce que je vais savoir

> ("Was this day was this night perhaps the day
> still waits for me in what I will find out")

In the second poem, the knowledge of self had been thwarted:

> Et je ne serai jamais que moi tant que je ferai une
>   différence entre le jour et la nuit
>   —"Deuxième Poème," concluding lines

> ("And I will never be anyone else but me as long as I
>   differentiate between day and night")

Similarly energies and desires had been dissipated without touching those around them, ignorant of their potential:

> Les désirs glissent et font des courbes allongées
>   pour se croiser sans toucher les
>   gens qui sont assis entre eux
>   "Septième Poème"

> ("Desires slide and form long curves
>   so they can pass each other without touching
>   the people who are sat among them")

Now desire is the key to knowledge and to power:

> Nos désirs sont les libérateurs du jour enfermé
>   dans l'inconnu que contient chaque jour
> Et dans la joie de la vie il nous suffit pour vivre
>   de voler de las vie et d'en donner voici

> ("Our desires are like the liberators of the day confined
>   in the unknown contained by every day
> And in the joy of living all we need to live
>   is to steal life and to give it here you are")

The relentless movement of time, "ce couloir à sens unique qui s'allonge entre hier et demain" of the seventh poem, is more ambiguous here, still moving forward but more disparate and undulating:

> Une forme une couleur une ombre une lumière
> enroulements de pourquoi et de parce que
> qui nous conduisent d'hier à demain jeu de la fa-
> randole serpentine qui court de
> l'entrée à la sortie

> ("A shape a color a shadow a light
> scrolls of why and because
> Which lead us from yesterday to tomorrow tricks of the serpentine
> farandole which winds between
> the entrance and the exit")

And from the midst of this it is possible to rescue a moment in time, to recapture youth:

> Et j'ai écarté la droite et la gauche pour pouvoir
> enfoncer ma jeunesse au milieu
> . . . .
> Et enfoncée au milieu entre la droite et la gauche
> ma jeunesse est bien en vie

> ("And I separated right from left to be able
> to drive my youth into the middle
> . . . .
> And driven into the middle between the right and left
> my youth is alive and kicking")

The quest is fraught with danger as the right and the left of time, past and future rush to converge in oblivion:

> mais les deux lignes
> Sont amoureuses l'une de l'autre et ma jeunesse
> en course va se faire étran-
> gler au somment de l'angle
> Mais non ma jeunesse en course est passée elle
> a ri et pour elle la droite s'est
> disjointe de la gauche

> ("but the two lines
> Are in love with each other and my youth
> in its swift passage will be choked

in the apex of the angle
But no my youth in its swift passage has passed by
it laughed and as far as it is concerned right
has broken apart from left")

The desired moment wins and is celebrated in a musical metaphor ("mélo-
dies," "lisses harmonies") now ready to be contemplated in pleasure, in
a moment out of time:

Eros	Thanatos
Desire for knowledge	The unknown, "le secret" (if not explored)
"nos désirs sont les	"du jour enfermé dans l'inconnu
libérateurs"	que contient chaque jour"
physical energy of the body	The inert, untouched by desire
Life ("voler/donner")	Death (as in earlier poems)
Movement of Youth	Passage of Time
	(deathly embrace "les deux lignes
	sont amoureuses l'une de l'autre")
"mélodies," "gracieuses	"jeu de la farandole serpentine"
ondulations," "lisses harmonies"	

Out of the frenzied dance of life, which paradoxically rushes toward
death, a moment of harmony, beauty, and love may be saved, made eternal, immortalized by the desire of the poet. As in the Proustian text Art
is the convergence of intuition (fleeting sensation) and of an effort of will,
so for Albert-Birot Poetry is a rush of sensual energy and elaborate
construction.

The Nature of the Sublime

In these first twelve poems where the poetic quest is established and
reaches this temporary celebration, a type of rising and falling pattern
may be discerned. The poet attempts to fulfill the potential of the self
and of language to secure a moment of the absolute, all the time aware
that he may fail, that indeed failure may be inevitable, and the poems
oscillate between the dangers and exaltations of such an adventure. This
pattern, where the poet appears to capture his eternal moment and the
truth of the self only to contradict that fulfillment, continues throughout
the rest of the collection. Poems 13 to 20, in particular, oscillate between
a celebration of the power of poetic creation and its failure to retain past
time and thus the complete self, and the sequence wavers between triumph and despair. In an effort to understand the nature of poetry and
man's creative potential, a return to origins is undertaken. Poems 21,
22, and 23 look to Albert-Birot's poetic ancestors; poem 24 is a further

questioning of the self; and poems 25 and 26 explore man as completely physical creature and man as creature of harmony with the universe. As the collection draws to a conclusion, poems 27 and 28 are poems of celebration. Poem 27 is a celebration of the self and of the power of the poem, and in poem 28 the body is again at one with the universe. The joy of this harmony with creation and between the ordinary events of everyday life and the extraordinary potential of the "poète-homme" (poem 32) builds to crescendo in the thirty-third poem—a poem of total exaltation yet falling in the last poem from certainty to uncertainty in this double movement that has been a dynamic of the entire collection.

In this sequence of poems, it becomes clearer that Albert-Birot's desire is not only one of an immortality such as poetry may offer its creator but that he seeks here to explore the spiritual needs of humanity and above all to understand and offer his reader the possibility of understanding what it is to create. The *Poèmes à l'Autre Moi* are more than a narcissistic quest and search for this knowledge of an individual identity. The desire that generates these poems is the ultimate search for knowledge, to create and to be in harmony with that creation, to be part of, and extension of, and simultaneously subsume, a creation created by the Self and creating the Self. A parallel with *Grabinoulor* is again apparent. The original title of *Poèmes à Dieu* is at once more apt and more misleading as the ambition of this collection becomes clearer. These are not poems dedicated to God, this is not a desire to have salvation conferred upon the individual by an exterior, superior being; it is the exploration of the interior that will bring about a kind of poetic redemption. Neither is it the poet attempting to take the place of God as master of his creation. The desire here is rather to have for the mortal self the relationship that humanity conceives God as having to his creation. This is the relationship humanity needs for a spiritual conception of the universe to confer upon God. This is to be inside and outside, bound up with yet separate from, discernible in every part of creation and yet apart, above it, and with the potential to direct its totality. Immortality is not to be found in the space of a poem on the page or in a book marked with the name of the poet. Immortality is an individual identity fused into perpetual creation. The last two verses of this thirty-third poem and climax of the celebration of poetic creation reveal this complex relationship between humanity, creator, and creation:

> Mensonge au front du livre Poèmes à l'autre moi ils
> sont de lui j'avoue et descendent sur moi mais j'ai
> cru qu'ils seraient de moi tel qu'on me voit tel
> qu'on me nomme et qu'ils iraient à lui comme si
> la prière était dans celui qui prie et non pas dans le
> Dieu que l'on veut

Me voici moi de toi en toi de moi autant que vie me
   permet vivant d'aller et c'est peut-être tant je
   l'aime que j'ai tout voulu et qu'elle a tout permis
   et je suis passé et je suis sorti de mon nom et je
   suis rentré dans mon nom et lettre à lettre ce livre
   s'était écrit

                    —"Trente-troisième Poème"

("Falsehood at the front of the book of Poèmes à l'autre moi they
   are by him I confess and they descend on me but I
   believed they would be by me as people see me
   as people name me and that they would go to him as if
   the prayer was inside the one who prays and not the
   God who is wanted
Here I am me of you in you of me as far as life
   allows me to go on alive and it is perhaps because I
   love it so much that I wanted everything and
   that it allowed everything and I passed by and I left my name
   and I returned to my name and letter by letter this book
   was written")

Inside and outside the name, the self, the poem, the problem of identity solved, the self made sublime, the other attained, the poem written.

In the recurrent themes and dominant figures, it is possible to read the continuation of the poetic quest between Eros and Thanatos and to appreciate more fully the generating forces of Albert-Birot's aesthetics. In the exaltation of the Self, the Word is celebrated as creation: "Le verbe lui le tout et le toujours" ("the word the everything and the always"). Absolute and timeless this at once confers being on the human: "aime et se prête à la personne elle aime" ("love and lends itself to the person it loves") and endows the human with divine potential despite the banalities of moral life ("Treizième Poème"). The power of man lies in language:

Pourtant mieux vaut l'ennui de naître et de mourir
Puisqu'on fait lever le soleil en disant il fait jour

("Yet better the boredom of being born and of dying
As you make the sun rise by saying it is daytime")

The poet is already in a particular state of grace—each individual has the power to make the sun rise by his articulation of the act. The poet communes with all humankind, past, present, and future, through the potential of the written word:

Et tous ceux d'avant et tous ceux d'après
Sont avec moi dans les signes-esprits
Que je trace de ma main
Et nous voici tous sur du papier

—"Quatorzième Poème"

("And all those before and all those after
Are with me in the signs-minds
That I draw with my hand
And here we all are on paper")

Yet the vacillation between such certainty and uncertainty made explicit in the final two poems, the beauty and danger of knowledge, the ambiguity of human desire run throughout the sequence. The aspiration to the divine is ambiguous, "archange" becomes "demon" twice in the opening lines of the "Quinzième Poème," and the poet is unsure of the truth of the knowledge he has acquired. Such uncertainty climaxes in poem 16 in a desire to be separated from the potential of the other self.[87] Mortal man is unable to bear the vicissitudes of human life without the poet and returns to claim the powers of the poetic imagination and the power of the Word, which is able to evoke the past in the present:

Envoie un peu d'été dans l'hiver
Afin de m'annoncer le printemps

Couche-moi
Berce-moi sur le passé mou velouté
Où je croirai entendre voir et prendre
Tout ce que tu m'as promis

—"Dix-septième Poème"

("Send a little summer into the winter
To let me know it is Spring

Lay me down
Cradle me on the soft velvety past
Where I will believe I can hear see and take
All that you promised me")

The everyday and the absolute, the man who walks in the streets of Paris and the sublimated self, must be reconciled. The possibility of transcending that everyday is plagued with the uncertainty of his ability to understand the truth of such an existence:

Tandis que je continue à traverser le petit aujour-
d'hui pour m'ébahir du grand demain

Mais que t'ai-je donc donné là ce Printemps ne
m'avait rien offert et je t'ai menti

—"Vingtième Poème"

("While I continue to make my way through the trifling here and now
to stand amazed at the great tomorrow
But what have I given you there this Spring
has not given me anything and I lied to you")

As if to ascertain poetry's capacity to unveil and express the truth, the sequence of three poems that follow invoke the poets who have gone before him, the "douces lumières poètes des pauvres Saints" ("Vingt-et-unième Poème") whose company he seeks, the "poètes des temps d'épée" ("Vingt-deuxième Poème") whom he invites to join him:

Venez avec moi vous aussi dans mon livre où l'on
voit souvent les choses des yeux
Comme dans les vôtres que nous faisons d'éter-
nité à force de contours et mystérieuses
A force de vérité trouvez ci votre aise y garde-
rons notre jeunesse jusqu'au poète suivant

("Come with me you also in my book where you
often see things with your eyes
As in your own that we create from eternity
with outlines and mysterious things
With truth make yourself comfortable here
and let us hold onto our youth here until the next poet")

The meeting of poets and figures of the past, in fact always present, will become a key feature of *Grabinoulor*.

The twenty-third poem invokes Charles de France and François (Villon) to confer divine status on the human artefact which is the book:

Et toi François feu de vie et vin de verbe je te
prie entre aussi dans mon écriture graissée
d'humain comme ajourée d'au-delà pour
que l'ange puisse entrer et sortir

("And you François fire of life and wine made from words I beg
you also enter my writing lubricated with
Humanity as if pierced with the beyond
so that the angel can come and go")

Despite the disparity between the poetry of Villon and his own

les tiens sont
tout grouillants de la Mort qu'il t'a plu
mettre vivante en eux

("yours are
crawling with Death which it pleased you
to put in them alive")

there is an appreciation of the eternal poetic quest that needs no conferral
of name to be validated:

Mais pardon toi pardon moi je trouble l'amitié de
nos poèmes en leur parlant de nous comme
si nous étions encore à eux et comme si
François ou Pierre ils étaient
encore à nous

("But forgive you forgive me I disturb the friendship
of our poems by speaking to them of us as
if we still belonged to them and as if
François or Pierre they were
still ours")

The identity of the poem is assured within itself and the lines that follow
reiterate the enigmas and dilemmas of the identity of the poet created in
language, a creation that is ever elusive:

Parce que rangées de lettres noires ils ont l'air
d'être immobiles dans un livre commençant
par notre nom sont-ils notre portrait ou
sommes-nous que la peinture

("Because they are lines of black letters they look
as if they are motionless in a book beginning
with our name are they our portrait or
are we merely the painting")

The expression of the dilemma is exactly that which we explored in the
parallel discourses of autobiography and self-portrait. The attempt to
capture a self, a living identity in writing or paint, is death bound for it
brings what is potentially immortal (and in movement) into the realm of
the human, the physical, and the flesh which is mortal:

Ce sont eux qui sont vivants et ces êtres faits de
verbe sont meurtris quand on veut les prendre avec filet de mots pour les tenir de près
et leur demander que dis-tu
Adieu poètes j'ai trop tourné pensée de vous elle
me conduirait à prendre nos poèmes avec
les mains comme mamelles en temps de
chair comme emmâlée gaude-mihi

("It is they who are alive and these creatures made of
words are murdered when you try to capture them
with a net for words to hold them close
and ask them what are you saying
Farewell poets I have turned over thoughts of you too much
they will lead me to cup our poems in
my hands as if breasts in times of flesh
made masculine gaude-mihi")

This is another paradox of artistic creation, it is necessarily touched by
the human, given value because human, but finally tainted and doomed
because human. The poet aspires to the realm of the spirit:

En livre que voudrais parfaire je mettrai ce moi
animé lettre à lettre souffle de souffle Fils de
Père pour l'offrir à ceux d'amour comme
à ceux qui le mettront en croix
—"Vingt-troisième Poème," concluding lines

("In a book that I would like to complete I will put this self
quickened letter by letter breath by breath Son
of the Father to give him to the ones filled with love as to
the ones who will put him on the cross")

There is a spiritual quest where the body may be sacrificed for entry into
the realm where the flesh no longer exists, The dilemma is poignantly
apparent here—sacrifice the human for the divine, the certainty of the
everyday for the uncertainty of a potential state of absolute, substitute
the body for the word. But to dispense with the human entirely invalidates
the quest; the value of poetic creation lies in the celebration of body
and spirit:

Ecrire est un acte religieux, hors toute religion. Ecrire, c'est accepter de se le
faire savoir, aux frontières de l'absurde et du précaire de notre condition. Ce

n'est pas croire, c'est être certain d'une chose indicible, qui fait corps avec notre essentielle.[88]

("Writing is a religious act, removed from any religion. Writing is to accept to make oneself known, at the limits of the absurd and of the precariousness of our condition. It is not to believe in; it is to be certain of an unsayable thing that forms one body with our essential being.")

On one side exists the human ("écrire," "faire," "acte," "corps," "absurde," "condition") whose quest ("faire savoir," "être certain") is to speak the "indicible." There can be no clearer statement on the quest of Albert-Birot.

The same themes and figures constantly occur; the same questioning is reiterated. The validity of expressing the self in writing is constantly challenged: "surface organisée en noir et blanc" ("a surface organized in black and white") ("Vingt-quatrième Poème"). The fear of deception, of not seeing the truth, of not telling the truth, is always present. The sequence is nonetheless full of the inescapable contrasts of the human condition, always present, the celebration of the physical, animal-life nature of the human with savage and erotic imagery:

> Et faut que chair à chair s'enroule
> Et que gorge étrangle des cris
> Que peau déchire et que sang perle
> Et faut que joie aille à la douleur
> Bête me veut bête me prenne
> Et que bête s'écroule en heur
> —"Vingt-cinquième Poème"

("And flesh must coil about flesh
And the throat must choke off the cries
Skin must tear and blood must well
And joy must run to sorrow
The beast wants me beast seizes me
And beast must collapse in good fortune")

This is the spiritual ideal toward which the poetic self strives. It is the unity with self and divine self in an exalted state of harmony:

> Et nous voici dans l'équilibre qui n'a ni veille ni
>   lendemain rien que de la lumière et moi nous
>   Et nous rêvons mon corps . . .
>   Et nous sommes heureux d'avoir des mots sur
>   les lèvres des mots divinités des lèvres
>   des lèvres roses déesses des mots

Et voici que dans notre chaleur d'être nous avons
encor créé ces vers image d'équilibre
qui nous ressemble davantage

—"Vingt-sixième Poème"

("And here we are in an equilibrium that has no night before
nor tomorrow nothing but light and myself us
And we dream my body . . .
And we are content to have words on
our lips words deities of the lips
lips pink goddesses of words
And in the heat of being we have
again created these lines image of equilibrium
which looks more like us")

Here the communion of self in language is no longer to be questioned;
the poet no longer troubled if the image is merely a deceptive surface:

Ils ont mon corps et notre espace mais ils n'ont
pas ses limites et partout comme nulle
part ils sont encore où il n'est plus
Verbe sans visage ils sont paysage et sa lumière
chaleur sans feu homme et Dieu mystère
du mouvement dans l'immobilité[89]

("They have my body and our space but they do not
have its limits and everywhere as nowhere
they are still there where it is no longer
Words without a face they are landscape and its light
heat without fire man and God mystery
of movement in stasis")

The quest of the poet is fulfilled in a creation of the self that is far
removed from the death bound self-portraiture into the expression of
which he has at first been lulled. The space of the poem and the nature
of its creative process allow the expression of a self removed into another
realm, the eternal and unchanging one he has so desired:

Lumière et moi voici donc achevée notre création tendrement arrondie nous qui nous
sommes créés dans l'espace un jour d'Eté
Sphérique et plein de ciel et nous retrouvons à
détour de désir notre infini dans la courbe
de ce poème qui nous recrée et continue

—"Vingt-sixième Poème"

("Light and myself so here it is completed our
creation lovingly rounded off we who

created ourselves in space one Summer's day
Spherical and bursting with sky and we find once more
in the course of desire our infinity in the curve
of this poem which recreates us and continues")

From mortal time, "un jour d'Eté," an infinite is achieved, that that infinite should have the shape of a circle is a constructing element of Albert-Birot's poetic universe we have already explored in our analysis of the contrast between the moment and the eternal in *La Guerre* and indicated throughout this study. These concluding lines further stress this act of creation, an act of will, akin to our perception of the divine will that created and directs the universe. The following poems reiterate in diverse expression this joy in creation and poetic creation, enjoying the moment, "bel instant" but preferring the "mon beau dieu-moi" able to confer:

> un agrandissement
> Où tout sera sans heure sans date et sans con-
> tour dans tout l'éternellement
> de sa réalité née
> —"Vingt-septième Poème"

> ("an enlargement
> In which everything will be timeless dateless and without
> outline in all the forever more
> of its born reality")

a celebration ending in the joy of a type of autoeroticism, returning us explicitly to the nature of this narcissistic quest which, we are reminded, is the basis of this quest in writing:

> Notre vie à l'encre noire ou bleue et l'autre à
> l'encre d'or et l'autre et l'autre
> qui n'est pas écrite
> On ne voit pas et l'on veut prendre pour s'offrir
> à soi beau vice de l'accouplement de soi à soi
> —"Vingt-septième Poème"

> ("Our life in black or blue ink and the other in
> golden ink and the other and the other
> which has not been written
> You don't see and you want to take to give yourself
> to the fine vice of coupling self with self")

Narcissus, we are reminded here, is both the subject and the object, the poet who undertakes the quest to express the self. From this desire for the self, the body is celebrated:

> Ma peau d'enfant ma peau d'homme ma peau d'a-
> mant vraie parure de joie que
> j'ai trouvée sur moi

> ("My skin of a child my skin of a man my skin
> of a lover true raiment of joy that
> I found covering myself")

Words are able to express, or come close to expressing, the "vérité visible," the body truly at one with the universe:

> Toi ma peau toute ma vérité visible tu mets déjà
> de l'âme à mes yeux à ma main à mes doigts
> Partie de l'Univers harmonisée dans l'espace
> quand je te vois tu me dis déjà du bien de moi
> Douce douce
> —"Vingt-huitième Poème," concluding lines

> ("You my skin my entire visible truth you are already
> putting my soul in my eyes in my hand in my fingers
> Part of the Universe harmonized in space
> when I see you already you say nice things about me
> Sweet sweet")

The body returns us to the work of the poet-artisan who must elevate the self from the banality of the everyday to this transposed realm. The sublime may be created through human knowledge, hard work and physical skill:

> Ouvrier je le suis moi aussi charpentier maçon
> sculpteur et je dresse et maçonne et sculpte
> ma certitude comptée et pesée souci
> de mes muscles
> Et je l'étreins la frappe la dompte au marteau et
> lui donne autre poids autre mesure ainsi que
> l'avais dit quand je l'ai d'abord regardée

> ("I am a worker also carpenter mason
> sculptor and I erect and build and sculpt
> my certainty reckoned and weighed concern
> for my muscles

And I grip it strike it subdue it with the hammer and
give it another weight other dimensions as
I said when I first looked at it")

It is the poet-artisan of *La Lune* who is able to reach a certainty of his ability and potential:

Et tandis que je l'ordonne elle m'affirme que je
suis comme elle m'affirme qu'elle est et
quand elle est belle selon ma beauté voici
Je me repose devant elle certitude qui est devant
moi certitudes l'une en face de l'autre . . .

("And while I put it in order it tells me that I
am as it tells me it is and
when it is beautiful in accordance with my beauty here it is
I rest before it certainty which is before
me certainties facing each other")

The sublimity of creation is not merely a spiritual ideal ("souffle de souffle"), it is perceptible in the everyday for the poet who has explored the nature of the self: "Ecrire est un acte religieux, hors toute religion." The twenty-ninth poem continues:

Alors on fait la gueule et l'on dit quel sal'temps
j'ai dix doigts je suis deux peut-être trois
mon chapeau est neuf et je n'ai
pas de parapluie

("So you pull a face and say what awful weather
I have ten fingers there are two of me perhaps three
my hat is new and I do not
have an umbrella")

Everyday human existence and the poetic sublime are not opposites but two perceptions of the same experience. The work of the artisan becomes the celebration of perfect unity of self with self, restating the physical and intellectual elements of the quest already explored. Yet in this final sequence, the dynamic life force is tempered with the knowledge that such perfect unity may be found only in death, that the exaltation of the self in verse is merely a poetic hope:

Malgré ma naissance et ma mort ne suis-je pas
un peu toi Grand Moi et n'es-tu pas ce qui sera
Peut-être suis-je une rature mais j'ai douceur à

me mettre en toi pour l'heure où
Temps m'effacera
—"Trente-et-unième Poème"

(Despite my birth and my death am I not
a little of you Great Self and are you not what will be
Perhaps I am a deletion but it is sweet
to place myself within you for the time
when Time will obliterate me")

We are returned unambiguously to the limits of existence and of creativity that we established at the beginning of this reading of the collection. The long thirty-second poem begins on the physical, mortal nature of man:

Eté d'espace oeuvre de chair
Hurle de désir sort de peau

. . . .

Mais tout et tout je poète-homme
Riche plus que Père je suis
De tout un corps et du mourir
—"Trente-deuxième Poème"

("Summer of space work of flesh
Howl of desire fate of skin

. . . .

But all and all I poet-man
Wealthy rather than Father I am
Above all a body and destined to die")

The word death is sounded several times:

Et souffle à souffle Mort me prend
Souffle à souffle de bouche et d'yeux
J'aspire Terre et Ciel et donne
Vie à Mort que Mort devra rendre

("And breath by breath Death takes me
Breath by breath with mouth and eyes
I breathe in Heaven and Earth and give
Life to Death which Death will have to return")

With death omnipresent there is the desire for more and for life to continue:

> Quand tout est pris tout prendre encore
> Quand tout est dit trouver le dire
> Qui tout ce qui reste dira
> Que sois tout quand tout s'en ira

> ("When everything is taken take everything again
> When everything is said find something to say
> Who will tell of everything that remains
> May you be everything when everything has gone")

In this desire for more, the poem repeats itself in its reconciliation of mind and body, and celebration of man's physicality:

> Indesserrable réalité des bras paix des épaules
> certitude des reins hommes on s'est connu
> plus grand que Terre

> ("Unyielding reality of arms peace of shoulders
> certainty of kidneys men we have known ourselves
> greater than the earth")

These lines are repeated towards the end of the poem. The body of the opening lines is celebrated throughout—"mains," "poids," "corps," "yeux," "genoux," "bras," "oreille," "bouche," "femelle," "mâle," "lèvres," "muscles," "pied," "épaules," "reins," "oeil," "jambes," "dents"—many words reiterated several times literally fleshing out the poem with no repulsion of the flesh despite its weight and attachment to the earth, for it aspires to the sky. The physical must act, experience the human condition, transpose it through deed and word both spoken and written to gain knowledge of the meta-physical.

The thirty-third poem we have returned to several times and offer little further analysis here. It is the high point of the collection, a point of unity, mind with body, self with self, reiterating every stage of the quest we have explored:

> Quand j'ai mis ma main sur moi je t'ai trouvé quand je
> t'ai parlé je t'ai vu alors ma chair d'homme enla-
> cée d'esprit a voulu mettre autour de toi la chair
> de la lettre et maintenant d'autres hommes vi-
> vants pourront peut-être dire je vois

> ("When I placed my hand on myself I found you when I
> spoke to you I saw you then my man's flesh interwoven
> with spirit wanted to wrap you around with the flesh

    of letters and now other living men
    will perhaps say I can see")

This is a restatement of the whole quest not only for knowledge of the
self but that the self should be transmitted in writing to the other who
will continue its creation. The poem ends on the fulfillment of this and
more, for the self is created in the poem and transposed into that other
realm which has a timelessness beyond that of the words on the page.
The self is written in the word but is not held there immobile, "lettre
morte," it passes through and beyond this form of human expression.
Nonetheless it is in the human realm that the collection opens and it is
with the human that it ends:

> En signes humains je dirai
> Moi qu'on représente à volonté par Pierre Albert-Birot
>   incipit, 'Premier Poème'

> ("Using human signs alone I will tell of
> Myself whom people describe ad lib as Pierre Albert-Birot")

> Saveur d'humain me fait
> Comme humain m'a fait mon humain fera
>   —incipit, "Trente-quatrième Poème"

> ("Sweet taste of humanity creates me
> As humanity has created me my humanity will create")

The "tout moi poème" is handed to the reader, and it is here the fragility
of this expression is revealed, the final word being one of silence and
death. The collection of the *Poèmes à l'Autre Moi* has again simultaneously presented the poet and the poem as one physically (remembering
that like *La Lune* this is another book that the poet typeset personally)
and brought into being a metaphysical transposition of the poet and his
creation that is at once generated from him and generates him—this two-
way process that bestows divine status. Despite the exaltation of the
poem that precedes this, the final lines reveal the terrible fragility and
uncertain fate of the poem that must continue to circulate in the mortal
world. Its perfection must be handed to the human body to be revitalized,
yet it is the nature of the human to be both life giving, "lèvres font vie
de vie" and death bound, "mais plus loin lèvres tuent." Any attempt to
express the self in language, a medium equally caught between the two
and inextricably linked to the human, must remain paradoxical, ambiguous and uncertain:

Eros		Thanatos
	Mortal	
The Human life-force	subject	The Human condemned to death
	The Poet	
"Tout moi poème"		"Tout moi poème"
Self as poem exalted		Self as poem (in silence on the page)

The word remains human, spoken and written, one self remains death bound, but the poet has discovered the potential of the Word and the Self to which he will continue to aspire: "le mouvement dans l'immobilité."[90]

THE ADVENT OF THE LOGOS

Within this collection the "poète-artisan" of *La Lune* is transformed by a desire for knowledge of the self articulated between the poles of exaltation and despair, between excess and silence, into the "Poète-Dieu," originator of this creation and that to which all creation will return, multiplying, glorifying, and rendering eternal. From the personal mythology of the man who would be poet of everyday existence, Albert-Birot moves through an interior experience which is at once solitary and universal to a poetic self engendering its own creation myths. The self and the universe are transposed into poetic text, a movement continued and intensified in the naming of all creation in *Les Mémoires d'Adam* and the recounting of creation from time immemorial in *La Belle Histoire*, all, as always, contained in and containing *Grabinoulor*, perpetual source, commentary, and prolongation of the rest of the poetic production. Returning to our opening remarks in this chapter, our own reading reveals a movement in the opposite direction to that of Follain's observation of Albert-Birot's "l'ajustement de soi à l'univers." It is rather a universe adapted to the self, as though the poet, realizing the impossibility of true and absolute communion with the greater forces outside himself, whatever name he chooses to bestow upon them, reverses the direction and realizes a universe within the self, the universe that is given form through poetic creation.

In the *Poèmes à l'Autre Moi*, poetry receives its sacralization by Albert-Birot: poetic production is "divine" in the sense that it allows a communion between humanity and creation, between humanity and universe, between humanity and humanity made God. The collection unfurls itself as in the space of a creation, through the Word; the poet's relationship to the cosmos is explored with the promise of a reconstruction of the universe to fulfill humanity's needs, a theme constantly returned to in the pages of *Grabinoulor*. As the individual embraces the universal, so the word becomes sacred.[91] It would appear that the self, having sought unity and nondivision in the poetic dialogue with the "Autre Moi," an appeal for fusion, is then able to intensify itself through constant multiplication in *Grabinoulor*. Indeed the dialogue with the Self has once again allowed the poet a chance to dominate his material (as in *La Lune*) and thereby discover the potential of his creativity. This "divine" aspect of the poet's ability has its source in the desire for the mastery over the ambiguous, proliferating, and constantly fleeing material that is language, the material explored and manipulated in *La Lune*. In the earlier collection, the poet stands like the artist or sculptor before the raw material, at the limit seeking integration with his creation. In the second major collection, the poet-artist-sculptor is fused with his material and such a creation receives divine status. Looking back to the origins of Albert-Birot's poetics, Apollinaire's text on the nature of creation, divinity, and painting here echoes and reverberates:

> Mais le peintre doit avant tout se donner le spectacle de sa propre divinité et les tableaux qu'il offre à l'admiration des hommes leur conféreront la gloire d'exercer aussi et momentanément leur propre divinité.
> Il faut pour cela embrasser d'un coup d'oeil: le passé, le présent et l'avenir. La toile doit présenter cette unité essentielle qui seule provoque l'extase . . .
> Le tableau existera inéluctablement. La vision sera entière, complète et son infini au lieu de marquer une imperfection, fera seulement ressortir le rapport d'une nouvelle créature à un nouveau créateur et rien d'autre.[92]

> ("But the painter must above all offer himself the spectacle of his own divinity and the paintings which he offers to men's admiration will confer upon them the glory also to exercise momentarily their own divinity.
> For this the past, the present, and the future must be embraced in one look. The canvas must present this essential unity which alone brings about ecstasy. . . .
> The painting will ineluctably exist. The vision will be complete and its infinity, instead of marking an imperfection, will only bring out the relation of a new creature to a new creator and nothing else.")

Yet Apollinaire's position is ultimately one that is radically different from that of Albert-Birot. The pursuit of the modern can be a process as estranging as it is liberating, a "fragmented and fragmenting avant-garde," and Apollinaire's poetry may be perceived as writing a lack of identity: "a poetics of the estranged and the decentered."[93] Our reading of Albert-Birot's production thus far leads us to conclude a position for the poet at the opposite pole. The experience of the avant-garde acts as catalyst, certainly a potentially fragmenting one, but Albert-Birot withdraws and rather than any negative influence upon his sense of identity, leads him to reinforce his own personal confidence in the status of the poet-creator,

strengthening his belief in the "myths of creativity," indeed perpetually
writing and re-writing his own creation myths. His experience of simultaneity and of synthesis, the fundamental aim of the modern artist as understood by Albert-Birot is that of the artist fused with and yet manipulating
time and space on the canvas, at the centre of his creation. In Albert-
Birot's case the original techniques of simultaneity and synthesis provide
a fertile foundation in his constant search for an Absolute. In the beginnings of his acclaimed "rebirth" as true creator, true poet, Albert-Birot
as painter is already Albert-Birot as philosopher-poet. His reflection on
the world and his relationship to it begin as expression on the canvas, for
the exercise of painting is a metaphysical contemplation.[94] In the *Poèmes
à l'Autre Moi*, which grows out of and intensifies this attitude toward
artistic expression, the poet develops a reflection on the nature of his
own identity and relationship to the world around him, on humankind's
identity and its position in the cosmos:

> Elle [la poésie] porte en elle l'espoir d'un nouvel ordre, d'un nouveau sens,
> dont elle doit imaginer l'instauration. Elle met tout en oeuvre pour hâter la
> venue du *monde* encore inexprimé, qui est l'ensemble de rapports vivants dans
> lesquels nous trouverions la *plénitude* d'une nouvelle *présence*.[95]

> ("It [poetry] carries in it the hope for a new order, for a new meaning, whose
> establishment it must imagine. It puts everything into action to hasten the
> coming of *a world* as yet inexpressed, which is the whole of the living relation-
> ships in which we would find the *plenitude* of a new *presence*.")

The words emphasized here by Starobinski are the keys to the passage
from the *Poèmes à l'Autre Moi* to *Grabinoulor*. Albert-Birot passes from
figurative self-portrait, to the expression of self through abstraction, to
the expression of self written explicitly into the poem, to the essence of
self expressed through poem. The Self speaks and the Word is made
present. The Word is spoken and the Self is made present. The advent
of the Logos makes the Word present. The poet is not merely the intermediary between God and the world; his word is the Word of God. Here
we finally join with those commentators on Albert-Birot who have also
perceived the philosophical implications of his work as he attempts to
elucidate the ambiguities and mysteries of existence, a quest that brings
him closer and closer to the eternal enigma: "Chez Birot, l'Homme est
Noyau Central et quasi Dieu, super-paganisme 'naturel' qu'ont rêvé quelques philosophes." ("In Birot's work, man is the central nucleus and
demi-god, a natural superpaganism that some philosophers have dreamed
of.") Using words, the poet extends beyond the philosopher: "Ces mots,
c'est tout son univers. . . . N'avons-nous pas dépassé toute philosophie?
La poésie n'est-elle pas toujours ou en deçà ou au delà?"[96] ("These words

are his entire universe. . . . Have we not gone beyond any philosophy? Is not Poetry always either on this side or the other of it?") Albert-Birot's attitude to creation and the world around him develops this spiritual vision such as is offered particularly in the *Poèmes à l'Autre Moi*: "Il parvient alors à une vision toute spirituelle de notre univers pseudo-matériel, vision qui transfigure cet univers et le rend à son origine et à sa destination première."[97] ("He therefore arrives at a totally spiritual vision of our pseudomaterial universe, a vision that transfigures this universe and returns it to its origin and its first destination.") Albert-Birot's vision, his looking at and reflection on the cosmos, is that of the artist/philosopher. This look that we have discovered through our detailed reading of the *Poèmes à l'Autre Moi* is at once life-drive and death-drive, the look that is simultaneously Eros and Thanatos, the look that is the essence of the ambiguity of all human existence, the look that will attempt to keep *Grabinoulor* in perpetual motion.

The reading of the "Poet-God" presents a number of problems, however. Is this then literature that reads literary creativity in its male definition as "fathering" of the text, where in the image of the divine creator the writer becomes the divine-author, the sole and unique origin and meaning of his work? If this were the only generating force at work in *Grabinoulor*, then the prose work would be a piece of nineteenth-century narrative and our reading of Albert-Birot's works as an integral and fundamental part of the literary texts of the twentieth century a pointless endeavor. The experience retains the consciousness of a potentially fragmented subject for poetry is necessarily reliant on 'l'écoute de l'Autre:"

> Le sujet, le moi, si fortement présent dans l'acte d'énonciation, ne reste pas seul en scène dans ce qu'il énonce: il fait largement place à l'autre, à ce qui requiert compassion, et il accepte que la conscience individuelle face au monde, se plie à l'exigence d'une *vérité* dont elle n'a pas le droit de disposer arbitrairement.[98]

> ("The subject, the self, so strongly present in the act of enunciation, does not remain alone on stage in what it enounces. It leaves a large place to the other, to he who requires compassion, and it accepts that individual awareness in the face of the world bends to the demand of a truth that it does not have the right to use arbitrarily.")

The experience of the fragmented subject has been explored diversely in the poetry of the twentieth century, and the *Poèmes à l'Autre Moi* reveal most poignantly Albert-Birot's modern consciousness. Is *Grabinoulor*'s dense narrative the antidote to such fragmentation, dialoguing internally, complete unto itself? Having analyzed the status of the self thus far, we must now turn our attention to his "épopée," its very description sitting incongruously within a modern perspective, and constantly bear in mind the question, what constitutes *Grabinoulor* as a modern text? Why should *Grabinoulor* be read as a key moment of the literature of the first half of our century? What, finally, does the reinsertion of such a text in the literary discourse of the twentieth century imply for our reading of its art?

5

Grabinoulor and the Seeking of Knowledge

croyez-moi son goût naturel est l'amour des histoires merveill-
euses ouvertes sur l'infini or la vérité c'est un mur à pic sur
lequel on se casse le nez vous savez bien que la vérité habite
au fond d'un puits alors vous voyez quel horizon
— *Les Six Livres de Grabinoulor*, V. 9, p. 693

("Believe me his natural taste is the love of stories that are
marvelously open onto infinity now the truth is a sheer wall
against which you come a cropper let me tell you that truth
lives at the bottom of a well so you see what a great horizon
it has")

On voudrait avoir la foudre
au bout des doigts
Et l'espace cette espérance
Et la lumière cette vitesse
Et plus encor
Alors on ferait le grand poème
qui ne s'écrit pas
Mais on n'a que des mots
Du papier
Et un désir

— "Excuses" in *Les Amusements Naturels*

("We would like to have lightning
At our fingertips
And space that aspiration
And light that speed
And still more
Then we would make the great poem
That doesn't get written
But all we have is words
Some paper
And a desire")

GRABINOULOR AS METATEXT

As has been indicated, most previous commentators have concentrated their efforts on this text, with a few of the poetry collections exciting sporadic interest. One of our aims here is to widen the scope of criticism of Albert-Birot's work as a whole and as such we have chosen to focus equally on certain other texts. Yet it is impossible and futile to work within Albert-Birot's poetic creation without *Grabinoulor*.[1] *Grabinoulor* is the key to the universe created by Albert-Birot, informing the other texts within its orbit and self-informing; it is the product of the application of theories of poetic creation and a theory in the process of being elaborated.[2] *Grabinoulor* constructs and is perpetually being constructed.

We have explored Albert-Birot's theoretical program contained within the initials of his literary journal *SIC*—"Sons," "Idées," "Couleurs"— these three letters, this one word, enclosed on three sides by a large "F" signifying "forme." We initially based our hypothesis on Albert-Birot's understanding of the creative process implied within the relationship between the invisible and the unutterable and the artist's quest to paint and speak them ("dire/peindre" in the first of the *Trente et un Poèmes de poche*). The immense scope of *Grabinoulor* encompasses all his experimentation to approach the impossible of the work of art; the absolute, the unknown, the invisible, and the unutterable are explored from every angle. It has been our intuition in this study that the apprehension of the poetic universe, of the time and space that structure this textual creation, will be informed by an attention to the visual. This visual takes many forms. An analogy with cubist practice is evident, its concern with presenting a greater "realism" close to Albert-Birot's understanding of the "sur-réel." This obviously has implications for the reading process—the reader must enter the space of the text that is *Grabinoulor* just as the spectator must enter the space of a cubist painting. Throughout *Grabinoulor* the discussion (for this is a narrative generated through dialogue) recurrently returns to the visual arts, and in the closing lines the words *peintre cubiste* echo. An awareness of the visual, of the color and form on the canvas, and of the words on the page is essential if we are to apprehend the universe within the canvas or the textual universe. The visual here is more concerned with structure than with the imagery. *Grabinoulor* speaks not only of itself and of Albert-Birot's poetics but of all literary creation:

> Texte infini, *Grabinoulor* est aussi un texte pluriel où convergent, à travers des éléments de structure capturés dans la littérature antérieure et contemporaine, l'épopée, le conte philosophique, le journal intime, la poésie futuriste, le roman

historique, le théâtre de marionnettes, la Bible et Dada. En même temps *Grabi-noulor* se donne aussi comme 'texte futur', puisque le 'maintenant' de la poé-tique nunique est un pur instant qui abolit la durée en la parcourant simultanément dans toutes ses directions.[3]

("An infinite text, *Grabinoulor* is also a plural text in which, through the ele-ments of structure taken from earlier and contemporary literature, the epic, the philosophical story, the diary, futurist poetry, the historical novel, puppet theatre, the Bible, and Dada converge. At the same time, *Grabinoulor* is offered also as a "future text," because the "now" of nunic poetics is a pure instant that abolishes duration by running through it simultaneously in all directions.")

When Albert-Birot writes of *Grabinoulor* "Ce livre est le prototype de l'espirit *SIC* et son premier chapitre a paru dans ma revue en juin 1918,"[4] ("This book is the prototype of the spirit of *SIC* and its first chapter appeared in my journal in June 1918.") he is writing of the work as a fundamental point of reference within a modernist discourse to which he never failed to adhere and of which, as for Apollinaire, cubism is the most perfect form and expression. The paradox nonetheless remains between the modern and the status and form(s) of *Grabinoulor* as "epic." The quest of the text is that of a reconciliation and assimilation of opposites as much as a theory of poetics and of artistic creation. The personal myth and Albert-Birot's voluntary identification with *Grabinoulor* is revealed as infinitely complex, far beyond a mere lyrical, poetic magnification of the poet's everyday.[5] The reader spirals into a narrative that not only speaks of creation, of immortality, of infinity but that desires to find and offer a form in which these may be made manifest. The reading proposed here is an attempt also to write of the voyage of discovery that this study itself has been.

The myth of Pierre Albert-Birot and of *Grabinoulor* (for the text itself has achieved its own type of mythic status, frequently alluded to but little known) is the point of departure for this final, yet ultimately principal section of our reading for which we may first provide an initial questioning with which to orientate an analysis of a multiform, multivoiced whole:

- What is the relationship between the act of (artistic) creation and the object that is created? How does this "creature" come into being? The original moment and movement of creation will be best exempli-fied by the discourse on painting that is maintained throughout the narrative, being the form of artistic creation most frequently com-mented on by Grabinoulor and his interlocutors.
- Why is it in a narrative form that the poet finds his most perfect and most adequate expression? Following on from a discussion of artistic creation in the visual arts, we will explore the space of *Grabinoulor*

as a geometric one, the narrative not only as the space of a cubist canvas but one where the generating figures of Albert-Birot's creative force resurge to provide the internal space and movement that constitute poetry, where the (re)organization of self and created universe takes place in external space and where the body of the poet and the text fuse most fully.
- What is the nature of the excess of this proliferating, nonpunctuated, yet structured narrative? How can we read the ever becoming of the narrative and the limitless being of *Grabinoulor?* The perpetual ever-expanding, all-encompassing present moment of the narrative is its excess, infusing the text with a spirituality, a meditation on the nature of the divine and the creator, of immortality and mortality, of art and the human condition. Does the never-ending quest for knowledge, which propels the narrative, confer on this the status of sacred text?

These first two problematics bring us close to the explorations already made here of Albert-Birot's two important poetry collections, the artisanal and corporeal aspects of poetry that are but the visible representation of a metaphysical impulse apparent in both *La Lune* and the *Poèmes à L'Autre Moi.* It is in the final questioning proposed here that we will most intimately seize the particular nature of *Grabinoulor* and of Pierre Albert-Birot as poet as we listen to the discourse of being and, in our final reading, the discourse of nonbeing, of what it means to be human.[6]

GRABINOULOR AS "EPIC" AND SACRED TEXT

The Voice, the Epic, and the Sacred

Within the "grabinoulorian" myth of the publication of the work itself, the story is told of how the publisher Denoël suggested this epic label to Albert-Birot for the 1933 edition and his pleasure in this idea. (The terms "roman" and "romancier" are anathema in the text of *Grabinoulor* where Grabi repeatedly pours scorn on both their authors and their readers.) For Albert-Birot his own advent into modernity, carrying with him his knowledge of Latin and Greek and his love of medieval literature, the idea of this ancient form being applied to a modern narrative immediately loses its ambivalence and rather becomes personally apt and particularly suitable for the construction the episodes take on increasingly in the second and third volumes. Once again the reading of the text to its small circle of admirers becomes more than a social and literary gathering, rather rendering the voice (Greek *epos*) and restoring the true epic status of the narrative.[7]

Todorov's consideration of the Odyssey as less the return of Odysseus to Ithaca, because this is its ending and therefore its death, but rather as its telling (Odysseus has the desire to narrate, the desire of a narrator), suggests for us also various readings of the text of *Grabinoulor* as epic.[8] In Todorov's examination of the construction of the epic, he stresses the action of the narrative as primordial, and he considers a literature where action is more important than the psychology of the characters, such as the *Decameron* and the *Arabian Nights*. Throughout *Grabinoulor* the major attribute of the hero is his constant movement: it is impossible to paint his portrait or to attribute any psychological traits. The reader can only be sure that he will move on to his next adventure. "On comprendra mieux le récit si l'on sait que le personnage est un nom, l'action est un verbe. Mais on comprendra mieux le nom et le verbe en pensant au rôle qu'ils assument dans le récit."[9] ("The narrative will be understood better if one knows that the character is a name, the action is a verb. However the name and the verb will be better understood by thinking about the role they assume in the narrative.") This is exactly the narrative of *Grabinoulor* where the eponymous hero "premier du nom" is ("the first to have this name") is above all the verb that perpetually moves him.

This constant momentum again recalls the construction of oral narratives, where the appearance of each new character indicates a new episode.[10] In Ancient Greek oral narrative, there was no plotting as in the structure of the prose form of the novel. The hearer was rather plunged *in medias res,* just as is the reader at the beginning of *Grabinoulor.* Similarly there was disregard for temporal sequence, a situation being narrated and later explained. *Grabinoulor* follows a similar sequencing, the narrator occasionally interrupting the narrative flow to quell the reader's disbelief or to explain how Grabi came to be in all places at once, for example. Even on a more superficial level, a comparison may be drawn that indicates that Albert-Birot is consciously referring to such literature, as the titles of volume III onward increasingly become short (although often enigmatic) résumés of the chapter reminiscent in tone of, for example, the *Decameron:* "Pour étudier la structure d'un récit, nous devons d'abord présenter cette intrigue sous la forme d'un résumé, où à chaque action distincte de l'histoire correspond une proposition."[11] ("To study the structure and the narrative, we must first present the plot in the form of a résumé in which each action distinct from the story corresponds to a proposition") Thematically the constant questioning of the existence of God and of the nature of the creation of the universe, in addition to being an artistic and personal preoccupation of the poet, is reminiscent of the medieval psyche where the biblical text is the point of reference. Furthermore the apparent ambiguity of this revival of ancient and especially medieval aesthetics may not be at such odds with Albert-Birot's will to modernity, for as Umberto Eco has pointed out, our own culture has much in common with that of the Middle Ages:

> A côté de cette entreprise massive de la culture populaire se déroule tout un travail de composition ou de collage exercé par la culture savante sur les détritus de la culture du passé. Prenons une boîte magique de Cornell ou d'Arman, un collage de Max Ernst ou une machine inutile de Munari ou de Tinguely: on se retrouvera au milieu d'un paysage qui n'a rien à voir avec Raphaël ou Canova mais qui a beaucoup à voir avec le goût esthétique médiéval. Dans la poésie on retrouve les rébus et les devinettes, les kennigam irlandais, les acrostiches, les tissus verbaux de citations multiples qui rappellent Pound et Sanguinetti; les jeux étymologiques de Virgile de Bigorre et d'Isidore de Séville qui resssemblent fort à Joyce (celui-ci le savait), les exercices de composition temporelle des traités de poétique qui semblent être un programme pour Godard et surtout le goût du recueil et de l'inventaire qui se concrétisent alors dans les trésors des princes et/ou des cathédrales où l'on recueillait indistinctement une épine de la couronne de Jésus, un oeuf trouvé dans un autre oeuf, une corne de licorne, la bague de fiancailles de St. Joseph, le crâne de St. Jean—à l'âge de 12 ans.[12]

("Beside this massive undertaking of popular culture unfolds a whole work of composition or of collage carried out by scholarly culture on the rubbish of the culture of the past. Take one of Cornell's or Arman's magic boxes, one of Max Ernst's collages, or one of Munari's or Tinguely's useless machines, and you find yourself in the middle of a landscape that has nothing to do with Raphael or Canova but that has a great deal to do with medieval aesthetic taste. In poetry you find the rebus and guessing games, the Irish kennigam, acrostics, verbal webs of multiple quotes reminiscent of Pound and Sanguinetti, the etymological games of Virgil of Bigorre and of Isidora of Seville that closely resemble Joyce (who was aware of this), exercises in the temporal composition of treatises on poetics that seem to be a program for Godard and above all the taste for the collection and the inventory that takes the form of the treasures of princes and cathedrals where a thorn from Jesus' crown, an egg found inside another egg, a unicorn's horn, St. Joseph's engagement ring, and the skull of St. John when he was twelve are indiscriminately gathered together.")

Read with Eco, *Grabinoulor* is at once medieval and intensely modern, for there is all the narrative: verbal games in which unfurls the relationship between the everyday and the marvelous, where the events of the everyday become literally fabulous, where Grabinoulor's incessant desire to look for disparate objects in the far-flung corners of the world become ancient quest and modern narrative, where the accumulation of events is an aesthetic both old and new, where Albert-Birot finds the perfect form: "Notre art, comme celui du Moyen Age, est additif et composite."[13] ("Our art, like that of the Middle Ages, is accumulative and composite.")

Yet more than merely accumulating, the essential of the narrative is its ever-becoming:

> Le récit qui parle de sa propre création ne peut jamais s'interrompre, sauf arbitrairement, car il reste toujours à raconter comment ce récit qu'on est en train de lire ou d'écrire, a pu surgir. La littérature est infinie, en ce sens qu'elle dit une histoire interminable, celle de sa propre création.[14]

> ("The narrative that speaks of its own creation cannot be interrupted, except arbitrarily, because there always remains to relate how this narrative, which we are in the process of reading or writing, came to be. Literature is infinite in the sense that it tells a never-ending story, that of its own creation.")

The constant returns and self-references in the narrative equally follow epic processes, as do the myriad epithets attributed to Grabinoulor. *Grabinoulor*, product of the era of print, dense narrative, a typographical block, revives the construction of the old oral narratives:

> The heroic and the marvelous had served a specific function in organising knowledge in an oral world. With the control of information and memory brought about by writing and more intensely by print, you do not need a hero in the old sense to mobilise knowledge in story form.[15]

Albert-Birot returns his hero to ancient forms, and his relationship to Poetry, which we uncovered in *La Lune*, continues to function in his prose narrative, taking poetry back to its origins as the memory of humanity. Albert-Birot's preface to *Grabinoulor*, where he insists upon the "souffle du poète" similarly takes on a new dimension, not merely a plea for acceptance of his unpunctuated and apparently author-directed prose but rather a call to read this as we would hear the epic adventures of the past, a call to remember other forms of narrative structure and heroes of greater dimensions.[16] Reading Albert-Birot's discussion of the text, however, the voice takes on a deeper, essential significance. This is not merely a justification for a difficult text, it is an indication of its nature. Punctuation is "une invention assez récente," and Albert-Birot makes clear that his writing looks back to the origins of poetry and disparages the progress made by the written word in line with reasoning and logic:

> Les premiers hommes qui aient écrit n'ont pas éprouvé le besoin de faire cette invention parce que ces hommes étaient des poètes et que la poésie—qui, elle, ne raisonne pas—n'a aucun besoin de marquer les temps qui correspondent à l'opération graduelle du raisonnement, et ce poème écrit était une chose en soi, fixation en quelque sorte du poème chanté (modulation sur quelque notes) qui ne prétendait absolument pas être une imitation du discours parlé.[17]

("The first men who wrote did not feel the need to invent this because those men were poets and poetry—which does not reason—has no need to mark out the moments that correspond to the gradual operation of reasoning, and this written poem is a thing in itself, a fixed form to a certain extent of the sung poem (a modulation on a few notes) that in no way claimed to be the imitation of spoken discourse.")

Little by little this imitation took place, the human mind "en son état naturel de tous les jours a des semelles de plomb et monte toujours l'escalier, marche après marche"—("in its natural everyday state has leaden soles and always climbs the stairs step by step") a gradual movement alien to Grabinoulor who crosses time and space at will and in every direction. He admits that punctuation is useful when making a reasoning clear to a reader: "Les virgules et les points l'empêcheront de s'essouffler au sens propre comme au sens figuré." ("commas and full stops prevent if from getting out of breath, in a literal sense as well as a figurative one.") Nonetheless there is a vast divergence between logic and poetic creation:

> Or il me paraît de la plus belle évidence qu'une conception d'ordre poétique ne peut être toute qu'une seule courbe et doit être, comme un pont d'une seule arche, lancée d'un seul jet, sans une brigue, sans une reprise. Le poète crée selon son rythme, avec sa masse verbale, une forme aussi pleine que cela lui est possible et là, ce n'est plus le souffle court de la logique et de la respiration qui commande, mais uniquement sa puissance créatrice, en un mot ce n'est pas le souffle du lecteur qui est à considérer, mais le souffle du poète.[18]

("It seems to me to be blindingly obvious that a conception of a poetic order can only be one curve and must be launched in a single spray, like a bridge with a single arch, without any detours or resumptions. The poet creates according to his own rhythm, with his verbal mass, a form that is as full as is possible, and there, it is no longer the short breath of logic and breathing that is in command, but only his creative force. In a word it is not the reader's breath that is to be taken into consideration but the breath of the poet.")

The narrative is continuous, infused with a life force: "Un bon coeur bat de naissance à la mort, un coeur qui a des points est une coeur malade" ("A healthy heart beats from birth to death, a heart that has full stops is a heart that is unwell.") Albert-Birot's remarks link body to voice, matter to mind, in a simile that strikingly resembles Bergson's *L'Energie Spirituelle:* "Or je crois bien que notre vie intérieure tout entière est quelque chose comme une phrase unique entamée dès le premier éveil de la conscience, phrase semée de virgules, mais nulle part coupée par des points."[19] ("I believe that our entire inner life is something like a unique sentence begun with the first awakening of the conscience, a sentence sown with commas but nowhere cut by full stops.") The text is written according to the personal rhythm of its creator, that is, a celebration of energy. The reader quickly adopts the pace inscribed: the more one reads, the easier it becomes, one's own breathing adopting the cadence. The reader enters into physical communion with the text: *Grabinoulor* is not only medieval epic, it is sacred text.[20] The jubilation of the text is energized by the breath, its vitalism a transcendence for, as we shall discover, the ultimate quest is the speaking of truth—the advent of the Logos of which *L'Autre Moi* speaks.

The Epic and Its Quest: The Sacred Text and Truth

Grabinoulor's search for the Holy Grail is an obvious illustrative episode of the text as both epic narrative and sacred text generated by a quest for truth. This serves equally as a classic example of the grabinoulorian narrative, for when Grabinoulor sets out to find the ultimate "objet de valeur," he becomes so involved in the adventure itself that he forgets the goal and loses interest in this one tale when there are so many others to be told. For him to have found it would have necessarily entailed "an end," and the true object of the quest can only be the narrative itself. The "perpetual present" of the text of *Grabinoulor*, always commented upon by its readers, is that also of the structure of the quest of the Holy Grail as read by Todorov where:

> La logique narrative implique, idéalement, une temporalité qu'on pourrait qualifier comme étant celle du "présent perpétuel." . . . Le discours n'est jamais en retard, jamais en avance sur ce qu'il évoque. A tout instant aussi les personnages vivent dans le présent, et dans le présent seulement.[21]

> ("Narrative logic implies, ideally, a temporality that could be qualified as being that of the 'perpetual present.' . . . The discourse is never behind or in advance of what it is evoking. At every instant also the characters live in the present, and only in the present.")

Todorov defines the quest of the Holy Grail as articulated between narrative (as above) and ritual, between the profane and the sacred, and between the deeds of the knights and the apparitions of the Grail:

> En revanche, la logique rituelle repose, elle, sur une conception du temps qui est celle de 'l'éternel retour'. Aucun événément ne se produit ici pour la première ni pour la dernière fois. Tout a été déjà annoncé, et on annonce maintenant ce qui suivra.[22]

> ("On the other hand, ritual logic rests on a conception of time that is that of the 'eternal return.' No event happens here for the first or for the last time. All has already been announced, and now what will follow is announced.")

The narrative of *Grabinoulor* unfolds according to these "logics," the deeds of Grabinoulor perpetually present, and the rituals of myth, legend, fairy tale, religion, although subverted, constantly returning. In Todorov's terms the first is a horizontal line, "le récit de contiguïté," the second variations piled up vertically, "le récit de substitutions."[23] It is this construction that is the very opposite of any one-dimensional narrative and that is the structure of the text of *Grabinoulor*—at first sight a block of linear narrative moving horizontally but through its quest structure accumulating variants, substitutions, establishing its own cyclical structure. It is the nature of the Round Table (or rather round tables in general) that excites Grabinoulor's interest in the Holy Grail:

Il trouve qu'elles n'ont ni commencement ni fin ce qui leur donne à ses yeux du moins quelque chose de cosmique . . . c'est donc par amour de la table ronde que Grabinoulor en vint à s'intéresser au verre de Jésus (IV, 8, p. 462)

("He finds that they have no beginning and no end which gives them in his eyes at least something of cosmic nature . . . it's therefore through the love of the round table that Grabinoulor comes to be interest in Jesus' glass")

Such a quest necessarily entails the recurrent poetic quest that generates all Albert-Birot's work. As for the Grail itself: "Il est très raisonnable d'y penser puisque de par sa nature sacrée et surtout par la quasi incassabilité de sa matière cet incommode verre à vin doit être quasiment éternel" ("It's very reasonable to think about it because through its sacred nature and above all through the virtual unbreakability of the material it's made of this impractical wine glass must be virtually eternal.") This ultimate quest is, therefore, at once material and spiritual: "et enfin peut-être raison dominante il aime retrouver ce qui est à jamais perdu" ("and finally perhaps the dominant reason he likes to recover what is lost forever").[24] It is in the fusion of the material and spiritual quest that Todorov sees the special nature of the search for the Holy Grail, for in itself and its maintaining of opposites it goes against our laws of logic:

Ceci et le contraire ne peuvent pas être vrais en même temps dit la logique du discours quotidien; *La Quête du Graal* affirme exactement le contraire. Tout événément a un sens littéral *et* un sens allégorique. . . . Le dynamisme du récit repose sur cette fusion des deux en un.[25]

("This and the opposite cannot be true at the same time says the logic of everyday discourse; *The Quest for the Holy Grail* affirms exactly the opposite. Each event has a literal meaning and an allegorical meaning. . . . The dynamism of the narrative rests on this fusion of the two in one.")

This maintaining of contradictions, which has always been the propelling force of all fantastic fiction,[26] is one of the generating forces of this narrative, and the problem of the apparently opposing limits of our existence will be constantly pursued: "Tout ce qui touche Grabinoulor est incroyable et c'est bien pour ça qu'il faut le croire" ("Everything that touches Grabinoulor is unbelievable, and that's why it must be believed.") (p. 463).

Finally the unique character of Grabinoulor's tale, set among the myriad of other tellings of the quest, must be upheld: "Mais à l'encontre des chercheurs à cheval d'autrefois ils ne perdirent aucun temps dans des aventures dont on puisse faire un roman non non à la recherche et pas d'histoires ils allaient à la moderne" ("But contrary to knights of old they didn't waste any time having adventures from which you could make a novel no no get on with searching and no nonsense they went on in the modern way.") Yet while commenting on itself in the process of relating, the narrative must be dissimulated as doing so:

> L'effort du récit de se dire par une auto-réflexion ne peut-être qu'un échec, chaque nouvelle déclaration ajoute une nouvelle couche à cette épaisseur qui cache le procès d'énonciation. Ce vertige infini ne cessera que si le discours acquiert une parfaite opacité: à ce moment, le discours se dit sans qu'il ait besoin de parler de lui-même.[27]

> ("The effort of the narrative to tell itself by means of self-reflexivity can only end in failure; each new declaration adds a new layer to this thickness, which hides the process of enunciation. This infinite vertigo will only end if the discourse acquires perfect opacity. At that moment, the discourse tells itself without it needing to speak of itself.")

This episode stands, therefore, as perfectly indicative of the structure of the whole text: a basic quest structure, thematically securing a literary filiation that is treated at once seriously and humorously, inviting us to read the text as epic and simultaneously reflecting on its differences through an ironic narratorial stance; an "eternal return" both thematically and structurally. Grabinoulor sets out, weaves a narrative both horizontally and vertically as he goes and returns to the place of departure, a cyclical time structure that remains ever present, a space that constantly expands out, sure of always being in the same place. Grabinoulor dominates time and space; he is man and monster in the terms with which Proust concludes his own epic narrative:

> Du moins, si elle m'était laissée assez longtemps pour accomplir mon oeuvre, ne manquerais-je pas d'abord d'y décrire les hommes (cela dût-il les faire ressembler à des êtres monstrueux) comme occupant une place si considérable, à côté de celle si restreinte qui leur est réservée dans l'espace, une place au

contraire prolongée sans mesure—puisqu'ils touchent simultanément, comme des géants plongés dans les années, à des époques si distantes entre lesquelles tant de jours sont venus se placer—dans le Temps.[28]

("But at least, if strength were granted me long enough to accomplish my work, I should not fail, even if the result were to make them resemble monsters, to describe men first and foremost as occupying a place, a very considerable place compared with the restricted one that is allotted to them in space, a place on the contrary immoderately prolonged—for simultaneously, like giants plunged into the years, they touch epochs that are immensely far apart, separated by the slow accretion of many, many days—in the dimension of Time.")

In such an immense text as *Grabinoulor,* the selection of an example episode has certain reductive features, yet as an introduction into the structure, the quest for the Grail, if obvious by its selection to provide an illustration of the narrative, does offer several ways to proceed, specifically offering a way forward for the voyage of discovery of which we spoke earlier. How can we read such a text then? Perhaps only through such a selection of individual moments constantly expanding out to embrace the whole of the text—not to a totalizing reading that would be impossible but with the potential to encompass a space that does justice to the text in its entirety: "Réduisons donc pour mieux agrandir, pour mieux accommoder un champ déterminé d'écoute et de vision."[29] ("Let us reduce then in order to better enlarge, in order to better accommodate a specific field of sound and vision") Remember in the reception of this text for what concerns its production there is no "part" of creation, that all creation is constantly present, and that the past is merely a linguistic invention, a pedantic use of language:

Je vis à l'intérieur de mon cycle et un cycle entier n'est qu'un même temps mon temps le tien le temps de nous les hommes du présent cycle et tout ce qui est en lui du commencement à la fin est vivant bien . . . il faut se décider à reconnaître que le passé n'est qu'une affaire de grammariens coupeurs de temps en tranches minces . . . le temps est le temps d'une seule pièce comme une boule et conviens avec moi qu'un homme de cinq mille ans est notre contemporain (V, 10, p. 701)

("I live inside my cycle and a complete cycle is but a same time my time yours the time of us men of the present cycle and all that is in it from the beginning to the end is living well . . . you must decide to recognize that the past is only the affair of grammarians cutters up of time into thin pieces . . . time is time of one single piece like a ball and admit with me that a man five thousand years old is our contemporary")

Having illustrated the epic nature of the text, the problem of reading has been approached but not solved. Because all time is present in one place within the narrative, so Grabinoulor and Furibar, their interlocutors, who range from figures from history, myth, literature, allegory, and the everyday, and, indeed, include the reader sometimes directly addressed, are equally constantly present. After this overview of the text as "epic," we can now elaborate a model of reading with which to proceed.

THE CIRCULAR SPACE OF THE NARRATIVE AND THE CIRCULAR SPACE OF READING: SPATIAL MODES OF READING

The space of *Grabinoulor* is one of concentric circles—from the central point of Grabinoulor's own body ripple out circles of his apartment; the street; Paris, France; the world; the universe; and that which is beyond. Each circle may be traversed in any time dimension, from the very origin of humanity to an indefinite point in the future.[30] Each time Grabi takes a new step outside himself, a new movement, the circles reverberate out, finally returning to the self of Grabinoulor.[31] Here we begin to apprehend the dynamics of the narrative for the point of return is in movement itself. Grabinoulor is not a fixed point of the narrative for the very nature of Grabinoulor is motion. There is no fixed point of the narrative. Grabi may pass polite conversation with M. Stop, but his attitude to his recurrent interlocutor is clear: "Au revoir M. Stop nous sommes très pressés pour l'instant ne manquez pas de revenir à un meilleur moment" (III, 1, p. 139) ("goodbye M. Stop we're in a hurry at the moment don't fail to come back at a more convenient time"). The narrative is in itself a paradox, a dense block of type endlessly proliferating, filling up all the space that contains and surrounds it: "Ecriture du 'hic et nunc' par excellence, l'écriture birotienne se base en effet sur l'occupation totale de l'espace, non seulement l'espace référentiel pour le personnage mais aussi de l'espace textuel."[32] ("Writing of the here and now par excellence, Albert-Birot's writing is based in fact on the total occupation of space, not only the referential space for the character but also that of the textual space.") Yet this does not bring movement to a halt, for the figure of the text is circular: "La circularité règle également la prolifération du langage qui devient ainsi une figure exemplaire de l'autogénération du texte."[33] ("Circularity equally rules the proliferation of language that becomes therefore an exemplary figure of the self-generation of the text.") And above all the circle is infinite and all-absorbing, self-generating, and whole, yet never complete and finished: "C'est seulement dans ce 'chant sphérique' que le poète retrouve son infini, création qui répond au moment de la création même du poète; autrement dit dans 'la courbe de ce poème qui vous crée et continue.'"[34] ("It is only in this 'spherical song' that the poet regains his infinity, a creation that responds to the very moment of creation of the poet; in other words in 'the curve of the poem which creates and continues you.'")

From what we perceive visually on the page, the linear narrative, we move into a different figural space, the space of desire.[35] In *Grabinoulor* the circle is an underlying abstract figure, the geometry of the narrative created in the space of the mind of the poet and in the mind of the reader. A progressive reading of Albert-Birot's work brings to the surface the deep significance of this figure: "Le texte est inscrit vis-à-vis du lecteur. . . . Le texte fait visage. Il est placé comme un visage en face de celui qui le lit. . . . Pour le message écrit, elle est aussi ce qui détermine les positions réciproques du visage du lecteur et du texte."[36] ("The text is inscribed vis-à-vis the reader. . . . The text made face. It is placed like a face opposite he who is reading it. . . . For the written message, it is also what determines the reciprocal positions of the faces of the reader and of the text.")

The circular space of creation meets the circular space of reading, also a space of concentric circles as the self of the reader opens out from the page, to the book, to the whole of literature, the universe around him, as he reads, returning back through those circles to the body of the reader, an entity like that of Grabinoulor himself that remains constant yet always in motion. To consider exactly how such a creation comes into being and remains ever-becoming, therefore the dynamics and generation of such a narrative, we propose a brief return to the very beginnings of Albert-Birot's contact with modernity and the visual arts of the period in an effort to understand how a new process of creation and a new process of reading are the fundamental source of such a text. For what the figure of the circle allows is in fact a reading of synthesis and simultaneity, key concepts of the avant-garde. We move from a chronology to a topology of reading as the breaking up of space allows new spatial models of reading to function, apparent in painting in the breaking up of perspective and in poetry in the experience of space on the page. The reading process (for both the visual arts and for poetry that became further aligned during this period) must necessarily respond to artistic productions constructed with the twin forces of simultaneity and synthesis working both on and in them. The centrifugal force is a double perception of the increased movement of the modern world exciting both exhilaration and the fear of fragmentation and loss of meaning. The centripetal force and particularly the force of the creative self offsets the danger inherent in the first. As poetry and painting move closer together, as new forms of expression are produced to match the new concepts of time and space, and as humankind's relationship to the modern world is explored and new ways to think the word become necessary, it is not only for the reading of poetry

that new reading strategies become necessary. The chronology of the
reading process, reinforced by the plot of the nineteenth-century novel
moving inexorably to its logical conclusion, is replaced in the novel also
by a topology of reading, an essentially twentieth-century aesthetic. The
reading of the novel, no longer necessarily linear and requiring more and
more a collaboration between writer and reader, an active participation
in the part of the reader, demands a similar effort to that demanded of
the reader of poetry. A new understanding of the world must engender a
new artistic language with which to speak that knowledge. The creators
of that new language must teach its functioning to new readers. In the
continual juxtaposition of disparate elements, a visual structure of reading is necessary to read an apparently linear verbal text. In *Grabinoulor*
the figure of the narrative is the circle, not the straight line, as initially
apprehended for this is a linear narrative created originally in the cubist
"état d'esprit," the poetic moment where past, present, and future are
eternally present.

"GRABINOULOR": "UN CHAOS GÉOMÉTRIQUE"

> encore un 'abstrait' et même ajouta Grabinoulor un presque vrai en dehors de
> toute figure objective c'est si j'ose dire la représentation de la 'bellicité' en
> quelque sorte **un chaos géométrique** et en certains endroits continua l'Ange je
> vois de bien telle matière surtout dans les blancs les gris et les noirs ce tableau
> est récent? point du tout je me suis amusé à le peindre voici tantôt trente ans
> en un temps où la peinture 'abstraite' était nommée par Apollinaire orphique
> il a d'ailleurs vu celui-ci avant de mourir (*Grabinoulor*, IV, 13, p. 528; our
> emphasis)

> ("another 'abstract' and even added Grabinoulor almost a real one without any
> objective figure it's if I dare to say the representation of 'bellicity' to some
> extent a geometric chaos and in certain places continued the Angel I see clearly
> such a subject in the whites the greys the blacks is the painting recent? not at
> all I amused myself by painting it almost thirty years ago at a time when
> 'abstract' painting was called by Apollinaire orphic what's more he saw this
> one before he died")

It has been an initial hypothesis of this study that it is the visual arts
that provide Albert-Birot's theoretical framework for his poetic production. In chapter 1 we analyzed *La Guerre*[37] as founding moment of a
poetics. In chapter 2 we particularly emphasized the importance of the
"dialogues nuniques" in *SIC* as the point where Albert-Birot truly enters
the aesthetics of modernity. The importance of the visual is evident in
the poetry of *La Lune*, and in the previous chapter, we discussed two

parallel modes of expression—self-portrait and autobiography. Within *Grabinoulor* the visual arts merit attention even in terms of frequency of reference alone.[38] These discussions are more than a metadiscourse on art theory and history, however. It is in these considerations that the process of artistic creation is explored and most significantly the organization of time and space not only on a canvas but in the narrative itself.

The hypothesis here is that the space of *Grabinoulor* is structured like the space of a cubist canvas, where the eye of the creator holds his creation at all times in all dimensions and where the figures of the circle and the straight line, uncovered as a generating force of Albert-Birot's artistic and poetic creation, produce a space that is concrete and symbolic, material and figurative. First we will consider the discourse on the visual arts in *Grabinoulor* to posit a theory of the way in which space is organized and second we will explore the implications of this "geometric space" for the reading of *Grabinoulor* as a whole, bearing in mind the new reading processes already in progress engendered by the new artistic language to speak the multidimensional space of modernity.

Artistic Creation and the Visual Arts

It is at the reception given by Grabinoulor for selection of guests from every area of human achievement throughout the ages (philosophers, leaders, artists, writers) that the most important discussions on art take place (Livre V, 6). It is the visual arts that are most thoroughly analyzed, particularly in the discussion between Cézanne and Raphael where the painter heralded by the cubists explains the principles of their techniques to the old master. Painting prior to cubism had remained in an elementary stage of its evolution where the artists had accepted to:

> se contenter d'une seule face de l'objet c'est donc peindre une image qui ment puisqu'elle prétend dire l'objet peint tandis qu'elle est bien loin d'en dire le quart . . . alors les cubistes se sont levés de leur siège et ils sont venus tourner autour du modèle et même si c'est un objet ils l'ont pris dans la main et bien étudié à tous les points de vue et dans tous les sens ciel s'écria Raphaël quel coup de génie je comprends! (. . .) vous voyez Raphaël quelle richesse pour le peintre qui va si bien connaître son modèle vivant dans l'espace et il va même le connaître intérieurement car rien ne l'empêche de l'ouvrir pour voir ce qu'il a dans le ventre alors avec les éléments que contient cette quasi totale connaissance il compose un tableau qui s'approche incomparablement plus près de la vérité que ceux des peintres assis et qui en outre est son oeuvre bien plus qu'une copie-imitation ah disait Raphaël songeur si j'avais connu le cubisme! (p. 636)[39]

("To content oneself with one side of the object is therefore to paint an image that lies because it claims to speak for the painted object while it is really saying less than a quarter about it . . . so the cubists got up from their seats and came to turn all around the model, and if it was an object they held it in their hands and studied closely all the points of view in every direction heavens cried Raphael what a stroke of genius what wealth for the painter who is going to know his model living in space so well and he will even know it internally for nothing stops him opening it up to see what it has in its stomach so with the elements contained in this almost total knowledge he composes a painting that is incomparably closer to the truth than those of seated painters and that is furthermore his own work much more than an imitation-copy ah said Raphael dreamily if only I had known cubism!")

The first quality necessary is the status of nonrepresentation and therefore of pure creation. The maxim of *SIC*, "L'Art commence où finit l'imitation," of several decades earlier, returns. Earlier in this same volume, Grabinoulor takes issue with Pascal whom he considers to be incapable of understanding true painting:

> Comment ne voyez-vous clairement que dans un tableau il y a l'objet plus le tableau et que ce n'est point l'objet peint qui est à regarder mais bien la façon dont il est peint et donc d'un très misérable objet le peintre va pouvoir faire un très beau tableau . . . la raison du peintre n'est pas de représenter il n'est pas un "représentateur d'objets" (V, 2, p. 586)

> ("How can you not see clearly that in painting there is the object plus the painting and that it is not at all the object that has been painted which is to be looked at but the way in which it has been painted and therefore from a very pitiful object the painter will be able to make a very beautiful painting . . . it is not a painter's lot to represent he is not a 'representator of objects'")

The discussion with Pascal is taken up in the last volume, where the philosopher is displeased with Grabi's earlier remarks that he is not interested in painting simply because: "j'ai dit autrefois que les peintres cherchent à nous intéresser aux choses qui ne nous intéressent pas dans la nature" (VI, 13, p. 934). ("I said along time ago that painters try to make us interested in things that don't interest us in nature.") Grabinoulor's answer introduces a key term into the discussion on the nature of artistic creation and one that takes us immediately back to the poetic creation of the *Poèmes à l'Autre Moi*. The subject matter of the painting is: "transformé en valeur picturale c'est-à-dire qu'il est devenu une oeuvre d'art . . . ce qu'il y a en lui de plus divin c'est le don de faire inventer" ("transformed into pictorial value that's to say that it's become a work of art . . . what there is in him that is most divine is the gift to invent.") The artist is thus "divine," and once again the words of Apollinaire echo.

Nonrepresentational art and the divine nature of true artistic creation have been covered time and time again in Albert-Birot's discourse within the framework of the avant-garde. Cézanne goes on to reveal new developments in art, however, reserving a value judgment because he confesses to knowing little about it. Nonetheless the potential of abstract art is to further an understanding, a knowledge of the world, and of the self:

> J'en ai eu seulement par oui-dire la donnée générale et je suis un peu perplexe car naturellement elle est tout le contraire du cubisme puisqu'il était lui la réalité quaisment totale du monde extérieur tandis que la nouvelle peinture est la réalité peut-être totale aussi du monde intérieur le nouveau peintre ne peint plus ce qui est en dehors de lui mais ce qui est en dedans de lui (6, p. 637)

> ("I only heard through hearsay the general facts, and I am a little perplexed because naturally it is the very opposite of cubism because that was the almost total reality of the external world whereas the new painting is perhaps also the almost total reality of the internal world the new painter no longer paints what is outside himself but what is inside him")

True creation takes place at some limit position between internal and external space. In the remarks that follow the creative principles we have previously identified in *La Guerre* are indicated, and most significantly a program also for the narrative of *Grabinoulor* itself is offered:

> Ce qui est là-dedans est-ce bon pour la peinture est-ce de la forme et de la couleur peut-on en faire un tableau m'est avis qu'on y trouve *douceur* et *violence amour* et *haine laideur* et *beauté* et *des tas de choses* de *même impalpabilité* peut-être peuvent-ils les *manifester* et les *poser* sur une toile *au moyen* des *sept couleurs* et *ces deux lignes mères la droite et la courbe* Dieu a fait encore plus difficile puisqu'il n'avait même pas ça peut-être disait Raphaël peut-être[40] (Ibid.; my emphasis, and previously quoted in chapter 1)

> ("What is in there is it good for painting is it form and color can you make a painting from it methinks that you find there gentleness and violence love and hate ugliness and beauty and lots of things and even impalpability perhaps they can be shown and put on a canvas by means of the seven colors and the two mother lines the straight line and the curved line God had an even more difficult job because he didn't even have that perhaps said Raphael perhaps")

The construction of the work of art is a series of contradictions, the expression ("manifester," "poser") of the impalpable ("l'indicible," "l'invisible") with a material ("les sept couleurs") and figures ("la droite et la courbe"), whose nature is excessive ("tas de choses") because it is generated through difference, through opposites ("douceur/violence"; "amour/haine"; "laideur/beauté") the most vital of which is conspicuous here by its absence. Poetry and art are between "two worlds," assigned sacred status in the new order dominated by man's scientific and technological knowledge. Art assumes an essential ontological function, a reflection on the condition of living and on man's spiritual needs.[41]

From the discourse of modernity generated through the early twentieth century avant-garde's preoccupation with humankind's new position in the world, already accorded divine status by Apollinaire, has developed a belief in the creative potential of humanity that exceeds the artistic program to give expression to the meeting point of inner and outer worlds that is the very origin of the world itself as Grabinoulor explains to Nature.[42]

> En un mot il suffit qu'ils aient du génie pour être quelqu'un dans le genre de Dieu car en somme si tu es la Mère des peintres Dieu est bien leur père c'est certainement (si certitude il y a) lui qui a fait le premier et le plus grand tableau connu et c'est non moins indiscutablement lui qui a eu le premier l'idée de projeter hors de soi ce que l'on a en soi ce qui a bien l'air de prouver que les peintres actuels qui te montrent si monstrueusement le dos sont les vrais peintres tandis que ceux qui n'ont d'yeux que pour toi ne sont que des souspeintres seulement Dieu ne pouvait pas se contenter d'un simple tableau à encadrer il a fait une sorte de sculpto-peinture dans laquelle on se promène à l'aise (V, 9, p. 686)

> ("In a word it's enough that they have some genius to be someone like God because all in all if you are the Mother of painters God is their father it's certainly [if there is any certainty] he who made the first and greatest known painting and it's no less indisputably he who was the first to have the idea of projecting outside yourself what you have inside which seems to prove that painters today who turn their backs so monstrously to you are real painters while those who only have eyes for you are merely subpainters only God couldn't content himself with a simple painting to frame he made a kind of sculpto-painting in which you can walk at ease")

The artistic process is a cognitive process, born of knowledge and understanding of self and world: "Tu es le désordre—le beau désordre si tu veux—et nous chère amie nous sommes l'ordre" ("You are disorder—beautiful disorder if you like—and we dear friend we are order") Grabinoulor tells Nature (V, 9, p. 683). The vocation of poetry and art is vitally implicated in the state of noncompletion of the world around us: "Tu n'es que l'ébauche d'un monde et qui plus est d'un monde anhumain sur laquelle nous travaillons et dont à grand ahan nous parvenons à faire un monde relativement achevé et à peu près humain" (V, 9, p. 683) ("You are only the sketch of a world and what is more of an anhuman world on which we work and from which with much striving we manage to make a world which is relatively finished and almost human")

It is through the principles of cubism's appropriation and reorganization of external form to abstraction's formulations of inner realities that the true creative process takes place. The artistic object must create a space at once imaginary and real, physical and metaphysical, where the dimensions of time and space may be reorganized and art, and therefore humanity, achieve their potential:

> Voici trente ans à peine qu'ils ont commencé à peindre comme qui dirait de la méta-physique c'est-à-dire à mettre en formes et en couleurs ce qui n'a ni forme ni couleur en un mot à tirer encore une fois une sorte de monde d'une sorte de néant in principis creavit . . . et divisit lucem a tenebris . . . encore une Genèse (V, 9, p. 687)

> ("Scarcely thirty years ago, they began to paint in a way that could be called metaphysical that's to say to put into forms and colors that which has neither form nor color in a word to draw forth once again a kind of world from a kind of nothingness in principis creavit . . . et divisit lucem a tenebris . . . another Genesis")

Finally, however, it is not on canvas that Albert-Birot will achieve his Genesis, his "sculpto-peinture" but in a narrative where Grabinoulor "se promène à l'aise," essence of true creation, poetic potential at a point between two worlds, between an internal and an external space, the world metamorphosed by desire into text.

The Cubist Space of *Grabinoulor*[43]

The space of *Grabinoulor* is one constructed as the space of a cubist canvas where "two worlds" meet and where the juxtaposition of disparate elements carries its own logic in the way Tzara writes of both modern poetry and cubist painting:

> Ce qui, aux yeux de la logique classique, pourrait sembler arbitraire est pourtant soumis à une rigueur intérieure d'un autre ordre, je veux dire à une logique poétique basée sur l'association des idées. C'est en grande partie d'elle que dépend la formation de l'image poétique. Dans la peinture cubiste, celle de Picasso en particulier, l'association des formes est un des facteurs essentiels à la constitution des images picturales dont le peintre organise la disposition dans le tableau. Et de même que la profondeur de l'espace n'est plus indiquée par les moyens de la perspective classique, les temps dans la poésie moderne n'ont plus recours à la succession chronologique habituelle, l'instant poétique ayant plus d'importance que le développement causal.[44]

> ("That which, in the eyes of classical logic, might seem arbitrary is, however, submitted to an internal rigor of another order, I mean to say to a poetic logic

based on the association of ideas. It is to a large extent on this that the formation of the poetic image depends. in cubist painting, Picasso's in particular, the
association of forms is one of the essential factors for the constitution of the
pictorial images whose arrangement the painter organizes in the painting. And
just as the depth of space is no longer indicated by means of classical perspective, so time in modern poetry no longer has recourse to the usual chronological succession, the poetic instant having more importance than causal
development.")

The discourse on the time-space interaction is a privileged one for the
avant-garde:

> Qu'il ait existé une correspondance intuitive entre le bouleversement par Ein-
> stein de l'espace et du temps absolu de Newton et la destruction de l'ordre de
> la perspective poussée à son terme par Picasso et Braque, c'est d'autant plus
> vraisemblable que de telles révisions de l'espace-temps surgissent parallèle-
> ment dans la prose de Joyce ou de Gertrude Stein, que Schönberg ou Stravinski
> se dégagent alors des structures traditionnelles de la musique, comme Max
> Jacob, Apollinaire, Reverdy, Blaise Cendrars de celle de la métrique française.[45]

> ("That there existed an intuitive correspondence between the disruption by
> Einstein of Newtonian space and absolute time and the destruction of the order
> of perspective pushed to its limit by Picasso and Braque is all the more likely,
> because such revisions of the time-space continuum spring up in parallel fash-
> ion in Joyce's or Gertrude Stein's prose, because Schoenberg or Stravinsky
> break away from traditional musical structures, just as Max Jacob, Apollinaire,
> Reverdy, Blaise Cendrars break with French meter.")

It is in the structuring of a new space-time dimension that modern poetry
and modern painting are at their closest.[46]

The chance meetings that generate the narrative as Grabinoulor moves
from encounter to encounter form their own "logique poétique" in the
way Tzara speaks of, relying not on causality but an unfolding that sus-
tains and holds together these elastic poetic instants:

> quand il s'agit du temps grabinoulorien c'est une durée . . . donc il y eut une
> durée entre le moment où se boxant il sortit de son imagination et l'instant
> comme qui dirait en caoutchouc très élastique où . . . il s'affirma qu'il était
> bien lui (III, 2, p. 140)

> ("When it's a question of grabinoulorian time it's a duration . . . therefore
> there was a duration between the moment when fighting with himself he left
> his imagination and the instant which you could say was made of very elastic
> rubber when . . . he could definitely say that he was himself")

The narrative is constantly potent, always able to engender, to dissemi-
nate. Its force is its potentiality of occurrence. Yet this implies a chaos,

an "anything might happen," which lacks the synthesis that the artistic act and the true artistic object requires. It is the ordering of the universe, of Nature (opposed to her "beau désordre"), which is the mark of humanity's divinity for Albert-Birot. *Grabinoulor,* for all its apparent proliferation in every direction, to every subject from the scatological to the divine, is not a chaos, it is a geometric chaos. It has order, and it has structure, based on its own internal logic and laws. Geometry, science of exactitude, becomes the perfect instrument for the manipulation of a potentially chaotic space, and we will return to a consideration of geometry later. In an early episode (Livre I, 2), which is frequently commented upon, the world is restructured by Grabi to restore the equilibrium of a statuette standing on a shelf in his apartment. In the first chapter of the final volume, Grabi once again carries out an experimental reorganization of the world where the countries and continents are given geometrical shapes.[47] When Grabinoulor visits the first Eden (not the biblical version but an anterior and for this narrative true paradise) and the original and most perfect Adam in IV, chapter 15 (p. 560), all is order and harmony, and Adam tells the hero "Seigneur Grabinoulor HOMME est inséparable de GEOMETRIE" (p. 560), ("Lord Grabinoulor MAN is inseparable from GEOMETRY") with which Grabi agrees, man being "un être si plein d'équilibre et de volonté." ("a being so full of equilibrium and will.")

Lyotard suggests that after Galileo: "Le langage dans lequel s'exprime le nouvel univers est celui de la géométrie." He argues that from this point on there is a geometrization of the field of vision.[48] For Lyotard Cézanne's revolution is the reorganization of a geometric space:

> C'est en effet par rapport aux règles de l'écriture géométrique de l'espace représentatif établies au sortir du premier quart du quinzième siècle, que l'espace cézannien accomplit sa fonction de déconstruction. C'est par rapport à une 'écriture' que la fonction critique, le travail de vérité du figural s'accomplit, elle consiste avant tout dans la déconstructon de cette écriture.[49]

> ("It is in fact in relation to the rules of the geometric writing of representative space established at the end of the first quarter of the fifteenth century that space in Cézanne's work achieves its deconstructive function. It is in relation to a 'writing' that the critical function the true work of the figural is achieved, it consists above all in the deconstruction of this writing.")

We have previously analyzed the forms of the straight and curved line in the structure of Albert-Birot's canvas *La Guerre.* In the first book of *Grabinoulor,* the two are respectively attributed to man and God. When "ce païen de Grabinoulor construit la Tour de Vie": "il n'y a que deux lignes—quelle misère pour des gens comme nous et il semble impossible d'espérer le moindre enrichissement—la courbe qui appartient mettons à

Dieu et la droite qui appartient à l'homme" (*Grabinoulor*, I, 7, p. 18).
("This pagan of a Grabinoulor builds the Tower of Life—there are only
two lines—what misery for people like us and it seems impossible to
hope for the least enrichment—the curved line that belongs let's say to
God and the straight line that belongs to man.") In the third volume, the
innate quality implied here is made clear: "vive la ligne courbe une vraie
âme immortelle ne peut pas s'accommoder de la pauvre ligne droite"
(*Grabinoulor*, III, 12, p. 253).[50] ("long live the curved line a real immortal
soul cannot make do with the poor straight line")

The opposition thus maintained between straight/curved, humanity/
God suggests the opposition between mortality and immortality which
we previously read as the Eros/Thanatos division and opposition in the
Poèmes à l'Autre Moi: "God" would be then he who creates and transcends his own geometric space. It is only God who may behold all
simultaneously and transcend the differences thereby instigated. We are
returned here to the program of creation in Cézanne's discussion of abstract art that encompasses all oppositions, ordering the excess and manipulating the material into "sept couleurs" (expression) and "ces deux
lignes mère la droite et la courbe" (form). "Dieu est le pur regard ubiqui-
taire perçant le système des oppositions, instituant le textuel sans ombre
et sans modèle; nous somme plongés dans la différence."[51] ("God is the
pure ubiquitous look piercing the system of oppositions, establishing the
textual without shade and without model; we are plunged into difference.") Grabinoulor enjoys within his own narrative such ubiquity, the
quality which his readers most frequently attribute to him, and the power
of science to order and control to which he aspires is similarly the discourse of God: "Géométrie, arithmétique, analyse . . . leur privilège pro-
vient de ce que ce discours mathématique est le même que celui dans
lequel Dieu dit le monde. Là se trouve la limite métaphysique à l'extension de l'arbitraire.[52] ("Geometry, arithmetics, analysis . . . their privilege
comes from the fact that this mathematical discourse is the same as that
in which God speaks the world. There is found the metaphysical limit
at the extension of the arbitrary.") In such a perspective, it is in the
geometrization of the universe that the poet becomes God. In his conversation with the Eiffel Tower, Grabinoulor comes closest to perceiving the
form of the creator: "ah certes il a ces droites et ces courbes tellement
artificielles ces pauvres et faciles courantes de géométrie élémentaire
tandis que moi j'ai la vraie ligne vivante" (V, 3, p. 603), the Tower says
of the Palais de Chaillot. ("ah certainly it has those such artificial straight
and curved lines those poor and simple shapes of elementary geometry
whilst I have the true living line") Above all the Tower (whom Grabi calls
Isabelle) insists: "je suis de la divinité la plus parfaite image que les
hommes aient jamais faite"; ("I am the most perfect image of divinity

that men have ever made") "Image de Dieu mais fille d'homme" ("Image of God but daughter of Man") (p. 606). The most perfect perception of God made by an age most unbelieving for: "elle nous a été donnée non par l'aspiration au divin mais par l'impératif des chiffres qui tout à fait sans en avoir l'air conduiraient alors plus sûrement à Dieu que toutes nos grandes spéculations intellectuelles ou spirituelles et donc ce serait l'existence de Dieu démontrée mathématiquement" (pp. 606–7). ("it has been given to us not through the aspiration to the divine but through the imperative of numbers which without at all seeming to do so would lead more surely to God than all our grand intellectual or spiritual speculations and therefore this would be the existence of God demonstrated mathematically.") This assimilation of God to the Eiffel Tower, although elaborated certainly with irony and humor, is nonetheless indicative of the way in which the space of the narrative of *Grabinoulor* is generated and structured. "Grabinoulor l'ubiquiste" is the poet/creator contemplating his restructured universe. The imaginary space, that is the space that comes into being at the limit point between two worlds, is the space that, transcribed, becomes the text, a space that is structured, coded geometrically.[53] Geometry is linked not only to structure but to the quest for truth and knowledge that motivates the entire text. In chapter 1 we discussed how abstraction is intensely subjective but can only be apprehended by rigorous analysis and how geometry plays a crucial role not only in the visual expression of cubism and abstraction but in Albert-Birot's writing as he seeks to express the enigma of the real and the problems of its representation, for example, the transposition of the apprehension of the real and simultaneously the structuring of the space of desire. The "poetic space" of *La Guerre* is assembled with geometric precision. Constructed with subjectivity and logic, with the imaginary and the real, the canvas, the poem, the narrative is generated. The structuring lines of *La Guerre* are those of this entire poetic universe.

The Imaginary Space of *Grabinoulor*

The canvas, the narrative, constructs its own space, which, in turn, contains it, holding within it the geometric chaos that brings it into existence. Simultaneously it opens out ceaselessly onto a more vast space, the space of the imagination. As the surface structure begins to fragment, the space and depth of the imagination rise to the surface. The border line between inner and outer, between "two worlds," is the place on which we now focus.

Grabinoulor with the sensibility of a poet understands and manipulates the line of difference between everyday reality and the inner reality of the imagination. When Furibar the complaining pragmatist takes issue with Grabi, his own poetic essence is his defense:[54]

> conviens-en là bien entre nous Grabi tu ne te nourris que de 'pas vrai' tout ce que tu dis tu l'inventes tout ce que tu prétends faire ne se passe que dans ton imagination et voilà bien le grand mot IMAGINATION tu ne te plais que dans ta nom de dieu d'i-ma-gi-na-tion j'en conviens Furibar le gros vrai quotidien m'emmerle par sa présence même et me réduit par sa limite tandis que je me déploie tout à mon aise dans l'illimité du vrai vrai qui brille dans l'imaginé lumineux là on a de la place c'est là qu'est le haut monde et le bas monde n'est que la matière brute dont notre imagination distillatrice fait l'oeuvre mettons si tu veux que ce bas monde est une vinasse dont le poète tire l'alcool ou encore de la vie ordinaire il fait de l'extraordinaire (V, 11, p. 710)[55]

> ("Admit it just between us Grabinoulor you only feed yourself on the 'not true' everything you say you make up everything you claim to do only happens in your imagination and there it is the great word 'IMAGINATION' you're only happy in your damned i-ma-gi-na-tion I agree Furibar the down to earth real everyday bugs me by its very presence and reduces me through its limitations whilst I spread myself to my heart's content in the limitlessness of the real real which shines in the glorious imagined there you have space it's there that is the upper world and the world down here is only the raw material out of which our distillery-imagination make the work of art let's say if you like that this world down here is a cheap wine from which the poet takes the alcohol or rather that from an indifferent wine he makes something quite different")

There could be no clearer explanation as to how Grabinoulor's own narrative is generated and of how access to the "greater space" is to be accomplished. The place of the imagination at the limit of two worlds can be represented diagrammatically by opposite semantic fields in this section of the text:

gros vrai quotidien	illimité du vrai vrai l'imaginé lumineux
on me réduit	je me déploie
limite	on a de la place
bas monde	haut monde
matière brute	oeuvre
vinasse	alcool
vie ordinaire	extraordinaire

The figuring of these two opposite fields could be represented in various ways—closed/open, passivity/activity, and, of course, the axes of death and life (horizontal/vertical) we have previously suggested: the Eros/

Thanatos opposition of the *Poèmes à l'Autre Moi* and the circles and straight lines of *La Guerre*.

Furibar remains unconvinced that poetry can ever be more than an illusion, removed from the reality of the everyday:

> vivre le vol plané en IMAGINATION mon pauvre Grabinoulor tu me fais rigoler rigole Furibar rigole je suis fier d'arriver à ce résultat non je ne veux pas rigoler il n'y a vraiment pas de quoi avec ta POESIE tu crois donner à la vie tout ce qui lui manque mais au vrai tu ne lui donnes rien du tout (V, 12, p. 725)

> ("to live the soaring flight in IMAGINATION my poor Grabinoulor you make me laugh laugh Furibar laugh I am proud of arriving at this result no I don't want to laugh there really isn't any need with your POETRY you think you're giving life everything it lacks but in truth you're not giving it anything at all")

Grabi of course disagrees: "puisque je le crois c'est une réalité oui eh oui quand tu as le cul bien enfoncé dans le coussin de ton fauteuil et que tu prétends faire un voyage inter-planétaire c'est une réalité oui Furibar je fais le voyage" (V, 12, p. 725). ("since I believe it it's a reality yes oh yes when your bum's nicely ensconced in your armchair and you say you're making an inter-planetary voyage that's a reality yes Furibar I make that voyage") Here Grabinoulor spells out the relationship of the poet to his poetry, of the creator to his creation. Man occupies an everyday space and yet has the potential as poet (and everyone has the potential to be a poet) to inhabit an unlimited poetic space that may exist continually and simultaneously but in a dimension removed.[56]

The body of Grabinoulor, an object within a textual space, set within a universal outer space, is in itself a space to explore:

> Dans ce jeu fait de réalisme quotidien et de surnaturel indissolublement mêlés à travers les apparitions les disparitions les fusions et les ineffables résurrections de Grabinoulor qui emplit l'univers et en même temps l'absorbe en lui-même, le pénètre et s'en pénètre, s'y dilate et s'y amplifie, et partout triomphe, étant la poésie même, à la fois libre et profonde qui se joue de la réalité en des prestidigitations magistrales[57]

> ("In this game made up of everyday realism and the supernatural inextricably mixed together through the appearances, disappearances, fusion, and ineffable resurrections of Grabinoulor who fills the universe and at the same time absorbs it into himself, penetrates it and is penetrated by it, is dilated and amplified there, and who triumphs everywhere being poetry itself, simultaneously free and with great depth and who plays with reality with masterful magic tricks")

Through the relationship of Grabinoulor to the narrative, we perceive the relationship of the poet to his creation: "il suffit que le corps propre n'ait plus de dimensions fixes pour que les objets perdent leur constance et l'espace ses coordonnées euclidiennes."[58] ("It is enough that the body itself no longer has any fixed dimensions in order for objects to lose their constance and for space its euclidian coordinates.") The text is at once part of the poet's body and an object that functions in a space external to it. The created object may be a mirror in which to view the self in the way in which a spatial reading of Freud's analysis of the Fort-Da game offers: "Ce schème a néanmoins ceci de remarquable qu'il implique une structure spatiale originelle correspondant à la projection dans l'espace de l'objet, à sa distanciation effective et à la création de la dimension de profondeur."[59] ("This schema has nonetheless this which is remarkable, it implies an original spatial structure corresponding to the projection in space of the object, to its effective distanciation, and to the creation of the dimension of depth.") What Sami Ali suggests is that this original relationship to the body in space is where a "here" and "there" are established, a new dimension in space. Through this game, the self is projected: "Les relations objectales se nouant à travers le jeu s'avèrent des projections de soi, sous-tendues par une structure imaginaire identique à celle de l'image spéculaire."[60] ("The relations outside the self joining together through the game turn out to be projections of the self, with beneath them a structure in the imagination identical to that of specular image.") This is equally the separation between the body of the child and the body of the mother, which the discourse of psychoanalysis continues to explore. It is also the move from the pleasure to reality principle, from the imaginary to the symbolic in Lacanian terms.[61] The two bodies thus separated in the world of everyday, the poet seeks to reassimilate them in the realm of the imaginary, for this is where wholeness may be restored. This is the most intimate relationship between the poet and his created object, once produced and given away, he then seeks reintegration. From *La Lune* to the *Poèmes à L'Autre Moi* to *Grabinoulor,* an inner space is given form, projected into an outside space where a new dimension of depth is created and where the poet may see his own image reflected. This is illustrated graphically by Albert-Birot's self-portrait which faces the opening page of the manuscript of Livre V: "Fantasmatique: le corps propre prenant le relai de l'objet absent restitue à celui-ci à travers l'image qu'il fait apparaître dans le miroir, une existence temporelle et spatiale quasi réelle."[62] ("Part of the fantasy: the body itself taking over from the absent object restores to it, through the image that it makes appear in the mirror, an almost real temporal and spatial existence.") The ways in which the child comes to organize space are the ways in which the artistic creation comes into being. Space is the product of the interaction between the

perceiving mind and the environment that surrounds him.[63] What becomes essential is the activity (compare our diagram of the semantic fields
of Grabi's defense of the imagination) of this spatial organization where
the body is pushed to the outside of its own limits toward a point of
coincidence with an exterior reality:[64]

> A travers ce mouvement qui va de la possession de l'espace à la possession
> par l'espace (c'est là assurément l'une des joies les plus pures du jeu fantasmati
> que), le sujet se dédouble, se divise, se fragmente: grand et petit, réel et irréel,
> il se perd parmi les illusions pour mieux se retrouver identique à lui-même."[65]

> ("Through this movement, which goes from the possession of space to the
> possession by space [and this is surely one of the purest joys of the fantasized
> game], the subject splits, is divided, is fragmented. Large and small, real and
> unreal, it becomes lost in illusions in order to refind its true self.")

At this "limit point," there is fragmentation. Here takes place the drama
of the identity of the creating subject. The proliferation of the narrative
of *Grabinoulor* is a quest for a return to wholeness. It is not only the
space of the universe that must be reorganized to the dimensions of the
imaginary; that imaginary space must be made to recoincide with the
creating subject. The body of the text holds the desire of the body of the
poet: "Parce qu'il se constitue à travers le corps propre, l'espace garde
toujours, en dépit de son élaboration rationnelle, un lien secret avec l'inconscient que révèlent, le cas échéant, des mouvements regressifs."[66]
("Because it is constituted through the body itself, space always retains,
in spite of its rational elaboration, a secret link with the unconscious
which, if need be, regressive movements reveal.") It is above all visually
that the workings of the unconscious may be apprehended: "L'étude des
fantasmes objectivés dans le graphisme parait un moyen privilégié pour
saisir sur le vif comment tout un monde imaginaire émerge et se déploie
à partir de ce point idéal, le sujet incarné."[67] ("The study of objectified
fantasies in graphics seems to be a privileged way to grasp on the spot
the way in which an entire world created in the imagination emerges and
unfolds from this idea point, the subject incarnate.") The structuring lines
of *La Guerre*, where the geometric space of the poet's imaginary is visually, physically constructed, are those of his whole poetic universe, the
curved line and the straight line, the infinite and the limited, the eternal
and the temporal, God and humanity, poetic space and the space of the
everyday: one and the same geometric structure.[68] Thus is constructed
the space that is appropriate to the desire, the motivating and propelling
force of the creative act and of the canvas/narrative itself. In the terms
of Lyotard, we have arrived at the matrix of the discourse: "et le fantasme
est la matrice de ce découpage, de cette mythique imposée désormais à

tout ce qui arrivera dans l'ordre de la réalité et dans l'ordre de l'expression."[69] ("and the fantasy is the matrix of this cutting up, of this mythical dimension imposed from now on on everything that happens in the order of reality and in the order of expression.") The time of the narrative, this "elastic moment" is born of the space thus constructed:

> Da là naît, sur le modèle de l'espace auquel il se convertit, un temps qui n'a plus d'orientation précise et qu'il faut bien qualifier d'imaginaire: traversable dans les deux sens comme si le futur était déjà là au même titre que le passé, il est capable de s'étirer ou de se ramasser sans que le mouvement illusoire par lequel il est parcouru n'atteigne l'éternité sous-jacente.[70]

("From there is born, according to the model of space into which it is converted, a time that no longer has any precise direction and that must be qualified as that of the imagination. Traversable in both directions as if the future was already there in the same way as the past, it is capable of elongating itself or rolling itself up without the illusory movement that runs through it attaining the underlying eternity.")

Or in Grabinoulor's own words: "allons Furibar réagis le temps est le temps d'une seule pièce comme une boule" (V, 10, p. 701). ("come on Furibar react time is time that is a single piece like a ball.") Grabinoulor, who strides across time and space dimensions at will, returning always to the same place and occupying an eternal present moment, is the embodiment of such an imaginary time: "Aucune nécessité n'ayant prise sur lui, il est à même, livré à la toute-puissance du désir, de rebrousser chemin, de s'immobiliser sur place et de tourner en rond. Le temps imaginaire est par excellence le règne de la répétition.[71] ("Without any necessity having a hold on him, he is able, delivered up to the all-powerfulness of desire, to turn back to himself, remain stationary, and go round in circles. The time of the imagination is the ultimate reign of repetition.") The exploration of this time and space made by Ali is a description dazzling in exactitude of the qualities of Grabi: "le propre de Grabi est de s'en aller ô bonheur d'être là ô bonheur d'être ailleurs et surtout là et ailleurs en même temps chère ubiquité embrassons-nous dit Grabi l'ubiquiste et ils s'embrassèrent secrètement" (III, 11, p. 223) ("the very nature of Grabinoulor is to move around oh the happiness of being there oh the happiness of being elsewhere and above all here and elsewhere at the same time dear ubiquity let us embrace each other says Grabinoulor the ubiquitist and they secretly embraced.") "Grabinoulor ne s'arrête pas bien entendu il tourne tout en faisant ses réflexions il tourne toujours—tourner en rond voilà bien l'infini à la portée des pieds" (V, 7, p. 661). ("Grabinoulor doesn't stop of course he continues to turn while thinking he is always turning—turning in circles and there is infinity within reach of his feet.") And when Grabinoulor finally disappears from the page, it is into his own desired imaginary space that he is projected: "laissons-le donc vivre où il lui plaît et sans fin malgré le POINT," (VI, 14, p. 944) ("let's leave him to live where he likes and forever in spite of the FULL STOP.") He disappears into a space, therefore, which is limitless "sans fin," not subject to the laws of the everyday, "le point."

The limitless space of the narrative of *Grabinoulor* allows a reorganization of time and space in a way finally more satisfactory for the creating subject than the dismantling and reconstruction offered by the space of the cubist canvas. It is paradoxically in prose, in an apparently linear narrative rushing toward its conclusion, the straight line of man, that the artist/poet finds the most perfect figure of his desired circle, the curved line of God. The immensity of the narrative of *Grabinoulor* strives to dissolve external time and spatial limits and construct a space where the reign of the inner creation is assured.

From the manipulation of physical space in the poetry of *La Lune*, the poet seeks to dominate his imaginary space, to give it expression. In the movement that such a narrative allows the poet/sculptor attempts to resolve the problem of how to breathe vitality into his creation.[72] The textual mobility of the unpunctuated prose allows a structure that retains its form while allowing mobility, essence of any life form.[73] The poet has created his perfect poetic substance. In the following sections of our exploration of *Grabinoulor*, we will investigate further how exactly this substance comes into being and finally explore the dynamics of that creature but this time in the perspective of the discourse of excess, which this dissolving of limits necessarily implies.

GRABINOULOR IS EXCESSIVE

Pourquoi donner des idées aux gens qui n'en ont pas bien que après tout ce soit à ceux-là qu'il conviendrait justement d'en donner—et instantanément il pensa qu'il y avait tout un traité à ecrire sur les excès et les limites de la générosité (*Grabinoulor*, IV, 8, p. 465)

("Why give ideas to people who don't have any although after all they're the ones to whom it'd be right to give some—and instantaneously he thought that there was a whole treatise to write on the excesses and limits of generosity")

The system of excess that operates in *Grabinoulor* has been perceived by several critics, most notably by M.-L. Lentengre, who suggests that food and sex keep the text moving, their function to be "adjuvants de forces motrices qui animent le personnage et le texte."[74] ("motor force adjuncts that drive the character and the text.") These are the obvious, outward systems of excess symptomatic of the functioning of the text as a whole, and these principal excessive activities have been further analyzed and categorized by N. Le Dimna, adding to "la nourriture" and "le sexe" that she perceives to be the third motivating force of the text, "la promenade," Grabinoulor, and the text itself being perpetually "en promenade."[75] All of these are, however, surface figures of excess, symptoms of a text whose whole narrative is excess. What is more these first two categories particularly are more characteristic of the early volumes than from Livre III onward where the global nature of the text changes, becoming more excessive in terms of length of chapters yet revolving less around carnal and alimentary excess than discussion and debate. What we would wish to suggest here is a way of looking at the excess of the narrative in a different way. Fundamentally our reading suggests that the motivating force of the narrative is a quest for knowledge (compare the exploration of space as knowledge in the previous section), a quest for truth (as in the epic), or at least truths of history, of legend, or artistic creation, of human existence, of the nature of humanity and the divine.[76] The nature of such a quest is that it is proliferating, self-perpetuating, excessive in itself, for it aims to be total, all-encompassing, and that excess is double-edged, for the nature of excess is both having and losing, the quest for knowledge is simultaneously a gathering up and a dissemination, accumulation and loss. The quest for truth opens onto the infinite and the eternal; it is never-ending, perpetually present yet also always incomplete, the goal constantly escaping. Within the multiplicity of a creation, which attempts to be all-encompassing, there must also be loss; underlying this is the threat to the identity of the subject within the discourse of excess, necessarily limitless and multiple, yet risking also disintegration. The state of excess is a problem of individual identity, of being.

Excess and "Jouissance"

The dynamic "joie de vivre" commented upon by virtually every reader of *Grabinoulor* is one side of this economy of excess and the original generating force as tirelessly reiterated by Albert-Birot himself, that is, Grabi born of the *Joie des sept couleurs* and infused with the "esprit *SIC*." This becomes an ethical, almost political stance of the hero who takes position against all the inhibiting forces that oppress human nature as he transgresses any natural laws which normally prevent humankind from taking total pleasure in the cosmos, enjoying every moment, every journey, and every chance encounter. Grabi's choice is one of an affirmation of life over inertia. (Here we return to life/death drive, Eros/Thanatos opposition.) The outward expressions of this would be those categories of his exploits previously perceived (food, sex, movement). The proliferation of the everyday and its perpetual transformation into the realm of the marvelous create a bidimensional textual space that constantly self-generates and pulses with a life force of human and super human energies. The constant debates between Grabi and his regular interlocutors and those making a guest appearance infuse the narrative with a voice, a breath, a physical presence; all communication becomes a medium of the manifestation of excess as each problem is presented, meditated on, countered, or supported. The eroticism of the early volumes is a revelation of the sovereignty of desire, the body, the witness, and the expression of this dynamism. Throughout the narrative the humor that constantly circulates ensures a hearty laugh in the face of any threat to this celebration of the life force. The narrative is therefore the place of all potentialities, the domain·of excess par excellence. It is the very process of creation, its constant amplification, its perpetual mobility is life itself.

Excess and Loss

For the narrative of *Grabinoulor* literature is also the place of the impossible, its material, language, too slow, the life force always more mobile.[77] The time of narration frequently is referred to by the narrator of *Grabinoulor* as constantly missing the essence of the event: "il ne faut pas croire que Grabinoulor ait mis pour préparer son beurre tout le temps qu'il a fallu pour faire les réflexions ci-dessus rapportées" (V, 1, p. 582); ("You mustn't think that it's taken Grabinoulor the same time to butter his bread as was needed to think the thoughts reported above") "on n'a pas écrit tout ce qui s'est dit ou a eu l'air de se dire au cours de cette entrevue mi-historique et comme toujours ce qui n'a pas été immobilisé sur le papier devait être le meilleur" (III, 6, p. 174); ("We don't write down everything that is said or that seems to be said in the course of this semihistoric interview and as always what has not been fixed on paper is sure to be the best") "on n'a pas eu le temps de dire que Grabi avait rendez-vous sous le marronnier avec Furibar" (III, 8, p. 183); ("We haven't had time to say that Grabi had an appointment under the chestnut tree with Furibar") "mais cependant qu'on mettait en écriture ces travaux de cervelle sur la relation des crèmes avec l'enciellement de l'esprit Grabinoulor bien entendu a mis les voiles" (III, 11, p. 226); ("But while we were putting in writing this brainwork on the relationship of cream with the heavenlifying of the mind Grabinoulor has of course flown") "car pour désembouler la pensée et l'étaler en une bande de mots il faut du temps et du temps et Grabinoulor naturellement était pressé" (IV, 4, p. 409); ("For to unravel thought and lay it out in a ribbon of words you need time and Grabinoulor was naturally in a hurry") "les mots en effet sur le papier ont l'air de représenter du temps mais dans le bec ce n'était plus rien tant il les sortit avec rapidité c'est-à-dire qu'en réalité sur le papier les mots sont entiers tandis que dans le bec il y en avait à peine la moitié enfin le tout fut si éclair" (IV, 9, p. 479) ("In fact words on paper seem to represent time but in his mouth it seemed nothing at all he got them out so quickly that's to say that in reality on paper words are whole where as in the mouth there's scarcely half of them indeed the whole thing was so fast") "tout cela est long à mettre sur du papier mais en action ce n'est rien c'est d'un seul regard" (V, 15, p. 753). ("All that takes a long time to put on paper but to do it's nothing just one look")

If the activity of Grabinoulor is even more mobile and subject to excess than is captured in the narrative, then his being is unlimited in the way perceived by Bataille: "Il y a dans la nature et il subsiste dans l'homme un mouvement qui toujours excède les limites, et qui jamais ne peut être réduit que partiellement."[78] ("There is in nature, and it subsists in man a movement that always exceeds the limits and that can only be reduced partially.") This constant excessive activity would have a tendency to fragmentation, and rather in the way that the artists of the avant-garde offset the danger of fragmentation in the speed of the modern world by combining the exploration of simultaneity with the techniques of a synthesis and the central importance of the "moi créateur" the narrator must constantly "contain" the proliferation of its creation.

It is furthermore this excess that breaks up the teleology of the narrative. Thus it is possible to speak of a geography of *Grabinoulor,* but not a history, and for this reason our analysis has considered its geometry, its figurative language that attempts to escape a limiting discourse and forge toward infinity. Here again danger threatens. Not only is the necessarily fragile identity of a subject, which knows no limits, liable to pass into fragmentation, into nonexistence, only its excess, its energy remaining, so might such a narrative not perpetually amass and affirm itself but lose everything and fall rather into nothingness. This "voyage au bout du possible" is, in Bataille's terms, "cette ligne de fracture qui traverse une infinité de plans, est constituée par une infinité d'expériences et obéissant à un besoin d'aventure illimité tend vers l'infini, vers "l'abîme" qui est le fond des possibles."[79] ("This break line, which crosses an infinite number of levels, which is constituted by a infinite number of experiences and obeying the need for unlimited adventure, tends toward infinity, toward the "abyss" that is the source of what is possible.") Thus this need for an unlimited adventure is the double edge of excess itself: life affirming and death orientated, the narrative of *Grabinoulor* functioning as we have read the *Poèmes à l'Autre Moi* between the poles of Eros and Thanatos, between the excess and silence of all existence, in the tension between which function both literature and life, the poles of human experience and the limits of literature. It is in the quest for knowledge that is the ultimate generator, simultaneously structuring and providing the dynamics of the text, that we may explore more closely these limit(less) experiences and approach a way of understanding one of the text's enigmas—immobility within constant mobility, *le dynamico-statique* (VI, 7, p. 869). (We have made several references to this state without commenting until now.) In a text that promotes dynamism as the expression of life, what is the status of the immobile? If the truth of life, of being, is excess, than when can we ever truly apprehend ourselves? When exactly does the subject come into being from the chaos of nonbeing, the ultimate chaos?

Excess and the Quest for Truth

From the possibility that there is truth the text emerges, and the question of truth is hermeneutic, metaphysical, and ethical—as it structures the narrative so it sacralizes it.[80] We are returned to the epic status of the narrative. Truth and falsehood are difficultly discernible, not functioning as opposites within the system of values but as two sides of the same manifestation. In the narrative of *Grabinoulor,* where each problem presented is viewed from several sides, where the illusions of myth and legend, of history and of the present, and of all the elements of human existence are offered up for examination as Grabi enters into discussion with the protagonists of these events, the quest for truth remains finally of ambivalent value: "ultimate truth" is both desirable and nondesirable, plunged as we are into a state of uncertainty, concerning our immortality and the truth of our existence. When Grabi meets our original ancestors, he is told: "et dans le tous-les-jours que vous considérez les sous-pères comme des pères je te le dis vous ne pouvez que vivre d'une vérité provisoire la vraie et définitive est pour plus tard" (III, 13, p. 269). ("and in the everyday you're considering the subfathers as fathers I'm telling you that you can only live on a provisional truth the real and definitive truth is for later") The way to find truth is in itself fraught with illusion and error. In his discussion with M. Loupar, "une loupe à la main," ("a magnifying glass in his hand") who complains of men preferring illusion when there is truth in the world, Grabi counters the argument:

en ne vivant qu'avec la vérité de votre loupe vous allez bien inutilement vous désespérer car cette vérité est un mensonge et c'est vous M. Loupar vous l'homme à la loupe qui vous nourrissez d'apparences (. . .) vous voyez la vérité grossie ce n'est donc pas la vérité grossir la vérité M. Loupar est une très grave forme de mensonge (IV, 13, p. 534).

("living only with the truth your magnifying glass provides you're going to make yourself desperate uselessly for that truth is a lie and it's you Mr. Magnifier you the man with the magnifying glass who lives on appearances . . . you see exaggerated truth is not the truth exaggerating the truth Mr. Magnifier is a very serious type of lie")

This is not the way to find the truth of existence. The eternal question of truth in art shows Grabi's aesthetics to be similar in tone to the maxims of *SIC,* as his invective against imitation in art makes clear: "cessez de nous faire croire que c'est vrai inventez que diable brassez la vérité de chaque jour et sachez y découvrir une sorte de vérité universelle des oeuvres" (IV, 14, p. 538) ("stop making us believe that it's true make up everyday truth what the hell fill it with hot air and know how to find in it a sort of universal truth of the work of art") and he goes on to rebuke readers and audiences satisfied with *ça:* "ils sont tous atteints d'imitatio- nisme aigu ou incurable" (p. 539). ("they are all afflicted with acute or incurable imitationism") Grabinoulor's very nature is assimilated to truth: "mais vous êtes Grabinoulor et tout le monde sait que vous êtes la vérité" (VI, 1, p. 793) ("but you are Grabinoulor and everyone knows that you are truth") Yet there are reservations also. The character of truth is a problem in itself, and the role imagination plays in everyday life should not and cannot be denied. (Compare its importance in the previous ex- change between Grabi and Furibar.) Man's powers of perception are fi- nally not adequate to discern truth from illusion as the exchange between Grabi and M. Lérudi makes clear:

La vérité est le plus grand danger qui nous attende sur la Terre (. . .) la vérité est que la Vérité n'est pas cette belle Vénus au miroir qu'on aperçoit quelquefois enjambant la margelle ah mais non pas du tout et remarquez en passant à quel point la vérité n'est pas le propre de l'homme puisque pour nous en montrer la figure il n'a rien eu de plus pressé que de recourir au mensonge et heureuse- ment ne vaut-il pas mieux à tout prendre rencontrer de temps en temps cette belle fille bien en chair (mais qu'on ne voit pas en chaire) et bien blanche et bien rousse plutôt que de voir gigoter au vent ça et là le squelette dur et sec et grinçant qu'est en vérité la Vérité oh je pense bien Grabinoulor pour moi personellement je préfère ça moi voilà cette Vérité que d'après vous nous n'aimons pas pourquoi l'avons-nous faite séduisante c'est tout naturel Lérudi cette séduisante Vérité imaginée correspond à notre 'air d'aimer' et en même temps à notre amour de refaire et d'inventer (V, 9, p. 693)

("The truth is the greatest danger on earth . . . the Truth is that truth is not that beautiful Venus looking in the mirror that you sometimes get a glimpse of astride the well ah no not at all and take note in passing just to what extent the Truth has nothing to do with man because in order to show us its face it was so anxious to turn to lies and fortunately isn't it better when all's said and

done to meet this beautiful plump white-skinned red-head from time to time
rather than seeing the hard dry skeleton wriggling about in the wind which is
in truth the Truth oh I think so Grabinoulor for me personally I prefer that
there's that Truth that according to you we don't like why then have we made
it so seductive it's totally natural Mr. Learned that seductive imaginary Truth
corresponds to our 'seeming to like' and at the same time our love of remaking
and inventing")

It is this constant demand for an absolute truth that may be dangerous
for men: "bravo aux religions primitives aux religions antiques qui pour
toutes les histoires fabuleuses qu'elles ont imaginées ne prétendaient pas
à LA VERITE mais à un équivalent poétique seul le christianisme dit je
suis l'absolu . . . il nous a tout dépoétisé" (V, 16, p. 775). ("bravo for the
primitive religions and the ancient religions which for all the fabulous
stories imagined by them never made a claim to TRUTH but to a poetic
equivalent only Christianity says I am the absolute . . . it has depoetized
everything for us.") This discussion takes place on the most important
and detailed philosophical debate of the text, while Grabi, Furibar and
Cherami are on their "world tour." Yet three pages later, for all its dangers, the quest continues. When the friends meet M. Stop, they cannot
halt their adventure (their "limitless adventure"): "nous chercons VERI-
TAS en marchant au grand air" (p. 778).[81] ("we're looking for VERITAS
while having a walk out in the fresh air.") In the mystery of existence,
the danger remains. We remain caught between the desire to know and
the safety of ignorance:

crois-moi Furibar perds-toi une bonne fois dans le 'ne pas savoir' c'est là
seulement qu'on peut vivre au grand air savoir où l'on en est mais mon vieux
c'est une situation désespérée évidemment Grabi évidemment mais comment
veux-tu qu'on ne sache pas puisqu'il y a le Grand Livre alors Furibar c'est
élémentaire on refuse de l'ouvrir nom de dieu c'est une idée comme une autre
mais quand on l'a déjà ouvert et bien on le referme et on se soutient qu'on ne
l'a jamais ouvert alors Grabinoulor la Vérité qu'en fais-tu la Vérité! mais mon
vieux il faut être au-dessus d'ça la Vérité on la refait sur commande c'est la
seule qui soit vivante l'autre c'est de fantaisie on la laisse aux écoliers qui
essaient de la coucher dans leurs devoirs que cette personne toute nue se
promène dans les écoles c'est une vieille habitude (VI, 2, p. 809)

("Believe me Furibar lose yourself for once in the 'don't know' it's only there
that you can live in the open air and know where you are but my old friend
it's a desperate situation evidently Grabi evidently but can it be that we don't
know since there's the Great Book then Furibar it's elementary you refuse to
open it Good God it's an idea but what about when you've already opened it
so you shut it again and you say you've never opened it so Grabinoulor what
are you going to do about Truth! but my old friend you must be above that

you remake Truth on demand it's the only sort which is alive the other sort is
a fantasy and we'll leave it to schoolboys who try to bed it in their homework
it's an old habit of this personnage to walk school corridors")

"Truth," equated again with traditional Christianity, is ironized, distanced
with humor. And when Furibar continues to want only truth, Grabi again
urges caution: "la vérité on ne sait pas trop comment c'est fait je voudrais
bien que tu me dises si elle a de beaux yeux la vraie vérité peut parfaite-
ment être prise pour un mensonage et le mensonge avoir tout l'air de la
vérité" (VI, 6, p. 854)[82] ("we don't really know what truth's made of I
should like you to tell me if it has lovely eyes the real truth can perfectly
well be taken for a lie and a lie seem completely like the truth.") Even if
we find "truth," what are we to do with it?

Nous voici en possession d'une vérité capitale entendu Grabinoulor mais maintenant que vas-tu faire de cette vérité-là et ce n'est certes pas la première fois
que Grabinoulor se trouve avoir une vérité sur les bras ce n'est donc pas la
première fois qu'il s'aperçoit que cette personne majestueuse—surtout quand
elle est capitale—est bougrement lourde et encombrante (VI, 8, p. 877)

("Here we are in possession of a capital truth agreed Grabinoulor but now
what are you going to do with that truth and it's certainly not the first time
that Grabinoulor finds himself lumbered with a truth so it's not the first time
that he notices that this majestic personnage—especially when it's capital—is
damned heavy and cumbersome")

The narrative is constructed on this ambivalence. We return again to
the position of the narrative as epic. The quest of the Holy Grail as read
by Todorov is structured as maintaining opposites. Similarly we have
identified *Grabinoulor* as a will to the position of God, inside and outside
creation, and able to sustain a system of oppositions without contradiction. It is the embodiment of the truth(s) perceived by Grabinoulor, as
when Grabi tries his last experimental reorganization of the continents
in the small hours of the morning so that no one notices: "c'est pourquoi
si le Livre de Grabinoulor n'avait pas fait cette révélation aucune Histoire
du Monde n'en aurait dit un mot" (VI, 11, p. 914) ("that's why if the Book
of Grabinoulor hadn't made this revelation no History of The World would
have said a thing about it.") The *Books of Grabinoulor* are the revelation
of truth: they are sacred, Bible. The "Livre de Grabinoulor" is "Le Grand
Livre." Yet all truth is illusion. And perhaps illusion should be cher-
ished—it is when Grabinoulor realizes that our way is scattered with lost
illusions that the narrative is threatened with immobility through his fear
of treading on these precious objects:

Dès qu'on bouge on risque le crime crime involontaire et même à bien dire crime quasi obligatoire d'accord mais crime tout de même aussi longtemps que Grabinoulor n'y avait pas pensé bien mais maintenant voici qu'il n'ose plus mettre un pied devant l'autre en un mot le voici réduit à l'immobilité et encore même quand il est assis qui sait s'il n'est pas assis sur une illusion perdue Grabinoulor à l'état de statue Grabistat 'for ever' fichtre la situation est grave Grabinoulor au point fixe la question ne peut même pas être posée (VI, 4, p. 839)

("As soon as you move you risk committing a crime an involuntary crime and even to be honest an almost obligatory crime agreed but a crime nonetheless as long as Grabinoulor didn't think about it fine but now he no longer dares to put one foot in front of the other in a word here he is reduced to immobility and even when he's sitting down who knows whether or not he's sitting on a lost illusion Grabinoulor in the state of statue Grabistat 'for ever' goodness the situation is serious Grabinoulor at the fixed point the question cannot even be posed")

Only when Grabinoulor finds a satisfactory solution in the plan to build a "Palais des Illusions Trouvées" (VI, 4, p. 839) can he move again: "Grabinoulor était si satisfait de cette solution qu'il reprit sa route à grands pas." ("Grabinoulor was so satisfied with this solution that he went striding along on his way again.") Truth, therefore, like excess, is both gain and loss. Truth is movement, unending quest. Grabinoulor wants to have and to hold, to reach truth but to keep those lost illusions also, to sustain contradictions.

Grabinoulor appears to be fighting against any intrusion of the void into the plenitude of existence, preferring excess to nothingness, a refusal to exclude, a desire to include everything. The problem of truth and illusion brings Grabinoulor to a most extreme situation, that of immobility, the *point fixe* where movement is made (temporarily) impossible.[83] Excess (here figured as movement) is brought up against the ultimate paradox truth/illusion and therefore brushes with nothingness, and non-being (here figured as immobility). Grabinoulor's state of immobility here brings our analysis to its next point of departure as we consider the nature of mobility and immobility within the problematics of excess and of truth previously structured: "quand on a la vérité c'est fini on ne peut pas aller plus loin on est entouré d'un mur on est emmuré *vitam impendire vero*" (V, 9, p. 693) ("when you've got truth it's finished you can't go any further you're surrounded by a wall you are walled up *vitam impendire vero*"). We are also returned to the problematics of *La Guerre* and to the *Poèmes à l'autre moi*—how to give form to a perpetually present moment that nonetheless retains its perpetual movement, "du mouvement dans l'immobilité" (poem 26).

MOBILITY AND IMMOBILITY

> homme et Dieu mystère
> mouvement dans l'immobilité
> > —Vingt-sixième poème', *Poèmes à l'Autre Moi*

> ("man and God mystery
> movement in immobility")

> Grabinoulor est une type qui ne tient pas en place
> afin d'être toujours dans la bonne société du présent
> ce mouvement perpétuel dans l'immobilité
> > —*Grabinoulor* III, 15, p. 302

> ("Grabinoulor is someone who never stays in one place
> to be in the good company of the present
> this perpetual movement in immobility.")

The ubiquity and perpetual movement of *Grabinoulor,* continually recurring as a definition of Grabi, is also a definition of the narrative itself. The immobility that is considered to be the most dangerous situation that Grabinoulor can experience is a threat also to the narrative:

> cependant qu'il hésitait entre la marche avant et la marche arrière mobile immobile entre deux points de l'espace . . . mais voilà bien le malheur c'est qu'à partir de l'instant où Grabinoulor se dit 'suis-je libre' il se trouva coincé à partir de l'instant entre ses deux points chacun lui soufflant à chaque oreille . . . mobile immobile c'était en définitive une situation extrêmement dangereuse que cette liberté si parfaitement équilibrée un pareil équilibre pourrait ne jamais se déséquilibrer cette immobilité pouvait être éternelle quelle affreuse aventure pour Grabinoulor c'eût été sa dernière (IV, 7, p. 448)[84]

> ("however he hesitated between walking forward and walking backwards mobile immobile between two points in space . . . but that's really the problem that from the moment when Grabinoulor says to himself 'am I free' he finds himself stuck between his two points both whispering in each ear . . . mobile immobile it was definitely an extremely dangerous situation this such perfectly balanced freedom such a balance could never become unbalanced this immobility could have been eternal what a terrible adventure for Grabinoulor it might've been his last")

The immobile would appear to be not merely an absence of life force but equivalent to a state of nonbeing, void, nothingness. Creation is generated from chaos, flux, the antithesis of immobility. Grabinoulor does not appear to be in such grave danger for he is a creature of language, and the nature of the material from which he is made is repetition, variation, an infinity of forms:

> comme vous le dites Lérudi capitales mais n'oubliez pas qu'il y a aussi les grands capitaines les grandes capitales les gros capitaux les beaux chapiteaux les petits chapeaux les grands chapeliers les gros capitalistes les lourdes cap-itations les vieux capitols les lâches capitulations les interminables chapitres les vins capitaux les gens bien capités et mêmes les rois décapités (VI, 3, pp. 828–29).

> ("as you say Mr. Learned capital [questions] but don't forget that there are also great captains great capitals great amounts of capital lovely capitals little caps large cappers fat capitalists heavy.capitations old capitols cowardly ca-pitulations interminable chapters capital wines people well-capped and even decapitated kings")

Paradoxically it is a process of language—the writing down of events—that threatens movement with immobility. The immobile (nothingness, the void, death) may be at the tip of the pen of the narrator: "on n'a pas écrit tout ce qui s'est dit on a eu l'air de se dire au cours de cette entrevue mi-historique et comme toujours ce qui n'a pas été immobilisé sur le papier devait être le meilleur" (III, 6, p. 174). ("We haven't written down everything that was said or seemed to be said in the course of this semi-historic interview and as usual what hasn't been fixed on paper is sure to be the best.") The portrait would equally be threatening:

> car est-il rien de plus immobile que la précision toute chose précise est vitrifiée que ces choses soient en présence ou en absence donc aucun portrait de Grabi-noulor qui nécessairement aurait l'air de mourir à la première tentative faite de lui donner une forme et une couleur puisqu'il se pense à mesure qu'il vit— ce qui est bien près d'être la même chose (III, 12, p. 245)

> ("because is there anything more immobile than precision every precise thing is vitrified whether these things are present or absent therefore no portrait of Grabinoulor who would necessarily appear to die at the first attempt made to give him a form and a color since he thinks himself as he lives—which is virtually the same thing")

Grabinoulor always successfully escapes the threat of immobility, which would mean ceasing to exist. The creature of language within the text appears secure in its state of ever-becoming.[85] Nonetheless an unease has set in, becoming gradually more apparent, a state of uncertainty where the "divine" qualities with which Grabi is invested may not continue to function. it is toward an exploration of this "unease," set within the explicitly "confident" narrative, that we are moving in the concluding remarks of this final chapter.

In the preceding section, we have attempted a reading of *Grabinoulor* within a broader discourse of excess such as that of Houdebine's suggestive exploration of Sollers and the texts of Bataille. All literature is, however, a moment of excess, generated between the limits of excess and of silence, excessive even when under the burden of such silence. In the tension between that which is being said, that which has already been said and is repeated, that which may be said, but differently, that which is still to be said, and that which remains unsaid, is covered over, between that which is disseminated (with the implications of both potentiality and of loss which that implies) and that which is distanced, literature comes into being. A narrative such as *Grabinoulor*, which apparently exhibits itself fully, dressed to excess and repeatedly showing, affirming itself as truth, is no exception. The poet Albert-Birot, who has worked his material in every form, is well acquainted with the nature of his own "pâte à création." Literature, the ultimate product of language, therefore, must behave like the material from which it is made—it is mobile (excessive, limitless) and immobile (silent, death bound). Even Grabinoulor, whose principal characteristic is movement, whose being is the form of the text, falls prey to this other side of the nature of language, here a bringer of doubt as when both Furibar and Bôfrizé query the validity of the reply from the "Creator": "il a suffit d'un homme et d'un tout petit diable pour qu'il reste coincé entre le oui et le non Grabinoulor coincé! lui qui n'a jamais assez de place en plein air" (V, 1, p. 578). ("It only took a man and a tiny devil for him to be stuck between yes and no Grabinoulor stuck! him for whom there's never enough space in the open air.") (This episode, where Grabinoulor enters into direct correspondence with the creator, will be commented on in the following section.) It is this constant movement of Grabi that constitutes his limitless being and the limitless being, the ever-becoming of the text itself as it holds forever present, in an eternally present moment, its creation: "pardon gros monsieur je suis Grabinoulor le parfait existant" (III, 13, p. 275); ("sorry vast sir I am Grabinoulor the perfect existing one") "assez assez que de jamais dit Grabinoulor qui préfère 'toujours'" (IV, 1, p. 368). ("enough enough what a lot of never says Grabinoulor who prefers 'always.'") Movement is therefore equivalent to being, to existing, to being present always. The notion of absence, of nonbeing, for example, when Grabinoulor is asleep, causes problems for the narration:

> Grabinoulor s'endormit et que voulez-vous faire d'un homme endormi même si c'est Grabinoulor on le voit mais il est absent c'est une absence présente avec volume et poids mais rien de plus quand on le regarde on ne peut même

pas dire "c'est" Grabinoulor quoique nous le disions pour ne pas avoir l'air de faire le malin mais en tout cas lui—si l'on pouvait employer un pronom personnel pour désigner une personne qui pour un temps n'est personne et d'ailleurs 'personne' n'a pas à être désigné mais zut on n'en finirait pas et il faut toujours finir pour en finir—donc en tout cas lui ne dit pas c'est moi ou s'il le dit c'est qu'il le rêve et rêver n'est pas jouer le rêve est un dire sans consistance des mollasseries tandis que l'homme éveillé à le dire solide car en effet le conscient c'est du grand dur (V, 11, p. 714)

("Grabinoulor falls asleep and what is there to do with a man who's asleep even if it's Grabinoulor you can see him but he's absent it's a present absence with volume and weight but nothing more when you look at him you can't even say 'it's' Grabinoulor even though we say it so as not to act clever but in any case he—if you can use the personal pronoun to refer to someone who for a time is no one and besides 'no one' isn't to be referred to but drat there's no end to it and you should always finish to be finished with it—so anyway he doesn't say it's me or if he does he dreams it and dreaming isn't playing fair dreams are sayings with no consistency lethargic lumps while the man who is awake has solid things to say for in fact the conscious is nice and hard")

The narrator secures the reader's complicity in the necessity of waking up Grabinoulor, this *nous* then ascertaining Grabi's existence and identity for the next few pages by entering into direct dialogue with him. (Grabi awakes affirming that we are anyway perhaps 'en perpétuelle conversation avec Dieu' thereby assuring our continuing identity.) In the same chapter, the problem of our existence during sleep is returned to and remains unresolved with an unexpected validation of these periods of nonbeing. When Grabi again goes to sleep, the narrator once again addresses the reader directly:

Vous êtes peut-être en train de vous dire avec humeur que Grabinoulor dort trop nous n'y pouvons rien il ne serait pas vivant s'il n'avait sa petite mort quotidienne et vous lecteur qui n'êtes pas content de le voir dormir peut-être lisez-vous encore quand depuis longtemps minuit a sonné voici une heure du matin puisqu'il dort profitez-en pour en faire autant fermez le livre tant pis pour l'auteur (V, 12, p. 723)

("You are perhaps saying crossly to yourself Grabinoulor sleeps too much we can't do anything about it he wouldn't be alive if he didn't have his daily little death and you reader who perhaps aren't happy to see him sleeping are you still reading a long time after midnight has struck it's one o'clock in the morning since he's sleeping take advantage of it to do the same close the book it's too bad for the author")

The two poles of our existence are to be respected and accepted, in the interests of the truth about our being:

S'il ne dormait jamais il lui manquerait quelque chose or à Grabinoulor il ne doit rien manquer combien de ces livres nommés "romans" vous déroulent des années de vie d'un tas de personnages qui ne dorment jamais vous n'y faites pas attention c'est entendu mais tout de même ces gens-là ne sont pas vrais et ne dites pas que le sommeil est du négatif dont on n'a que faire dans un livre car il est en fait aussi positif que l'état de veille (pp. 723–24)

("If he didn't sleep he'd be missing something and Grabinoulor mustn't be missing anything how many books called 'novels' unfold for you years of the lives of loads of characters who never sleep and you don't take any notice agreed but all the same these people are not real and don't say that sleep is something negative which has no place in a book because it is in fact as positive as being awake")

Importantly there is a point in the narrative when Grabinoulor himself is absent, he has departed in search of the "Corps Alpha," and the string of visitors are received by an increasingly bad-tempered Furibar, each expressing his amazement. First M. Lérudi, whose quest for knowledge has always met with Grabi's immediate interest; "c'est la première fois que ça m'arrive il est toujours là quand je viens le voir et il me semblait tout à fait impossible qu'il pût ne pas y être Grabinoulor absent c'est quelque chose qui ne se conçoit pas" (IV, 12, p. 505) ("it's the first time that's happened to me he is always there when I come to see him and it seemed to me totally impossible that he could not be there Grabinoulor absent it's something that cannot be conceived") Yet Furibar understands the nature of Grabi's own quest, for he is not only in search of the Corps Alpha but simultaneously of the knowledge of what it is not to be present, not to be:

maintenant il veut que cela se conçoive et il a voulu savoir ce que c'est de ne pas être là il en avait assez d'être toujours présent partout il veut que quelque chose se passe malgré son absence et voilà bien l'affaire Monsieur Furibar moi il me paraissait impossible qu'il se passât quelque chose quand il n'est pas là (IV, 12, p. 505)[86]

("now he wants it to be conceived and he wanted to know what it is not to be there he'd had enough of always being present everywhere he wants something to happen in spite of his absence and well what a business Mr. Furibar it seemed impossible to me that anything could happen when's he's not here")

The creation generated through and by him, however, continues in much the same way, Furibar copiously taking notes of what the visitors wanted so that the narrative itself continues to move and grow. Yet the consternation of the protagonists continues as Mme de la Monnaye asserts that if

Grabinoulor can be absent, then indeed we are plunged into a great state of uncertainty:

> je n'avais jamais pensé que Grabinoulor pût ne pas être là j'en suis toute bouleversée rien que de pronouncer son nom c'est une présence alors on n'en revient pas qu'il n'y ait personne ah mon dieu où va le monde si Grabinoulor se met à ne pas être là partout (IV, 12, p. 507)

> ("I never thought that Grabinoulor could not be there I'm completely thrown by it just saying his name is a presence so you can't get over the fact that there's no one there oh dear what's the world coming to if Grabinoulor takes to not being everywhere")

Like the protagonists, as each of us faces the absence of Grabinoulor so we face our own absence, we are brought face to face with our own mortality.

Furibar remains ironical about the proceedings: "j'ai noté mais si le défilé continue c'est un livre que Grabinoulor va trouver en revenant cent pages de conneries faut-il tout de même qu'il les aime pour s'être fait une pareille collection de fêlés" (IV, 12, p. 509). ("I've noted it down but if the procession continues it'll be a book that Grabinoulor is going to find when he gets back a hundred pages of damned rubbish he must really like them to have collected around him such a bunch of nutcases.") Despite the prevailing humor, it is, of course, Oscar Thanatou who points out the seriousness of such an occurrence: "ne pas être là c'est être un peu mort" ("not being there is to be a bit dead") (IV, 12, p. 510). The text refrains from a total death, just a partial one is admitted. Grabinoulor returns unscathed and the witness of extraordinary events: "il attend de l'extra-ordinaire d'ailleurs il en attend toujours son état normal est d'attendre l'anormal" (IV, 12, p. 513). ("he is expecting the extraordinary what's more he always expects it his usual state is to expect the unusual")

In Livre VI his disappearance is once again prepared; first the narrator assures his own and Grabi's status within the narrative (VI, 13, p. 929), and then he tells us that Grabi has been away for six months: "Grabi a voulu vivre un peu en dehors de son livre pour voir sans doute si on est mieux ou moins bien dedans" (VI, 13, p. 929). ("Grabi wanted to live a little outside his book to see no doubt if one is better or not inside") Yet he continues to affirm that this would not be an absence, for what can exist without him?

> Il est évident pour tout le monde que Grabinoulor ne peut pas disparaître de la circulation—qui circulerait encore s'il ne circulait plus (VI, 13, p. 929)

> ("It's obvious for everyone that Grabinoulor cannot disappear from circulation—who would still be circulating if he was no longer circulating")

To be is, therefore, to be eternally present in an eternal present as Grabi tells Ange Olivier: "comme Bôfrizé et comme vous-même je ne m'occupe pas du temps je suis toujours dans l'eternité présent perpétuel bravo Grabinoulor vous parlez comme un ange" (IV, 13, p. 526). ("like Bôfrizé and like yourself I don't bother with time I am always in eternity bravo Grabinoulor you speak like an angel") To be absent, therefore, is to be out of circulation, out of the eternal circular movement of the narrative itself. It is to be in the void in nothingness, outside the ever-becoming of creation. At the end of the dinner with the condemned man, a conversation takes place on the nature of essence and existence. Grabinoulor is seized by a strange desire:

> Il était si bien lancé qu'il en venait même à l'ETRE celui qui par définition n'existe pas tant il est et puis soudain il se dit mais si un jour il lui prenait l'étrange envie d'exister . . . ce serait plus commode pour faire son portrait (V, 12, p. 733)[87]

> ("And there was no stopping him he even came to BE he who by definition doesn't exist he so much is and then suddenly he said to himself but what if one day he was seized by the strange desire to exist . . . it would be more convenient to do his portrait")

Grabinoulor, therefore, does not exist but simply is. Can we draw a distinction between existence, ordinary, mortal existence in time and the state of being, presumably outside the limits of time and space, which is the state of Grabinoulor himself. Is this the state to which we can aspire? Is it through literature, through artistic creation that such a salvation is obtainable: salvation for author, reader, and art itself? There is nothing new or original about such a questioning and such a hope (equally dealt with at great length by the Proustian text). Before we can offer some tentative replies in our concluding remarks to this chapter, we should briefly consider the relationship between creator, creature, and the process of creation as explored within the narrative of *Grabinoulor*.

CREATION AND THE DIVINE

> Je suis arrivé à la conviction qu'un grand roman, une grande pièce, un grand poème, un grand tableau ne peut atteindre certaines dimensions formelles sans poser la question ou de l'existence ou de la non-existence de Dieu . . . Cette question peut être explicite ou implicite: dans tout ce qui porte sur le vide, sur le noir du noir, l'absence de Dieu est fortement ressentie, il y a un poids de l'absence. (George Steiner, Interview, *Le Monde des Livres*)[88]

("I have come to the belief that a great novel, a great play, a great poem, a great painting cannot achieve certain formal dimensions without posing the question of the existence or nonexistence of God. . . . This question may be explicit or implicit. In everything concerning the void, the darkness of darkness, the absence of God is felt hard, there is a weight of absence")

God and Adam

Albert-Birot's fascination with Michelangelo's painting of God creating Adam is above all with the infinitesimal space between the finger of the creator and that of his creation.[89] In that space lies all potential. In this work of art is explored the moment of beginnings and the beginnings of all art, all creation. Yet a beginning inherently carries within it an ending, therefore, it is the act of creation, not the created "object" itself, which is invested with never ceasing potential—an act, a process, that must be perpetually sustained so that the implied ending may never be reached.

Adam plays an important role in Albert-Birot's poetic mythology; Adam is for him above all the first poet, waking to a new creation every day, and naming that creation:

Voilà pourquoi il a écrit *Les Mémoires d'Adam*. Ne pouvant supporter de n'avoir pas été le premier à découvrir le monde, puisqu'il sait bien qu'il le découvre chaque jour, ce qui revient à dire qu'il l'invente, il parle au nom de ce personnage absolument candide: Adam, un personnage, qui veut tout, un avaleur de contraires.[90]

("That is why he wrote *The Memoirs of Adam*. Being unable to bear not being the first to discover the world, because he knows well that he discovers it every day, which comes down to saying that he invents it, he speaks in the name of this absolutely candid character: Adam, a character, who wants everything, a swallower of opposites.")

Through naming, through the word, the world may be appropriated. In the process of creation, which the biblical story tells and which Albert-Birot retells in his own way, is mirrored the coming into being of the work of art, The story of Adam is the story of the poet himself: "Ce premier homme, Albert-Birot le trouve au fond de lui-même avec ses visions, ses étonnements, ses gestes primaries, homme tout neuf qui transcrit le mémorial et si quelque humour s'y montre, il sort de la vie même."[91] ("This first man, Albert-Birot finds him in the heart of himself with his visions, his wonderments, his primary gestures, a completely new man who transcribes the chronicles and if some humor shows, it comes from life itself.") More than this Albert-Birot here touches upon the universals of mankind, desires, and their figurations, which are the constants of poetry. The appearance, the "presence" of the first man instigates the quest for knowledge:

> La nature entière est *phénomènes*—que la présence du premier être vivant a transformé pour partie en *signes* ou *signaux* et dont une partie a été transformé en *information* par cet être vivant pour sa survie. . . . Aussi l'expérience de l'ignorance ne mène-t-elle qu'à l'erreur et l'expérience de l'erreur qu'à la confusion. C'est donc qu'il existe une raison maximale, qui fait passer de l'inconnu au connu, du connu au réel, du réel au vrai *Logos*."[92]

> ("The whole of nature is made of *phenomena*—that the presence of the first living being transformed in part into *signs* or *signals* and a part of which was transformed into information by this living being for its survival. . . . What is more does not the experience of ignorance only lead to error and the experience of error only to confusion? It is, therefore, that there exists a maximal reason, which leads the way from the unknown to the known, from the known to the real, from the real to the true Logos.")

Adam enjoys a privileged relationship with his creator; he becomes the breath and voice of God's power, physical embodiment of the transcendental. The metadiscourse of *Grabinoulor,* ontological, ethical, political, is an endeavor to embrace the knowledge of the universe, truths that mean absolute knowledge: "J'ai inventé un mot qui représente toutes ces choses vues, ce mot dont je suis très fier est VERITE, le mot est le grand mot: dès que je le prononce je n'ai plus rien à désirer" (*Les Mémoires d'Adam,* p. 11) ("I've invented a word that represents all these things that are seen, this word of which I am very proud is TRUTH, the word is the great word. No sooner than I pronounce it, I have nothing more to desire.") Yet again to no longer desire would paradoxically mean the end of all knowledge.

When Grabinoulor makes his journey to visit Adam, it is in an attempt to understand both the nature of God and of Man.[93] In a text with multiple references to Adam,[94] it is in Livre IV, 15, that the principal adventure takes place, for Grabi discovers that there were two Adams, two Edens, and that the state of the "Adam antérieur" is perfection itself, where the singular is a plurality and complete unto itself: "Seigneur Adam vous avez raison l'homme pluriel est pour moi une révélation et après cette révélation je vois l'humanité plus grande" (IV, 15, p. 558). ("Lord Adam you are right the plural man is a revelation for me and after this revelation I see humanity as greater") Further on he understands that the presence of Eve would pose a problem: "c'est le réduire au singulier un et un ce n'est plus que banal pluriel par adjonction" (p. 559). (it's to reduce him to the singular one and one is nothing more than a banal plural by addition") This original Adam is the model of human control over his environment; all is ordered in this original Eden, and on the pedestals of the statues that foretell the history of Adam's future descendants, science dominates:

> Chacune des quatre faces du dé est couverte de lignes et de formules gravées mais tellement couverte que tout se touche et se mélange afin sans doute qu'il soit à peu près impossible de lire pourtant Grabinoulor croit bien voir dans tous ces fouillis linéaires et graphiques de la physique de la chimie de la mécanique (IV, 15, p. 561)[95]

> ("Each of the four sides of the dice is covered in engraved lines and formulae but so covered that everything runs into everything else no doubt to make it nearly impossible to read nonetheless Grabinoulor thinks he can see in this linear and graphic mess physics chemistry mechanics")

In the "Paradis postérieur," all is in disorder: "c'était bien le Paradis auquel chacun pourrait s'attendre c'est-à-dire quelque coin de terre sauvage" (IV, 15, p. 567) ("it really was the Paradise that each one of us would expect that's to say some wild spot.") We are returned to the geometrization of creation and to its paradox. The chaos of creation must be ordered. The "geometric chaos" we have explored, yet we must also retain its chaotic energy and impulse, its potency. The anterior Eden, for all its geometric and perfect beauty, is a sterile place, the posterior one for all the uncouth nature of Adam's and Grabi's disappointment is a place of energy represented in the text by sexuality. Creation is again at a limit position, attempting to reconcile opposites, to contain excess, to express what it is to exist in the human condition while aspiring to a manifestation of perfection, of order, of the sacred.

The space of creation must be, although structured, in constant flux, in constant evolution, to survive. In an episode to which we have previously alluded, Grabinoulor is dissatisfied, and having had the validity of the reply in his letter to the Creator thrown into uncertainty, his next step is to bring about, with Furibar and Bôfrizé,[96] an idea he has had before— to create a new being himself, for here surely the enigma of the act of creation would be revealed. The episode ends in farce, for two chapters later, the "products," begun in movement and darkness, have already come to life and left leaving a short message: "sommes trop pressés pouvons pas vous attendre tous nos regrets de ne pas connaître créateurs" (V, 3, p. 599). ("in too much of a hurry couldn't wait for you deepest regrets at not knowing our creators") Furibar resents their ingratitude, but Grabinoulor is apparently indulgent: 'je ne suis pas loin de trouver tout à fait naturel qu'aussitôt vivants ils aient été pressés de vivre sans perdre leur temps à dévisager de points d'interrogation comment se fait-il que nous vivions et qui nous a donné la vie' (V, 3) ("I almost find it natural that no sooner were they alive that they were in a hurry to live without wasting their time staring at question marks and asking how is that we're alive and who gave us life") Grabinoulor's own Adam has escaped him. However the fundamental question, the question that underlies all other questionings in the narrative, is posed here with clarity seen though Grabi appears to dismiss it as unimportant. His disparaging attitude belies the importance of the question—in the words of Steiner used as our epigraph to this section: "l'absence de Dieu est fortement ressentie, il y an un poids de l'absence.' In a narrative where the questioning of the basic elements of human existence are constantly sought and debated, are indeed the narrative's very raison d'être; the unease and uncertainty below the surface confidence becomes more and more apparent. The proliferation of the quest for knowledge turns around and around a void. The presence of the text covers an absence.

Grabinoulor and God

The recurrent questioning of M. Keskedieu forces Grabinoulor to take his own position with regard to the creator and that position is a critical one. When M. Keskedieu asks: "ne pensez-vous pas qu'il soit le plus grand poète du monde" (III, 11, pp. 229–30) ("don't you think that he's the greatest poet in the world") Grabi's reply is sardonic; it is perhaps true he admits: "mais un peu malheureusement il s'est laissé devenir dramaturge." ("but rather unfortunately he let himself become a playwright")

M. Keskedieu never abandons the challenge, and he offers a proposition of the nature of the supreme identity as zero: "zéro c'est l'éternel ni temps ni espace rien tout rien zéro égal singulier et pluriel" (IV, 10. p. 488). ("zero is the eternal neither time nor space nothing at all nothing zero equals singular and plural") Despite the protestations of Bôfrizé, Grabinoulor is in agreement: "c'est peut-être en effet la façon la plus élégante de 'voir' Dieu." ("it's indeed perhaps the the most elegant way of 'seeing' God') Bôfrizé perceives this as the end of everything. Grabinoulor is the infinite potential of creation: "zéro le parfait indivisible et immultipliable et insoustractif" (p. 489). ("zero the indivisible and unmultipliable and unsubtractable") The zero represents the eternal and the void together. It is the reconciliation of the final paradox.[97]

The divinity of the zero occurs in *Rémy Floche, employé*. Rémy considers the nature of the number 1–10:

Et toi enfin mon cher 0 ta figure affirmative me plaît, vraie forme divine qui contient les deux infinis, celui de droite et celui de gauche, celui du oui et celui du non. Que tu es beau dans ton immobilité qui affirme avec la même impassibilité j'existe ou je n'existe pas. (p. 135)

("And you at last my dear 0 I like your affirmative face, true divine form which contains the two infinities, that of the right and of the left, that of yes and that of no. How beautiful you are in your immobility which affirms with the same impassiveness I exist or I don't exist.")

Right and left, yes and no, existence and nonexistence all contradictions are contained and reconciled.

If the Eiffel Tower is perhaps the existence of God proved mathematically (as previously considered), M. Keskedieu also considers other calculations to find Him: "ah certes si j'étais mathématicien l'opération en serait grandement facilitée car avec une suite de spéculations mathématiquement bien tassées et une bonne série d'équations je pourrais dire il est là comme un astronome le fait pour un astre" (V, 4, p. 615). ("ah certainly if I was a mathematician the operation would be greatly facilitated for with a series of mathematically piled up speculations and a good series of equations I could say he is there like an astromonist does for a star") Once again the well ordered may triumph over chaos and lead to knowledge. In an equation the elements are reconciled to each other to produce an answer and here to construct a presence. Mathematics and science transform the unknown into the known, offering exactitude for uncertainty.

M. Lérudi's proposition for the creation of the universe turns to the scatological, the very opposite of M. Keskedieu's tormented searching. The secret is, according to Lérudi, that it was during a great banquet held by the creator when "l'Infini tout entier retentissait de joie," ("the whole of Infinity was ringing with joy") and at the end of which "il se sentit trop plein et voulut s'alléger donc il se débarassa très abondamment par toutes les sorties" (V, 13, p. 739). ("he felt too full and wanted to lighten himself therefore he very abundantly got rid of it all by all the exits") Grabinoulor is impressed by this[98] "une cosmogonie qui se pose." ("a cosmogony is coming into being") For Grabi, however, the creator must remain artist and poet-artist as we have already explored: "c'est . . . indiscutablement lui qui a eu le premier l'idée de projeter hors de soi ce que l'on a en soi (V, 9, p. 686). ("it's undisputably him who first had the idea to project outside oneself what one has inside oneself") God is an abstract artist, a return to the discourse of the visual arts. Yet Grabi never ceases to complain about what God is lacking, for the imagination of God must be extremely poor if this is the creation we have to show for it. It is Furibar who begins by chastising the creator for "la lumière incolore," ("uncolored light") but Grabi does not find it so surprising: for anything different to have come into being it would have taken "un inventeur bourré d'imagination" (VI, 8, p. 876), ("an inventor with oodles of imagination") and clearly this is not the case. Furibar continues:

> "je ne m'explique absolument pas quand nous hommes avons les sens esthétique poétique spéculatif et même métaphysique tellement développés comment il a pu lui tellement en manquer" (VI, 8, p. 876).

> ("I can't explain it at all how when we men have our aesthetic poetic speculative and even metaphysical senses so developed how he could have been so lacking in them")

The natures of God and man are diametrically opposed in Grabinoulor's reply:[99] "l'inventeur et l'inventé s'opposent quasiment comme la tête et la queue l'un s'arrête à la physique l'autre commence à la métaphysique. . . . Dieu est le matérialisme en personne tandis que l'homme est le parfait idéaliste" (VI, 8, p. 876). ("The inventor and the invented are opposed almost like the head and the tail the one ends with the physical and the other begins with the metaphysical . . . God is materialism in person whilst man is the perfect idealist")

The idea is repeated in the final chapter of this last book: "le matérialisme par excellence c'est Dieu et le parfait idéaliste c'est l'homme" (VI, 14, p. 942). ("materialism par excellence is God and the perfect idealist is man")

Grabi is constantly disappointed in the universe as it exists. When he offers to help the "Eternel," the Creator of our universe during this voyage through space, the "Eternel" goes about it his own way anyway:

> tant pis c'est son affaire à l'Eternel et Grabinoulor tourne le dos lui aussi laissant le Vieux Décorateur faire son boulot à son idée et à son temps d'ailleurs Grabinoulor est souvent d'avis que le plus simple est de considérer ce provisoire comme du définitif c'est une fichue manie que d'y chercher des différences supprimons ces nuances et nous pouvons ainsi continuer à vivre en paix cependant que l'Eternel continue à tâtillonner (IV, 1, p. 383).

> ("too bad it's the Eternal's own business and Grabinoulor also turned his back leaving the Old Decorator to get on with his job his own way and in his own time besides Grabinoulor is often of the opinion that the simplest thing is to consider this provisional world as though it were definitive it's a damned mania to look for differences in it let's suppress these nuances and we can thereby carry living in peace while the Eternal carries on with his persnickety touching up")

A superficial reconciliation of contradictions is "supprimons ces nuances." What we think of as temporary may in fact be everlasting. Man

is full of creative potential even though what is created may fall short of
our aspirations; if created in freedom and originality, those creations may
reach superhuman status. Listening to the concert created by the musicians who refuse to follow a score, each playing to his own inspiration,
Grabi reflects on such creation:

> c'est peut-être ça la vraie grande et surnaturelle musique au moins là il n'y a
> ni sentiment ni peinture ni description littéraire ni philosophie *ce chaos sonore*
> *est dégagé du terrestre et de l'humain pourquoi ne serait-il pas au-dessus*
> *plutôt qu'au dessous d'une "oeuvre" d'un "travail" raisonnable affaibli terres-*
> *trifié par le choix l'ordre et le mesure* un peu comme les mondes créés forment
> un Univers moins cosmiquement grand que *le primordial chaos pâte à créa-*
> *tions* (V, 8, p. 680; my emphasis)

> ("that's perhaps it the true great and supernatural music at least there's no
> feeling or painting or literary description or philosophy this sonorous chaos is
> freed from the earthly and the human why shouldn't it be more rather than
> less than a 'work of art' a 'work' which is reasonable weakened earthified by
> choice order and timing rather how created worlds form a Universe less cos-
> mically great than the primordial chaos the stuff of creations")

Grabi is aware that such a reasoning would imply that the material would
be more beautiful than the artistic object and would possess valuable
qualities beyond its production. The message for the divine creator, who
is man, poet, painter, musician, is clear nonetheless: to write, paint, orchestrate a creation whose very structure retains the chaos of its origins,
a "chaos géométrique," Grabi's description of *La Guerre* and "un chaos
sonore," the state to which the narrative of *Grabinoulor* aspires. Such a
creation will perhaps assure the status of the poet as divine, immortal,
eternal, the ideal of the thirty-third poem of the *Poèmes à l'Autre Moi*.
Grabi's own reflection on the best possible expression of the divine form
most significantly takes up an expression in music once again:

> Dieu serait encore mieux personnifié par le son depuis une seule note jusqu'à
> la plus compliquée des polyphonies selon qu'on voudrait Dieu réduit à sa plus
> simple expression ou dans sa forme la plus complexe et la plus impénétrable
> (IV, 5, p. 423)

> ("God would be even better personified by sound from a single note to the
> most complex polyphony according to whether you wanted God reduced to
> his simplest expression or in his most complex and most impenetrable form")

These are key words not only for the concept of the creator as defined
in the text, but for the text itself—polyphonic, complex, impenetrable.
The nature of creator and creation are fused as the narrative constantly

proliferates its voices, its density, its interminable lines of enquiry, its conflicting points of view, its ambiguities. As we suggested early on in this chapter, the narrative to retain its potency must constantly move, and in all directions yet be structured by its own internal logic. This remains within the realm of the poet's potential. Humankind may also be Divine in its creative potential, yet the fundamental difference between God and humanity remains—the recurrent question of immortality versus mortality, the circle and the straight line, the forces of Eros and of Thanatos. Even though Grabinoulor has been unable to find the "Empire des Morts" and is mainly convinced that death does not exist and constantly evades the questioning of M. Oscar Thanatou[100] on the subject, certainty remains elusive. Is it essential for the narrative that these fundamental oppositions, the final set of contradictions, remain sustained? Is the question of death in fact vital? Do we need death to "be"?

GRABINOULOR AND THE HUMAN CONDITION

> avant d'envisager l'Etre il faut
> compredre le non-Etre
> —*Grabinoulor,* III, 12, p. 251

> ("before contemplating Being you must
> understand non-Being")

> cette dualité de l'Etre et le non-Etre
> pas moyen de sortir de là
> —*Grabinoulor,* IV, 12, p. 503

> ("this duality of Being and non-Being
> there's no way out of it")

In our earlier section on geometric space, the curved line has been assimilated to God and the straight line to Man: "vive la ligne courbe une vraie âme immortelle ne peut pas s'accommoder de la pauvre ligne droite" (III, 12, p. 253). ("long live the curved line a true immortal soul cannot make do with the poor straight line") The earlier analysis of the figures of *La Guerre* is again validated as revealing the fundamental structures of Albert-Birot's poetics. The problem is unresolved—the human imagination and powers of reflection may be greater, yet God enjoys the eternal, while humanity is condemned to death. Grabi and Furibar argue as to humanity's potential to immortality when they discuss the states of sleep and drunkenness that Furibar considers to be "petits mourirs" and Grabi "un avant-goût de super-vie voire d'immortalité . . . être ivre c'est sur-être et sur-être c'est être immortel" (IV, 8, p. 460) ("a foretaste of superlife indeed immortality . . . to be intoxicated is to super-be and to super-be is to be immortal") Furibar also remains unconvinced by the progress of science as defined by M. Lérudi:

> ces biologistes les voilà qui parlent déjà de nous donner une relative immortalité oh relative évidemment mais tout de même ça fera toujours plaisir . . . d'ailleurs potentiellement elles sont immortelles nos chères petites cellules (IV, 11, p. 499)[101]

> ("you have those biologists who are already talking about giving us a relative immortality oh evidently relative but all the same it'll be very nice . . . besides our dear little cells are potentially immortal")

He insists on a better answer:

> mais oui non sommes-nous immortels car vous parlez là de l'immortalité des bras et des jambes et moi c'est l'autre l'immortalité celle qu'on ne voit pas qui m'intéresse (IV, 11, p. 499)

> ("but yes or no are we immortal because you're speaking there of the immortality of our arms and legs and it's the other immortality the one you don't see that interests me")

On a visit to Venus where the origins of man may be discovered, Grabi asks the first men why we have lost our certitude in our immortality. The answer is simple: When man was sure of being immortal, he found the temporary, experimental life of no worth and hurried to rid himself of it: "sortir au plus vite du provisoire pour entrer dans cette si belle et si chere immortalité" (IV, 11, p. 501). ("get out of the provisional as quickly as possible to get into this so lovely and so dear immortality") Their state of certainty was, therefore, changed:

> pour eux toujours toujours du peut-être et jamais jamais du certain en un mot il n'y aura là rien d'officiel . . . n'étant pas sûr du tout de l'immortalité ils se payent de la petite vie tant qu'ils peuvent (IV, 11, pp. 501–2)[101]

> ("for them always always perhaps and never never certainty in a word there be there nothing official . . . not being at all sure of immortality they enjoy this little life as well as they can")

If there can be no unquestionable certainty in life, then Grabi seeks for a certainty that death does not exist, and therefore logically humankind must be immortal. In Livre I, he is amazed that, after his unsuccessful quest for the "Empire des Morts" despite consulting Virgil and Dante, that men have believed in death for so long, and instead a belief in the continuing life and interrelationship of all the elements of the cosmos is affirmed:

> Grabinoulor vit bien que sa mère était la rose qui s'épanouissait à côté de lui la forêt qu'il traversait les oiseaux qui volaient les enfants qui jouaient les amoureux qui passaient la lumière qui les éclairait et alors il eut beaucoup de joie et admira le monde (I, 6, p. 17).[102]

> ("Grabinoulor saw very clearly that his mother was the rose blooming beside him and the forests he was walking through and the birds flying and the children playing the lovers passing by the light illuminating them and then he was filled with joy and he admired the world")

The proof of death as a definitive state is constantly refuted: Poire as a mature person may be dead, but Grabi can still meet him as an adolescent. What is more: "et puis est-il bien mort qu'en savez-vous avez-vous été à son enterrement ce qui au surplus ne serait pas une preuve tout à fait suffisante un personnage ne meurt pas si facilement et puis en tout cas il ressuscite à volonté" (III, 6, p. 38 and III, 10, p. 307). ("and then is he really dead what do you know about it did you go to his funeral which what's more it wouldn't be sufficient proof a person doesn't die so easily and then in any case comes back to life at will") Every myth and belief concerning death is considered and reworked. For Grabinoulor, death remains at best a bad joke: "je pense que la mort est une dernière plaisanterie du dernier mauvais goût" (III, 6, p. 175), ("I think that death is a final joke in the worst possible taste") "Grabinoulor jugeant la mort une absurdité inacceptable inventée par tout le monde Grabinoulor tient pour tout à fait naturel que la mort n'existe pas parce qu'il trouve ça trop bête" (III,10); ("Grabinoulor judging death an inacceptable absurdity invented by everyone Grabinoulor thinks it totally natural that death doesn't exist because he finds it too silly") "L'Empire des Morts est invention qui ne tient pas debout" (III, 13, p. 277) ("The Empire of the Dead is an invention that doesn't hold water.")

If humanity would only recognize the fallacy and stand together against the illusion, the concept of death would be abolished. Individually human-kind has said quietly "que ça nous embêtait de mourir" (IV, 6, p. 441). ("that's it's a nuisance for us to die") It is a question of the will of the individual and of the collective:

> à condition que nous soyons tous mais dans le vouloir là dans le vouloir à fond dans le vouloir fait de vouloir vouloir et tous absolument tous les hommes qui

sont sur la Terre il faut que le refus soit aussi bien en nous que le besoin de
respirer et que tous lancent le "contramen" (IV, 6, p. 442)[103]

("on condition that we all have the will the will completely the will made of
the wanting to want and all absolutely all the men on earth and the refusal
would have to be part of us like the need to breathe and everyone would have
to launch the 'contramen'")

Grabi's plan is ultimately to begin again with a different type of humanity: "il fallait recommencer une création," and although his method of
mass suicide to start afresh is abandoned, the message is clear—man is
a mortal creature with a will to immortality. The question is how to go
about this correctly, a question reiterated time and time again:

on a eu tort simplement de considérer la mort comme un état définitif il fallait
ne pas y croire et lui donner l'habitude de ne pas être éternelle (IV, 7, p. 453)

("we were simply wrong to consider death as a definitive state we shouldn't
have believed in it and have given it the habit of not being eternal")

la douleur est en voie de disparition puisque la mort de par notre volonté ne
sera plus la mort (IV, 7, p. 454)

("pain is in the process of disappearing since death through our will will no
longer be death")

The argument between Grabinoulor and Furibar concerning sleep and
drunkenness, when Grabi remains the eternal optimist and Furibar pessi-
mistic, begins with Furibar's frustration with man's compliant attitude
toward death:

Ils sont furieux d'être mortels et ils n'osent pas penser à la mort tant l'idée
seule les met à l'envers mais avant d'avoir la mort ils ont la vie—c'est la règle
et sans une seule exception—eh bien ils ont inventé cent trucs pour ne pas
vivre . . . ils sont enchantés de mourir tous les soirs et ce n'est pas rien tous
ces petits mourirs-là (IV, 8, p. 460)[104]

("They are furious at being mortal and the very idea sends them haywire so
they don't dare think about death but before having death they have life—
that's the rule and there's no exception—so they've invented loads of ways
not to live . . . they're delighted to die every night and it's not just nothing all
these little dyings")

Grabi remains convinced of the will to immortality: "ce n'est pas un bout
de mort qu'ils cherchent mais un avant-goût de super-vie voire d'immor-

talite." ("it's not a piece of death they're looking for but a foretaste of super-life even immortality") Not even the word *mort* suggests to him mortality: "ceux qui l'ont inventé sont sûrement des peuples nés avec l'immortalité dans la téte" (V, 14, p. 745) ("they who invented it are surely peoples born with immortality in their heads") Yet after the experience he has with the Chevalier Evran whom he rescues from his own funeral because "à vrai dire puisqu'il s'agit de la mort il n'y a aucune raison de s'arreter" (VI, 2) ("to tell the truth since it's a question of death there's no reason to stop") we learn a secret of Grabinoulor's—whenever he passes a church he checks to see that it is not he who is being buried (p. 818).

Contradictions surface concerning death, and its nonexistence does not prevent Grabi conversing with those who are apparently dead,[105] most notably with the Unknown Soldier (who turns out to be an old childhood friend of his) who reveals something of great interest to Grabi: "un mort n'a qu'un désir se dégonfler pour entrer vivement dans l'absolu impensé" (V, 7, p. 664) ("a dead man has only one desire to deflate in order to enter lively into the unthought absolute") Grabi, sidetracked by the fate of this most famous of the dead, regrets not to have questioned him more closely on the nature of this state:

> J'aurais dû lui demander quelques explications sur cet "absolu impensé" ce n'est pas clair mais on sent qu'il doit y avoir là quelque état de perfection ainsi donc ceux qui meurent très volontiers fait preuve d'un goût très prononcé pour l'absolu et on ne peut le nier c'est avoir bon goût (V, 7, p. 665)

> ("I should've asked him for some explanations about this 'unthought absolute' it's not clear but you feel that there must some state of perfection in it so those who die very willingly prove to have a very pronounced taste for the absolute and you can't deny that's to have good taste")

For an absolute, therefore, for some state of perfection, would death be worth risking? A state implies a condition no longer in flux, no longer in movement. Immobility is a life-threatening force as we have previously explored. A state of perfection where contradictions are reconciled? Nothing is resolved. Can salvation be secured by a participant in the human tragicomedy, simultaneously derided and made sublime.

There are more contradictions: as the narrative progresses, Grabinoulor becomes increasingly despairing of his fellow men, not in fact imbued with divine qualities, but alien to his ability to make the ordinary extraordinary:

> la matière pour eux n'aboutit qu'à la merde d'accord Grabi mais les gens aiment la merde parfait grand bien leur fasse moi Furibar je n'en puis fabriquer un peu que—si j'ose dire—pour ma 'consommation' personnelle (IV, 11, p. 710)

("For them matter ends only in shit agreed Grabi but people like shit perfect good may it do them Furibar I can only make a bit for—if I dare say it for my personal 'consumption'")

Creation may not be such a salvation, merely an addition to the excess already in production that finally serves no purpose and as merely the excrement of living matter, is less a hope than an expression of an inevitability. Grabi's plans for the amelioration of the world of men are for once forgotten:

Je ne vis pas pour les 'gens' d'accord Grabinoulor mais alors pour qui vis-tu? probablement pour moi comme tout vivant et j'y ajoute l'Univers par dessus le marché c'est une bonne idée Grabinoulor avec ça tu peux te foutre de ta solitude et puis tout de même n'oublie pas que je suis là et que je n'ai été mis au monde que pour gueuler et pour t'aimer[106] (IV, 11, p. 710)

("I don't live for 'people' alright Grabinoulor but who do you live for then? probably for myself like all living beings I'll add the Universe on top of that it's a good idea Grabinoulor with that you can not give a damn about your solitude and then all the same don't forget that I'm here and I was only brought into the world to bawl my head off and to love you")

There is at this moment no communion, solidarity, brotherhood in humanity; each individual is left alone to suffer, a moment of existential doubt and suffering never commented on by readers who (desire to?) read only the positive in Grabinoulor's verve and life force. The diatribe of Grabi against the rest of the human race is not an isolated moment in the narrative. In the first chapter of Livre VI, Grabi and Furibar argue about the former's continuing fantastic ideas; Grabi refuses to conform:

moi Grabinoulor je suis ce désemmerdeur et si les gens "sérieux" me tenaient pour beaucoup plus sérieux qu'eux-mêmes le monde entier serait un monde mondé comme l'orge ce qui serait d'ailleurs trop une vingtaine de cogitoirs bien désinfectés c'est bien suffisant que tous les autres bouffent de la merde à pleine cervelle tous ces emmerdés-là ils puent comme de juste et on les laisse tomber c'est la vingtaine qui compte alors Grabinoulor tu vis pour vingt personnes ou Furibar tout au plus et c'est déjà beau.[107] (VI, 1, p. 802)

("Me Grabinoulor I'm this un-pain in the neck and if 'serious' people took me more seriously than themselves then the whole world would be a world hulled like barley which would be what's more too much a couple of dozen well disinfected brain boxes is well sufficient let all the others stuff their minds with shit all those damned nuisances stink as they should and you just forget them it's the couple of dozen that count so Grabinoulor you live for about twenty people yes Furibar maximum and that's just right")

Grabi begins to relinquish his role as a savior, a different sort of comprehension taking precedence:

> Il devrait bien laisser à d'autres le soin de sauver le monde c'est-à-dire qu'en finale vérité lui commençait à en avoir marre que le monde se dédémerdouillarde après tout pourquoi serait-ce toujours Grabinoulor le sauveur (VI, 7, p. 872)

> ("He should leave the task of saving the world to others that's to say that when it comes down to it he was beginning to have enough let the world un-get itself out of its own bloody mess after all why should it always be Grabinoulor the savior")

A life's work then may remain isolated; a work of art will not save the world, and although Grabi himself may remain immortal, there is no message of a universal truth in art—Grabi offers no revelation to his readers, the quest for truth that has continued to motivate and sustain the narrative reveals only this—that finally what we write against, what we create against either in art, in other work, in love, in our investment in others or in self, in pursuit of good or evil, is the nothingness that may at any point engulf it. Grabi continues to walk "vers l'inconnu" (VI, 3, p. 824) because the quest for knowledge is unending, even as he becomes even less sure of its utility. Even as the narrative draws to its (perhaps always provisional) ending, there is no lack of projected excursions and plans. Grabi still walks in hope and curiosity, avoiding any temporary obstacles.[108] Yet a new tone would seem to have taken hold of Grabinoulor, philosopher—one that has been sown here and there throughout the narrative, alluded to fleetingly, distanced, ironized, among the celebrations of movement and being.

The salvation, if salvation there is within *Grabinoulor,* is that man continues to create, not without despair and disillusion, but with them, despite the knowledge that "nous avons cette mort dans la peau que nous désirons tant cet idéal-néant" (IV, 11, p. 494) ("we have this thing death under the skin we so desire this ideal-nothingness") The words are those of Furibar. Grabi disagrees, but Furibar is not the antithesis of Grabinoulor. He is one and the same just as being and nonbeing, excess and silence, truth and illusion, are not opposites but unbearably close:

> Il y a donc eu, dans l'espoir de la conscience vivante la plus pure, la génération de l'Homme et très vite, et très sournoise, la différenciation. . . . Notre vie, ce n'est donc pas seulement l'état présent de la mort, repoussé (le redire!), ni du Paraclet, ni le demi-rêve demi-réel, c'est l'obligation éthique, *le chaos maîtrisé* ou c'est une agonie.[109]

("There was therefore, in the hope of the most pure living conscience, the generation of Man, and very quickly, and very underhand, differentiation. . . . Our life is therefore not only the present state of death, put off (to say it again!), nor is it as Paraclete says, half-dream half-real, it is ethical obligation, chaos mastered or it is agony.")

Grabinoulor is such an obligation, a seeking of knowledge, a statement of life, a poetic act, a presence in the face of absence, a "chaos géométrique," "chaos maîtrisé," produced with jubilation in the knowledge of suffering.

The poet-philosopher knows that being and nonbeing are not opposite poles of our existence but are situated just each side of a fine dividing line. The life force with which all the works of Albert-Birot reverberate pulses not because they are written against death, the void, nonbeing but as an attempt to encompass, to embrace it, perhaps to fill it, to nullify it. Impossible quest for at any moment excess may topple over into a nothingness that we can never begin to think. The value of the work lies finally in its sustained quest, not to deny those aspects of existence that we think of as opposites but to reconcile them because they live so closely together. In its continued creation, an aspiration to an infinity in the knowledge of nothingness, a narrative of both extraordinary and human proportions is brought into being.

> il est vrai qu'il faut bien nourrir l'amour et Grabinoulor en marchant toujours de ce beau pas d'un homme qui aime le pain de la terre se disait qu'il y a tout de même des divertissements à la périphérie oui mais il n'y a pas que du bon pain et des divertissements comme il n'y a pas que la périphérie et sur l'autre côté de sa face il tortillait une légère grimace ah que la contradiction lui est chère mais Grabinoulor regarde en même temps le Nord et le Sud et il dit que la contradiction n'existe pas Grabinoulor est tout face le dos est pour les pauvres ce qui explique approximativement comment il est à la fois au centre et à la circonférence et même ailleurs (III, 3, p. 149)

("It's true that you need to feed love well and Grabinoulor always walking with that fine stride of a man who loves the earth's bread was saying to himself that all the same there are amusements on the periphery yes but it's not only good bread and amusements just as there isn't only the periphery and on the other side of his face he twisted his face into a slight grimace ah how dear contradiction is to him but Grabinoulor looks at the same time at the North and the South and he says that contradiction doesn't exist Grabinoulor is all face the back's for other poor people which approximately explains how he is at the center at the circumference and even elsewhere at the same time")

At the limit point, *Grabinoulor* comes into being, at the meeting point of internal and external space, a space that coincides with the desire of

the poet—metadiscourse on every aspect of the human condition, ultimate creation of the poet's universe. Throughout this epic the human,
the value of the human, continues to celebrate itself even when in mortal
danger—it dares to be. Grabinoulor is of the status envisaged by George
Steiner (with whom we opened this chapter): "Et sur le plan artistique,
le salut pourrait aujourd'hui venir d'une bouffée d'un rire profondément
sérieux, d'une danse nietzschéenne durant le désespoir.[110] ("And on the
artistic level, salvation could come today in a profoundly serious outburst
of laughter, in a Neitzschean dance during despair.") "Un rire sérieux"
is an apt description of *Grabinoulor,* vital, compassionate, derisory, human. It is a gamble in the way Steiner clarifies his own stance in the face
of the problem that confronts any search for meaning in the last years of
the twentieth century:

> La déconstruction a eu le grand mérite de jeter le gant. Elle nous a dit: vous
> postulez à tort qu'il y a quelque part une réassurance du sens: de même qu'il
> y a dans la perspective classique *un point de fuite où toutes les parallèles se
> réjoignent,* votre point de fuite à été Dieu. . . . *Je parie sur la réalité d'un lien
> entre le mot et le monde, entre le sens et l'être*—il peut être indirect, oblique,
> infiniment compliqué, mais il existe. Ça reste un pari bien sûr. Mais si on ne
> le tient pas, plus rien ne tient.[111]

("Deconstruction has had the great merit of throwing down the gauntlet. It
says to us: you postulate wrongly that there is the reassurance of meaning
somewhere. Just as there is in classical perspective a vanishing point where all
the parallels join, your vanishing point is God. . . . I gamble on the reality of
a link between the word and the world, between meaning and being—it may
be indirect, oblique, infinitely complex, but it exists. It remains a gamble of
course. But if you don't have that, nothing holds up any longer.")

The quest for knowledge implies a belief that there is a meaning to be
found. Yet definitive answers constantly elude Grabinoulor as the myriad
threads of the narrative undermine any possibility of certainty. Truth is
everywhere and nowhere. Born of and into a conception of modernity
that seeks to understand the world and humankind's place in it, Grabinoulor also appears to stand at the limit of the postmodern sensibility
where there is no meaning among the plethora of signs. Grabinoulor's
unlimited adventure is undertaken not only in the knowledge that the
line, at any moment, risks being broken and humanity may perhaps never
aspire to the circle, but that the tentative toward meaning constantly
escapes us in a universe where the ultimate *point de fuite,* where the
parallels coincide, where being and meaning are one, can never be
reached:

Grabinoulor heureux d'avoir des jambes bon coeur et bonne rate s'en allait s'en allait avec un tel entrain et l'esprit tellement "ailleurs" qu'il s'engagea de ce pas sur le chemin de l'Infini quelle promenade même pour un homme qui marche bien et *encore arrivera-t-il jamais à ce point unique où les parallèles se rencontrent?* (III, 17, p. 364; my emphasis)

("Grabinoulor happy to have legs a strong heart and a good spleen was going along and going along with such gusto and his mind so 'elsewhere' that he took like this the path of Infinity what a walk even for a man who walks well and still will he ever reach this unique point where parallels meet?")

Conclusion: Order and Chaos

Tout ce qui vit est mouvement, le bonheur comme le malheur,
des corps qui bougent ce n'est que l'apparence du mouvement,
le mouvement réel est le mouvement de l'esprit.
—*Rémy Floche, employé*, p. 127

("All that lives is movement, both happiness and unhappiness,
bodies which move are only movement in appearence, real
movement is the movement of the mind.")

THE notion of movement was originally perceived in this study as the
development of painter to poet and the coming to an understanding of
the necessity of new forms of expression within the prevailing artistic
climate of modernity. The concept of movement, however, quickly becomes all-encompassing for the poet as he explores the life force (and its
opposite) of his poetry, the flux of time, human identity, and humankind's
relationship to the cosmos. The textual universe created by Pierre Albert-
Birot is a universe in perpetual movement. This is an aesthetics concerned with the processes of artistic creation, with the coming into being
of the artistic object as much as with its completion. Although the dynamics of his work are directed toward a state (the vanishing point where
parallel lines meet?) where conflicts are resolved and order and harmony
are restored, he simultaneously flees that same state, which carries within
it a notion of fixity and ending. In the introduction we spoke of the alchemical process of poetry. In his ceaseless recombination of the elements, the transformation of matter, the quest for the reconciliation of
opposites and the celebration of the divine spark in the human, Pierre
Albert-Birot is the poet-alchemist in tireless search of the symbolic
gold—Grabinou*lor*, the Philosopher's stone that represents redemption
through unity both physical and spiritual. Through poetic creation the
poet may retrieve a lost relationship with the cosmos and simultaneously
elevate humanity to divine status.

The reading of *La Guerre* revealed this life's work to be conceived at
a moment of historical, social, artistic, and personal fragmentation and
rupture; the work then moves ever forward in an attempt to recoup the
whole, to recover a complete identity, a quest for a mode of living and
creating. *Grabinoulor* is driven by a will to continuity and wholeness, a

330

discourse of excess, the embracing of a totality from before a point of origin to beyond the point of the infinite. What is to be read between these two poles is an extended meditation on the human condition, on living the everyday with the knowledge of the constraints of death, on the role of the artist and writer, on humanity's spiritual needs and aspirations. The creative production of Albert-Birot is generated by the double quest for knowledge of self and knowledge of the world begun in painting and continued in poetry and narrative, a metadiscourse on the development of human knowledge and the history of ideas, science, and the arts on the ways in which man thinks of himself and the world around him. This is a work that elaborates a new order in the form of a "geometric chaos" where the essential system of opposites may be transcended but their vital impulse retained and where the inadequacies (and at best misconceptions) of our partial understanding of the human condition may be made sublime in the true knowledge toward which the poet strives. Yet nothing is ever resolved in the universe of Pierre Albert-Birot: chaos—order—chaos—order to perpetuity.[1] This is an intuition of the positive force of chaos and its part in the functioning of the universe, a new order simple and complex, pattern and structure which allows a vital return to disorder: "s'ordonner dans le désordre, chaque tableau sera un temps de la création du monde en création perpétuelle."[2] ("to be ordered in disorder, each painting will be a time of the creation of the world in perpetual creation.")

In sculpture and in painting, Albert-Birot first confronts the real. In the reflection on the visual arts, particularly through the visual language of cubism which allows a reassembling of the elements in a new order, he initially articulates his understanding of the creative act in the canvas of *La Guerre*, matrix of a poetics and existential truth. From here he moves to work incessantly on verbal language. His entire poetic itinerary is a perpetual and continually progressive work on and through language, a constant rewriting and reorganizing of systems, and a working and reworking of his poetics, of the processes of creation, of the processes of thought. It is this work on language and on the search for an adequate form of artistic expression in language that demands a place for Albert-Birot among the great literary adventurers of the twentieth century, in the theater, in poetry, in the narrative, all seeking to render the experience of modern human existence. The experimentation of *La Lune* is not merely a reveling in the potential of his new material. In the *Poèmes à l'Autre Moi*, we have read a poet exploring a subjectivity and producing an essentially modern discourse on the position of the subject in relation to the other and to language, raising questions concerning artistic creation and identity, identity and language—how the self is formed, forged through language, how the artistic self uses that language to create. In

Grabinoulor the poet continues to exploit as fully as possible the linguistic resources available to him, yet the object of his quest constantly eludes him. Grabinoulor may find provisional answers—but others are constantly available. This is not an untroubled and transparent relationship to language and to knowledge despite the constant celebration of the medium. It is a reevaluation of language just as the social, institutional, intellectual, and even geographical systems analyzed in the narrative of *Grabinoulor* are constantly reworked and reordered. Albert Birot's jubilation in the creative process is offset by other conflicts. The constant repetition of the quest in *L'Autre Moi*, and in *Grabinoulor* reveals rather an awareness riddled with doubt yet still desiring fulfillment. Here is the true beauty of a lifetime's work.

The reading of Pierre Albert-Birot gives access to the major challenges of contemporary art and culture, questioning our relationship to ideologies, both artistic and political. In his refusal to be assimilated into the movements of futurism and surrealism and his insistence on remaining apart from politics, he forces the reader to reassess the relationship of the individual creator to artistic history, the social individual to collective history.[3] This is a work that resists easy categorization and as such provides a rich corpus for the further study of the processes of artistic creation.[4] The network of questions raised by the study of Albert-Birot's oeuvre proliferates as does the work itself, always in movement, always in conflict, and always and necessarily in paradox. Here we have established the necessity of an understanding of the practice and discourse of the visual arts for the genesis and subsequent structure of both his poetry and the narrative of *Grabinoulor*. We have alluded to but not developed the way in which these works interact with the practice of music. This is an essential area for further study to assess the impact of *Grabinoulor* on the development of the novel. Grabinoulor is a creature of language: the nature of the material from which he is formed is repetition, variation, and an infinity of forms as is the potential of any musical note. "Le poète est un prêtre architecte sculpteur et musicien" (*Grabinoulor*, I, 8, p. 26). ("The poet is a priest architect sculptor and musician.") Within the theoretical framework of the visual arts, we have explored the architect and sculptor. The musician is yet to be explored in more detail. The poet/musician practices his scales, reworks well-known melodies, introduces innovation, and varies his score between harmony and dissonance. The rhythm of the narrative in the nonpunctuated prose of *Grabinoulor* provides highs and lows, pauses and accelerations as in the time of the musical score. Equally we have sought to understand the divine status of the poet who communes with the universe outside himself through prolonged reflection on the self, transcending human limitations.[5] The processes of art and alchemy explored by poets and novelists throughout the centuries would provide other avenues of exploration for the understanding of place of the material and of the spiritual in the creative act.[6] The autobiographical project of Albert-Birot analyzed here in detail in the *Poèmes à l'Autre Moi* also necessitates development and particularly a consideration with the other self-reflective adventures of the twentieth century. We have referred briefly to other poets and writers in the course of this study—a reading with certain of them, most notably Michaux, Leiris, Perec, Queneau, Tardieu, Perros, would produce a further elucidation on the most insistent questions of the literature of the twentieth century.

I have insisted throughout this study that Albert-Birot's work must be "globally" viewed. His expressed intention in the final poem of the *Trente et un poèmes de poche* that there should be no separation between this work and what was to follow is sustained. The poetry collections and *Grabinoulor* run parallel in time and are poetically bound together. The theater of Albert-Birot, as we insisted at the beginning of our study, requires further investigation providing as it does another discourse on and reading of the poetry of Albert-Birot as poetry becomes drama and vice versa. I hope to have presented the diversity of Albert-Birot's creative production while seeking to sustain a particular line of enquiry to understand its structure and functioning. The impact of this work, which is simultaneously a personal poetics, a universal quest, and a project for the assessment of the twentieth century, is only beginning to be understood. Since this book went to press, two major conferences have been held—one at Cerisy-la-Salle in Normandy, the other at the Universite de Paris-Y Nanterre. This project is indeed beginning to be read.

Notes

PREFACE

1. During the 1960s, around the time of the poet's death in 1967, and the early 1970s, a number of literary journals dedicated special issues to Albert-Birot. Among these are several articles that provide valuable insights into his works, although these are intermingled with homages to and *témoignages* of the man himself. The most notable of these is *F* 2–3 (1972), which provides a broad outline of aspects of Albert-Birot's work and suggests several areas for investigation. Details of articles and academic work on Albert-Birot are to be found in the bibliography. In Britain there exists only one other thesis to date. David Balhatchet's, "A Critical Study of *Grabinoulor* by Pierre Albert-Birot," submitted to the Board of Medieval and Modern Languages and Literature for the degree of D.Phil., University of Oxford, 1987, which comprises a comprehensive thematic analysis of the figure of the circle in *Grabinoulor* and highlights a number of key linguistic aspects in the appendices. The appendices include studies of wordplay; phonetic and semantic considerations; word creation; shifts of meaning due to spelling and register changes; periphrasis; personification; imagery; and the use of adaptations and parodies of well-known expressions and texts. In America one Ph.D. thesis has been written: V.J. Marottoli, "Futurism and its Influence on the French poet Pierre Albert-Birot," University of Connecticut, 1974. At the time of writing, there is no complete work of critical theory on the works of Albert-Birot. A collection of three essays by Nicole Le Dimna, *Jeux et Enjeux chez Pierre Albert-Birot. Lectures de "Grabinoulor,"* (Chieti, Italy: Maria Solfanelli, 1989)—which includes a stylistic analysis, a structural survey of an illustrative episode of *Grabinoulor,* and a very suggestive reading of the same text with Bakhtin's notion of "carnival"—serves as a good introduction to *Grabinoulor.* The essential starting point for the work in its entirety is the recent monograph of Albert-Birot by Marie-Louise Lentengre, *Pierre Albert-Birot, L'Invention de Soi* (Paris: Editions J.-M. Place, 1993). There are several useful reference points in the Rougerie republications of the poetry and theater, which contain invaluable presentations and postfaces by Arlette Albert-Birot. The year 1992 also saw the publication of a new edition of *La Lune ou le livre des poèmes* with notes by Arlette Albert-Birot, again published by Rougerie. Jean Follain's monograph in the Seghers's "Poètes d'aujourd'hui" series (1967) remains a comprehensive survey and appreciation of the work as a whole, including photographs, facsimiles, and illustrations.

2. With regard to Surrealism, see the work done by Germana Orlandi Cerenza and Marie-Louise Lentengre in their early seminal articles:

> Le seul surréalisme qu'il s'attache à suivre donc, en dehors de toute école et en opposition avec toute école et dont il se sentit membre, réside dans l'exploration de la surréalité, à travers l'imagination, c'est-à-dire un surréalisme de toujours qui signifie aller au-delà de la réalité en faisant appel à l'imaginaire.

"Pierre Albert-Birot: un surréaliste hors du 'chateau,'" typescript translation of
the article that appeared in Italian as "Pierre Albert-Birot, un surrealista fuori
del 'Castello'" in "Surréalisme/Surrealismo," *Quaderni del novecento francese 2*,
[Roma: Bulzoni; Paris: Nizet, 1974], pp. 75–95, Germana Orlandi Cerenza, available in the Fonds Albert-Birot).

> ("The only surrealism which he endeavours to follow and of which he feels himself a
> member therefore, is removed from and in opposition to any school, and consists of the
> exploration of surreality, through the imagination, that is to say a surrealism which has
> always existed and which means going beyond reality by calling on the imagination.")

Marie-Louise Lentengre sees Albert-Birot's concept of *sur-réalité* as linked to
his own theory of *nunisme*:

> . . . remettre le chef d'oeuvre de Pierre Albert-Birot dans sa différence, c'est-à-dire de
> montrer brièvement en quoi il participe d'une poétique originale qui sut formuler son
> propre concept de surréalité, dans le contexte de l'Esprit Nouveau à l'entour des années
> 1916–1918, une poétique baptisée par le poète du nom du 'nunisme.'

(M.-L. Lentengre, *"Grabinoulor* ou le triomphe de l'imaginaire" in "La lettera-
tura e l'immaginario," Problema di semantica e di storia de lessico franco-italiano,
Atti del XI Convegni della Società per gli studi di lingua e letturatura francese
[Verona, 16, 1982], p. 163)

> (". . . to place Pierre Albert-Birot's masterpiece in its difference, that is to say to show
> briefly how it is derived from an original poetics which managed to formulate its own
> concept of surreality in the context of the Esprit Nouveau around 1916–1918, a poetics
> given the name *nunism* by the poet.")

3. The most thoroughly researched work on this period is the monograph by
M.-L. Lentengre already referred to and an earlier critical article by her, "Aux
sources de la métamorphose de *SIC:* la rencontre de Gino Severini et Pierre
Albert-Birot," (Firenza: Leo S. Olchki Editore, 1987). For the poet's own account,
see especially "Naissance et vie de *SIC*" in *Autobiographie*, suivi de *Moi et moi*,
(Troyes: Librairie Bleue, 1988, pp. 45–62).
4. An extremely useful reading of the paradoxes inherent in the concept of
the avant-garde is to be found in Antoine Compagnon's *Les Cinq Paradoxes de
la modernité* (Paris: Seuil, 1990). He begins by commenting on the fundamental
paradox of modernity that affirms and denies art at the same time, rupture itself
constituting tradition, and on the vicious circle of every avant-garde "le conform-
isme du non-conformisme" (p. 9). He defines the birth of modernity as the identification of the new as value and goes on to explore five paradoxes of the aesthetics
of the new. His consideration of the perspective of Baudelaire (quoting the end
of "Voyage": "Au fond de l'inconnu pour trouver du *nouveau*") ("into the depths
of the Unknown, in quest of something new"; translation by Francis Scarfe, London: Anvil Press Poetry, 1986, p. 247) provides an interesting and fruitful criterion
with which to read the position of Albert-Birot. Baudelaire stands at a different
limit of the notion of the modern, an affirmation of the idea of progress, of the
superiority of the modern that is not the aesthetics of change and negation supported by the avant-gardes of the twentieth century. In Compagnon's view we
habitually confuse "modernity" and avant-garde, the first being "la fondation
d'une tradition nouvelle" ("the foundation of a new tradition") and the second
"négation de toute tradition" ("the negation of any tradition") (p. 163). The per-

spective offered here is one to which we will return in our analysis of Albert-Birot's painting, *La Guerre* (1916) and our treatment of aspects of *SIC*.

CHAPTER 1. IDENTITY, *LA GUERRE*, AND THE STRUCTURES OF A POETICS

1. *Autobiographie*, suivi de *Moi et moi*, (Troyes: Librairies Bleue, 1988). The autobiography dates from 1952 when Albert-Birot was seventy-six years old and focuses mainly on his childhood in Angoulême and the early years of training and study in Paris. See bibliography for details of interviews, lectures, and conferences given both by and on Albert-Birot.

2. As a sculptor Pierre Albert-Birot had been the pupil of Falguière, having registered in his atelier on 24 January 1892. He also frequented the studio of Gerôme, and Gustave Moreau agreed to correct some of his sketches. Critical notices on his sculptures include such remarks as these: "L'émoi de M. Birot mérite une sérieuse attention. Il témoigne chez son auteur de rares facultés d'observation et d'une science d'exécution fort remarquable . . . une oeuvre de premier ordre, simple, largement exécutée, très impressionnante" (Article of 31 May 1903, which appeared in the *Chronique de St Jean D'Angely; Annales La Rochelle, Gazette des Bains de Mer de Royan, Journal d'Oléron, Courrier de Rochefort* (Fonds Albert-Birot). ("M. Birot's emotion deserves serious attention. It is testimony to its creator's rare faculty of observation and rather remarkable knowledge of how to give this form . . . a first-rate piece of work, simple, amply executed, very impressive.") In *Gil Blas*, 3 April 1903, A. Dayot wrote that *La Veuve* was one of the works of that year that maintained "le prestige du Salon des Artistes Français." *La Veuve* was bought by the state and now stands in the cemetery at Issy-Les-Moulineaux. *Les Ames simples* is outside the Eglise St. André in Angoulême.

3. The earliest poem existing in the Fonds Albert-Birot dates from December 1900 and is entitled "La Solitude."

> Nous étions en novembre. Engourdi par la brise
> J'allais triste et rêvant.
> . . . .
> Une femme imposante au vêtement tout noir
> Lentement descendait sous la brume du soir.
> Emu, je contemplai cette noble attitude
> Et les larmes aux yeux, je vis la solitude.
>
> ("It was November. Numbed by the breeze
> I walked along sad and dreamy.
> . . . .
> An imposing woman dressed all in black
> was slowly coming down the street in the evening mist.
> Moved, I contemplated her noble attitude
> and with tears in my eyes, I saw solitude.")

The "widow" appears later in the play *La Dame enamourée* and in the person of Eugénie in the final chapter of *Grabinoulor* I.

4. Lentengre, *Pierre Albert-Birot*, particularly chapters 1, 2, and 3 collectively entitled "La vie anonyme."

5. See Lentengre, *Pierre Albert-Birot*, for biographical details that provide more information behind such an analysis. She presents a type of summary of the emotional ruptures Albert-Birot experienced up to his meeting with Germaine, who was to be his first wife, that is, the abandonment by his father of the young Pierre and his mother, bringing to an abrupt halt a happy childhood (hence the move from Angoulême to Bordeaux to Paris); the estrangement of his first mentor, Philippe Allaire, after the older man's marriage; the death of his friend, the painter Georges Bottini; the loss of the latter's sister, Marguerite, the mother of Albert-Birot's four children, who abandoned them and their father, marrying another man in 1909; the opposition of the family of Hélène Chapelain to marriage with an artist who already had a family and little money. The poet's solitary existence continued. In 1913 he married Germaine de Surville, who enthusiastically supported his venture with *SIC* and his theater company, *Le Plateau*, throughout the twenties. She died in 1931, and the poet remained alone until his meeting with Arlette Lafont in 1956, who was to become his second wife. In later interviews Albert-Birot recognized that this excessively solitary existence had led to the ignorance and consequent neglect that surrounds his work.

6. At an exhibition of Albert-Birot's paintings (as complete as has ever been mounted) at Angoulême, a number of self-portraits were presented: *Autoportrait* (sketch) (ca. 1896); *Autoportrait* (1903); *Autoportrait* (1914); *Pierre Albert-Birot et les siens* (1915); *Autoportrait* (1935). A simple pencil sketch is to be found in the manuscript of *Grabinoulor* at the opening of Volume IV. (Exhibition held at the museum of Angoulême, 28 June–15 October 1969, organized by Robert Guichard, "Conservateur au musée"; catalog compiled by Arlette Albert-Birot, preface by J. A. Catala.)

7. Arlette Albert-Birot, "Pour un art poétique," *F*, 2–3, p. 38.

8. This impetus from the visual unsurprisingly constantly recurs in Albert-Birot's relationship to his creativity. Arlette Albert-Birot has often remarked on his fascination with two paintings in particular: Michelangelo's *God Creating Adam* from the Sistine Chapel, their fingertips almost touching, with an infinity between them; and a reproduction of Adam and Eve in the Garden of Eden by Cranach, which Albert-Birot always kept on his desk and which survives in the Fonds Albert-Birot. It is this insight that inspired the final part of the present study, which seeks to explore Poet as Creator and Adam as Poet.

9. Alfred Victor Espinas, born in 1844 at Saint-Florentin, friend of Mallarmé with whom he corresponded when the former went to Paris to continue his studies. See Lentengre, *Pierre Albert-Birot*, chapter 3, for the poetry exchanged between them. He also translated in 1874 Spencer's *Principles of Psychology* with Théodule Ribot. Espinas began teaching at the Sorbonne in 1894 and became "professeur adjoint" in 1899. He became a member of "l'Institut" in 1905. His major works are *Les Sociétés animales* (1877), *La Psychologie expérimentale en Italie* (1880), *Histoire des doctrines économiques* (1892), *Les origines de la technologie en Grèce* (1897), and *La Philosophie sociale aux XVIIIe siècle et la Révolution* (1894). He died in 1922.

10. Lentengre points out the closeness of Espinas's language in *La Philosophie sociale du XVIIIe siècle et la Révolution* and the early slogans of *SIC*: "L'exaltation de la volonté, le vitalisme optimiste qui éclatent dans les premiers fascicules de *SIC* et traversent toute l'oeuvre d'Albert-Birot, ne sont pas un emprunt à la doctrine futuriste, mais une interprétation personnelle de la pensée

d'Espinas," *Pierre Albert-Birot*, p. 62. ("The exaltation of the will, the optimistic vitalism that burst from the first issues of *SIC* and are present throughout Albert-Birot's work, are not borrowings from futurist doctrine but a personal interpretation of Espinas's thought.") We are in total agreement with Lentengre on this point, having read *SIC* as first and foremost a self-affirmation. See our analysis of *SIC* in chapter 2 of this study. It is certainly unlikely that Albert-Birot was familiar with the futurist manifesto published in *Le Figaro* in 1909.

11. *1915*, included in the "Documents" section of the facsimile edition of *SIC*, Jean-Michel Place, Paris, 1980. Again various versions can be found among Albert-Birot's papers.

12. Lentengre's analysis considers the real metamorphosis of *SIC* to have occurred only after the meeting with Severini, who contributes to the second issue and inspires Albert-Birot's "conversion" to the superficially more futurist-inspired and influenced approaches from n° 3 onward. She sees the difference between *1915* and *SIC* as being at first only visual and superficial as regards content, with just a change in style: "En fait, la différence profonde entre le projet de *1915* et le premier numéro de *SIC*, se situe uniquement sur le plan de style, à la fois graphique et verbal" ("Aux sources de la métamorphose de *SIC*," p. 24, and repeated in her monograph). ("In fact the fundamental difference between *1915* and the first issue of *SIC* is only at the level of both the graphic and verbal style.") She quotes convincingly from two anterior versions of the "sorte de manifeste" in *SIC* n° 3 (March 1916) (JMP, p. 18), one more in the style of *1915* and an intermediary text closer to the tone of *SIC:* "L'idéologie est réduite au slogan, l'image implicite du moi comme 'isolé' ou 'égaré' disparaît, tandis que le monde moderne vient nominalement s'affirmer." ("Ideology is reduced to a slogan, the implicit image of the self as 'isolated' or 'lost' disappears, while the modern world begins nominally to affirm itself.") Severini's exhibition was held at the Galerie Boutet de Monvel, 15 January to 1 February 1916. A lecture by the Italian painter preceded it, entitled "Les arts plastiques et la science moderne."

13. The influence of Georges Achard, friend of the poet and of his mother, particularly after their arrival in Paris, certainly had some bearing on Albert-Birot's "unseeing" of modern art. It was on Achard's advice that Albert-Birot entered the atelier of his own "maître" Falguière. Achard himself exhibited for the first time in 1894 and continued to exhibit regularly until 1935. Albert-Birot is disparaging about his lack of originality although he admits that during these formative years he had caught "le virus de l'anti-nouveauté" and remained convinced, like Achard, that "nouveauté est erreur" (*Autobiographie*, p. 33). In a talk given a few years before his death, Albert-Birot again presents the paradox:

> Quelques difficultés se présentent pour accorder, surtout du point de vue littéraire, mon amour des grandes oeuvres du passé et mon amour intuitif des choses nouvelles, ce qui fait que j'ai passé toutes ces années de première et seconde jeunesse avec Homère, Eschyle, Virgile, Lucrèce, comme avec des textes roman des Xe, XIe et XIIe siècles et quelques poètes du XVe et du XVIe siècle: Villon, Maurice Scève, d'Aubigné. Et bien entendu, j'étais l'ami de Montaigne.

(Talk and readings at the "Théatre des Poètes," Conservatoire National d'Art Dramatique, 31 October 1964. André Lebois talked on the evolution of Albert-Birot's work while the poet gave readings from the *Iliad*, the *Eumenides*, the *Aeneid*, *Prose de Sainte-Eulalie*, "le premier texte poétique, ou à peu près, que nous connaissons en français" ("more or less the first poetic work known in French"); le *Jeu d'Adam, Sermon de Maurice de Sully.*) ("A few difficulties are evident, especially from a literary point of view, to reconcile my love for the great works of the past and my intuitive love for new things, which means that I spent much of my early life with Homer, Aeschylus, Virgil, Lucretius, and with the late Latin texts of the tenth, eleventh, and twelth centuries and a few fifteenth- and sixteenth-century poets: Villon, Maurice Sève, d'Aubigné. And naturally I was Montaigne's friend.")

The influence of medieval literature, apparent also in the work of Apollinaire, Reverdy, and Max Jacob, who integrated it with a modern expression, makes an interesting comparison here.

14. Albert-Birot, "Le théâtre en vers," *Scoenia*, 26, 1 September 1910, p. 101.

15.

> La modernité, c'est le transitoire, le fugitif, le contingent, la moitié de l'art, dont l'autre moitié est l'éternel et l'immuable. . . . En un mot, pour que toute modernité soit digne de devenir antiquité, if faut que la beauté mystérieuse que la vie humaine y met involontairement en ait été extraite.

(Baudelaire, *Le Peintre de la vie moderne*, vol. 2 [Paris; Gallimard, 1976], p. 695) ("Modernity is the transitory, the fleeting, the contingent, one half of art, whose other half is the eternal and the unchangeable. . . . In a word, for modernity to be worthy of becoming antiquity, the mysterious beauty that human life gives to it unintentionally must have been extracted.") This is quoted by both Compagnon, *Les Cinq Paradoxes*, and Lentengre, *Pierre Albert-Birot*, who notes also Apollinaire's much-quoted piece from *Les Peintres cubistes:* "On ne peut pas transporter partout avec soi le cadavre de son père." (Paris: L. C. Breunig and J.-Cl. Chevalier, Hermann, 1965), pp. 46–47. ("You cannot carry your father's corpse with you everywhere you go.")

16. *La Guerre 1916*, oil on canvas, 125.5 x 118 cm, Musée d'Art Moderne, CGP, Paris. CAM 1977.639. Exhibited at the Tate Gallery, 1980: "Abstraction: Towards a New Art, Painting 1910–1920." Reproduced in Serge Fauchereau, *Peintures et dessins d'écrivains* (Paris: Belfond, 1991), p. 123, and in Richard Cork, *A Bitter truth: Avant-Garde Art and the Great War* (London: Yale University Press, 1994), p. 146.

In the archives of the Courtauld Institute, London, are a charcoal and white chalk sketch inscribed *La Guerre*, P. A.-Birot, 1917 (55 x 44 cm). Exhibited in Milano, Galeria Milano, 1976, *Pittori Scrittori/Scrittori Pittori*, and a pastel signed by initials only, 57 x 49 cm., *La Guerre*, 1916. Exhibited in Milan as above and Modena, 1977. A further pen and india ink and white gouache signed and dated 1916 (14 x 25.5 cm), entitled "Mammelles," using the same forms of triangles and circles, was sold at Sotheby's, 1 December 1976.

17. Dominique Baudouin, "La Panthère Noire," Espaces, Documents XXe siècle, n° 5, 1975, p. 29. Here he is commenting on Albert-Birot's "Moulin à poèmes" (in *Les Amusements naturels*, 1983, p. 107), which he identifies as performing the function of a symbol of creation within the schema of Albert-Birot's poetic universe:

> Il obéit à son mouvement expansif par cercles concentriques grandissants: ou mieux encore, grâce à des poussées, des percées, des percées ou des approfondissements nouveaux, qui le portent dans une sphère plus vaste, plus lointaine ou plus étrange. ("It obeys its expansive movement through ever-greater concentric circles, or rather through surges, breachings or the plunging of new depths, which carry it into a vaster sphere, further away and more strange.")

18. A number of other commentators have referred to the importance of the visual arts for Albert-Birot's work, but there are no previous in-depth analyses. See, for example, Yves Seraline, "Des arts plastiques à l'écriture," *F*, 2–3, pp. 44–46, originally written for the exhibition in Angoulême, June-November 1989, and previously referred to, first published in *La Charente libre*, 17 September 1969, or the comments made by Daniel Abadie and Hubert Juin in the radio program "Une vie, une oeuvre," 1986 (see bibliography for details).

19. The collection made by Serge Fauchereau, in the book of drawings and paintings by writers in which *La Guerre* figures is ample testimony to the ways in which writers approach visual expression. The reasons for expression in each medium and the losses and gains entailed pose a more difficult question to both production and reception. The analyzing of Albert-Birot's itinerary goes some way also to exploring what is at stake in crossing the "boundaries" between the arts.

20. Pierre Albert-Birot, "Au bras de poésie," Lecture, Paris, 1965. Typescript available in the Fonds Albert-Birot. The analogy with musical composition is also one to which we will return at the end of this study.

21. Pierre Albert-Birot, notebooks available for consultation in the Fonds Albert-Birot. These sketches and aphorisms are collected together in the *Pages sans titre* by François Norguet, in a limited edition of 150, Paris, 1979 (editions hors commerce).

> Les premiers développements et les études de thèmes . . . proviennent du carnet où Pierre Albert-Birot prépara, de mars à juillet 1916, les numéros 3 à 7 de *SIC*; l'ordre chronologique des dessins, difficile à préciser, diffère vraisemblablement peu de l'ordre thématique adopté ici: spirales, tourbillons, hélices, triangles, ensuite associés dans des constructions de type "cubiste." (Accompanying notes.)

> ("The first developments and studies of themes . . . come from the notebook in which Pierre Albert-Birot prepared, from March to June 1916, numbers 3 to 7 of *SIC*. The chronological order of the drawings, difficult to date precisely, probably differs little from the thematic order adopted here: spirals, vortices, helices, triangles, which are then put together in 'cubist'-type constructions.")

Further sketches contained in this collection were originally found in the notebook for *SIC* nos 8–14 and, while no doubt relating to *La Guerre*, also reveal the working through for the forms of *Femme Nue dans une salle de bain* (*SIC* no 8/9/10) and *Intimité* (*SIC* no 12), eventually engraved on wood and showing Albert-Birot's engagement with a cubism already opening out onto abstraction. The interest of the mathematician Norguet in these sketches is equally revealing of the relationship between mathematics and aesthetics. It is not, however, our intention to discuss the visual in mathematical terms. Here geometry is considered for the crucial role it plays in the art of cubism and abstraction as it seeks to express the enigma of the problem of representation.

22. Vassily Kandinsky, quoted on the CGP information leaflet on his work.

23. On the question of the problems facing any "visual poetics," see especially the collection of articles in *Style*, no 22, summer 1988, "Visual Poetics," concerned with establishing various interpretative strategies for such an endeavor in all its manifestations—the word-image interaction, rendering verbal texts visually or reading the visual and expressing it in verbal language.

24. It is beyond the scope of this study to develop this point concerning the interaction between poetry and painting. Nonetheless the artistic context of the period is very much present in the reading adopted here.

25. Albert-Birot, interview with José Pivin, typescript, p. 6.

Albert-Birot is not alone in such an expression towards the outbreak of war, which is personal and not what we would now see as socially and historically conscious: "Le temps de la création de *SIC* ce n'était pas un temps gai, il y avait la guerre, mais la foi dans les possibilités créatrices était grande et sincère" (Gino Severini, *La Barbacane* 7, special issue dedicated to Albert-Birot, p. 100). ("The time during which *SIC* was being created was not a happy time, there was the war, but the faith in creative possibilities was great and sincere.")

26. We are particularly indebted to the rigorous study by J.-M. Floch, *Petites Mythologies de l'oeil et de l'esprit*, (Paris-Amsterdam: Hadès-Benjamin, 1985), in which, among other analyses, he proposes a semiotic reading of Kandinsky's *Composition IV*, formulating new ways of seeing/reading the work of art and of linking the verbal and the visual. The title obviously acknowledges Merleau-Ponty's *L'Oeil et l'esprit*. Modern criticism must be interdisciplinary, given the nature of the modern artistic object, whatever its form. Floch proposes a methodology with which to explore such création and precise critical tools with which to approach the notion of abstraction. His approach differs from both that of Barthes and that of Greimas, who have been mainly concerned with the figurative in film, painting, and so forth. See Floch also in his article "Les Langages planaires," in *Sémiotique. L'Ecole de Paris* (Paris: Hachette, 1982). A semiotic reading such as that elaborated by Floch to read the visual by putting in place codes of expression for images and specific visual categories allows an apprehension of the relationship between form and content (see *Petites Mythologies*, p. 200).

27. Floch, *Petites Mythologies*, p. 203. Floch's starting point does differ in that *Composition IV* has no connotative title, apart from perhaps a musical analogy in the use of the term "composition."

28. This danger has been highlighted by Floch: "Il n'a jamais été question au cours de cette étude de 'réduire' le tableau à ces oeuvres figuratives, de le lire 'comme si' son caractère abstrait et les différences d'expression plastique qu'il implique étaient des choses négligeables.," ibid., p. 441. ("There has never been any question in the course of this study of 'reducing' the painting to these figurative works, of reading it 'as if' its abstract character and the differences in visual expression that this implies were negligible.")

To do this Floch divides his analysis into five sections, dividing the canvas into three sections and examining the signifying units of each of the three parts and making a correlation between structure and expression before offering a theory of the construction of a "semisymbolic" meaning generated by the work. Given the nature of the composition of Albert-Birot's canvas, equally inviting a structural division into three sections, the application of Floch's methodology could be made directly in a more technical analysis.

29. Compare Floch, *Petites Mythologies*, p. 43: "On peut ainsi essayer de diviser cet espace en unités discrètes provisoires, grâce à quelques oppositions visuelles prises comme critères de découpage et produisant des ruptures de continuité dans l'étendue." ("One could therefore try to divide this space into provisional discrete units by taking some of the visual oppositions as criteria for such a cutting-up and thereby producing ruptures in the continuity of the overall space.")

30. Albert-Birot's rejection of surrealism is rooted in the privileging of the unconscious mind in creation to the exclusion of all other elements:

Pour moi je pense que de tout temps les poètes ont cherché leur vie ET dans le conscient et dans le subconscient, l'un complète l'autre. N'a-t-on pas toujours vu les poètes demander à l'ivresse de leur ouvrir la porte de l'Inconnu. Seulement ce n'est pas l'inconnu sous-conscient qui'ils recherchent, mais l'inconnu sur-conscient, ils veulent aller au maximum d'eux-mêmes mais plutôt en hauteur qu'en profondeur. . . . Oui, plus j'y pense, plus je m'assure qu'un poème est un tout qui contient et du conscient et de l'inconscient, c'est un composé et non un corps simple. (Pierre Albert-Birot, letter to Léo Tixier, 2 November 1949)

("Personally I think that poets have always sought their life both in the conscious AND in the subconscious, the one complements the other. Haven't we always seen poets asking ecstasy to open the door of the Unknown to them? Only this is not the subconscious unknown they seek, but the superconscious unknown, they want to go to their greatest limit, but in height rather than depth. . . . Yes, the more I think about it, the more certain I am that a poem is a whole which contains something of both the conscious and the unconscious, it is a composite body, not a simple one.")

There are echoes of Rimbaud at the gate of *l'ivresse*, echoes of Baudelaire seeking *l'Inconnu*,. Yet Albert-Birot remains skeptical of any artificial ways of opening up the subconscious, and there is rather a poetic state, a state of grace to which the poet accedes naturally, a *sur-réalité*, a state beyond reality entered through the *sur-conscient*, a creative tool and a source of poetic jubilation. This letter is reproduced in full in the article by G. Orlandi Cerenza, "Un surréaliste hors du château."

31. Compare Floch, *Petites Mythologies*, p. 45.

32. Severini, 1913 Manifesto, "The Plastic Analogies of Dynamism," reproduced in Umbro Appollonio, *Futurist Manifestos* (London: Thames & Hudson, 1973), p. 123.

33. Reproduced in Appollonio, p. 91.

34. "Le thème de la spirale se retrouve longtemps après dans 'l'Etude poétique au 100.00ème' qui clôt les 'Cent et quelques poèmes ordinaires' des *Amusements Naturels* (Denoël, Paris, 1945), et dans le "Moulin à Poèmes" (*De Temps à temps*, n° 3, 1955)" (Collection "Pages sans titres," accompanying notes). ("The theme of the spiral is found again much later in the 'Poetic study to the 100.000th,' which closes the 'Hundred and a few ordinary poems' in the *Amusements Naturels* (Paris: Denoël, 1945), and in the "Poem mill'" (*De temps à temps*, n° 3, 1955.) Dominique Baudouin has already pointed out the importance of the figure of the "Moulin à Poèmes."

35. Although Albert-Birot had had contact with Gustave Moreau, it is unlikely that he met any of the later Fauve painters. It is in the use of color as structure that the techniques of the Fauvists differ from those of the Impressionists concerned with the rendering of the effects of light.

36. Dora Vallier, *Du Noir au Blanc. Les couleurs dans la peinture,* (Caen: L'Echoppe, 1989), p. 7; our emphasis.

In this collection of three articles, Dora Vallier uses the linguistic model as elaborated by Jakobson to explore the functioning of painting. See particularly "Malévitch et le modèle linguistique en peinture," pp. 9–26. Originally published in *Critique*, Paris, n° 334, March 1975.

37. Albert-Birot, "La Peinture absolue," *Synthèses* 123, (1951): pp. 111–15.

38. André Lebois, preface to *Grabinoulor* (Paris: Gallimard, 1964).

39. Jean Follain, *Pierre Albert-Birot*, Compare also Paul de Vree on *Grabinoulor:* "Léger, lumineux, lumnivore, voici le transparent Grabinoulor," in "Pierre Albert-Birot, de groene dichter," *De Tafelronde*, XII, Antwerpen, 1964, translated unpaginated section added to the reference copy in the Fonds Albert-Birot. ("Light, luminous, lumnivorous, this is the transparent Grabinoulor.")

40. Dora Vallier, *Du Noir au blanc*, p. 47.

41. Braque, quoted by Vallier (p.53), in an interview by her, "Braque, la peinture et nous," originally published in *Cahiers d'Art*, 24, no. 1 (October 1954): p. 16. "Or dès qu'il y a stabilisation de la vision, il y a effet d'espace" (p. 53). ("As soon as vision is stabilized, there is the effect of space.")

42. Margaret Davies, "La notion de la modernité," *Cahiers du 20ème siècle*, n° 5. (Paris: Klincksieck, 1975), pp. 9–30.

43. Robert Delaunay, *Du Cubisme à l'art abstrait*, (Paris: SEVPEN, 1957), p. 15. Delaunay's theories of color, particularly that of "le contraste simultané," were based on that of the chemist Chevreul, whose classification of colors led him to construct a chromatic circle that showed the whole spectrum of colors and the relationship between them. On the analogy between colors and words in their respective language systems, especially Vallier's vigorous analysis which, following the Saussurian and Jakobsonian models, identifies the equivalent of *phonèmes*, the three primary colors red, blue, and yellow, from which the others of the spectrum can be made: "Ces trois couleurs étant irréductibles à d'autres plus simples et étant invariables dans leur relations réciproques peuvent être considérées comme des phonèmes" (Vallier, *Du Noir au blanc*, p. 13). ("These three colors, being irreducible to others which are simpler and being invariable in their reciprocal relations, can be considered as phonemes.")

44. Dora Vallier, pp. 11–12.

45. The black, white, and gray system of the right-hand side of *La Guerre* is certainly like the cubist palette. In her linguistic model, Vallier forms the "triangle chromatique," PTK, of these three colors as opposed to the "triangle chromatique" of red, blue, and yellow, which correspond to the vowels A, U, and I. See pp. 17–18.

46. Vallier, *Du Noir au blanc*, p. 62.

47. Floch calls this the elaboration of a semisymbolic meaning. The analysis moves from an initial intuition to an understanding of the structures that underly the effects which produced that intuition. See Floch, op. cit., and also in "Les Langages planaires," pp. 202–3.

48. In pointing this out we are reminded particularly of Balla's *Optimism and Pessimism* (1923), where the forms and organization of the canvas are reminiscent of Albert-Birot's *La Guerre*, but where the simple color contrasts of blue and black in binary opposition leave the spectator in no doubt that the work sets up a confrontation between the impulses of negative and positive forces.

49. Compare also that most famous of triangles, the Eiffel Tower, whose sex has caused much debate between artists and poets. Grabinoulor converses with the Tower, of female gender, whom he calls "Isabelle" *(Grabinoulor*, V, 3).

50. Floch's analysis leads him at this point to a consideration of the dynamics of Kandinsky's creation within the framework of a basic four-term semiotic square—vie/non-mort//mort/non-vie, suggesting that the circuit of death, nondeath, life, nonlife is representative of the reading of the particular canvas he has studied, the conflict between and victory of life over death being a constant of Kandinsky's work (see Floch, *Petites Mythologies, p. 73*).

The aim of the use of the semiotic square is to make visible the differences and relationships within the text in order to discover possible meanings. It is a tool to aid the discovery of the organization of the "text," how the text is generated, the visible signs of the dynamics of the text. Developed by A. J. Greimas (*Du Sens*, [Paris: Seuil, 1970]), it is an attempt to offer suggestions for the perception of meaning. The semiotic square is an elementary structure of signification:

Since meaning is diacritical any meaning depends on oppositions and this four-term structure relates an item to both its converse and its contrary (black: white::non-black::-non-white). This basic configuration holds also, Greimas argues, for the simplest representation of the meaning of a text as a whole. It is grasped as a correlation between two points of opposed terms. This structure can either be static or dynamic, depending on whether the text is read syntagmatically or paradigmatically: that is, as narrative or as lyric. (Jonathan Culler, *Structuralist Poetics*, [London: Routledge & Kegan Paul, 1975], p. 92)

51. See, for example, J.-M. Adam, *Le Texte narratif* (Paris: Nathan, 1985). In his discussion of the semiotic square, he offers examples of both circuits of "revolt"—for example, *Le Père Goriot*, and of "resignation"—for example, *Anna Karenina*, as classic dynamics of the narrative form (p. 143).

52. Floch prefers the term "nonfigurative" both for Kandinsky's work and for the historical perspective of the development of painting (*Petites Mythologies*, p. 76). It is a term that also seems more appropriate here. In the next chapter, we discuss Albert-Birot's theoretical statements on the visual arts.

53. See also, for example, the "Chroniques," poems collected in *La Lune*, several of which were first published in *SIC*. These are discussed in this study in chapter 3.

Chapter 2. Pierre Albert-Birot, *SIC*, and the Avant-Garde: Collective Adventure and Voyage of Self-Discovery

1. See, for example, the studies by Balhatchet and Lentengre previously referred to. Note especially V. Marottoli, "Futurism and Its Influence on the Poet Pierre Albert-Birot," Ph.D. thesis, University of Connecticut, 1974, which treats the question in depth, and an article by Giovanni Lista, "Le Futurisme de Pierre Albert-Birot," *Les Cahiers Bleus*, Troyes, n° 14 (winter/spring 1979), which seeks to establish *SIC* within the aims and expression of futurism in France.

2. *SIC* has been republished three times in the series of facsimile editions of avant-garde journals by Jean-Michel Place, most recently in 1993. The edition of *SIC* (Editions J.-M. Place, Paris, 1980) with which we will be working includes a foreword by Arlette Albert-Birot; the advance publicity for the proposed journal *1915* (which immediately predates *SIC*); the program of the "Manifestation *SIC*" for the production of Apollinaire's *Les Mamelles de Tirésias* on 24 June 1917, which includes a sketch by Picasso, a woodcut by Matisse, poems by Max Jacob, Jean Cocteau, Pierre Reverdy, and Albert-Birot; and the sole issue of *Paris*, a literary journal created by Albert-Birot in November 1924, with poems by the editor and an article by Roch Grey on Apollinaire's surrealism.

This edition contains an invaluable index of the names of the contributors and of their contributions by title, an index of all names referred to throughout *SIC*, an index of all works referred to, and a thematic index. These appendices read like a reference list of the major poets, artists, literary movements, and artistic developments of the first half of the twentieth century. Apart from the numerous contributions of Albert-Birot himself, the most frequent contributors are Apollinaire, Aragon, Perez-Jorba, Reverdy, Soupault, and Tzara. Our references throughout this chapter are to this edition, using the abbreviation JMP followed by the page number.

3. The concept of an avant-garde in art and literature is a feature of the notion of modernity in general and has been prominent throughout the century, particularly in France. In France what is termed the avant-garde approach is evident in all branches of intellectual and artistic activity. See especially A. Compagnon, *Les Cinq Paradoxes*, for a discussion of these two concepts. See also "The Concept of the Avant-Garde," an essay by John Weightman in *The Concept of the Avant-Garde, Explorations in Modernism* (London: Alcove Press, 1973), pp. 13–37. In this essay he traces the heritage of the tabula rasa from Socrates, indicating Montaigne and Descartes, the thinking of the French Enlightenment as presenting human life as a process in time, and the poet-thinker Valéry as exponents of the procedure. The modern use of the term avant-garde as metaphor appears to date from the nineteenth century (first by French political movements around 1845), and the first uses of the term in literature and art go back only to the Romantic movement. Just as the notion of modernity originates in a wider philosophical view of the universe, so, too, does the notion of the avant-garde. It indicates the replacement of a medieval belief in a finished universe by the modern scientific view of a universe evolving in time, and affecting political and social thinking long before it penetrated into literature and the fine arts. The problem in the thinking of Albert-Birot is evident and is a source of the development of his individual creativity. Weightman suggests that the ideas of the avant-garde may be an attempt to escape from the dilemma of a perpetual movement by finding some substitute for eternity—that is, some god movement. This would certainly seem to be a valid statement on the work of Albert-Birot, which develops from his contact with the avant-garde and the fascination with the speed of the modern world to a personal quest for artistic and spiritual fulfillment contained within the work of creation. We deal with this aspect of his work in the final chapter of this study.

4. Lentengre sees *SIC* as originally a purely personal program, and she sees the significance of the title isolated from the preoccupations of the avant-garde:

> Ces généralités (sons, idées, couleurs, formes) n'ont pour l'heure aucune parenté intentionelle avec la synthèse des arts moderniste, elles ne sont rien d'autre que l'expression de la personnalité artistique polymorphe d'Albert-Birot, versé dans les trois arts que représentent les idées (poésie), les couleurs (peinture) et les formes (sculpture) auxquelles s'ajoutent les sons qui étaient l'art de Germaine. ("Aux sources de la métamorphose de *SIC*," p. 21)

> ("These generalities [sounds, ideas, colors, forms] do not have for the moment any intentional relationship with the synthesis in modern art, they are nothing more than the expression of Albert-Birot's polymorphic artistic personality, versed in the three arts represented by ideas [poetry], colors [painting], and forms [sculpture] to which sounds are added which were Germaine's art.")

This is undoubtedly true, yet he had begun to breathe "l'air du temps," and our argument here treats the question differently, attempting to give *SIC* its status as both a historical and an artistic document as well as a personal statement.

5. "L'Esprit Nouveau" is Apollinaire's general statement on modernity. We will discuss this later with regard to Albert-Birot and his own "state of mind," and to the value of the modern and innovation in artistic creation.

6. For example, in *SIC* n° 8/9/10, August–October 1916, Apollinaire is interviewed by Albert-Birot on "Les Tendances nouvelles," followed by the reproduction of a woodcut by Severini, one of Albert-Birot's "poèmes-simultanés" ("Le Raté-poème à deux voix"), his theoretical considerations on his *théâtre nunique*,

followed by two of his typically aphoristic "Réflexions": XXV, "Chercher c'est vivre, trouver c'est mourir" ("To seek is to live, to find is to die"); XXVI, "Une oeuvre d'art doit être composée comme une machine de précision" ("A work of art must be composed like a precision machine") and a piece of a musical composition by the futurist musician Pratella.

The content of a later issue is indicative of the development and changing face of *SIC* as it comes of age. For example, nº 40/41, February/March 1919, includes reviews and critical pieces by Louis Aragon and the Catalan poet and editor Perez-Jorba (who also compiled the first monograph of Albert-Birot, see bibliography for details), a section of Reverdy's novel *L'Imperméable* (published in installments over several issues), poems by Raymond Radiguet, a piece of prose by Roch Grey, and a short piece by the sculptor Ossip Zadkine with a photograph of one of his sculptures, a poem by Albert-Birot ("Chronique d'hiver," one of a series of "chronique" poems, some of which detail artistic events of the period), and an extract from his play *Matoum et Tévibar, Histoire édifiante du vrai et du faux poète,* and finally a musical manuscript reproduced from *Dada 3.*

7. On the importance of "contextual analysis" for the theories and productions of modern artists, see the introduction in Herschel B. Chipp (contributions by Peter Selz and Joshua C. Taylor), *Theories of Modern Art: A Source Book by Artists and Critics* (Berkeley, Los Angeles, London: University of California Press, 1968). We will be using this as a framework for our analysis of *SIC* as a source document.

8. "Il y a qu'en 1915, je me suis trouvé, c'est venu. . . . Voilà tout le programme de ma vie" ("I only found myself in 1915, it came to me. . . . There is the whole program of my life") after reading the opening words of *SIC* in the radio interview with José Pivin. Typescript, Fonds Albert-Birot, p. 10.

9. W. B. Chipp, *Theories of Modern Art,* p. 2.

10. Ibid., pp. 2–3. Commenting on these criteria, Chipp adds: "The points of study outlined above would attempt to define an ideological context for the documents, thus extending their meaning, and hopefully would eventually lead to a deeper understanding of the art. According to this method, a document is seen not only as a theoretical view of an artistic problem but also as the product of broad environmental conditions" (p. 6). As this suggests this approach has been widely used in art history, yet it appears to us to be more broadly applicable, allowing both the context and the intrinsic qualities of the text to be revealed. It would seem a particularly perceptive way to approach a document such as *SIC*, whose individual qualities have been neglected in a too easy categorizing of it.

11. For a discussion of the effect of the war on the artists of the period, see Kenneth Silver, *Esprit de corps. The Art of the Parisian Avant-Garde and the First World War 1914–1925,* (London: Thames and Hudson, 1989; translated into French very aptly as *Vers le retour à l'ordre,* Paris Flammarion, 1991). Silver exhaustively documents and discusses the effect of war on a modernism born of a group that contained disparate national origins, residing in Montmartre and Montparnasse. Most of the French originators left for the front, leaving behind a handful of "foreigners" (who became suspect) and some Frenchmen whose daily lives became difficult in the patriotic fervor. The artistic establishment seized the moment and delivered onslaughts against the degeneration of French art in the prewar years caused, they believed, by foreign influences (for example, the lecture by Tony Tollet in Lyons in 1915: "De l'Influence de la corporation judéo-allemande des marchands de tableaux sur l'art français," quoted by Silver, *Esprit de Corps,* p. 8. Silver refers to *SIC* and other magazines of the period, notably

Le Mot and *L'Elan*, as seeking to challenge the reactionary wave by a defense of modernism, whose rhetoric nonetheless offers a vision of France after the war very close to that of the right-wing politicians (see pp. 29–31)).

12. As Michel Décaudin points out in the radio program "Une vie, une oeuvre," France Culture, 27 February 1986, dedicated to Albert-Birot, during such periods of "frémissement intellectuel et esthétique chacun a son système" ("intellectual and aesthetic activity, each one has his system") (Typescript, Fonds Albert-Birot, p. 4), with very often little difference between each theory. He considers Albert-Birot's concept of "nunisme," worked out theoretically in *SIC* particularly with regard to the theater, to be the poet's form of "modernity." As we will be discussing later, this is an early expression of the "modern" for Albert-Birot, a moment and a step toward an individual production.

13. Interview with Pierre Berger, "Les Lettres françaises," 1057 (3 December 1964).

14. Radio Program with Pierre Béarn, "Douze minutes avec un poète," Emission de Pierre Béarn, "Vers juin ou juillet 1950," Typescript, Fonds Albert-Birot, and published in *La Passerelle*, n° 24, hiver '75–'76.

15. "Naissance et vie de *SIC*," p. 49. Also quoted in the preface to *SIC*, Eds. J.-M. Place, p. VI.

16. "Naissance et vie de *SIC*," pp. 48–49. Also quoted in the preface to *SIC*, Eds. J.-M. Place, p. VI.

17. The inclusion, continued and transformed, of a classical cultural heritage into modern expression is a feature that will be essential to Albert-Birot's creativity, as we have indicated in our first chapter. We have here an expression of the apparent paradox of the position of Albert-Birot at this moment—a literary journal proclaiming essentially modern intentions with a title heralding such a program in Latin, conceived by a poet/editor educated in nineteenth-century artistic values with a love of classical and medieval art forms. The belief in the assimilation of what is considered best in an artistic heritage into the new brings Albert-Birot closer to Apollinaire's expression of *l'esprit nouveau* than the aggressive attitudes of futurism or dadaism. Painting moved toward a "new classicism" after the war, as France sought to reconstruct its cultural values. Albert-Birot's is a personal stance apparent throughout his work.

18. Albert-Birot was, of course, conscious of the self-imposed program: "Le oui catégorique latin. C'était aussi tout un programme. Chacune des lettres était l'initiale des mots: sons, idées, couleurs." Interview with Guy Le Clech in *Le Figaro Littéraire*, n° 1061, 18 August 1966. ("The categoric Latin yes. It was also a whole program. Each of the letters was the initial of the words: sounds, ideas, colours.")

19. Radio interview with José Pivin, op. cit., typescript, p. 10.

20. Michel Décaudin, "L'avant-garde autour d'Apollinaire," *Information Littéraire*, n° 3, Paris, 1969. Note the opposing view of Lentengre, which we have indicated in note 4 above.

21. Discussing Derain's woodcuts for Apollinaire's *L'Enchanteur pourrissant*, Pierre Daix indicates the heritage the woodcut brings with it: "Intimement liée à l'invention de l'imprimerie, la gravure sur bois est celle dont le style se marie le plus heureusement à l'aspect d'un feuillet imprimé, mais sa tradition typographique s'est vite perdue pour se confondre en quelque sorte, depuis le XIXᵉ siècle, avec celle de la gravure sur métal" ("Intimately linked to the invention of printing, wood engraving is the thing whose style goes best with the aspect of a printed page, but its typographic tradition was soon lost so as to become confused to a

large extent, since the nineteenth century, with metal engraving.") (Pierre Daix, *Journal du Cubisme*, Editions d'Art Albert Skira, Paris, 1982, p. 62). As for *Les Soirées de Paris*, the directors Apollinaire and Serge Férat would be among the most frequent contributors to *SIC* and indeed influential on Albert-Birot himself. There is some irony in the choice of Gothic lettering to present a magazine concerned with the dissemination of modern art and literature. Although we use the term Gothic lettering here, we are not suggesting more than an attitude to such a heritage.

22. These are Albert-Birot's "Les éclats," n° 28, April 1918, and "Chronique d'éte," n° 30, June 1918; Germaine Albert-Birot's "1er chant des *Mamelles de Tirésias*," n° 33, November 1918.

23. Albert-Birot's own short resumé of his literary activity written in 1932, unpublished (Fonds Albert-Birot). Such bold statements coupled with an artistic isolation are common in Albert-Birot's comments on the period.

24. "Naissance et vie de *SIC*," p. 49.

25. Collected in *La Lune ou le livre des poèmes*. Chapter 3 is an analysis of this collection. ("poem-posters" and "poem-placards")

26. Serge Fauchereau, *La Révolution cubiste*, Denoël, Paris, 1982, p. 172.

27. "Une revue, c'est la naissance et la vie des choses. Un livre, c'est par définition quelque chose de "fini," une revue par contre est toujours en train de se chercher, se créer. En lisant une revue sa conception et sa perception des choses se ressentent. Pourquoi tel ou tel texte est-il là? Il faut lire, voir ces textes à leur place, faire sentir la vie et l'esprit de la revue." (Jean-Michel Place on the nature of the literary journal and of his work of republishing such documents, interviewed by Debra Kelly in *La Chouette*, n° 22, special issue on surrealism, London, July 1989, p. 1). ("A journal is the birth and life of things. A book is by definition something that is "finished." A journal, on the other hand, is always in the process of seeking itself, of creating itself. When you read a journal, its conception and perception of things are felt. Why is such and such a text there? You have to read, see these texts in their place, make the life and the spirit of the journal felt") It is, of course, the very nature of a magazine to grow, turn in new directions, and reflect the present moment.

28. For example, there is the issue devoted to the staging of *Les Mamelles de Tirésias*, n° 18, June 1917, and the special issue dedicated to the memory of the recently deceased Apollinaire, n° 37/38/39, Jan.-Feb. 1919.

29. The contributors who may be termed collaborators by the nature and frequency of their contributions are discussed in our section "Other Voices."

30. *The Times Literary Supplement*, 6 June 1980, pp. 635–40. The article is introduced thus: "We asked a number of writers what they considered to be the role of the literary magazine in their country and how well they felt this role was being fulfilled today." It contains answers from Raymond Williams, George Steiner, Maurice Nadeau, Masolino d'Amico, Irving Howe, John Weightman, Gabriel Josipovici, Robert Pinsky, David Bromwich, Lewis Nkosi, and Michael Rutschky, covering America, Britain, France, Italy, Germany, and Africa. For the original indication of this article, see the Ph.D. thesis on the journal *Adam International* by Vanessa Davies, King's College, London, 1987. This framework is a much more specific one than the more general considerations used earlier for the analysis of source documents.

31. Albert-Birot found the funding for *SIC* in the state benefit he received when declared unfit for service. Intellectually and creatively *SIC* had run its course for the poet/editor in 1919, but more pragmatically the war had ended and

the normal pressures of day-to-day life had resumed. In contrast to the continuing and consistent publication of *SIC* through personal funding, Reverdy's *Nord-Sud* stopped when there was no more outside assistance and indeed had a much shorter existence than that of *SIC*, being paid by Doucet for one year only.

32. Steiner, "The role of the literary magazine". He argues that a literary journal satisfies both a psychological need and a particular type of creativity.

33. This relationship to the material of the created object will be discussed in detail in the following chapter. Albert-Birot followed the printing process of *SIC* very closely and with much interest.

34. Again see Kenneth Silver, *Esprit de Corps*, for a convincing presentation of the ensuing diverse paths of the prewar avant-garde, and the way in which creativity continued at the front although in a very different way from Paris, remaining in fact more radical in the trenches.

35. The indexes of the J.-M. Place edition of *SIC*, to which we have referred throughout, are invaluable for such a survey, facilitating, for example, an assessment in terms of theme or by name (magazines, writers, critics, etc.).

36. Michel Décaudin et E. A. Hubert, "Petit historique d'une appellation: 'cubisme littéraire,'" in "Cubisme et Littérature," special issue of *Europe*, juin-juillet, 1982, p. 10.

37. The term "points de ralliement" ("rallying points") is Décaudin's "Petit historique," p. 9. The reading by Kenneth Silver of this period is again relevant here. He charts, for example, the rise of Jean Cocteau to the forefront of the avant-garde in the void of these years, and especially interesting is the evolution of Picasso from cubism to a new classicism during the period of the war. At various points during these years, artists and writers did indeed rally together—for example with "Art et Liberté," an association of artists for the defense of artistic freedom, whose manifesto was signed by, among others, Matisse, Severini, Albert-Birot, Van Dongen, Rouault, Brancusi, and Lhote (Silver, *Esprit de Corps*, p. 184).

38. For the influence of Severini at this time, see chapter 1 of this study and particularly M-L. Lentengre, "Aux sources de la métamorphose de *SIC*," and her monograph *Pierre Albert-Birot*.

39. See, for example, the work of the critic and writer on Italian futurism, Giovanni Lista, previously alluded to. He places Albert-Birot in what he terms the "second wave" of the avant-garde, and he considers both Albert-Birot's inheritance and his autonomy vis-à-vis the ideas of Marinetti and Severini ("Le Futurisme de Pierre Albert-Birot,"). Lista discusses both Albert-Birot's painting and his theater from the viewpoint of futurist theory, which he considers developing due to his contact with futurism. Lista also stresses the iconography of *SIC* in a futurist perspective, but he is dismissive of what he calls Albert-Birot's *poésie cubiste*, which he terms "ornamentale" and failing to constitute a "véritable solidarité plastique" (p. 42). Lista's analysis of *La Guerre* considers it to be a similar experiment to that of Balla's "peinture conceptiste," and he concludes by adding his own views on Albert-Birot's development. He sees the poet moving away from his avant-garde position from 1918 onward. He draws a parallel between this movement and that of the French position in general with regard to futurism, which he considers to be an essentially Italian movement only, because the French reject its more radical cultural and ideological concepts (p. 49).

40. Severini's exhibition "Première Exposition Futuriste d'Art Plastique de la Guerre et d'autres oeuvres antérieures," previously referred to in connection with its impact on Albert-Birot and his commentary in *SIC* n° 2 (JMP, pp. 14–15),

was certainly the most radical demonstration of prewar artistic techniques set within the context of the war. It shows the avant-garde to be vitally active at the beginning of 1916. His is certainly the most rigorous attempt to examine the war situation in a pictorial language developed in the prewar period. Nonetheless in the following months, Severini also followed the general artistic trend in Paris toward more traditional expression, the "new classicism," in his portrait of his wife and *Motherhood* (1916). See Silver, p. 86, for more precise details on the changes in Severini's life and artistic style.

41. Certainly the Italian futurists themselves seem to consider *SIC* as continuing to diffuse futurist ideas in Paris, as indicated by the letter from Prampolini, which is published together with the designs for the production of Albert-Birot's *Matoum et Tévibar* in Rome. In that letter he details the performance and his own "costumes architectroniques-dynamiques" for the king and queen and the "architecture lumineuse" that he designed. The issue incidentally sees a return to the rhetoric of the posterlike editorial page.

42. Apollinaire also recognized the importance of Marinetti's ideas for his own typographical experimentation and his earlier *poèmes-conversations.* Yet both Apollinaire and Albert-Birot differ from the Italian most notably concerning the position of the self within the creative process. Marinetti advocates the "death of the literary I" and the destruction of syntax, removal of punctuation, "condensed metaphors," "compressed analogues," telegraphic images, and a new orthography that will lead to a total destruction of "meaning" within the text and thereby the destruction of the creative self: "My technical manifesto opposed the obsessive 'I' that up to now the poets have described, sung, analysed and vomited up" ("Destruction of syntax—Imagination without strings—Words-in-Freedom," in Apollonio, *Futurist Manifestos,* pp. 95–106, and quoting from p. 98). As Bergman has noted, in many futurist works, "le moi est absent, le désordre au maximum," P. Bergman, *Modernolatria e Simultaneità,* Coll. Studia Litterarum Upsaliensa, n° 2, Svenska Bokförlaget, Stockholm, 1962, pp. 190–91. In the poetry of Apollinaire and of Albert-Birot, the creative self is never absent, acting as a force of synthesis and therefore closer to the techniques of cubism.

43. As Timothy Mathews has pointed out in his appraisal of futurism with regard to Apollinaire, there is contained in the futurist enterprise a naive attitude toward the relationship between object and language, as they appear to attempt to make signifier and signified coincide: "We need to be suspicious of any project that attempts to equate language with experience rather than to represent the displacement that language exemplifies and fails to encompass" (Mathews, *Reading Apollinaire,* p. 222; see also p. 170 for a discussion concerning this attempt to eradicate the difference between signifier and signified, which in his opinion actually emphasizes the fundamental lack at the center of the sign).

44. Philippe Soupault, *Vingt mille et un jours.* Interview with Serge Fauchereau, Paris Belfond, 1980, p. 16; also mentioned on p. 36.

45. The first issue of the new series (n° 18) reproduces Picasso's *Violon, verre, pipe et ancre* (painted in the spring of 1912) as its frontispiece. On *Les Soirées de Paris* and the visual arts, see Alexandre Pariogolis, "Les constructions cubistes dans *Les Soirées de Paris,*" *Revue de l'Art,* n° 82, Editions du CNRS, 1988, pp. 61–74.

46. Apollinaire's answer to the final question of the interview: "Allons-nous vers un art complexe ou simple?" can only underline the fact that this is a meeting between kindred spirits: "Je vous ai parlé de simplicité tout à l'heure, simplicité d'expression s'entend, pour atteindre à une plus grande perfection. Mais pour ce

qui est de la complexité elle sera en rapport avec la richesse intérieure du poète ou de l'artiste" ("Are we moving toward a complex or simple art form?") ("I spoke to you just now about simplicity, by that I mean the simplicity of expression, to attain a greater perfection. As for complexity, it will be in relation to the internal richness of the poet or artist." (JMP, p. 59 and previously quoted)

47. This event is covered anecdotally in "Naissance et Vie de *SIC*,". A later lecture concerning the play, given in the 1960s, reiterates many of the same points ("A propos du drame surréaliste d'Apollinaire"; see bibliography for details). Albert-Birot's enthusiasm was complete: "Le succès en a été très grand et selon l'esprit nouveau qui s'oppose à ce vieux pessimisme. . . . Les romantiques au visage sinistre avaient beau prendre leur mine des plus mauvais jours, on sentait le rire lyrique de l'auteur emporter leur lamentable sottise comme le vent emporte une feuille morte dans son tourbillon vainqueur" (JMP, p. 138). ("Its success was very great and in accordance with the *esprit nouveau* that is in opposition to that old pessimism. . . . It was no use the Romantics with their sinister faces wearing their worst expressions, the author's lyrical laughter carried away their lamentable stupidity as the wind carries off a dead leaf in its conquering whirlwind.") See *SIC* nᵒ 19–20, juillet-août 1917, JMP, pp. 14–152 for extracts from the press concerning the play and attacks on *SIC* from the conservative establishment:

> Au moment où la presse d'opinion manque de papier, où les journaux indépendants se voient menacés de disparaître, où la Pensée libre est traquée, on voit imprimée, luxueusement, avec des caractères neufs et élégants, une revue qui s'appelle *SIC* et où, pantins déliquescents du cubisme intégral, des clowns de la plume comme Albert-Birot et Jean Cocteau saccagent misérablement le papier accordé avec tant de parcimonie aux écrivains qui ont l'orgeuil de combattre pour une idée. Que les artistes me pardonnent, que le lecteur m'excuse, trois mots surgissent en guise de point final sous ma plume—et je les lance à la face de ces bateleurs: Ah! les cochons! (Léo Poldès, *La Grimace*, 7 juillet, 1917; JMP, pp. 151–52).

> ("At a time when the critical press is short of paper, when the independent newspapers see themselves threatened with disappearence, when free Thought is hunted down, we see being printed, luxuriously, with new, elegant characters, a journal that is called *SIC* and in which the decaying puppets of integral cubism, clowns of the pen like Albert-Birot and Jean Cocteau, miserably wreck the paper given with such parsimony to writers who have the pride to battle for an idea. May the artists excuse me, may the reader excuse me, three words spring from my pen by way of a final full stop—and I throw them in the faces of these buffoons: Ah! The swine!")

SIC is therefore a place of conflict and dissent, a resuscitation of the "Querelle des Anciens et Modernes" raging around *Les Mamelles*, echoing the first night of *Hernani*. It clearly enjoys its notoriety, publishing the attacks as a further justification of its activities.

48. Max Jacob: "Perigal-Nohor"; Jean Cocteau: "Zèbre"; Pierre Reverdy: "Mao-Tcha"; and Pierre Albert-Birot: "Poème en rond."

49. Often associated also with with "cubisme littéraire," a label he rejected in favor of his own term "poésie plastique," Reverdy's work with the visual in poetry uses typographical disruption but creates its effect with the eye and mind of the reader/spectator by the use of space on the page. See, for example, Serge Fauchereau, *La Révolution cubiste*, pp. 180–81, for an analysis of two versions of the poem "Espace." The "transposition" of cubist techniques into poetic creation led predictably enough to the application of the terms *cubisme littéraire* or *poésie cubiste* to the work of Apollinaire, Reverdy, Max Jacob, and Albert-Birot

(see M. Décaudin et E. A. Hubert, "Petit historique"). The label was refuted by the poets, especially vehemently by Reverdy, and accepted only by Max Jacob with reference to the prose poem: "Théorie lapidaire: alors que toutes les proses en poème renoncent à être pour plaire, le poème en prose renonce à plaire, pour être. C'est quelque chose comme un tableau cubiste" (quoted by Décaudin and Hubert, "Petit historique", p. 14). ("A succinct theory: while all prose in poetic form renounces merely being to please, the poem in prose renounces pleasing in order to be. It is something like a cubist painting.") Reverdy's refusal of the term is published in *Nord-Sud*, n° 10, December 1917, and Albert-Birot criticizes Lefèvre's use of the term *"cubisme littéraire"* in *SIC*, n° 25, January 1918: "On reste quasi muet en présence d'une aussi total incompréhension" (JMP, p. 191). ("We remain almost dumb in the face of such total incomprehension.")

50. The indexes of the facsimile edition provide a very useful indication of the proliferation of literary and artistic journals of the period, serving both the avant-garde and the establishment (JMP, unpaginated, "Index des Revues Citées"). Albert-Birot's "Etc" gives indications as to the characters of each of these.

51. *L'Imperméable* is an experimental prose piece: "Les coupes et décalages suivent tous les mouvements de la pensée et de la voix. Le récit se morcelle en un jeu de notations aux arêtes trop dures, trop nettes pour se fondre en un flou impressioniste; chaque ligne, chaque plan reste net, prenant appui sur l'ensemble avec justesse. Regardez la page, lisez-la: quel équivalent plus précis peut-on imaginer à un tableau "synthétique" de Braque ou de Picasso. Reverdy traite un récit avec la même poétique qu'un poème" (Fauchereau, *La Révolution cubiste*, p. 177). ("The breaks and gaps follow all the movements of thought and of the voice. The narrative is divided up into a game of notations, the bones of which are too hard, too clear for it to dissolve into an impressionist blur; each line, each plane remains clear, supporting itself with precision on the whole. Look at the page, read it: what more precise equivalent can one imagine to a 'synthetic' painting by Braque or Picasso. Reverdy treats a narrative with the same poetics as a poem.")

52. "Le cubisme n'étant pas un procédé mais une esthétique et même un état d'esprit doit avoir forcément une corrélation avec toutes les manifestations de la pensée contemporaine. On peut inventer isolément une technique, un procédé, on n'invente pas de toutes pièces un état d'esprit" (Juan Gris in "Chez les cubistes," *Bulletin de la vie artistique,* n° 6, January 1925, collected in "Ecrits de Juan Gris," Juan Gris, D. H. Kahnweiler, Gallimard, 1946, p. 203, and quoted by Fauchereau, *La Révolution cubiste,* pp. 23–24). ("Cubism was not a procedure but an aesthetics, and even a state of mind must necessarily have a correlation with all the manifestations of contemporary thought. You can invent a technique, a procedure in isolation, but you cannot invent a whole state of mind.")

53. Although he clearly welcomed their contributions, Albert-Birot takes up a position with regard to these movements that would be the attitude of a lifetime: "à travers un demi-siècle au cours duquel se succèdent, du surréalisme au nouveau roman, des mouvements et des recherches auxquelles Albert-Birot n'est pas personnellement mêlé et par lesquels, pourtant, il ne se laissera pas dépasser" (René Lacôte, "Chroniques de Poésie," *Les Lettres Françaises,* n° 1051, 29 octobre–4 novembre, 1984). ("Through half a century in the course of which the new novel succeeded surrealism, movements and research with which Albert-Birot personally did not involve himself and by which, nonetheless, he did not allow himself to be overtaken.")

54. Just how close this is to Albert-Birot's exploration of language and poetic creation will become startlingly apparent in chapter 3.

55. Tzara's poems published in *SIC* are testimony to the renewed vigor in the visual impact and the format of Tzara's work, which appeared radical to young poets of the time:

> Les poèmes de Tzara publiés par *Nord-Sud* et *SIC* nous étonnaient. Un autre ton que ceux des poètes de cette époque, influencés par Guillaume Apollinaire, Pierre Reverdy et Blaise Cendrars. . . . Bouleversement. Ces poèmes nous libéraient de nos influences. Jamais ceux que nous admirions n'auraient osé bousculer la syntaxe et le vocabulaire comme Tzara le proposait avec autorité et sans regrets.
>
> (Philippe Soupault, *Vingt mille et un jours*, p. 49).

> ("Tzara's poems published by *Nord-Sud* and *SIC* astonished us. They had a different tone from those of the poets of the time, influenced by Guillaume Apollinaire, Pierre Reverdy, and Blaise Cendrars. . . . We were totally bowled over. These poems freed us from our influences. Those whom we admired would never have dared to upset the syntax and the vocabulary as Tzara was proposing with authority and with no regrets.")

56. Pierre Albert-Birot, letter to Tzara, published in Michel Sanouillet, *Dada à Paris* (Paris: Pauvert, 1965). It is interesting to note that Apollinaire, a naturalized Frenchman, would not contribute to Dada, which was international and challenging to France's cultural chauvinism during this period (letter of 6 February 1918 to Tzara, Sanouillet, *Dada à Paris*, p. 98).

57. Pierre Albert-Birot, interview with Fernand Pouey, "Quand ils avaient le diable au corps" (Une série d'entretiens avec Pierre Albert-Birot, recueillis par Fernand Pouey, n⁰s I–IX, *Arts-Spectacles*, Paris, 5 June to 2 August, 1952). Although Albert-Birot seems to have misunderstood the positive attitude of Dada that lay behind its provocations in the face of the absurdity of the war, it is undoubtedly true that the two projects are widely divergent. On the aims of Dada, see, for example, Willy Verkauf, "Dada—Cause and Effect," and Marcel Janco, "Creative Dada," in *Dada Monograph of a Movement*, ed. Willy Verkauf, New York: St. Martin's Press; and London: Academy Editions, 1975. The prevalent metaphor of construction in postwar France is an important one.

58. Aragon is not the only creative and critical collaborator to *SIC*. Another good example is the Catalan poet J. Perez-Jorba, also editor of the Franco-Catalan review *L'Instant*. His collaboration begins in February 1918, n° 26, and he is both creatively and intellectually a source of artistic and "political" support for Albert-Birot during the years of *SIC*. As with *Dada*, Albert-Birot acknowledges Perez-Jorba's own magazine:

> *L'Instant* revue franco-catalane fondée et dirigée par le poète Perez-Jorba compte déjà plusieurs numéros et il ne m'a pas été donné de saluer ici sympathiquement cette publication intelligente. Malgré le manque de place je ne veux pas y faillir aujourd'hui. C'est une oeuvre qui s'annonce sérieuse consciencieuse et compréhensive et c'est bien là l'oeuvre que pour ma part j'attendais du noble homme qu'est Perez-Jorba.
>
> (*SIC* n° 31, October 1918)

> ("*L'Instant*, a Franco-Catalan journal founded and run by the poet Perez-Jorba, can already count several issues, and I haven't yet had a chance to greet here in a friendly way this intelligent publication. Despite the lack of space I don't wish to fail in this today. It's a work that announces itself as serious, conscientious, and comprehensive, and it's exactly the work that I personally expected from the noble Perez-Jorba.")

He frequently refers to and praises *L'Instant* in his rubric "Etc. . .," although he does call for more intransigence with regard to some of the contributors. On

SIC's "thermomètre littéraire," *L'Instant* figures at n° 7 on a scale between 0 and 11, an equal rating with *La Raccolta, Noi, Valori Plastici* n° 1, and *J'ai tué* (Cendrars). What should be particularly noted here is that in those issues where Perez-Jorba's reviews appear (for example, n° 40/41 and 42/43), *SIC*'s "Etc. . ." column, where Albert-Birot usually exercises his own critical voice, is either small or nonexistent. As with Aragon, there is evidence in these later issues of Albert-Birot's entrusting the critical faculties of *SIC* to other minds.

59. A breakdown looks like this:

SIC issue n°	31	No "Etc . . .," although Perez-Jorba's *L'Instant* is referred to.
	32	No "Etc . . . ." No criticism by Aragon.
	33	No "Etc . . . ."
	34	No "Etc . . . ."
	35	No "Etc . . . ."
	36	"Etc . . ." moved from its usual place at the end of *SIC* and containing only acknowledgments of other artistic journals.
	40/41	"Etc . . ." in usual place. Journals only.
	42/43	No "Etc . . . ."
	44	Journals only.
	45/46	No "Etc . . . ."
	47/48	Journals and books reviewed.
	49/50	Very long "Etc. . . ."
	51/52	No "Etc . . . ."
	53/54	No "Etc . . . ." Final issue.

60. These contributions by Aragon make the text published in *L'Infini*, n° 31, automne 1990, pp. 124–28 (extract from an unpublished manuscript to be published with preface and notes by Marc Dachy) all the more surprising and incongruous. Aragon's attack on Albert-Birot is savage and malicious, undermining and ridiculing his position in the avant-garde and disparaging of the status of *SIC*. The facts point to a rather different attitude at the time. His contributions are critical, opinionated pieces, and he clearly considered *SIC* to be a platform from which to make his voice heard. Albert-Birot found himself under attack from poets around Aragon during the time of *SIC*'s publication—most notoriously by Theodore Fraenckel, who sent a poem signed Jean Cocteau, published in issue n° 17, May 1917, "Restaurant de nuit" (JMP, p. 135). The first letters of each line spell out "PAUVRES BIROTS," an attack to which Albert-Birot subsequently replied in *SIC* n° 18, June 1917. Jacques Vaché refers to the incident in a letter to Fraenckel dated "Lundi 4 juin": "Est-ce que tous les collabos de *SIC* mystifient ensemble M. Le Birot?" (collected in *Jacques Vaché. Soixante-dix-neuf Lettres de Guerre*, assembled and presented by Georges Sebbag [Paris: J.-M. Place, 1989, no pagination], letter 41).

61. In a 1974 article, "Pierre Albert-Birot, un surréaliste hors du château," Germana Orlandi begins to establish Albert-Birot's position with regard to the surrealist movement that followed him. Orlandi particularly comments on remarks made by Albert-Birot in a letter, which she reproduces in full, in response to

questions asked him by a researcher proposing a study on the origins of surrealism (letter to Leo Tixier). She also comments on an article by Albert-Birot entitled "Mon bouquet au surréalisme," which appeared in Ivan Goll's *Surréalisme*, one issue only, October 1924. The letter is especially revelatory, with Albert-Birot giving the "Freudianism" and subconscious elements of surrealism short shrift. Several researchers have quoted from this letter, and we are loath to cite Albert-Birot extensively. We have previously indicated his statement of his attitude to the working of the poet's conscious and subconscious mind, and consequently to the *imaginaire*, and to the poet the idea of *a sur-conscient* (as opposed to *l'inconnu sous-conscient*) extended to one of the poetic recreation of a *sur-réalité*.

Note also Marie-Louise Lentengre's "Grabinoulor ou le triomphe de l'imaginaire," for its important point concerning the *revolt* of surrealism and its giving value to negation, compared with the "valeurs productives et affirmatives de l'art," which is the basis of Albert-Birot's "nunisme" (p. 184). This is equally true of the poet's stance with regard to Dada, of course.

62. Claude Abastado, "Jeux et visée d'un texte parodique," *Grabinoulor*," F, 2–3, pp. 77–78.

63. Pierre Albert-Birot, interview with Pierre Béarn, op. cit., typescript, p. 4.

64. P. Albert-Birot, "Mon bouquet au surréalisme,". Compare also the remarks made by him and quoted in the preface by André Lebois to the Gallimard edition of *Poésie 1916–1924:* "Chacun de ceux qui étaient là a fouillé au fond de lui-même pour y découvrir sa vérité. Nous n'avons pas créé une école, mais de la poésie" (p. III). ("Each one of those who were there searched his heart of hearts to discover his truth there. We did not create a school, but poetry.")

65. Pierre Albert-Birot, "Ismisme," *L'Intransigeant*, 6 February 1930.

66. Ibid.

67. Apollonio, *Futurist Manifestos*, pp. 74–88. Extracts from Luigi Russolo, "The Art of Noise," 11 March 1913 (capitalization as in the original). Published as a booklet by Direzione del Movimento Futurista, Milan, 1 July 1913, written to Pratella, "great Futurist composer." Giovanni Lista, "Le Futurisme de Pierre Albert-Birot," comments on futurist music: "Première théorisation d'une 'musique concrète,' le bruitisme de Russolo revendiquait tous les bruits, de la percussion au cri humain, comme manifestation immédiate de la matière qu'il fallait opposer à l'idéalisme artistique et abstrait" (p. 41). ("An initial theorization of a 'concrete music,' Russolo's 'bruitism' claimed that all noise, from percussion to the human cry, was the immediate manifestation of matter which had to be opposed to artistic and abstract idealism.")

68. Russolo, "The Art of Noise." Giovanni Lista sees especially the influence of Marinetti: "C'est encore une idée qui relève d'un certain matérialisme. Car il s'agit d'une attitude absolument anti-wagnérienne, laquelle au lieu d'idéaliser le flux musical, met au contraire en évidence sa source matérielle ainsi que le travail qui produit l'action sonore." "Le futurisme de Pierre Albert-Birot," p. 41. ("It is again an idea that comes from a certain materialism. Because it is a question of an absolutely anti-Wagnerian attitude, which, instead of idealizing the musical flux, shows on the contrary its material source as well as the work that produces the sonorous action.")

69. Compare, for example, Albert-Birot's own "Poèmes à crier et à danser" in *La Lune ou le livre des poèmes*. Giovanni Lista notes this element also: "Mais il y a peut-être une nuance de primitivisme à souligner chez elle, à ce sujet, ainsi que, plus tard, un effort d'adéquation de sa musique bruitiste à la fabulation et à la sensibilité pseudo-enfantine dont relève *Matoum et Tévibar*," "Le futurisme de

Pierre Albert-Birot," p. 41. ("But there is perhaps a nuance of primitivism to emphasize in her work, as well as later an effort to make her 'bruitist' music appropriate for the tale and pseudo-childlike sensibility which gives rise to *Matoum et Tévibar*.")

70. For example, Germaine Albert-Birot: *Les Mamelles de Tirésias*, Choeur de l'Acte II, *SIC* n° 21–22, September/October 1917; "Le 1er chant de *Matoum et Tévibar*," cover of *SIC*, n° 33, November 1918; *Matoum et Tévibar*, Cris, Rythmes, Bruits, *SIC* n° 42–43, March/April 1919.

71. Fauchereau, *La Révolution cubiste*, pp. 124–25, commenting on the music of Les Six: Durey, Poulenc, Tailleferre, Auric, Milhaud, and Dutheil.

72. Extract from an article by M. Luciani in *La Voce*, Florence, in *SIC* n° 17, May 1917.

73. Gauguin had already used the term "musical" to describe his paintings in the 1890s. Kandinsky makes comparisons with music in his *Du Spirituel dans l'Art*. Compare also the *Disques* of Delaunay and the *Fugues chromatiques* of Kupka.

74. The series of six lectures given by Leonard Bernstein at Harvard University in 1973 and grouped together in a book of the same title, *The Unanswered Question* (Cambridge, Mass., 1976), gives a full and fascinating insight into the development of modern music toward what he terms the "delights and dangers of ambiguity" in the twentieth century. He also surveys the interaction between music and poetry from the Romantic Revolution onward and the culmination of the "crisis" of music in such work as that of Stravinsky or Schoenberg.

Grabinoulor reflects on the nature of music in just such a way when listening to a concert created by musicians who refuse to follow the score (Livre V, pp. 159ff.), an episode that we will discuss in our final chapter.

75. In an article (unpublished) dated 13 février 1914, "L'esthétique de la mode," Fonds Albert-Birot, the poet, writes of fashion as the reflection of the mentality "d'un individu, d'une époque, d'un peuple. Il est la manifestation la plus directe de l'état de l'esprit." ("of an individual, of an era, of a people. It is the most direct manifestation of the state of mind.")

And women are artists as they dress themselves: "recherche de couleurs et de formes des recherches d'harmonie." ("research into colors and forms, research into harmony"). An analogy with music also suggests itself here. In the context of the period, we might consider the work of Sonia Delaunay, who worked with material for fashion and furnishings in styles and patterns that reflect and interact with her work on canvas. For a study of fashion and culture, see Roland Barthes, *Système de la Mode* (Paris: Seuil, 1967).

76. The problem of the isolation of the poet from the crowd he should be able to address is a continuing preoccupation for Albert-Birot. His play *Larountala* deals with the noncommunication between the individual and the masses, while "La Légende" deifies the speaker of the poem who becomes the object of worship by the crowd. In a newspaper article for *L'Intransigeant*, 27 May 1925, entitled "Les Jeux, les poètes, la foule," he writes: "Au commencement était le verbe, c'est-à-dire n'est-ce pas, qu'au commencement il y avait accouplement entre le poète et la foule." ("In the beginning was the word, that is to say, is it not, that in the beginning there was the bringing together of the poet and the crowd.") Newspapers, he suggests, are perhaps a method of mass circulation that could help remedy the situation, but Albert-Birot still holds on also to the idea of posters for the streets made by poets for which he originally intended his *poèmes-pancartes* and *poèmes-affiches* collected in *La Lune ou le livre des poèmes*.

Poetry must be a living entity: "Qu'on rende le poète à la foule/Le temps est venu." ("Let the poet be given to the crowd/The time has come.") Such a position between the individual and the collective is interesting, given the initial problem between the Self and the Other we have identified in chapter 1 for Albert-Birot's creative beginnings. After the collective adventure of *SIC*, it would seem that the poet retreats before the idea of artistic collaboration with other creators, but the exchange between individual creator and the "general collective" remains primordial.

77. For example, in the interview with Apollinaire, issue 8/9/10, août-septembre-octobre 1916: "Pensez-vous que la guerre doive modifier les mouvements d'avant-garde et dans quel sens? Pensez-vous que la guerre elle-même puisse inspirer des oeuvres dignes d'intérêt?" (JMP, p. 58). ("Do you think that war should change avant-garde movements and in what way? Do you think that war itself can inspire works worthy of interest?") That this is an artistic preoccupation of Albert-Birot himself we have indicated several times. We have also previously alluded to Kenneth Silver's evaluation of the period where the war instigates a "return to order" among the artists of the period and where the discourse of the left-wing avant-garde and the right-wing establishment do not differ much in tone.

78.

"Pas besoin de cinq lignes, la guerre marquera le vrai départ d'une ère nouvelle."

"Prêchez, prêchez le modernisme pendant que nous sommes dans les tranchées.
Vous faites comme nous votre devoir de Français. Prêchez le modernisme!
C'est tout ce que j'ai à dire." (JMP, p. 24)

("No need for five lines, the war will mark the real departure for a new era.")

("Preach, preach modernism while we are in the trenches.
You are doing your duty as a Frenchman just as we are. Preach modernism!
That's all I have to say.")

Silver indicates these replies at the beginning of his chapter 2, op. cit., p. 28. Gabriel Boisy, who replies in *SIC*, n° 4, was the editor in chief of *Commoedia* (JMP, p. 31): "Elle [la guerre] mesure les hommes entre eux et d'elle surgit une nouvelle noblesse." ("It [war] measures men among themselves and a new nobleness springs from it.")

79. "Prenant à son tour en considération le rapport entre l'art et la guerre, Albert-Birot a synthétisé ses convictions à ce sujet dans une page de *SIC*, à l'apparence anodine, mais néanmoins importante pour comprendre sa pensée. La Guerre y est directement associée aux recherches cubistes et futuristes. Leur produit commun serait pour Albert-Birot la volonté, synonyme d'ordre et de style, qu'il a assimilée à l'art lui-même. En risquant une exégèse on peut affirmer qu'il y a pour Albert-Birot une complémentarité entre la force destructrice de la guerre et les recherches formalistes du cubo-futurisme. L'énergie libérée par la première doit aboutir, grâce à l'esprit d'avant-garde, à une nouvelle composition de toutes les données" (G. Lista "Le futurisme de Pierre Albert-Birot," p. 37). ("Taking in its turn into consideration the relationship between art and war, Albert-Birot synthesized his convictions on this subject in a page of *SIC*, of anodyne appearance, but nonetheless important to understand his thought. The war is directly associated with cubist and futurist research. Their common product would be for Albert-Birot will, synonymous with order and style, which he assimilated to art

itself. At the risk of exegesis, one can affirm that there is for Albert-Birot a complementarity between the destructive force of the war and the formalist research of cubo-futurism. The energy freed by the former must end in, thanks to the avant-garde spirit, a new composition of all the elements.")

As Kenneth Silver points out, this is true not only of Albert-Birot, and he suggests a similar conviction as the reason why the productions of those artists actually at the front continue with "cubist" techniques longer than those of artists remaining in Paris, *Esprit de Corps*, p. 80, on the "nascent aesthetic conservatin home and the thriving pictorial radicalization at the Front."

80. "L'Esprit nouveau et les poètes," November 1917, published in the *Mercure de France*, November 1918 (*Oeuvres Complètes de Guillaume Apollinaire*, vol. 3 ed. Michel Décaudin [Paris: Gallimard, 1966], p. 900). The lecture has been criticized by supporters and enemies of Apollinaire alike. The young poets (the later surrealists particularly) were suspicious and disappointed with the nationalistic tone and treatment of the old concept of the traditional role of the poet as guide and unveiler of "truth." For Albert-Birot, of course, the assimilation of traditional literary values (and indeed the patriotic tone adopted ab initio by *SIC*) into new forms of research validated his own project and quest.

81. This is the form also of the Socratic dialogues, and the influence of classical philosophy on Albert-Birot is obvious in his choice of the representation of master and new disciple in a type of initiatory ritual. In chapter 4 we will explore the dialogism of the poetic text as an aspect of contemporary poetry.

82. The series of "Dialogues nuniques".

Issue n° 5 (May 1916)	"Devant les peintures modernes"
6 (June 1916)	"N'importe ou"
7 (July 1916)	"En marche"
8/9/10 (Aug/Sep/Oct 1916)	"Autour du monde"
11 (Nov 1916)	"Continuent"
14 (Feb 1917)	"Dans une salle chauffée"
16 (April 1917)	"Vos papiers?"
18 (June 1917)	"A la pêche"
21/22 (Sep/Oct 1917)	"Monologue nunique. Conclusion"

83. This problem of temporality, and particularly the expression of "durée" in the work of art, brings Albert-Birot close to Bergson, and necessarily, of course, to Proust, formulated, however, very differently. Bergsonian principles of the many layered dynamism of experience are equally clearly evident in this thinking, influential as he was for the whole of the avant-garde. His theories of change, relativism, and flux made Bergson the most important philosopher of the prewar period, and his notion of the "élan vital" is essential for an understanding not only of Albert-Birot's work but that of the whole period.

Kenneth Silver remarks that such a philosophy of change, chance, and fluctuation was "out of step with wartime ideology" (p. 216) and as such is indicative of the reactions taking place between pre- and postwar aesthetics. That a quotation from Bergson is taken as an epigraph for the complete edition of *Grabinoulor* (Jean-Michel Place, 1991) is especially fitting.

84. According to Cendrars, the poet is concerned with the task of deciphering and reassembling, a process of analysis and of synthesis: "C'est la tâche de déchiffrer (analyse) et puis de rassembler (synthèse) qui est la force élastique qui se

tend à la rencontre de l'univers qui revient au seul poète" (Cendrars, quoted by M. Davies, "La notion de la modernité," p. 28.) ("It is the task of deciphering (analysis) and then of reassembling (synthesis) that is the elastic force which strives to meet the universe and which returns only to the poet.") The analogy with cubist technique is self-evident.

85.

> J'ai dit que je dirais ce que je dis que je dirai
> Mais je n'ai jamais dit ce que j'ai dit que je dirai
> Et je dis toujours autre chose
> ô POEME ARCHITECTURE DE PENSEE
> —Poème XVI, *Trente et un Poèmes de poche* (p. 27)

("I've said that I'd say what I say I will say / But I have never said what I've said that I'll say / And I always say something else / OH POEM ARCHITECTURE OF THOUGHT")

Our final chapter will explore both the construction of *Grabinoulor* and the myths of creation continually reworked by Albert-Birot.

The analogy with architecture is one that other writers have found equally suggestive for the creation of the work of art and particularly for a comparison with forms of "la poésie plastique":

> La page est une image. Elle donne une impression totale, présente un bloc et des strates de noirs et de blancs, une tache de figure et d'intensité plus ou moins heureuses. Cette deuxième 'manière de voir' non plus successive et linéaire et progressive comme la lecture, mais immédiate et simultanée, permet de rapprocher la typographie de l'architecture.

> ("The page is an image. It gives a total impression, presents a block with strata of black and white, the mark of a figure and an intensity that is more or less felicitous. This second 'way of seeing', no longer successive and linear and progressive like reading, but immediate and simultaneous, allows an analogy between typography and architecture.") (Paul Valéry, *Oeuvres*, vol. II [Gallimard: Pléiade, 1960], p. 1247, and quoted by Georges Longrée, *L'expérience idéo-calligrammatique d'Apollinaire* [Paris: Touzot, 1985], p. 263.)

The image of building became a metaphor for French art after the war, emphasizing the reconstruction of a new France and a crucial aspect of Parisian artistic discourse. See, for example, Silver, *Esprit de Corps*, p. 382. He quotes Roger Bissière in "Le Reveil des cubistes" in *L'Opinion*, 15 April, 1916: "Il serait temps de mettre de l'ordre dans tout ce chaos et de bâtir" ("It is high time to put some order into all this chaos and to build"), condemning those who have experimented without constructing and calling on those artists to put these materials together "pour élever une vaste et solide maison" ("to raise a vast, solid house"). Equally the idea of cubism moving from analysis, which fragments and destructs, to synthesis, which unifies and constructs, is in line with postwar artistic theory (pp. 346–47). He also quotes Albert-Birot's same "dialogue nunique."

86. See especially our final chapter on *Grabinoulor*. Note also *La Belle Histoire* and *Les Mémoires d'Adam* (see bibliography for details) for Albert-Birot's creation myths.

87. This is essential to the argumentation of this study. From the attention paid to the visual arts in *SIC*, through the complex structure of *La Guerre*, is born a whole poetic program.

88. For example, see the early *De la Mort à la Vie*, subtitled *essai dramatique* (see bibliography). For all its failings, the dramatic poem shows clearly "un goût aussi pour sortir le texte du livre, le projeter, créer le courant avec un public qui écouterait, regarderait le poème." ("A taste also for taking the text out of the book, projecting it, creating a current with the public who would listen to it and would look at the poem.") Arlette Albert-Birot and Didier Plassard in the notes to *Albert-Birot, Théâtre VII*, Rougerie, as yet unpublished. Typescript, Fonds Albert-Birot, p. 20. These notes are particularly revelatory covering the early ideas on theater, the developments and changes in these, the interest in the use of marionnettes that began in childhood, and the experimental theater group "Le Plateau" set up in 1929. There are a number of academic studies on aspects of Albert-Birot's theater (see bibliography for details), most notably D. Plassard's work on *Larountala*. Poetry and drama are inextricably linked: "Un poème n'est pas tout à fait du théâtre, mais c'est déjà une indication" (*SIC* n° 6, p. 48) ("A poem is not quite theater, but it is already an indication.") Both the circus and the theater are preoccupations also of the artists of the period. In the 1920s particularly, Picasso, Braque, Gris, and Léger designed sets and costumes for theatrical productions (remembering also *Parade*). We have by necessity excluded the theater from the corpus under examination here. It is an essential area for any understanding of Albert-Birot's work as a whole and deserves in itself a full-length study. The works indicated here and in the bibliography provide a good starting point, and this is certainly an area for further exploration. In this insistence on stage production and on the dramatic nature of poetry, Albert-Birot is a precursor of both Artaud and Tardieu.

89. This idea of the *dédoublement* of actors is recurrent in the theater of Albert-Birot, and particularly in *Larountala*. Indeed "doubles" are apparent throughout Albert-Birot's work and are discussed by Marie-Louise Lentengre, *Pierre Albert-Birot*, pp. 213–28, "Le poète et ses doubles."

The adaptation of Robert Pinget's *Monsieur Songe* (Editions de Minuit) for the stage by Anne-Brigitte Kern, directed and staged by Jacques Seiler for "Le Théâtre Aujourd'hui" in Paris, London, and New York, uses the same technique to great dramatic effect to present visually the double-sidedness/contradiction of the "everyday" Monsieur Songe and Monsieur Songe the writer at his desk.

90. Of more impact than these purely theoretical statements are Albert-Birot's dramatic works themselves. *Matoum et Tévibar* appears serialized in *SIC*, and *Larountala*, his most complex and innovative drama, is published by him "Aux Editions SIC." The importance of the staging of *Les Mamelles de Tirésias* is fundamental, and Albert-Birot begins writing his own plays immediately afterward: "La pièce d'Apollinaire fut fondamentale dans l'élaboration dramatique de Albert-Birot" (A. Albert-Birot and D. Plassard, *Théâtre VII*, p. 93) ("Apollinaire's play was fundamental in the dramatic elaboration of Albert-Birot"). It is this theatrical event that crowns *SIC*'s achievements in the eyes of its founder: "Nous sommes ici à peu près au point culminant de *SIC*, la revue entre, est déjà entrée, dans sa période de grande activité. Elle est présente partout, elle organise à chaque instant des séances littéraires. . . . De plus, depuis décembre 1916 se prépare le grand événement, le drame d'Apollinaire" ("Naissance et Vie de *SIC*," pp. 55–56) ("We arrive here at virtually the pinnacle of *SIC*, when the journal enters into, has already entered into, its period of great activity. It is present everywhere, it organizes at every moment literary events. . . . What is more, since December 1916 the great event is being prepared, Apollinaire's drama.")

Note Albert-Birot's insistence on the *action* of *SIC*. It should be remarked that

not all of the avant-garde was as enthusiastic, some publicly dissociating themselves from such "fantaisies" in *Le Pays*, June 1916 (quoted by Silver, *Esprit de
Corps*, pp. 166–67), among them Severini.

91. In 1920 Albert-Birot put together a series of theoretical pieces and scenar-
ios in *Cinéma*. A new edition supplemented with notes and some unpublished
material assembled by Arlette Albert-Birot is due for publication (see
bibliography).

92. In this *SIC* is very much the child of its era. Woodcut illustrations prolifer-
ate in poetry collections—for example, Derain's illustrations for Apollinaire's
L'Enchanteur pourrissant. The poet considered the woodcut the most apt medium
for harmony with the printed text.

93. "La Légende" is published in *Poésie 1916–1924* (Paris: Gallimard, 1967).
This central figure is a statue who speaks of a recurrent theme in Albert-Birot's
poetry: the poet who brings joy and light to the world. Compare *Matoum et
Tévibar*, where the head of Matoum "le vrai poète" is illuminated as he speaks
his poetry:

> Car le fils du Poète
> Est gendre de votre terre
> et dieu de la lumière
>
> (p. 459)

("Because the son of the Poet / is the son-in-law of your earth / and god of light")

94. Albert-Birot, "Naissance et Vie de *SIC*," p. 53.

95. The oil on canvas executed after this sketch belongs to the Tate Gallery
collection (London). The interpenetration of planes is an attempt to capture the
fusion of object and environment as they dynamically interact. It is a basic principle of the futurist aim of representing the velocity of the modern world in poetry
and on canvas. In accordance with this, they developed a concept of dynamic
motion as opposed to a static concept of reality (see, for example, Boccioni's
"Absolute Motion and Relative Motion" and Severini's "The Plastic Analogies
of Dynamism 1913," both included in Apollonio, *Futurist Manifestos*,). Dynamism
for the futurists is a general law of simultaneity and interpenetration of objects,
and theirs is a whirling, spinning universe celebrating the new rhythms imposed
by advancements in science and technology. Such an experience is represented
on canvas by shape and color. In poetry techniques were developed to remove
writing from linearity and successivity by giving dynamic simultaneous expression to the words on the page. The futurist enterprise is to offer a direct transposition of our experience of the dynamism of the world, whether through visual or
verbal language, and it is toward the elaboration of such a language system that
their energies are directed. (See also the *Founding Manifesto of Futurism 1909*
and the *Technical Manifesto 1910*, signed by the painters Boccioni, Carrà, Russolo, Balla and Severini, Apollonio, *Futurist Manifestos*)

96. Pierre Francastel, *L'Image, la vision et l'imagination. De la peinture au
cinéma*, (Paris: Denoël-Gonthier, 1983), p. 237.

97. Severini later saw cinema as the privileged medium for the expression of
movement: "Les peintres ont compris que ce n'était pas le but de la peinture
d'exprimer un corps qui se déplace puisque le cinéma pouvait le faire." (In "L'objet filmique et l'objet plastique," Francastel, *L'Image*, p. 244.) ("The painters
understood that it wasn't the goal of painting to express a body in movement
because cinema could do it.")

98. Georges Longrée develops the argument that the poem is an attempt by

Apollinaire to rid himself of the dissatisfaction of which he is aware when attempting to render cubist research in prose form in his critical writings. See Longrée, *L'Expérience idéogrammatique*, particularly chapter 4, "Le Monument de Rien à Picasso" where the poem is analyzed in some detail (pp. 174–92). He further suggests that it is through such an interaction that Apollinaire finds a more satisfactory way of talking about the aesthetics and effects of cubism.

99. Once again this reveals his position as close to that of Apollinaire, particularly with regard to the complexity of the cubist present moment and its relation to memory and to eternity. For an in-depth discussion, see T. Mathews, *Reading Apollinaire: Theories of Poetic Language* Manchester (Manchester University Press, 1989). The futurists' concern is with the dynamism of the present moment. Cubist research rather fixes that present moment within an eternal moment, and it is toward such an endeavor that Albert-Birot, as poet, will move.

100. "A literary review generally arises out of the need felt by a handful of writers to gather forces around a new idea, some aesthetic concept of which their books are to be an illustration and of which they mean their audience to be the beneficiaries. The review opens up the way to this audience, preparing it, shaping it in advance: this is what the Symbolists did with the *Revue Blanche* and the Surrealists with *La Révolution Surréaliste*" (Maurice Nadeau, contribution to the article "The role of the literary magazine," *The Times Literary Supplement*, p. 637).

"A vital literary magazine needs a point of view, a championing of some cultural or even social cause, not yet won or already lost. It needs some sharply-accented view of 'the situation'—and of course there always is a 'situation'" (Irving Howe, "The role of the literary magazine," p. 637).

101. The term is Pierre Albert-Birot's in *SIC* n° 36, December 1918, on *Couleur du Temps*, drame de Guillaume Apollinaire (JMP, pp. 276–77), where he criticizes *Art et Liberté* for the staging of the play without, of course, the direction of Apollinaire himself: "Non la chose était irréalisable, il fallait tout simplement publier et encore pour cela attention—ce canevas de pièce avec beaucoup d'autres travaux inachevés qu'on trouvera sans doute dans ses papiers; c'est là que les esprits qui en sont dignes eussent été chercher COULEUR DU TEMPS, l'étudier et l'aimer dans la pureté, dans la paix du livre." ("No, the thing was unrealizable, they should have just published it, and even that was a problem—this framework for a play along with many other unfinished works that you could no doubt find in his papers; it's there that the minds which are worthy of it should have looked for COULEUR DU TEMPS, studied it, and loved it in its purity, in the peace of the book.") Albert-Birot had, of course, signed the original manifesto of *Art et Liberté*.

102. Letter to Léo Tixier.

103. Interview with Fernand Pouey.

104. Interview as above.

105. George Steiner, "The role of the literary magazine," p. 639.

106. Interview with Barbara Wright for the BBC, 1966, Typescript, Fonds Albert-Birot, p. 17.

107. Guy Sorman, *Les Vrais Penseurs de notre temps* (Paris: Livre de Poche, 1991), p. 364.

Chapter 3. *La Lune ou le Livre des Poèmes:* The Manual of a Poetics

1. "Le recueil est composite mais il contient vraiment toutes les recherches d'Albert-Birot dans cette période où, littéralement, il est en train de naître à lui-

même" (Arlette Albert-Birot, "Ravengar en cage," *La Chouette*, n° 23, London, 1990, p. 49). ("The collection is a composite, but it truly contains all Albert-Birot's research during this period when he is, literally, being born to himself.") Page references to *La Lune* are to *Poésie 1916–1924*, présentation et notes de Arlette Albert-Birot (Mortemart: Rougerie, 1992). The original edition was printed by the author himself, ed. Jean Budry (Paris, 1924). See also *Poésie 1916–1924* (Paris: Gallimard, 1967), which also includes *Trente et un poèmes de poche, Poèmes quotidiens, La Joie des sept couleurs, La Triloterie*.

In her preface and notes to *La Lune*, Arlette Albert-Birot provides considerable detail on the circumstances in which the poet produced the collection, her aim being to furnish "des informations anecdotiques" rather than a critical appraisal. Nonetheless a "reading between the lines" of the story of the composition of *La Lune* reveals much about Albert-Birot's poetics and his approach to poetic production. The term "anecdotal" is not to be disparaged, for the story contained therein is a compelling and significant one.

2. These early collections are the *Trente et un poèmes de poche, Poèmes quotidiens, La Joie des sept couleurs*, and *La Triloterie*, which opens with "La Légende," a long "poème narratif" that incorporates both Albert-Birot's experimental "poèmes à crier et à danser" and interacts with his research into dramatic productions, simultaneously exploring poetry's original functioning with ritual and myth and celebrating the possibilities and euphoria of poetic communication. As previously stated we are leaving aside for the purposes of this study the consideration of Albert-Birot's dramatic productions that flourished during this period (see bibliography). We would wish to point out, however, that they are an integral ingredient in his creativity and not merely a parallel "accompaniment" to his poetic works. They were all originally published in the Editions SIC, 1917–1918. In chapter 2 we noted Léopold Survage's accompanying drawing for "La Légende," printed in *SIC*.

3. The original edition of the *Trente et un poèmes de poche* published in the Editions SIC was indeed a small (14.5 × 11.5) pocket collection. It is available for consultation in the Fonds Albert-Birot. In several of the poems all the elements of his later production are already present, transposing the elements of the everyday into the universal poetic and often with a very deliberate arrangement on the page.

4. Albert-Birot had found a small printing workshop on the Boulevard Saint-Jacques, and Arlette Albert-Birot provides a vivid account of Albert-Birot's passion: "Albert-Birot suivait passionnément le travail de composition de sa revue, caractères levés, bien sûr, plomb, bois, lettres ornementales, bois gravés complétant une page de proclamation. Devant l'intérêt manifesté par le couple Albert-Birot, Rirachovsky ne tarda pas à leur suggérer de s'équiper' (Preface to *La Lune*, p. 9). ("Albert-Birot passionately followed the work of the composition of his journal, raised characters, of course, lead, wood, ornamental letters, woodcuts finishing off a page of proclamations. Seeing the interest shown by the Albert-Birots, Rirachovsky soon suggested that they should get equipped themselves.")

The printer Rirachovsky lived at 50, Boulevard Saint-Jacques, near to the couple's home on the Rue de la Tombe-Issoire. It should be noted that, contrary to frequent misconceptions, Albert-Birot never printed *SIC* himself.

The acquisition of the press (probably at the beginning of the summer of 1922, according to Arlette Albert-Birot's account) was particularly important for the publication of Albert-Birot's work for the theater: *Le Bondieu* (1922), *Les Femmes pliantes* (1923), and *Image* (1924).

5. See especially the *Autobiographie*, on the printing and publishing of *La Lune*.

6. The poets of the period were aware of the book and the poem as an object in itself, which circulates, exchanges hands, is handled and looked at. Thus they fabricated these objects in a way that our society of mass production has frequently deformed. To read a reproduction of "La Prose du Transsibérien" is not a comparable experience to a contact with the original foldout. A moment of literary history and the project of the whole surrealist aesthetic may be tangibly and visually apprehended in the "lettre-collage" made by Breton for Jacques Vaché (see the reproduction and reconstitution of the circumstances of each section by Georges Sebbag, *L'imprononçable jour de sa mort. Jacques Vaché Janvier 1919*, Paris Editions Jean-Michel Place, 1990).

7. Roger Cardinal, Preface to *Figures of Reality*, (London: Croom Helm Barnes and Noble, 1981), p. 12. His objective in this book is "to isolate some of the typical manifestations of this phantom and to set them out, for clarity's sake, in the form of a series of simplified models."

8. As Arlette Albert-Birot remarks, "Quelques clefs nous permettent de mieux comprendre un ouvrage composite dont l'auteur a pleinement conscience qu'il est, pour lui, dans le secret de son âme, un livre de passage" (Preface to *La Lune*, p. 11). ("A few clues help us to understand better a composite work, which, as the author is fully aware in the bottom of his heart, is a book that is also a rite of passage.")

9. Arlette Albert-Birot, "Ravengar en cage," p. 53: "N'oublions pas que le poète se prénomme Pierre, et qu'il ne lui déplut pas d'être assimilé au Pierrot lunaire." ("Let us not forget that the poet's first name is Pierre, and that he it was not displeasing to him to be compared with moonlike Pierrot.")

10. Ibid., p. 50. The novel was immediately translated into French after its publication in 1901. In it the narrator tells of his journey to the moon through the invention by the scientist Cavor, of "cavorite."

11. Albert-Birot, acceptance speech for the Prix Cazes in 1936, speaking on the need of all of us to change the world and to build one more fitting to our personal spirit. Radio, "Voix de Paris," 25 March 1936 (our emphasis).

12. Arlette Albert-Birot, preface to *La Lune*, p. 11.

13. Robert Caillois, *Art Poétique*, (Paris: Gallimard, 1958), p. 130, quoted by Georges Jean, *La Poésie* (Paris: Seuil, 1966).

14. Georges Mounin, *Poésie et Société* (Paris: P.U.F., 1962), p. 271, p. 86, quoted by Georges Jean, *La Poésie*, p. 51.

15. Of the three "chroniques" that did not appear in *SIC*, "Chronique Sardinique" was written before the publication of the journal and prefigures this type of poetry (used with greater skill in the later poems). "Chronique Jazz" was written after *SIC*'s demise, the theme being, of course, indicative of a new twenties passion. Taking *SIC* as an indication of dating, the poems would therefore appear to be arranged in more or less chronological order. It is not until the 1950s, with his *Autobiographie*, that Albert-Birot will seek once again to establish his position within literary and artistic history.

16. Georges Mounin, Poésie *et Société*, p. 76, quoted by Georges Jean, *La Poésie*, pp. 28–29.

17. And indeed explicitly:

> Or comme j'écris non pas seulement
> Pour ceux de maintenant
> Mais surtout pour ceux de l'avenir
> —"Chronique d'hiver," *La Lune*, p. 44

("Since I am writing not only / For those now / But above all for those in the future")

18. One immediately thinks here of the work of Francis Ponge and George Perec. The novel has used this juxtaposition to great literary and political effect from *The Tin Drum* to Don Delillo's chronicling of America, with countless examples in between.

19. Compare also the end of "Vernissages," questioning *SIC*'s presence:

> Qu'avait-il à faire ici en effet
> Pour vivre heureux vivons cachés
> Et mettant cette maxime en pratique
> Je suis allé promener mes yeux
> Aux Champs-Elysées
> Où les enfants achetaient pour cinq sous
> Les ballons verts les,ballons bleus
> Thérésiasques mamelles
> Et j'ai regardé Guignol
>
>   —*La Lune*, p. 23

> ("What was it doing here in fact
> To live happily live hidden
> And putting this maxim into practice
> I went to walk my eyes
> On the Champs-Elysées
> Where children were buying for five pence
> Green balloons blue balloons
> Theresiasque breasts
> And I watched Punch and Judy")

The ambiguity of Albert-Birot's position is ended. He remains a solitary figure within a collectivity, and the poem is premonitory of the way he would live after *SIC*. Note also the child within himself that the poet nurtures here and in other poems:

> Quel est enfant blond qui court en riant après ces billes de couleurs? *mes billes*
> C'est moi
> Et quel est le poète qui écrit ce poème?
> Cet enfant blond qui courait en riant après ses billes de couleurs
>   —Poem XV. *Trente et un poèmes de poche*, p. 26

> ("Who is that blond child who is laughing while running after those colored marbles?
> *my marbles*
> It's me
> And who is the poet who is writing this poem?
> That blond child who was laughing while running after his colored marbles")

In the child's relationship to play and to language there is the space of creation, as the child escapes from the rules of "reality" and language into his own universe. Compare the importance of childhood experience in the project of Proust, the poetry of Queneau, in particular *Chêne et chien*, at once autobiography, diary, novel in verse form, and the autobiographical quest of Leiris, to take but three obvious examples from a twentieth century obsessed with the nature of selfhood.

20. These "divers poèmes du même genre" of the second part of the section's title were not easily incorporated into a suitable place within the collection, ac-

cording to Arlette Albert-Birot's assessment of the composing of *La Lune*. He certainly wished to include them because they appear in the first draft of the table of contents and had been published in *SIC*. They were not to be confused, however, with the true "poèmes" that would constitute the later section. The first of these "divers poèmes" is the "Epistre à mes dévoués détracteurs." Indeed Albert-Birot had been attacked by the critics belonging to the conservative literary establishment and by the more provocative members of the avant-garde, particularly the future adherents of the surrealist movement (for example, Vaché's disruption of *Les Mamelles de Tirésias* and the poem sent by Fraenkel to *SIC* under Cocteau's name).

21. André Lebois, preface to *La Lune*, p. VII.

22. Arlette Albert-Birot, notes to *La Lune*, p. 11.

23. Arlette Albert-Birot, preface to *La Lune*, p. 13. The "apprenticeship" of parody again offers a parallel with Proust in *Pastiches et Mélanges*.

24. See particularly the details and the discussion offered by Georges Longrée in his book on Apollinaire's "calligrammes": *L'Expérience idéo-calligrammatique d'Apollinaire*, chapter 2, pp. 92–100 in particular. Longrée discusses the idea of a universal language, which pervaded the last quarter of the nineteenth century, both as a utopian ideal inspired by political, commercial, and social needs, and in the light of a precedent for visual poetry because several of the proposed systems used symbols instead of phonic signifiers.

25. Arlette Albert-Birot, preface to *La Lune*, pp. 13–14.

26. Georges Jean, *La Poésie*, pp. 49–50.

27. See the preface to the collection by Arlette Albert-Birot for more information on this.

28. In several radio programs, for instance, the participants attempt to read them aloud while Albert-Birot corrects them. In the interview with "Jeunesses Poétiques" (Fonds Albert-Birot), the poet enthusiastically explains his intentions to the two young interviewers. See bibliography for details of radio and other interviews.

29. Albert-Birot, interview with José Pivin, p. 16. The term "mots collés" also suggests the technique of "papiers collés," again one that belongs to the visual arts.

30. Albert-Birot, quoted by Jacques Vallet in a talk given at the Collège Philosophique, "Hommage à Pierre Albert-Birot," 15 December 1965.

31. "Derrière la fenêtre" montre qu'il met à profit la lecture des manifestes marinettiens. Par rapport au poème 'La Kouan'inn bleue' . . . on constate le passage à la thématique urbaine prônée par le futurisme et à la recherche d'une vision multipliée qui impose la suppression de la ponctuation et l'association analogique directe." Giovanni Lista, "Le Futurisme de Pierre Albert-Birot," p. 32. ("'Derrière la fenêtre'" shows that he knows how to put to good use his reading of Marinetti's manifestos. In comparison with the poem 'La Kouan'inn bleue', . . . one notices the passage to the thematics of the city advocated by futurism and to the research on multiple vision that imposes the suppression of punctuation and direct analogous association.")

32. Blaise Cendrars, "Contrastes," *Du monde entier au coeur du monde* (Paris: Denoël, 1957), p. 84; Guillaume Apollinaire, "Les Fenêtres" in *Calligrammes*; Robert Delaunay, *Fenêtres* series, 1912–14.

33. In the interview with José Pivin, p. 16, Albert-Birot insists that the poem should be seen and read out loud together.

34. The poems in *La Lune* that use this technique are:

"Jeunesse," p. 312 (*SIC* n° 5, May 1916)
"Un homme qui passe," p. 313 (appeared in *SIC* n° 6, June 1916 as "Un homme qui pense")
"Jardins publics," p. 314 (*SIC* n° 11, November 1916)
"Crayon bleu," p. 315 (*Procellaria* n° 4, summer 1917; *Dada* n° 3, December 1918)
"Rasoir mécanique," (*Dada* n° 2, December 1917)
"Le Raté," (*SIC* n° 8/9/10)
"Balalaïka," (*SIC* n° 16, April 1917)
"Lundi" (*SIC* n° 24, December 1917, as a "poème-imagé"; *NOI* n° 5/6/7, January 1917, not "imagé" as in *La Lune*)

In the last two, the technique is used to a much lesser extent and after this is no longer used.

35. For example, Delaunay's various *Formes circulaires* and *Contrastes simultanés*. Compare also the "courserotativeenmusiquedeschevauxdebois" ("rotatingraceinmusicwoodenhorses") with *Manège à cochons*, 1922.

36. Compare Aragon on the importance of the "collage" in twentieth-century art forms: "Nous ne vivons pas dans un monde abstrait. Il y a des problèmes qui ne s'abordent que par le détail. Les collages sont un détail de première grandeur" (*Les Collages* (Paris: Hermann, 1965), p. 22; quoted also by F. Van Rossum-Guyon in *Vitalité et Contradictions de L'Avant-Garde* (Paris: Librairie José Corti, 1988), p. 85. ("We do not live in an abstract world. There are problems that can be tackled only by detail. Collages are a detail of the highest order.")

37. "Le Raté" in *SIC* 8/9/10 is the first of this type published there.

38. The status of the spoken word is a constant in Albert-Birot's work, his poetry, and his dramatic production. In *Grabinoulor* it is dialogue that frequently moves the narrative along, as Grabi is addressed by various interlocutors. This use of dialogue in the nonpunctuated text again demands active participation by the reader, because the question of to whom the words should be attributed is frequently ambiguous. Compare also the "dialogues nuniques" of *SIC* and the dialogue with the self in the *Poèmes à l'Autre Moi* and *Moi à Moi* published with the *Autobiographie*.

39. Interview with José Pivin, p. 27. In the manuscript, however, no distinction is made between the two voices, according to Arlette Albert-Birot's notes to *La Lune*, This concept of "simultaneous voices" is used by Julio Cortázar, for example, in the *Livre de Manuel*, translated by Laure Guille-Bataillon (Paris: Gallimard, 1974; original title: *Libro de Manuel*). Within a prose text composed in several parts of an assemblage of newspaper articles, advertisements, poems, etc., a section uses a "second voice" inserted between the lines of the text in small typeface (pp. 131–37). Cortázar was certainly familiar with the work of the surrealists.

40. As indicated in the notes composed by A. Albert-Birot for *La Lune*.

41. Albert-Birot indicates Lettrism in his lecture "Au bras de la poésie," 1964. Note especially the interest and appreciation of Albert-Birot's work by Henri Chopin for his own work on "la poésie sonore," and in his articles (see bibliography).

42. Interview with Jeunesses Poétiques, p. 6.

43. Compare the poets around Hugo Ball: "Ball and his friends had hit upon a crucial discovery, namely that the more a poet may retreat from conventional forms of communication, the more he may unleash the power of words to address our unconscious being" (Robert Cardinal, *Figures of Reality*, pp. 99–100).

44. Interview with Jeunesses Poétiques, p. 7.

45. Giovanni Lista, "Le Futurisme de Pierre Albert-Birot," p. 41.

46. Ibid., p. 41.

47. For Albert-Birot, however, the poem was unambiguously "primitive" rather than "modern": "Il m'est venu à l'idée de faire des recherches vers ce qu'on pouvait appeler une poésie pure, ou une poésie, comment dirai-je, qui serait pure du fait de son primitivisme, du fait de sa simplicité, et en somme je suis revenu à l'homme des cavernes. J'ai pensé que l'homme, à son début, le paléolithique, n'est-ce pas, vraiment l'homme des cavernes, dans toute l'acception du mot, sentait déjà, bien entendu, il avait des sensations, des sentiments, il éprouvait de la joie, de la peine, etc." Interview with Jeunesses Poétiques, p. 6. ("I had the idea of carrying out some research toward what could be called a pure poetry, or a poetry, how shall I put it, which would be pure because of its primitivism, because of its simplicity, and all in all I returned to the cave man. I thought that man, originally, paleolithic man, truly the cave man, in every sense of the word, already felt, of course, he experienced sensations, feelings, he felt joy, grief, etc.")

48. See, for example, Henri Béhar, p. 50, on Ball's "langage dépouillé de son pouvoir de signifier et dont toute la puissance est dans le rythme, intonation ou le cri. . . . En termes jakobsiens on dira que la fonction de communication a laissé le pas aux fonctions phatiques, connatives, émotives, métalinguistiques du langage." ("language stripped of its power of meaning and whose power is in the rhythm, the intonation, or the cry. . . . In Jakobson's terminology one would say that the communicative function ceded its place to the phatic, connotative, emotive, metalinguistic functions of language.")

49. Compare the "Poète-Inconnu" in *Grabinoulor* III, 8, who considers whether it is possible to create a new poetic language composed solely of syllabic variations.

The quest for immortality is one of the dynamics of the narrative, as we shall discover in chapter 5.

50. Roland Barthes, *Essais Critiques IV, Le Bruissement de la langue*, (Paris: Seuil, 1984), pp. 93–94.

51. Ibid., p. 94.

52. Albert-Birot in "A propos du drame surréaliste d'Apollinaire." See bibliography for the lectures and talks given by Albert-Birot.

53. Barthes, *Essais Critiques*, pp. 94–95.

54. See especially "La Légende." This long poem closes *SIC* and is to some extent Albert-Birot's final statement here on his avant-garde activity. As Barthes goes on to indicate, this exploration of language toward such a Utopia continues to be a mark of, for example, the work of Philippe Sollers. The reference is doubly significant, given Sollers's nonuse of punctuation in a text such as *Paradis*, whose initial impact of a dense narrative block is the same as that of *Grabinoulor*.

55. Roland Barthes, *Essais Critiques*, p. 97. In this comparison with Barthes, it is worth remembering that he also was a painter, and indeed a musician.

56. In this perspective, note also *La Joie des sept couleurs*, not analyzed in depth here, where the poet celebrates nature and modern life with the same breath. The poem is significant here, conceived concurrently with some of the poems of *La Lune* and immediately predating *Grabinoulor*. The poem works both visually (printed in capitals throughout and interspersed with the dense "blocks" of poetry we have previously alluded to) and vocally. The voice and the eye call the body into the reception of the poem. The sign on the page is not a "lettre morte" but a sign of life.

57. We also begin to see here how the poetics reveal to us what we grasped intuitively at first, that Albert-Birot must move toward a more intense exploration

of his own subjectivity, his individual identity, after the collective adventure of the avant-garde. As his work moves inexorably to the work of the *Poèmes à l'Autre Moi*, so must our own study. His poetics in movement, and poetics of movement, is the journey in the creation of a creativity.

58. In the work of Albert-Birot it is not only poetry that must live and breathe: "Je vous ferai entendre l'enregistrement que j'ai fait dernièrement d'un chapitre de *Grabinoulor* dont quelques personnes ont entendu parler. J'ai fait cette lecture dans le rythme même que j'entendais en l'écrivant" (Albert-Birot, "A propos du drame surréaliste d'Apollinaire,"). ("I will let you hear the recording I made recently of a chapter of *Grabinoulor,* which a few people have heard about. I did this reading in the same rhythm I heard as I wrote it.") This is actually crossed out on his manuscript for the reading but remains a valuable indication of how *Grabinoulor* is literally inspired. The effect of hearing *Grabinoulor* read out loud by Jean Follain at the "Dîners Grabinoulor" is described in its physical sensation by Marcelle Janet: "Ce soir nous boirons la poésie en cent et mille gouttes, et en fleuve, lorsque la voix de Jean Follain soulèvera d'un souffle les faits et dits heroïques de Grabinoulor" (*La Barbacane*, 7, p. 63), a memory of hearing Jean Follain read the text in November 1967. ("This evening we'll drink poetry in a hundred thousand drops, and in floods, when the voice of Jean Follain breathes life into the heroic deeds and words of Grabinoulor.") Compare also Marie-Jeanne Durry, *La Barbacane*, p. 54: "La Poésie était sa respiration." Marcelle Janet goes on to communicate the breath and rhythm of the narration:

Il conte sur le rhythme oral de la narration, usant de toutes les libertés et désinvoltures d'une phrase exhalée, puis suspendue; posée un instant sur deux ou trois syllabes, relancée à loisir, battant à peine la mesure sur un complet rapide, attrapant au vol une assonance en écho. Phrase respirante qui soumet le souffle aux humeurs et couleurs du récit. Conter vif sans se presser, conter bref avec tous les détours de l'école buissonnière; art difficile, allure naturelle de Pierre Albert-Birot. (*La Barbacane*, 7, pp. 64–65)

("He tells the story with the oral rhythm of narration, using all the freedom and the casualness of a sentence uttered and then left hanging, stopped for a moment on two or three syllables, then leisurely started again, scarcely keeping time on a rapid sentence, catching in full flight an echoed assonance. A breathing sentence that puts the breath in the service of the humor and colors of the tale. Telling a story without rushing, cutting a long story short with all the tricks of the truant. A difficult art, and the natural pace of Pierre Albert-Birot.")

59. W. J. Ong, *Orality and Literacy: The Technologising of the Word* (London: Methuen, New Accents Series, 1982), p. 32.

60. Ibid., p. 33. Ong refers the reader to his own work *Interfaces of the Word* (Ithaca and London: Cornell University Press, 1977), pp. 230–71.

61. Ibid., p. 75. Ong's book traces the development of literature from its origins in an oral-based culture and assesses the changes due to the printing of the word and the implications for human communication.

62. Again Ong's observations are richly suggestive:

For God is thought of always as "speaking" to human beings, not as writing to them. . . . The spoken word is always an event, a movement in time, completely lacking in the thing-like repose of the written or printed word. In Trinitarian theology, the Second Person of the Godhead is the Word, and the human analogue for the Word here is not the human written word, but the human spoken word. God the Father "speaks" his Son: he does not inscribe him. Jesus, the Word of God, left nothing in writing, though he could read and write (Luke 4: 16). "Faith comes through hearing," we read in the Letter to the Rom (10: 17). "The letter kills, the spirit gives life" (2 Cor. 3: 6).

(Ong, p. 75, section entitled "Orality, Community and the Sacral"). The Trinity returns again and again in the *Poèmes à l'Autre Moi* and in *Grabinoulor*.

63. In this recuperation of the spoken text, Albert-Birot also calls upon the heritage of the medieval literature with which he was so familiar, the originally oral nature of "texts" that we now perceive as written having been studied by medievalists such as Paul Zumthor. Albert-Birot is therefore inserting his work also into his own literary heritage and reminding the reader not only of the origins of humanity and the status of the word, but also of the origins of our literature. See Paul Zumthor, *La lettre et la voix: de la "littérature" médiévale* (Paris: Seuil, 1987).

64. See Yves Delègue, "La Littérature ventriloque" in *Poétique* (Paris: Seuil, November 1987), p. 482. He suggests that the "texte-voix" is such a "texte-limite": "situé à la limite du lisible et de l'intelligible, comme s'il s'agissait de recueillir l'audible pur." From a colloquium on "La Voix," Strasbourg, 14/15 March 1987. ("situated at the limit of the legible and the intelligible, as if it was a case of capturing the audible in its pure state.")

65. "When I hear I gather sound simultaneously from every direction at once, I am at the center of my auditory world, which envelops me, establishing me at a kind of core of sensation and existence" (Ong, *Orality and Literacy*, p. 72).

66. Ong, *Orality and Literacy*, p. 73. Compare this to Apollinaire's "Lettre-Océan" where the poet is likened to the Eiffel Tower, receiving and emitting sound waves. The "myth" of the Eiffel Tower is, of course, a potent symbol of modernity for the poets and painters of the period, which again changes perception of the space of the world.

67. Ong, *Orality and Literacy*, pp. 31–32: "There is no way to stop sound and hold sound. If I stop sound I have nothing—only silence, no sound at all."

68. For example, the final poem of the *Poèmes à l'Autre Moi*, which we will consider in more detail in the following chapter:

> Tout moi poème
> Mais vient-il jusqu'aux lèvres parlantes
> Qui ne l'ont jamais vu
> Ont-elles forme pour lui
> Ou lèvres hélas lui font corps
> Lèvres font vie de vie
> Mais plus loin lèvres tuent

> ("All myself poem
> But is framed by eloquent lips
> That have never laid eye on him
> No they assume a shape for him
> Or do lips alas form one body with him
> Lips create life from life
> But further on lips can kill")

69. "Print encourages a sense of closure, a sense that what is found in a text has been finalized, has reached a state of completion. This sense affects literary creations, and it affects analytic, philosophical, or scientific work" (Ong, *Orality and Literacy*, p. 132).

70. See *L'écriture: théories et descriptions* (Brussels: De Boeck Universitaire,

Collection Prisme, 1985), by Jacques Anis with J.-L. Chiss and Ch. Puech, for a consideration of handwritten, printed, and computer-screen texts.

71. Critical opinion on the validity of such a separation is varied and conflicting: "Je poserai donc que la typographie n'est pas isolable, qu'elle participe de, et réalise, chaque fois comme la syntaxe, le lexique, ou l'information . . . un ensemble théorique-pratique qui accomplit à la fois un statut du langage et un effet de sens" (Henri Meschonnic, *Critique du Rhythme* [Paris: Verdier, 1982], p. 304). ("I will posit, therefore, that typography cannot be isolated and that it is part of and realizes, just like syntax, vocabulary, or information . . . a theoretical-practical whole that simultaneously fulfills a language status and an effect of meaning.")

For critics such as Laparcherie, Bassy, and Goldenstein who have worked on the "calligrammes" of Apollinaire, it is possible and desirable to isolate the "scriptuaire" and the "phonique" in poetry, which explicitly privileges its visual impact. In a recent work by theoreticians of linguistics (J. Anis, *L'Ecriturè*), just such an autonomous status is sought for the written text (see particularly their "Avant-propos," p. 5, and the section "Le graphématique autonome"). Here they include all written texts, not just those which exhibit to an intense degree their visual aspect as in "poésie plastique" and concrete poetry: "L'espace graphique manifeste la structuration du texte, il rend visibles les unités textuelles: vers, strophes, parties, titres, il fournit des lieux aux effets de sens" (p. 205). ("The graphic space manifests the structuring of the text, it makes the textual units visible: lines, stanzas, parts, titles, it provides the support for the effects of meaning.") For these theorists graphic space is validated as an "object in itself" to be explored, and for them such a theory as Lyotard's on figurality *(Discours, Figures)* is to be questioned because it prevents us from looking at graphic space in its own right (pp. 30–31). These arguments are situated within the speculations of Derrida on the privileging of the voice over the written in the Western philosophical tradition (e.g., in *De la grammatologie*).

72. See particularly A.-M. Bassy, "Forme littéraire et forme graphique: les schématogrammes d'Apollinaire," *Scolies*, Cahiers de recherche de l'ENS, III, IV, 1973–1974), pp. 161–207; J.-P. Goldenstein, "Analyse de l'article de A.-M. Bassy," *Revue des Lettres Modernes* (Guillaume Apollinaire 13), n° 450–455 (1976), pp. 173–82; *Que Vlo-ve?*, Bulletin de l'Association des Amis de Guillaume Apollinaire, Actes du Colloque de Stavelot (1977), n° 29–30, juillet-octobre 1981, dedicated to the study of Apollinaire's "Calligrammes." Most critics have attempted to categorize the diverse "calligrammes," particularly Goldenstein in his "Pour une sémiologie du calligramme" (*Que Vlo-ve?*); Willard Bohn in "Imagination plastique des calligrammes" (ibid.), and Pénélope Sacks in "La Mise en page du calligramme" (ibid.). Sacks's ideas are expanded in *Calligramme ou écriture figurée: Apollinaire inventeur de formes* (Paris: Minard, 1988), where she convincingly examines simple and complex figures that are either closed onto their internal space or open out onto external space, not only distinguishing between circular, cruciform, rectangular, and figural shapes but offering a useful distinction between "calligramme," "sonogramme," and "pictogramme." She refers incidentally to Albert-Birot's work in *SIC* and indicates "Métro" and the first "poème à crier et à danser" (pp. 211–12). The limited production of Albert-Birot's visual poems makes a categorization like this of less value than for the multiple creations by Apollinaire. Nonetheless this final categorization (pp. 184–93) is equally useful in identifying the varying features of Albert-Birot's work in this domain.

73. In addition to the research above, we would like to point out the work of

Georges Longrée, "Du poème symboliste au calligramme: 'Lettre-Océan' ou le déroulement du topologique" (*Que vlo-ve?*), and his book *L'Expérience idéo-calligrammatique d'Apollinaire* to which we have previously referred; Margaret Davies, "La Mandoline, l'oeillet et le bambou" (*Que vlo-ve?*), and in her *Apollinaire* (Edinburgh: Oliver & Boyd, 1964); and the work of Timothy Mathews in *Reading Apollinaire*, which although not ostensibly dealing with *Calligrammes* presents *Alcools* in the light of Apollinaire's contact with cubism. There are further references to relevant articles in the bibliography.

74. Anis, *L'Ecriture*, p. 173.

75. Compare, for example, Floch subverting McCluhan's "message": "Le message est le médium," "Les langages planaires," p. 206.

76. Anis, *L'Ecriture*, pp. 204–5.

77. Ibid., pp. 212–13. Mallarmé, *Oeuvres complètes* (Paris: Pléiade, Gallimard, 1945, p. 455).

78. For a richly suggestive reading of these texts, see Pénélope Sacks in the article previously referred to. Particularly interesting is her perception of the "formes éclatées" (e.g. "Lettre-Océan") and the "formes fermées" (e.g., "Coeur couronne et miroir") and her reading of the circular form in Apollinaire's work. The same forms are at work in the creations of Albert-Birot.

79. We do suggest, however, that a comparative study would considerably further our understanding of "la poésie plastique" in all these poets. Albert-Birot does not hesitate to use the term "calligramme" for his own work (interview with José Pivin, p. 17).

80. J.-P. Goldenstein, *Guillaume Apollinaire*, 13, p. 180. ("at the crossroads of readability and visibility"). Compare the term "vilisibilité" adopted by Anis, *L'Ecriture*, and in his article "Vilisibilité du texte poétique," *Langue Française* 59, Larousse, 1983.

81. "Le calligramme exploite les propriétés visuelles du langage écrit et les possibilitiés sémantiques de la forme visuelle" (W. Bohn, *Que vlo-ve*, p. 2). ("The 'calligramme' exploits the visual properties of written language and the semantic possibilities of visual form.")

82. Arlette Albert-Birot, *Silex*, n° 10, 1976, p. 4. Compare other references to Albert-Birot as artisan—Max Pons, *La Barbacane*, 7, p. 9; Yanette Deletang-Tardif, La Barbacane, 7, pp. 49–50; Claude Abastado, *Silex*, 10, p. 13.

83. G. Lista, "Le futurisme de Pierre Albert-Birot" p. 42.

84. "Reposoir" did not appear in *SIC* but was published in *El Cami*, Barcelona, n° 6, 2nd year, June 1918. (See A. Albert-Birot's notes to *La Lune*)

85. The first of these is a celebration of a train journey, which sets up an opposition between the sadness of those who are left as the train departs and the joy of arriving for the passengers. The train journey might be read as a favorite futurist-inspired theme, but in the poem there is no attempt to represent the movement of the train. The journey between "DEPART" and "ARRIVEE" is made only in the perceiver's imagination. The second of the "poèmes-dessins" in *La Joie* functions in a similar way, although it is more lyrical in content. The following "dessins" recall sketches—the flowers behind the garden fence and—one of the most intricate of Albert-Birot's visual poems—the dialogue between the shadow of the tree and the road across which it spreads its shade in the sun. The first is a lament for freedom, the second a dialogue of love, the road sharing its passion between the sun and the shadow. The final "poème-dessin" belongs also to the preliminary category where the visual unambiguously reflects the verbal message: composed in the shape of an airplane, it celebrates this man-

made invention that fulfills an age-old desire. The airplane is, of course, another privileged theme and image of the artistic discourse of the period.

86. How to situate the work of art with relation to the everyday is a major concern of twentieth-century art, given the difficult relationship to "reality," which characterizes the century. The everyday is "la grande découverte du vingtième siècle" ("the great discovery of the twentieth century"), according to J.-L. Houdebine in *Excès des langages* (Paris: Denoël, 1984), in discussing Joyce, Céline, and Sollers. The textual collage or collage in painting at once sets up a relationship between external "reality" and the created reality of the work of art. It emphasizes the nature of the production as a fiction, a something made. See especially the article "Le Collage comme concept et comme pratique dans l'avant-garde et le roman français contemporain," in *Vitalité et contradiction de l'avant-garde*, pp. 87–93.

87. G. Apollinaire, "La Peinture moderne," *Chroniques d'Art*, p. 273.

88. Ferdinand Léger, "Les réalisations picturelles actuelles" in *Les Soirées de Paris*, July-August 1914. Also quoted by G. Longrée, pp. 154–58.

89. Collage is a device exploited in the work of the "nouveaux romanciers"— for example, Butor in *Mobile* or Simon in *Le Palace*, although Pinget's work uses this type of conversational "sound collage" in many instances.

90. Information leaflet on cubism, Centre Georges Pompidou, Musée d'Art Moderne, 1989, on Braque's work with lettering in particular. My emphasis.

91. Arlette Albert-Birot, notes to *La Lune*,
For the framework of the "pancartes," he used the expertise of Rirachovsky, the printer of *SIC*. Ian Hamilton Finlay made a poster of the "Paradis" poem in 1954 (Arlette Albert-Birot, *La Lune*). A reproduction also hangs in the Library of the Taylor Institute, Oxford. Grabinoulor points out the "poèmes-pancartes" to Ange Gabriel who visits him in his apartment (*Grabinoulor* IV, 13). Albert-Birot decorated the walls of his own apartment with them.

92. If Albert-Birot never proposed to publish his visual poems separately, there is evidence to indicate that many of them were linked directly to exhibitions of the poetry. In 1921 one exhibition catalog lists as exhibited: "Série d'images populaires," "Série de Haï-Kaïs," "Poèmes-Affiches," "Poème-Rébus," "Poème carré," "Poèmes à crier et à danser," "Poème extrait de 'La Lune au plafond,'" "Poème Cavalcade," "Idéogramme destiné au 'tombeau' de Guillaume Apollinaire," "Dentelle," et "Rosace." There were readings by Greta Prozor of "Les invectives contre l'automne," *La Joie des sept couleurs*, "La Légende," and some of the *Poèmes quotidiens* read by Jean d'Yol. This exhibition took place from 26 November to 3 December 1921 in the gallery of Pierre and Dolly Chareau, Rue Nollet, Paris. Greta Prozor was an actress whose voice Albert-Birot much admired and for whom he had written *Image*. The following year his work was exhibited at the gallery of Berthe Weill, Rue Lafitte, from 8 to 16 June: "Ecrits au pinceau et à l'encre de chine noire sur fort papier d'arches, peints en blanc ou sur fonds outremer ou noir, les poèmes étaient présentés comme des oeuvres graphiques" (Arlette Albert-Birot, preface to *La Lune,*). ("Written with a brush and Indian ink on strong paper, painted in white or on an ultramarine or black background, the poems were presented like graphic works.") The works exhibited were similar to those of the previous year, and it is here that "Ode" was displayed on a rotating column. Not only poems of overt typographical disruption or "prowess" (such as "Dentelle") are exhibited, but also several of the aphoristic poems such as "Haï-Kaïs," "Images Populaires," and "Poèmes blancs" (from *La Lune*).

93. The charge that these are merely "decorative" without any true "plastic"

status is frequent: "En réalité chez Albert-Birot tout comme chez Apollinaire et les autres, la visualisation de l'écriture suit une esthétique plutôt décorative où s'incarne, de façon très significative, l'un des visages de ce penchant vers le 'gracieux,' produisant des broderies de salon dépourvus d'une véritable solidité plastique, que Boccioni indiquait polémiquement comme une tendance toujours présente au sein de l'art français" (G. Lista, "Le futurisme de Pierre Albert-Birot," p. 42). ("In reality in Albert-Birot's work, just as in Apollinaire's and the others,' the visualization of writing pursues a rather decorative aesthetics in which, in a very significant way, one of the faces of this taste for the 'graceful' is incarnated, and which produces decorative embroidery without any real plastic solidity, which Boccioni indicated polemically as a tendency always present at the heart of French art.")

"Nous passons de même sur les calligrammes qui sont prouesses techniques d'un typographe amateur . . . mais, réduits à l'aune des lignes ordinaires, ne valent guère mieux que les mêmes exercices du gros Guillaume. Le jeu n'en vaut plus la chandelle" (Bernard Jourdan, *Critique*, n° 177, February 1976). ("We'll leave aside the calligrammes, which are examples of the technical prowess of the amateur typographer . . . but which, reduced to ordinary lines, are worth no more than the same exercises carried out by portly Guillaume. The game does not stand up to scrutiny.") Certainly we would not wish to deny the elements of the ludic at work in such endeavours, and the obvious delight that Albert-Birot experienced in the process of hand printing. Our contention here is that in the manipulation of space and in the convoking of the body there are more serious considerations in operation. Henri Chopin is more sure of Albert-Birot as precursor of "concrete poetry" than of Mallarmé and of Apollinaire, who are frequently evoked in such a context: "La poésie concrète est graphique, les graphies de Pierre (contrairement aux calligrammes) l'étaient" (Henri Chopin, "Le contenu d'un contenant," p. 26). ("Concrete poetry is graphic poetry, and Pierre's graphic poetry [contrary to the 'calligrammes'], was just that.")

94. Arlette Albert-Birot, notes to *La Lune*, Albert-Birot describes such poems as "acrobaties techniques" in a typescript of a kind of autobiographical résumé dated 1932 (Fonds Albert-Birot). The choice of vocabulary is revealing, for beneath the ludic and the clownesque, acrobats risk their lives, relying on their own skill for the entertainment of others and in so doing come face to face with themselves. The preface to *Larountala*, which uses acrobats in its "mise en scène," makes an explicit analogy between the circus and language: "j'aime les culbutes des clowns mais j'aime autant plus les culbutes des mots." ("I love clowns' somersaults but I love just as much the somersaults of words.") The reader must follow these disorientating spins and tumbles, whether the poet is working at the extremes of sound or of vision: "Devant les changements de rythmes constants, ces mots désarticulés en syllabes et en caractères, le lecteur est forcé de descendre dans les rouages internes du langage et d'en éprouver le fonctionnement par la vue, l'ouïe et l'intelligence à la fois' (Denis Rigal on the poetry of e. e. cummings, *Sud*, 19, 1976, p. 661: he notes that cummings also admired clowns and mime artists). ("Faced with the constant changes of rhythm, these words dislocated in syllables or characters, the reader is forced to go down into the internal workings of language and to experience the way it functions, using sight, hearing, and intelligence all at the same time.")

See also the prose piece *Le Funambule* by Jean Genet, in which the risks of the tightrope walker becomes the metaphor of the risks of the creative artist (*Le

Funambule in *Oeuvres complètes*, Vol. V, Gallimard, 1979, originally published in "L'Arbalète," 1958).

95. Arlette Albert-Birot, notes to *La Lune*, These "blocks" of poetry that make up the majority of the final part of *La Lune* are also a form of the prose poem, a form practiced particularly by Reverdy and by Max Jacob, in connection with which he reputedly first used the label "poésie cubiste." Note also the poem "Métro," previously discussed, where a block of print represented the observing self of the poet.

96. Compare the projects of Queneau and Perec and the "models" and "rules" applied to language by the techniques of L'OULIPO to explore its infinite possibilities.

97. The term "contour" is the terminology of W. Bohn in his article to which we have previously referred.

98. Arlette Albert-Birot, notes to *La Lune*, She goes on to offer a key to the rebus: "Les fleurs dans leur vase ont l'air bête et (petit à) petit meurent. La Rose au milieu du salon pose elle attend que vous lui disiez qu'elle a grand R." ("The flowers in the vase look silly and bit by bit die. The Rose in the middle of the living room is waiting for you to tell it that it looks imposing.")

99. J.-F. Lyotard, *Discours, Figure*, p. 300.

100. "La présence de lettres ou mots dans le rébus, bien loin de l'éclairer, porte à son comble la confusion du textuel et du figural," Lyotard, ibid., p. 304. ("The presence of letters or words in the rebus, far from shedding light on it, bring to its height the confusion of the textual and the figural.")

101. Lyotard, *Discours, Figure*, p. 307.

102. Ibid.

103. G. Lista's disparaging remarks on the visual poetry of Albert-Birot do, however, serve to illustrate the vast difference between his personal enterprise and that of the futurists, and the fact that any assimilation of his work and indeed of the whole enterprise of *SIC* into futurist concepts can only be superficial: "La recherche gestuelle, l'intensité dynamique et la tension agressive, la polyphonie du psychique et du concret, le matérialisme qui impose la corporéité du support et du signe, c'est-à-dire tout ce qui faisait pour Marinetti le noyau même de l'esthétique futuriste de l'écriture, s'évaporent pour laisser la place, chez Albert-Birot comme chez Apollinaire, à une attitude auto-célébrative où l'auteur cherche à charmer le lecteur en secondant son goût au moyen d'un jeu graphique qui oscille entre les divertissements du baroque et la joie de la forme miniaturisée" ("Le Futurisme de Pierre Albert-Birot", p. 42). ("Gestural research, the dynamic intensity and aggressive tension, the polyphony of the psychological and of the concrete, the materialism that imposes the bodily form of the support and of the sign, that is to say, everything that made up for Marinetti the very crux of the futurist aesthetics of writing, evaporates to cede its place, in Albert-Birot's work as in Apollinaire's, to a self-celebratory attitude where the author seeks to charm the reader by following his taste by means of a graphic game that oscillates between the amusements of the baroque and the pleasure of the miniature form.")

That the enterprise of both Apollinaire and Albert-Birot are more seriously concerned with the exploration of language and the relationship of poetic object to space is obviously a fundamental assumption of this study and as such is opposed to such a position.

104. Henri Chopin, "Le contenu d'un contenant," p. 12.

105. Compare Virginia La Charité, *The Dynamics of Space: Mallarme's "Un*

coup de dés n'abolira le hasard" *(Lexington, Ky.: French Forum Publishers, 1987).*

106. It is here that our insistence on the importance of the concept of simultaneity and its artistic procedures within the general context of modernity becomes more clear. The language of simultaneity is explored by both artists and poets from Mallarmé onward. "Ainsi, le simultanéisme est l'un des exemples privilégiés de la circulation des modèles de cette époque. . . . A cet égard, les recherches engagées dans le simultanéisme et 'la poésie plastique' inventent une perspective multiple sur l'espace et le temps," Gaëtane Lechevalier, "Un nouvel état de l'intelligence," *La Chouette,* n° 24, London, 1990. ("Therefore, simultaneity (the use of simultaneous action) is one of the privileged examples of the circulation of the models of this period. . . . In this respect research into simultaneity and 'plastic poetry' invents a multiple perspective on space and time.")

107. Even if the reader/spectator must reconstitute, decipher linearly afterward, he or she is privy to the act of creation in its multiplicity: "Lecteurs et spectateurs réalisent eux-mêmes cette 'mise en scène' spirituelle dont parle Mallarmé. Cette écriture sublimée instaure une dynamique entre deux lectures, l'une horizontale (ordre des successivités), l'autre verticale, polyphonique (ordre de la simultanéité)," G. Lechevalier, "Un nouvel état," p. 30. ("Readers and spectators realize themselves this spiritual 'production' of which Mallarmé spoke. This sublimated writing sets up a dynamic between two readings, one horizontal [successive order], the other vertical, polyphonic [simultaneous order].")

In the article previously referred to, W. Bohn also stresses the importance of the theory and practice of simultaneity: "Il reste à rapprocher l'imagination plastique d'Apollinaire de sa théorie et de sa pratique du simultanéisme. Car il n'y a pas de doute que la poésie visuelle est née des mêmes expériences simultanéistes que 'Les Fenêtres' et 'Lundi Rue Christine.' En dépit de différences évidentes de forme et d'inspiration, le calligramme, le poème simultané et le poème-conversation incarnent tous le même concept de base" (W. Bohn, p. 14). ("It remains to bring together the visual dimensions of Apollinaire's imagination with his theory and his practice of simultaneity. For there is no doubt that visual poetry is born of the same simultaneity experiments as 'Les Fenêtres' and 'Lundi Rue Christine.' In spite of the obvious differences in form and inspiration, the calligramme, the simultaneous poem and the poem-conversation all embody the same basic concept.") This position is indicative of our own. Bohn does not share the view of A.-M. Bassy that Apollinaire's "calligrammes" are abstract signs that function only as symbols and have nothing to do with painterly techniques (Bassy, "Forme littéraire et forme graphique: les schématogrammes d'Apollinaire," *Scolies,* n° 3–4, 1973–74, pp. 200 and 196). It is in the same perspective that our theory on the visual poems of Albert-Birot has taken form.

108. Ong, *Orality and Literacy,* p. 81. Ong refers readers also to his other work, *Interfaces of the Word,* 1977, pp. 230–71.

109. One of the aims of visual poetry appears to be to make word and object coincide, to destroy the space between signifier and signified. Yet a deep unease has set in between word and object, and the poet is forced time and time again to confront the paradox at the heart of language. The effect of print reinforces this reification of the word in the shift that occurs from sound to visual space. (Timothy Mathews, *Reading Apollinaire,* explores this with regard to the project of the futurists. Also compare Denis Rigal on e.e. cummings, as previously referred to. "Introduire la vie, qui est le sens, là où il n'y en avait pas, elle témoignent d'un effort pour résorber l'arbitraire du signe que nul poète n'a jamais

vraiment accepté.") ("To introduce life, which is meaning, there where there was none, is testimony to an effort to break down the arbitrary nature of the linguistic sign, which no poet has ever really accepted.")

110. Ong, *Orality and Literacy*, p. 129.

111. Compare also the later collection *La Panthère Noire*, made up of poems explicitly represented as links and pieces on such a chain and graphically illustrating this concept. The chain is not to be laid out in a series but to be clasped together in a circle and made complete.

112. Albert-Birot on the task of the poet (interview with José Pivin, p. 18).

113. Albert-Birot on the thought of Einstein and considering this to be equally a definition of poetry. (Interview with José Pivin.)

Chapter 4. The *Poèmes à L'Autre Moi:* The Reflection on/of the Self

1. All translations of these extracts of the *Poèmes à L'Autre Moi* in this chapter are by Sue Rose to whom I extend my thanks once again.

2. Dominique Baudouin, "Pierre Albert-Birot, Poésie, Langage, Mythe," *Sud* 19 (1976), pp. 5–11.

3. Jean Follain, pp. 31–32 Follain continues his richly suggestive image of "la solitude peuplée" of Albert-Birot to which we referred in the first chapter. See also "La Solitude peuplée de Pierre Albert-Birot," *F*, 2–3, 1972.

4. Ibid., p. 44.

5. Ibid., p. 32.

6. André Lebois, *Poésie 1916–1924*, p. 20, for example.

7. *Rémy Floche, employé* (see bibliography for details). Lebois, p. 20.

8. Max Pons, *La Barbacane*, 7, p. 9.

9. G. Orlandi, preface to *Matoum et Tévibar*, p. 52. She notes as parallel texts to this Baudelaire's *Spleen et Idéal*, Mallarmé's internal drama of creation in "Le Cygne," and Apollinaire's "Thérèse-Tirésias."

10. Ibid., p. 52. Arlette Albert-Birot also opens her commentary on the integral edition of *Grabinoulor*, (Paris: Jean-Michel Place, 1991), with the concept of the double (p. 947).

11. G. Bachelard, *La Poétique de la Rêverie*, (Paris: PUF, 1960), p. 8.

12. G. Orlandi, *Matoum et Tevibar* p. 54. Of these "doubles" it is on several levels that these function—Matoum, "le vrai poète" (the true poet) and Tévibar, "le faux poète" (the false poet), are phonetically echoes of Grabinoulor and Furibar. Grabinoulor is himself a "double being," living at once an ordinary existence and one extraordinary, outside the confines of human time and space. Furibar, his negative opposite, has equally two faces, carrying at one point Toutenrose on his back. In the textual space of *Grabinoulor*, time and space are multidimensional as these existences run parallel, meet and diverge.

13. On the concept of the double in Albert-Birot's work, see M.-L. Lentengre, "Les appétits hyperboliques de Grabinoulor," p. 147, p. 104, and Bernard Jourdan, "Approche de Pierre Albert-Birot ou le poète double," commentary on *Grabinoulor, Adam, Poèmes à l'Autre Moi*, and *La Joie des Sept Couleurs*, "cet autre moi perpétuel," in *Critique*, n° 177 (February 1972).

14. Jean Follain, "Pierre Albert-Birot dit PAB, dit Grabinoulor," *Cahiers bleus* 15 (1979), p. 7.

15. On this see Arlette Albert-Birot, "Un style de vie poétique, une entrée au

ciel," *Le Monde* (16 March 1988), an idea that she repeats in her commentary on *Grabinoulor*, 1991, p. 947.

16. This autobiographical project may take the form of either prose or poetry. In the twentieth century, the "nouveaux romanciers" continue their questioning of the status of fiction with their explorations of the (im)possibility of writing one's life. Problems of time and memory are recurrent in the autobiographies of, for example, Duras, Robbe-Grillet, and Sarraute. The dialogic nature of such a questioning (and compare again Sarraute) recurs again and again, and the poetic quest of poets as diverse as Guillevic:

> Qui te dira
> Si ton poème
> Est poème?
> —(*Art poètique*, Gallimard, Paris: 1989)

> ("Who will tell you / If your poem / Is poem?")

Tardieu (*Monsieur, Monsieur*) and Bonnefoy: "Et vois, tu es déjà séparé de toi-même" (*Hier Régnant Désert*, 1958, Paris: Gallimard, 1982, with preface) ("And see, you are already separated from yourself") use the moi/toi division overtly, but all such quests for identity and origins are founded on "l'écoute de l'Autre."

The exploration of the self in language by Michel Leiris is the revolutionizing of the autobiographical form. The psychoanalytical approach of Lacan rereading Freud in terms of language and identity provides a theoretical and critical framework with which to read these dilemmas of the construction of the self.

17. Dominique Baudouin, "Une lecture des *Poèmes à l'Autre Moi*," *F*, 2–3, p. 105.

Here he identifies the movement and extent of synthesis between the two selves as one between body and soul, their union being accomplished "dans un équilibre lumineux hors du temps" ("in a luminous balance outside time"). There is certainly an element of mysticism in the quest. However our analysis here proposes to focus on the work of language and the construction of the self rather than to explore the quasi-religious thematics that would be another possible reading of the text.

18. It is in this perspective that a parallel may be drawn between Albert-Birot and one of the goals of the surrealists despite his protestations against their ideas and aims, again situating his work within the aesthetic of the twentieth century. The idea of a type of transposition of the self and the focus on the subject at the center of the artistic creation began in *Les Champs Magnétiques* where: "the discovery of a form of verbal expression in which the poetic self excitingly occupies the centre of the universe exerting an ever-widening circle of influence" (J. H. Matthews, *Towards a Poetics of Surrealism*, [New York: Syracuse University Press, 1976], p. 52). It is one of the desires of the surrealists "to possess more than Man's situation in the world guarantees him, and to see what he does not yet possess, by means of poetic action" (p. 25).

19. The surrealist revolution aimed at both action and creation, "poetic action." Existential thinking promoted literature's social and political responsibility for the individual and the collective, responsibility for the act. The dilemma of the project of *SIC* returns here, promotion of the collective endeavor failing because of an inability to accommodate its coexistence with personal discovery—a conflict of twentieth-century literature essential for any understanding of the work under analysis here.

20. The concept of "le faire poétique" is taken here in the sense defined by Lorand Gaspar:

Ce qui importe, c'est le processus, le faire poétique. Il faudrait rendre compte de cette tentative de porter à la parole ce qui est hors langage; d'utiliser le langage pour faire entendre ce qu'il n'est pas dans son pouvoir de dire (*Sud*, hors série, 1983, "Espaces de Lorand Gaspar," textes réunis et présentés par Roger Little, p. 32).

("What is important is the process, the poetic act. This attempt to bring to the spoken word what is outside language must be taken into account; this use of language to make heard what is not in its power to say.")

Lorand Gaspar's search for origins is a quest to express the "invisible," the "indicible," as is Albert-Birot's.

21. J.-M. Adam, *Le Texte narratif,* (Paris: Fernand-Nathan, 1985), p. 202.

22. This idea of parallel modes of expression is one that we want to stress. It is not our intention to replace one by the other or to form any sort of hierarchy: "Ecriture et peinture ne sont pas deux langues hiérarchisées, mais deux modes d'expression parallèles, chacun des deux peut servir à éclairer l'autre, voire à le traduire, mais ne peut le remplacer—pas plus que la traduction ne peut remplacer l'original" (Christian Delacampagne in "Regards, Miroirs, rêverie" in *Corps Ecrit* 5 [Paris: P.U.F., 1982], p. 150). ("Writing and painting are not two languages organized in a hierarchy, but two parallel modes of expression, each of which can serve to throw light on the other, even to translate it, but which cannot replace it—no more than a translation can replace the original.")

23. Albert-Birot, "La Peinture absolue." Albert-Birot's pronouncement is remarkably similar to that of the philosopher J.-F. Lyotard: "Ce que le tableau montre, c'est le monde en train de se faire. . . . De ce point de vue, le tableau est le plus étrange des objets quand il remplit la fonction dont la dote la peinture moderne: c'est un objet où se montre l'engendrement des objets, l'activité transcendantale même" (*Discours, Figures*, p. 28). ("What the painting shows is the world in the process of creating itself. . . . From this point of view, the painting is the strangest of objects when it fulfills the function that modern painting bestows on it. It is an object where the creation of objects is shown, transcendental activity itself.") Our analysis of *La Guerre* has shown just such "un monde en train de se faire," a poetics in formation, a poetic universe in formation, the birth of a poetic self, a transposition of the present personal/artistic/historical moment into the eternal moment of Art. *La Guerre* is the genesis of a world for Albert-Birot, a genesis referred to time and time again.

24. See also the discussion on modern art and poetry in *Grabinoulor*, V, 6.

25. Paul Valéry, *Oeuvres*, I, p. 232, and quoted by Anne Boyman, *Lecture du Narcisse: sémiotique du texte de Valéry*, (Montréal, Québec: Didier, 1982), Série 3, Vol. VI, p. 32. Also quoted by Béatrice Didier, "Autoportrait et Journal intime," *Corps Ecrit* 5, p. 189.

26. We are indebted to the above work by A. Boyman for the concept "Narcisse-sujet," "Narcisse-écrivain." See particularly, Ch. II, "Le Narcissisme," pp. 23–24, and in her close textual analysis of Valéry's "Fragments du Narcisse." Commenting on a remark by J. Bellemin-Noël in "Le narcissisme des Narcisse (Valéry)," *Littérature* 6, (1972), p. 34, the critic makes clear how the mechanism works for "Self" and "Writer":

"Le coup de maître de Valéry," écrit J. Bellemin-Noël, "consiste à faire parler la 'narcissisité' même," c'est-à-dire que Valéry ne traite pas le mythe de Narcisse de façon allusive, décorative ou incidentelle, mais saisit le mécanisme narcissique (du sujet et de l'écrivain), dans ce qu'il a de plus universel et essentiel."

("Valéry's master stroke," writes J. Bellemin-Noël, "consists in making 'narcissisity' itself talk, that is to say that Valéry does not treat the myth of Narcissus in an allusive, decorative or incidental way, but he grasps the narcissistic mechanism (of the subject and of the writer) in what it has that is most universal and essential.")

This is the mechanism that we have identified earlier as the quest for identity, generating a writing that is increasingly self-conscious.

27. Boyman, *Lecture du Narcisse*, p. 33.

28. Paul Valéry, "Sur les Narcisse," *Paul Valéry vivant, Cahiers du Sud* 24–25, n° spécial, p. 283, quoted by Boyman, p. 32.

29. Valéry, *Cahiers*, VIII, p. 241, quoted by Boyman, p. 32. It should be noted also that there are several sketches of hands and faces in the *Cahiers*, 29 volumes (Paris: C.N.R.S., 1957–61) just as Albert-Birot made his numerous self-portraits, including a sketch to be found in the manuscript of *Grabinoulor*.

30. It should be noted that Albert-Birot's original title was *Poèmes à Dieu*, which he changed on the advice of his publisher (verbal assurance from Arlette Albert-Birot). The changed title is, however, more indicative of a collection that is essentially an exploration of the self and not an address to a being of ambiguous religious nature outside the self.

31. Philippe Sollers, *La Littérature et l'expérience des limites* (Paris: Seuil, 1968), p. 67, "Littérature et totalité." Of all the quotations we could have chosen to support our statements on the general nature of twentieth-century fiction, Sollers intervenes most aptly in any work on Albert-Birot, choosing as he has to work without punctuation in *Paradis* with extensive and ongoing narrative.

32. Edgar Morin, *Le Paradigme perdu: la nature humaine,* (Paris: Seuil, 1973), p. 112, quoted by Boyman, p. 5.

33. Boyman, *Lecture du Narcisse*, p. 8.

34. It is interesting to note that among the myriad figures from myth who intervene in *Grabinoulor,* Narcissus (in name anyway) makes only three very brief appearances: *Grabinoulor* III, ch. 6; ch. 11; V, ch. 9, thus, never meriting a long conversation with Grabinoulor.

35. Several of these are collected in the Fonds Albert-Birot. See also the *Autobiographie*, front cover, for the reproduction of an early sketch.

36. Albert-Birot's *Autobiographie* seeks the answer to this to some extent in his exploration of family and childhood that makes up the major part of the text. Yet less than an experience of the search for origins in which the reader participates as is the case, for example, in the autobiographies of Leiris, Sarraute, Duras, or Robbe-Grillet, the effect here remains merely that of an anecdote without a questioning of the nature (and weaknesses) of memory. What does this suggest? Perhaps that the question of "Who am I?" which all writers face at some time, is to be found elsewhere in his work. That these writers associated with the "nouveau roman" turned their attention to the writing of the self after the challenges of fiction and the representation of "reality" in language raises further complexities around the questioning of the "practice of writing" (Stephen Heath). Although deeply aware of the medium of language in his poetic and fictional works, Albert-Birot displays a surprising naïveté when using the autobiographical form, never questioning whether it is possible to write "the story of my life," even more astonishing after the problems of writing the self explored in *L'Autre Moi*. The

poems are a more ambiguous project that the *Autobiographie*, a slim and evasive piece of writing that dates from 1952 when the poet was seventy-six years old.

37. Here we concentrate particularly on an article, very personally written and yet generally thought-provoking. "Regarder un autoportrait," pp. 136–46 in *Corps Ecrit* 5, "L'Autoportrait."

38. Lejeune, "Regarder un autoportrait," p. 135.

39. Even the use of certain colours, style, etc., would require prior knowledge on the part of the viewer to recognize the painter's "self." Note also the point that a discourse always surrounds paintings, for example, Butor, *Les Mots dans la peinture*, p. 5. "Toute notre expérience de la peinture comporte en fait une considérable partie verbale. Nous ne voyons jamais les tableaux seuls, notre vision n'est jamais pure vision." See also Ch. Delacampagne, *Corps Ecrit* 5, 'Regards, miroirs, rêverie," p. 149. ("The whole of our experience of painting is made up of a considerable verbal part. We never see paintings alone, our vision is never pure vision.")

Taking up Butor's idea: "Notre regard est toujours orienté, modulé, façonné par des mots. Cela, qui demeure vrai pour la peinture en général, l'est encore plus vivement pour ce genre très particulier que constitue l'autoportrait." ("Our look is always directed, modulated, fashioned by words. And this, which remains true for painting in general, is even more so for this very particular type which is self-portraiture.")

Compare also the irony of Robert Pinget: "Il serait piquant de faire son autoportrait en le signant d'un autre nom. Pour dérouter les amateurs futurs et dégoûter les portraitistes de leur talents de faussaires" (*Du Nerf*, Minuit, 1990, pp. 14–15). ("It would be entertaining to do one's self-portrait signing it with another name. To throw future art lovers off the scent and also to disgust portraitists of their talent as forgers.")

40. Lejeune, "Regarder un autoportrait," p. 136.

41. Lejeune, "Regarder un autoportrait," p. 138. His example is the Norman Rockwell *Triple Self-portrait* (1960) where reproductions on the canvasses of Dürer, Rembrandt, Picasso, and Van Gogh make this type of artistic "intertextuality" explicit. In the context of Albert-Birot's work, the example of Picasso is particularly revealing—of all artistic production, the disorientation felt by the spectator before the self-portraits and portraits is perhaps the most spectacular and most revealing, undermining and making us rethink as it does not only our relationship to reality but to self.

42. Lejeune, "Regarder un autoportrait," p. 140.

43. Lejeune, "Regarder un autoportrait," p. 141.

44. Ibid., p. 141.

45. Lejeune, p. 141.

46. "Le peintre est là, le pinceau à la main. Il a peint, il peindra (sur une toile que je ne vois pas, et qui est justement celle que je regarde). Mais en ce moment il ne peint pas. Il se regarde. Et ce regard *vaut pour* la peinture. Moi qui ne sais pas peindre, je trouve là un biais 'existentiel' pour entrer (m'imaginer entrer) dans l'activitié de l'artiste. De même le lecteur de Proust privilégie l'expérience de la réminiscence, qu'il peut partager avec le narrateur, sans bien saisir qu'elle n'est qu'une métaphore de l'activité, invisible mais omniprésente, qui le sépare de lui: l'écriture" (Lejeune, "Regarder un autoportrait," p. 142). ("The painter is there with his brush in his hand. He has painted, he will paint [on a canvas which I cannot see and which is precisely the one I'm looking at]. But at this moment he is not painting. He is looking at himself. And this look is equivalent to painting.

I who do not know how to paint, I find here an 'existential' device to enter [to imagine myself entering] into the artist's activity. Just as the reader of Proust privileges the experience of reminiscence, which he can share with the narrator, without fully grasping that it is only a metaphor for the activity, invisible but omniscient, that separates him from him—writing.")

47. Lejeune, "Regarder un autoportrait" p. 142.

48. Lejeune, "Regarder un autoportrait" p. 145.

49. An episode in *Grabinoulor* is strikingly relevant here—Grabi's letter to the creator, whose reply touches upon the nature of creation: "Le propre du Créateur est d'être toujours créant," and Grabi must continue to search for the truth: "Il faut en effet que vous gardiez pour vivre le plaisir de toujours la chercher c'est-à-dire pour que vous soyez un peu semblable à moi toujours cherchant comme je suis toujours creánt" (*Grabinoulor*, V. I, pp. 575–76). ("The character of the Creator is to be always creating.") ("You must indeed retain in order to live the pleasure of looking for it that is to say in order for you to be a bit like me always looking as I am always creating.")

This we will explore more fully in the next chapter on *Grabinoulor.*

50. Didier, *Corps Ecrit* 5, p. 170.

There is a play on words with "Pierre," the poet's first name meaning also "stone."

51. Lejeune, "Regarder un autoportrait" p. 143. It is interesting to note that there is no "self-sculpture" of Albert-Birot but several pieces of his children. Also sculpture was, as we have already noted, very much the way he made his living as opposed to the removal from the everyday that writing allowed him, despite its being a medium in which he was a very skilled craftsman.

52. Ch. Delacampagne, *Corps Ecrit,* 5, p. 149.

53. *Grabinoulor,* V, I, p. 576. We will return to this in the following chapter. Compare also the dialogic questioning of Nathalie Sarraute in various texts, *Enfance* for example, given our autobiographical context, or the later *Tu ne t'aimes pas.*

54. *Grabinoulor,* V, I, p. 576. The way in which *Grabinoulor* seems here to inform *L'Autre Moi* is an important area for exploration. In many ways *Grabinoulor* is indeed a reading program for the poetry collections. Yet this program functions in both ways—*Grabinoulor* equally enriched by a reading of *L'Autre Moi.* Above all it is an intense indication of the complexity of Albert-Birot's oeuvre in its totality and an illustration of how a lifetime's work is generated.

55. La "modernité," désignée comme telle depuis la "coupure" du dix-neuvième siècle, désigne donc principalement une littérature qui, se distanciant d'elle-même, se regarde et s'analyse comme objet linguistique. Cette distance qui permet la prise de conscience de l'objet, est la condition nécessaire pour que l'écriture jusqu'alors "innocente" devienne une écriture consciente d'elle-même ou narcissique.

("Modernity, indicated as such since the 'break' of the nineteenth century, refers principally therefore, to a literature which, distancing itself from itself, looks at itself and analyzes itself as a linguistic object. This distance that allows the object to become aware of itself is the necessary condition for writing which was up until then 'innocent' to become a writing aware of itself or narcissistic.") Boyman, *Lecture du Narcisse,* p. 11. In support of her statement, Boyman quotes Barthes in *Le Degré zéro de l'écriture* (Paris: Seuil,1953), p. 11 (charting the progression from Chateaubriand, Flaubert, to Mallarmé) and Foucault in *Les Mots et les choses* (Paris: Gallimard, 1966), p. 313:

Elle (la littérature) n'a plus alors qu'à se recourber dans un perpétuel retour sur soi, comme si son discours ne pouvait avoir pour contenu que de dire sa propre forme: elle s'adresse à soi comme subjectivité écrivante, où elle cherche à ressaisir, dans le mouvement qui l'a fait naître, essence de toute littérature: et ainsi tous ses fils convergent vers la pointe la plus fine singulière, instantanée, et pourtant absolument universelle—vers le simple acte d'écrire.

("It [literature] has then only to curve up in a perpetual return to itself, as though its discourse could have no other content that its own form. It addresses itself as writing subjectivity, where it seeks to grasp again, in the movement that gave birth to it, the essence of all literature; and so all the threads converge toward the most singular, instantaneous point that is nonetheless absolutely universal—toward the simple act of writing.")

56. Boyman, *Lecture du Narcisse*, p. 16. Prior to establishing this distinction, the critic discusses her idea in the light of Jakobson's "poetic function" (p. 15) to define the narcissistic text more precisely: "Cette fonction, qui met en évidence le côté palpable des signes, approfondit par là même la dichotomie fondamentale des signes et des objects" (*Essais de linguistique générale* [Paris: Minuit, 1963], p. 218). "Cette fonction comporte une attitude introvertie à l'égard des signes verbaux" (*Questions de Poétique* [Paris: Seuil, 1973], p. 485). ("This function, which makes clear the palpable side of signs and objects, deepens by the very act of doing this the fundamental dichotomy of signs and objects.") ("This function is comprised of an introverted attitude toward verbal signs.")
57. Boyman, *Lecture du Narcisse*, p. 16.
58. Boyman, *Lecture du Narcisse*, p. 16.
59. Compare Boyman, *Lecture du Narcisse*, p. 34. "Si le narcissisme constitue, à la base, le lien entre les deux pôles oppositionnels pulsion de vie/pulsion de mort, il faut comprendre que la problématique narcissique n'est pas linéaire mais qu'elle se présente plutôt comme un cycle: cycle, car le mouvement d'aliénation, de perte et de désir qui la définit est un mouvement sans véritable résolution, qui ne peut être envisagé que dans les termes d'une quête perpétuelle." ("If narcissism constitutes, at its basis, the link between the two opposing poles life drive/death drive, it must be understood that the narcissistic problem is not linear but that it presents itself rather like a cycle. It is a cycle because the movement of alienation, of loss and desire, which defines it is a movement without any real resolution, can only be envisaged in terms of a perpetual quest.)
60. Boyman, *Lecture du Narcisse*, p. 40.
61. Ibid., p. 43.
62. Boyman, *Lecture du Narcisse*, p. 43, quotes Lévi-Strauss at the end of *L'Homme nu, Mythologiques* IV (Paris: Plon, 1971), p. 621.

L'opposition fondamentale, génératrice de toutes les autres qui foisonnent dans les mythes . . . est celle même, qu'énonce Hamlet sous la forme d'une encore trop crédule alternative. Car entre l'être et le non-être, il n'appartient pas à l'homme de chosir. Un effort mental consubstantiel à son histoire, et qui ne cessera qu'avec son effacement de l'univers, lui impose d'assumer les deux évidences contradictories dont le heurt met sa pensée en branle et, pour *neutraliser leur opposition, engendre une série illimitée d'autres distinctions binaires qui, sans jamais résoudre cette antinomie première, ne font, à des échelles de plus en plus réduites, que la reproduire et la perpétuer.* (My emphasis.)

("The fundamental opposition, generator of all the others that flourish in myths . . . is the very one articulated by Hamlet in the form of a still too credulous alternative, because it is not given to men to choose between being and nonbeing. A mental effort consubstantial to his history, which will only end with the abolition of the universe, imposes on him the two contradictory pieces of evidence the clash of which sets his thought in motion and, to neutralize their opposition, engenders a limitless series of other binary distinctions that, without ever resolving this original antinomy, merely, on a more and more reduced scale, reproduce and perpetuate it.")

It should be noted, as we pointed out in our analysis of *La Guerre*, that the "structure profonde" uncovered with a reading of a Greimassian semiotic model reveals just such a structure of basic binary oppositions.

63. Boyman, *Lecture du Narcisse*, p. 44.

She continues: "C'est grâce au lien vertical de l'axe paradigmatique permis par le rapport de rupture et paradoxalement de connexion entre manifeste/latent ou connotation/dénotation, que le lecteur pourra traduire la surface dans le langage horizontal ou linéaire du nouvel axe syntagmatique qu'est la profondeur du texte." ("It is thanks to the vertical link of the paradigmatic axis allowed by the relation of rupture and paradoxically of connection between the manifest/latent and connotation/denotation that the reader will be able to translate the surface into the horizontal or linear language of the new syntagmatic axis which is the deep structure of the text.")

64. This is close to the problematic explored by George Steiner. Also implied is the modern preoccupation with the relationship between man and the city.

65. We have already referred to the fact that Albert-Birot was fascinated by the Michelangelo painting of God creating Adam in the Sistine Chapel. (Verbal assurance by Arlette Albert-Birot.) This will be further commented on in chapter 5. It was the space between the finger of God and the finger of Adam, infinitesimal and yet unbreachable, which was the source of such a fascination—the space between divine and human where creation takes place.

66. Boyman, *Lecture du Narcisse*, p. 92, on Valéry's "Narcisse," lines 259 and 261–67.

67. André Green, "L'interprétation psychanalytique des productons culturelles et des oeuvres d'art," *Critique sociologique et critique psychanalytique*, Bruxelles Editions de l'Institut de Sociologie, 1975.

68. *Grabinoulor* I, p. 49. The etymologist explains the origin of the name "Birot" to Grabi, who recognizes it as that of a twentieth-century poet whose name is inscribed into a wall:

LE POETE PIERRE ALBERT-BIROT
A ETE CONCU EN ALGERIE
IL EST NE ICI

(THE POET PIERRE ALBERT-BIROT
WAS CONCEIVED IN AGERIA
HE WAS BORN HERE)

Among the theories of the origins of the name of Grabinoulor himself is Bernard Jourdan's anagram:

NOU(S) ALBER(T) BIRO(T)

("Approche de Pierre Albert-Birot ou le poète et son double," p. 132.) This translates as "We Albert-Birot."

69. Paul Mathis, *Le Corps et l'écrit*, Paris: Aubier Montaigne, 1981, p. 122.

70. Compare, for example, Follain's "La solitude peuplée de Pierre Albert-

Birot" or Lentengre's monograph where she considers the poet's solitary existence before and after the adventure of the avant-garde (both previously extensively referred to).

71. Boyman, *Lecture du Narcisse* p. 27.

72. Bertrand Ogilvie, *Lacan. Le Sujet* (Paris: P.U.F. "Philosophie," 1987), in section titled "Lacan: la formation du concept du sujet. 1933–49"), p. 107, quoting Lacan in *Ecrits* (Paris: Seuil, 1986), and comparing Lacan's *Séminaire I*, p. 88. In writing the subject strives toward that imaginary unity shattered at the "mirror stage" by the entry into the Symbolic. There is a clear parallel here with the autobiographical project of Michel Leiris. The reconstitution of the self as text can be read as a will to wholeness, a return to the ultimate place of origins. Another way of reading the fundamental structure not made explicit here would be the tension between unity and rupture, initially around the mother. The figure of the father is not explored here but again could be investigated as a primal other that provokes alienation and the loss of the original maternal object, thereby creating perpetual desire.

73. Compare Lacan, 'L'homme se voit, se conçoit autre qu'il n'est', Lacan, *Séminaire I*, p. 14. ("Man sees himself, conceives of himself other than he is.) Albert-Birot is exploring the concept of the subject that Lacan will analyze later. These theoretical concerns set out analytically the problematic already explored in the creative act. This "story of my face" occurs again and again in literature: in Sartre's *La Nausée*, very famously in the opening of Duras's *L'Amant* in the context of autobiography, and in *The Picture of Dorian Gray*, where the face becomes the place of the fantastic.

74. B. Ogilvie, *Lacan*, p. 112.

75. Ibid., p. 113.

76. Ogilvie, *Lacan*, p. 113.

77. Ibid.

78. Lacan, "Quelques réflexions sur l'Ego," published 1953 (dating from 1951) in *Journal International de psychanalyse*, Paris vol. 34, pp. 11–17. Quoted by Ogilvie, *Lacan*, p. 116. The texts that develop the concept of the "stade du miroir" are collected in the appendix, p. 119.

79. J. Starobinski, *L'Oeil vivant*, (Paris: Gallimard, 1961), p. 14.

80. Ibid.

81. See particularly the article by Y.-A. Favre, "Pierre Albert-Birot ou le langage en fête," Colloque de Cadiz, 'Dada, Surrealismo: Precursores, Marginales y Heterodoxes, University of Cadiz 1988, where *Grabinoulor* is read exclusively as the incarnation of the Pleasure Principle, suggesting this to be the generating force of Albert-Birot's work. This is indeed a valid reading but a partial one for the whole oeuvre is propelled by contradictory forces.

82. Boyman, *Lecture du Narcisse*, p. 31.

83. Note also the prevalence of Angels in *Grabinoulor*: Grand-Amour, the lover of Eugénie, the extended visit of Gabriel, L'Ange Olivier, and l'Ange Grabinoulor.

84. The reference to "L'Intran" is to the newspaper of the period *L'Intransigeant*. Note the Apollinairian tone of the idea of newspapers bringing the citizen of Paris in contact with the farthest corners of the world. The idea of the everyday being a vehicle for the transition from the trivial to the sublime is explored extensively by Georges Perros: "La poésie est dans la rue, dans le ruisseau" (*Papiers Collés*, II, p. 100) quoted by Lorand Gaspar in his preface (1988) to the 1967 Gallimard edition of *Une Vie ordinaire*. ("Poetry is in the street, in the gutter.")

Une Vie ordinaire, "roman poème," is yet another autobiographical/poetic explanation of the self and a detailed parallel reading with *L'Autre Moi* would be fruitful
in this problematic of the self in language. The opening line: "On m'a bien dit que
j'étais né," echoes the first poem of *L'Autre Moi;* the long poem is just such a
dialogue with self and other, ending on the uncertainty and mortality of the human
condition. ("According to them I was born.")

85. This problem of the "safety" of the everyday, of ignorance, is a problematic explored particularly by Robert Pinget in a text such as *Quelqu'un.* The
narrator, insecure in his identity, dogged by poor memory, continues nonetheless
to spin a web of language for beyond lies the void and death. The details of
human daily life, the banalities of social intercourse, and the comforting and
uncomfortable myriad human activities are proliferated in all their glorious trivial-
ity in the narrative, yet the words move closer and closer to silence as the narrative draws to a close, excess tilting over into nothingness: "J'ai voulu trop faire
. . . et total c'est la mort qui entre" (*Quelqu'un*, p. 222). ("I wanted to do too
much . . . and the net result is it's death that enters.")

86. Compare our analysis of the status of the printed word in chapter 3.

87.

> Je voudrais m'en al-ler sans moi . . .
> je veux
> jus-qu'à demain au moins me sé-parer de je
>
> ("I would like to go a-long without myself
> I want
> Un-til tomorrow at least se-parate myself from I.")

Both this and poem 18 are set to a musical score, reminding us of the programme of *SIC* and of the place of the voice as explored in *La Lune.* The totality
of Albert-Birot's poetic exploration is constantly present, and the potential of
music as the absolute of human creation is returned to in *Grabinoulor.*

88. Georges Perros, *Papiers Collés* II, p. 113, chosen as an epigraph by Lorand Gaspar to his preface for *Une vie ordinaire*, p. 7.

89. The concept of "le mouvement dans l'immobilité" is one that is taken up
at significant moments in *Grabinoulor* and that we will explore in the following
chapter. The constant interaction between these two texts is evident here in the
detail of the expression and the key idea to an understanding of Albert-Birot's
work. See chapter 5, section 6, "Mobility and Immobility." Grabinoulor himself
is referred to as "ce mouvement perpétuel dans l'immobilité," III, 15. (This perpetual movement in immobility/in stasis.)

90. As a postscriptum to this reading of the poems, we would like to indicate
an unpublished poem dating from around 1962–63 when the poet is almost ninety
years old. In a mood of despair and anguish he refers explicitly to both the
exaltation and uncertainty of every poetic quest, and *L'Autre Moi* in particular:

NIET! NIET!

> Où est celui que j'appelais moi-même encor mieux l'autre moi
> Lequel des deux inventa les trente et quatre poèmes
> Moi ou l'autre moi
> Disons qu'il fait trop froid aujourd'hui pour le savoir
> Ne suis ni moi ni l'autre moi
> Hélas hélas que reste-t-il alors

Un non moi qui se souvient d'un moi
Et d'un autre moi
Qui recevait le soleil
Mais ce n'était pas le même
La preuve en est que je faisais de la lumière en écrivant
Tandis qu'aujourd'hui
Tout ce que j'écris
Est gris
Et le serait encor
Même si j'écrivais à l'encre d'or

("Where is the one whom I called myself more accurately the other self;
Which of the two invented the thirty-four poems
Myself or the other self
Let us say that it is too cold today to know
I am not myself nor the other self
Alas alas what is left then
A non self who remembers a self
And an other self
Who welcomed the sun
But this was not the same
The proof is that I created light by writing
While today
Everything I write
Is gray
And would still be gray
Even if I were writing in golden ink")

"Moi," "autre moi," "non-moi,"—being, the sublime, nonbeing—these are all elements of the collection we have analyzed.

91. This sacralization of the poetic text is to be found also in the poetry of Bonnefoy with whom we have already made a parallel. Starobinski reads Bonnefoy's poetry less as the narcissistic reflection of the self than the seeking for an understanding of man's relationship to the world. Albert-Birot's self-reflection is equally a reflection on the nature of this relationship to the world, for from the inner experience an art that may be communicated comes into being: "Le sacré, s'il ne doit pas disparaître, se réfugie dans l'expérience "intérieure," se lie à l'acte de vivre, à la communication, à l'amour partagé—et prend ainsi pour demeure le sensible, le langage, l'art" (J. Starobinski, preface to Bonnefoy, *Poèmes* [Paris: Gallimard, 1982], p. 10). ("The sacred, if it is not to disappear, takes refuge in interior experience, is linked to the act of writing, to communication, to shared love—and so takes as its abode the sensory, language, art.)

92. Apollinaire, *Chroniques d'Art*, (O.C. IV, pp. 16–17).

93. Timothy Mathews, "Apollinaire and Cubism?" in *Visual Poetics*. Note Mathews's current work in progress on alienation in modern French literature and painting. He sees Apollinaire's later work as a consequence of the poet's involvement with and interpretation of Cubism and Orphism and argues that "the post-modern subversion of the I and the ego, its decentering of the subject, seeks to undermine the myth of creativity itself in an effort to uncover the relations binding the present to history." Mathews notes his differences to Marjorie Perloff's work on these points. In the poetics of estrangement and alienation that Mathews assigns to Apollinaire, it would appear that the poet never takes up the divine role that he advocated: Albert-Birot embraces the call to divinity wholeheartedly.

94. Compare Ch. Delacampagne in *Corps Ecrit,* p. 151, where he notes the devalorization of painting by philosophy: "la peinture donne une représentation sensible des idées, la philosophie une repésentation purement intellectuelle des intelligibles" ("painting gives a perceptible representation of ideas, philosophy is a purely intellectual representation of what is intelligible.") Remembering also Starobinski's remarks where the sacred takes refuge in "le sensible, le langage, l'art." Delacampagne goes on to examine the relation between painting and philosophy, specifically in terms of the self-portrait, the reflection on and expression of the self as metaphysical meditation: "La question de l'autoportrait ne cesse de nous reconduire vers le problème entre peindre et philosopher, c'est-à-dire vers leur profonde unité" (ibid., p. 159). ("The question of the self-portrait never ceases to take us back to the problem between painting and philosophizing, that is to say, to their profound unity.")

95. J. Starobinski, preface to Bonnefoy's *Poèmes,* p. 11.

96. Roger Roussot, *Barbacane* 7, p. 94. It should be remembered that during his early years in Paris training as a sculptor, Albert-Birot attended classes in philosophy at the Sorbonne and Collège de France (see Introduction).

97. Ibid.

98. Starobinski, preface to Bonnefoy's *Poèmes,* p. 12. Again he is discussing the relationship of Bonnefoy to his creation, and yet the reading is strikingly appropriate for the work of Albert-Birot between *L'Autre Moi* and *Grabinoulor.*

CHAPTER 5. *GRABINOULOR* AND THE SEEKING OF KNOWLEDGE

1. David Balhatchet's thesis (see bibliography) gives an idea of the immensity and scope of this proliferating text, written continuously from 1917 to the early 1960s. The early part of his thesis also charts the various problems of publication that *Grabinoulor* has been subjected to, detailed also by Albert-Birot himself in his "Les Malheurs de Grabinoulor" and included in the preface to the 1933 edition (Denoël et Steele) of Livres I and II. The 1991 integral edition includes a "Historique de l'édition de *Grabinoulor*" (pp. 951–53) and a bibliography of the various sections and chapters that have been published sporadically from 1918 to the definitive edition, Editions Jean-Michel Place, Paris, November 1991.

2. Previous readers of Albert-Birot's work recognized a similar position: "C'est je crois, cette énorme épopée qu'il faut scruter le plus attentivement. Tout me paraît s'y trouver. Les clefs ainsi que les motivations majeures de l'écriture pabienne" (Max Pons, "Connaissance de Pierre Albert-Birot," *F,* 2–3, p. 16). ("It is, I believe, this enormous epic that must be scrutinized the most attentively. Everything seems to me to be in there. Here are the keys to, as well as the major motivations of Albert-Birot's writing.") This early insight is here developed into a more rigorous critical analysis. The emphasis on *Grabinoulor* as epic is essential to our own preliminary section on the text.

3. M.-L. Lentengre, "Les appétits hyperboliques de Grabinoulor," p. 18.

4. Albert-Birot in his letter to Léo Tixier. It is equally as Arlette Albert-Birot points out in her preface in the 1991 edition, the aesthetic of "L'esprit nouveau," an aesthetics of surprise (see Apollinaire's "L'Esprit nouveau et les poètes."

5. Albert-Birot answered to the name of Grabinoulor or Grabi as his hero is frequently referred to in the narrative. The text encourages this familiarity be-

tween Grabi and his interlocutors and indeed between Grabi and his readers. On another level the concept of myth is extremely powerful in the reading proposed here:

> Le mythe raconte une histoire sacrée; il relate un événément qui a lieu dans le temps primordial des 'commencements'. Autrement dit, le mythe raconte comment, grâce aux exploits des Etres surnaturels, une réalité est venue à l'existence, que ce soit la réalité totale, le Cosmos, ou seulement un fragment. . . . Dans la plupart des cas, il ne suffit pas de connaître le mythe de l'origine, il faut le réciter; on proclame en quelque sorte sa science. On la montre. (M. Eliade, *Aspects du Mythe* [Paris: Gallimard, Collection "Idées," 1963], p. 15, quoted also by G. Jean, *La Poésie*, pp. 29–30.)

> ("Myth recounts a sacred story; it relates an event that takes place in the primordial time of "beginnings." In other words, myth recounts how, thanks to the exploits of supernatural Beings, a reality came into existence, whether this is the total reality, the Cosmos, or simply a fragment. . . . In most cases, it is not enough to know the myth of origins, it must be recited; you proclaim, as it were, your knowledge.")

The reciting of *Grabinoulor* at the "dîners Grabinoulor" lends an extra mythic dimension to the creation and the reception of the narrative as the narrative body fuses with the human body, the word becomes flesh, and true creation is revealed. Compare our concluding remarks to chapter 4 on the advent of the logos in the *Poèmes à l'Autre Moi*.

6. Albert-Birot would appear to be an archetypal poet in the way that Virginia La Charité considers Mallarmé:

> Basically, Mallarmé is an archetypal poet, drawing on all human expressions of creation from classical myth to the Bible to plastic art, even fashion. . . . If there is religious thinking in his work, it is not that of Pascal, the Romantics, Baudelaire or even Verlaine; rather he assigns to poetry the role that poets of the decades and centuries before him traditionally assigned to God. Mallarmé makes a religious act of poetry in the sense that he ascribes to it the principles of coherence, order, beauty, harmony, unity and synthesis. He does not poeticize in the manner of the Romantics, nor does he wrestle with God and Christianity in the manner of Baudelaire. (*The Dynamics of Space: Mallarmé's "Un coup de dés n'abolira jamais le Hasard,"* [Lexington, KY.: French Forum Publishers, 1987], p. 119)

The heritage of both Mallarmé and Baudelaire echo in the work of Albert-Birot, but neither of these two poetic projects anticipate exactly the work under analysis here. Albert-Birot is a poet without orthodox religious belief but with a faith in the vocation of the poet to explore the spiritual in human existence.

7. W. Ong in *Orality and Literacy,* discusses the epic and orality with reference to the Homeric epic (for example, p. 21) and agrees with Havelock that the beginnings of Greek philosophy were tied in with the restructuring of thought brought about by writing, in a culture hitherto entirely oral (pp. 27–28). The paradox of the epic and the modern, resolved for Albert-Birot himself, continues to be problematic for our reading here.

8. T. Todorov, *Poétique de la prose,* (Paris: Seuil, 1971), for example, p. 30.

9. Ibid., p. 57.

10. Ibid., pp. 36–37.

11. Ibid., p. 49.

12. Umberto Eco, *La Guerre du Faux,* Paris eds. Grasset et Fasquelle, 1985, Section II, "Le Nouveau Moyen Age," pp. 87–116 (quoting here from p. 112). Eco discusses our epoch as a new Middle Ages not only artistically but historically

and politically also. Compare the medieval/modern status of his own *The Name of the Rose*. The reading of *Grabinoulor* by way of Bakhtine's reading of Rabelais in Nicole Le Dimna's study, "La Sage Folie de Grabinoulor," is also to be paralleled here. The Rabelaisian aspects of the text have been noted by several commentators.

13. Eco, *La Guerre du Faux*, p. 114.

14. Todorov, *Poetique*, p. 29, returning here to his discussion of the Odyssey. The self-conscious narrative of the "nouveau roman" has invented nothing new, self-reflexivity having been a generating force from the origins of literature.

15. Ong, *Orality and Literacy*, pp. 70–71. The writer considers the development of the modern hero and anti-hero as a direct consequence of the printing process.

16. Grabi's own encounter with Gutenberg is an interesting one where the hero chastises the father of the printing process for destroying the unique value of each literary creation. Gutenberg believes himself to have bestowed endless riches on mankind:

> Les livres Grabinoulor les livres les livres y penses-tu! j'y ai pensé Gutenberg et bien pensé oui les livres voilà ta mauvaise action tu as VULGARISE tu as tué les oeuvres en les reproduisant à volonté mille dix mille cent mille fois de cette réalité vivante et unique comme un être tu as fait des "exemplaires" . . . or une oeuvre une grande oeuvre de mots est l'étoile du poète toute créée par mystérieuse procuration cette étoile pour garder toute sa valeur doit demeurer unique dès qu'il y a reproductions il n'y a plus qu'étoiles fabriquées (VI, 12, pp. 919–20)

> ("Books Grabinoulor books books think about it I've thought about it Gutenberg and thought about it well yes books that's your evil deed you've VULGARIZED you've killed works of art by reproducing them at will a thousand ten thousand a hundred thousand times from this living and unique reality like a human being you've made "copies" . . . well a work a great work of words is the poet's star created by mysterious procuration and this star to keep its value must remain unique as soon as there are reproductions there are only fabricated stars")

There is a personal note in this, of course, when Grabi "the great unread" continues: "il tombe sous le sens que plus l'oeuvre est haute moins elle a de lecteurs et ensuite plus elle est à tout le monde plus elle perd la puissance et l'unicité." ("It stands to reason that the more lofty a work is, the less readers it has and then that the more it is everyone's reach, the more it loses its strength and its uniqueness.")

The epic hero laments the demise of his peers: "As writing and eventually print gradually alter the old oral poetic structures, narrative builds less and less on 'heavy' figures, until, some three centuries after print, it can move comfortably in the ordinary human world typical of the novel. Here in the place of the hero, one eventually encounters the anti-hero." (Ong, *Orality and Literacy*, p. 71.) See also chapter 6, particularly "Oral memory—the story line and characterization," p. 131 onward.

17. Albert-Birot's "La Langue en barre," published as an appendix to *Les Six Livres de Grabinoulor*, pp. 961–63. The quote is from page 961.

18. Ibid., p. 962.

There is a startling contemporary comparison to be made in the work of Philippe Sollers. His introductory remarks to *Paradis* take up not only the same ideas, but the same vocabulary:

Pourquoi pas de ponctuation visible? Parce qu'elle vit profondément à l'intérieur des phrases, plus précise, souple, efficace; plus légère que la grosse machinerie marchande des points, des virgules, des parenthèses, des guillemets, des tirets. Ici, on ponctue autrement et plus que jamais, à la voix, au souffle, au chiffre, à l'oreille; on entend le volume de l'éloquence lisible! Pourquoi pas de blancs, de paragraphes, de chapitres? Parce que tout se raconte et se rythme à la fois maintenant, non pas dans l'ordre restreint de la vieille logique embrouillée terrestre, mais dans celle merveilleusement claire et continue, à éclipses, des ondes et des satellites.

("Why no visible punctuation? Because it is living deep down inside the sentences, more precise, supple, effective, lighter than the heavy machinery that produces full stops, commas, brackets, speech marks, dashes. Here punctuation is done in another way and, more than ever, with the voice, the breath, with figures, with the ear. The volume of legible eloquence is heard! Why are there no spaces, paragraphs, chapters? Because everything is recounted and finds its rhythm at the same time, not in the restrained order of old earthly, muddled logic, but in a logic that is marvelously clear and continuous, that of eclipses, waves, and satellites.")

The encyclopedic, all-embracing nature of the narration also has a striking parallel and Sollers's description of his work would be eminently applicable to *Grabinoulor:*

Pourquoi pas une histoire mais cent mille histoires? Parce qu'il n'y a plus à simuler et à encadrer, mais à faire déferler, le plus amplement, minutieusement et rapidement possible, la narration et sa mémoire qui vont de l'horreur au comique, du constat de mort répété à l'état mystique, de l'information critique à la méditation catastrophique, du biologique au métaphysique en passant, par la dérision, l'obscénité, et bien entendu, le tragique. (Philippe Sollers, inside front cover of *Paradis*, [Paris: Seuil, 1981]).

("Why not one story but a hundred thousand stories? Because there is no longer anything to simulate and to frame, but to unfurl, as widely, as meticulously, as rapidly as possible, the narration and its memory that go from the horrible to the comic, from the reporting of death to the mystical state, from critical information to catastrophic meditation, from the biological to the metaphysical by the way of derision, obscenity, and, of course, the tragic.")

There are important differences also—*Paradis* does not obey the rigorous syntax of *Grabinoulor* and relies more on rhythm and repetition for its construction, although the juxtaposition of words, which generates the musicality of the text, is to be found frequently also in *Grabinoulor*. Philippe Forest describes the "posture prophétique" of *Paradis*, its status as a sacred text: "Le nouveau texte prophétique qui appelle l'apocalypse que nous vivons." ("The new prophetic text which summons the apocalypse which we are living.") (Philippe Forest, remarks made in a research seminar, "Sollers Tel Quel, un romancier français au Paradis," Birkbeck College, November 1991). See also his book, *Philippe Sollers*, (Paris: Seuil, 1993).

19. Henri Bergson, *L'Energie spirituelle*, chosen as epigraph to the *Six Livres de Grabinoulor.*

We have previously discussed the importance of Bergson for the aesthetics of the avant-garde during the first decade of the twentieth century and the particular parallel to be made with the vitalism of the work of Albert-Birot.

20. When Albert-Birot describes in "La Langue en barre" how the text should be read out loud, his description is that of a litany:

Je ne veux point d'intonations, je ne demande point au lecteur d'être expressif, il n'a qu'à lire ces pages avec un minimum d'intelligence évidemment indispensable et un maximum d'articulation, sur un seul ton, et sa lecture devra être, si l'on veut, un ronronnement qui déterminera dans l'esprit de l'auditeur le spasme poétique, si, bien entendu, cet auditeur est sensible, et s'il ne s'oppose pas à se mettre en état de bonne réceptivité.

("I do not want any intonation, I do not ask the reader to be expressive, he only has to read these pages with a minimum of intelligence which is obviously indispensable and a maximum of articulation, in one tone, and his reading will have to be, if you like, a purring that will determine in the mind of the listener the poetic spasm, if, of course, this listener is not opposed to putting himself in a state of good receptiveness.")

Albert-Birot appears to advocate a state of passive reception—to receive the sacred text and hear its message.

21. Todorov, *Poétique*, p. 71.

22. Ibid.

23. Compare Todorov, Poétique, pp. 73–74: "La construction cyclique de substitions s'oppose à nouveau à la construction unidirectionelle et contiguë." ("The cyclical construction of substitutions is in opposition again to the one-directional and contiguous construction.")

24. A parallel with Proust is irresistible here, *A la recherche du temps perdu, Le Temps retrouvé,* the titles indicating that this also is a quest, a quest in time, in memory for something that has been lost and, once found, endows the seeker with eternal life. The Holy Grail manifests itself in many forms. Todorov's narrative structure (horizontal/vertical) is, of course, applicable here also—another immensely dense narrative stretching out linearly but equally cyclical.

25. Todorov, *Poétique*, p. 67.

26. See, for example, the argument of Kathryn Hume on the mimetic impulse and the fantastic impulse in literature in *Fantasy and Mimesis. Responses to Reality in Western Literature,* (New York and London: Methuen, 1984), chapter 1.

27. Todorov, *Poétique*, p. 29.

28. *Le Temps retrouvé,* concluding lines. *Time Regained,* trans. Andreas Mayer (London: Chatto and Windus, 1931); this edition is 1970, p. 474.

29. Houdebine, *Excès de langages,* (Paris: Denoël, 1984), p. 322. The writer is considering here how to approach the "souffle hyperbolique" of the text of Sollers's *Paradis,* similarly unpunctuated. Houdebine chooses to follow a voice in the thread of the narrative: "Disons que dans la polyphonie du roman, je suivrai plus particulièrement la trace d'une voix, dont toutefois le récurrence est telle qu'elle assure au moins de ceci: que qui ne l'entend pas n'entend rien." ("Let us say that in the polypony of the novel, I will follow most particularly the trace of a voice, the recurrence of which is such that it assures at least this—that he who does not hear it hears nothing.") From here Houdebine is able to construct a set of formulations for possible access to the text.

30. This constant return to the body seems at the very opposite pole to such an abstract system as that, for example, of Descartes. The body/mind opposition seems clear in the act of creation—not "Je pense donc je suis," but more "Je crée / je bouge donc je vis." ("I think therefore I am") ("I create / I move therefore I live")

31. Again see the thesis of David Balhatchet on the significance (thematically) of the circle in *Grabinoulor* and in other literary works. Here my emphasis is on the structuring force of the circle and its implications for the reading process.

32. Nicole Le Dimna, "La sage folie de Grabinoulor," in *Jeux et Enjeux chez Pierre Albert-Birot*, p. 45.

33. M.-L. Lentengre, "Les appétits hyperboliques de Grabinoulor," p. 140. Lentengre gives the episode of the repeated actions of the clowns in a circle in *Grabinoulor*, II, 18, as a "mise-en-abyme" of the text as a whole.

34. Mary Ann Caws, "Le Chant sphèrique de Pierre Albert-Birot," *F*, 2–3, p. 35. The circular aspect of Albert-Birot's text and its recurrence in his poetry is frequently commented on (other than in the extended analysis of Balhatchet), for example, Dominique Baudouin on *Les Poèmes à l'Autre Moi:* "Verbe poétique qui unifie en une création sphérique le spatial et l'infini" (*F*, 2–3, p. 113). ("Poetic word which unifies in a spherical creation the spatial and the infinite.") He takes his "moulin à poèmes" "poetry mill" as symbolic of his entire creation "une autre spirale cosmique" ("another cosmic spiral").

35. Compare J.-F. Lyotard, p. 112, commenting on "le rapport de l'espace scriptural au corps propre du lecteur." ("the relationship of scriptural space to the reader's own body") He suggests: "Le corps est induit à prendre certaines attitudes selon que lui est offert un angle ou un cercle, une verticale ou une oblique." ("The body is induced to take up certain attitudes according to whether it is offered an angle or a circle, a vertical or an oblique.") The parallel with our reading of *La Guerre* in chapter 1 is extremely important.

36. Lyotard, ibid., p. 213, commenting on Mallarmé's "Un coup de dés."

37. In an extended episode in Volume IV, Grabinoulor gives one of his visitors, Ange Olivier, a tour of his Paris apartment and points out this canvas, immediately recognizable as *La Guerre*, in particular. Ange Olivier also comments on two poems hanging on the wall that are reproduced in the text itself. Grabi explains: "ah ça ce sont des poèmes-pancartes que j'eusse aimé voir dressés le long des routes en panneaux de quatre mètres sur trois" (IV, 13, p. 527). ("ah that they're bill-board poems which I would've liked to see set up along the road on boards measuring four metres by three") They appear in the text as they were originally printed in *La Lune*. That these are a selection of the paintings that hung on Albert-Birot's own walls is no surprise, and they may still be viewed in the Fonds Albert-Birot.

38. This is not to ignore or deny the metadiscourse on poetry, and there are certain episodes that should be briefly highlighted as a source for further reflection. In Livre III, 8, p. 185, Grabi meets "le Poète-Inconnu" (the unknown-poet) and discovers his poetry machine: "La machine transformera toute cette matière élémentaire en un poème complexe" ("the machine will transform all this elementary matter into a complex poem"), and a discussion ensues on the nature of true and false poetry and on those qualities necessary for the true poet—"Poète-Ingénieur" (engineer-poet), "Poète-Mécanique" (mechanic-poet), theoretician, and chemist: "ce qui lui avait permis de concevoir sa machine de telle sorte que les mots à l'intérieur soient en perpétuelles combinaisons et réactions entre eux c'est merveilleux fabuleux miraculeux lumineux vertiginieux" (p. 186). ("which had allowed his machine to be conceived in such a way that the words inside are in perpetual combinations and reactions between themselves it's marvelous fabulous miraculous luminous vertiginous.") What is particularly relevant in the discussions on poetry is that they frequently reflect the discourse of painting and essentially so when considering the development of modern poetry. At the reception given by Grabinoulor for scholars, artists, and great men from every era and branch of human knowledge (V, 6), Grabinoulor and Lamartine discuss modern poetry, "la vraie poèsie" ("true poetry"):

Vous mettez en écriture l'essence de cette situation en somme nous n'avons donné que l'aspect extérieur nous n'avons fait que souligner l'apparence que tout le monde peut voir tandis que vous vous donnez la réalité intérieure enfin quoi nous avons donné le corps et vous en vrais dieux vous donnez l'âme mais Monsieur de Lamartine comme vous voici renseigné oui c'est Guillaume Apollinaire qui vient de me raconter tout ça quelle révélation hélas bien tardive (p. 649)

("You put into writing the essence of this situation all in all we only rendered the external aspect we only emphasized the appearance that everyone can see whilst you you at last render the internal reality we rendered the body and you like real gods you render the soul but Monsieur de Lamartine how well informed you are yes it's Guillaume Apollinaire who just told me all that what a revelation alas a rather late one")

Apollinaire, also a guest and in Grabi's opinion the only person able to explain such a thing is: "le poteau-frontière ou le poste-frontière entre le passé et l'avenir entre les temps anciens qui vont d'Homère à la fine point Baudelaire Rimbaud Mallarmé." ("The border post or the border transmitter between the past and the future between the ancient times which go from Homer to the highest point Baudelaire Rimbaud Mallarmé.") Lamartine discusses the poets after Apollinaire:

"Et ceux qui les suivent se sont plus avant encore envolés dans le chant qui ne "dit" pas pour dire bien davantage enfin les poètes d'aujourd'hui savent ce que Poésie est ce qui ne veut pas dire qu'ils la tiennent mais ils l'ont vue et maintenant bien sûr ils ne cesseront plus de courir après toutefois pour être juste il convient de dire que dans tous les temps les poètes ont eu un semblant d'intuition de ce que doit être la vraie poésie seulement pour les poètes du présent siècle c'est une réalité largement consciente (ibid.)

("And those who follow them took off even higher in the song which does not "say" to say it better well today's poets know what Poetry is which doesn't mean to say they've got it but they've seen it and now of course they won't stop running after it but to be fair it should be said that in every era poets have had some intuition of what true poetry should be only for poets in the present century it's a generally conscious reality")

Enthusiastic, Lamartine decides: "Un jour réincarné bien qu'incarné j'écrirai 'Le Lac' sans lac" (p. 650). ("One day when I'm reincarnated I'll write "The Lake" without the lake.")

39. The conversation between Cézanne and Raphaël includes a damning indictment of surrealism as the history of art is related:

Ils ont fait aussi la peinture surréaliste sorte d'élucubrations subconsciolittéraires qui ne touchent en rien les fondamentales recherches picturales et sont d'ailleurs peintes par des peintres affreusement "pompiers" qui peignent ces soi-disant surréalités beaucoup plus mal que Meissonier ou Bouguereau ne peignaient leur pseudo-réalité alors Cézanne pourquoi me parlez-vous de ces peintrillons de fausee originalité parce que s'ils n'étaient pas brillants ils étaient horriblement bruyants laissons ce bruit Cézanne parlez-moi plutôt du cubisme ça c'est quelque chose (V, 6, p. 637)

("They also did surrealist painting a sort of subconscioliterary wild imaginings that have nothing to do with fundamental pictorial research and that are what's more painted by terribly "pretentious" painters who paint these so-called surrealities much more badly than Meissonier or Bouguereau painted their pseudo-reality so Cézanne why are you telling me about these painterlings and their false originality because if they weren't brilliant they were horribly noisy let's leave this noise Cézanne rather tell me about cubism that really is something")

40. Enthusiastic about these explanations, Raphaël creates his first "abstract" on a napkin. Unfortunately in true grabinouloresque fashion, Hep, Grabi's servant, throws it away while clearing up.

41. In chapter 4 we quoted Starobinski from the preface to Bonnefoy's *Poèmes* on the relationship between art and the sacred in the contemporary world. The concept of "between two worlds" is taken from the title of the preface: "La poésie, entre deux mondes." Starobinski's reading of Bonnefoy provides a suggestive interaction with the attitudes of Albert-Birot and the paradoxes that face poetry in the twentieth century:

> Telle est, me semble-t-il, la condition paradoxale où se trouve la poésie, depuis moins de deux siècles: condition précaire, puisqu'elle ne dispose pas du système de preuves qui assure l'autorité du discours scientifique, mais en même temps condition privilégiée où la poésie assume consciemment une fonction ontologique—je veux dire, toute une réfléxion sur l'être—dont elle n'avait pas eu à porter la charge et le souci dans les siècles antérieurs. Elle a, derrière elle, un monde perdu, un ordre dans lequel elle était incluse, et dont elle sait qu'il ne peut revivre. Elle porte en elle l'espoir d'un nouvel ordre, d'un nouveau ·sens, dont elle doit imaginer l'instauration. (pp. 10–11)

> ("Such is, it seem to me, the paradoxical position in which poetry has found itself for at least the last two centuries. It is in a precarious position because it does not have at its disposal the system of proof that assures the authority of scientific discourse, but at the same time it is a privileged condition in which poetry assumes consciously an ontological function—I mean by that a whole reflection on being—the burden and concern of which it did not have to carry in earlier centuries. It has, behind it, a lost world, an order in which it was included and which it knows cannot be brought back to life. It carries with it the hope of a new order, of a new meaning, whose institution it must imagine.")

The ontological and spiritual quest of poetry requires also a parallel with the work of Henri Michaux, and although there are at the same time enormous differences between his writing closer to Blanchot's "écriture du désastre" than to Albert-Birot's vitalism, the emphasis on the subjectivity, the presence of the body, the quest for truth in movement, rhythm and excess demand equally a parallel exploration: "J'écris pour me parcourir. Peindre, composer, écrire, me parcourir. Là est l'aventure d'être en vie" (Michaux, *Passages* [Paris: Gallimard, 1950], p. 142). ("I write to travel all over myself. Painting, composing, writing, traveling myself. There is the adventure of being alive.")

42. Grabinoulor is discussing painting with nature (V, 9), each accusing the other of selfishness. Nature's one consolation in mankind had always been the painters who had clearly adored her in their imitations of her but had now appeared to have abandoned her. Grabinoulor argues for this as a development of art. Nature remains unconvinced: "Adieu Grabinoulor amuse-toi bien avec tes créateurs de ronds et de carrés soi-disants abstracteurs de quintessence" (p. 688). ("Farewell Grabinoulor enjoy yourself with your creators of circles and squares so-called quintessential abstractionists"). This is an extremely important discussion on the role of art, the representation of reality, and the role of the artist.

43. No other commentators have analyzed the narrative in this way; only one reviewer (on Barbara Wright's translation, see bibliography for details) makes the comparison: "Neither is this just a collection of random fantasies, or an exercise in self-indulgent optimist: the story pulses urgently to suggest ways in which the world might be rearranged to enhance its brightness and openness" (Kevin Taylor,

in *Poetry Nation Review*). This particular reviewer comments particularly on the "statuette" episode in Livre I, 2 and its significance for the book as a whole:

> In this way the book serves as a meditation on dimension, spatial and temporal. It is concerned with centres, (locating and inventing and then exploring the objects and ideas we hold as centres of references), with lines, curves and angles . . . and with time. . . . These ideas are related throughout to images of copulation, which are seen as transcending time, involving the ultimate coming-together of curves and straight lines: superimpositions of two centres creating a third.

The assimilation of the basic figures of the curve and the straight line to sexuality is an important point but applicable only to Livre I and, to some extent, to Livre II.

The allusions to cubism outside the theoretical discussions are frequent. Ange Olivier expresses his delight in cubism in the visit previously indicated and in abstraction also:

> Mais vous avez là un tableau cubiste ma parole ça c'est de la peinture moi je vous avoue que la peinture ne commence à m'intéresser vraiment à partir de l'école cubiste oh l'impressionnisme je ne peux pas le voir enfin cubisme vint et j'aime aussi beaucoup ce que vous nommez si drôlement la peinture abstraite vraiment je ne connais rien de plus surprenant que cette volonté de mettre l'abstrait en plastique il n'y a que les hommes pour aller jusque là (IV, 13, p. 525)

> ("But you have there a cubist painting my word now that's painting I must admit that painting only really begins to interest me fron the cubist movement onward oh impressionism I can't stand it finally cubism came along and I also like very much what you call so funnily abstract painting I know nothing more surprising than this will to give form to the abstract only men would go to those lengths")

When Grabi meets Vie in IV, 3, p. 403, she resembles "un parfait tableau cubiste." ("a perfect cubist painting)." It is significant that the life force should have the energy of a cubist canvas. Finally an allusion to cubist painting appears in the final lines of the final volume of *Grabinoulor:* "ce qui ne l'empêche pas de se mettre à sourire à la pensée inattendue qui lui passe quelque part par la tête qu'il met Xeuxis devant un tableau de peintre cubiste mais qu'en pense Xeuxis cela ne nous regarde pas". ("which doesn't prevent us from smiling at the unexpected thought which goes through his head that he can put Xeusis in front of a cubist painting but what Xeusis thinks about it is none of our business"). It is after this comment that the narrator loses Grabi from sight and the hero, the narrator, and the reader are left finally to their own devices. (p. 943).

44. Tristan Tzara, *Oeuvres Complètes* 4, p. 398 and quoted by Serge Fauchereau in *La Révolution cubiste*, p. 170.

We recall also Albert-Birot's own insistence on the difference between "l'écrit logique" and "la conception poétique" ("La Langue en Barre," previously quoted.)

45. Pierre Daix, *Journal du Cubisme*, (Paris: Editions d'Art Albert-Skira, 1992). By spring 1913 he argues: "Ce n'était plus le cubisme qui bouleverse la peinture, c'est le nouvel espace pictural qui écartèle les peintres" (p. 96). ("It is no longer cubism that turns painting upside down, it is the new pictorial space that tears the painters apart.") Compare also Albert-Birot on Severini's paintings: "Jusqu'ici un tableau était une fraction dans l'étendue, et qu'il devient avec vous une fraction dans le temps" (*SIC*, n° 2, JMP p. 15) and quoted by us in chapter

2. ("Until now the painting was a fraction in space, and with you it becomes a fraction in time.")

46. All commentators on Albert-Birot's work have something to say about the nature of time in *Grabinoulor* and in his work as a whole, for example, Jean Follain, *Pierre Albert-Birot*, p. 27: "Albert-Birot en marche se sent dans un éternel présent" ("Albert-Birot when waking feels himself to be in an eternal present"), and p. 36: "Grabi fait ses voyages en durée et étendue avec la volonté de toujours se retrouver au coeur du présent" ("Grabi makes his journeys in time and space with the will to always being at the heart of the present"); Arlette Albert-Birot, *La Barbacane* 7: "Son existence entière aura été une lutte joyeuse avec Kronos" ("his whole existence was a joyful struggle with Kronos"); Jean Rousselet, ibid., p. 90: "Un pied dans la préhistoire et l'autre dans l'illimité de l'avenir ("one foot in prehistory and the other in the unlimited space of the future"); Claude Abastado, "Jeux et visées", p.73: 'Le temps illimité et réversible des exploits est enchâssé dans le présent de l'existence banale' ("the unlimited and reversible time of the exploits is embedded in the present of banal existence"). It is in this final quote that we come close to the perspective explored here, the idea of an imaginary space-time that is created, structured.

47. A constant generative force of the narrative is Grabinoulor's will to change an imperfect world made by a creator with neither foresight nor imagination. David Balhatchet examines exhaustively Grabinoulor's taste for "cosmic manipulation." Grabinoulor continues to work for the "greater good" of humankind in a world where Nature is at worst hostile and at best indifferent. He does, however, become less and less impetuous in his projects as the narrative progresses, and he is forced to acknowledge the conservative side of human nature becoming eventually disillusioned with his fellow man. Starobinski's preface again stresses a similar point:

L'essor de la physique mathématique prolongé par celui de la technique, a tout ensemble accru la sécurité matérielle des hommes, et déplacé le lieu de la nature au service des hommes (des désirs humains, en ce "bas monde"), mais ils ont dû, par cela, renoncer à contempler les objets naturels, les choses singulières—laissant ainsi en déshérence tout le territoire où ce qui nous environne est perçu dans sa couleur, sa musique, sa consistance palpable. (p. 9)

("The expansion of mathematical physics prolonged by that of technical development, together increased the material security of men, and displaced the place of nature in the service of men [of human desires in this world 'here below'], but by doing that, the had to renounce the contemplation of natural objects, remarkable things—thereby escheating the whole domain where what surrounds us is perceived in its colors, its music, its palpable consistency.")

48. J.-F. Lyotard, *Discours, Figure*, p. 181 and p. 186.
Grabi's own interaction with Galileo is one of the few unsuccessful missions in the text. In the final volume, Grabi sets off to find Galileo regarding the rotation of the world (VI, 12). Once again he must have truth: "à savoir au juste quel est celui qui a réussi à la faire tourner même en admettant que nous ne sachions jamais comment il s'y est pris et si c'est effectivement Galilée" (p. 923). ("To know exactly who it was who managed to make it turn even while admitting that we'll never know how he did it and in fact it's Galileo)." The astonishing thing is that Grabi is unable to find him:

on veut dire par là qu'en fait de Galilée il n'a recontré que le vide et c'est sur ce vide qu'il s'est cassé le nez . . . c'est peut-être la première fois que pareille mésaventure lui advient on sait en effet qu'il a toujours pu avoir à volonté des entretiens particuliers avec les personnages soi-disant plus ou moins anciens auxquels il avait à dire des choses plus ou moins sérieuses déçu et assez furieux il se met à chercher or chercher c'est profondément désagréable (ibid.)

("We mean by that that in fact all he found of this Galileo was the void and it's against this void that he came a cropper . . . it's perhaps the first time that such a mishap befalls him we indeed know that he has always been able to have personal meetings at will with so-called more or less ancient personnages to whom he had more or less serious things to say disappointed and rather angry he began to search and searching is deeply disagreeable").

For the first time Grabi does not fulfill his quest for a source of knowledge.

49. J.-F. Lyotard, *Discours, Figure,* p. 164, in the section "Positions du discours et neutralisation de l'espace."

He continues by commenting on both Bergson and Freud: "L'un et l'autre, néanmoins admettent à des titres divers le rôle du langage dans l'organisation de l'espace 'adulte'" (p. 165). ("Each of them admit nonetheless in different ways the role of language in the organization of adult space.")

50. Compare also the poem "Ophiolâtre" by Albert-Birot, published in *Le Mensuel littéraire et poétique,* Bruxelles, n° 189, November 1990, p. 7 (not in a collection at this point in time).

Ophiolâtrie

un poème (1959) [extrait]

Si les paysages étaient serpents souples souples il s'enrouleraient
Nature notre vieille amie ne serait que volutes et souples lovées
Monde ne serait que douces douces courbes amoureuses de l'homme
Qui lui-même tout en arrondis serait doux doux amoureux du Monde
Les mots eux-mêmes seraient ronds un beau poème en écriture serait
Serait une ou des pages d'inégaux cerceaux les uns aux autres
Plaisamment enchaînés ainsi notre âme bulle si satinée nature
Ne craindrait ni les déchirures ni même espérons-le les égratignures
Il est bien certain que l'amour cet e dans l'o cette boucle dans l'ove
N'est que rondeur à rondeur et les planètes n'ont-elles pas cherché
Leur bonheur dans la sphéricité et ne sont-elles pas toutes amoureuses
De la sphère d'à côté interminable Univers scintillant miracle d'amour
La chose est bien prouvée Terre notre Terre est un monde raté
Il fallait que fût grosse d'eau Planète Mer et que fussions-nous
Un poisson supérieur alors tout n'était que courbes glissades et profondeurs
Et un jour il nous eût été donné de rêver la dure et impossible droite

Ophiolatry

a poem (1959) (extract)

If landscapes were supple supple serpents they would curl and curl
Nature our old friend would be all volutes and supple coils
The World would be all soft soft curves in love with man
Who himself would be all soft soft rondures in love with the World
Words themselves would be round a beautiful handwritten poem would be
Would be one or several pages of unequal circles pleasantly interlinked
So that our soul that bubble which by nature is so silky
Would not have to fear wounds or even let us hope scratches
It is quite certain that love that e in the o that loop in the ovum

Is only a roundness to a roundness and did not the planets
Look for their joy in sphericity? and are they not all in love
With the nearby sphere? the interminable Universe that scintillating miracle of love?
It has been clearly proved the Earth our Earth is a failed world
When Planet Sea became pregnant with water and we were
A superior fish then everything was all glissades and depths
But one day we were given the possibility of dreaming the hard impossible straight line
(Translation by Barbara Wright, unpublished, 1995.)

Dominique Baudouin reads the symbolism of the two lines in the same way and emphasizes their importance for the work as a whole: "Il faudrait tout relire pour saisir les mille nuances de ce vaste réseau où s'entrecroisent l'axe de la mort et de la vie" (*Espaces*, p. 39). ("You would need to reread the whole thing to grasp the thousands of nuances of this vast network in which the axes of life and death intersect each other.") His point reiterates the need for our insistence on these in the present study.

51. Lyotard, p. 182.

52. Ibid., p. 187. Compare also here the work of writers like Raymond Queneau and Georges Perec.

53. Compare the terminology of J.-L. Houdebine in *Excès de Langages*, p. 328: "La codification du représentable (et donc de l'imaginaire)" ("The codifying of what is representable [and therefore of the imagination].)" Houdebine discusses the mathematics of Cantor and the principle of infinity in the work of Duns Scot to elaborate a problematic of infinity both mathematically and philosophically. He quotes Cantor: "Tout dépend de la *position* du fini par rapport à l'infini, si le fini précède, il passe dans l'infini et y disparaît $(1 + =)$ s'il cède le pas au contraire et prend place après l'infini, il subsiste et se continue avec celui-ci en un infini nouveau, parce que modifié $(+ 1 = (+ 1))$"; et Duns Scot: "C'est le fini qui présuppose l'infini, et non l'inverse" (p. 360). ("Everything depends on the position of the finite in relation to the infinite, if the finite precedes, it passes into the infinite and disappears $[1 + =]$ if it gives way on the other hand and takes its place after the infinite, it subsists and continues itself with this infinity in a new because modified infinity $[+ 1 = [+ 1]]$; and Duns Scot says "It is the finite which presupposes the infinite and not the opposite.")

54. On a structural level, the dialogues that take place between Grabi and various interlocutors (some becoming themselves important protagonists, for example, M. Lérudi, M. Stop, M. Keskedieu, M. Oscar Thanatou) are extremely important. The most notable of these is, of course, Furibar, not as opposite exactly of Grabi but whose opinions always differ. We are reminded of the quote taken from J.-M. Adam (*Le Texte narratif*, p. 202) at the end of chapter 4 on the dialogic nature of narrative, modeled "sur l'écoute d'un Autre."

55. Another paradox of the text arises here. We have clearly insisted on the importance of the body for the narrative generation (c.f. earlier the mind/body opposition we referred to). Here, however, the body would appear to be merely "unwelcome luggage" when the mind/imagination takes on a superior status in poetic creation. This is in direct opposition to the insistence on the "artisanal" aspect of poetry.

56. J. H. Matthews sees one of the main values of surrealism as the reintroduction of the marvelous into daily possibilities (*Towards a Poetics of Surrealism*, p. 151, for example). From an original point of agreement, Albert-Birot and the surrealists diverge greatly in methods of producing this and attitude toward it.

57. Henri Chabrol, *Alternances 44*, ("Souvenirs et témoignages de Albert-Birot"), p. 17.

58. In the discourse of psychoanalysis, the relationship between the imaginary and our awareness of space is through the body: "L'intuition primordiale de l'espace est par essence imaginaire puisq'elle implique la possibilité d'une mise en ordre fondée sur la spatialité du corps propre" (Sami Ali, *L'Espace imaginaire*, [Paris: Gallimard, 1984], p. 23). ("The primordial intuition of space is through the essence of the imagination because it implies the possibility of on ordering founded on the spatiality of the body.") Thus the apparent paradox between mind (imagination) and body is reconciled where knowledge is gained through the exploration of space.

59. Ibid., p. 47.

60. Ibid., p. 53.

61. Yves-Alain Favre in his article previously referred to describes Grabi as the pleasure principle incarnate. This would seem only partially true because his relationship to the reality principle is a complex one: he operates between the two and not wholly in the realm termed by Lacan the Imaginary.

62. Sami Ali, *L'Espace imaginaire*, p. 57.

63. Ali quotes Piaget: "L'espace est donc le produit d'une interaction entre l'organisme et le milieu, dans laquelle on ne saurait dissocier l'organisation de l'univers perçu de celle de l'activité propre" (p. 80). ("Space is therefore the product of an interaction between the organism and the environment, in which you cannot disassociate the organization of the perceived universe from that of the activity itself.")

64. Compare Ali, *L'Espace imaginaire*, p. 81: "Tout se passe donc comme si le fait d'avoir un corps suffisait pour qu'un monde, tant soit peu organisé, émerge et continue à s'imposer en tant qu'une présence réelle et imaginaire tout ensemble." ("Everything happens as though merely having a body was enough for a world, however poorly organized, to emerge and to continue to impose itself as both a real and imaginary presence.") In Ali's terms a centrifugal force opposes the "égocentrisme" of the subject and pushes the body beyond its limits "au point de le faire coïncider avec la réalité extérieure prise dans sa totalité." ("At the point of making it coincide with eternal reality taken as a whole.")

65. Ibid., p. 123.

66. Ibid., p. 86.

67. Ibid., p. 86.

68. Compare Ali's analysis of the fundamental dimension of space in Lewis Carroll's *Alice in Wonderland* and *Through the Looking Glass* as he explores "l'imaginaire carrollien" (Part 4 of *L'Espace imaginaire*)

69. J.-F. Lyotard, *Discours, Figure*, p. 249.

70. Sami Ali, *L'Espace imaginaire*, p. 242. Ali's theory continues that time is limited to the conscious mind, space to the unconscious.

71. Ali, *L'Espace imaginaire*, p. 243. Ali also quotes Bergson: "Nous projetons le temps dans l'espace" ("we project time into space"). Once again the importance of the thought of Bergson is evident.

72. The presence of the body and the exploration of the perception of movement and space again suggest a parallel with the poetry of Henri Michaux: "Je suis de ceux qui aiment le mouvement, le mouvement qui rompt l'inertie, qui embrouille les lignes, qui défait les alignements, me débarasse des constructions. Mouvement, comme désobéissance comme remaniement" (*Emergences-Résurgences*) [Paris: Skira, 1972], p. 65). ("I am the kind of person who loves

movement, movement that breaks inertia, that mixes up lines, that undoes alignments, rids me of constructions. Movement as disobedience, as reshaping.") It
is through poetry that limits dissolve as for Albert-Birot and the disobeying of
these limits and their *remaniement* brings to mind also Grabi's penchant for
cosmic manipulation, disobeying the "rules" of man's condition.

73. We have previously indicated the way in which this unpunctuated prose
functions and the differences and similarities with some of the texts of Philippe
Sollers.

74. M.-L. Lentengre, "Les appétits hyperboliques de Grabinoulor," p. 143.
Compare also other references to these excesses: "Le système gastrologique de
Grabinoulor obéit à la double loi de l'ubiquité et de l'excès" ("the gastrological
system of *Grabinoulor* obeys the double law of ubiquity and excess") (ibid., p.
140) and "L'ubiquité et l'excès déterminent une survalorisation des pulsions"
("Ubiquity and excess determine an over-valuing of the drives") (p. 151).

75. Nicole Le Dimna, "La Sage Folie de Grabinoulor," pp. 73–94, "La Trin-
ité grotesque."

76. The final lines of the text indicate that this is what Grabinoulor would be
doing should he return, leaving the reader with a final set of enigmas:

> nous qui avions tant de questions à lui poser nous n'en avons peut-être jamais les répon-
> ses enfin on peut toujours en inscrire quelques-unes ici peut-être y répondra-t-il si ayant
> une certaine nostalgie de son livre il y revient un soir donc Grabinoulor au jour de ton
> retour tu nous diras s'il y a de la pensée sans penseur si la pensée a quelque étendue si
> un principe peut être conclusion *quid* des fleurs tristes qui n'ont de parfum que la nuit
> (VI, 14, p. 944).

> ("we who had so many questions to ask him we'll perhaps never have the answers well
> we can always write some of them down here perhaps he'll reply to them if feeling a
> certain nostalgia for his book he returns one evening so Grabinoulor the day you come
> back you can tell us if thought exists without the thinker if thought takes up any space
> if a principle can be a conclusion *quid* about the sad flowers who only have any fragrance
> at night")

77. Any discussion of the excesses of literature, of the excesses of human
existence must necessarily refer to the work of Bataille, in its form (and thematics)
very different to the text under study here, yet there are parallels to be made.
For Bataille literature finally fails, excess is not a state but a moment, and it
cannot be captured in the written word where finally it remains a verbal game.
For Bataille the *geste* itself of writing can be the only real experience of excess
within the context of literature. It is in this perspective that Michaux enjoys also
the *geste* of painting.

78. Georges Bataille, *L'Erotisme*, Minuit, 1985, p. 46.

79. Georges Bataille, *L'Expérience Intérieure*, O.C.V., 1981, p. 19, 34.

80. The question of truth has motivated two of the great critical voices of our
century: Barthes's examination of the force of the hermeneutic code in literature
and Derrida's "undoing" of the truth of the text, of the truth behind every sign
that functions only in "différance." Where, what is "truth" is a question both
sacred and profane, always implicitly calling on the (non)existence of God.

81. It is here that the reader may apprehend the recurring nature/status of
the text. Above all it is the *mise-en-scène* of a questioning—philosophical, metaphysical, ethical, political, ontological. The "grand tour," like the search for the
Holy Grail, is privileged moments of the narrative, where its underlying nature
may be read also on the surface.

82. Furibar is not fooled by Grabi's reticence, awaiting the usual discourse on art: "ah non mon vieux Grabinoulor je te vois venir tu vas me parler de l'ART et déclarer ex cathedra que c'est le peintre des cavernes qu'est la vérité et non le peintre photographe" (VI, 6, p. 854). ("ah no my dear old Grabinoulor I can see you coming you're going to talk to me about ART and declare ex cathedra that it's the cave-man painter who has the truth and not the painter photographer")

83. It is Furibar who echoes the voice of the narration as he complains about the relative immobility of the world as we know it, an immobility due to the paucity of the Creator's imagination:

> tout est réglé une fois pour toutes irrévocablement c'est d'une pauvreté d'imagination à vous donner la jaunisse et quelle paresse et quel goût servile de l'immobilité de la bonne vielle habitude de l'éternel déjà-vu au lieu d'une manifestation de vie ardente toujours à la recherche de la nouveauté et de l'imprévu (IV, 10, p. 484)

> ("everything is decided irrevocably once and for all it shows a poverty of imagination which is enough to make you sick and what laziness and what a servile taste for immobility good old habit the eternal old hat instead of a manifestation of passionate life always in search of novelty and the unexpected")

Furibar is allied as closely to Grabi to movement; when he tries to rid himself of his own double/opposite, Toutenrose, the struggle risks never ending because of their equality: "les forces étant apparemment égales cet équilibre eut peut-être été le définitif mouvement perpétuel" (III, 14, p. 296). ("the forces being apparently equal this equilibrium could perhaps have been the definitive perpetual movement").

84. The most obvious manifestation of the 'mobility' of the narrative of *Grabinoulor* is its *non*punctuation (a term more apt here than *un*punctuated). This nonpunctuation invites a wide range of readings and raises many questions that we are indirectly dealing with in this analysis but not according here a major area of analysis—it nonetheless obviously must be commented upon. Both Grabinoulor and the narrative avoid and disagree with M. Stop:

> tout le monde est d'avis que dans l'Ecriture un petit mort de temps en temps c'est agréable . . . on ne rencontrera pas le moindre petit mort dans ce livre trop vivant M. Stop le coeur bat sans arrêt d'un bout à l'autre de la vie et comme un coeur mon livre ne s'arrêtera de battre qu'à sa fin (*Grabinoulor* IV, 9, p. 467)

> ("everyone is of the opinion that in Writing a little death from time to time is nice . . . you won't find the least dead person in this book M. Stop our heart beats without stopping from one end of life to the other and like a heart my book will only stop beating at the end")

M. Stop first appears in III, 1, p. 139, where Grabi bids a hasty good-bye to his new "friend" and the narrative picks up, as always thereafter, exactly where it had been interrupted. *Grabinoulor* is constituted by words that move in freedom without the constraints of punctuation as M. Stop complains: "plusieurs fois j'ai essayé de rentrer mais vous êtes toujours entouré d'une si massive muraille de mots" (III, 5, p. 159) ("I've tried several times to get in but you're always surrounded by such a huge wall of words"). The eternal and the infinite to which Grabinoulor aspires and which is his very state of being can only function in such a nonpunctuated text. The heart beats, life pulses, and as J.-L. Houdebine comments: "Là est la signification essentielle de l'absence de signes de ponctuation (marques visibles s'il en est), qui multiplie d'autant une ponctuation vivante invisible, son battement rythmé au plus près de sa propre répétition" (*Excès de langages* p. 235, n. 58.) ("Here is the essential meaning of the absence of punctuation marks [visible marks if there ever were] that multiplies an invisible living punctuation, beating in rhythm with its own repetition.") There is a case for suggesting that M. Stop represents a "real" break in the writing of the narrative:

ah bonjour M. Stop vous arrivez bien c'est en effet le moment de s'arrêter car voici les pompiers laissons-les passer oh ils ont beau être encore loin moi j'ai l'oreille fine (IV, 7, p. 452)

bref Grabinoulor lui-même après le petit assassinat de M. Stop . . . il resta comme ça dans le vide pendant près de huit jours terrestres comment pourrait-il après cela savoir exactement où il en était lorsque le dit bourreau par son coup de hache avait traché net le fil de ses idées . . . il n'y avait ni à faire ni à dire Grabinoulor avait été un trou pendant huit jours (IV, 5, pp. 427–28)

(ah hello Mr. Stop you've arrived just at the right time it's indeed the moment to stop because here are the firemen let them go past oh it's no use them still being a way off I have sensitive hearing")

(in short Grabinoulor himself after the little assassination by Mr. Stop . . . he stayed like that in the void for nearly an earthly week could he know after that exactly where he was when the executioner with the blow of his axe had sliced right through the thread of his ideas . . . there was nothing to say or to do Grabinoulor had been a hole for a week")

85. The thesis of David Balhatchet explores the verbal aspects of the text in a way that would be very suggestive for a further questioning of the text suggested here: the generation of words by words themselves, neologisms, etc. Despite Grabi's proclaimed horror of "re" ("renaître revenir redevenir" [V, 10, p. 700]) episodes are constantly returned to, often in other guises, and repetition becomes regenerative.

86. Arlette Albert-Birot reads this as Pierre Albert-Birot consciously writing, preparing in writing his own disappearance. "Néanmoins l'angoisse passe, légère certes; désolation d'un monde sans ce porteur de rêve, projection secrète de la future absence du poète, triomphe provisoire d'Oscar Thanatou" (Preface to *Les Six Livres de Grabinoulor,* p. 949). ("Nonetheless the anguish passes, a slight anguish certainly, the distress of a world without this bearer of dreams, secret projection of the future absence of the poet, provisional triumph of Oscar Thanatou.")

87. There is no "description" of Grabinoulor in the narrative, and the famous sketch of Grabi by Géa Ausbourg shows his suit of clothes with no face. The closest we come to a portrait is when Grabi visits Absurdie: "cet homme à visage ovale yeux bleus nez moyen bouche moyenne et menton rond signe particulier néant (attention ce portrait de Grabinoulor est vu un peu trop largement ne pas s'y fier pour donner son signalement d'abord il a des tas de signes particuliers" (*Grabinoulor* V, 15, p. 756) ("this man with the oval face blue eyes medium-sized nose medium-sized mouth and round chin distinguishing features nothing [be careful this portrait of Grabinoulor is too general don't trust it to give his particulars what's more he has loads of distinguishing features]"), which the reader is not given. The fact that it is impossible to draw Grabi's portrait contrasts very interestingly with Albert-Birot's attraction to portraits (especially of his first wife)

and indeed to self-portraiture, one of which (as previously remarked upon) is included within the manuscript of *Grabinoulor*. Even more remarkable is our previous quote when the portrait is unambiguously linked to the immobile and therefore to death.

88. George Steiner wrote in an article on him, "Le Pari de George Steiner," *Le Monde de Livres* (11 January 1991), p. 17 (propos recueillis par J.-F. Duval).

89. Arlette Albert-Birot provides personal testimony to the poet's fascination with the painting:

> Pab avait toujours sous les yeux l'image de la célèbre création de l'homme, peinte par Michel-Ange pour la Sixtine. L'espace qui séparait le doigt de Dieu du doigt d'Adam le bouleversait. Infime et pourtant infini. N'est-ce pas ainsi qu'il a tenté de se situer lui-même face à sa création poétique? (Arlette Albert-Birot, *Caractères* 20–21 [Paris, 1976], p. 16)

> ("Pab always in front of him the image of the famous creation of man, painted by Michelangelo for the Sistine Chapel. The space which separated God's finger from Adam's shook him to his core. Tiny yet infinite. Is it not like this that he tried to situate himself in relation to his poetic creation?)

In Livre II, 29, Grabinoulor is described exactly as Adam in the Michelangelo painting as a prelude to an erotic encounter: "il convient de considérer que jusqu'ici Grabinoulor est resté tout en souplesse tel que Michel-Ange a peint Adam au sortir du doigt de Dieu" (p. 121) ("it would be right to consider that up until now Grabinoulor remained flaccid like Michelangelo painted Adam at God's fingertip"). Compare Kandinsky on the same scene: "The contrast between the acute angle of a triangle and a circle has no less effect than that of God's finger touching Adam's in Michelangelo. And if fingers are not only anatomy or physiology but more—namely pictorial means—the triangle and the circle are not only geometry, but more—pictorial means" (V. Kandinsky, *Reflections on Abstract Art*, 1931). The quote and analogy bring us back to Albert-Birot's own *La Guerre* and the relationship between triangle and circle—one death bound, one eternal. (It should be noted, however, that the point is that there is no contact between the finger of God and Adam, the very crux of Albert-Birot's own fascination.)

90. Yanette Deltang-Tardif, *La Barbacane* 7, p. 50. The "swallowing" of opposites, the containing of all paradoxes to overcome them, has been one of our underlying themes. This text is an important complement to *Grabinoulor*. The space of creation in Albert-Birot's universe is constructed along the double axes of the human condition—vertical open to the infinite, projected toward the eternal, horizontal, like the plot of a novel, moving inexorably toward death. The spatialization of *Les Mémoires d'Adam* is elaborated on these two axes, and the contradiction of human existence generates an entire poetic oeuvre as an attempt to reconcile this difference. Dominique Baudouin reads in the article already referred to *La Panthère noire*, perhaps the most lyrical of Albert-Birot's collections as such a reconciliation: "Sur ces dernières visions se nouent les deux axes de la condition humaine, horizontale et verticale, pessimisme tragique de la mort, optimisme et cosmique de la vie" (Baudouin, p. 37) ("On these last visions the two axes of the human condition join, the horizontal and the vertical, the tragic pessimism of death, the cosmic optimism of life"). This is finally a more satisfactory reading of the impulse of Albert-Birot's poetry too often read only in its dimension of a celebration of life and one that we will continue to pursue in our own analysis. There are always contradictions within the narrative as the problem

is being worked out, as when Grabi and Furibar discuss the vertical and horizontal axes of existence: "debout tu es mort mets toi sur le dos tu entres dans le maintenant perpétuel" (III, 12) ("stood up you are dead lie on your back you enter in the perpetual now"). The *Mémoires d'Adam* deserve close analysis which space does not permit here. The attempt to reconcile differences and thereby attain some kind of transcendence cannot be stated too emphatically.

91. Jean Follain, *Pierre Albert-Birot* p. 34. Follain insists upon the importance of *Les Mémoires d'Adam:* "Ce livre peut apparaître comme un avant-dire à toute sa poésie" (p. 140) ("this book can seem like a foreword to all his poetry"). Follain reads Adam as another "self" of the poet: "Cet autre moi, Albert-Birot le projette, certes, en son Adam, dans un monde encore vierge, mais il nous sera plus intensément et diversement présent dans ce monde habité de tous temps où vient s'ébattre ce personnage au nom de Grabinoulor" (p. 35) ("This other self, Albert-Birot projects it certainly into his Adam in a still untouched world, but it will be more intensely and diversely present for us in this world inhabited forever where this character called Grabinoulor comes to frolic.")

This naming of the world is a metaphysical as well as a linguistic problematic. See, for example, G. Longrée, *L'Expérience idéogrammatique*, chapter 3, on Apollinaire's use of neologisms as a will to autonomy, an absolute. See Balhatchet's linguistic survey for the variety of the neologisms, etc., used by Albert-Birot throughout *Grabinoulor*.

92. Boris Rybak, *L'Identité humaine* (Paris: J.-M. Place, 1990), p. 13. Compare the way in which André Mora talks about Albert-Birot's work: "Nous serons toujours les Adams de la curiosité sans laquelle le monde n'eût pas existé" ("En hommage à PAB," *Alternances*, n° 44 [Caen, 1959], p. 21. ("We will always be curious Adams without whom the world would not have existed.")

93. In the poetic works, Albert-Birot journeys again to the origins of humanity, to the poetry of the first men in *Les Amusements Naturels* (1945), and very importantly to before the creation of the world itself in *La Belle Histoire* (1966), which relates the coming into being of the creation with which we think ourselves familiar, or "à la manière pabienne comment on passe de RIEN au tout" ("in the pabian way how you pass from NOTHING to everything") (Arlette Albert-Birot): the first words of the long narrative poem being "RIEN—déjà quatre lettres de trop" ("NOTHING—already four letters too many"). Lorand Gaspar's *Sol Absolu*, (Paris: Gallimard, 1972), provides a parallel in the telling of a Genesis, his beginning in "SILENCE" and "RIEN." It is a fundamental poetic impulse to (re)create the universe and then to name it.

94. For example, I, 13 (p. 30): "il était Adam que Dieu venait d'animer" and in touch with the infinite; IV, 9 (pp. 476–77) ("it was Adam into whom God had just breathed life"). When Grabinoulor gets out of bed, he feels completely new, like Adam:

en qualité de premier homme qu'il se trouva tout dépaysé dans cette chambre . . . il s'offrit le plaisir d'être Adam . . . il voyait les choses que personne au monde n'aurait jamais su voir et certes il en a vu des choses quasiment incroyables et tout à fait extraordinaires

("in his capacity as the first man he found himself all disorientated in this bedroom . . . he gave himself the pleasure of being Adam . . . he was seeing things that no one in the world had ever seen and he certainly saw almost unbelievable and totally extraordinary things")

In VI, 13, Grabi once again visits Adam and Eve. The twelth-century play *Le Jeu d'Adam* was put on by Albert-Birot's theater company "Le Plateau," and the program features in his short-lived magazine *Le Plateau,* n° 2 (May 1929). The actors were those who usually figured in Albert-Birot's theatrical presentations: Diable—Claude Cahun; Eve—Solange Roussot; Adam—Roger Roussot.

95. Recent scientific theory, however, would rather subscribe to the theory that the apparently well ordered in creation is generated by and returns to chaos. The "pâte à création" is chaotic energy, a chaotic impulse that may only be temporarily ordered and logical. The implications of this for all quests for knowledge is, of course, fascinating and devastating.

96. Bôfrizé is one of the little devils who come to visit Grabinoulor from their Gothic cathedrals to complain that no one fears them any more (IV, 9). They become fond of each other, and Bôfrizé remains Grabi's constant companion for a time, living in his pocket, frequently disagreeing with Grabi until their final major argument when he disappears (V, 8).

97. J.-L. Houdebine, *Excès de langages,* considers various works of literature and philosophy that may appear very different but are all propelled by a principle of infinity, including Sollers's *Paradis* to which we referred: "L'être infini je répète l'être infini tout est dans cette pointe l'infini vraiment infini" (*Paradis II,* [Paris: Seuil, 1986], p. 265) ("The infinite being I repeat the infinite being everything is in this point the truly infinite infinity")

98. Grabi considers at one point that the irrefutable evidence that God exists could revolve around the fact that we have hairs up our nose (VI, 6, p. 857). If they grow of their own accord, God does not exist; if they were put there, this is absolute proof of his existence: "l'éternelle question de l'Eternel est enfin résolue c'est définitivement entendu il existe" ("the eternal question of the Eternal is at last resolved it's definitively agreed that he exists").

99. That God and man can never coincide is presented in a different way during the "World Tour" where Grabi, Furibar, and Cherami never stop debating—a philosophical walk rather than sightseeing tour. There should be two Gods, one for the earth and one for Humanity because there is clearly no harmony between the two (V, 16). In *Les Mémoires d'Adam,* there are two Creators who converse with Adam—the Dieu-de-Droite and the Dieu-de-Gauche, the "Double-Dieu."

100. It is in Livre III that M. Oscar Thanatou makes most of his appearances. Grabi's replies are elusive when he is asked what he thinks about death: "comment déjà M. Oscar mais j'arrive juste repassez dans huit jours je vais y réfléchir (III, 1, p. 140); "je suis justement très occupé avec la Vie" (III, 15, p. 318). ("what already M. Oscar but I've only just got back come by again in a week I'm going to think about it"); ("I'm precisely very busy with life"). He eventually sends Thanatou off to see Lazarus, but Oscar is no dupe: "vous tenez à vous débarasser de Thanatou car vous ne voulez pas avoir compris que ce qui m'intéresse c'est de savoir ce qu'un vivant pense de la mort" (IV, 9, p. 466) ("you're determined to get rid of Thanatou because you don't want to understand that what I'm interested in is to know what a living man thinks about death"). Yet Grabi's certainty sometimes wavers: "Grabi savait qu'on peut mourir presque pour de bon ou au moins pour toute la vie" (III, 2, p. 141) ("Grabi knew that you can die almost for good or at least for a lifetime"). He still argues his point: "comment M. Thanatou comment n'avez-vous jamais compris que sans résurrection la mort n'est qu'une simple hypothèse ou si vous préférez un style plus poétique sans résurrection la mort c'est de la blague" (III, 8, p. 182) ("what Mr. Thanatou what haven't you

still understood that without resurrection death is only a hypothesis or if you prefer a more poetic style without resurrection death is just a joke").

101. Boris Rybak offers a reading of man's existence as the acknowledgment of our capacity for renewal and our fragility:

> Or l'Univers est donc un espace de phénomènes jusqu'à la singularité que fut l'apparition du premier être vivant, puisque celui-ci se distinguait de la masse des inertes (forces et matières) par le fait qu'il était capable d'opérations de transformations récurrentes des inertes dans une permanence individuelle et dans une descendance; l'état vivant installé métabolisait donc les inanimés et les transformait en sa propre substance, à quoi s'ajoutait la pérennité—en même temps qu'il se caractérisait par sa fragilité, comme être *vivant* donc passible de mort. (*L'Identité humaine*, p. 18).

> ("The Universe is therefore a space of phenomena up until the singularity that was the appearance of the first living being, because this distinguished itself from the mass of inert forces and matter by the fact that it was capable of operating recurrent transformations of inert material in an individual permanent state and in its descendants; the established living state metabolized therefore inanimate matter and transformed it into its own substance, to which durability was added—at the same time it was characterized by its fragility as living being and therefore liable to die.")

The reading of the human body and its state of being by this professor and surgeon is striking as are the questions it poses for a scientific reading of the questions pursued in *Grabinoulor*—the status of the real and the nature of being, what it means to be human.

102. Translation by Barbara Wright, *The First Book of Grabinoular*, p. 19.

103. Albert-Birot's quest/will impulses in the narrative are fundamental, of course, in semiotic theory. This is not then a "theory" applied in retrospect but a narrative which implies (anticipates) critical readings of the second half of the twentieth century. The way in which these readings are related to the development of science is again evident when read with Rybak:

> Il y a un bien intrinsèque à l'être et par l'être et un mal également intrinsèque selon l'être; dans la logique du système humain marqué par les étapes d'histoire, le cheminement a conduit à l'aujourd'hui plus agonisé que vécu dans l'esprit immédiat et la chronicité de la chair. Cette "force des choses," qui est la pression évolutive, ajoute, par ces faits réalisés, à la difficulté homéostatique de l'être en tant que tel—un médecin, Xavier Bichat, dans sa fréquentation avec la maladie et la mort, a pu l'exprimer sans doute mieux qu'un introspectif: *"La vie est l'ensemble des fonctions qui résistent à la mort."* Autrement dit, *l'Homme pour se maintenir comme être, vit un travail résistant* dans tous ses accidents aussi menus qu'ils soient, puisque si ce travail résistant cessait, l'être et l'êtravoir pourrait se perdre—comme il en va dans l'autisme mais aussi dans la tromperie de l'hédonisme. (Rybak *L'Identité humaine*, p. 65, my emphasis)

> ("There is something good intrinsic to being and through being and something bad equally intrinsic according to being; in the logic of the human system marked by stages of history, the path has lead to a today that is more agonized than lived in the immediate mind and the chronicity of the flesh. This 'force of circumstances,' which is evolutive pressure, adds, through the realization of these facts, to the homeostatic difficulty of being as such—a doctor, Xavier Bichat, in his frequentation of illness and death, managed to express it no doubt better than an introspective person: 'Life is all the functions which resist death.' In other words, man, to maintain himself as being, lives the work of resistance in all troubles as small as they may be, because if this work of resistance were to end, the being and the 'êtravoir' (Beinghaving) could be lost—as happens in autism but also in the illusion of hedonism.")

104. Once again Albert-Birot's modernity is apparent—modern in a way not only conceived by the avant-garde but revealing the preoccupations of the later part of the century. The parallel with Perec becomes more and more apparent: "cent trucs pour ne pas vivre" *(La Vie mode d'emploi).* Also more fundamentally in the constant treatment of space, of classification *(Penser/Classer),* of the autobiographical *(Je me souviens),* of the will to exhaust the possibilities of the narrative in order to contain, to have, to hold, to escape the void.

105. For example, there is Grabi's telephone conversation with "la marquise" where he is not allowed to use such words as "espérer" (to hope) (VI, 5). In chapter 11 of the same book, Grabi writes a letter to Death about doctors, who despite continually saving those that Death has marked for himself, appear to be tolerated (VI, 10). He does not receive a reply. The letter to Death counterbalances his missive for the Creator. The absence of the former's reply is especially significant.

106. That this is a painful cry from the heart of an Albert-Birot living himself in solitude and his work unknown and ignored for the most part can be in little doubt. This is a moment of existential anguish, self-doubt, and doubt in the value of his life's work.

107. Again it is difficult not to read this as Albert-Birot's personal criticism of a world that has remained indifferent to a creation that has sustained his own individual life and given pleasure to a few others around him. It is a testimony also of a man who witnessed the first half of the century and beyond. The violence of the diatribe and his indignation make a parallel with Céline extremely pertinent. Both writers moved to an extreme position by human failings, although in the case of Albert-Birot this is not sustained.

108. There are three endings to *Grabinoulor:* the manuscript breaks off in midsentence a few pages before the first typescript by Albert-Birot himself. In the "Historique de l'édition de *Grabinoulor,*" *Les Six Livres de Grabinoulor,* Arlette Albert-Birot explains these. With the original typescript is an alternative manuscript ending—with no full stop.

109. Rybak, *L'Identité humaine,* p. 96; my emphasis.

110. George Steiner in "Le Pari de George Steiner," *Le Monde des Livres,* p. 17.

111. Ibid., my emphasis. Compare especially the work of the semiotician Greimas who has striven to develop a method to account for meaning in all its complexity, to account for all the forms, positive and negative, of signification within the economy of human life. Grabi is constantly deconstructing power systems, but the task of the critic is to uncover the coming into being of a poetic universe and therefore the meanings even of deliberate deconstructions.

CONCLUSION

1. Une oeuvre est un ordre et une norme. Acte de révolte contre le Créateur, selon Pierre Albert-Birot, elle affirme un système de valeurs face au chaos ou au non-sens. Ecrire, c'est instituer un monde, récrire, c'est mettre ce monde en question. (Claude Abastado, "Jeux et visés d'un texte parodique: *Grabinoulor" in F,* 2–3, p. 67)

("A work of art is an order and a norm. An act of revolt against the Creator, according to Pierre Albert-Birot, it affirms a system of values in the face of chaos and nonmeaning. To write is to establish a world, to rewrite is to put this world into question.")

Abastado's seminal article on *Grabinoulor* recognizes the order/chaos dynamic by identifying the effects of the parodying of recognizable textual formulas, the subversion of genres, and the ironical stance of the narration. Indeed it is the supreme irony of a text that disparages logic while rigorously generating argument and counterargument toward an always provisional conclusion.

2. P. Albert-Birot, "La peinture absolue."

Compare the framework of scientific research into chaos theory. Without a detailed analysis of such a parallel, which is outside the scope of this study, we wish to draw attention to the way in which Albert-Birot's search for meaning leads to the building of a temporary complex order, and in the process reflects the way in which many scientists believe that the multiple phenomena of the universe behave.

3. There are necessarily moments of convergence between the individual and the collective, and one of the aims of this study has been to situate Albert-Birot in relation to surrealism and futurism (see particularly chapter 2). In general concerns Albert-Birot does, from time to time, realign with the Surrealist movement:

> This is one of the most important discoveries of the first Surrealist Manifesto has to share with those who really hear its message: the fascination with language lies in its being a less than adequate instrument and, at the same time, the most readily available means by which Man may assert his freedom from controls, socio-political, ethical, moral, literary and artistic. (J. H. Matthews, *Towards a Poetics of Surrealism*, p. 77)

It is in the detail of the way this is to be accomplished that Albert-Birot diverges completely, and it is this that makes us question our commonly held assumptions concerning what is the "sur-real."

> 4. Nous avons affaire à une oeuvre inclassable, qui suscitera de nombreuses thèses et à laquelle nous pouvons désormais prendre plaisir car l'esprit de notre époque se prête fort bien à ce genre de somnambulisme éveillé et pleinement assumé. (Alain Bosquet, "La joyeuse épopée de Pierre Albert-Birot," *Le Quotidien des Livres*, January 1992)

> ("What we have here is an unclassifiable work which will give rise to numerous theses and in which we can take pleasure because the spirit of our times lends itself well to this type of sleepwalking while awake and which is totally accepted.")

The reception by the French media's critical establishment of the integral edition of *Grabinoulor* in November 1991 was a celebration of the restoration of this "lost" masterpiece to the panorama of twentieth-century literature, seizing immediately on the jubilation and energy of the work. This study has sought to understand the impulses that generate this energy and the processes of its creation.

5. There are specific moments in the narrative when Grabinoulor ponders on the nature of music and the divine, considering music as the form most suitable for the expression of the divine, simultaneously simple and complex (see chapter 5). In V, 8 (p. 680), Grabinoulor listens to the concert created by musicians who refuse to follow the score, each playing to his own inspiration and contemplating this "chaos sonore" as perhaps the form of true creation.

6. The alchemist seeks to unify the dynamic oppositions that he believes to be the foundation of the spiritual world. Redemption is achieved through unity. An interesting example is Michel Leiris's early surrealist narrative *Aurora*, which clearly shows the attempt to reconcile all differences and the quest for truth and knowledge.

Bibliography

Primary Sources: The Works of Pierre Albert-Birot

The Fonds Albert-Birot contains, in addition to the manuscripts and first editions of the works referred to, numerous typed interviews and talks with transcribed text, the correspondence of the poet, and the unpublished work, as well as articles, special issues, and academic works. We are indebted to Arlette Albert-Birot for so generously making this available.

Grabinoulor

Livre, I, chapitre 1, *SIC,* 30 (1918)

Livre I, chapitre 8, *ValoriPlastici,* 2–3 (1919)

Le premier livre de Grabinoulor. Paris: Editions SIC, 1921

Livre II, chapitre 17, *La quinzaine de Pierre Albert-Birot,* 1 (1926)

Grabinoulor épopée, premier et deuxième livres. Paris: Denoël et Steele, 1933, Prix Cazes, 1936

Livre I, chapitre 16, *Le Centaure,* 4 (1933), 1–2

Livre II, chapitre 21, *Le Centaure,* 6 (1934), 3–4

Livre IV, chapitre 1, *Maintenant,* 2 (1946), 194–203

Grabinoulor-Amour, Preface by André Lebois "Passeport pour l'île Albert-Birot," Mortemart: Rougerie, 1955

Grabinoulor à Paris, Le Mercure de France (June 1957), 262–66

Livre I, chapitre 1, *Ou, cinquième saison,* 19 (1963), 33–34

Livre II, chapitres 2, 3 et 8, *Cyanuur,* 15 (1964)

Grabinoulor, nouvelle edition revue et augmentée, preface by Jean Follain. Paris: Gallimard, 1964; selections from Livres I, II and III; 'La Langue en barre,' P. Albert-Birot. Appendix "Grabinoulor au Palais—Lettre à un avocat"

Livre IV, chapitre 1, *Synthèses,* 224 (January 1965), 385–95, presented by Stélios Castanos de Médicis. Original text up to seventh line of p. 395 "tout Grabinoulor que tu sois." There follows seven lines especially written for the occasion by Pierre Albert-Birot.

Livre I, chapitres 16, 22, 26, *Cahiers du Sud* (February-March 1965), 93–108

Livre III, chapitre 1, *Journal des poètes,* 5 (May 1965)

Livre III, chapitre 2, Editions de la revue *Strophes,* (December 1965)

Livre V, chapitre 2 (extraits), *La Barbacane,* 3 (1965)

Livre I, chapitres 9, 12, 16, Livre II, chapitre 19, in *Pierre Albert-Birot*, J. Follain, coll. 'Poètes d'aujourd'hui. Paris: Seghers, 1967, pp. 156–69

Livre III, chapitre 4, *La Barbacane*, 7 (1968), 113–28

Livre III, chapitre 9, *Métamorphoses* (4) (1968); (1) (1969)

Livre IV, chapitre 9, *F*, 2–3 (1973), 131–45. Special issue Albert-Birot

Livre VI, chapitre 14, *Sud*, 19 (3) (1976), 31–39. Special issue Pierre Albert-Birot, e.e. cummings

Livre III, chapitre 10, *La Barbacane*, 19–20 (1977–78), 9–30

Livre I, chapitre 16, *Le Temps parallèle*, 21 (June 1979), 27–30

Livre I, chapitres 5, 9, 12, 14, *Cahiers bleus*, 15 (Summer 1979), 55–65

Livre II, chapitre 22, *Corps Ecrit*, 25 (March 1988)

Les Six Livres de Grabinoulor. Paris: Editions Jean-Michel Place, 1991. Postface by Arlette Albert-Birot, "De l'éveil au point final" pp. 947–50; "Historique de l'édition de *Grabinoulor*," pp. 951–54; "Première préface—Les Malheurs de Grabinoulor" (1933), pp. 955–58; "Second préface—Les Nouveaux Malheurs de Grabinoulor" (1955), pp. 959–80; "La Langue en barre," pp. 961–63; Index des noms des personnages; Index des noms de lieux.

Grabinoulor: Translations

Book III, extracts from chapters 1 and 2, translated by Barbara Wright, *Form*, n° 8, (September 1968), pp. 22–25

Das erste Buch von *Grabinoulor*, Übersetzt aus dem Fransösischen and herausgegeben von Eugen Helmule, Text und Kritik. Munich, 1980

Grabinoulor, Book I, chapters 1, 2, 3, 4, 6, translated by Barbara Wright, *Atlas Anthology III*. London: Atlas Press, 1985

The First Book of Grabinoulor. Translated and preface by Barbara Wright; postface by Arlette Albert-Birot. London: Atlas Press, 1986. Prix Scott-Moncrieff, 1987, for the best translation from French

The First Book of Grabinoulor. Translated and preface by Barbara Wright; preface by Barbara Wright; postface by Arlette Albert-Birot. Illinois: The Dalkey Archive Press, 1987

Works in Prose

Cinéma. Drames-Poèmes dans l'espace (avec notes de l'auteur). Paris: Editions SIC, 1920

Le Catalogue de l'antiquaire, handprinted by the author. Paris: Editions Jean Budry, 1923

Rémy Floche, employé. Paris: Editions Denoël et Steele, 1934

Les Mémoires d'Adam et les pages d'Eve. Paris: Editions Balzac, 1943

Les Mémoires d'Adam suivi des *Pages d'Eve*, Ed. du Dauphin. Paris, 1948

Autobiographie, Cahiers bleus, 14 (1) (1979), 5–23

Les Mémoires d'Adam et les pages d'Eve. Postface by Arlette Albert-Birot. Paris: Editions de l'Allée, 1986

Rémy Floche, employé. Postface by Arlette Albert-Birot. Paris: Editions de l'Allée, 1987

Autobiographie suivi de *Moi et moi.* Preface by Arlette Albert-Birot. Troyes: Librairie Bleue, 1988

Le Catalogue de l'antiquaire, suivi de *Deux millions et demi.* Thaon: Amiot-Lenganey, 1993

Works in Prose: Unpublished

L'homme coupé, histoire invraisemblable des dix derniers hommes sur la Terre (due to be published by Editions La Barbacane, Bonaguil, 1996)

La plus belle histoire du monde, conte pour enfants

Et tzimm et tzoumm, ou les vacances miraculeuses, roman pour enfants

Fauteuil tournant, roman

Mon ami Chronos, essai de philosophie poétique

Splendeurs, suite et fin de "Rémy Floche"

Le Conte pour un jeune Dieu

Temps et sujets, lettres échangées entre Roch Grey et Pierre Albert-Birot

Affaires d'état, essai

Le Célèbre Témoignage

Voyage de noce

Les Petits Papiers de Gabriel

Cinéma, suivi de *Monsieur Poire et Madame Coeur parmi les oiseaux et les fleurs,* new edition with notes and previously unpublished material collected by Arlette Albert-Birot, to be published in 1996

Theater

Matoum et Tévibar. Histoire édifiante et récréative du vrai et du faux poète, drame pour marionnettes. Paris: Editions SIC, 1919

Larountala, polydrame en deux parties. Paris: Editions SIC, 1919

L'Homme coupé en morceaux, drame comique en trois actes pour acrobates, jongleurs et équilibristes. Paris: Editions SIC, 1921

Le Bondieu, drame comique en cinq actes, un prologue et quatre intermèdes, handprinted by the author. Paris: Editions SIC, 1922

Les Femmes pliantes, drame comique en trois actes, handprinted by the author. Paris: Editions SIC, 1923

Monsieur Poire et Madame Coeur parmi les oiseaux et les fleurs, idylle tragicomique. *Films* (11 October 1923)

Image, premier drame tragique, handprinted by the author. Paris: Editions Jean Budry, 1924

La Barbe-Bleue. Deuxième drame tragique, handprinted by the author. *La Quinzaine de Pierre Albert-Birot.* Paris, 1926

L'Homme coupé en morceaux. Drame comique, in *Réalités secrètes.* Mortemart: Rougerie, 1956

Plutus ou le dieu des riches. Comédie en deux tableaux, libre transposition d'Aristophane. Mortemart: Rougerie, 1969

Théâtre I, volume comprising *Matoum et Tévibar* and *Larountala.* With preface by Robert Abirached, remarks by Arlette Albert-Birot. Mortemart: Rougerie, 1977

Théâtre II, volume comprising *L'Homme coupé en morceaux* and *Le Bondieu*. Remarks by Arlette Albert-Birot. Mortemart: Rougerie, 1978

Théâtre III, volume comprising *Les Femmes pliantes* and *Image*. Remarks by Arlette Albert-Birot. Mortemart: Rougerie, 1978

Théâtre IV, volume comprising *Plutus* and *Matoum en Matoumoisie*. Remarks by Arlette Albert-Birot. Mortemart: Rougerie, 1979

Matoum et Tévibar, critical edition by Germana Cerenza Orlandi. Milan-Paris: Istituto editoriale Cisalpina, Nizet, 1979

Théâtre V, volume comprising *La Dame enamourée* and *Le Mariage tiré par les cheveux*. Remarks by Arlette Albert-Birot. Mortemart: Rougerie, 1980

Théâtre VI, volume comprising *Le Petit Poucet*, *Barbe-Bleue*, and "des pièces-études"—*Loulia*, *Banlieue*, *Silence*, *La Discorde*, *Deux scènes enfantines* ("La Promenade en auto" et "La Leçon de danse"), *Babi-baba*, *Guignol veut s'enrichir*, *L'Anguille*, and *Les Mains*. Remarks by Arlette Albert-Birot. Mortemart: Rougerie, 1980

Théâtre VII, with detailed notes by Arlette Albert-Birot and Didier Plassard, and a the complete text of a dramatic adaptation: *Le Cantique des cantiques* to be published by Rougerie 1996

Theater (Unpublished)

La Chatte, drame radiophonique

L'Empire des Morts, drame radiophonique

Le Fer à cheval, drame radiophonique

Translations

"Parmenide" de Platon, lithographies de Serge Pliakoff. Paris: La Rose des Vents, 1964

Et patati et patata. French adaptation of the poems of Krista Bendova, based on a translation from Slovak by Zdenka Datheil. Grund, 1966.

Poetry

De la mort à la vie, essai dramatique. Paris: Librairie Léon Vannier, éditeur, A. Messein successeur. 1905

Le Dernier Chant d'Yseult. Transcription byAlbert Birot. *La Poétique* 43 (1 February, 1909)

Trente et un poèmes de poche, with a *Poèmeprèfaceprophétie* de G. Apollinaire. Paris: Editions SIC, 1917

Poèmes Quotidiens. Paris: Editions SIC, 1919

La Joie des sept couleurs, poème orné de cinq poèmes-paysages hors-texte. Paris: Editions SIC, 1919

La Triloterie. Paris: Editions SIC, 1920. The collection comprises "La Légende," "Les Invectives contre l'automne," "En marge du Rubaiyat d'Omar Khayam."

Quatre poèmes d'amour. Hand printed by P. and G. Albert-Birot. Paris: Editions SIC, 1922

Les Soliloques napolitains, with eight illustrations by Jean Lurçat, "Danzig 1822," restricted sale only. Paris, 1922. The sixteen poems appear in *La Lune* under the title "Le Palais des mirages."

La Lune ou le livre des poèmes. Hand printed by P. and G. Albert-Birot. Paris: Editions Jean Budry et Cie, 1924

Poèmes à l'Autre Moi. Hand printed by P. and G. Albert-Birot. Paris: Editions Jean Budry et Cie, 1927

Ma morte, poème sentimental suivi d'*Un souvenir du poète André Marcou,* restricted sale only. Hand printed by P. Albert-Birot. Paris, 1931

Deux poètes. Deux poèmes, Albert Birot ("La Colombe"), Jean Follain ("Vieille Europe"). Hand printed by P. Albert-Birot. One hundred signed and numbered copies. Paris: Editions des Canettes, 1936

Le Cycle des douze poèmes de l'annéé. Hand printed by Albert-Birot each month from October 1936 to September 1937. Paris: Editions des Canettes, 1937

Amenpeine. Trente poèmes élégiaques. Hand printed by P. Albert-Birot. Paris: Editions des Canettes, 1938

La Panthère noire. Poème en 50 anneaux et 50 chaînons. Hand printed by P. Albert-Birot. Paris: Editions des Canettes, 1938

Miniatures. Trente jeux prosodiques. Hand printed by P. Albert-Birot. Paris: Editions des Canettes, 1939

Les Amusements naturels, "L'Iliade," "Les Euménides," "Le Mystère d'Adam." Des traductions et cent cinquante poèmes nouveaux. The collection is divided into three parts: Greek, Roman, Modern. The last section is subdivided as follows: "Cent et quelques poèmes ordinaires"; "Silex, poèmes des cavernes"; "Poèmes de midi et demi." Paris: Editions Denoël et Steele, 1945.

Cent dix gouttes de poésie. Paris: Editions Pierre Seghers, 1952

Dix poèmes à la mer suivi de *Tout finit par un sonnet,* poème en six parties, pour F [Florentin] M [Mouret] et ses amis, restricted sale only. Paris, 1953–54

Poèmes à l'Autre Moi. Paris: Caractères, 1954. This edition contains only thirty-two poems; poems 16 and 17, set to music by the poet, are missing.

Graines. Poèmes-missives. Genève: Editions du Club du poème, 1965

Silex, poèmes des cavernes. Frontispiece de Zadkine, avant-propos de Max Pons. Bonaguil: Editions des Cahiers de la Barbacane, 1966

La Belle Histoire. Poème narratif. Illustrated by Staritsky. Veilhes (Tarn): Editions Gaston Puel, 1966

Poèsie 1916–1924. Preface by André Lebois. Collection comprising *Trente et un poèmes de poche; Poèmes quotidiens, La Joie des Sept couleurs, La Triloterie, La Lune ou le livre des poèmes.* Paris: Gallimard, 1967

Cent nouvelles gouttes de poésie. Bonaguil: Editions des Cahiers de la Barbacane, 1967

Merci quand même mon bon Daimon. Le dernier poème de Pierre Albert-Birot. Engraving by Staritsky. Printed in October 1967 on the author's printing press

Mes galaxies, poèmes, unpublished extracts in Jean Follain, *Pierre Albert-Birot,* collection "Poètes d'aujourd'hui." Paris: Seghers, 1967, pp. 173–79

"Beau-fixe" suivi de *"Cri."* Hand printed by Arlette Albert-Birot on the author's own printing press, engravings by Staritsky. Paris: Editions SIC, 1968

Le Train bleu. Preface by Pascal Pia, lithography by Jacques Spacagna. Paris: Editions Guy Chambelland, Poésie Club, Librairie St. Germain-des-Prés, 1970

Aux trente-deux vents. Poèmes des jours ombreux. Frontispiece by Nicolas Schöffer. Foreword by Henri Chopin. Paris: Editions SIC, 1970

Fermeture hebdomadaire. Illustrated and printed by Pierre-André Benoit. Alès, 1970

Le Pont des Soupirs, suivi de *Dix sonnets et une chanson* et de *Isis.* Paris: Les Editeurs Français Réunis, 1972

Six quatrains de Chantilly. Engravings by Staritsky, hand printed by Arlette Albert-Birot on the author's own printing press. Paris: Editions SIC, 1973

Long cours suivi de *La Grande Couronnée.* Mortemart: Rougerie, 1974

Distance suivi de *Vingt poèmes,* with presentation by Arlette Albert-Birot. Mortemart: Rougerie, 1976

Les Poèmes du dimanche. Engravings by Staritsky, hand printed by Alain Sanchez for the centenary of Albert-Birot. Paris: Editions SIC, 1978

Poésie 1927–1937, collection comprising *Poèmes à l'Autre Moi* and *Le Cycle des douze poèmes de l'année,* presentation by Arlette Albert-Birot. Mortemart: Rougerie, 1981

Poésie 1931–1938, collection comprising *Ma morte* and *Amenpeine.* Mortemart: Rougerie, 1982

La Queue au diable, suite de quatre poèmes, livre-objet by Alain Roger. Saint-Pierre-la-Vielle: L'attrape-science, 1982

Poésie 1938–1939, collection comprising *La Panthère noire* and *Miniatures.* Mortemart: Rougerie, 1982

"Physicalité," *Corps écrit.* Paris: PUF, 1983

Pierre Albert-Birot, Vreckové basne (anthology). Translation and postface by Valér Mikula, Brastislava: Kruh Milovnikov Poézie, 1983

Poésie 1945–1967, collection comprising *Les Amusements naturels* and *Deux cent dix gouttes de poésie.* Paris: Rougerie, 1984. Only the modern part of *Les Amusements naturels* is republished. "Carte postale," "Les Fleurs bleues," and "Moulin à poèmes" have been added. The *Deux cent dix gouttes de poésie* are the fusion (desired by the poet) of *Cent dix gouttes de poésie* and *Cent nouvelles gouttes de poésie*

Mon palais, including the facsimile of the manuscript with ten drawings by Michel Mousseau, and remarks by Arlette Albert-Birot, "Discours sur la méthode." Caen: Editions Le Pavé-Christian Dorrière, 1985

Poésie 1954–1966, volume comprising *Dix poèmes à la mer, Tout finit par un sonnet,* and *La Belle Histoire,* chronological bibliography and alphabetical index of Albert-Birot's published collections. Mortemart: Rougerie, 1985

Poésie 1916–1920, volume comprising *Trente et un poèmes de poche, La Joie des sept couleurs, Poèmes Quotidiens* and *La Triloterie,* Mortemart: Rougerie, 1987

Moi et moi in *Autobiographie,* Troyes: Librairie Bleue, 1988

Sept poèmes, with an etching by Michel Mousseau. Roubaix: Editions Brandes, 1989

Poésie 1916–1924, La Lune ou le livre des poèmes. With preface and notes by Arlette Albert-Birot. Mortemart: Rougerie, 1992

Translations (Poetry)

Gedichte 1916–1924, Ubersetzt aus dem Franzosischen und herausgegeben von Eugen Helmlé, Text und Kritik. Munich, 1985

There are a considerable number of poems that have been published in literary magazines (most notably *Sud* and *La Barbacane*). A complete list is cataloged in the Fonds Albert-Birot. Unpublished work is also available for consultation there.

Articles by Pierre Albert-Birot

"De l'originalité." *La Poétique* 6 (1905), 166–67

"Le théâtre en vers." *Scoenia* 26 (1910), 100–2

Preface to *L'Homme coupé en morceaux*, 1920 (In *Théâtre II*)

"Guignol école dramatique." *Les Cahiers idéalistes*, nouvelle série, 2 (1921)

Preface to *Femmes Pliantes*, 1922 (in *Théâtre III*)

"Mon bouquet au surréalisme." *Surréalisme*, 1 (October 1924), republished in *Europe*, (November-December 1968), 475–76

"Les jeux, les poètes, la foule." *L'Intransigeant* (May 1926)

"Réponse à une enquête d'Edouard Dujardin sur l'anti-poésie." *Les Cahiers idéalistes* 14 (1926), 14–15

"Les Mots." *L'Intransigeant* (December 1929)

"Ismisme." *L'Intransigeant* (February 1930)

"Anno oetatis." *Le Centaure* 12 (March 1932); *Jeunesse 1932*, special issue of the journal comprising March and May's issues (Spring 1932)

"*Les Mamelles de Tirésias*, Guillaume Apollinaire," special issue of *Rimes et Raisons* (1946), La Tête noire, Albi

"A propos d'cubes." *Art d'aujourd'hui* 3–4 (1953), 77

"Hommage à Jean de Boschère." *France-Asie* 87 (1953), 703

"Naissance et vie de SIC." *Les Lettres nouvelles* 7 (1953), 843–49; also in *Autobiographie*. Troyes: Librairie Bleue, 1988, pp. 45–62

"Max," *Roepling*, special issue on Max Jacob. Editions Jan Van Spaendonck, Tilburg (February 1954), 67–70

"G. A." *Le Flâneur des deux rives* 4 (1954)

"Petite historique du Poèmepréfaceprophétie." *Le Flaneur de deux rives* 7–8 (1955)

"La Langue en barre," in *Grabinoulor-Amour*. Limoges: Rougerie, 1955, pp. 55–60; republished in *Grabinoulor*. Paris: Gallimard, 1964, pp. 11–15 and *Les Six Livres de Grabinoulor*, J.-M. Place, 1991, pp. 961–63

"La Peinture absolue." *Synthèses* 123 (1956), 111–15

"A propos du drame surréaliste d'Apollinaire." *Marginales* 62–63 (1958), 29–39

"Mon cher Pierre Reverdy." *Le Mercure de France* 1181 (1962), 303–5

"Réaction de Pierre Albert-Birot." *Les Cahiers du Refus* 1 (1962)

"Le Poète aux dents blanches." *Entretiens*, hommage à Pierre Reverdy 20 (1962), 131–35

"Dialogue avec Zdenka Datheil." *Le Musée vivant* 25–28 (1965)

Preface to *Les Galets gris* by Michel Nicoletti. Brussels, 1966

"Max," introductory note to Max Jacob's *L'Homme de cristal*, revised edition. Paris: Gallimard, 1967

Correspondence

"Lettres de Pierre Albert-Birot à Jean Follain." *Cahiers bleus* 4 (1976), 51

There is a considerable amount of correspondence as yet unpublished in the Fonds Albert-Birot.

Literary and Artistic Magazines founded and edited by Albert-Birot

SIC, 54 issues, Paris, January 1916–December 1919

Paris, one issue only, Paris, November 1924

La Quinzaine de Pierre Albert-Birot 4 issues, Paris, April–June 1926

Le Plateau, programme-revue, 1, March 1929; 2, May, 1929

SIC, reprint, Chroniques des Lettres françaises, Paris, 1973; Editions Jean-Michel Place, republished 1980 and 1993; facsimile edition, which also contains *Paris* and the program for *Les Mamelles de Tirésias*

Interviews and Talks on and with Albert Birot

Radio "Voix de Paris," 25 March 1936. Prix Cazes

"Interview de Pierre Albert-Birot le solitaire," by Lois Dubrau, *Le Journal des poètes*, 10, Brussels, 1947

"Douze minutes avec . . . Pierre Albert-Birot," program presented by Pierre Béarn, O.R.T.F., 1950; published in *La Passerelle*, 24 (1975–76)

"Quand ils avaient le diable au corps," "Le petit frère de Dada," "Un grand coup de poing au théâtre réaliste," "Avez-vous lu *Grabinoulor*," "Faut-il recourir au scandale," five interviews with Pierre Albert-Birot by Fernand Pouey, *Arts*, (June–July 1952)

Interview with Georges Pitoëff jnr, O.R.T.F., program for the Near-East, May 1956

Interview wtih Les Jeunesses Poétiques, Knokke le Zoute, Belgium, September 1963

Nicolas Lemarin et Pierre Longchamp interview Pierre Albert-Birot, Paris, 1963

"La Saison vivante," program presented by Jean-Michel Minon, with Liliane Becker and Pierre Albert-Birot, RTB, 1964

"Au Bras de Poésie," Musée d'Art et d'Histoire, Geneva, 2 April 1964 Conversation with Pierre Albert-Birot at the Conservatoire national d'art dramatique, 31 October 1964

"Entretien avec Pierre Albert-Birot," by Pierre Berger, *Les Lettres françaises*, 1057, December 1964

Interview with Dolly Steiner recorded after a session of the *Théâtre des poètes* on Pierre Albert-Birot, France-Inter, 31 October 1964

Readings by André Lebois, Michel Décaudin, Jacqueline Bellas, Henri Pevel, Radio Toulouse-Pyrénées, 25 January 1965

"Visite à Grabinoulor" by Robert Abirached, *La Nouvelle Revue française*, 13a, March 1965

"Causerie sur Guillaume Apollinaire" by Pierre Albert-Birot at the lycée Paul Eluard in Saint-Denis, 1965 (unpublished)

"Hommage à Pierre Albert-Birot," organized by Jacques Vallet, Collège Philosophique, December 1965

Interview with Barbara Bray, BBC, 16 June 1966

"Grabinoulor—A Study of Pierre Albert-Birot," compiled, translated, and introduced by Barbara Wright, BBC, 22 June, 11 July 1966

"Suffit-il d'avoir cinquante ans pour voir ses mérites reconnus? On découvre aujourd'hui Pierre Albert-Birot, l'homme qui lança le surréalisme," *Le Figaro Littéraire*, 1061, August 1966

"Entretien avec le poète Pierre Albert-Birot," by Jean-Marie Péret, *Sud-Ouest Dimanche*, 4 September 1966

Interview with José Pivin, "Au cours de ces instants," O.R.T.F., 30 April 1967, 2 July 1967

"Le Bureau de Poésie," André Beucler, R.T.F., 1967

Causerie devant les étudiants de la Sorbonne, 2 June 1967 (unpublished)

Les matinées littéraires de Roger Vrigny, billet de J.-F. Noël, n° 9, "l'Homme coupé en morceaux," 1978, Radio France/France Culture

"Les Nuits Magnétiques," Jean Daive et Pamela Doussaud, O.R.T.F., 20 December 1979

"Une vie, une oeuvre," Hubert Juin, with Daniel Abadie, R. Abirached, Arlette Albert-Birot, Michel Décaudin, Germana Orlandi, Didier Plassard, France Culture, 27 February 1986

"Panorama," France Culture, "Rémy Floche, employé" presented by Jacques Duchateau with J.-P. Salgas, Nadine Vasseur, Gilbert Lascault, Anne Portugal, 12 February 1987

"Cinquante ans de poésie," Arlette Albert-Birot, Maison Française d'Oxford, November 1988

"Panorama," France Culture presented by Jacques Duchateau, "Pour Grabinoulor," with Nicole Vasseur, Arlette Albert-Birot, Jean-Pierre Salgas, Gilbert Lascault, 26 December 1991

"Pour Pierre Albert-Birot," Readings and Round Table directed by Madeleine Renouard (with Arlette Albert-Birot, Hélène Cazes, Marcel Benabou, Michel Chaillou, Dominique Noguez, Jean-Michel Place, Jean Roudaut, and Jean-Pierre Salgas, Centre Georges Pompidou, Paris, 15 February 1992 (Exhibition 5–17 February)

"Poésie sur parole," presented by Andre´ Velter with Arlette Albert-Birot, readings by Janine Souchon and Yves Graffey, France Culture, 4–9 May 1992

"Les Arts et Les Gens" and "Une exposition en vedette: Pierre Albert-Birot," presented by Pierre Descargues with Arlette Albert-Birot and Valère Bertrand, readings by Christian Alers, France Culture, June 1992

"PAB et Grabinoulor dans La Lune," Galerie Michlèle Heyraud, Paris, staged by Claude Debord with Janine Souchon, Albert Bohbot, Claude Debord, Yves Graffey, 12 June 1992

"Pour célébrer Pierre Albert-Birot," Round table discussion at the Maison de

La Poésie, Paris with Arlette Albert-Birot, Marie-Louise Lentengre, Barbara Wright, Madeleine Renouard, Jean-Michel Place, Debra Kelly, Hélène Cazes, and Christophe Bussein, 16 November 1993

"Spectacle Grabinoulor" staged by Monique Dorsel with Dominique Delforge, Monique Dorsel, Yves Bical, Joachim Defgnée, Jacques Delforge, 16 and 17 October 1993, Maison de La Poésie, Paris

STUDIES OF THE WORKS OF PIERRE ALBERT-BIROT

Books

Perez Jorba, J. *Pierre Albert-Birot*. Paris: Bibliothèque de l'Instant, 1920

Follain, J. *Pierre Albert-Birot*, collection "Poètes d'aujourd'hui." Paris: Seghers, 1967

LeDimna, N. *Jeux et enjeux chez Pierre Albert-Birot. Lectures de "Grabinoulor."* Chieti, Maria Solfanelli. 1989

Lentengre, M.-L. *Pierre Albert-Birot. L'Invention de soi.* Paris: J.-M. Place, 1993

Special Issues of Literary Magazines Devoted to Albert-Birot

L'Année poétique, 1934

Maintenant, 2 (1946)

Alternances, 44 (1959)

Ou,cinquième saison, 19 (1963)

Courrier international d'études poétiques, 47 (1963)

De Tafelronde, 11 (1964)

La Barbacane, 7 (4) (1968)

Form, 8 (1968)

F, 2–3 (1972)

Silex, 10 (1976)

Sud, 19 (1976)

Cahiers Bleus, 15 (1979)

Atlantiques, 70 (1992)

Articles

Abastado, Claude. "Jeux et visées d'un texte parodique: *Grabinoulor*," *F*, 2–3 (1972), pp. 67–78

Abirached, Robert. "Viste à Grabinoulor," *La Nouvelle Revue Française* 25 (March 1965), pp. 568–72

———. Préface, in *Pierre Albert-Birot: Théâtre I*. Mortemart: Rougerie, 1977, pp. 7–17

Albert Birot, Arlette. "Un style de vie poétique," *Le Monde des livres*, supplement to n° 7208, Paris (16 March 1968), p. IV

———. "Pierre Albert-Birot et le surréalisme." *Europe* 475–76 (November-December 1968), 100–2

————. "Dans le sillon de Pierre Albert-Birot." *La Barbacane* 7 (1968), 13–19

————. "Sous le signe de Grabinoulor." *La Barbacane* 11–12 (1971)

————. "Avant-propos." *F,* 2–3 (1972), 3–4

————. "Pour un art poétique," *F,* 2–3 (1972), 36–43

————. "Pierre Albert-Birot, *SIC* et le futurisme." *Europe* 55 (1975)

————. "Pierre Albert-Birot typographe." *Silex* 10 (1976)

————. "Pierre Albert-Birot et le théâtre." *Cahiers bleus* 14 (1979), 62–64

————. "Pierre Albert-Birot le dompteur du temps." Postface to *Les Mémoires d'Adam,* Pierre Albert-Birot. Paris: Editions de l'Allée, 1986

————. "Un pied dans un soulier trop court." Postface to *Rémy Floche, employé.* Paris: Editions de L'Allée, 1986

————. "Making Friends with Grabinoulor." Translated by Barbara Wright, preface to *The First Book of* Grabinoulor. London: Atlas Press, 1986; Illinois: Dalkey Archive Press, 1987

————.Presentation of *Poésie I* Rougerie. Mortemart, 1987

————. "Tu leur diras—un leitmotiv de l'oeuvre" suivi de "La Plume en or." *Jointure* 16 (1987)

————. "Pierre Albert-Birot." *Le Cri des Gueux,* (1988)

————.(With Didier Plassard.) "Pierre Albert-Birot et l'acteur en carton." *PUCK 1 (1988)*

————. *"SIC* et *Nord-Sud."* Centenaire de Reverdy, Colloque d'Angers-Sablé-Solesmes, University of Angers, 1990

————. "De l'éveil au point final" in *Les Six Livres de Grabinoulor.* Paris: Jean-Michel Place, 1990

————. "Ravengar en cage." *La Chouette* 23 (1990)

————. "Pierre Albert-Birot." *Le Cri des Gueux* 12 (1991), 16–22 (including two unpublished poems: "Un poème" (1959) and "Niet! niet!" [1962–63])

————. Notes to *La Lune ou le livres des poèmes.* Mortemart: Rougerie, 1992

————. (With Didier Plassard.) Notes to *Théâtre VII,* to be published by Rougerie

————. "Albert-Birot et les beaux-arts: survol rapide." *Atlantiques* 70 (1992)

Alyn, Marc. "Le retour de Pierre Albert-Birot." *Le Figaro Littéraire* (1 January 1968), p. 21

Aragon, Louis. "Pierre Albert-Birot." *L'Infini* 31 (Autumn 1990)

Aubray, Thérèse. "Quelques mots sur une amitié." *Alternances* 44 (March 1959)

Audejan, Christian. "Pierre Albert-Birot, Grabinoulor." *Esprits* 333 (1964), 1057–58

Aveline, Claude. "Grabinoulor s'éveille." *La Barbacane* 7 no. 4 (1968), 20–24

J.B. "Grabinoulor par Pierre Albert-Birot." *Syndicats* (1964)

Bachelard, Gaston. "Deux lettres à Pierre Albert-Birot." *Alternances* 44 (1959); reprinted in *Silex,* 10 (1976)

————. "Pierre Albert-Birot vu par Bachelard." *Silex* 10 (1976), 2

Bann, Stephen. "The work of Pierre Albert-Birot." *Form* 8 (September 1968), 21–32

Baudouin, Dominique. "Une lecture des Poèmes à l'Autre Moi." *F,* 2–3 (1972), 101–16

——. "'La panthère noire' de Pierre Albert Birot." *Espaces,* documents du XXe siècle 1 (1975), 28–40

——. "Pierre Albert-Birot: poésie, langage, mythe." *Sud,* 19 no. 3 (1976), 5–11

Béarn, Pierre. "Pierre Albert-Birot." *Alternances* 44 (March 1959)

——. "Lorsque on n'est pas un technocrate." *La Barbacane* 7 no. 4 (1968), 25–28

——. "Douze minutes avec Pierre Albert-Birot." *La Passerelle* (1975–76), 32–37

Béhar, Henri. "Pierre Albert-Birot" in *Le Théâtre dada et surréaliste.* Paris: Gallimard, 1979, pp. 87–97

Bellejoie, Narcisse. "Cette poésie" *Silex* 10 (1976), 29

Bellino, Pierre. "Grabinoulor par Pierre Albert-Birot." *Le petit bara* (July 1933)

Berger, Pierre. "Entretien avec Pierre Albert-Birot." *Les Lettres Françaises* 1057 (1964)

Betove, , "J'ai connu Pierre." *Alternances* 44 (1959)

Beucler, André. "Le Pab qui me séduisit." *La Barbacane* 7 no. 4 (1968), 29–32

Bofa, Gus. "Grabinoulor." *Le Crapouillot* (December 1933)

Bosquet, Alain. "'Présentation de Aux trente deux vents' de Pierre Albert-Birot." *La Table ronde* 92 (1955), 21–28

——. "'Grabinoulor," un livre en avance sur son époque," *Le Monde* 6187 (5 December 1964)

——. "La joyeuse épopée de Pierre Albert-Birot." *Le Quotidien des Livres* (January 1992)

Bray, Barbara. "Grabinoulor Rides Again." *The Sunday Times,* 28 Maruch 1965

Brezekowski, Ian. "Grabinoulor nakolacji, *Kurer Paranny,* (1937)

Burgos, Jean. "Pour un portrait de Pierre Albert-Birot." *F,* 2–3 (1972), 7–15

Calle-Gruber, Mireille. "Grabinoulor—ces jeux du vraisemblable." in *L'Effet—Fiction de l'illusion.* Paris: Nizet, 1989, pp. 71–97

Carlton, Lake. "Textes de Pierre Albert-Birot," in *Baudelaire to Beckett, a Century of French Art & Literature.* Austin, Texas, University of Texas at Austin 1976

Cassou, Jean. "Pierre Albert-Birot, Grabinoulor." *Cahiers d'Art* 4 (1933)

——. "Pierre Albert-Birot au temps de SIC." *Alternances* 44 (1959)

Caws, Mary-Ann. "Le chant sphéerique de Pierre Albert-Birot." *F,* 2–3 (1972), 34–35

Cazes, Hélène. "Grabinoulor." Bulletin critique du livre français, (April 1992)

Chabrol, Henri. "Sur le ton de La Fontaine," *Alternances* 44 (1959)

Chaillou, Michel. "Un Maldoror heureux." *Le Monde* (3 January 1992)

Chapelain-Midy, Roger. "Sans doute il n'a jamais su." *La Barbacane* 4 (1968), 35–37

Chopin, Henri. "Notes à propos de l'oeuvre de Pierre Albert-Birot." *Courrier du Centre International d'Etudes Poétiques* 47 (1963), 13–18, reprinted in *De Tafelronde* 11 (1964), 4–8

——. "Voir Pierre Albert-Birot." *La Barbacane* 7 no. 4 (1968), 38–42

——. "L'avant-garde?" *F,* 2–3 (1972), 19–27

Clancier, Georges-Emmanuel. "Carte d'identité de Monsieur Grabinoulor." *F,* 2–3 (1972), 79–80

Cluny, Claude-Michel. "Stèle pour P.A.B." *La Quinzaine Littéraire* 35 (1967)

———. "Pierre Albert-Birot: Poésie 1916–1924." *La Nouvelle Revue Française,* 31 (1968), 1087–88

Collette, Jean. "Grabinoulor le magnifique." *L'Instant* (28 November 1991)

Cornwaulh, Joël. "SIC pour: Sons, Idées, Couleurs." *Atlantiques* 70 (1992)

———. "Grabinoulor in extenso," interview with Arlette Albert-Birot. *Atlantiques* 70 (1995)

Crumb, Daniel. "Pierre Albert-Birot et Angoulême." *Atlantiques* 70 (1992)

F.D. "Grabinoulor." *Le Rempart* (23 April 1933)

Datheil, Raymond. "Une lettre de Raymond Datheil." *La Barbacane* 7 no. 4 (1968), 43–47

Décaudin, Michel. "Un temoin: Pierre Albert-Birot." *L'Information Littéraire* 3 (1969), 121–23

———. "De l'utilité de Pab au théâtre." *F,* 2–3 (1972), 47–54

Delahaye, Robert. "Nous autres usagers des chemins." *Alternances* 44 (1959)

De La Mort, Noël B. "Lettre de Paris." *Le Paysan du Sud-Ouest* (27 August 1933)

———. "Pierre Albert-Birot, Grabinoulor." *La Province d'Alsace* (15 September 1933), reprinted in *La Voix Française, organe des intérêts français au Maroc* (30 September 1933)

———. "En parlant de Grabinoulor avec Pierre Albert-Birot." *La Voix Française, organe des intérêts francais au Maroc* (7 October 1933)

———. "Pierre Albert-Birot, Grabinoulor." *Action Nationale* (Tunis) (15 October 1933)

Deletang-Tardif, Yanette. "Présence de Pierre Albert-Birot." *La Barbacane* 7 no. 4 (1968), 48–51

Della Faille, Pierre. "Présence de Pierre Albert-Birot." *Alternances* 44 (1959)

Denuit, Désiré. "Pierre Albert-Birot, Grabinoulor." *Terre Wallonne* (October 1933)

Dermée, Paul. Compte rendu de *Trente et un poèmes de poche. Nord-Sud,* 4–5 (1917)

Dewalhens, Paul. "En relisant Grabinoulor de Pierre Albert-Birot." *Alternances* 44 (1959)

———. "Grabinoulor plus vivant que jamais." *L'Essai,* 31 (1965), 5–6

Dubrau, Louis. "Interview de Pierre Albert-Birot, le solitaire." *Le Journal des poètes* (Bruxelles) 10 (1947)

Dujardin, E. "Grabinoulor." *Le Mercure de France* (1 July 1920)

Dunoyer, Jean-Marie. "Mort du poète Pierre Albert-Birot." *Le Monde* (26 July 1967)

———. "Pierre Albert-Birot, le précurseur." *Le Monde des Livres,* supplement to n° 7208, 16 March 1968, pp. IV–V

Durry, Marie-Jeanne. "C'était voilà un peu plus de deux ans." *La Barbacane* 7 no 4 (1968), 53–55

Eichorn, Linda. "The Voice of a New Age: P. Albert-Birot and *SIC.*" *Library Chronicle of the University of Texas at Austin* 35 (1986), 45–60

R.F. "Grabinoulor." *Le Rempart* (23 October 1933)

Favier, Anne. "Grabinoulor enfin complet." *Livres Hebdo,* 47 (22 November 1991)

Favre, Yves-Alain. "Adieu à Pierre Albert-Birot." *Etudes Charentaises* 7 no. 1 (1968), 303–6

———. "Pierre Albert-Birot ou le langage en fête." Colloque de Cadiz "Dada, Surrealismo: Precursores, Marginales y Heterodoxes." University of Cadiz, 1988, 23–25

Follain, Jean. "Contes et fantaisies: Grabinoulor." *Nouvelle Revue Française* (November 1933), 773–76

———. "Pierre Albert-Birot, grand vivant." *La Barbacane* 7 no. 4 (1968), 57–61

———. "La solitude peuplée de Pierre Albert-Birot." *F*, 2–3 (1972), 5

———. "Pierre Albert-Birot, dit Pab, dit Grabinoulor." suivi de "Lettres de Pab à Follain." *Cahiers bleus* 15 no. 3 (1979), 19–30

Gasser, Viviane. "Pierre Albert-Birot qui fût essentiellement poète, ami d'Apollinaire et pionnier du surréalisme." *Tribune de Genève* (28 July 1967)

Gandon, Yves. "Pour Monsieur Pierre Albert-Birot." *L'Intransigeant* (26 April 1933)

———. "La page arrachée de Grabinoulor." *L'Intransigeant* (28 April 1933)

Gayan, Louis-Guy. "Le combat du rêve contre le réel." *Sud-Ouest* 893 (4 September 1966)

Gonzague Frick, Louis de. "Du pyrogène au pyrsephore." *Alternances* 44 (1959)

Gregh, Fernand. "Pierre Albert-Birot a eu le tort." *Alternances* 44 (1959)

Grindea, Miron. "Grabinoulor." *The New York Times Literary Supplement*, 2 March 1965

Guillaume, Louis. "Présentation de Pierre Albert-Birot." *Les Lettres* 21–22 (1954)

———. "Le premier drame tragique de Pierre Albert-Birot: Image." *Alternances* 44 (1959)

———. "Le 5 avril 1967." *La Barbacane* 7 no. 4 (1968), 59–61

Guillemain, Bernard. "Pierre Albert-Birot et l'esthétique du présent." *Alternances* 44 (1959)

Harlong. "Dans le tunnel." *Gringoire* (8 September 1933)

Helmle, Eugen. Postface to the German translation of the First Book of Grabinoulor. Translated by Petra Timpe, Munich, Text & Kritik, 1980

Hoffmeister, Adolf. "Présentation de Pierre Albert-Birot et traduction d'un ensemble de 'Trente et un poèmes de poche.'" *Host* (Prague, 5 (1922)

Humeau, Edmond. "Quel sens aurait la ponctuation?" *Arts* 16 (Janurary 1953)

Israel, Madeleine. "Grabinoulor" in "Les livres par M.I." (May 1933)

Jacob, Max, "Souvenirs et critque," *Les nouvelles littéraires* 13 (May 1933)

———. "Lettre à Pierre Albert-Birot du 16 juillet 1943." *Alternances* 44 (1959)

Janet, Marcelle. "Nous présentons Grabinoulor." *La Barbacane* 3 (1965)

Jans, Adrien. "Pierre Albert-Birot et le premier surréalisme." *Le soir* (Bruxelles), 12 November 1964

Jasseron, C. "Pierre Albert-Birot, Grabinoulor," *La République Lyonnaise*, 11 November 1933

Jean, Georges. "Connaissez-vous Pierre Albert-Birot?" *Le Français d'aujourd'hui* 29 (1975), 83–88

Jean Raymond. "Préface des Femmes pliantes." *Le Monde des Livres*, supplement to n° 7208 (March 1968), III

Jourdan, Bernard. "Approche de Pierre Albert-Birot ou le poète et son double." *Critique* (1962), 121–33

———. "Grabinoulor." *Les Livres,* Bulletin Bibliographique mensuel, 8 (1965)

———. "Pierre Albert-Birot jusqu'ici." *La Barbacane* 7 no. 4 (1968), 69–72

———. *"Rémy Floche employé* et l'exorcisme." *F,* 2–3 (1972), 81–84

Ker-Frank-Houx. "De quelques poètes et chinois." *Ariste* (2), 7–8 (1919)

Labrusse, Françoise. *Théâtre à la Maleherbe.* Thaon: Amiot-Lenganey, 1992. (Account of the staging, with photographs, of five plays by Pierre Albert-Birot.)

Labrusse, Hughes. "Ad Unguem." *Sud* 19 no. 3 (1976), 12–24

———. "Le 'Oui' de Jean Follain à Pierre Albert-Birot." *Cahiers bleus* 15 no. 3 (1979), 33–35

Lacôte, René. "Chronique de poésie: Pierre Albert-Birot." *Les Lettres Françaises* 1051 (29 October–4 November 1964), 9

Laffont-Bompiani (coll.). "Grabinoulor" in *Dictionnaire des Oeuvres,* Vol. 3. Paris: Bouquins Robert-Laffont, 1986, pp. 269–70

Lafont, (Albert-Birot) Arlette. "Loin des foules: rétrospective "SIC," *La table ronde* 129 (1958), 169–72

———. "Souvenir de Roch Grey." *Alternances* 44 (1959)

———. "Présentation de Pierre Albert-Birot." *Between Poetry and Painting* (October–November 1965), pp. 24–27

L'Anselme, Jean. "Présentation de PAB avec choix de poèmes en francais, anglais espagnol, arabe." *Brèves nouvelles de France* 39 (1978), 31–42

Lassaque, Roger, 'La joie du verbe et des "sept couleurs"', *F,* 2–3 (1972), 89–100

Lebois, André. "Pierre Albert-Birot, l'artificier silencieux." *Quo vadis* 53/54/55 no 1 (1953), 80–93

———. "La poésie de Pierre Albert-Birot." *Le Mercure de France* 318 (June 1953), 239–45

———. "Passeport pour l'île Albert-Birot." in *P. Albert-Birot: Grabinoulor-Amour.* Limoges: Rougerie, 1955, pp. 9–41

———. "Pierre Albert-Birot," *Le goëland* (March 1956)

———. "Pierre Albert-Birot ou la joie d'écrire." *Courrier du Centre International d'Etudes Poétiques* 47 (1963), 3–6

———. "Grabinoulor redivivus." *Le Tyrse* (June 1965), 317–27

———. "Pierre Albert-Birot." *Les Lettres Françaises* (2 August 1967), 3–4

———. Preface, in *Pierre ALBERT-BIROT, Poésie 1916–1924.* Paris: Gallimard 1967, pp. I–XVII

———. "Pierre Albert-Birot, Saint Chamarand et Germain Nouveau." *La Barbacane* 7 no. 4 (1968), 73–80

———. "Transfiguration du réel dans les lettres d'aujourd'hui," in *Littérature V* (February 1957), 21–45

———. "L'aventure humaine et son épilogue: Pierre Albert-Birot dans Le train bleu.'" *F,* 2–3 (1972), 117–26

———. "Pierre Albert-Birot: grand maître d'optimisme et d'énergie." *Revue des Lettres* 2 no. 2 (1976), 14–18

———. "Une étude pour le centenaire de Pierre Albert-Birot." *Le journal des poètes* (Bruxelles), 7 (1976), 3–5

Le Clec'h, Guy. "On découvre aujourd'hui Pierre Albert-Birot, l'homme qui lança le surréalisme." *Le Figaro Littéraire* 1061, (18 August 1966), 2

Le Dimna, Nicole. "Grabinoulor faits de style." Pescara, *C.L.U.A.*, University of Pescara, 1985

———. "Une description créatrice, l'accident du pont de bois en Grabinoulor." Pescara *C.L.U.A.*, University of Pescara, 1985. Collected in Le Dimna, *Jeux et enjeux chez Pierre Albert-Birot*

———. "*Pierre Albert-Birot, créateur de forme(s) nouvelle(s).*" *Hommage à Rimbaud*. University of Pescara, 1991

Lentengre, Marie-Louise. "Grabinoulor, epopea surrealista?" *Il Verri*, 12 no. 2 (1978), 138–50

———. "Les appétits hyperboliques de Grabinoulor." *Lectures* 2 (1979), 137–61

———. "Grabinoulor ou le triomphe de l'imaginaire," extract from "La letteratura e l'immaginario,' Problemi di semantica e di storia del lessico franco-italiano, Atti dell'XI Convegno della Società Universitaria per gli studi di lingua e letteratura francese, Verona, 14 and 16 October 1982, pp. 163–71

———. "Aux sources de la métamorphose de 'SIC', la rencontre de Gino Severini et Pierre Albert-Birot," *Francofonia*, Studi e richerche sulle letterature di lingua francese, 13, Autumn 1987

———. "Au commencement était le cri." *Atlantiques* 70 (1992)

Leperlier, Francois. *Claude Cahun. L'Ecart et la Métamorphose.* Paris: J-M Place, 1992, pp. 82–110

Lepape, Pierre. "Une épopée surréaliste." *Paris-Normandie,* 4 December 1964

Linze, Georges. "Grabinoulor par Pierre Albert-Birot." *Anthologie* 1 (1933)

Lista, Giovanni. "Le futurisme de Pierre Albert-Birot." *Cahiers bleus* 14 no. 1 (1979), 27–50

Marcel, Gabriel. "Grabinoulor par Pierre Albert-Birot." *L'Europe nouvelle* 805 (1993), 669–70

———. "Pierre Albert-Birot." *Le Centaure* 8 (1931), 1–3

Marcou, André. "Projecteur à un poème de Pierre Albert-Birot." *Journal des poètes,* 12 (1932)

Margerit, Robert. "Souvenir de Grabinoulor," *F,* 2–3 (1972), 61–66

Marion, Louise. "Pierre Albert-Birot et moi." *Alternances* 44 (1959)

Marissel, André. "Pierre Albert-Birot," in *Littérature de notre temps* IV. Paris: Casterman, 1970, pp. 9–12

Massat, René. "Notre ami Grabinoulor." *Alternances* 44 (1959)

Matthys, Francis. "Grabinoulor—l'intégrale enfin." *La Libre Belgique* 21 (November 1991)

Mauriac, Claude. "Grabinoulor de Pierre Albert-Birot." *Le Figaro,* 2 November 1964

Maury, Pierre. "Grabinoulor. Un point c'est tout!" *Le Soir de Bruxelles,* 21 November 1991

Medicis, Stelios Castanos de. "'Grabinoulor par Pierre Albert-Birot'" suivi du premier chapitre du quatrième livre. *Synthèses* 224 (1965), 385–95

Miguel, André. "Grabinoulor ou la liberté." *Cahiers du Sud,* 381 (1965), 100–4

Miomandre, Francis de. "Pierre Albert-Birot." *Nouvelles Littéraires* 8 (1956)

Montagne, Alfreyd. "Question aux "pauvres Birots.'" *Modernisme et compréhension*, 2 (1917)

———. "J'accuse Monsieur Birot." *Modernisme et compréhension* 3 (1917)

Mora, André. "En hommage à Pierre Albert-Birot." *Alternances* 44 (1959)

Mouren, Gaston. "Grabinoulor par Pierre Albert-Birot." *Cahiers du Sud* (December 1933), 817–18

Nicoletti, Michel. "La délicatesse." *La Barbacane* 7 no. 4 (1968), 81–84

———. "Au bout du monde." *F,* 2 (1972), 6

———. "L'impossible résumé de *Splendeurs,*" *F,* 2–3 (1972), 85–88

Normand, Claude. "Chronique d'un lecteur." *Silex* 10 (1976), 10–13

Noulet, Emilie. "Chronique de la poésie: *Poèmes à l'autre moi.*" *Synthèses* 100 (1954), 276–79

Orlandi Cerenza, Germana. "Pierre Albert-Birot: un surrealista fuori del Castello,'" in P.A. Jannini, *Surrealismo presentazione.* Rome, Bulzoni, Paris, Nizet, 1974, pp. 75–95

———. "Pierre Albert-Birot" in *I Contemporanei, Letteratura francese* 2. Edited by M. Colesanti and L. de Nardis. Rome: Lucarini, 1977, pp. 31–42

———. "Marinetti e Albert-Birot." *SI e NO,* quaderni di letteratura e d'Arte 2. Rome: De Luca, 1979

———. "Futurismo e Cubismo letterario," in "La fortuna del Futurismo in Francia." *Avanguardia storiche.* Collected and edited by P.A. Jannini. Rome: Bulzoni, 1979

———. Introduction to Matoum et Tévibar. *Diccionario della letteratura mondiale del novocento,* vol. XI. Rome: Paolini, 1984

———. "Poetiche d'avanguardia del primo novocento francese," in *Dal Romanticismo al Surrealismo.* Rome: Bulzoni, 1984

———. "Perennità e utopia del teatro di Pierre Albert-Birot." *Sipario,* 520 (1992)

Orloff, Chana. "Pierre Albert-Birot, né cent ans trop tôt," *Alternances* 44 (1959)

Parrot, Louis. "Grabinoulor." *Jeunesse, Talence* (October 1933), pp. 97–100

Pellerin, J., and G. Picard. "Pierre Albert-Birot," in *Figures d'aujourd'hui.* Illustrated by Chana Orloff. Paris: D'Alignan, 1923, pp. 29–33

Peret, Jean Marie. "Entretien avec le poète Pierre Albert-Birot." *Sud-Ouest,* 893 (1966)

Perez Jorba, J. "Pierre Albert-Birot, poeta nunista." *Messidor* 3 (1918), 37–39

———. "Sobre la novela del porvenir." *El Diagrafico* (August 1921)

Pia, Pascal. "A l'entour d'Apollinaire." *Le Carrefour* 1059 (1964), 18

———. "Chaque amateur de poésie." *La Barbacane* 7 no. 4 (1968), 85–87

———. "Avant-propos," in Pierre Albert-Birot. *Le Train bleu.* Editions Guy

Plassard, Didier, *L'Acteur en effigie. Figures de l'homme artificiel dans les théâtres des avant-gardes historiques.* Paris: L'Age d'homme, 1992, pp. 177–189

———. "Pierre Albert-Birot: le théâtre à l'état naïf." *Atlantiques* 70 (1992)

Pons, Max. "Pour une approche de Pierre Albert-Birot." *La Barbacane* 7 no. 4 (1968), 7–11

———. "Dans la lumière de Pierre Albert-Birot." *La Barbacane* 7 no. 4 (1968), 109–11

———. "Connaissance de Pierre Albert-Birot." *F,* 2–3 (1972), 16–18

————. "Lire Pierre Albert-Birot." *Cahiers bleus* 4 (1976), 80–81

————. "Avez-vous lu Pierre Albert-Birot?" *Sud* 19 no. 3 (1976), 29–30

————. "Pierre Albert-Birot année 100." *La Barbacane* 17–18 (1976), 53–58

————. "Pierre Albert-Birot l'éveilleur." *Cahiers bleus* 15 no. 3 (1979), 39

Pouey, Fernand. "Une série d'entretiens avec Pierre Albert-Birot." *Arts* (1952), 362–70

Poulaille, Henri. "Pierre Albert-Birot." *Germinal,* (June 1933), reprinted in *L'équipe des arts et des lettres* 2 (1939)

Proïa, Francois. *Di qua e di là dall'imagine. Letteratura e cinema nelle avanguardie francesi del primo Novecento.* Chieti: Solfanelli, 1992. Contains "Documenti; tre sceneggiature inedite di Pierre Albert-Birot: *Voyages de noces, D'après La Triologie d'Eschyle, Les Heures à Paris,*" 185–204

Roch, Grey. "Pierre Albert-Birot." *Maintenant* 2 no. 2 (1946), 186–93

Root, Waverly Lewis. "A modern Rabelais." *Chicago Daily Tribune* (European edition), 7 August 1933

Rousselot, Jean. "Un grand poète authentique: Pierre Albert-Birot." *Proximités* 2, dated approximately by Arlett Albert-Birot 1939–46

————. "Le nonagénaire amoureux." *Les Nouvelles Littéraires* 2083 (3 August 1967)

————. "Pierre Albert-Birot, homme de la vraie joie." *La Barbacane* 7 no. 4 (1968), 89–90

————. "Pierre Albert-Birot et la convenance du dire," in *Mort ou survie du langage.* Paris-Bruxelles: Editions Sodi, 1969

————. "Pierre Albert-Birot ou l'écriture réinventée." *F,* 2–3 (1972), 28–33

————. "Grabinoulor et l'espace." *Sud* 19 no. 3 (1976), 25–28

Roussot, Roger. "C'était en 1926." *La Barbacane* 4 (1968), 91–99

Roudaut, Jean. "Grabinoulor." *Magazine Littéraire,* 70 (November 1972), 56–57

————. "Introduction à Grabinoulor." *Cahiers bleus* 15 no. 3 (1979), 49–51

————. "l'Epopée de Grabinoulor." *Magazine littéraire,* no. 295, (January 1992)

Rudler, G. "Grabinoulor de M. Pierre Albert-Birot." *L'Echo de Londres,* 15 June 1933

Sabatier, Robert. "Pierre Albert-Birot" in *Histoire de la poésie française, XXème siècle,* vol. II. Paris: Albin Michel, 1982

Salmon, André. "Si la société des gens de Lettres." *Alternances* 44 (1959)

Schoffer, Nicolas. "Mes souvenirs." *Alternances* 44 (1959)

Senechal, Christian. "Présentation de Pierre Albert-Birot." *Poésie* 2 (1934), 23–30

Seraline, Yves. "Des arts plastiques à l'écriture." *F,* 2–3 (1972), 44–46

Seuphor, Michel. "J'ai connu Albert-Birot." *Alternances* 44 (1959)

Severini, Gino. "Pierre Albert-Birot et *SIC.*" *La Barbacane* 7 no. 4 (1968), 100–2

Sitta, Carlo-Alberto. "Ricordo di PAB." *La gazetta di Modena,* 4 June 1968

————. "Tascabili feriali cronachistiche poesie di Pierre Albert-Birot." *Carte segrete* 16 (1971), 72–86

————. "L'épopée de Grabinoulor." *Il Caffé,* series 6, 6–7 (1973–74). Contains the translation by the author of chapters 1 and 2 of Book I

Smiday, Paul. "Grabinoulor de Monsieur Pierre Albert-Birot." *Temps,* 19 August 1922

Survage, Léopold. "J'ai fait la connaissance de Pierre Albert-Birot." *Alternances* 44 (1959)

Treich, Léon. "Grabinoulor." *Paris Magazine* (August-November 1933)

Truc, Gonzague. "Pierre Albert-Birot, Grabinoulor." *Balsac*, 1 July 1933

Ulmann, Paul. "Je suis heureux que." *Alternances* 44 (1959)

Vandercammen, Edmond. "Grabinoulor ou l'homme qui était sorti de son imagination." *Le rouge et le noir* (4 October 1933)

Verdone, Mario. "Le anticipazioni magiche di Pab" (with a previously unpublished leter from Prampolini to Albert-Birot). *Il Dramma* 11–12 (1971), 99–101

Verdone, Mario. "Prologo collage in un atto d'après Pab." *Il Dramma* 11–12 (1971), 104–7

Verhesen, Fernand. "La courbe de ce poème qui nous recrée Pierre Albert-Birot." *Courrier du Centre International d'Etudes Poétiques* 47 (1963), 7–12

Virmaux, Alain. "Pierre Albert-Birot et le cinéma." *F*, 2–3 (1972), 55–60

Vree, Paul de. "Pierre Albert-Birot: de groene dichter." *De Tafelronde* 11 and 1 (1964), 2–3

Wagneur, Jean-Didier. "Grabinoulor et Furibar." *Libération*, 26 December 1991

Wetterwald, Denis. "Grabinoulor, place à la Birotique." *Politis* 1825 (1992)

Wright, Barbara. "A French Translation: *SIC*, Pierre Albert-Birot, *Grabinoulor*." *Times Literary Suppliment*, 18 February 1965

———. "Pab on l'aimait." *La Barbacane* 7 no. 4 (1968), 103–4

———. Introduction to the translation of *Grabinoulor* Book 1, Chapters 1, 2, 3, 4, and 6, in *Atlas Anthology* III. (London: Atlas Press, 1985), pp. 10–12

Zadkine, Ossip. "Cher, tu es l'ennemi." *La Barbacane* 7 no. 4 (1968), 105–6

Academic Studies

("Dissertation" indicates masters level and "thesis" indicates doctorate, but it should be noted that the requirements vary widely between countries.)

Ingenbleek, N. "Monographie de Pierre Albert-Birot." Dissertation, Université Libre de Bruxelles, 1957–58

Lassaque, R. "La Joie des sept couleurs." Dissertation supervised by M. J. Durry, Sorbonne, 1968

Marottoli, V.J. "Futurism and Its Influence on the French Poet Pierre Albert-Birot." Ph.D. thesis, University of Connecticut, 1974

Plassard, D. "Pierre Albert-Birot: idées sur le théâtre (le surréel à la scène)." Dissertation, University of Caen, 1979

Timpe, P. "Untersuschungen zur Epischen Fiktion Pierre Albert-Birots am Beispiel von Grabinoulor. Dissertation, University of Bielefeld, 1980

Basile, M. "Introduction à l'oeuvre de Pierre Albert-Birot." Dissertation, University of Bologna, 1980–81

Carol, N. "Lecture de 'La Joie des sept couleurs." Dissertation supervised by P. Brunel and A. Albert-Birot, University of Paris IV, 1985

Montanari E. "Introduction à la lecture de 'Grabinoulor' de Pierre Albert-Birot." Dissertation, University of Bologna, 1987

Ricci, R. "Pierre Albert-Birot e il teatro." Dissertation, University Gabriele d' Aminzio, 1987

Balhatchet, D. "A Critical Study of *Grabinoulor* by Pierre Albert-Birot." Doctoral thesis submitted to the Board of Medieval and Modern Languages and Literatures, University of Oxford, 1987

Bagnost, V. "Pierre Albert-Birot et Guillaume Apollinaire. Le théâtre de l'esprit nouveau, 1917–1920." Dissertation supervised by Daniel Debreil, University of Paris III, 1992

Kelly, D. "The Works of Pierre Albert-Birot: A Poetics in Movement, a Poetics of Movement." Doctoral thesis submitted for the degreee of Ph.D. University of London, 1992

Leary, Joanna, "A Study of Pierre Albert-Birot's *Catalogue de l'Antiquaire.*" Dissertation, Birkbeck College, University of London, 1994

Chaussinand, Laurence, "Une étude de *Rémy Floche, employé* par Pierre Albert-Birot." Dissertation Birkbeck College, 1995

Fabre, Guillem, "La Digression Grabinoulorienne: étude à partir *du Troisième livre.*" Dissertation supervised by Claude Debon, University of the Sorbonne-Nouvelle-Paris III, 1995

BIBLIOGRAPHICAL REFERENCES

(This is not a general biblography and contains details only of books referred to in this study.)

The Avant-Garde; The Visual Arts

Books

Apollonio, Umberto. *Futurist Manifestos.* London: Thames and Hudson, 1973

Aragon, Louis. *Les Collages.* Paris: Hermann, 1965

Bergman, P. *Modernolatria e Simultaneità.* Stockholm: Coll. Studia Litterarum Upsaliena, n° 2, Svenska Bokförlaget, 1962

Bohn, Willard. *The Aesthetics of Visual Poetry.* Cambridge, 1986

Briosi, Sandro & Hillenaar, Henk, *Vitalité et Contradictions de l'avant-garde,* Paris, Librairie Jose Corti, 1968

Butor, Michel. *Les mots dans la peinture.* Geneva: Les Sentiers de la Creation, 1989

Chipp, Herschel B. (with contributions by Peter Selz and Joshua C. Taylor). *Theories of Modern Art. A Source Book by Artists and Critics.* Berkeley, Los Angeles, and London: University of California Press, 1988

Compagnon, Antoine. *Les Cinq Paradoxes de la modernité.* Paris: Seuil, 1990

Daix, Pierre. *Journal du cubisme.* Paris: Editions d'Art Albert Skira, 1982

Davies, Margaret. *Guillaume Apollinarie.* Edinburgh and London: Oliver Boyd, 1964

Delaunay, R. *Du cubisme à l'art abstrait.* Paris: Francastel, Sevpen, 1957

Fauchereau, Serge. *La Révolution cubiste.* Paris: Denoël, 1982

———. *Peintures et desins d'écrivains.* Paris: Belfond, 1991

Francastel, Pierre. *L'Image, la vision et l'imagination*. Paris: Denoël-Gauthier, 1983

Kandinsky, Vassily. *Complete Writings on Art*. Edited by Kenneth C. Lindsay and Peter Vargo. Boston: C. K. Hall, 1982

Lista, Giovanni. *Futurisme, Manifestos—Proclamations—Documents*. Lausanne: L'Age d'Homme, 1973

Longrée, Georges. *L'Expérience idéo-calligrammatique d'Apollinaire*. Paris: Touzot, 1985

Marinetti, Filippo. *Les Mots en liberté futuristes*. Milan: Edizione Futuriste di "Poesia," 1919

Mathews, Timothy. *Reading Apollinaire. Theories of Poetic Language*, Manchester: Manchester University Press, 1987

Matthews, J. H. *Towards a Poetics of Surrealism*. Syracuse, N.Y.: Syracuse University Press, 1976

Perloff, Marjorie. *The Futurist Moment. Avant-Garde, Avant Guerre and the Language of Rupture*. Chicago and London: University of Chicago Press, 1986

Sacks, Pénélope. *Calligramme ou écriture figurée: Apollinaire, inventeur de formes*. Paris: Minard, 1988

Sebbag, Georges. *Jacques Vaché. Soixante-dix-neuf lettres de Guerre*. Paris: J.-M. Place, 1989

———. *L'imprononçable jour de sa mort. Jacques Vaché Janvier 1919*. Paris: J.-M. Place, 1989

Silver, Kenneth. *Esprit de Corps. The Art of the Parisian Avant-Garde and the First World War 1914–1925*. London: Thames and Hudson, 1989

Soupault, Philippe. *Vingt mille et un jours, Entretiens avec Serge Fauchereau*. Paris: Belfond, 1980

Vallier, Dora. *Les Couleurs dans la peinture*. Caen: L'Echoppe, 1989

Verkauf, Willy, ed. *Dada, Monograph of a Movement*. New York: St. Martin's Press; London: Academy Editions, 1975

Weightman, John. *The Concept of the Avant-Garde, Explorations in Modernism*. London: Alcove Press, 1973

Articles

Bassy, Alain-Marie. "Forme litteraire et forme graphique: les schématogrammes d'Apollinaire." *Scolies,* Cahiers du recherche de l'Ecole Normale Supérieure, 3–4 (1973–74), 161–207

Breunig, L.-C., and J.-C. Chevalier. "Apollinaire et Les Peintres Cubistes.'" *Revue des Lettres Modernes,* 104–7, Guillaume Apollinaire 3 (1964), pp. 8, 9, 112

Chevalier, J.-C. "G. Apollinaire. Rôle de la peinture et de la poésie dans l'élaboration d'une poétique." *Revue des Lettres Modernes,* pp. 217–22; Guillaume apollinaire 8 (1969), pp. 97–107

Clark, J.-G. "Delaunay, Apollinaire et les *Fenêtres." Revue des Lettres Modernes,* Guillaume Apollinaire 7, 1968

Davies, Margaret. "La notion de la modernité." *Cahiers du 20ᵉ siècle,* Klincksieck, Paris, pp. 9–30

Debon, Claude. "'L'Ecriture cubiste' d'Apollinaire." *Europe* 638–39 (1982), 118–27

Décaudin, Michel and E. A. Hubert. "Petit historique d'une appellation: 'cubisme littéraire.'" Cubisme et Littérature, *Europe* (1982), 10

Décaudin, Michel. "La Nouveauté des calligrammes dans l'oeuvre d'Apollinaire." *Le Flâneur des deux rives* 4 (1954), 38–40

——. "L'Avant-garde autour d'Apollinaire." *Information Littéraire* 3 (1969)

Drost, Wolfgang, and Géraldi Leroy. "La Lettre et la figure: La littérature et les arts visuels à l'époque moderne." Heidelberg: Actes du ler colloque des Universités d'Orléans et de Siegen, Universitätsverlag, 1989

Goldenstein, J.-P. Review of A.M. Bassy, "Forme littéraire et forme graphique: les schématogrammes d'Apollinaire." *RLM* 450–55, Guillaume Apollinaire, 13, (1976), pp. 173–82

Gris, Juan. "Chez les cubistes." *Bulletin de la vie artistique* 6 (1925)

Guiney, Mortimer. "Cubisme, littéraire et plastique." *Revue des sciences humains*, vol. XXXVI, 142 (1971), 269–81

Kelly, Debra. "Place au surréalisme!" *La Chouette* 22 (1989)

——. "Et moi aussi je suis peintre: Poetry, Painting and the Manipulation of Typography." *La Chouette* 23 (1990)

Laparcherie, J.-G. "Ecriture et lecture du calligramme." *Poétique* 50 (1982)

Lechevalier, Gaëtane. "Un nouvel état de l'intelligence." *La Chouette* 24 (1990)

Léger, Ferdinand. "Les réalisations picturelles actuelles." *Les Soirées de Paris* (July–August 1914)

Malraux, André. "Des origines de la poésie cubiste," in *La Connaissance* 1 (1920), 38

Orlandi Cerenza, Germana. "Futurismo e Cubismo letterario," in *La Fortuna del Futurismo en Francia*. Roma: Bulzoni, 1979

——. "Cubismo letterario," in *Letteratura Francese Contemparanea*, vol. 1, "Le correnti d'avanguardia," Rome, Lucarini Editore, 1982

Parigolis, Alexandre. "Les constructions cubistes dans *Les Soirées de Paris*." *Revue de l'Art* 82 (1988)

Severini, Gino. "Symbolisme plastique et symbolisme littéraire." *Le Mercure de France* 1 (1916)

Will-Levaillant, F. "La lettre dans la peinture cubiste," in *Le Cubisme*. Saint-Etienne: CIEREC, 1973

Special Issues of Magazines

Que vlo-ve? Actes du 8ᵉ colloque "Apollinaire et la peinture," 21–22 (1979)

Que vlo-ve? Actes du 9ᵉ colloque "Lecture et interprétation des Calligrammes," 29–30 (1981)

Revue des Lettres Modernes, "Apollinaire, le cubisme et l'esprit nouveau," 69–70 (1962)

Art d'aujourd'hui, "Le Cubisme," May–June 1953

Langue Française, "Le signifiant graphique," 59 (1983)

Littérature, "Graphies," 46 (1982)

Littérature, "Voix et figures du poème," 59 (1985)

L'Esprit Créateur, "The Poet as Art Critic," 22 (4) (1982)

Visual Poetics, "Style," 22 (2) (1988)

General Critical Theory; Philosophy; Psychoanalysis

Books

Adam, J.-M. *Le texte narratif,* Paris: Editions Fernand Nathan, 1985

Ali, Sami. *L'Espace Imaginaire.* Paris: Gallimard, 1984

Anis, Jacques, with J.-L. Chiss and Ch. Puech. *L'Ecriture: théories et descriptions.* Brussels: De Boeck Universitaire, 1985

Bachelard, Gaston. *La Poétique de la rêverie.* Paris: P.U.F., 1960, 1978

Barthes, Roland. *Le Degré zéro de l'écriture.* Paris: Seuil, 1972

——. *Critique et vérité.* Paris: Seuil, 1966

——. *Système de la mode.* Paris: Seuil, 1967

——. *Essais Critiques IV, Le Bruissement de la Langue.* Paris: Seuil, 1984

Bataille, Georges. *L'Erotisme.* Paris: Minuit, 1985

——. *L'Expérience Intérieure,* in *Oeuvres Complètes, V,* Paris, Gallimard 1981

Benvenuto, B., and R. Kennedy. *The Works of Jacques Lacan. An Introduction.* London: Free Association Books, 1986

Bernstein, Leonard. *The Unanswered Question: Six Talks at Harvard.* Cambridge: Harvard University Press, 1976

Boyman Anne. *Lecture du Narcisse: sémiotique du texte de Valéry.* Montréal, Québec: Didier, 1982

Cardinal, Roger. *Figures of Reality.* London: Croon Helme Barnes & Noble, 1981

Coquet, J.-C. *Sémiotique. L'Ecole de Paris.* Paris: Hachette, 1982

Culler, Jonathan. *Strucuralist Poetics.* London: Routledge & Kegan Paul, 1975

Derrida, Jacques. *La Dissémination.* Paris: Seuil, 1972

Eco, Umberto. *La Guerre du Faux.* Paris: Grasset et Farquelle, 1985

Eliade, Mircea. *Aspects du mythe.* Paris: Gallimard, 1963

Floch, J.-M. *Petites mythologies de l'oeil et de l'esprit.* Paris-Amsterdam, Hadès-Benjamin, 1985

Foucault, Michel. *Les Mots et les choses.* Paris: Gallimard, 1986

Greimas, A. J., et al. *Essais de sémiotique poétique.* Paris: Larousse, 1972

Houdebine, Jean-Louis. *Excès de langages.* Paris: Denoël, 1984

Hume, Kathryn. *Fantasy and Mimesis. Responses to Reality in Western Literature.* New York and London: Methuen, 1984

Jakobson, R. *Essais de linguistique générale.* Paris: Minuit, 1963

——. *Questions de poétique.* Paris: Seuil, 1973

Jean, Georges. *La Poésie.* Paris: Seuil, 1966

Lacan, Jacques. *Ecrits.* Paris: Seuil, 1986

La Charité, Virginia. *The Dynamics of Space: Mallarmé's "Un coup de dés n'abolira jamais le hasard."* Lexington: French Forum Publishers, 1987

Lévi-Strauss, Claude. *L'Homme nu, Mythologiques IV.* Paris: Plon, 1971

Lyotard, Jean-Francois. *Discours, Figure.* Paris: Klincksieck, 1971

Mathis, Paul. *Le Corps et l'écrit.* Paris: Aubier Montaigne, 1981

Merleau-Ponty, M. *L'Oeil et l'esprit.* Paris: Gallimard, 1984
Meschonnic, Henri. *Critique du rythme.* Paris: Verdier, 1982
Morin, Edgar. *Le Paradigme perdu: la nature humaine.* Paris: Seuil, 1973
Mounin, Georges. *Poésie et Société,* Paris: P.U.F., 1962
Ogilvie, Bertrand. *Lacan. Le Sujet.* Paris: P.U.F., 1987
Ong, Walter. *Orality and Literacy: The Technologising of the Word.* London: Methuen, 1982
――――. *Interfaces of the Word.* Ithaca and London: Cornell University Press, 1977
Rybak, Boris. *L'Identité humaine.* Paris: J-M Place, 1990
Sollers, Philippe. *La Littérature et l'expérience des limites.* Paris: Seuil, 1968
Sorman, Guy. *Les Vrais Penseurs de notre temps.* Paris: Livre de Poche, 1991
Starobinksi, Jean. *L'Oeil vivant.* Paris: Gallimard, 1966
Todorov, T. *La Poétique de la prose.* Paris: Seuil, 1971, 1978
Zumthor, Paul. *La Lettre et la voix: de la 'littérature' médiévale.* Paris: Seuil, 1987

Articles

Anis, Jacques. "Vilisibilité du texte poétique." *Langue Française* 59 (1983)
Bellemin-Noel, Jean. "Le Narcissisme des Narcisse." *Lettérature* 6 (1972)
Delègue, Yves. "La littérature ventriloque." *Poétique,* (November 1987)
Floch, J.-M. "Les langages planaires," in *Sémiotique: L'Ecole de Paris,* Paris, Hachette, 1982
――――. "Sémiotique visuelle et statut sémiotique des éléments visuels du discours théâtral," *Degrés* 13 (1978)
Green, André. "L'interprétation psychanalytique des productions culturelles et des oeuvres d'art." *Critique sociologique et critique psychanalytique,* Editions de l'Institut de Sociologie, Bruxelles, 1975
Mounin, Georges. "Qu'est-ce que 'le langage visible'?" *Semiotica* 3–4 (1981), 383–89
Rigal, Denis. "La poésie de e.e. cummings." *Sud* 19 (1976)

Special Issues of Magazines

Corps Ecrit, "L'Autoportrait," 5 (1982)
Langue française, "La Ponctuation," 45
TLS, "The Role of the Literary Magazine," 6 June 1980

Creative Works by Other Writers

Apollinaire, Guillaume. *Oeuvres complètes.* Edited by Marcel Adéma and Michel Décaudin. Paris: Bibliothèque de la Pléiade, 1965
――――. *Les Peintres cubistes.* Edited by Leroy C. Breunig and Jean-Claude Chevalier. Paris: Miroirs de l'art, 1965
Baudelaire, C. *Oeuvres complètes.* Edited by Claude Pichois. Paris: La Pléiade, 1975

Bonnefoy, Yves. *Poèmes.* Paris: Gallimard, 1982

Céline, Louis-Ferdinand. *Romans.* Edition introduced and annotated by H. Godard. Paris: Bibliothèque de la Pléiade, Gallimard, 1981, 1988

Cendrars, Blaise. *Du monde entier au coeur du monde.* Paris: Denoël, 1957

Cortázar, Julio. *Le Livre de Manuel.* Translated by Laure Guille-Bataillon. Paris: Gallimard, 1974

Gaspar, Lorand. *Sol absolu.* Paris: Gallimard, 1972

——. *Approches de la parole.* Paris: Gallimard, 1978

Guillevic, Eugène. *Art poétique.* Paris: Gallimard, 1989

Jacob, M. *Le Cornet à dés.* Paris: Poésie, Gallimard, 1967

Jarry, Alfred. *Ubu Roi,* etc. Paris: Editions Noël Arnaud & Henri Bodillon, 1978

Mallarmé, Stéphane. *Oeuvres complètes.* Edited by Henri Mondor and G. Jean-Aubry. Paris: Bibliothèque de la Pléiade, 1951

Michaux, Henri. *Passages,* Paris: Gallimard, 1950

——. *L'Infini turbulent.* Paris: Mercure de France, 1957

——. *Emergences, Résurgences.* Paris: Skira, 1972

Perec, Georges. *Les Choses.* Paris: Julliard, 1965

——. *Un homme qui dort.* Paris: Denoël, 1967

——. *Espèces d'espaces.* Paris: Galilée, 1974

——. *Tentative d'épuisement d'un lieu parisien.* Paris: Christian Bourgois, 1975

——. *Alphabets: cent soixante-seize onzains hétérogramifiés.* Paris: Galilée, 1976

——. *La vie, mode d'emploi.* Paris: Hachette, 1978

——. *Je me souviens.* Paris: Hachette, 1978

——. *Penser/classer.* Paris: Hachette, 1985

Perros, Georges. *Papiers collés I, II, III.* Paris: Gallimard, 1960, 1973, 1978

——. *Une vie ordinaire.* Paris: Gallimard, 1967; new edition 1988 with "Avant-propos" by Lorand Gaspar

Pinget, Robert. *Quelqu'un.* Paris: Editions de Minuit, 1965

——. *Monsieur Songe.* Paris: Editions de Minuit, 1982

——. *Du nerf.* Paris: Editions de Minuit, 1990

Proust, Marcel. *A La Recherche du temps perdu,* 3 vols. Edited by Pierre Clarac and André Ferré. Paris: Bibliothèque de la Pléiade, Gallimard, 1954

Queneau, Raymond. *Bâtons, chiffres et lettres.* Revised, augmented edition. Paris: Gallimard, 1965

——. *Chêne et chien,* suivi de Petite cosmogonie portative et de *Le Chant du Styrène.* Paris: Gallimard, 1969

Rabelais, Francois. *Oeuvres complètes.* Paris: Garnier, 1962

Sarraute, Nathalie. *Enfance.* Paris: Gallimard, 1983

——. *Tu ne t'aimes pas.* Paris: Gallimard, 1989

Sollers, Philippe. *Paradis.* Paris: Seuil, 1981

——. *Paradis II.* Paris: Seuil, 1986

Tardieu, Jean. *Le Fleuve caché. Poésies 1938–1961* (with preface by G.E. Clancier). Paris: Gallimard, 1968

———. *La Part de l'ombre. Proses 1937–1967* (With preface by Yvon Belaval). Paris: Gallimard, 1972

Tzara, Tristan. *Oeuvres complètes.* Annotated by Henri Behar. Paris: Flammarion, 1975

Valéry, Paul. *Cahiers,* 29 vols., Paris: C.N.R.S., 1957–61

———. *Oeuvres.* Paris: Gallimard, 1960

Index